PERSONNEL

The Management of People at Work

The Management of People at Work

5th Edition

DALE S. BEACH
Rensselaer Polytechnic Institute

Macmillan Publishing Company
New York

Collier Macmillan Publishers
London

copyright © 1965, 1970, 1975, and 1980
by Dale S. Beach
A preliminary portion of this book was copyrighted © 1963 by
Dale S. Beach.

Macmillan Publishing Company
866 Third Avenue, New York, New York 10022

Collier Macmillan Canada, Inc.

Library of Congress Cataloging in Publication Data

Beach, Dale S.
   Personnel: the management of people at work.

   Includes bibliographies and indexes.
   1. Personnel management. I. Title.
HF5549.B32   1985   658.3   84-9698
ISBN 0-02-307060-9 (Hardcover Edition).
ISBN 0-02-946010-7 (International Edition)

Printing: 1 2 3 4 5 6 7 8   Year: 5 6 7 8 9 0 1 2 3

ISBN 0-02-307060-9

To the Memory of My Beloved Wife Shirley

Preface

The fifth edition of *Personnel: The Management of People at Work* includes a thorough updating of the text and the addition of important new topics.

This book has been designed for use in courses in personnel management, human resource management, management-employee relations, and related courses in college and university programs in business administration, management, labor and industrial relations, public administration, and industrial and management engineering. It is also suitable for use in management development programs and as a reference for executives, personnel managers, and supervisors in both private and public sector work organizations.

The management of people is an integral part of the process of management. It is really the heart of management. Getting out production and managing people are inseparable. There must be a partnership between the managers and specialists in the personnel department and operating managers throughout the enterprise. Training in human resource management is necessary not only for those pursuing careers in personnel but also for those planning careers in the various functional areas of management (production, finance, marketing, engineering, administration, and the like) and in general management.

In the 1980s American industries have faced critical challenges from abroad to their ability to compete and survive. In addition, the American economy has experienced low growth in productivity and little or no real-wage growth since the early 1970s. The entire process by which the workforces in thousands of establishments are nurtured and managed is a key determinant in the vitality of American enterprises, both public and private.

The personnel-human resource function has assumed greater stature in business firms throughout the world. Personnel executives possess very substantial influence in shaping organization-wide policies and programs. Top executives have learned that effective personnel programs and processes are essential to the attainment of corporate objectives.

One of the new features of this edition is a chapter on Employee Rights. This covers protection of one's job (employment-at-will issue), due process and just cause, freedom of speech and whistle-blowing, privacy, off-the-job behavior, and protection against layoff. Among other important new topics added to the fifth edition are the following: special problems facing women in the workplace (including sexual harassment and comparable worth), the Japanese system of management, quality circles, stress on the job, the Hackman-Oldham job design model, U.S. Supreme Court decisions dealing with employee benefits and discipline, new information on labor–management relations (including attitudes of workers toward unions), duty of fair representation, character of labor movement, and research on differences between union and nonunion organizations.

Additionally, this edition contains an elaboration and updating of previous topics, such as illegal questions in the employment process from the standpoint of equal employment opportunity, labor negotiation dispute resolution methods, grievance arbitration, union-management cooperation, public sector collective bargaining, impact of the Occupational Safety and Health Act upon injury rates, positive reinforcement theory, and quality of working life.

Many new figures and tables have been added to the text. References and statistical and survey data have been updated. The suggestions for further reading contained at the end of every chapter have been made current.

The fifth edition contains four new case problems. In the *Instructor's Manual*, objective exam questions for every chapter and teaching notes for each case can be found.

Finally, the fifth edition has been redesigned in order to facilitate the presentation of information and ideas. Color has been used to highlight important elements and passages, and thus should help to make the book more accessible to students and other users.

The author wishes to express his sincere appreciation to those whose constructive suggestions and help have aided in the development of this book. Professor Clifford E. Smith of Iowa State University, Professor Marvin Katzman of George Washington University, and Professor Nathan Himmelstein of Essex Community College reviewed the manuscript for the fifth edition and offered many useful ideas. The following individuals also offered valuable advice which is sincerely appreciated: Professors Joseph H. Culver (University of Texas), Alan Cabelly (Portland State University), Thomas R. Masterson (Emory University), Gary C. Raffaele (University of Texas-San Antonio), James Reinemann (College of Lake County), Eugene E. Holmen (Essex Community College), Eric Stein (City College of Chicago), Raymond L. Hilgert (Washington University), Robert G. Roe (University of Wyoming), T. Roger Manley (Florida Institute of Technology), Newton B. Green II (University of New Hampshire), and G. E. Parker (St. Louis University). I also thank Mr. Bill Matthew for his suggestions.

I wish to thank Alison Scheer for her especially competent work in typing and preparation of the manuscript for the fifth edition. She has been very helpful.

One final note: Throughout the text I have tried to provide for rhetorical equality between the male and female pronouns. Sometimes the pronoun *he* is used, sometimes *she*, and at times, *he or she*.

D. S. B.

Contents

PART I   MANAGEMENT AND THE PERSONNEL FIELD · 1

1 Management, Employees, and the Personnel Field   3

Important issues in the 1980s • Management • A look at personnel
management • The labor force in America • Evolution of theory and
practice of personnel management • General observations • Questions
for review and discussion • Suggestions for further reading

2 Philosophy, Principles, and Policies   23

Ethics and managerial philosophy • Organization objectives • Managing
people at work • Personnel policies • Questions for review and
discussion • Case problems • Suggestions for further reading

3 The Personnel Function   42

Terminology • Who does personnel work? • Staff role of the personnel
department • Personnel (human resource) functions • Survey data •
Organization for the personnel function • Questions for review and
discussion • Case problems • Suggestions for further reading

PART II ORGANIZATION AND JOBS 61

4 Organization 63

Approaches to the study of organization • Organization structure • Delegation and decentralization • Line and staff • Bureaucratic and organic systems of organization • Questions for review and discussion • Case problem • Suggestions for further reading

5 Job Design and Analysis 85

Job design • Job information and personnel management • Analyzing jobs-obtaining job information • Functional job analysis • Administration of the job analysis program • Questions for review and discussion • Exercise • Suggestions for further reading

PART III EMPLOYMENT AND DEVELOPMENT OF PEOPLE 107

6 Human Resource Planning 109

Reasons for human resource planning • The planning process • Conclusion • Questions for review and discussion • Case problems • Suggestions for further reading

7 Recruitment and Selection 128

Labor market considerations • Recruitment and selection policy issues • The employment process • Sources of people • The selection process • Selection procedure • Auditing the recruitment and selection effort • Questions for review and discussion • Suggestions for further reading

8 Testing, Interviewing, and Assessment Centers 148

Selection testing • Fundamental guides to testing • Testing concepts • Developing a testing program • Types of tests • The selection interview • Psychological foundations for interviews • Types of interviews •

Preparing for the interview • Conducting the interview • Common pitfalls in interviewing • Assessment centers • Questions for review and discussion • Case problems • Suggestions for further reading

9 Equal Employment Opportunity   177

The situation of nonwhites and Hispanic Americans • The situation of women • EEO laws and regulations • Older workers and age discrimination • The handicapped • Impact of EEO upon personnel activities • Sexual harassment • Comparable worth • Reverse discrimination • Questions for review and discussion • Case problem • Suggestions for further reading

10 Performance Appraisal and Management by Objectives   204

Basic considerations in appraisal • Appraisal methods • Problems in rating • Appraisal and personal development • Management by objectives • Issues and perspectives • Questions for review and discussion • Case problems • MBO exercise • Suggestions for further reading

11 Career Development   231

Career development processes and concepts • Career planning • Career management • The smaller organization • Questions for review and discussion • Suggestions for further reading

12 Training   243

Training in the organization • The learning process • Training methods • Training programs • Employee Orientation Content • Evaluation of the training effort • Questions for review and discussion • Case problem • Suggestions for further reading

13 Management and Organization Development   262

Nature of management development • Planning and administering the program • Development through work experience • Formal training courses • Organization development • Interventions • Concluding observations • Questions for review and discussion • Case problem • Suggestions for further reading

14 People and Motivation   293

Human behavior fundamentals • Motivation • Human adjustment • Significant motivation theories • Morale and productivity • Applying motivational concepts • Questions for review and discussion • Case problems • Suggestions for further reading

15 Quality of Working Life   319

The nature of work • Contemporary problems of American workers • Quality of working life • Strategies for improvement • Concluding comments • Questions for review and discussion • Suggestions for further reading

16 Leadership, Supervision, and Management Systems   332

Nature of leadership • Foundations of leadership • Authority and power • Leadership style • Situational factors • Supervision • Pattern of effective supervision • Management systems • Japanese system of management • Concluding observations • Questions for review and discussion • Case problems • Suggestions for further reading

17 Participative Management   357

Role of participation in the organization • Research into participation • Conditions for effective participation • Types of participation • Worker's participation—European style • Questions for review and discussion • Suggestions for further reading

18 Discipline   371

Approaches to discipline • Administering the disciplinary program • Rules and penalties • Questions for review and discussion • Case problems • Suggestions for further reading

PART V — LABOR-MANAGEMENT RELATIONS   385

19 Unions and Management   387

Motivation to join unions • Motivation to reject unions • Attitudes of working people toward unions • Development of unions • Union organization and functions • The AFL-CIO • Independent unions • Union objectives and behavior • Character of American labor movement • Impact of the union upon management • Union-management climate • Questions for review and discussion • Suggestions for further reading

20 Collective Bargaining   409

The nature of collective bargaining • The legal framework of collective bargaining • Structure for collective bargaining • Negotiating the agreement • Subject matter of collective bargaining • Subject matter of union-employer agreements • Public sector collective bargaining • Dispute settlement and strikes • Differences between union and nonunion organizations • Questions for review and discussion • Case problems • Suggestions for further reading

21 Grievances and Arbitration   442

Nature of complaints and grievances • Why have a grievance procedure? • Grievance settlement for unionized employees • Grievance arbitration • Grievance settlement for nonunion employees • Questions for review and discussion • Case problems • Suggestions for further reading

PART VI — FINANCIAL COMPENSATION   459

22 Compensation Administration   461

Rationale of financial compensation • Principal compensation issues • Wage criteria • Wage policy and principles • Job evaluation • Job Evaluation Systems • Establishing the pay structure • Administration of pay within ranges • Wage surveys • Compensation for professionals • Compensation for managers • Questions for review and discussion • Exercise • Suggestions for further reading

23 Individual and Group Incentives 492

Direct wage incentives • Types of incentive pay plans • Human and administrative problems • Incentives and labor-management cooperation • Profit sharing • Lincoln Electric incentive system • Conclusions • Questions for review and discussion • Case problems • Suggestions for further reading

PART VII   SECURITY 519

24 Health and Safety 521

Occupational Safety and Health Act • Occupational disease • Occupational safety • Causes of accidents • Components of safety and health program • Worker's compensation • Health services • Stress on the job • Mental health • Questions for review and discussion • Case problem • Suggestions for further reading

25 Benefits and Services 552

Types of benefits and services • Why adopt benefit and service programs? • Significant benefit and service programs • Alternative work schedules • Questions for review and discussion • Case problem • Suggestions for further reading

PART VIII   EMPLOYEE RIGHTS 573

26 Employee Rights 575

Protections created by law • Job protection • Due process and just cause • Freedom of speech and whistle-blowing • Employee privacy • Off-the-job behavior • Protection against layoffs • Questions for review and discussion • Suggestions for further reading

PART IX PERSPECTIVES 589

27 Personnel Management in Perspective 591

Personnel (human resource) management as a career • Accomplishments and continuing needs • Questions for review and discussion • Suggestions for further reading

NAME INDEX 603
SUBJECT INDEX 605

PERSONNEL The Management of People at Work

PART I

Management and the Personnel Field

Management, Employees, and the Personnel Field

This book is about the management of people at work. Although humans have for centuries collected into groups to form durable organizations for the purpose of accomplishing mutual goals, it is only in recent years that an organized body of knowledge has developed encompassing the theory and practice of personnel management— also called human resource management. This is partly because scientific and systematic inquiry into most branches of science has occurred primarily within the past hundred years. Work in the physical and life sciences occurred somewhat earlier and at a more rapid rate than in the social sciences. Personnel management, which is an applied, professional field of work as well as an academic discipline, derives much of its foundations from the social sciences, which have really emerged in the main since 1900. The principal social sciences which have contributed to the development of personnel management are psychology, industrial sociology, labor economics, political science, and cultural anthropology. The professional disciplines of management and public administration have also made their contributions. To the foregoing must be added the important accomplishments made by personnel management practitioners in industry, governmental organizations, and consulting firms.

Now it is certainly true that people engage in many endeavors long before the scientists come along to provide the theoretical explanations. To a certain extent this has been so in the field of personnel management. Frederick W. Taylor and his disciples were designing and installing wage incentive plans long before the modern sociologists and social psychologists developed theories to explain the complex motivational and social factors involved. Workers have been hired and fired for centuries without benefit of formal theory to guide those in charge. Even today a great deal that comprises the field of personnel management is based upon the accumulated trial-and-error experiences of countless employers. But the research studies of scientific investigators are gradually adding to the fund of knowledge available to the management practitioners. They are entering firmer ground when they make decisions in regard to organization, hiring, training, compensation, discipline, and supervision. The management of people at work is partly an art and partly a science. Undoubtedly for many generations to come, the successful manager will still have to rely upon a good deal of judgment, intuition, and trial-and-error in directing the work force. But more and more the manager can come to decide on actions and predict consequences as a result of applying scientific knowledge.

So far we have related the recent emergence

of personnel management as a distinct field of endeavor and as an academic discipline concurrent with the recent development of the social sciences. But there are other and quite different reasons as well. The farmer who manages his own family farm with the help of his wife and children has little need for the knowledge and skills of personnel management. The master craftsman who runs his own shop in town with the help of one or two people to make wagons, shoe horses, print newspapers, or to make clothes has little need to employ sophisticated personnel management techniques. Until the latter part of the nineteenth century the economic activity of the United States was primarily centered upon agriculture and the handicrafts and trading of the country village. The financial tycoons were just beginning to put together their industrial empires in the late nineteenth century. The technology of mass production did not arrive until the early twentieth century. The point being made here is that personnel management problems did not really become pressing until we had large aggregations of people working together in one organization, and the American economy did not reach the point of widespread large-scale organizations until the twentieth century.

In the small establishments of yesteryear employee relations problems were handled largely on an informal basis between the owner and the individual employee. Elaborate organization structures did not exist. Personnel policies were rarely reduced to writing. Rather they evolved through practice and custom. Hiring arrangements were very simple. Psychological tests did not exist. The new employee learned by watching fellow workers. Accident prevention programs and safety engineering were practically nonexistent. Because management was not recognized as a distinct field of endeavor or as a profession, management training was also nonexistent.

IMPORTANT ISSUES IN THE 1980S

- *High unemployment and declining industries.* Nationally the unemployment rate has fluctuated between 6 and 10 per cent for many years. Even in periods of economic expansion the unemployment rate has stayed in the 6 to 8 per cent range. Automobile, steel, textiles, wearing apparel, and rubber have been declining industries in the United States. Hundreds of thousands of jobs have been lost permanently. These industries have been unable to meet foreign competition successfully.

  Frequent and persistent layoffs have caused both labor and management to search for ways to increase the viability of the firms, to retain workers, and to enhance job security.
- *Shift toward service industries.* Over the past 20 years or so, our economy has shifted, in terms of employment, markets, and investment, toward service industries. Telecommunications, recreation, banking, food service, lodging, insurance, education, health care, and government have become major growth industries. Employment in manufacturing, by comparison, has grown very little. This has important implications in terms of the mix of skills needed in service establishments, training requirements, propensity to unionize, and job design.
- *The productivity challenge.* Closely related to the problem of persistent unemployment and declining industries is recognition by management, labor, and government policymakers of the need to make American industry more competitive and to increase productivity.

  One method of accomplishing these twin objectives is labor-management cooperation and participative management. Other methods are to upgrade the quality of the labor force and of management by means of comprehensive training programs. Still other means are to develop new modes of organization and of management leadership.

- *Growth of high technology firms and industries.* New businesses and new firms are being created in the high technology area. These businesses are helping the economy grow, are providing new jobs especially for professionals and technicians, and are providing new products and services.

  One characteristic of high technology companies is rapid change. This causes severe stress upon the members of such organizations and this poses a responsibility to the personnel–human resources department to develop programs to help people cope.

- *Employee rights.* Various forces (employees, unions, writers, the courts, legislatures, and managers) are gradually taking action to enhance employee rights in the workplace. These newer rights include protection against unjust discharge, right of due process appeals in adverse action cases, right to a reasonable measure of privacy, and right to self-expression. These emerging rights are coming soon after employees have gained the right (through legislation) to a safe and healthful workplace and to nondiscrimination in employment.

- *Increasing litigation in the employment relationship.* Unions and employers have shown an increasing propensity to file charges against one another before the National Labor Relations Board. Increasingly, grievances are taken all the way to arbitration. Litigation in the area of equal employment opportunity has expanded.

- *Career opportunities.* With a better educated workforce have come demands for more meaningful jobs, for more opportunities for promotion, and for career development programs.

- *Insufficient opportunities for a better educated workforce.* The percentage of the labor force in the United States holding college degrees has steadily increased over the years. Unfortunately many of these college graduates have been forced to take jobs that do not utilize their full skills and talents. This leads to disappointment and frustration. There is a pervasive need to upgrade job content and to enrich jobs.

- *Safety and health.* The widespread use of toxic substances in industry poses a special health hazard to employees. Often symptoms of disease may not appear until years after initial exposure. There is a need by employers to devote more money and attention to industrial hygiene and prevention of occupational disease.

- *Assimilation of women into the workplace.* Women have been moving into jobs once dominated by men. Old barriers are falling. As this assimilation evolves the issues of comparable worth (equivalent pay for men and women) and of sexual harassment on the job have become significant. Working mothers have needs for maternity leaves and benefits, job sharing, flexible work schedules, and child care centers for preschool children.

- *Equal employment opportunity.* Although equal employment opportunity laws have been on the books since the mid-1960s, there still exists a considerable gap in the job opportunities and in annual earnings between whites and blacks and between men and women. In the individual company, management must devote continuing attention to making job opportunities available to protected minorities and women and to providing opportunities for training and promotion.

- *High-talent personnel.* In recent years increasing numbers of technical and professional personnel have been employed in work organizations. Employers need to adapt their personnel programs to meet the special needs of these high-talent people. These adaptations can include such actions as new incentives and forms of recognition, ample opportunities for development, challenging job assignments, and special career paths.

Terminology—Work Organization

Issues, problems, and principles involved in the management of people at work are common to all kinds of organizations: factories, offices, retail stores, hospitals, government agencies, and educational institutions. To emphasize this universality the term *work organization* will be used frequently throughout this book. It is a general term selected to apply to all kinds of establishments or organizations whether they be private business enterprises, governmental organizations, or nonprofit private bodies. It excludes social and religious bodies. In order to provide for a variety of language the terms *company, corporation, enterprise,* and *establishment* will be used from time to time.

MANAGEMENT

To a considerable extent the manager of today has achieved his or her position because of knowledge, skill, and ability and not because the control of financial assets has entitled him or her to a seat in management. Although there are thousands of family-owned businesses in this country, these are predominantly small in size. The vast majority of medium- and large-sized enterprises are directed by hired professional managers. The corporate form of business enterprise coupled with the diffusion of stock ownership, such that a single individual rarely has a controlling interest, has led to a separation of ownership from management. The board of directors selects a chief executive officer or president who in turn selects the top executive team. Our industrial technology has become extremely complex. The managerial skills required to guide the modern corporation are likewise complex. These and other factors have resulted in the development of a professionalization of management. Although managers are actually hired employees, as a class they tend to identify their interests closely with those of the owners of the business. Top management considers the welfare of the corporation and its own welfare as identical on most issues.

In the field of public administration, as a consequence of the merit or civil service system, the vast majority of the administrative personnel are selected on the basis of well-defined standards of competence. This system is most advanced at the federal level and least at the municipal level. In contrast to the private business system the policy-making positions at or near the top are filled by either popular election or by political appointment.

Thus far we have spoken of management as a group or class of people. Management also connotes a distinct kind of activity or process. *Management is the process of utilizing material and human resources to accomplish designated objectives. It involves the organization, direction, coordination, and evaluation of people to achieve these goals.*

In analyzing the work of management, Newman and Summer state that the total task of management can be divided into organizing, planning, leading, measuring, and controlling.[1] Koontz and O'Donnell view the functions of management as planning, organizing, staffing, directing, and controlling.[2] Harbison and Myers have attempted to include the frames of reference of both economists and industrial management writers by listing the functions of management as (1) the undertaking of risk and the handling of uncertainty; (2) planning and innovation; (3) coordination, administration, and control; and (4) routine supervision.[3] Although in the very small firm all of these functions may be performed by the owner, in a com-

---

[1] William H. Newman, Charles E. Summer, and E. Kirby Warren, *The Process of Management* (Englewood Cliffs, N.J.: Prentice-Hall, Inc., 1972), pp. 11–14.

[2] Harold Koontz and Cyril O'Donnell, *Principles of Management: An Analysis of Management Functions*, 5th ed. (New York: McGraw-Hill Book Company, 1972), pp. 46–49.

[3] Frederick Harbison and Charles A. Myers, *Management in the Industrial World: An International Analysis* (New York: McGraw-Hill Book Company, 1959), p. 8.

pany of any reasonable size these tasks are dispersed among various members of the entire management team.

If one studies the day-to-day activities of a manager, it will be found that he or she devotes a high percentage of the time to interacting with other people. In preparing plans he or she must consult colleagues and subordinates. In organizing managers must work closely with subordinates to define and guide the relationships among them. Managers accomplish results *through* and with others. They lead, persuade, and influence. At times they conduct and at other times they participate in decision-making conferences. The practicing manager must be skilled in the art of human relations. He or she spends a great deal of time communicating with others, mostly through face-to-face contact.

Management involves the act of accomplishing results through other people. The skilled space technology manager does not personally design a spacecraft. The manufacturing executive does not personally build automobiles. The university president does not teach. The role of the manager is to assemble the best work team he or she can obtain and then to provide a supportive motivational environment to guide that team to accomplish agreed-upon objectives.

The essence of management is the activity of working with people to accomplish results. It involves organizing, motivating, leading, training, communicating with, and coordinating others. Lawrence A. Appley, President of the American Management Association for many years, has written that management is the development of people and not the direction of things. He maintains that management and personnel administration are one and the same.[4]

Now the reader should not jump to the conclusion that the successful manager need only possess knowledge and skills in the fields of personnel management and human resources.

[4] Lawrence A. Appley, "Management the Simple Way," *Personnel,* Vol. 19, No. 4 (January 1943), pp. 595–603.

This person must also be trained in other fields, such as the technology of the particular industry, management science and administration, planning, and personal communication skills. In addition, the modern-day executive must have knowledge of the economic, social, and political environment in which he or she lives and works. The degree of competence a manager must have in these areas is determined primarily by the particular circumstances of job, company, level in the organization, and geographical location. Notwithstanding these other areas of competence demanded of the manager, his or her "world" is primarily one of human interaction.

A LOOK AT PERSONNEL MANAGEMENT

Personnel (or human resource) management is challenging and often exciting work. It comprises an amazing variety of activities. To introduce the reader to the field of personnel management we shall here give several samples of activities involved in the "management of people at work." The samples given below are not meant to be all-inclusive of the personnel field. They are given to provide the "flavor" of the human resource activities that occur in work organizations. Later chapters of this book will contain in-depth treatments of the topics suggested in the items to follow.

- A supervisor meets with a group of three new employees to welcome them to the department, to introduce them to fellow employees, to show them the layout and facilities, and to generally orient them to their new situation.
- A middle-level manager conducts management-by-objectives meetings with each of the supervisors working in her department. In these private meetings the manager and the subordinate discuss job objectives, perfor-

mance measures, and work accomplishments in a mutual problem-solving manner.

- The personnel director receives many pieces of information, directly and indirectly from the employees, which reveal serious discontents and frustrations. The employees claim that the front-line supervisors practice favoritism and discrimination. Many employees have been discharged arbitrarily. There is some evidence that employees are reacting to this situation with a high rate of absenteeism, outspoken complaining on the job, and some talk of inviting a union to organize the employees. In cooperation with other top-level executives the personnel director makes plans to systematically assess the state of morale by means of an attitude survey. He contemplates establishing a comprehensive organization development effort to improve understanding among management and the employees and to generally enhance organizational effectiveness.
- A supervisor and her employees are convened to receive official recognition and an award from the president of the company for achieving new production goals.
- Management wishes to do a better job of identifying those persons within the organization who have high potential for success in managerial positions. With assistance from a consultant, the personnel department creates an assessment center for selecting managers.
- The company and the union have just finished bargaining their first labor agreement. A permanent labor–management committee, composed of an equal number of representatives from the union and the company, has been established to meet monthly to discuss and resolve employee relations problems. Both parties have high hopes that this committee will become an effective instrument for problem solving.
- The supervisor of benefits and services (a member of the personnel department) makes a comprehensive study of the current employee benefits (health insurance, pension, life insurance, dental insurance, paid leaves, and so on). Management wishes to ascertain whether the current schedule of benefits is adequate to meet employee needs and if it is competitive with that provided by other firms.
- A production supervisor devotes special attention to an employee whose performance has seriously declined over the past several weeks. She holds private meetings with the individual to determine the cause of the decline and to work out a corrective program of action.
- The supervisor of health and safety (a member of the personnel department) participates with members of the engineering department in planning the installation of new production equipment to insure that it meets health and safety standards.
- Representatives of the personnel and the industrial engineering departments and of various operating departments hold a series of meetings to plan the redesign of various production jobs. The goal is to enrich these jobs to enhance both productivity and employee satisfaction.

The foregoing activities, which comprise but a part of the whole of human resource management, demonstrate that personnel work is carried on both by the members of the personnel department and by the other members of management throughout the enterprise.

The responsibility of the personnel department is to formulate personnel policies in cooperation with other members of top management, to plan and develop personnel programs, to carry out certain personnel service activities (such as analyzing jobs, interviewing and testing job applicants), and to insure that the entire range of personnel activities are performed effectively throughout the entire organization.

The responsibility of the other supervisors and managers in all the departments and divisions of the organization is to manage their own work forces to achieve performance goals and to maintain employee well-being. These managers play a key role in performing such human resource responsibilities as employee orientation and training, performance appraisal, communications, leadership, discipline, grievance handling, and maintenance of workplace health and safety.

Constructive and sound management of an enterprise's human resources is crucial to effective organizational performance. If management neglects this responsibility the enterprise may founder.

THE LABOR FORCE IN AMERICA

The United States has experienced great economic progress over the past one hundred or so years. This has occurred through the process of industrialization which converted a largely agricultural nation in the nineteenth century into a very complex, advanced industrialized society in the twentieth century. Important features of our industrialized economy have been vast capital investment in plant and equipment, mass production and continuous production processes, sophisticated managerial and organizational methodologies, and rapid technological advances.

How has the American worker fared during this process of industrialization and economic growth? What changes have occurred in the nature and composition of the labor force?

The labor force includes the noninstitutional population, sixteen years of age and over, who are employed plus all those who are unemployed but who are actually seeking work.

Rising Status of Labor

The average working man or woman in the United States has risen to unprecedented heights in terms of standard of living, educational attainment, freedom of opportunity, and voice in affairs. Let us briefly examine some of these matters.

Standard of Living. The best measure of improvement in the level of living of working people is the change in "real wages" between two periods. Real wages show the relative purchasing power of wages in terms of a base period when changes in the price level have been canceled out. Bloom and Northrup have tabulated weekly earnings of production workers in manufacturing from 1914 through 1975 in terms of 1967 dollars. Real weekly earnings went from $36.27 in 1914 to $114.88 in 1975. Thus, 1975 earnings were 3.17 times as much as 1914 earnings.[5]

However, real earnings in the private non-agricultural sector of the economy actually peaked in 1972 and drifted downward slowly after then. This downward drift has been caused by a very low rate of productivity growth in the economy and by high rates of price inflation.

Shorter Work Time. In 1850 the average work week for all industries was 70 hours. Since the 1940s the average work week has hovered around 39–40 hours. The greatest reductions occurred between 1900 and 1947.

Prior to 1940 paid vacations for hourly paid workers were rare. Sometimes they received a week off in the summer but without pay. Salaried employees, however, often got a paid vacation. By the 1970s nearly all classifications of workers (except those in agriculture and construction) received paid vacations. Vacation policies for hourly paid and salaried employees have become nearly identical. Typically an employee receives a two-week paid vacation after one year of service, three weeks after ten years, and four weeks after twenty years.

Before World War II major national holidays were frequently observed in private industry but

[5] Gordon F. Bloom and Herbert R. Northrup, *Economics of Labor Relations*, 8th ed. (Homewood, Ill.: R. D. Irwin, Inc., 1977), p. 399.

without pay. As of the mid-1980s, the prevailing practice was to grant about 10 paid holidays per year.

Thus, we can see that on the average the American worker devotes fewer hours per week and fewer days per year to the job. This does not necessarily mean that people sit idle during the remaining waking hours. They may consume them in a variety of ways, such as engaging in more recreational pursuits, working around the house, commuting longer distances to work, or holding an additional part-time job. But there can be no doubt that this added time off the job has given the American worker greater freedom in determining what he or she does with life.

More education. There has been a long-term trend toward increased educational attainment for the population. In 1981 18.3 per cent of the civilian labor force had completed four years or more of college. About 77 per cent of the labor force had graduated from high school.[6] The higher educational attainment has contributed to better jobs and higher income for the people involved.

Expectations and Demands. Aside from those changes that can be clearly documented with statistical data, it seems clear also that modern workers as a group or force in society have greater expectations and greater wants than did their forebearers of a few generations ago. They want better homes, cars, food, and clothing than could be obtained years ago. Many things considered luxuries years ago are now held to be necessities. Parents expect their children to finish high school and even obtain some college or technical institute education. They expect to spend more and more on services and recreation. This continual drive for more and more can be explained in terms of the psychological theories of motivation. As more basic needs for the necessities of life are satisfied, humans strive to satisfy higher social and egoistic drives. The fulfillment of these cannot be directly measured. Generally in these psychological and social areas human wants are never satisfied—people always want more.

Today employees expect to have a greater voice in their own destiny at their place of employment. A considerable share of the labor force has found union membership to be an avenue for this expression. Through the collective bargaining process, workers make greater demands upon management not only for such material things as higher wages and more fringe benefits but also for fair treatment, freedom from discrimination, and a say-so in matters affecting them. To a considerable extent the ideals of political democracy, which are so much a part of the American culture, have seeped into the workplace. Management in recent years has come to be interested in and to pay attention to the ideas of its employees. The techniques for providing for employee participation have been many. Among these are collective bargaining, consultative supervision, democratic leadership, labor-management cooperation, productivity bargaining, and suggestion systems.

Changing Composition of the Labor Force

Over the years a great many changes have occurred in the way people earn a living. In the mid-nineteenth century four out of five persons who worked for a living worked for themselves. Most were farmers, shopkeepers, and craftsmen. By the last quarter of the twentieth century, nine tenths of the labor force worked for someone else. Thus we are a nation made up primarily of wage and salary earners.

There has been a long-term trend of increases in white-collar employment, both in absolute numbers and in percentage of the labor force. In 1900 white-collar workers constituted only 17.6 per cent of the total labor force. By

---

[6] U.S. Department of Labor, *Employment and Training Report of the President, 1982*. Washington, D.C. Table B-14.

TABLE 1-1. Occupational Distribution of the Labor Force from 1900 to 1982.

Occupation	1982	1960	1940	1920	1900
White-collar:	53.7%	43.3%	31.1%	24.9%	17.6%
Professional and technical	17.0	11.8	7.5	5.4	4.3
Managers and administrators	11.5	8.8	7.3	6.6	5.8
Clerical	18.5	15.1	9.6	8.0	3.0
Sales	6.6	7.6	6.7	4.9	4.5
Blue-collar:	29.7	38.6	39.8	40.2	35.8
Craft	12.3	14.2	12.0	13.0	10.5
Operatives	12.9	19.4	18.4	15.6	12.8
Nonfarm laborers	4.5	5.0	9.4	11.6	12.5
Services	13.8	11.6	11.7	7.8	9.0
Private households	1.0	2.8	4.7	3.3	5.4
Farm workers	2.7	6.4	17.4	27.0	37.5

Source: Table 1 in Chapter 1, "The Survival of Work" by S. A. Levitan and Clifford M. Johnson, contained in *The Work Ethic—A Critical Analysis,* edited by J. Barbash, R. J. Lampman, S. A. Levitan, and G. Tyler. Madison, Wis.: Industrial Relations Research Association, 1983. Reprinted by permission.

1982 they represented 53.7 per cent of the labor force. By contrast blue-collar workers have declined from a peak of 40.2 per cent of the labor force in 1920 to only 29.7 per cent in 1982. Also the percentage of the total labor force who are farm workers has declined dramatically since 1900. See Table 1-1.

Within the foregoing broad occupational groups, the occupations showing the most striking rate of growth are those in the professional and technical category. In 1900 they comprised only 4.3 per cent of the total labor force. By 1982 they represented 17.0 per cent of the total. There has been an especially rapid increase in the number of scientists, engineers, and technicians employed in industry and government.

Another long-term trend has been the decline in the number and percentage of unskilled workers. More and more tasks formerly performed by unskilled laborers have been taken over by machines. Dropouts from high school can usually qualify for nothing but unskilled jobs and these opportunities are disappearing.

In 1900 the total labor force in the United States consisted of 83 per cent males and 17 per cent females.[7] A woman held a paid job only if she were unmarried or widowed. Few jobs were open to women in those days. Those who held jobs were commonly employed as domestic servants, as needle trades workers, or as clerks in stores. By contrast in 1979, 41.5 per cent of the labor force was made up of women.[8] Several forces have operated to dramatically increase the number and percentage of women in the labor force in recent years. Among these have been a decline in the fertility rate since the late 1950s, fewer children born and expected by women,

[7]Gertrude Bancroft, *The American Labor Force: Its Growth and Changing Composition* (New York: John Wiley & Sons, Inc., 1958), p. 34.

[8]U.S. Department of Labor, *Handbook of Labor Statistics 1980,* Bulletin 2070, Washington, D.C., Table 2.

increasing availability of household labor-saving applicances, equal employment opportunity actions by the Federal government, and the women's liberation movement. Once-sharp distinctions between men's occupations and women's occupations are disappearing. Women now hold jobs as jockeys, telephone linewomen, soldiers and sailors, astronauts, engineers, executives, and university professors.

Women, however, still have a long way to go before they achieve parity with men. Despite all the progress women have made in recent decades, women still earn, on a weekly or annual basis, only about 60 per cent of the average for men. This disparity is primarily caused because women are concentrated in the lower-paying occupations.

EVOLUTION OF THEORY AND PRACTICE OF PERSONNEL MANAGEMENT

One of the best ways to understand the present is to examine the past. The past is our prologue. We shall trace the various managerial theories and practices relating to the treatment and direction of employees from the early 1800s to the present. In studying these developments, it is important for the reader to keep in mind that at any one period there existed a variety of ideologies and practices. The diverse movements do not fit into a neat package of unified philosophies and practices commencing at one point in history and ending clearly at another.

The people contributing to the development of the personnel management field have had varied backgrounds and professions. An important group have been the university scholars, writers, and researchers who have pushed back the frontiers of knowledge. A large amount of soundly based experimentation and research has been conducted by these people in areas such as small-group theory, organization theory, motivation, morale, productivity, leadership, personnel testing, fatigue, accidents, and personnel evaluation.

Another significant group of contributors have been the management practitioners themselves: industrial executives, personnel specialists, and consultants. These have been active in such fields as work measurement, wage incentives, job evaluation, organization design, industrial training, executive development, and union-management relations.

A third group have been government legislators and administrators who have shaped and administered public policy in the areas of wages, hours, collective bargaining, workmen's compensation, unemployment, and equal employment opportunity. These programs have had a decided impact upon the management of people at work in private business.

A fourth and final group of influential people have been the leaders of organized labor: Samuel Gompers, John L. Lewis, Philip Murray, Walter Reuther, George Meany, and their followers. In a large measure, their influence in the personnel field has been felt through labor legislation advocated by organized labor and through management policies and programs adopted in response (and sometimes in opposition) to union initiative.

Early Philosophies

The United States followed somewhat after England in becoming an industrialized nation. It was not until 1880 that the less than 50 per cent of the American labor force was engaged in agriculture. Being culturally close to the British, American entrepreneurs tended to adopt many of the British attitudes toward workers.

One of the pioneer industrialists was Robert Owen (1771–1858), a Scottish textile manufacturer, who in 1813 wrote a book entitled *A New*

View of Society. If Owen were alive today he would be called a paternalistic employer. He built model worker villages by his cotton mills at New Lanark, Scotland. He built decent health and sanitation facilities in his factories and established schools for children and workers. Eventually he abolished child labor in his mills. Owen's views and practices contrasted sharply with those of the majority of employers in that period, for he took a genuine interest in the welfare of his people. He advised other manufacturers to devote as much attention to their "vital machines" (that is, workers) as they did to their inanimate machines.

Andrew Ure, in his *Philosophy of Manufacturers,* published in London in 1835, praised the factory system over the coexisting cottage or putting-out system of home production. He defended the widespread use of child labor in the textile industry against the then current public criticism. He was a spokesman for the prevailing belief of members of the entrepreneurial class that workers left to themselves were lazy and ignorant. But factory employment improved their morals and health and gave them higher wages then could be obtained in agriculture or cottage production. He denounced any combination of workers (that is, unionization) as a product of agitators who caused violence and crime.

Others whose works have a bearing on early managerial thought were Adam Smith, who wrote the *Wealth of Nations* in 1776, and Charles Babbage, who wrote *On the Economy of Machinery and Manufactures* in 1832. Smith emphasized that if each individual worked for economic self-interest, the greatest good would accrue to society. Babbage subscribed to Smith's ideas. In addition, he concentrated upon developing such principles of manufacturing as the division of labor. Babbage emphasized mutuality of interests between employer and workers. Hard work and high productivity were a source of good wages for the worker and high profits for the employer. In this book he advocated the adoption of such motivational techniques as wage incentives, profit sharing, and plans of employee participation in the establishment of shop rules. Babbage like Ure, however, was opposed to unions of workers.

Scientific Management

Frederick W. Taylor was the real father and driving force behind the scientific management movement.[9] He and his followers Frank and Lillian Gilbreth, Henry L. Gantt, Morris L. Cook, and Harrington Emerson exerted a profound effect upon management thought and practice not only in the United States but throughout the world.

Although Taylor created a number of important shop management techniques, such as time study, methods study, functional foremanship, standardization of tools, a differential piece-rate system, instruction cards for workers, and a cost control system, he proclaimed that scientific management was primarily a mental revolution on the part of workers and management alike and not simply a set of efficiency devices.

Taylor preached cooperation between labor and management but in a different way from that of most modern writers. He believed that by scientific measurement of work (that is, time study), specification of the best method, selection and placement of the right worker in the right job, and establishment of an appropriate wage, the source of most of the conflict between management and labor would be removed. The increased output, higher wages through wage

[9]A full explanation of Taylor's contributions and impact would be beyond the scope of this book. The interested reader may wish to consult the following works: Frederick W. Taylor, *Principles of Scientific Management* (New York: Harper and Row, 1919); Robert F. Hoxie, *Scientific Management and Labor* (New York: Appleton-Century-Crofts, 1915); George Filipetti, *Industrial Management in Transition,* rev. ed. (Homewood, Ill.: Richard D. Erwin, Inc., 1953), chs. 2 and 3.

incentives, and higher profits for the employer would cause harmony to prevail.

Implicit in Taylor's consulting activities and writings was a full acceptance of the "economic man" concept that dominated management thinking for such a long time, both before and after his time. This is the notion that people are primarily motivated to maximize economic gain. The concept further holds that each person is individualistic in nature. It ignores the social and psychological drives of people.

In his book entitled the *Principles of Scientific Management*, Taylor asserted that no single element of his system constituted scientific management, but rather it was the entire program and philosophy that was its hallmark. He summarized this as (1) science, not rule of thumb; (2) harmony, not discord; (3) cooperation, not individualism; and (4) maximum output, in place of restricted output.[10]

The scientific management movement has had a great impact upon management—employment relationships and upon management in general. It contributed greatly to the professionalization of management. It elevated management by plan, system, and design while causing management by hunch and intuition to decline. It brought the engineer into a more active role in designing man–machine systems and even entire factory production systems. The work measurement and wage incentive systems introduced by the scientific management pioneers have become accepted practice (with improvements, of course) throughout a large segment of industry. Not only have these contributed to higher productivity, lower unit costs, and higher take-home pay, but they have "muddied the waters" of labor–management relations and caused innumerable disputes. The emphasis upon differences in worker abilities and a scientific selection of employees laid the groundwork for the widespread acceptance of the industrial psychologist and his selection testing programs.

[10]Taylor, op. cit., p. 140.

Welfare Movement

In the early 1900s the welfare movement became fairly widespread in American industry. This movement aimed to uplift the physical, hygienic, social, and educational conditions of working-class people for their own benefit and to make them better employees. Many factors contributed to the interest of employers in welfare programs. As corporations grew, top management became more distant from the workers and there occurred a decline in the tenor of relationships. Social reformers and writers had for some time awakened the general public to certain exploitive and sweatshop conditions of the factory system. Many towns that grew up around a single local industry lacked essential housing and decent community facilities. Thus, corporate executives perceived a need and an opportunity to improve the well-being of their people as a positive value in itself and as a way of generating greater employee loyalty and possibly greater productivity.

These early welfare programs included health facilities; wash-up and locker facilities; lunchrooms; recreation facilities for employees and their families; libraries, schools, and classes in English for immigrants; disability and group insurance, and pension programs; and savings and legal aid programs.

By the 1920s welfare work in industry had declined and become somewhat discredited. Some companies operated their programs in a highly paternalistic manner and continued them only as long as the workers evidenced genuine appreciation. Other employers offered these benefits to their employees to placate them into accepting long hours, low wages, and bad working conditions. In short, opportunism and expediency were the motives of some businessmen. Executives became disillusioned when baseball and horseshoe-pitching leagues, company picnics, reading rooms, savings associations, and company housing did not increase productive efficiency. Employees became disillusioned when they sensed that employer interest in them was not always genuine.

Employment Management

Prior to the 1911–1920 decade, the hiring of workers was performed principally by line supervision. In effect the foreman did his own hiring and firing. At about this time a number of forces began to operate that demonstrated to top management in American corporations the need for establishing a specialized department to handle employment management.

Frederick W. Taylor had emphasized the need for proper selection and placement of workers on jobs for which they could become superior producers. A number of researchers had demonstrated the very considerable costs associated with high labor turnover. World War I created a demand for the hiring of many thousands for work in defense production factories. War production alone caused the creation of a great number of employment departments in industry. About this time a feeling developed among top managements that foremen were overburdened with problems of production, training, maintenance, and other supervisory duties and that they should be relieved of the responsibility for hiring and firing. There was considerable criticism in the management literature of that period of the "rough and ready" manner in which foremen had performed the employment function.

Thus employment management departments sprang up throughout industry around the time of World War I. In 1912, the first employment managers' association was formed in Boston. In 1915 the Amos Tuck School of Dartmouth College offered the first training program for employment managers. The employment departments performed the functions of recruiting, selection, job placement, and record keeping. In some concerns their responsibilities also included training, grievance handling, welfare program administration, and final decision

making on discharges for hourly workers. These early employment departments were the forerunners of the modern personnel or industrial relations department.[11]

Industrial Psychology

Industrial psychology had its beginnings in 1913 when Hugo Munsterberg (the father of industrial psychology) published his *Psychology and Industrial Efficiency.*[12] Major contributions to the professional practice of personnel have been made by industrial psychology in personnel testing, interviewing, attitude measurement, learning theory and training, fatigue and monotony studies, safety, job analysis, and human engineering (now commonly called *human factors analysis.*) Of all these areas, the major application of the knowledge and techniques of industrial psychology has been in testing for employment, job placement, promotion, and training. Psychologists have made a major contribution, over the years, by their adherence to careful experimentation, rigorous research designs, and use of sophisticated statistical methods.

As a rule, even today, only the very large corporations employ professionally trained psychologists on a full-time basis. But the knowledge, findings, and skills of industrial psychology have been applied rather extensively through education, publication, and consultation services.

Health and Safety

The passage of worker's compensation laws by most of the states occurred in the 1910–1920 period. These laws hold the employer financially

---

[11]A detailed explanation of the development of the employment management activity in industry is contained in Henry Eilbirt, "The Development of Personnel Management in the United States," *Business History Review,* Vol. 33, No. 3 (Autumn 1959), pp. 345–364.

[12](Boston: Houghton Mifflin Company, 1913).

responsible for all injuries occuring to workers while on the job. Employers since that time have been required to carry insurance to compensate injured workers for medical expenses, loss of weekly earnings while off the job, and for loss of earning power due to permanent physical damage. Because premium rates are adjusted upward or downward to reflect the accident experience of a company, this has served as an incentive for the employer to eliminate the causes of accidents in the plant.

The passage of these laws was a prime force causing employers to take positive steps to reduce and prevent work injuries and to organize company health programs. Thus, we saw the creation of such positions as safety engineer, safety director, company physician, industrial nurse, and medical director. In more recent years the position of industrial hygienist has been added by many large companies.

In 1913 the most influential nationwide organization devoted to the promotion of occupational safety was formed. This is the National Safety Council, a nonprofit organization devoted to research, education, technical service, and publication in the field of safety. It is a membership organization composed largely of manufacturing, public utility, and transportation companies, as well as insurance companies in the liability and worker's compensation fields.

The fields of industrial hygiene and industrial medicine have grown up during the same era as the accident prevention movement. Both the American Industrial Hygiene Association and the Industrial Medical Association have worked to improve conditions of health at the workplace.

Concerned about a significant nationwide increase in work injury frequency that took place between 1960 and 1970 and about the prevalence of occupational diseases, Congress enacted the Occupational Safety and Health Act (OSHA) in 1970. It provides for Federal safety and health standards, government inspections of workplaces, and a system of citations and penalties.

Unionism and Management Reactions

Efforts by American workers to form trade unions to represent their interests in dealings with employers became very widespread and intense commencing in the mid-1880s. In this era, and indeed for many years thereafter, the principal efforts of the unions were directed toward getting the employers to recognize them and to bargain over wages, hours, and other employment conditions.

All through the years, and even up to the present time, employers generally have not taken kindly to unionization of their workers. Basically entrepreneurs and managers opposed unionism for their workers because such action constituted a serious challenge to their authority. With the enhanced bargaining power derived from unified action and the ever-present threat of a strike, a union was in a position to demand a voice in wage-rate determination; job assignments; promotion, transfer, and layoff policies; work schedules; working conditions, work loads, and many other vital factors. When a union entered the picture, the authority of the employer was no longer supreme. In addition, union demands exerted a strong impact upon the cost of doing business.

During the 1920s managements in American industry, acting both individually and in concert through their various associations, launched a great ideological campaign against unions. This took the form of open-shop campaigns, company-established unions and welfare capitalism (paternalism). The main features were education, training, indoctrination, and welfare programs.

Then came the Great Depression, the formation of the CIO, intensified union-organizing activity, and the passage of the National Labor Relations Act (Wagner Act) in 1935. The Wagner Act signified positive encouragement of collective bargaining as public policy. Peaceful means via National Labor Relations Board elections were instituted to settle the violence-fomenting issue of union recognition.

Not until the late 1930s and the 1940s did American management begin to develop a sophistication and maturity in the field of labor relations. Faced with the near inevitability of dealing with unions on a permanent basis, corporations established such positions as vice-president of labor relations and industrial relations director. Commencing in the 1940s, a number of major universities established industrial relations centers or schools that engaged in the triple functions of research, adult education extension activities, and on-campus undergraduate and graduate instruction. As people have become trained in the disciplines of labor economics, industrial relations, and human resources, and have taken responsible positions in industry, the field has become professionalized to a large extent.

In the 1960s unionization of government employees at the federal, state, and local level spread rapidly. This was initially fostered by President Kennedy's Executive Order 10988 of 1962, which required Federal government agencies to recognize as exclusive bargaining agents unions that, by a secret ballot, have been shown to represent a majority of the unit.

Unionism has had a number of tangible influences upon the management of personnel. Among these have been the adoption of sound employee grievance handling systems, almost universal acceptance of arbitration to resolve conflicts of rights, due process discipline practices, expansion of employee benefit programs, liberalization of holiday and vacation time off, clear definition of job duties, and job rights via seniority. Also union pressures have forced management to install rational, defensible wage structures. Decision making in these and related areas has tended more and more to become a joint consultative process between management and union.

In the 1980s, certain contradictory forces have emerged. One points toward more conflict whereas the other points toward collaboration. Some companies have filed for Chapter 11 bankruptcy primarily in order to break union contracts. Many firms have acquired great sophistication in repelling union organizing drives. On the other hand, there has been renewed interest in labor-management cooperation as a way of making American industrial companies more productive and competitive.

Labor Laws

Commencing with the enactment of workmen's compensation laws in most of the states by 1920, government legislation has increasingly become an instrument for improving the conditions of working men and women. Labor laws have exerted a profound effect upon the way human resources have been managed within work organizations. Below is a chronological listing of the principal Federal labor laws which regulate labor-management relations and personnel practices.

a. National Labor Relations Act, as amended (Wagner Act—1935 and Taft–Hartley Act—1947): Guarantees to employees the right to form unions of their own choosing; requires employers to bargain with unions certified as bargaining agent by the National Labor Relations Board.

b. Fair Labor Standards Act—1938 (amended many times): Establishes a minimum wage and premium pay for hours worked in excess of 40 in a week.

c. Labor–Management Reporting and Disclosure Act—1959: Regulates the internal governance of labor unions and provides certain member rights.

d. Equal Pay Act of 1963: It is illegal to pay women less than men (or men less than women) where they are doing work that requires equal skill, effort, and responsibility.

e. Title VII—Equal Employment Opportunity (of Civil Rights Act of 1964) as amended by Equal Employment Opportunity Act of 1972; Executive Order 11246—1965 as amended: Both of these laws and the executive order prohibit discrimination in employment on basis of race, color, religion, sex, or national origin. They apply to hiring, testing, upgrading, pay, benefits, training, and other conditions of employment.

f. Age Discrimination in Employment Act of 1967, as amended: Prohibits discrimination against employees, 40 through 69 years of age, in regard to hiring, discharge, retirement, pay, and conditions of employment.

g. Occupational Safety and Health Act—1970: establishes specific health and safety standards in the workplace and provides for Federal (or in some cases state) enforcement.

h. Rehabilitation Act of 1973: Requires private employers having Federal government contracts to take affirmative action to hire and advance qualified handicapped persons.

i. Employee Retirement Income Security Act of 1974: Establishes standards for the operation of pension plans and protects employee rights to their pensions.

Rational Wage and Salary Administration

Years ago wages were set for individuals in a very haphazard manner. A person's pay frequently depended upon the strength of his personal ties to his boss, whether he had been hired during a period of business prosperity or recession, and a crude guess by management of the going rates in the local area. Increases in pay after a man had worked for a period of time were often based upon whim and expediency. Although this untenable situation still exists in some companies, the trend for the past thirty-five years has been toward rational, systematic pay administration.

Two major driving forces behind this movement have been the pressures generated by unions and the War Labor Board of World War II. Although the systems of logic of unions and those of management are often opposed in rela-

tion to wage determination, it has been clear that union pressures both at the bargaining table and through the grievance procedure have induced management to adopt a well-thought-out, defensible compensation program. In certain industries, such as steel, the union and managements have cooperated jointly to administer a job evaluation program. When it was called upon to resolve labor disputes and later when it was called upon to administer the wage stabilization program, the War Labor Board formulated a number of sound principles that were used in arriving at wage decisions in companies. In many cases the Board directed that companies establish formal wage structures, job evaluation programs, and reasonable pay administration policies.

Today industry has pretty well accepted the principles of basing internal wage differentials upon differences in job content, having a formal job-grade structure, and surveying the labor market area to ascertain going rates for jobs of equivalent content.

Education

Employee Training. Although the apprenticeship system of training workers has existed for centuries, it provided formalized training only for the small minority of workers who were in the skilled trades. Widespread training of production workers, and to some extent of foremen, began during World War II, with the Training Within Industry program. This program was designed to develop employee skills in manufacturing industries for the war effort. Many thousands received training in the three principal TWI programs of Job Instruction Training (JIT), Job Methods Training (JMT), and Job Relations Training (JRT). The principles and techniques developed in the Training Within Industry program have had a great impact upon industrial training in the years since. Industrial executives have learned that employees do not learn new jobs and new skills simply by watching others and by trial and error. The time required of the average person to reach acceptable performance can be significantly shortened by placing him in a proper training environment.

Management Development. Since the early 1950s American industry has devoted a great deal of time and money to formal management development programs. This has been owing to several factors. There has been a growing recognition that management is an emerging profession that depends upon a distinctive body of knowledge and teachable skills. Years ago businesspeople assumed that by working long years as an individual contributor, whether as a craftsman, clerk, or engineer, a worker would develop the necessary abilities to function as a supervisor or executive. Such an assumption proved to be false. Prospective managers must be placed in the proper environment involving both on-the-job and classroom learning experiences if they are to develop managerial skills.

Management development activities have taken many forms. They have included personnel assessment, performance appraisal, counseling, job rotation, and special assignments. They have included a large variety of in-service training courses, university programs, and conferences and seminars run by professional associations, consultants, and industry associations. A great many schools of management and schools of business at universities have been conducting special, nondegree, management education programs for middle and upper levels of management. Both the American Management Association and The Conference Board give a variety of management education short courses and seminars.

Organization Development

In the 1960s a new field of activity, namely organization development, was created. Objectives of organization development are to facilitate problem solving on the job and to improve the quality of decisions, to accomplish change more effectively, to reduce destructive conflict and make it more productive, to increase commitment to organization objectives, and to foster collaboration among individuals and groups. Organization development is often guided by an outside consultant having trained in applied behavioral science. Among the methods he or she may use are sensitivity training (laboratory training), managerial grid workshops, team building, confrontation meetings, survey feedback, change in organization structure, job enrichment, and process consultation.

Organization development is related to management development. However, management development focuses mainly upon improving the performance of managers as individuals, whereas organization development seeks to improve the overall performance of entire groups, departments, and the organization as a whole.

Human Relations and Behavioral Science

Management's interest in human relations commenced, for the most part, in the 1940s, especially after World War II. Many factors operated to cause this development at that time. The rapid expansion of unionism in the late 1930s and early 1940s caused management everywhere to be more sensitive to the problems and needs of its work force. Management could not ignore festering human problems and employee complaints because the union would not let these issues go unnoticed. Some managements saw the rise of unionism as a challenge to provide so sound a personnel program and so enlightened a leadership that their employees would find no need for a union.

Another factor causing management interest has been the rising educational attainment of the labor force. Educated employees demand better leadership. Industry and government have been employing more engineers, scientists, and technicians and fewer unskilled workers. The gulf separating managers from employees has narrowed. Educated employees want to contribute their ideas in the managerial decision-making processes.

Starting in the 1940s, academics in our universities produced a great body of published material dealing with human relations in industry. Much of this was based upon a growing body of research evidence.

The research experiments of Elton Mayo and his Harvard University colleagues at the Hawthorne Works of the Western Electric Company in Chicago from 1927 to 1932 created the theoretical and intellectual foundations of what we call the human relations movement. Human relations advocates in both the universities and industry advanced a number of propositions. They showed that the enterprise was a social system. The informal work group developed its own norms and standards and was a source of worker control. Human behavior has both its rational and nonrational components. Feelings and values are legitimate and important concerns of the manager. Human relations principles were turned into practice by means of supervisory training programs which emphasized concern for the worker, the need to be supportive and friendly, and the desirability of consulting employees on matters affecting them.

By the early 1960s the term "human relations" faded in popularity and the modern term "behavioral science" replaced it. Behavioral science is much more than a new label for a set of older concepts. Behavioral science is a branch of the social sciences. It consists of the disciplines of cultural anthropology, psychology, and sociology. *Behavioral science is essentially the scientific study of human behavior.* Modern behavioral science tends to emphasize sophisticated research and experimental designs. Educated managers in industry have shown a keen interest in trying to apply many of the important findings and prescriptions that have emanated from behavioral research and theorizing.

Modern behavioral science has tended to be normative and value-oriented. It is also humanistic and exhibits an optimistic view of the nature of people and their potentials. It tends to emphasize genuine employee participation in decision making, group methods of supervision, and concern for the development of interpersonal skills.

Significant contributors to behavioral science applied to work organizations have been Douglas McGregor, Frederick Herzberg, Rensis Likert, Abraham Maslow, Chris Argyris, Robert R. Blake, and Jane S. Mouton.[13] These people could be called the modern pioneers. They are now being followed by a second generation of important contributors.

GENERAL OBSERVATIONS

This chapter has explained the relatively recent emergence of personnel management as a distinct field of endeavor. We have examined the nature of management, both as a field of activity and as a group or class of people. It was shown that management involves working with and through others to accomplish organizational objectives. A manager alone does not operate a machine, design products, or wait on customers (except in an emergency). He or she creates the environment in which employees can work effectively to accomplish the goals of the enterprise and at the same time obtain substantial satisfaction of their needs.

[13]Douglas McGregor, *The Human Side of Enterprise* (New York: McGraw-Hill Book Company, 1960); Frederick Herzberg, *Work and the Nature of Man* (Cleveland: World Publishing Company, 1966); Rensis Likert, *The Human Organization* (New York: McGraw-Hill Book Company, 1967); Abraham Maslow, *Eupsychian Management: A Journal* (Homewood, Ill.: Richard D. Irwin, 1965); Robert R. Blake and Jane S. Mouton, *The Managerial Grid* (Houston, Texas: Gulf Publishing Co., 1964); Chris Argyris, *Integrating the Individual and the Organization* (New York: John Wiley & Sons, Inc., 1964).

We noted some important issues in the 1980s that affect the management of people at work. We have provided an introduction to the management of people at work (or human resource management) by giving several examples of personnel management activities that illustrate the rich variety and challenge it entails.

An analysis of the changes that have occurred in the American labor force over the past several decades gives us a better picture of the situation encountered by the modern executive who must establish realistic policies for managing a work force. Perhaps most notable of these developments have been the rising standard of living enjoyed by American workers and their greater educational attainment. The modern work group is in a position both to expect more from the employer and to make substantially greater contributions to the running of the business than was its counterpart of two and three generations ago.

We have traced the developments in theory and practice of managing people in work organizations. Management has gained, over the years, a more realistic appreciation of the great worth and potentialities of its work force both in terms of individuals and the group as a whole. Because people are truly the most precious resource of any company, management has evolved rather elaborate programs for developing, maintaining, motivating, and caring for its work team.

Questions for Review and Discussion

1. Explain the reasons for the relatively recent emergence of personnel management as a specialized, professional area of management and as an academic discipline.
2. Define the term *management*. What are the functions of management?
3. Based upon your knowledge of personnel management to this point, what kinds of knowledge, skills, and training are necessary for successful performance in this field of work?
4. Why do you think such a large number of Federal labor laws such as the National Labor Relations Act, equal employment opportunity laws, and the Occupational Health and Safety Act have been enacted? Do you think such laws are necessary or would a system of "voluntarism" work just as well?
5. What effect has the higher educational attainment of the labor force had upon management-employee relationships?
6. Why has there been a long-term decline in the percentage of unskilled in the labor force, whereas the number of white-collar workers has increased greatly?
7. Describe prevailing philosophies of entrepreneurs and economists during the nineteenth century as they relate to management, work, and workers.
8. What was the "scientific management movement"? What has been its effect upon the field of personnel management?
9. Describe the relationship of the following to personnel management theory and practice:
   a. The growth of unions
   b. Human relations and behavioral science
   c. Rational wage determination
   d. Industrial psychology

Suggestions for Further Reading

Ellig, Bruce R. "The Impact of Legislation on the Personnel Function," *Personnel*, Vol. 57, No. 5 (September–October 1982), pp. 49–54.

George, Claude S., Jr. *The History of Management Thought*, 2nd ed. Englewood Cliffs, N.J.: Prentice Hall, Inc., 1972.

Ginzberg, Eli, Daniel Q. Mills, John D. Owen, H. L. Sheppard, and M. L.

Wachter. *Work Decisions in the 1980s.* Boston: Auburn House Publishing Co., 1982.

Ling, Cyril C. *The Management of Personnel Relations: History and Origins.* Homewood, Ill.: Richard D. Irwin, Inc., 1965.

Merrill, Harwood F., ed. *Classics in Management,* Rev. ed. New York: American Management Associations, 1974.

Mills, Ted. "Human Resources—Why the New Concern?" *Harvard Business Review,* Vol. 53, No. 2 (March–April 1975), pp. 120–134.

Schneider, Harold L. "Personnel Managers Look to the 80s," *Personnel Administrator,* Vol. 24, No. 11 (November 1979).

Sovereign, Kenneth. *Personnel Law.* Reston, Va.: Reston Publishing Company, Inc. 1983.

"A Work Revolution in U.S. Industry," *Business Week* (May 16, 1983), pp. 100–110.

Philosophy, Principles, and Policies

The pattern of beliefs, attitudes, and values of those who establish and manage an organization sets the tone for that enterprise in all of its relations with its customers, employees, shareholders, suppliers, and the public at large.

Executives, especially businessmen and women, sometimes hold that they are practical people who handle each problem on the basis of its merits and of the situation. If asked to express their philosophy of management, many would be hard-pressed to articulate a unified, consistent set of guiding principles. Yet whether they express their philosophies or not and whether they are always fully aware of it or not, those who manage the work organizations of our society usually possess some fundamental beliefs about the nature of man and his behavior in an organizational context. To a considerable extent each enterprise possesses a distinctive personality or character. Often this business character is a reflection of the person who founded the firm, as is the case of Thomas Watson and the International Business Machines corporation or of George Eastman and the Eastman Kodak Company. In other cases the corporate character seems to transcend the personality of any one man, as with the former Bell Telephone System (American Telephone

and Telegraph Company). But in any event a particular image or character comes to one's mind at the mention of any of these companies.

In this chapter we shall examine the roles of philosophy and ethics in shaping the character of an organization, with particular reference to the management of people. The basic beliefs and assumptions that managers hold regarding the nature of man and the behavior of people in organized group activity determine the methods and procedures they employ to accomplish organizational objectives. We shall examine also the important issue of organizational objectives, especially with reference to a business enterprise. In guiding the affairs of a company, executives apply a certain philosophy or set of guiding principles to achieve the goals of the organization. If the goals are unclear or contradictory the business may founder. Likewise if the philosophy or creed of those in charge is confused or in conflict with prevailing standards of morality in the society of which it is a part, then again the enterprise is likely to fail.

Finally we shall examine the subject of personnel principles and policies. We shall discuss the necessity for creating a set of sound personnel policies and for communicating and applying these throughout the organization.

ETHICS AND MANAGERIAL PHILOSOPHY

Ethics, which is a set of moral principles, should play a very significant role in guiding the conduct of managers and employees in the operation of any enterprise. Although there are those who would say that any action that optimizes profit and that conforms to the established laws of the land is justified, such a standard is clearly insufficient. The traditional "ethics of the market place" are no longer adequate behavior in our society, if indeed they ever were.

Ethics is concerned with what is right and what is wrong in human behavior. It is normative and prescriptive, not neutral. It addresses the question of what ought to be. Ethics refers both to the body of moral principles governing a particular society or group and to the personal moral precepts of an individual.

From what source do people derive their moral principles? One major source has been the doctrines—primarily religious and political—that have been promulgated over the years since the beginning of recorded history. Significant among these have been the Mosaic Ten Commandments, the Athenian principles of democracy and individual excellence, the British conception of individual justice under the law, the U.S. Declaration of Independence, the Bill of Rights of the U.S. Constitution, and the United Nations Declaration of Universal Human Rights. Another source is the values and norms of a given society. These are related to religious teachings, custom, and tradition, and vary from society to society. Among mankind in Western Europe and North America the principles of human dignity, personal freedom, and the rights of private property ownership have been highly valued. A further guide to ethical conduct is the codes and standards formulated by particular organizations, professions, fraternal groups, and business groups. Thus such diverse organizations as the American Medical Association,

Rotary International, The National Electrical Manufacturers Association, The Association of Consulting Management Engineers, and a great many corporations have drawn up formal statements of ethical standards to guide the conduct of their members.

Some people subscribe to a utilitarian reference in determining what is right and what is wrong. They hold that a proposed course of action be judged from the standpoint of the greatest good for the greatest number of people. From this point of view there are few absolute standards and each issue must be judged by studying its impact upon all affected parties.

Simple moralistic and religious precepts such as the "golden rule," while desirable as a foundation, are seldom sufficient to guide human decisions that often require an evaluation of several competing interests. Should salary increases be based upon merit or seniority? In order to provide jobs for racial minorities, should an employer reject qualified nonminority individuals who are competing for the same limited job openings?

We must recognize that generally accepted values change over time. Child labor in industry was widely accepted in the United States until the middle 1930s. Today it is not only illegal but it is so widely rejected as to be scarcely a subject for conversation. Countless occupations were closed to women and blacks on a de facto basis until the mid-1960s. Prior to this time employers justified discrimination in their own minds. But since the 1960s there has been a pronounced shift in public sentiment toward equal employment opportunity.

Because the business community exercises such a pervasive influence upon the economic, political, and social life of the American society, the general public has a right to expect high standards of moral conduct not only from business executives as individuals but also from the corporation itself as an entity. A chief executive officer cannot absolve his corporation from accountability for the acts of major executives who behave in a grossly improper fashion simply by saying that they violated company policy.

There are countless situations arising every day in the big corporation that put individuals to the test of ethical conduct. These are but a few:

1. Although management has a legal right to discharge a long-service employee who violated a certain company rule, should it do so in the instant case?
2. Are the advertising claims for a particular consumer product likely to mislead the public?
3. Is it proper for a top executive of a corporation to own a controlling interest in a principal supplier?
4. Does a large corporation that is the principal source of employment in a town have any moral duty to consider carefully the impact of its planned factory shutdown upon the town's economy and the lives of the population?
5. Is it ethical to seek actively to destroy the local union with which the employees have cast their lot because it interferes with the unrestrained operation of the business.

Public concern with ethical (and unethical) conduct in business and government is high. Transgressions by persons occupying high office tend to generate waves of public indignation, and well they should. Following the price-fixing conspiracy by major corporations in the electrical industry, Luther Hodges, Secretary of Commerce in President Kennedy's administration, convened a Business Ethics Advisory Council in 1961 to formulate a code of business ethics. Scandals—major and minor—do occur throughout each year. The fraudulent activities of the Equity Funding Corporation of America, which operated in mutual funds and insurance, were brought to light in 1973. Hundreds of millions of dollars were involved in illicit transactions. The uncovering of illegal corporate political contributions to president Richard Nixon's re-election campaign in 1972 (this information emerged from the Watergate investigations), opened up further investigations by the U.S. Department of Justice and the Securities and Exchange Commission. The general public learned for the first time that many of America's most respected and powerful corporations had, for a number of years, made illegal campaign contributions to candidates for United States public offices and had engaged in widespread foreign bribery to obtain business contracts from governments throughout the world.

More and more we see discussion of ethical issues in articles in management journals. One wonders whether the general level of morality and ethical behavior is rising or declining among personnel in our organizations—public and private. Measurement is difficult in this area but qualitative evaluations have been offered by various observers. Clarence Walton offers the view that personal morality in America is declining yet the level of moral performance of institutions is rising. He attributes the improvement in organizational morality to the internally enforced standards and controls of the formal organization upon the individual members. In other words the bureaucracy has been a positive force for righteous conduct.[1]

ORGANIZATION OBJECTIVES

The objectives of an organization are the results it wants to achieve. In place of the term *objectives*, executives sometimes speak of the terms *goals* or *purposes*. These three words are essentially synonymous when used in this context.

It is important that the leaders of an organization clearly establish its objectives and that

[1]Clarence C. Walton, *Ethos and the Executive* (Englewood Cliffs, N.J.: Prentice-Hall Inc., 1969), pp. 107–109.

the members of that organization agree upon these as desirable ends to be achieved. In democratically oriented organizations the members are expected to help shape the objectives.

Why is it important that the objectives of an organization be clearly established and agreed upon? There are many reasons for this.

1. Human beings are goal-directed. People must have a purpose. They must have something to work for. Announced organizational goals provide meaning to work.
2. Objectives serve as standards against which to measure performance.
3. If the participants in the organization have been sufficiently educated so that they believe in the objectives, then there is less need for close control of their behavior. Such education promotes voluntary cooperation and coordination. Self-regulated behavior is achieved.
4. Objectives stand out as guidelines for organizational performance. They help set the tone for action by participants. They also help establish the "character" of the organization.

Objectives of the Business Enterprise

In our discussion of organizational objectives, we shall concentrate upon the business enterprise because it stands as the cornerstone of productive activity in our society.

Fallacy of Profit as Sole Objective. Oftentimes we will hear employers or business executives assert that the only justification for the existence of their companies is to make a profit. This is lauded as the noblest of business objectives and is held to be consistent with the statement of Adam Smith, who described capitalism as a system in which every individual must have freedom to pursue his or her own economic self-interest and that in so acting, the natural forces

of competition would take hold to achieve the best interests for society as a whole. In talking in this vein the business executive may concede that his company has certain responsibilities it must meet, but these are all viewed as distinctly subsidiary to the primary goal of profit.

If a woman starts her own business concern and if she is the sole proprietor, her goal very likely may be to make as good a living for herself and her family as possible. In deciding whether she is making a good living, she would undoubtedly lump together the salary she draws from the business with the profit. Our sole proprietor may have subsidiary motives, such as engaging in a kind of business she enjoys and achieving respect from her employees and from the general public, but all in all, economic gain is still probably her most important goal.

Now if a business becomes incorporated and a number of shareholders acquire interests in the firm, then there is a tendency for the executives in charge to assume that the primary objective of operating the corporation is to make profits for these owners. This condition often prevails when the members of one family are major stockholders and are also active in the management.

But when a corporation grows substantially in size, when the ownership becomes diffused among many stockholders, none of whom possesses a controlling interest, and when the direction of its affairs is entrusted to a group of hired professional managers, we can say that the situation has changed substantially. The situation is especially changed when we are talking about a medium- or large-sized corporation that represents a concentration of great economic, social, and political power. Such a corporation may be the principal source of jobs, the major payer of property taxes, and, through its purchasing function, a major consumer in the area. As a group the managers may occupy positions of leadership in such organizations as the school boards of education, community chest, service clubs, charitable institutions, and religious bodies. Thus, the corporation may directly and indirectly exert vast power in a community, a region, or even the nation. The national influence is especially apparent in the case of large corporations that have plants throughout the country and in the case of large corporations that do a substantial portion of their business with the Federal government.

Proper Role of Profits. For the modern corporation profits are not an end in themselves. Profit is no more the only goal of a corporation than is eating the only goal of man. Profits, like food, are necessary for the continued existence of a business in a free enterprise economy. It must make profits to attract investment capital. Profit should be looked upon (1) as an incentive to produce goods or to perform services and (2) as one important guide for measuring the success of a firm.

However, profit and related monetary measures, such as costs and sales, should not be used as the sole measures of performance in an organization. Rensis Likert has presented some convincing arguments for using other measures in addition to these. He maintains that management can show a very favorable record in the short run by using pressure-oriented supervision and close controls when measured by conventional performance figures of output, cost, and profits. But the good record may be achieved at the expense of a depletion of human resources so that in the long run the whole organization may suffer. In addition to employing the usual measures of profits, costs, product quality, and technical efficiency, Likert argues in favor of evaluating the performance of an organization in terms of such factors as extent of member loyalty, extent to which the organization's objectives are compatible with members' own goals, level of members' motivation, amount of anxiety felt by people in the organization, character of the decision-making process, and adequacy of the communication process.[2]

Goals of a Modern Publicly Owned Corporation

Whereas the tendency formerly was to view the objectives of the corporation solely from the standpoint of its owners, now scholars and business executives conceive of the matter in much broader terms. A business enterprise has multiple goals and multiple interest groups who are intimately involved and who have legitimate rights and interests. The stockholders want a good return on their investment, the employees want job security and adequate wages, the customers want a product or service of specified quality, delivered on time and at a fair price. Suppliers want the firm to treat them fairly and pay prices that permit them to exist, and the community expects the modern company to be a good corporate "citizen" and to use its power in a way that advances the interests of the general public. The professional managers who direct the affairs of the enterprise are expected to balance the interests of all parties to the best advantage of all. A survey by the *Harvard Business Review* of approximately 3,500 corporate executives (primarily middle- and top-level managers in a wide variety of industries) revealed that a substantial majority believe that a corporation's duty is to serve as fairly and equitably as it can the interests of four sometimes competing groups—owners, employees, customers, and the public.[3]

It is pretty widely recognized that a business corporation really has multiple objectives. These may be viewed in the framework pre-

---

[2]Rensis Likert, *New Patterns of Management* (New York: McGraw-Hill Book Company, 1961), chs. 5 and 13.

[3]David W. Ewing, "Who Wants Corporate Democracy?" *Harvard Business Review*, Vol. 49, No. 5 (September–October 1971), pp. 146–147.

sented in the preceding paragraph, in which it is held that the corporation seeks to serve the wants and needs of the various interest groups that are vitally affected by it. Eells and Walton have expressed the objectives of the corporation as (1) profit making; (2) service; (3) social responsibility; and (4) survival.[4]

In *The New Industrial State* John Kenneth Galbraith devotes his attention to the very large American corporations and their interaction with our economic system. He has coined the term "technostructure" to designate that complex whole of managers, staff experts, professionals (engineers and scientists), and administrators who really make the key decisions and control the affairs of the corporation. From the standpoint of the technostructure, the goals of the corporation in rank order priority are (1) survival and a secure level of earnings; (2) greatest possible rate of growth as measured in sales; (3) technological virtuosity that creates new products, jobs, and customers; and (4) social goals such as building a better community, schools, public health, and the like.[5]

Social Responsibilities. Increasingly in recent years spokespersons for business and for the public have emphasized that business firms must bear substantial social responsibilities. We live in a very interdependent world. Urban crises, air and water pollution, strikes, plant shutdowns, and expansions of employment all have significant impacts upon both business and the general public. Few would now deny that private industry has a real stake in the welfare of the people and the nation. The enthusiasm with which top executives across the country contributed to the National Alliance of Businessmen, which was launched in 1968 to help solve the problem of the hard-core unemployed, attests to this recognition of their real social responsibilities.

The Committee for Economic Development is a private organization of corporate presidents and board chairpersons and university presidents that prepares policy recommendations based upon research and informed discussion. Its report dealing with corporate social responsibilities generally endorses business activities that help improve our society. It lists ten major areas in which companies in the aggregate are performing in the public and social area. These are economic growth and efficiency, education, employment and training, civil rights and equal opportunity, urban renewal and development, pollution abatement, conservation and recreation, culture and arts, medical care, and government. Under the heading of employment and training the report lists (1) active recruitment of the disadvantaged; (2) functional training and remedial education; (3) provision of daycare centers for children of working mothers; (4) improvement of work/career opportunities; and (5) retraining of workers affected by automation or other causes of joblessness.[6] Of course, not every corporation can provide substantial efforts in all of the ten major areas.

The Xerox Corporation grants paid leaves of absence to limited numbers of its employees to devote up to a year's time to social welfare projects ranging from aiding the mentally retarded to assisting exconvicts to resume life in their communities.

Schools of business and of management at a large number of universities now offer courses variously titled Management and Society or Business and Its Environment. These explore

---

[4]Richard Eells and Clarence Walton, *Conceptual Foundations of Business*, rev. ed. (Homewood, Ill.: Richard D. Irwin, Inc., 1969), pp. 534–537.

[5]John Kenneth Galbraith, *The New Industrial State* (Boston: Houghton Mifflin Company, 1967). Galbraith asserts that profit maximization is not a goal of the technostructure because it does not benefit this group once a level of earnings has been achieved that is sufficient to placate the stockholders. For the technostructure, growth is all important because it benefits this group with more jobs, more promotions, and more pay.

[6]*Social Responsibilities of Business Corporations* (New York: Committee for Economic Development, 1971).

the interrelationships of private business and the public. Among the issues they cover are business and government, business values and ideology, ethics and social responsibility, social power and responsibility, consumerism, minority and female job rights, and ecology.

Because of increased concern with social action programs by private business concerns, some leaders in the field have begun to undertake a systematic assessment of these activities. This work is just beginning. Mostly the top managements of individual companies have been asking such questions as What are we doing now? What should we be doing? How much does it cost? What results have we achieved? It is very difficult for a company really to measure what impact it has had in certain social areas. Thus, it may be hard to prove that a company's efforts to improve the quality of health care or of education in a community have had any demonstrable success. But an inventory of what a firm is actually doing and a frequent monitoring of this work ought to provide some qualitative gauges. And with time, top management, the employees, and the public can gain an appreciation of what is being done and where it is leading.[7]

Public and Nonprofit Organizations

When we think of public and nonprofit organizations we refer to such entities as government, the military, schools and colleges, hospitals, and charitable and philanthropic foundations. The profit motive does not exist in such institutions. Generally the motive of service to the organization's constituents is paramount. Other goals may be survival, stability, economy of operation, efficiency, and growth. But just as with the corporation, the goals are multiple, not unitary.

[7]For ideas on conducting a social audit of a company see Raymond A. Bauer and Dan H. Fenn Jr., "What Is a Corporate Social Audit?" *Harvard Business Review*, Vol. 51, No. 1 (January–February 1973), pp. 37–48.

MANAGING PEOPLE AT WORK

The way managers treat and deal with their subordinates in order to accomplish the multiple objectives of the organization is determined primarily by management's system of beliefs about the nature of man and about the determinants of cooperation in an organized endeavor. The fundamental assumptions that leaders hold condition their actions. How will they go about seeking performance from others? Will they trust people? exert tight control? centralize decision making? Or will they create the conditions by which people can create, achieve, and assume responsibility?

We shall portray two dissimilar frames of reference. One will be called the "traditional" or "authoritarian" philosophy. Certain principal components of this philosophy have also been referred to as "Theory X," the pessimistic view of man, and the bureaucratic approach to organization and management. The other school of thought we shall designate as the "modern" or "human resource" philosophy of management. This has also been given such appellations as "Theory Y," supportive management, management by integration and self-control, System 4 management, and the optimistic view of man. It should be clear upon reading these two descriptions that they represent wholly contrasting systems of belief. In actual practice the attitudes and behavior of business executives can be scaled along a continuum. Undoubtedly some clearly belong to the traditional camp, whereas others are entirely in the modern camp; but probably many managers also hold beliefs derived from both schools of thought. Some are also on the middle ground in their attitudes and day-to-day behavior.

Traditional (Authoritarian) Philosophy

An early and rather widespread view of man is that he is selfish, rebellious, and uncooperative.

Left to his own devices he tends to act in a mean and base manner. Therefore, the leader must be ruthless and strict in the way he controls men, even to the point of harshness. The classic spokesman for this type of reasoning was the Florentine nobleman and political philosopher Niccolò Machiavelli. He stated that the "end justifies the means." A prince or ruler must put aside such questions as integrity, morality, and honor. He should follow any tactics that will maintain himself in power and preserve the state or the army. Machiavelli asserted that it was desirable for the ruler to *appear* to be straightforward, humane, clement, and trustworthy but that he should always be ready to follow the path of evil if the occasion should arise. He should have a spirit to adapt to the varying winds of fortune.[8]

Thomas Hobbes in his *Leviathan* (1651) asserted that men are acquisitive, and seek power and prestige. They want what their neighbor possesses. Therefore, man must submit to the authority and law of a ruler and the state to regulate and constrain these avaricious and selfish tendencies.[9]

Another underlying theme has been "social Darwinism" or survival of the fittest. During the nineteenth century Herbert Spencer, the British philosopher, derived social implications from Charles Darwin's biological theory. He preached the doctrines of individualism, liberty of action, and survival of the fittest. He claimed that the weak, the infirm, and the intemperate must fall by the wayside. Ultimately only superior human beings would survive. This process would evolve toward a superior type of society.

The ideas Adam Smith propounded in his *Wealth of Nations* in 1776 have served for two hundred years as the basis of our capitalistic system. He argued that the wealth of a nation was best served when everyone pursued self-interest in the utilization of energy and capital. Government should not interfere in the economic system. Each person may seek as much private gain as possible, but the forces of competition in a free market will serve as a self-regulating mechanism. According to Adam Smith, the "invisible hand" of the market place, that is supply and demand and the price mechanism, provided a just allocation of scarce resources. Like Spencer, Smith glorified individualism and the pursuit of one's self-interest. Unrestrained competition and profit maximization ultimately resulted in the public good even though the individual entrepreneur sought only his own private gain.

In the field of employment relationships there are many who maintain that the company is in business to make a profit. The strongest and best-run firms survive; the inefficient ones fail. Likewise, among employees, individualistic competition is emphasized. The rewards go to the best producers, who are retained and promoted; those who are less efficient are demoted, laid off, or discharged.

In a capitalistic society in the Western world, the basic moral values to be derived from hard work, self-denial, saving, and pursuit of monetary gain have been preached, directly or indirectly, over the years. Max Weber has written a classic study in tracing the blending of the ideas of capitalism and those of Protestantism. In certain regions of Europe and in the United States this synthesis has resulted in the practice of the aforementioned behavior. It has been considered a necessary virtue.

During the late nineteenth and early twentieth centuries, a great deal of both fiction and nonfiction was written publicizing the assertion that those who rose to the top in industry did so because of hard work, perseverance, superior innate abilities, and greater energy. It was felt that abundant opportunity existed in America for anyone to achieve personal and economic success if he tried hard enough. If a person did not succeed in the business world, if he forever

---

[8] Niccolò Machiavelli, *The Prince,* Thomas G. Bergin, trans. (New York: Appleton-Century-Crofts, Inc., 1947). Machiavelli wrote this work in the year 1513.

[9] Thomas Hobbes, *Leviathan* (Indianapolis: The Bobbs-Merrill Company, Inc., 1958).

remained a laborer or a clerk, it was because he was lazy, noncompetitive, and unimaginative.

People in the Organization. According to Douglas McGregor, the traditional managerial view regarding people in a work organization is that the average worker has an inherent dislike of work, avoids responsibility, lacks ambition, and wants to be closely directed. Faced with this fundamental "fact" the only course open to management is to exercise close control and to coerce and threaten workers in order to get them to exert sufficient effort to attain organizational objectives. McGregor has labeled this managerial philosophy "Theory X."[10] In fact, if managers continually treat their subordinates as if these assumptions are actually true, this pattern of management can be self-validating. If one deals with subordinates as if they are indolent shirkers who cannot be trusted to behave responsibly, then they will tend to act that way, especially in an authoritarian environment.

A basic tenet of the traditional point of view is that the authority of the employer is supreme, the authority is synonymous with power, and that authority comes from the top and is transmitted down through the organization structure. Authority and controls are the basic integrating force. Control is exercised through command. The power and right to make decisions must be centralized at the top.

In such a system the front-line supervisor is viewed as an agent of higher management. His or her job is to obtain obedience to orders received from the boss. He or she tells subordinates what to do and how to do it. He or she is expected to exercise close supervision over their activities. He or she tends to be highly production-centered, not people-oriented. The supervisor is expected to meet production goals, control costs, and maintain proper product quality.

[10] Douglas McGregor, *The Human Side of Enterprise* (New York: McGraw-Hill Book Company, 1960), ch. 3.

Efficiency is enhanced when the organization is carefully defined and when job duties and responsibilities are clearly specified. Employees are expected to assume neither fewer nor more responsibilities than contained in their job descriptions. Maximum efficiency is achieved when policies, procedures, rules, and methods are clearly spelled out. The emphasis is upon fitting the person to the job rather than adapting the job to the individual. Standardized, predictable performance is the goal. This is the essence of the bureaucratic model of organization.

The motives that are tapped are primarily the lower-order needs: physical and economic security. In practice people are induced to produce through "the carrot and the stick." This means monetary incentives on the one hand and threats, fear, and the specter of discharge on the other hand. The response of the employees to such leadership can be either hostility or docile compliance. Actually those who rebel against authoritarian leadership tend to drift away from the organization; those who remain respond in a conforming sort of manner. They learn to accept it and gain certain economic and security satisfactions. They occupy a dependency relationship to their superiors and to the employer generally.

Authoritarian or Theory X management is very widespread and pervasive. It is standard in all military forces and is very common in private business, industry, and in government bureaucracy. It often is effective in achieving performance up to a certain level. It frequently achieves satisfactory results especially in the short run. But it seldom elicits real enthusiastic response from the organization members. High achievement, creativity, and a feeling of self-responsibility are sacrificed in favor of a moderate level of predictable and regimented performance.

Paternalism. A fairly common variant of traditional, autocratic management is paternalism. This is basically benevolent autocracy. Management treats its employees well by providing job security, decent working conditions, and adequate pay. In return the employees are expected to be cooperative, loyal, and productive. A dependency relationship is created. The organization members are expected to be docile and do what they are told. As long as they stay in their place, they will be taken care of adequately. But the people are not expected to stand on their own two feet and make decisions for themselves. There is little delegation of authority and responsibility in a paternalistic enterprise. As in the bureaucratic autocracy, decision making and influence are tightly held at the top. In the paternalistic enterprise people are taught to expect that the organization will take care of them in time of trouble if they themselves have been loyal to the organization.

Role of the Union. Traditionalists in management generally do not accord a real place for a union in their thinking. They tend to feel that the authority of management should be supreme and that if a union represents the employees, it will try to restrict management's freedom of action. If a union has won bargaining rights and certification as a result of a National Labor Relations Board election, then management will certainly recognize the union and bargain over wages, hours, and other conditions of employment as required by law, but there will be no attempt by management to open up to bilateral determination any subjects that are not absolutely required by law. In effect the union will be confined to as small a role in the affairs of the business as possible.

Modern (Human Resource) Philosophy

The modern philosophy of management is based upon an optimistic view of the nature of women and men. They are considered to be potentially creative, trustworthy, and cooperative. They are not inherently predatory. They are not predisposed by inheritance or instinct to be either mean or good. Rather their behavior reflects the character of their life experiences as they mature. People have potential for growth, achievement, and constructive action with others. It is the job of management to nurture and tap these productive drives.

The writings of such behavioral scientists as Douglas McGregor,[11] Rensis Likert,[12] Chris Argyris,[13] Frederick Herzberg,[14] and Blake and Mouton[15] are richly illustrative of this modern school of management thought. This philosophy is somewhat ahead of actual practice in industry, although executives in the more progressive organizations are generally familiar with these ideas on the intellectual level and some have applied them in their day-to-day activities. As indicated previously, this pattern of management has been variously called "Theory Y," supportive management, and management by integration and self-control. Rensis Likert calls it "System 4" management.

Advocates of this school of thought hold that people possess innate capacity for exercising initiative, accepting responsibility, and making worthwhile contributions. They do not inherently dislike work. Work can be a meaningful, satisfying experience. Employees will actively work for the goals of the organization when such behavior is compatible with their own goals. This demands an integration of the goals of the organization with those of the individual. Commitment to organizational objec-

[11] Ibid.

[12] Rensis Likert, *The Human Organization: Its Management and Value* (New York: McGraw-Hill Book Company, 1967).

[13] Chris Argyris, *Personality and Organization* (New York: Harper and Row, 1957); and *Integrating the Individual and the Organization* (New York: John Wiley & Sons, Inc., 1964).

[14] Frederick Herzberg, *Work and the Nature of Man* (Cleveland: The World Publishing Company, 1966).

[15] Robert R. Blake and Jane Mouton, *The Managerial Grid: Key Orientations for Achieving Production Through People* (Houston: Gulf Publishing Company, 1964).

tives is a function of the rewards associated with their accomplishment. Although external controls may be available, it is felt that the best control of employee behavior is self-control. Management should share information and objectives with subordinates. It is also advised to establish a climate where employees may contribute toward decisions affecting the business in those areas where they possess competence.

What is the role of the front-line supervisor under supportive, or Theory Y, type of leadership? He is expected to build a team that has a strong sense of responsibility for getting work done. He also is expected to represent his group to higher management as well as represent organizational needs to his people. He goes to bat for his employees when warranted. He has trust in them and they trust him. He tries to understand their problems. He is both people- and production-centered.

Whereas traditional management depends primarily upon economic motivation and "the carrot and the stick," Theory Y holds that all motives—economic, social, egoistic—must be activated. The employee is most highly motivated to work when the motivation is intrinsic—that is, the person derives satisfaction from doing the work itself. Emphasis is placed upon activating the higher motives of responsibility, recognition, achievement, and innovation. People are taught to accept responsibility and exercise self-control. External discipline and control are minimized when employees and supervisors control their own behavior. They evidence a high degree of commitment to the company and its programs.

Some critics have mistakenly asserted that the style of management we have been describing is soft or ineffective. They say that management relinquishes its responsibility to run the business. Manifestly this charge is not true. Modern supportive management seeks to enlist the full creative energies of all organization members. It is more of an open system. Information is widely not narrowly shared. Under authoritarian leadership the planning and controlling are done by top management and the doing is carried out by the employees. But the more modern approach involves a wider spectrum of members in the planning, doing, and controlling processes. Nevertheless, management still bears full and final responsibility for guiding the enterprise and achieving results.

How widely have the concepts we have been discussing become accepted by management practitioners? An interesting research project bearing on this subject has been conducted by Haire, Ghiselli, and Porter, all of the University of California. By means of a questionnaire they surveyed the attitudes of 3,000 managers in fourteen different countries throughout the world. They probed four areas of the manager's belief system: (1) belief in the individual's innate capacity for initiative, individual action, and leadership; (2) belief in the value of sharing information and objectives; (3) belief in participative management; and (4) belief that individual control should be by self-control rather than control by supervisors. The results of their survey revealed a paradoxical condition. Rather generally the managers surveyed believed in shared objectives, participation, and individual control; yet they tended to have serious doubts about the capacity of people to demonstrate initiative, individual action, and leadership. The situation is paradoxical because the first premise above is a precondition for applying concepts 2, 3, and 4. The researchers conclude that their findings reveal a basic lack of confidence in the abilities of other people and that democratic leadership cannot succeed unless executives come to believe that lower-level personnel are capable of making worthwhile contributions at the decision-making level.[16]

Authority in the organization is viewed in a

[16] Mason Haire, Edwin E. Ghiselli, and Lyman W. Porter, "An International Study of Management Attitudes and Democratic Leadership," Symposium Paper A9a, *International Management Congress*, CIOS XIII, 1963.

less absolute manner. The traditionalist maintains that authority is a fixed body of legitimate rights and powers that reside in the board of directors and the president of the organization. These are delegated down through the chain of command as required. The behavioral view is that authority and power become effective only when people accept them. A manager's influence and ability to get results are highly dependent upon the kind of relationships she or he builds up with subordinates, peers, and superiors. Three managers may appear in the same level in the organization chart and yet each may effectively possess quite different amounts of authority and influence.

One practical manifestation of the human resource or modern approach to management is "management by objectives." Management by objectives is a system of management in which there is genuine collaboration between managers and their subordinates in developing performance goals and performance measures, and in evaluation of performance on an ongoing basis.[17]

Role of the Union. Although not all writers of the modern school discuss unionism, a few do. The newer view accords a more significant role for the union than does the traditional philosophy of management. The union is not looked upon as the "enemy" or as a force that exists to make management's job more difficult. Rather it is recognized that for many sound reasons the union plays a very vital part in representing the interests of the employees. The process of managing the work force in an organization is probably the most important of all management functions. The holding of discussions with elected union leaders to make mutually satisfactory decisions on such issues as wage rates, work loads, transfers, safety, and employee suggestions is viewed as a legitimate way of managing the work force.

[17] The concept of management by objectives was originally formulated by Peter Drucker in *The Practice of Management* (New York: Harper and Row, 1954), ch. 11.

Traditional vs. Modern—Which Approach?

It is perhaps safe to say that the vast majority of executives in work organizations throughout the world lean closer to the traditional philosophy of management than to the modern view. This is evidenced both by their beliefs and their practices. Acutally, it is somewhat more true of their practices than their beliefs. Many profess to believe in self-discipline, self-control, participation, group methods of leadership, management by objectives, development of subordinates' abilities, and the like, yet they continue to deny their people true opportunities for assuming responsibilities and for growing in the organization. Philosophically they hold that they would like to trust people more and grant more discretion to their subordinates; yet they continue to hoard company information and centralize decision making.

It seems reasonable to assume, however, that as the level of education of people in work organizations continues to rise and as more highly talented people enter industry, executives will come to grant greater autonomy and discretion to their people. Also as younger generations of managers rise in the business world, they will gradually apply more of these concepts of modern management, which they absorbed while in college and from participation in management education programs.

Tannenbaum and Davis do see a trend toward acceptance of Theory Y (McGregor) or System 4 (Likert) as a philosophy and style of management. They assert that growing evidence suggests that humanistic values not only resonate with an increasing number of people, but also are highly consistent with the effective functioning of organizations built on the newer organic model. Among the specific value changes that they believe are occurring are the following: (1) away from negative evaluation of individuals toward confirming them as human beings, (2) away from fearing differences among people toward accepting and utilizing them, (3) away from maskmanship and game playing toward authentic behavior, (4) away from distrusting people toward trusting them, and (5) away from primary emphasis upon interpersonal competition toward a much greater emphasis upon collaboration.[18]

PERSONNEL POLICIES

A policy is a plan of action. It is a statement of intention committing management to a general course of action. When management drafts a policy statement to cover some feature of its personnel program, that statement may often contain an expression of philosophy and principle as well. Although it is perfectly legitimate for an organization to include philosophy, principles, and policy in one policy expression, it is well for the thoughtful student of personnel management to be able to separate the expression of principle from the policy statement.

The following is a statement of principle or objective in regard to the health and safety of company personnel:

> It is the intention of the company to provide a safe plant and a healthful working environment.

It can readily be seen that such a statement is quite general. A policy statement on the other hand is more specific. It commits management to a rather definite course of action, as shown in the following statement:

> Our policy is to institute every practical method for engineering safety into our processes and equipment, to provide protective clothing where necessary, to train employees in safe operating procedures, and vigorously to enforce estab-

[18] Robert Tannenbaum and Sheldon A. Davis, "Values, Man and Organizations," *Industrial Management Review,* Vol. 10, No. 2 (Winter 1969), pp. 67–86.

lished safety rules. Our policy is to provide a healthful plant by giving adequate attention to cleanliness, temperature, ventilation, light, and sanitation.

A policy does not spell out the detailed procedures by which it is to be implemented. That is the role of a *procedure*. A procedure is really a method for carrying out a policy. A policy should be stated in terms broad enough for it to be applicable to varying situations. Lower-level managers who apply policy must be allowed some discretion in carrying out the policy. The circumstances in Department A may differ from those in Department B; hence a rigid, excessively detailed policy statement might cause an injustice if supervision were not granted some latitude.

Why Adopt Definite Policies?

Many organizations of all types have never created a set of personnel policies. Top management has never been sufficiently aware of the hazards of operating without them nor of the advantages to be gained from establishing a sound group of policies. Why should an organization have clearly established policies?

1. The work involved in formulating personnel policies requires that management give deep thought to the basic needs of both the organization and the employees. Management must examine its basic convictions as well as give full consideration to prevailing practice in other organizations.
2. Established policies assure consistent treatment of all personnel throughout the organization. Favoritism and discrimination are thereby minimized.
3. Continuity of action is assured even though top management personnel change. The president of a company may possess a very sound personnel management philosophy, he may carry the policies of the organization

in his head, and he may apply them in an entirely fair manner. But what happens when he retires or resigns? The tenure of office of any manager is finite. But the organization continues. Policies promote stability.

4. Policies serve as a standard of performance. Actual results can be compared with the policy to determine how well the members of the organization are living up to professed intentions.

5. Sound policies help to build employee enthusiasm and loyalty. This is especially true where the policies reflect established principles of fair play and justice and where they help people grow within the organization.

Policies Should Be in Writing

Although this proposition may seem self-evident, countless companies have never bothered to reduce their practices, customs, and traditions to writing. In fact many executives actually are opposed to writing the personnel policies on paper and disseminating them to all concerned. They contend that such action would tie their hands and limit their freedom of action. Now if these executives mean that it would prevent the continued application of expediency and inequitable treatment, the answer is yes, it would. But if they reject management by expediency and intend to abide by reasonable principles, then the answer is no. Written policies do not so tie the hands of management that it cannot use some discretion and flexibility in handling particular cases. Policies are stated in broad terms. They are designed to aid the operation of the business, not impede it.

Written policies let everyone know just what kind of treatment she or he can expect to receive from management. They let one know where one stands. Only when policies are reduced to writing can they be communicated to all employees.

In large organizations containing many dispersed plants, written policies are almost a ne-

cessity. They insure reasonably consistent treatment throughout the company on such matters as pay, promotion, transfer, layoff, pension rights, insurance benefits, training opportunities, and grievance handling.

Formulating Personnel Policies

If the chief executive officer of a company should decide that the time has come to prepare a comprehensive statement of personnel policies, what should the content be? How does management decide what its wage policy or its hiring policy should be? Policies are not created in a vacuum. There are five principal sources for determining the content and meaning of policies. These are (1) past practice in the organization; (2) prevailing practice among other companies in the community and throughout the nation in the same industry; (3) the attitudes and philosophy of the board of directors and top management; (4) the attitudes and philosophy of middle and lower management; and (5) the knowledge and experience gained from handling countless personnel problems on a day-to-day basis.

Because people are free to resign from their jobs and take employment elsewhere and because any company must make its employment opportunities attractive enough to recruit new people into the business, management must so design its personnel policies that they reflect current good practice. If all other companies grant two weeks of paid vacation after a year's employment, then it would be unsound for a firm to grant no paid vacation. Likewise, if prevailing practice is to pay a 10 per cent premium to those who work the evening and midnight shifts, then a company that hopes to attract and retain qualified people must do something similar.

The actual work of formulating the written expressions of company personnel policy generally will be done by the personnel director, who will study existing documents, survey industry and community practices, and interview other executives within the organization to collect appropriate information. The actual and final decisions on the substantive content will, in most instances, be made by the president and the board of directors. Although the entire statement of personnel policy could be prepared by a very small group at the top of the structure or even by the president alone, there is considerable merit to the practice of bringing members of middle management (or even lower management in very small organizations) into the deliberations. These people can make particularly valuable contributions when it comes to evaluating the advantages and disadvantages of existing practices. And, of course, if these members of the management team are consulted, they will tend to support the fruits of their efforts when it comes to applying the policies.

Communicating Policies

The statement of the personnel policies does little good if it is locked in the company president's desk. It must be communicated throughout the organization.

All members of management, including shop foremen and office supervisors, are vitally concerned because they must interpret and apply the policies. Not only must the policies be communicated to all management personnel, but also a real education program should be set up to teach them how to handle various personnel problems in the light of the newly enunciated policy. A policy is worthwhile only when it is carried out on a day-to-day basis.

Many organizations publish and disseminate their personnel policies to all supervisors and managers by means of policy handbooks. These handbooks are often in looseleaf form to facilitate the insertion of new and changed policies. Often these books contain information on implementation of policies as well.

The most common way of informing nonsupervisory employees is by means of the employee handbook. But to achieve real understanding this should be followed up with an oral explanation and interpretation generally by first-line supervision.

Questions for Review and Discussion
1. What role should ethics play in the management of a business corporation?
2. Discuss possible ethical and policy implications of the following:
   a. Choosing individuals for promotion when there are whites, minorities, and females to select from
   b. Possible actions by managers when their subordinates challenge the propriety of certain orders or directives given to them
   c. The contemplated closing down of a plant due to declining profit margins where the plant is the principal employer in a community
   d. Determining the size of pay increases to be granted to salaried employees in a department
3. Why is it desirable for management to clearly establish the objectives of the organization?
4. Discuss the role of profit in the context of corporation objectives.
5. How do the goals of the family-owned company typically differ from those of the large, professionally managed, publicly owned corporation?
6. How might top management of a corporation translate a concern for social problems in the community into action?
7. Describe the "traditional" concepts of the nature of man and the ways of managing people in a work organization.
8. Describe the "modern" philosophy of the management of people.
9. What is "management by objectives"?
10. Why should an organization establish a definite set of personnel policies? Why should they be in writing?
11. Do policy statements "tie the hands" of management?

PROBLEM 1

Ms. Carson, having just finished her junior year in college, obtained a summer job as a teller in the branch office of the Central City Commercial Bank. She was majoring in social science in college. This was her second summer with the bank; however, she was new to this particular branch.

This branch office was located in a declining commercial-residential section of the city. Much of the housing was substandard and a substantial number of the residents were either retired and subsisting on their monthly Social Security checks or else they were living on meager incomes or on welfare.

The first month on the job was uneventful as Ms. Carson became adjusted to the routines of cashing checks, processing deposits, counting money, and reconciling the day's figures. Her relations with bank customers, fellow employees, and her supervisor were cordial.

One of the many services provided by this bank was that of a collection agent for the Mid-State Gas and Electric Company so that residents could conveniently pay their monthly bills. Ms. Carson observed that invariably power company customers paid their bills about the second week of each month and that they were required to pay a 5 per cent penalty. The power company bills stipulated this penalty on all accounts paid after the first of the month. When she advised a number of individuals that they could save this penalty charge by paying before the first day of the month, they explained that they could not afford to pay their electric bills until they had received their welfare or Social Security checks. These usually arrived on the third or fourth day of each month. Ms. Carson felt that these unfortunate people were not in a position to readily pay the 5 per cent penalty and that they were caught up in a huge impersonal system.

Having a social conscience and a desire to help these poor customers in some small way, Ms. Carson decided to write a letter to the Mid-State Gas and Electric Company. She wrote the letter on her own time at home one evening and addressed it simply to the "President" of the power firm. In the letter she pointed out that a great many of the persons paying their bills at this particular bank were impoverished and were subsisting on either Social Security or welfare checks that arrived on the third or fourth day of the month. It would be very dersirable if his company could change the date before which bills must be paid, without incurring a 5 per cent penalty, from the first to the tenth day of the month. Ms. Carson closed her letter by saying that this slight adjustment in the due date would probably cause little difficulty to the Gas and Electric Company but that it could give company officials a real sense of satisfaction by knowing that they had helped many unfortunate people in the community.

Ms. Carson never received a direct reply from the Mid-State Company. Instead, about ten days later, she was summoned to see Mr. Webster, the personnel director, at the main office of the Central City Commercial Bank. It was Mr. Webster who had hired her both last summer and this one and Ms. Carson had always considered him a warm, friendly person. She was unprepared for the harshness of his manner at this time.

Mr. Webster told her that the bank president had just received a letter from the president of the Mid-State Company threatening to remove its bill collection business (and possibly all its accounts) from the bank and to place it with a competitor bank because of the improper letter one of the bank's employees (Ms. Carson) had sent to him. The Mid-State president had considered it impertinent for one of the bank's employees to tell it to change its business practices for the convenience of certain customers whose cause Ms. Carson chose to champion. Mr. Webster told Ms. Carson that this was a very grave matter and that she must immediately write a letter of apology to the Mid-State president. Failure to do so would make it necessary for him to discharge her.

After recovering from her initial shock at the storm that had been raised over her simple letter, she countered by stating that she thought large companies ought to be socially conscious and responsive to the problems of people in the community. Mr. Webster replied that a private business was not a social welfare agency. He further stated that it was inappropriate to discuss social issues at this time. The problem at hand was the threat to the bank's relations with an important account. Would she or would she not write the letter?

Ms. Carson complied with this order and drafted a letter in Mr. Webster's office. His secretary immediately typed if for Ms. Carson's signature.

Ms. Carson went back to her job as a teller at the branch office and finished out the summer. Nothing more was said of the incident.

Questions

1. Was it improper for Ms. Carson to send the letter to the president of the gas and electric company? Discuss.
2. Evaluate the reaction of the president of the gas and electric company to her letter. How would you have reacted?
3. Evaluate the response of the president of the Central City Commercial Bank and particularly that of Mr. Webster in this case.
4. Is a social conscience on the part of the management of a private business enterprise compatible with traditional business practices?

PROBLEM 2: FILLMORE BUILDING SUPPLY AND LUMBER COMPANY

The Fillmore Building Supply and Lumber Company is a family-owned concern that has been in business for 80 years. There are three groups of people in the company: (a) the president, treasurer, and vice-president who are members of the Fillmore family, (b) the department supervisors and salesmen, and (c) sales clerks, office clerks, truck driver, mill equipment operators, truck loaders, and lumber handlers. Total employment is about 50.

Most of the third group above have a high school education or less. Their wage rates are only slightly above the federal minimum wage. The company has no pension plan, no company-paid health insurance, no group life insurance, and no lunch room. There is no formal wage structure. The rest rooms are dirty. Employees receive only a one-week paid vacation each year. Turnover among employees in the third group and among salesmen is very high.

Management treats the employees in a condescending manner. Supervision often prods the employees to work harder. A typical supervisor's remark is, "It's about time you guys did an honest day's work." Workers are not trusted. They are given little job discretion or responsibility.

Two years ago a few of the workers tried to form a union to improve wages and working conditions. Before the organizing attempt got off the ground the two leaders of the attempt were fired. This chilled employee interest in a union.

The employees show little loyalty toward the company. They generally do not work hard. Hard work, they reason, will do them no good. A typical employee comment is, "Hey, they are paying me minimum wage so it is only fair that I give them minimum work."

The unemployment rate in the area has been high for many years.

The Fillmore Company has a reputation in the community for selling high-quality building supplies and lumber. It is a profitable business.

Questions
1. Why do you suppose the management shows so little concern for the employees?
2. Can a management that is exploitive of its employees be profitable? How? Is profitability the best measure of a company's performance? Discuss.
3. If the employees appear to be lazy and unproductive, does this condition justify the Theory X behavior of management?
4. Do you think the kind of low-wage, exploitive policy of the Fillmore Company is common in America? Discuss.
5. What factors might change the management style and policies at Fillmore?

Suggestions for Further Reading

Eells, Richard, and Clarence Walton. *Conceptual Foundations of Business*, 3rd ed. Homewood, Ill.: Richard D. Irwin, Inc. 1974.
Foulkes, Fred K. *Personnel Policies in Large Nonunion Companies*. Englewood Cliffs, N.J.: Prentice-Hall, Inc., 1980.

Goodpaster, K. E., and J. B. Matthews, Jr. "Can a Corporation Have a Conscience?" *Harvard Business Review*, Vol. 60, No. 1 (January–February 1982), pp. 132–141.

Gorlin, Harriet. "An Overview of Corporate Personnel Practices," *Personnel Journal*, Vol. 61, No. 2 (February 1982), pp. 125–130.

Likert, Rensis. *The Human Organization: Its Management and Value.* New York: McGraw-Hill Book Company, 1967.

McGregor, Douglas. *The Human Side of Enterprise.* New York: McGraw-Hill Book Company, 1960.

Purcell, Theodore V. "A Practical Guide to Ethics in Business," *Business and Society Review*, Vol. 13 (Spring 1975), pp. 43–50.

Steiner, George A., and John F. Steiner. *Business, Government, and Society: A Managerial Perspective*, 3rd ed. New York: Random House, 1980; chs. 13, 14, 21, 22.

3

The Personnel Function

The work of personnel management pervades the entire organization. Personnel work must be carried on in the company too small to justify a separate personnel department. In larger establishments that do contain personnel departments, personnel management activities are performed by both operating managers and the staff personnel unit.

In this chapter we shall explore the terminology common to this field of endeavor, the personnel functions performed in organizations, the staff role of the personnel-industrial relations department, the division of authority and responsibility between line management and the staff personnel department in regard to the principal personnel functions, and organization of the personnel unit.

TERMINOLOGY

Over the years there has been some diversity in business practice in naming the function that is concerned with handling employment relationships. When specialized departments were first created in the 1920s and 1930s to handle the administration of the personnel program, they were usually called personnel departments. As a result of the rapid growth of unions in the 1930s and 1940s, many companies added the responsibilities of labor contract negotiations, contract administration, and grievance handling to the other activities of the personnel department. When this labor relations activity was combined with the personnel management work, many companies adopted the term *industrial relations* to apply to the new, enlarged function. This practice became especially prevalent in manufacturing companies, where the word *industrial* implied the concept of manufacturing and hence was deemed appropriate. In government, in hospitals and schools, and in nonmanufacturing industries such as trade and finance the term personnel department is very commonly used. This term is employed even when the employees are represented by a union and the labor relations function is prominent.

Another frequently encountered term is *employee relations*. In current practice, then, the three terms—*personnel management, industrial relations,* and *employee relations*—are generally synonymous. If we wish to make fine distinctions, we can say that *industrial relations* is most often used in manufacturing firms, especially where the employees are heavily unionized and labor-management relations represent a substantial portion of the total function. The term *personnel department* or *personnel office* is used more commonly in nonmanufacturing organizations and in organizations where either the workers are nonunion or only a moderate portion are unionized. The term *employee relations* is often applied to both union and nonunion situations and to manufacturing and nonmanufacturing. In very recent years some corporations have used the term *human resources* to designate their personnel departments.

What is the content of this work? What functions are included under the designation *industrial relations* or *personnnel management*? It encompasses the activities of recruitment and employemnt, human resource planning, employee training and management development, organization planning, organization development, wage and salary administration, health and safety, benefits and services, union-management relations, equal employment opportunity, and personnel research.

Looking at the matter from the standpoint of a field of knowledge or an academic discipline, we find that the terms *personnel management* or *personnel administration* have become widely accepted to designate that field concerned with all of the aforementioned topics plus applied human behavior areas such as supervision, motivation, work group behavior, communication, and managing change. In recent years schools of buisness administration and of management in universities have begun calling this academic area *human resources management* or *management of human resources.* The Academy of Management, which is a scholarly and professional society composed largely of university faculty members in schools of business and of management, changed the designation of its "manpower management" division to "personnel/human resources" division in 1975.

There are many departments, institutes, and schools of industrial relations (or industrial and labor relations) at colleges and universities throughout the country. These units carry on research, teaching, and extension programs in the whole broad areas of labor economics, organizational behavior, collective bargaining, labor law, income security, personnel administration, and labor union history and administration.

In order to be most accurate in describing this function or field of work in the business organization, it would perhaps be best to use the combined term *personnel management-industrial relations.* For the sake of conciseness, we shall use the term *personnel management* (or just *personnel*) and the term *industrial relations* interchangeably.

WHO DOES PERSONNEL WORK?

The very small company that employs, say, twenty-five or fifty people has no personnel department. Personnel policies and practices are generated by the president. Line management does the hiring, the training, the disciplining, and the firing. It establishes the rates of pay. Because the problems of production and sales usually seem more pressing to the employer, she or he generally does not develop a well-rounded, comprehensive personnel program. Decisions regarding employees are commonly made under the pressure of the situation without full regard for the long-run consequences.

In the larger organization it is not possible for the president and the line managers to handle adequately the many complex personnel management problems without specialized knowledge and help. Therefore, a personnel department must be established.

Now to the unsophisticated person it may seem that the creation of a separate staff personnel department is no different from the establishment of any other staff or service activity, such as engineering, purchasing, or advertising. If a company has grown to the point where functionalization becomes necessary, it can split off all product and equipment design work from line management and concentrate these duties in an engineering department. All relations with suppliers and the processing of purchase orders can be centralized in a purchasing department.

But personnel management is different from other staff specializations. Personnel management pervades the entire organization. Every individual who guides and directs the work of others, from the shop foreman all the way up to the corporation president, does personnel work. Now the nature of this work changes somewhat as one goes up the ladder of the organization structure. But regardless of level, every manager is truly a practicing personnel manager.

Consider for a moment the personnel management responsibilities of a first-line supervisor whether in factory or office. They are as follows:

Participate in the selection of new employees.
Orient new employees to their environment, organizational requirements, and their rights and privileges.
Train employees.
Provide face-to-face leadership.
Appraise performance.
Coach and correct.
Counsel.
Recommend pay increases, promotions, transfers, layoffs, and discharges.
Enforce rules and maintain discipline.
Settle complaints and grievances.
Interpret and communicate management policies and directives to employees.
Interpret and communicate employee suggestions and criticisms to higher management.
Motivate subordinates and provide rewards for good performance and behavior.
Eliminate hazards and insure safe working practices.

It is not truly possible to separate the human relations and personnel functions of operating management from day-to-day problems such as getting out production, controlling costs, and meeting quality standards. Many personnel problems arise during the course of directing the work force and giving orders and instructions.

STAFF ROLE OF THE PERSONNEL DEPARTMENT

The personnel (or industrial relations) department operates in an auxiliary, advisory, or facilitative relationship to other departments in the organization. Any staff unit, whether it be personnel or otherwise, exists to help the line or operating departments do their work more effectively. It has been created in the first place to take advantage of specialized talent and knowledge.[1]

The personnel department generally performs the following roles:

1. Policy initiation and formulation.
2. Advice.
3. Service.
4. Control.

Let us examine each of these activities.

Policy Initiation and Formulation. The executive in charge of the personnel department (who may be called the personnel director, the industrial relations director, or the vice-president in charge of personnel) is the one individual most actively involved in policy creation. It is his or her responsibility to propose and draft new policies or policy revisions to cover recurring problems or to prevent anticipated prob-

---

[1] Line and staff concepts are discussed further in Chapter 4, "Organization." Line positions and departments are those without which the organization could not function even for a day. In a manufacturing company those who make the product and those who sell it are considered line. In a department store, buying and selling activities are considered line. In a college the faculty members are line, whereas such individuals as the dean of students, manager of purchasing, and the controller are staff.

lems. Ordinarily these are proposed to the president of the company, and it is upon the latter's authority that the policy is actually issued. When proposing a new or revised policy the personnel director must analyze problems that have occurred in the past, survey other companies to determine how they handle similar situations, discuss the matter with colleagues and subordinates, and give due consideration to the prevailing philosophy in the organization. In effect he or she does all the necessary research and staff work, but in most cases the new policy is actually authorized by the president and/or the board of directors. On small policy matters the personnel director alone ordinarily may determine and institute policies.

Advice. A major portion of the activities of those engaged in staff personnel work is in the nature of counsel and advice to line managers. Countless examples can be given. A shop foreman may be confronted with a grievance over distribution of overtime. Another foreman may have a problem employee who she feels should be disciplined or even suspended. How should she go about doing this? At the time of the annual review of all salaried personnel for possible pay increases, the personnel manager plays a key role in advising operating managers on the administration of the program. An apparent concerted slowdown may occur in the assembly department. It may have been instituted by the union in retaliation for the cutting of piece rates the week before. How should production supervision handle this situation?

In all of the foregoing examples the personnel directors and their staffs are expected to be fully familiar with personnel policy, the labor agreement, past practice, and the needs and welfare of both the company and the employees in order to develop a sound solution. Successful personnel specialists must be people-centered. They must be sensitive to the feelings, wants, and motives of other people. At the same time they must continually be cognizant of their obligation to preserve the structure and functioning of the organization. In fact, this really is the essence of personnel management. Management must seek to so direct and coordinate the efforts of the people that the goals of the organization are achieved while at the same time providing need satisfactions for the members of that organization.

In carrying out the advice-giving role, the members of the personnel department do much more than simply supply oral advice to other members of the organization. Advice also includes the preparation and communication of bulletins, reports, and procedural guidelines for the interpretation and implementation of policy. For example, the personnel department issues explanatory statements regarding the implementation of equal employment opportunity policy, compliance with the Occupational Safety and Health Act, and the application of a new union-company labor agreement.

Service. The service responsibilities of the personnel department are apparent when one examines such things as the employment, training, and benefits functions. The tasks of recruiting, interviewing, and testing job applicants are performed in the personnel office. Training programs are planned, organized, and often staffed through the personnel office. The personnel group must see that adequate instructional materials and facilities are available. Once pension and insurance programs have been set up, all claims must be processed through the personnel department. The maintenance of adequate employee records is a service function that permeates all functional specialties within the personnel field.

Control. The personnel department carries out important control functions. It monitors the performance of line departments and other staff departments to insure that they conform to established personnel policy, procedures, and practices. The control function of the personnel department is quite comparable to the activities of a quality control group that measures product variables to insure conformance to engineering specifications or to the activities of the auditing staff that inspects accounting records to ascertain conformance with prescribed standards.

What are some examples of the control functions of the personnel–industrial relations department? There are many. Company policy may declare that all salaried employees shall be appraised as to performance and potential at least once a year. If certain supervisors fail to transmit their performance appraisal reports to the personnel office when required, then a follow-up is clearly required. A control activity of particular contemporary importance is that of monitoring operating departments and divisions to insure their compliance with Federal and state nondiscrimination and affirmative action programs.

As part of a continuing program for bringing the safety message to production workers, foremen may be expected to conduct a brief weekly safety meeting for their workers. If some foremen fail to do so, a member of the personnel department (usually the safety director) will certainly bring this matter to their attention. If discussion with the parties involved yields no direct improvement, then the safety director will generally bring the issue up with the foremen's immediate line superior.

A common form of staff control over line management personnel is *procedural control.* This means that managers and supervisors must follow established procedures in carrying out certain personnel management actions. For example, in order to discharge an employee who has allegedly committed a serious violation of a company rule, line supervision may have to follow a clearly defined procedure. Depending upon the particular circumstances, this may involve submitting written evidence, obtaining testimony of witnesses, notifying the union, and granting the person a full hearing.

To raise an employee's salary the supervisor generally must abide by certain procedures.

This may involve submitting a performance rating form at the time of the request, keeping the size of the increase and the total salary within prescribed limits, and doing this at certain designated times of the year.

Many times the personnel unit will conduct continuing audits of the line departments. Examples are measures of accidents, grievances, absenteeism, voluntary quits, and disciplinary actions. Quite often the control activities of a staff unit, such as the personnel department, require that it exert pressure upon line managers and supervisors. If the control work is not done with proper regard for the need to build a cooperative, healthy relationship with line personnel, serious dissension can occur. Personnel managers and their staff should exert their principal efforts toward counseling and educating line supervisors regarding the need for following established policies, procedures, and practices. The errant supervisor should be permitted to correct his or her ways first. If all attempts at persuasion fail, then, of course, the problem must be discussed with higher management.

PERSONNEL (HUMAN RESOURCE) FUNCTIONS

Just what is the content of personnel activities? As stated before, personnel management activities are carried on both by the staff personnel department and by operating management in the course of directing the activities of the work force. Let us now examine the principal personnel functions and note the more common division of responsibilities between the staff personnel unit and operating, or line, management. It should, however, be borne in mind that variation from the pattern described may occur in particular companies because of special circumstances.

Employment

This function includes recruitment, selection, and induction into the organization. The initial decision to add someone to the payroll is made by line management. It is also its responsibility to determine the content of the job to be performed and the employee qualifications necessary to perform the job satisfactorily. Very commonly, statements of job content and employee qualifications have been previously worked out jointly between line management and the personnel unit. These are recorded in the form of job descriptions and job specifications. The personnel department must develop and maintain adequate sources of labor. It must also set up and operate the employee selection system, which may include interviews, selection tests, a medical examination, and reference checks. Quite commonly the role of the personnel group is one of screening with the final decision to hire or reject being made by the supervisor who requested the new employee. However, in the case of a large-scale hiring program of unskilled or semiskilled workers, the personnel department is commonly granted full and final authority to make the hiring decision.

The new employee's supervisor bears important responsibilities for introducing her or him to the new work environment. This is often called *orientation* or *indoctrination*.

Transfer, Promotion, Layoff

For these tasks the personnel department serves primarily in a coordinative capacity. When employees are moved from one department to another either because of the needs of the business or because of individual requests, the personnel records may be studied to ascertain that they possess the requisite skills. Layoffs typically are processed by the personnel department to insure that the proper order of preference is followed. This can become quite complicated if combinations of job, departmental, and plant-wide seniority rights must be observed. When a vacancy occurs in a position, it may be filled by promotion from within or by direct hiring from outside the company. This decision is often made jointly between the personnel director and the executive in charge of the department where the vacancy has occurred. Many companies have established policies to cover matters of this type. The actual final decision as to which candidate is chosen for the promotion is largely made by the executive in whose unit the vacancy has occurred.

Training and Development

On-the-job training and coaching are performed by the line supervisor or by a specially designated employee who acts in the role of an instructor. It is the responsibility of the personnel–industrial relations group to determine training needs in cooperation with line management. Once the needs are established, the personnel training specialists must design a program to accomplish the desired results. If the program takes the form of in-service classroom courses, it usually is administered by the personnel unit.

Coaching, performance appraisal, and post-appraisal counseling, job rotation, understudies, and special broadening assignments are largely executed by operating managers but coordinated by a central personnel staff.

For those enterprises that are engaging in an organization development activity the personal manager or the personnel specialist serves in a consulting role to an operating department. He plans programs in cooperation with managers of operating departments, diagnoses "people" problems, conducts various workshop type programs, and provides feedback to the managers about ongoing problems.

Compensation Administration

The work of designing and installing a job evaluation program is handled, for the most part, by the personnel department with some consultation with line managers. The decision to adopt a particular pay structure with pay grades and fixed minimums and maximums for the grades is a top management responsibility.

The day-to-day work of analyzing jobs, evaluating their dollar worth according to a formal job evaluation plan, and maintaining suitable records is a staff personnel function.

Periodic wage and salary surveys of the labor market area are conducted by the personnel specialists, but any firm decision to raise or change the entire pay schedule is practically always reserved for the chief executive officer of the organization.

Health and Safety

A significant part of an occupational health program is the identification and control of agents within the working environment that can cause occupational disease. Some agents can be gases, dusts, fumes, toxic chemicals or metals, noise, heat, radiation, biological substances, and stress. Industrial hygienists are employed to identify and control such hazards to health.

Other important elements of an employee health program are pre-employment medical examinations, periodic examinations for those working on jobs having exposure to occupational disease-causing agents, rendering of first-aid, treatment of minor ailments such as colds and headaches, and providing health education information. Small companies typically hire physicians, nurses, and industrial hygienists only on a consulting or part-time basis. Large firms tend to be staffed with full-time personnel in these areas.

The safety program is directed toward the prevention of work injuries. The main elements are engineering, education, and enforcement.

The safety director, who is usually a member of the personnel department, works closely with the plant engineering unit to have machines and equipment properly guarded. New production processes and machines must be so designed and constructed that the possibility of human injury is remote. Employee safety education is a cooperative program conducted by both the staff safety director and all foremen. The safety director must prepare safety displays, distribute safety leaflets, and develop safety instructional material. Every foreman must instruct his or her people in how to perform their jobs safely. He or she may also be called upon to run a weekly safety meeting. Enforcement of safety rules is primarily a responsibility of every foreman.

Strong emphasis has been given to the health and safety function since the enactment of the Occupational Safety and Health Act in 1970. Of course, progressive companies recognized this to be an important area of management responsibility long before the adoption of this Act.

Discipline and Discharge

Discipline has two principal meanings. In the first sense it means "training that molds or corrects." This means the achieving and maintaining of orderly employee behavior because the people understand and believe in the established codes of conduct. The second meaning of the term *discipline* refers to punishment of wrongdoers.

The supervisor, whether in factory or office, must bear primary responsibility for training people to abide by the rules of behavior and for initiating punishment for the few whose conduct deviates from the norm.

The personnel department commonly assumes the responsibility for formulating the list of necessary rules together with the range of penalties for each offense. Frequently this list of rules and penalties is discussed and cleared with high-level line management before it is issued and communicated throughout the organization.

Most commonly, actual approval by the personnel department has to be obtained before an employee may be discharged. The reason is that discharge is a very severe penalty and should be used only when a very clear case can be shown. In addition, it is especially vital to achieve companywide uniformity in the handling of such cases.

Labor Relations

When a union has been certified by the National Labor Relations Board, as the result of an election, as the sole and exclusive bargaining agency for the employees, then management must bargain with it in regard to wages, rates of pay, hours of work, and other conditions of employment. The principal tasks involved in handling labor relations are contract negotiation, contract interpretation and administration, and grievance handling.

The personnel–industrial relations staff plays a very significant role in labor–management relations. The director of industrial relations usually serves as a key member of the bargaining team, often acting as chief management spokesman. In operating on a day-to-day basis under the terms of the labor agreement, line supervision often finds frequent occasion to consult the personnel staff regarding such matters as allocation of overtime, handling of transfers and layoffs, and the application of contract work rules.

Although nearly all grievance procedures as spelled out in the labor contract specify that the front-line supervisor shall be the first to hear and act upon an employee grievance, in all but the most routine cases the supervisor typically consults the personnel office before giving an answer. The personnel department is very commonly listed as either the second or third management step in the grievance procedure. In effect the personnel department representative is given line authority to make a binding settlement.

The personnel–industrial relations staff is granted such great authority in grievance handling in order to insure due regard for precedent and plantwide consistency of action. In addition, many grievances have plantwide or even companywide implications. Mishandling of a case could cause grave consequences.

Benefits and Services

Included under this category are pensions, group life insurance, hospital and medical insurance, sickness leave pay plans, supplemental unemployment compensation, loan funds, credit unions, social programs, recreational programs, and college tuition refund plans.

The actual decision to establish or to expand these programs is nearly always made by top line management upon the advice and consultation of the personnel staff. The actual design of pension and insurance programs requires a great deal of technical knowledge. These programs are generally worked out in conjunction with insurance companies or insurance consultants. After these plans are installed, the day-to-day processing of claims is handled by the personnel department.

Organization Planning

Organization planning requires the development of a concept of a company as a structure or system. It may require the delineation of the concepts of centralization or decentralization in terms of executive behavior and the locus of decision-making authority. The organization planning staff must prepare organization charts and position guides. It must counsel the chief executive officer and line management on organization theory and practice and with respect to company reorganization and expansion.

Originally this activity was carried on primarily in the office of the corporation president. And the president still has final responsibility in this area. But the growing complexity of large-scale enterprises and the increasing sophistication of organization theory has caused organization planning to emerge as a specialty in itself. The personnel office gathers data, does research, prepares plans, and gives advice to the office of the president in this vital area.

Organization Development

A Conference Board survey conducted in 1975 revealed that organization development has emerged as a major personnel activity since an earlier investigation in 1965.[2] Organization development (often called, simply, OD) is a general approach for improving the effectiveness of an organization that utilizes a variety of applied behavioral science methodologies. Among the objectives of OD are to increase the level of trust and supportiveness among people in the organization, enhance interpersonal skills, make communication more open and direct, directly confront problems, and to tap the knowledge of all who can contribute to problem solutions wherever they may be in the organization.

Consultants are often involved in OD work. They work jointly with management to collect data, diagnose problems, and work out solutions. Typical kinds of OD activities or interventions are confrontation meetings, team building, survey feedback, conflict resolution, T-group or laboratory training, and managerial grid exercises and projects.

Human Resource Planning

Another new function that has emerged in recent years is human resource planning (also

[2] Allen R. Janger, *The Personnel Function: Changing Objectives and Organization*, Report No. 712 (New York: The Conference Board), 1977, p. 48.

called manpower planning). Sometimes a specific person or office has this as its primary responsibility; more commonly the responsibilities are shared by several people within the corporate personnel unit. Human resource planning is the process by which a firm insures that it has the right number of qualified persons available at the proper times, performing jobs that are useful to the organization, and which provide satisfaction for the individuals involved. The principal elements involved in human resource planning are as follows: (1) goals and plans of organization; (2) current human resource situation including skills inventory; (3) human resource forecast including comparison of projected future demand for employees with projected supply; (4) designing programs to implement the plans (recruitment, selection, performance appraisal, transfer, promotion, training, motivation, compensation); and (5) audit and adjustment.

Many companies confine their human resource planning activities to those kinds of skills that are more commonly in short supply and that require a long development time. These are personnel in the managerial, professional, technical, and skilled trades fields.

Information and research data generated by manpower-planning specialists are made available to personnel officers and operating executives in the divisions and plants. The implementation of the plans is, of course, a collaborative activity among personnel officers and many operating managers throughout the organization.

Equal Employment Opportunity

Several Federal laws have caused both public and private employers to place great emphasis upon equal employment opportunity. Among these laws and regulations are Title VII of the Civil Rights Act of 1964 as amended, Executive

Order 11246 (1965) as amended, Equal Pay Act of 1963, and Age Discrimination in Employment Act of 1967. Employers are not allowed to discriminate in regard to race, color, sex, national origin, religion, or age. Government regulations require companies having more than 100 employees, or more than 50 employees if the company holds a government contract or subcontract, to designate an official to be in charge of the equal employment opportunity function and to serve as a point of contact with the government compliance agency.[3]

Very commonly the chief personnel executive in a company (that is, the individual in charge of the entire personnel department) bears the major responsibility for insuring that the organization complies with the various equal employment opportunity laws and regulations. She or he often delegates the day-to-day detailed administration to someone within the personnel department who either specializes in this field of work or who performs these duties along with others such as the employment function. Usually the chief executive officer (CEO) of a company, whether she or he be called the chairman of the board or the president, plays a key role in the formulation and implementation of equal employment policy.

In the Conference Board survey mentioned earlier, 97 per cent of the companies surveyed stated that equal employment opportunity had emerged as a major personnel function since 1965.[4]

Personnel and Behavioral Research

Although most companies do not conduct research in the personnel and behavioral area, there are some pacesetting firms which have done so. Among these are General Electric, In-

[3] Ibid., p. 83.
[4] Ibid., p. 40.

ternational Business Machines, General Motors, American Telephone and Telegraph, Procter and Gamble, and Texas Instruments. A major area of experimentation in recent years has focused on ways of simultaneously improving worker productivity and increasing the quality of working life. Other important areas for investigation are employee attitudes and motivation, predicting success in management, and organizational relationships.

Personnel Information Systems

Today, many organizations have staffs of people trained in mathematical analysis, computers, and management information systems. Some companies have applied these capabilities to personnel work. Among the applications have been human resource planning, skills inventories, employee benefits analysis, and productivity studies.

SURVEY DATA

A Bureau of National Affairs survey of 750 establishments (including manufacturing companies, nonmanufacturing businesses, and nonbusiness organizations such as educational institutions, hospitals, and government agencies) shows the broad range of activities performed by personnel departments. See Table 3-1. The data presented in this table also demonstrate that personnel activities tend to pervade the entire organization and are not carried out solely by the personnel department. For example, 54 per cent of the establishments centralize all the recruiting/interviewing/hiring activity in the personnel department. In 46 per cent of the establishments this activity is shared with other organizational units.

TABLE 3-1. Activities Handled by the Personnel Department.

| Activity | Per Cent of All Companies (750) | | | |
| | Extent of Personnel Department's Responsibility | | | No Such Activity at Company/Facility |
	All	Some	None	
Personnel records/reports/information systems	90	11	—	—
Unemployment compensation administration	87	9	2	1
Insurance benefits administration	85	11	3	*
EEO compliance/affirmative action	83	16	1	1
Personnel research	82	4	*	14
Wage/salary administration	80	19	1	*
Workers' compensation administration	79	13	7	1
Pre-employment testing	68	8	1	22
Tuition aid/scholarships	65	19	5	11
Job evaluation	65	32	2	2
Retirement preparation programs	61	12	3	24
Health/medical services	61	14	9	16
Promotion/transfer/separation processing	60	39	1	*
Induction/orientation	59	40	2	*
Vacation/leave processing	57	35	8	—
Pension/profit-sharing plan administration	56	27	9	8
Employee assistance plan/counseling program	55	18	2	25
Recreation/social/recognition programs	54	34	6	6
Recruiting/interviewing/hiring	54	46	*	—
Complaint/disciplinary procedures	50	47	1	1
Attitude surveys	50	9	2	40
College recruiting	47	14	3	37
Outplacement services	46	4	1	49
Union/labor relations	46	17	2	36
Employee communications/publications	45	33	17	4
Relocation services administration	45	17	4	34
Safety programs/OSHA compliance	44	38	17	2

TABLE 3-1. (Continued)

Activity	Per Cent of All Companies (750)			
	Extent of Personnel Department's Responsibility			No Such Activity at Company/Facility
	All	Some	None	
Executive compensation administration	43	30	17	10
Human resource planning	42	48	2	9
Supervisory training	41	47	7	5
Suggestion systems	35	19	9	37
Management development	34	49	8	10
Food services	33	6	29	33
Performance evaluation, nonmanagement	32	56	10	2
Community relations/fund drives	31	37	28	5
Thrift/savings plan administration	30	12	9	50
Career planning/development	27	40	3	30
Security measures/property protection	25	20	52	3
Management appraisal/MBO	22	49	11	18
Stock plan administration	21	11	10	58
Organization development	21	48	11	20
Payroll processing	17	29	53	1
Productivity/motivation programs	16	53	11	20
Skill training, nonmanagement	15	47	30	8
Public relations	14	32	49	5
Library	12	4	40	44
Administrative services (mail, phone, messengers, etc.)	12	15	72	2
Travel/transportation services administration	8	24	48	21
Maintenance/janitorial services	8	9	81	3

*Less than 0.45 percent
Source: ASPA-BNA Survey No. 46, *Personnel Activities, Budgets, and Staffs: 1982–1983*. Reprinted by permission from *American Society for Personnel Administration*, BNA survey, copyright 1983 by The Bureau of National Affairs, Inc., Washington, D.C.

ORGANIZATION FOR THE PERSONNEL FUNCTION

The executive in charge of the personnel department must be a member of the top management team. With assistance from members of the department he or she must set up management development programs, develop compensation plans for executives, advise the chief executive officer on compliance with equal employment opportunity regulations, and establish a viable relationship with the union which represents the hourly-paid employees. These are but a partial list of the many major executive responsibilities of the chief personnel officer in an organization. Truly the personnel department serves the entire organization. The executive in charge must have sufficient stature in the organization to be a trusted advisor and member of top management and to design and implement a really effective personnel program.

The top personnel executive should report organizationally to either the chief executive officer or the chief operating officer. Commonly in business organizations these officials are called the chairman of the board of directors and the president, respectively. Because the quality of the human resources determine the success of an enterprise, the executive in charge of personnel should be involved in top management meetings at which enterprise strategy, plans, and programs are formulated. In terms of job titles the top or senior executives in charge of personnel most commonly holds the title of vice-president. The term director (of personnel) is also frequently used.

Unfortunately, the presidents of some companies are ignorant of the proper role of a personnel department; hence they relegate it to a low level in the organization and staff it with unqualified people. This sometimes happens in small companies. Just because a supervisor gets along well with others and has accumulated many years of company experience, this does not mean that he is the ideal choice for personnel manager. Some company presidents have the erroneous notion that personnel work is primarily one of record keeping, keeping the workers happy, running the employment office, and arranging the annual Christmas party. With such an attitude, the company is bound to acquire a third-rate personnel program.

Personnel management and industrial relations are an emerging profession. A great many colleges and universities offer complete programs of study in this field. Some offer specialized degrees in industrial relations. The field contains a vast body of knowledge, much of which is derived from sound research, and a considerable body of literature. There are a number of professional societies throughout the country representing practicing personnel managers and specialists. When looking for someone to head the personnel–industrial relations program, a company president would be well advised to seek an individual who possesses a proper professional background in terms of education and work experience.

Organization for a Medium-size, Single-establishment Company

Figure 3-1 shows the sections comprising a typical personnel department in a single-establishment company having employment in the range of, say, 2,000–5,000 persons. The principal functions carried out in each of these sections are shown on this organization chart. Each section would be headed by a manager or supervisor and would contain personnel specialists such as job analyst, employment interviewer, safety engineer, and training specialist as required. In this example, it is assumed that certain categories of the work force, such as all the production and maintenance employees, are represented by a union; hence a labor relations section is included on the chart.

How large a personnel staff is necessary to service an organization of, say, 3,000 employ-

FIGURE 3-1 The Organization and Functions of a Personnel Department.

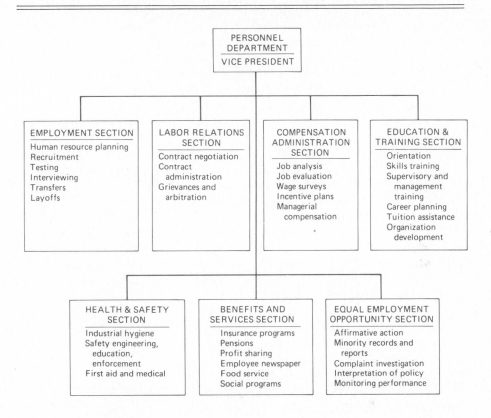

ees? The answer depends to a considerable extent upon the attitude of top management, which really determines how comprehensive a personnel program is to be carries on. Some companies have no formal training for either their employees or their managers. They may have no job evaluation system and never conduct a real area wage survey. They may provide only marginal first-aid facilities and have an inadequate safety program. With such an approach to personnel management, a company may get by with a very small personnel department and thereby save considerably on salaries. But it would certainly suffer in terms of lowered efficiency, more work injuries, lower morale, and more human relations problems.

Surveys reveal the number of people employed in personnel departments, on the average, per 100 employees in the work force of the entire enterprise. A 1983 survey by the American Society for Personnel Administration and the Bureau of National Affairs showed that the ratio of total personnel staff for every 100 employees was 1.1. The ratio of managerial/professional/technical staff in the personnel department per 100 employees in the workforce was 0.6. Thus, in the 3,000-employee company in our example there would be 18 persons in the managerial, professional, and technical categories in the personnel department. Total personnel staff (including clerical people) would be 33.[5]

[5]ASPA-BNA Survey No. 46, *Personnel Activities, Budgets, and Staffs: 1982–1983*. Washington, D.C.: The Bureau of National Affairs, May 26, 1983.

Large Divisionalized Companies

Very large corporations generally have many establishments scattered throughout the United States and in foreign countries. Organizationally they typically contain three broad levels of management: (1) top corporate headquarters; (2) division management; and (3) plant management. They are often decentralized in the sense that each division and plant manager has profit-center accountability. He or she possesses general authority and responsibility over the unit in order to obtain the results desired, and has nearly all the staff services such as personnel, purchasing, engineering, and accounting under his or her jurisdiction in order to realize the goals of the unit. Thus, these large firms have a personnel–industrial relations group at corporate headquarters and at each of the plants. They may also have units at the division level.

The personnel director at the plant level typically reports to the plant manager. He or she receives policy direction and technical guidance from the headquarters group, and is responsible for administering the personnel program in the plant. This personnel director holds a rank equivalent to that of other major executives in the plant, such as the chief engineer, controller, and the manager of manufacturing.

Questions for review and discussion

1. "The activities involved in personnel management pervade the entire organization. They are not performed solely by those in the personnel department." Explain the foregoing.
2. Explain the following four roles performed by a personnel–industrial relations department:
   a. Policy initiation and formulation.
   b. Advice.
   c. Service.
   d. Control.
   Give examples for each of these.
3. Name and give the content of the principal personnel–industrial relations functions.
4. Describe the staff role of the personnel department.
5. Explain the duties and responsibilities of the personnel department and of line supervision with respect to the following functions:
   a. Employment.
   b. Training and development.
   c. Safety.
6. At what level in the organization structure should the executive in charge of the personnel–industrial relations department be situated? Discuss.
7. In a multiplant company do you think it would be practical to have the personnel manager in each plant report directly to the corporate personnel vice-president? Discuss.

CASE PROBLEMS

PROBLEM 1

Recently 700 employees of a county nursing home and the county home for the aged (two public facilities located on the same plot of land) voted overwhelmingly to be represented by a union. The collective bargaining unit includes a great variety of employee groups from custodial and maintenance to professional nurses and social workers. Upon being interviewed after the union had won bargaining rights, the employees claimed that arbitrary and inconsistent treatment by the supervisors comprised the main reasons for their voting in the union. They charged flagrant favoritism and discriminatory treatment. They also charged that the supervisors made it a practice to discharge employees for inconsequential reasons or without adequate prior warnings. Employees were subject to frequent criticism by their supervisors in regard to their job performance. Even though many of the supervisors had been promoted from the "ranks," many of them seemed to abuse their authority in dealing with their subordinates.

Top managers in both "homes" were genuinely surprised when they first learned, during negotiations, about the serious and widespread employee discontent.

Question
1. Assuming that there is substantial truth to the employee complaints, what does this indicate about the quality of personnel management in the two institutions? Specifically what seems to be wrong? What should be done to correct the conditions?

PROBLEM 2

The Latham-Craft Company manufactures several lines of wood and metal products consisting of kitchen bowls, toys, croquet sets, and lawn furniture. The firm has been in business fifty years and is family-owned, the president being a major stockholder. Its branded items are well established in the market place. The company has earned a profit (though usually modest) for all but one of the past ten years. It employs a total of 350 people, of whom fifty are in the white-collar and managerial group. The production and maintenance employees are represented by a union.

The executive organization consists of the president, to whom report the sales vice-president, chief engineer, office manager, purchasing manager, director of product research and quality control, treasurer, and the plant superintendent. Sixteen factory foremen and two production control coordinators report to the plant superintendent.

The company is beset with a number of problems in regard to the management of its work force. The rate of employee turnover is high. This is caused by a high rate of voluntary quits and of discharges because of disciplinary problems and absenteeism. The company pays its production and maintenance employees rates that are equal to the average for the wood products industry but considerably below the going rates in its community, which contains companies in the automobile, electrical, and steel industries.

The hiring of new workers is handled jointly by the purchasing manager, who does the initial screening, and the production superintendent, who makes the final hiring decision. Both complain frequently about the caliber of help they are able to obtain. Most are young men with little training and experience who have failed to finish high school. The probationary period as spelled out in the union agreement is sixty days. The purchasing manager does little or no checking into the background of the new hires. His reasoning is that the company invests little in them during their first few weeks on the job, and if they should prove unsatisfactory, they can be discharged easily.

The accident rate in the plant has been very high for several years. Most of the injuries occur when the employees get their fingers or hands caught while operating or servicing the machines. The company president has become concerned about the rising cost for workers' compensation insurance, because the premium is based upon the actual loss experience in his plant. The foremen complain that whenever they try to suspend a worker for a serious infraction of a safety rule the company management usually backs down and rescinds the action in the face of pressure from the union business agent.

All of the present group of foremen have been promoted from the ranks of hourly paid employees. They have never received any formal training in supervision. They view their role as one of primarily pushing the workers to get out production. Very few exercise initiative or assume responsibility for seeing that housekeeping is improved, maintenance work is done on time, or that improved methods are instituted in their departments. The foremen are somewhat demoralized. They see few opportunities for advancement or even for salary increases. The company has no system for evaluating the performance of any of its managerial or clerical employees. There is no formal salary structure. If a worker has been doing a good job, if she or he has received no increase in pay for a long time, and if she or he complains firmly enough to the boss, he may receive a token pay increase.

The company does have a hospital and medical insurance plan as well as a pension plan. Claims are handled by the office manager.

For many years the company made small interest-free loans to employees to help them purchase necessary household items, for extraordinary sickness expenses, and the like. This policy was finally abandoned because of the administrative burden and because of the ill will generated when management denied a loan it felt was not justified. Recently there has been a rash of garnishments of employees' pay initiated by local small loan companies because employees have failed to repay their loans.

Questions
1. What appears to be the central problem in this company?
2. What organizational change or addition might be made to help solve the problem?
3. What personnel programs would you recommend be adopted?

Suggestions for Further Reading

Desatnick, Robert L. *The Expanding Role of the Human Resources Manager.* New York: American Management Association, 1979.

Janger, Allen R. *The Personnel Function: Changing Objectives and Organization* (Report No. 712). New York: The Conference Board, 1977.

Kaumeyer, Richard A., Jr. *Planning and Using a Total Personnel System.* New York: Van Nostrand Reinhold, 1982.

Langer, Steven. "The Personnel/Industrial Relations Function," *Personnel Journal*, Vol. 62, No. 7 (July 1983), pp. 540–543.

Ornati, Oscar A., Edward J. Giblin, and Richard Floersch. *The Personnel Department: Its Staffing and Budgeting.* New York: American Management Association, 1982.

Wolf, William B. (ed.). *Top Management of the Personnel Function.* Ithaca: New York State School of Industrial and Labor Relations, 1980.

Yoder, Dale, and Herbert G. Heneman, Jr. *ASPA Handbook of Personnel and Industrial Relations* (Vol. VIII), *Professional PAIR*. Washington, D.C.: The Bureau of National Affairs, Inc., 1979.

PART II

Organization and Jobs

4 Organization

Organization and the management of people at work are intimately related. The genesis of organization occurs when two or more people unite to achieve a common goal. If, for example, four friends decide to build a camp in the mountains to be used as a base for hunting and fishing trips, they must organize into a smoothly functioning team. The foremost organizational steps that these four friends must take are as follows: (1) decide their specific objectives for a camp in terms of location, cost, size, and design; (2) allocate different tasks to the individual persons according to their interests and abilities; and (3) develop the pattern of relations among the four individuals. This will involve designation of the person who will be in charge of the project, communication, coordination of efforts, and group and individual decision making. If the people in this group know one another well and are compatible, the problem of creating a smooth working team that successfully gets the camp built may not be particularly difficult. However, if one switches his thinking to the level of the large-scale organizations that have tended to become increasingly dominant in our society, he may appreciate that more careful planning and more complex organizational arrangements are required to make them function

properly. To initiate, operate, and regulate entities having thousands of members is no simple managerial problem. Consider the organizational problems involved in managing the military forces of the United States with its millions of men and women in uniform; the United States government itself, with its countless departments, bureaus, agencies, and services; or the great business corporations, such as General Motors, International Business Machines Corporation, and Eastman Kodak.

In order to function effectively, a large organization must systematize its way of doing things into plans, policies, procedures, rules, departments, specific jobs, and so on. A definite hierarchy of officials, managers, and supervisors must be established. The flexibility and informality characteristics of the small organization do not exist in large systems. On the other hand, the large organization exhibits greater stability than the small one.

In this chapter we shall explore several of the principle approaches that have been developed for the study of organization. We shall examine the issues of organization structure, delegation, decentralization, line and staff, and bureaucratic and organic systems of organization.

Organization Defined

An organization is a system, having an established structure and conscious planning, in which people work and deal with one another in a coordinated and cooperative manner for the accomplishment of recognized goals.

When we speak of an organization as a system, we mean that it consists of many interdependent constituent parts and that there are subsystems within the whole system. When we speak of structure, we mean that there is a degree of formality involved and that the members have designated roles to play. Conscious planning implies rationality, direction, and choice. People work in organizations in a coordinated and cooperative manner. Their behavior is not undirected and random. The activities are purposeful and goal seeking. The goals may be determined by concensus of involved parties both within and outside the organization or they may be set by fiat by one or more authority figures. The foregoing features distinguish an organization from a temporary grouping of people, an informal group, a friendship group, a crowd, a tribe, or a clan.

The process of organizing involves dividing all the work that has to be accomplished and assigning it to individuals, groups, and departments. This includes division of activities by level of authority and responsibility and also division of work across the establishment into different kinds or types. It entails the utilization of mechanisms for coordinating the efforts of individuals and groups. The relationships among members must evolve and become productive. Authority, responsibility, delegation, consultation, decision making, communication, and conflict resolution are all part and parcel of organization.

Examining the definition of organization and its amplifying ideas, one will conclude that it has wide application to all fields of endeavor. It includes not only business enterprises, but also government, the military, colleges and schools, churches, and such community service organizations as the Boy Scouts, Rotary, Kiwanis, and YMCA.

APPROACHES TO THE STUDY OF ORGANIZATION

Let us trace the evolution of theories of organization as these have developed since the early years of the twentieth century.

Classical

The earlier works have been designated the classical or traditional theories of organization and management. They belong to three main categories: (1) scientific management; (2) administrative management; and (3) the bureaucratic model of organization. Let us examine each in turn.

Scientific Management. The founder of this movement was an American engineer and management expert, Frederick W. Taylor (1856–1915).[1] He did not create a general theory of organization; rather he propounded a number of related techniques and philosophies derived from his extensive management and consulting experience. He was primarily concerned with manufacturing management and efficiency. He initiated and developed systematic job study, time study, standardization of the job, task specialization, setting of a measured quota of work, wage incentives to induce high output, and careful worker selection and training. He advocated maximum worker productivity rather than restriction of output. He proposed the use of science in managing the shop.

Taylor removed the work-planning responsibility from the employee and assigned it to a

[1] Taylor's views are given in his *Principles of Scientific Management* (New York: Harper and Row, 1919).

management specialist. He proposed a system of factory management called functional foremanship. Although it never took hold, it served as a forerunner of the expansion of staff planning and control in the factory.

The scientific management movement spread throughout the United States and Europe. Industrial leaders saw it as a way to higher productivity, greater profits, lower costs, and better control of the worker–machine system. Philosophically it was based upon the Protestant ethic, economic man, rational man, and the competitive view of man.

Administrative Management. Whereas scientific management focused upon the organization from the level of shop management, the administrative management theorists looked at the organization from the top down. Among its leaders were Henri Fayol, a French industrialist; Luther Gulick, an academician and public administration specialist; Lyndall Urwick, a British consultant and theorist; and James D. Mooney and Alan C. Reiley, General Motors executives.[2]

The administrative management theorists promulgated universal principles of organization and management. Although they each expressed their universal principles somewhat differently, the following represents a synthesis of their main propositions:

1. Specialization of function and division of labor are necessary for efficiency.
2. Coordination of functions and people is to be performed by the manager of each unit.
3. The responsibility and authority of each supervisor and manager must be clearly delineated. There must be a clear line of authority

[2]Henri Fayol, *General and Industrial Administration,* trans. by Constance Storrs (London: Sir Isaac Pitman & Sons, Ltd., 1949); Luther Gulick and Lyndall F. Urwick, eds., *Papers on the Science of Administration* (New York: Institute of Public Administration, Columbia University, 1937); James D. Mooney and Alan C. Reiley, *Onward Industry* (New York: Harper and Row, 1931).

from the top to the bottom of the structure (chain of command). Authority emanates from the top and flows downward through the organization. Responsibility must equal authority. Each person shall have only one boss (unity of command).

4. Orders, information, and complaints should flow primarily along the lines of the chain of command and there should be no bypassing of an individual manager in the chain of command.
5. The number of direct subordinates that one person can effectively supervise is limited to five or six, although the number may vary according to circumstances (span of control). Later formulations by some writers of the classical orientation reject a specific number as a universal limit but do hold that there is a limit, with the exact number depending upon many underlying factors that affect the complexity of the manager's job.
6. First design the organization and the jobs and then find the people to fit these jobs. Do not shape the job to fit the abilities and interests of the individual.

Bureaucratic Model. The concept of bureaucracy as a model of formal organization was originated by the great German sociologist Max Weber, who did most of his writing during the 1900–1920 period. In looking at the development of civilization through the broad sweep of history, Weber viewed the world, especially industrialized societies, as becoming progressively more rational and secular. In constructing and operating the institutions upon which man is dependent for the necessities of life, mankind tended to base its actions more and more upon knowledge, rational decision making, and technology and less and less upon mysticism and the occult. Weber's ideas concerning bureaucracy were but a part of his total social theory based upon the study of religion, capitalism, industry, and the political structure of society. He viewed bureaucracy as the most efficient instrument for operating large-scale enterprises, both public and private.[3]

The principal features of bureaucracy are (1) clear-cut division of labor and a high degree of specialization; (2) each lower office is under the control of a higher one (hierarchy); (3) a system of rules impersonally administered; (4) employment and assignment to positions based upon qualifications, not nepotism or favoritism; (5) job security for employees; and (6) extensive use of records, documents, and files.

Critique of the Classical View. Undoubtedly the classical theories of organization contain much that is of merit. In propounding their theories, the classical writers were giving what they observed to be truths about well-run and successful enterprises. Many establishments, both public and private, have been operated generally according to the principles formulated by these writers.

Yet in recent years the classical concepts and propositions have been subjected to attack by contemporary theorists, primarily those of the behavioral science school of thought.

One major criticism has been that classical theory represented a mechanistic view of men and women in the organization. They were expected to be pliant and submissive—to do what they were told. Job performance as to both quantity and quality was highly standardized. The scope of job responsibilities was to be narrow. Individuality in the work role was to be minimized. Motivation to work was based primarily upon money incentives and authoritarian leaders. Scant attention was given to attitudes, morale, and group relationships. Excessive emphasis was placed upon fitting the person to the job. They did not allow that individual to shape the job in accordance with that individual's special skills and abilities.

Authority tended to be viewed as a quanti-

[3]Max Weber, *The Theory of Social and Economic Organization,* trans. by A. M. Henderson and Talcott Parsons (New York: The Free Press of Glencoe, 1964).

fiable entity that could be measured out and assigned to managers. If a manager had authority, she or he was also presumed to have power equivalent to that authority. Generally ignored were the dynamic aspects of power and influence, and the political aspects of an executive's role. Implicit was the notion that officials were all-seeing and all-knowing just because they had been assigned formal authority.

Behavioral Science

The early contributors in this field, who did their work from the late 1920s through the early 1950s, have been called the human relationists. They were not called behavioral scientists in those days. They were primarily psychologists and industrial sociologists who belonged to university faculties. Private industry was their laboratory.

The research investigations of Elton Mayo and his Harvard University colleagues at the Hawthorne Works of the Western Electric Company in Chicago from 1927 to 1932 marked the beginning of the human relations movement. This series of studies demonstrated the key importance of group pressures, social relations, and attitudes toward supervision and the job as determinants of group productivity.

Whereas classical organization theorists focused upon task, structure, and authority, human relationists emphasized human dimensions. The enterprise was viewed as a social system as well as an economic-technical system. The informal work group was identified as a major source of worker control. Both the formal organization structure created by management and the informal organization that just evolved had to be taken into account in explaining how and why an enterprise functioned as it did.

While traditional writers viewed the authority of the boss and pay as prime motivators, the human relations school emphasized the importance of psychological and social factors in shaping employee behavior.

Many human relations theorists held that participation in management planning and decision making yielded positive effects in terms of both morale and productivity.

Managers were told that human behavior in the company had both its rational and nonrational components. Feelings, sentiments, and values were legitimate and necessary concerns of the manager.

The impact of the human relations school has been great. Countless management-training programs in both industry and government have contained a heavy component of material in human relations, that is, in motivation, morale, leadership, interpersonal communication, counseling and listening skills, and group dynamics. Managers have been sensitized to the importance of the human dimension.

However, the human relations movement has had its share of critics. Much of the criticism pertains to the way it has been operationalized in industry. The charge has been made that the human relationists were soft in their demands upon workers, that human relations emphasized manipulation of the worker, that it ignored the influence of unions, and that it overlooked the effects of technology and the economic environment upon the organizational system.

The modern contributors have rejected the human relations label for themselves. Instead, they call themselves behavioral scientists, organizational psychologists, organization theorists, and organization development specialists. Because of the large number of contributors to this growing field, we can refer to only a few of the leaders here. The works of Douglas McGregor, Rensis Likert, Frederick Herzberg, Warren Bennis, and Chris Argyris are significant and generally representative of this field.[4]

Although each of these leaders makes his own unique contributions, there are unifying and consistent themes among their works. They exhibit an optimistic view of the nature of man. They believe in his basic goodness. They believe that high performance can better be achieved by self-direction and self-control than by rigid bureaucratic regulation. Rather than fragmentation of work and narrow job definitions, they propose job enrichment. Positive motivation (not punitive), supportive leadership, and group methods of supervision are emphasized. They hold that the desirable organizational climate is one in which employees and managers can be more open, genuine, and trusting of others. Collaboration and teamwork are preferable to the all-too-common destructive interpersonal competition that we witness in business enterprises.

Systems View

General systems theory has become popular in the past twenty-five years because of its apparent ability to serve as a universal model of systems including diverse physical, biological, social, and behavioral phenomena. Systems theory is rather abstract. Theorists seek generalizations that help explain the functioning of various entities and processes.[5]

A system is an organized whole, consisting of interrelating and interdependent parts. Organization theorists treat organizations as systems. They examine the relationships among the ele-

---

[4]Douglas McGregor, *The Human Side of Enterprise* (New York: McGraw-Hill Book Company, 1960), and *The Professional Manager* (New York: McGraw-Hill Book Company, 1967); Rensis Likert, *The Human Organization* (New York: McGraw-Hill Book Company, 1967); Frederick Herzberg, *Work and the Nature of Man* (Cleveland: World Publishing

Company, 1966); Warren Bennis, *Changing Organizations* (New York: McGraw-Hill Book Company, 1966); and Chris Argyris, *Interpersonal Competence and Organizational Effectiveness* (Homewood, Ill.: Dorsey Press, 1962).

[5]For sources on general systems theory applied to organization and management, see Richard A. Johnson, Fremont E. Kast, and James E. Rosenzweig, *The Theory and Management of Systems*, 3rd ed. (New York: McGraw-Hill Book Company, 1973); *Academy of Management Journal*, Vol. 15, No. 4 (December, 1972), entire issue devoted to systems theory.

ments of the organization, the systems and subsystems of the organization, and interaction with other systems in the environment.

There are several important systems concepts that apply to organizations. Human organizations are predominantly *open systems*. This means that they interact with various elements of their environment. A business corporation, for example, interacts with many external groups such as customers, suppliers, the public, and various levels of government. It is affected by economic, social, and political forces. The business firm, in turn, affects the external groups with which it interacts.

Organizations tend toward a *dynamic or moving equilibrium*. The members seek to maintain the organization and to have it survive. They react to changes and forces, both internal and external, in ways which often create a new state of equilibrium and balance. *Feedback* of information from a point of operation and from the environment to a control center or centers can provide the data necessary to initiate corrective measures to restore equilibrium.

Organizations and the world of which they are a part consist of a *hierarchy of systems*. Thus, a corporation is composed of divisions, departments, sections, and groups of individual employees. Also the corporation is part of larger systems such as all the firms in its industry, the firms in its metropolitan area, and perhaps an association of many firms from many industries such as the National Association of Manufacturers.

Interdependency is a key concept in systems theory. The elements of a system interact with one another and are interdependent. Generally a change in one part of an organization affects other parts of that organization. Sometimes the interdependencies are not fully appreciated when changes are made. A change in organization structure and work flow in one department may unexpectedly induce changes in departments that relate to the first department.

Systems theory contains the doctrine that the whole of a structure or entity is more than the sum of its parts. This is called *wholism*. The cooperative, synergistic working together of members of a department or team often yields a total product that exceeds the sum of their individual contributions.

Systems theory helps organize a large body of information that might otherwise make little sense. It has made major contributions to the study of organization and management in recent years. Systems theory aids in diagnosing the interactive relationships among task, technology, environment, and organization members. Practitioners have adopted the system's conceptualization in designing, building, and operating management information systems and automation processes. Systems concepts have been applied in project and matrix organization designs.

However, systems theory applied to organization has its limitations. It is in its early stages of development. It does not, at present, comprise a consistent, articulated, coherent theory. Much of it constitutes a high level of abstraction. To be really useful to the professional practice of management, its spokespersons and leaders must move down to a more concrete and operationally useful range.

ORGANIZATION STRUCTURE

Organization implies structure. The total work to be carried on must be grouped by kind or type into divisions, departments, sections, and units. Likewise the work must be grouped into different levels; that is, the managerial hierarchy must be set up and defined. Means must also be devised to provide for coordination and integration of people and their activities.

Grouping Activities by Kind

There are five basic ways of grouping work activities. They are by (1) function, (2) location or geographical area, (3) product, (4) customer or client, and (5) number of persons. Let us examine each of these.

Function. Grouping activities according to similar work, skills, knowledge, and orientation is the most widely used of all bases of departmentation. This is done with both "brain work" and manual work. Thus, companies group all the engineers together into an engineering department and all the personnel specialists into a personnel department. Electricians may be grouped together in the electrical section of the maintenance department. Departmentation by *process* is closely akin to functional grouping. Thus all electroplating, machining, and electronic data processing may be grouped into separate departments. Figure 4-1 shows a manufacturing firm organized by function and process specialization.

Location and Geographical Area. Sales forces are typically organized by this method. Thus, a company may have a sales office in San Francisco to cover the western part of the country, one in St. Louis to cover the Midwest, and one in New York City to take care of the East. Automobile manufacturers locate assembly plants in different parts of the country and in foreign lands. Other examples are the U.S. Postal Service, Internal Revenue Service, and the Federal Reserve System. The usual reasons for organization by location are to get close to clients to obtain business and provide good service or to get close to sources of raw materials to minimize transportation costs.

Product. This method is very common in the manufacturing field. The General Electric Company, for example, has over one hundred

FIGURE 4-1 Chart Showing a Manufacturing Firm Organized by Function and Process.

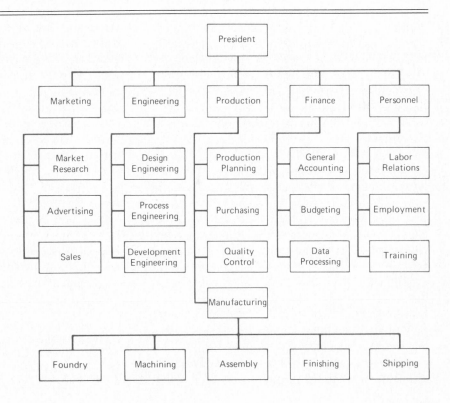

separate product departments. Examples are the Power Transformer Department, Large Lamp Department, and the Silicone Products Department. Because GE also has a decentralized management structure, these product departments are self-contained in that they have their own engineering, sales, purchasing, accounting, and employee relations units as well as the production units.

In American industry there has been a strong trend toward product departmentation in recent years. Originally, many companies were organized functionally, but as they grew the problems of coordination and achieving a unified effort became so difficult that they set up product divisions with functional units within their divisions. While product departmentation gains unified accountability for performance of product lines, it does entail the possible disadvantage of duplication of effort by staff groups in each product department.

Customer or Client. A sales force may be divided into those calling on government agencies, industry, and private individuals. The lending units of a bank may be specialized along the lines of a small installment department and a commercial department. This type of specialization may be advantageous if the personnel must cater to the special needs of particular classes of customers.

Number of Persons. Oftentimes there are large numbers of employees who are doing the same thing, working in the same general location on the same products and for the same clients. Yet it is necessary for administrative control purposes to set up units, sections, and departments. Thus, in the Army, personnel are organized into squads, platoons, companies, battalions, and the like. In a large office one hundred clerks who are doing identical work may be grouped into four separate sections with a supervisor for each.

In considering all of the foregoing bases for grouping activities it ought to be noted that rarely does one enterprise adopt only one pure form. Rather, it uses a combination. And as technology and environmental influences dictate, it may change from one mode to another.

Project and Matrix Organization

The project form of organization is a combination of the functional and the product types of structures. It has been variously called *project management, program management, product management,* and *matrix organization.*[6] It came into prominence in the 1960s when the United States Department of Defense and the aerospace industry began using it extensively. For many years companies engaged in manufacturing and selling consumer goods have had product managers who pilot particular products from the initial development stage through manufacturing, market testing, and ultimate sales to the consuming public. A product manager's role is that of a planner, coordinator, initiator, expediter, and persuader. She or he has substantial responsibility for the success of the product but normally possesses little formal authority.

The pure functional form of organization is often inadequate to meet the problem of obtaining synchronized effort on large complex projects and in situations in which product lines become diverse, market competition changes rapidly, and time schedules are tight. In such situations in which the functional departments are coordinated only at the level of top management, one finds that bottlenecks occur too often, there is confusion on priorities, project planning is inadequate, and too many problems get bucked upstairs to top management for resolution. To meet these difficulties, project and matrix forms of organization have been developed. Oftentimes projects have a finite duration. They

[6] For sources on project management, see David I. Cleland and William R. King, *Systems Analysis and Project Management,* 3rd ed. (New York: McGraw-Hill Book Company, 1983); Jay R. Galbraith, "Matrix Organization Designs," *Business Horizons,* Vol. XIV, No. 1 (February 1971), pp. 29–40.

are created, they live, and they terminate. One does not necessarily need the same people on a project throughout all phases of the work. By using project management, people can be shifted around as needed but they always retain their functional department home.

Project management can take a variety of forms. The three principal kinds are (1) staff project manager; (2) matrix; and (3) line project manager. Intermediate forms using task forces and committees are also used.

The staff project (or product) manager may be created when some general manager of a plant or division appoints an assistant to coordinate one or more products that are designed, made, and marketed by the functional departments. This product manager would have staff coordinative and advisory responsibility but possess little formal authority over functional departments. For example, in a food products company she might be a product manager in charge of a line of new breakfast foods. She would have responsibility for coordinating and expediting product development, planning, food production, scheduling, cost control, test marketing, and advertising.

Matrix organization constitutes an overlay of horizontal authority and responsibility relationships on top of a functional structure. Figure 4-2 shows a matrix organization for a division of a corporation that has three major projects being carried on simultaneously. People remain in their functional departments of engineering, manufacturing, and marketing, but work on their respective projects. In fact, some of these functional specialists may devote parts of their time to all three projects. The project managers, in a sense, are competing with one another for the time and talents of the people in the functional departments. The project managers have responsibility for planning, funding and budget, scheduling, performance standards, completion dates, and customer relations. They must insure unified effort by all who work on

FIGURE 4-2 A Matrix Organization.

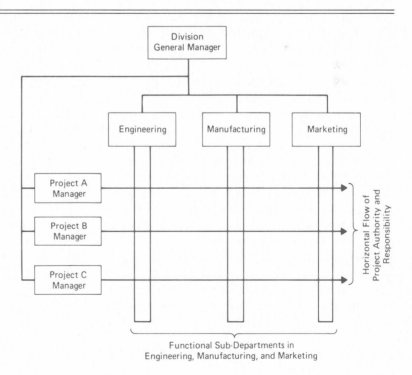

their project. They resolve conflicts that may disrupt progress. Usually they have more responsibility than formal authority; hence they must get results by means of persuasion, informal influence, and appeals to cooperation. In many companies, they do have project budget money and this gives them a source of power. The managers of the regular functional departments, on the other hand, provide specialized personnel to work on the project. They must maintain a capability of personnel and systems in terms of the state of the art. They perform the personnel administration functions of selection, training, performance appraisal, salary administration, promotion, and the like.

Several large corporations have adopted the matrix form of organization in recent years. Among these are General Electric, Equitable Life Assurance, TRW Systems, Citicorp, Dow Corning, and Shell Oil.[7]

The third type of arrangement places the people necessary to complete a project under the full authority of a project manager for the duration of that project, which may be for six months or a year or more. This is line project management because the manager is directly in the formal line hierarchy. The manager has full authority and responsibility for project performance. Of course, she may still have to negotiate with other departments for the use of special services that are costly and must be shared by many departments.

Project and matrix forms of organization are quite advantageous for the kinds of situations we have described. However, there are problems with their use. The professionals and supervisors working in such an environment must accustom themselves to dual authority and a dual information and reporting system. This is particularly true in matrix organization. The process of forming and disbanding project teams can be unsettling to some people. A premium is placed upon collaboration and constructive conflict resolution. Opportunities for

---

[7] *Business Week,* (January 16, 1978), pp. 82–83.

divergent pulls on the people abound. Thus, there exists a special challenge to the leadership skills of the managers.

Grouping Activities by Level

The grouping of work into different levels in the organization is another form of specialization. All manual work may constitute the bottom level in the organizational hierarchy. Supervision of this manual work makes up the foreman level; coordination and control of departmental operating and staff functions represent middle management; and policy making and overall direction of the business make up the top management level. Figure 4-3 shows a partial organization chart of a large manufacturing corporation. This chart shows typical functions, levels of management, and formal channels of authority. Including the board of directors, there are seven levels of management.

An important (but by no means exclusive) path for downward and upward communication is through the formal channel of authority. Orders, information, instructions, and requests for data flow down through the levels in the hierarchy. Information about work in progress, suggestions, questions, complaints, and grievances flow up the line. An important reason for not skipping intermediate supervisors when communicating is that they must know what is going on in their units. Their position, value, and status are strengthened if they serve as vital and essential links in the vertical channel of communication.

For an organization to work effectively there must be a great deal of lateral communication as well as vertical. If a worker has completed making certain items that are now ready for inspection, generally he need only notify the floor inspector that the work is complete. It would waste much time if he had to notify his foreman who would in turn pass the request up the structure until a single manager over both production and inspection was reached. This

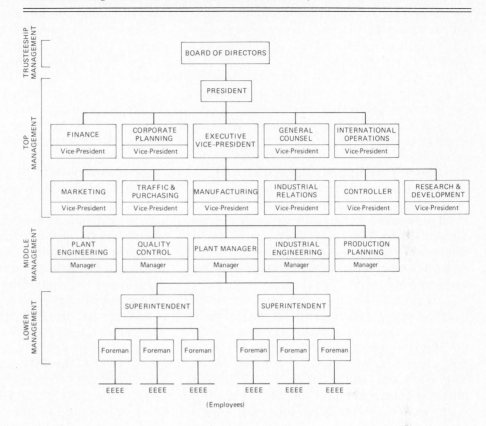

Levels of Management

manager would then tell the supervisor of inspection to have an inspector examine the product. Such a procedure is, of course, too cumbersome. Indeed lateral communications and discussions should be encouraged. The settlement of many problems at subordinate levels reduces the burden on higher executives.

Levels of Management

If a very capable and promising first-line supervisor were promoted rather rapidly up the organization ladder, he would find that the nature of his activities would change. Although he would be a manager both as a first-line supervisor and later as a member of middle or top management, the emphasis given to the different segments of the management function would be materially altered. To be successful as he rises in the hierarchy, he must adjust his behavior, outlook, and general orientation. Front-line supervisors devote a high proportion of their time to immediate direction and interaction with their subordinates. Top management, on the other hand, spends a high percentage of its time on planning, policy development, forecasting, and participating in meetings. All levels perform the five management functions of planning, organizing, staffing, leading, and controlling; however, the emphasis given to each and the nature of the specific tasks within each major function are different.

If we look at a large manufacturing corporation, what generalizations can we make to describe the work and behavior of the principal levels?

Lower Management. The term *lower management* includes assistant foremen, foremen, general foremen, and office supervisors. They instruct employees in the methods of performing their jobs, assign and reassign employees to specific jobs and tasks, and take prompt action to overcome delays and breakdowns in the production process. Definite production schedules of a short-term nature (daily and weekly) are assigned to them from higher authority. Their authority to make expenditures for capital improvements (tools, equipment, and so on) is extremely limited. As far as personnel actions are concerned, they have some limited say in selection of their subordinates, can assign minor disciplinary penalties, and have great authority in evaluating employees. They generally have full authority to take whatever steps are necessary to get production out on time. They can requisition materials and supplies, authorize overtime work, obtain maintenance and inspection services, and request technical assistance if necessary.

Middle Management. In the multiplant corporation the term *middle management* includes supervisory and executive personnel in production, sales, engineering, accounting, and other functional fields both within the plants and at corporate headquarters. Titles such as manager of industrial engineering, plant controller, assistant plant manager, and district sales manager are typical. No sharp lines of demarcation exist between lower and middle management. The terms are relative. Middle managers transmit and sharpen up information and orders from top management. They help solve major difficulties when lower supervisors experience trouble. They operate within the policies and programs set by higher officials but shape them to fit the particular needs of their departments. They evaluate performance results in accordance with the program and standards established for them. Considerable time tends to be spent in meetings with colleagues of similar rank.

Authority over such personnel matters as selection, training, changes of status and position, and settlement of grievance and disciplinary problems is considerable.

Top Management. In the business corporation this includes the president, vice-presidents, and major executives. In the large organization it covers the top two levels and sometimes the third level below the board of directors. Top executives are concerned with corporate strategy and the formulation of both long- and intermediate-range plans and programs. The chief executive officer provides an integrating function for the entire organization. She or he gives it direction and purpose. She or he must balance the internal interests of the firm with its external environment. The top executive team must concern itself with the survival and growth of the organization. Group decision making through committees and meetings is common. Considerable time is devoted to deliberation and reading of reports. The world of the top manager involves a lot of contact with the public and outside groups, such as government officials, trade association personnel, and other business executives. Business travel tends to be rather frequent. Authority and responsibility in monetary and personnel matters are very great and actions are only checked by higher authority (for example, the board of directors) at relatively long intervals.

Trusteeship Management. For a business corporation, the board of directors serves a trusteeship function by overseeing the direction of the business for the benefit of the stockholders, who are the owners. It decides upon the proper distribution of profits: for dividends, for retention in the business for expansion, and for paying off indebtedness. In both business and nonbusiness organizations, the board of directors also bears important trusteeship responsibilities for the employees, clients or customers, and the public. It must be remembered that it is at the discretion and indulgence of the public, operating through government, that private organizations exist.

Other vital functions of a board are the establishment of objectives, selection of the president and other top executives, approval of overall budgets, and auditing of results. The board must continuously review the operations of the organization and insure that it is viable and being run properly. If necessary it can replace the top executive team.

Boards of directors typically are composed of both insiders and outsiders. Insiders are major executives such as the president and key vice-presidents who have day-to-day operating responsibilities. Outside members do not work for the corporation. They may be major stockholders or people such as bankers, lawyers, and professionals who have an expertise that can be valuable to the firm. Although many boards are composed predominantly of insiders, management authorities generally hold that it is most desirable to have a substantial portion of outsiders on any board. They can act as an independent review of the performance of the management group.

DELEGATION AND DECENTRALIZATION

Because the single individual at the top of a pyramidal structure cannot do all the work of the organization himself, he delegates work to his immediate subordinates; they in turn redelegate part or all of this work to their subordinates and so on down to the nonsupervisory employees. There are three components of delegation.

1. Assignment of duties and functions to be performed.
2. Giving of authority to the subordinate sufficient to accomplish the results expected. Illustrations of the granting of authority are the right to purchase materials, the right to engage the services of an outside consultant, the right to hire employees, and the right to speak for the company in public.
3. Holding the subordinate accountable or responsible, the superior expects the subordinate to carry out conscientiously the work assigned.

In every organization that has multiple levels of management, successive delegations must take place. The question is not whether it shall occur but rather to what degree it should occur. By and large, the successful manager is one who leans toward more delegation rather than less. Delegation has these advantages: (1) It unburdens the executive or supervisor from the details of subordinates' jobs. This means that the superior has more time for planning and overall direction of his department and that his subordinates are encouraged to exercise broader decision-making responsibilities for their own work. (2) Because the subordinates exercise their own judgment and handle their activities on their own, they tend to generate greater commitment, enthusiasm, and pride in their work. (3) Delegation is a way of training subordinates to take on varied and larger projects and responsibilities. They learn to plan more effectively and evaluate their own work when they know that their immediate superior trusts them and is not going to make every decision for them.

In delegating work to those below him in the organization, the executive does not evade his own responsibility for the work. If the captain of a ship delegates the job of guiding the vessel through intricate waterways to a pilot and if that pilot runs it aground, the owners of the ship will hold the captain responsible. If the cashier of a commercial bank embezzles $100,000 from the bank, the bank president and board of directors are ultimately held accountable for this action. The fact that a superior is held accountable (within reason, of course) for the behavior of employees is necessary for the orderly operation of the organization.

One of the problems occurring most frequently in connection with delegation is that executives are reluctant to delegate adequately to their subordinates. Delegation requires giving freedom to the employee to exercise initiative to get the job done. The superior must place confidence in subordinates. She or he must recognize that they will not carry out each and every assignment precisely as she or he, the boss, would. In delegating, the boss should not then stand over subordinates to control their every action.

Decentralization

Decentralization means placing the authority and decision-making power as close as possible to the level at which the work is done. As many functional specialties as are necessary to accomplish results are placed under the manager in charge of that organizational unit. Decentralization is really delegation on an organization-wide basis. Delegation involves superior-to-subordinate relations on a person-to-person basis; decentralization relates top management to lower-level organizational units. If an enterprise is centralized, most decisions, both major and minor, are made by the president and top management. On the other hand, in a decentralized approach division and departmental managers are granted considerable authority to run their own units as they see fit as long as they achieve the desired results.

What are the advantages of decentralization (relative to centralization)?

1. It permits quicker decision making. The managers who are closer to the work have the authority to take action.
2. Problems of coordination, communication, and red tape are reduced. If a product design problem comes up, it is not necessary to delay making a decision in order to contact a centralized engineering department.
3. Autonomy of subordinate units permits greater experimentation and flexibility to meet new conditions.
4. It encourages subordinates at every level in the structure to exercise greater initiative and ingenuity. Ideas do not have to be sold to top management before they can be tried.
5. It insures the development of more capable managers. They have had ample opportunity to "sink their teeth" into problems. Middle and lower managers are not messengers in the hierarchy. They have learned to stand or fall on their own decisions and actions.

Decentralization is not an unmixed blessing. Local units may fail to utilize the expert services that staff units at headquarters have to offer. There is a danger of duplication of effort by local units. For example, a marketing or personnel problem may be tackled from scratch in one plant, whereas another plant may have spent thousands of dollars to successfully solve the same problem. The problem of control is made more difficult under decentralization.

Factors Governing Decentralization or Centralization

Whether a particular enterprise should be managed on a centralized or a decentralized basis depends upon a number of factors. The absolute size of the firm in terms of dollar volume of sales, number of plants, and number of employees is an important factor. It is very difficult to coordinate day-to-day decision making in a huge corporation. Efficiency may be enhanced by making the subordinate units semiautonomous. Another important factor is the nature and history of the firm. If it has only one product line and has grown primarily from within, then the company is more likely to remain centralized.

On the other hand, if a firm is engaged in the making of diverse and unrelated products and if it has grown by acquisitions and mergers, it is much more likely to be decentralized. It appears that speed and adequacy of decision making, flexibility, and efficiency are enhanced through decentralized operations for very large, multi-product, diverse, and complex businesses.

It is very difficult to maintain centralized authority and control in a business that has branches and units scattered throughout the country and the world. This is particularly true if these units must deal directly with customers and the general public and must take prompt action on complex problems.

Some management functions are more amenable to decentralization than others. In the large multiplant company, such functions as purchasing, traffic, cost accounting, quality control, plant engineering, and personnel tend to be decentralized. Yet financial planning and resource allocation may be reserved for the very highest level of decision making and control. Marketing may or may not be decentralized depending upon the nature of the markets and the variety of products.

Human relations factors also are important. Talented division and departmental executives often are unwilling to accept close domination from their organizational superiors. They desire independence. They want to run their own show and to be rewarded for what they are able to accomplish in their own units. Innovation and adaptability are encouraged by decentralization. If every contemplated action must first be approved by the front office, frustration and hostility tend to be byproducts.

LINE AND STAFF

In very small organizations all the employees and supervisors are line personnel. But as organizations grow, it becomes necessary to employ specialists who give technical advice and provide services to line personnel. Thus, a personnel director can help a superintendent with his training, safety, and grievance-handling problems. A production engineer may design a fixture for a machine. In this case the factory supervisor might have neither the time nor the knowledge to design the item himself.

In organizations the following kinds of positions may exist. These are

A. *Line*
B. *Staff*
 1. Specialized staff and service staff
 2. "Assistant-to" staff
 3. General staff

Line positions and personnel are directly involved in doing the work for which the organization was created. Generally the enterprise could not function, even for a day, without these activities. In a manufacturing concern, manufacturing and selling are considered line functions. Line personnel would be workers, foremen, superintendents, plant managers, and the president. In a department store both buying and selling are line functions. In a university devoted to the discovery and dissemination of knowledge, the faculty is line.

Specialized staff and service staff are closely related in their roles and responsibilities. They are also the most widespread of the various staff types. Specialized staff departments provide planning, advice, and control functions for the entire organization. Industrial relations and personnel, engineering, research and development, legal counsel, and auditing are examples of specialized staff groups. Such units are usually composed of people who are technical experts in their fields. They frequently are professionals and technicians. In addition to providing advice and control functions for all departments of a company, specialized staff units located at the level of top management also bear heavy responsibilities for policy formulation. Thus the office of the vice-president of personnel would formulate policies in regard to executive compensation, recruitment, training, labor relations, organization development, manpower, and benefit programs.

Service staff aids the organization predominantly in a physical sense. Examples of service staff are purchasing, maintenance, inspection, a real estate department for property acquisition, and a stenographic pool. Like specialized staff, service staffs serve the organization as a whole.

In actuality a sharp distinction between specialized and service staffs is not possible nor really necessary. Many of the sections within a personnel department are engaged more in rendering services than they are in policy planning, advice, and control. This is true for the employment office and for the unit that administers pension and insurance benefits. Some service staff units give technical counsel and perform control functions. This is true for quality control and purchasing. In Figure 4-4 the personnel department is shown as having a dotted-line staff relationship with other line and staff departments within the company.

"Assistant-to" staff is depicted in this figure in the position of executive assistant to the president. The "assistant-to" position is created to relieve an executive of burdens. It can be found at any level in the organization and there may be more than one assistant reporting to an executive. The President of the United States has several staff assistants: a press secretary, a military aide, assistant for Congressional relations, economic advisor, speech writers, and many others. The assistant to the president is apparently a growing phenomenon in American business. Assistants-to serve in the capacity that their bosses desire. Some are special-purpose (for example, speech writers or public relations), but many are broad-gauge. The broad-gauge ones often perform such assorted tasks as reviewing and commenting upon staff reports before they go to the chief, handling a multitude

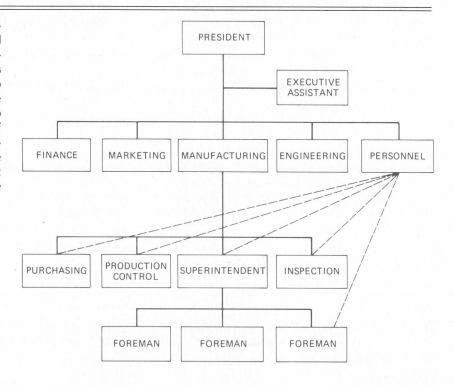

FIGURE 4-4 A Partial Organization Chart to Show Line and Staff Positions and Their Relationships. The dotted lines from the personnel office to the various departments in the manufacturing division and to the foreman show the flow of specialized advice, aid, service, and communication. The personnel office does not give direct orders to these individuals.

of administrative details, making special investigations, serving as a sounding board for the chief's ideas, and in general serving as one whom the executive can confide in.

General staff, although seldom used in private business, is widely employed in military forces throughout the world. It is also fairly common in government. It is similar to assistant-to staff in its organization position. However, instead of providing help to one executive, general staff consists of a group of experts who operate an office. It is used primarily for planning. The Prussian general staff, organized by Scharnhorst in the early nineteenth century, was a complete advisory service coordinated under a single head, the chief of staff. As a result of inefficiencies during the Spanish–American War in 1898, Elihu Root, the Secretary of War under Presidents William McKinley and Theodore Roosevelt, created the general staff device for the United States Army.

Relations Between Line and Staff

Problems can arise out of the interactions between staff specialists and line personnel. A staff engineer, for example, may have the responsibility to increase the output of a production process. In so doing the engineer may give instructions to operators and foremen that may appear to be in conflict with directives given by the shop superintendent. This is the problem of dual authority. Also, a major mission of many staff groups is to diagnose problems and devise improvements in processes and procedures. Staff initiates change. Line personnel often desire stability not change. They may resent intrusion by staff personnel into their domain. By gathering data on the performance of operating units and reporting deviations from standards to top management, staff serves as an instrument for control. Line personnel may resent implied criticism contained in staff reports.

In order to function effectively staff units need the full support of top management. Staff safety and health managers, for example, cannot effectively reduce occupational injuries and illnesses unless they have the full backing of higher management.

Staff and line personnel should consult and collaborate with one another. They should share credit for improved plans and results.

BUREAUCRATIC AND ORGANIC SYSTEMS OF ORGANIZATION

The model of organization that has guided the thinking of managers for over fifty years has been the bureaucracy. This has been true even though they may not have knowingly adopted the bureaucratic design. The prescriptions of classical organization theory affected the thinking of managers through many sources: practical articles in trade journals and management handbooks, books on management policy and practice, attendance at seminars and conferences, and by copying older organization forms such as the military.

More recently another model of organization has come into prominence. This is the organic or the organic-adaptive pattern. It has particular relevance to complex, high-technology organizations operating in a changing environment.

Bureaucracy

The principal identifying features of a modern bureaucracy are the following:

1. *Formal authority.* Authority to command is formally assigned and regulated.
2. *Autocratic authority.* The authority system is essentially autocratic. Obedience to superiors is a condition of employment.

3. *Positional authority.* It resides in the office, not the person.
4. *Chain of command.* Orders, communications, and appeals flow vertically through the official hierarchy of offices.
5. *Job duties.* These are clearly defined.
6. *Employee qualifications.* These are clearly defined.
7. *Employee selection.* Based upon qualifications, not personal friendship or nepotism.
8. *Specialization of work.* Activities logically grouped by specialization of function. Narrow job jurisdictions.
9. *Education and training.* Occupations require specialized skills and training. Much training provided within the organization.
10. *Professionalization of management.* Administration handled by trained experts.
11. *Records and reports.* Extensive use of records, reports, documents, files.
12. *Procedures and rules.* Methods of work highly standardized. Rules of behavior are elaborate and impersonally administered.
13. *Job security.* Substantial job security in return for loyalty and subordination of individual goals to larger goals of the organization.
14. *Promotion from within.* Based upon qualifications and seniority. This is to recognize good performance, promote harmony, and enhance morale.
15. *Decision and planning aids.* Mathematical models, electronic computers, sophisticated accounting and financial techniques.

The bureaucracy is pervasive throughout our economic and political system. Most large-scale organizations—whether they be manufacturing concerns, banking firms, or governmental agencies—exhibit many or most of the characteristics of bureaucracy. The bureaucracy tends toward permanence. Its viability does not depend upon a single executive or group of executives. Executives and employees alike are replaceable.

In addition to being relatively permanent and stable, the large bureaucracy tends to build a reputation for consistency of action. The emblem of one of our largest insurance companies is a picture of the Rock of Gibraltar. This conveys integrity, stability, and permanence. The client can expect to receive uniform, consistent treatment. A meal in a Howard Johnson restaurant in Boston is essentially the same as in a Howard Johnson restaurant in Buffalo.

For the production of a standardized product or service on time, day-in and day-out, throughout the years, the bureaucratic form of organization cannot be surpassed. Its effectiveness for this kind of mission is high.

On the other hand, there are distinct disadvantages. There tends to be excessive sanctification of procedures and rules by the employees. They are taught to work in conformity with detailed procedures and regulations that are issued by higher authority. The purpose of these regulations is to insure uniformity in accomplishment of the objectives of the company. However, the intermediate and lower-level functionaries often look upon rule compliance as an end in itself. They do not realize that the rules are means to an end and not ends in themselves. When sanctification of the rules becomes excessive to the point of interfering with goal accomplishment and serving the needs of clients and employees, then we have the familiar case of "red tape." Red tape is the label applied to the routing of a client's case through excessively slow and cumbersome channels. The bureaucracy is inefficient for meeting the special problems that a client might have. It is inefficient in reacting to change.

The forces that maximize routine efficiency often militate against new methods and ideas. Foremost among these is the autocratic authority structure. Functionaries are rewarded for doing what they are told, not for suggesting changes in programs developed by their bosses. Most policies, programs, and plans are formulated from "on high" and lower-level personnel are indoctrinated to comply. Responsibility tends to be shifted upward. Problems that fall outside the narrow limits of one's jurisdiction are referred

Organization and Jobs

upward until they come to a manager who feels she or he has sufficient authority to render a decision.

Regimentation and monotony are other hallmarks of the bureaucracy. Narrow job roles, standardization of work, mass production techniques, and lack of employee responsibility for planning and control of his own job all contribute to the monotony.

Organic System

A newer model of organization is the organic or organic-adaptive system.[8] Features of the organic system are

1. Job definitions are less rigid and narrow than in the bureaucracy. These can shift over time as conditions and job incumbents change. There is less emphasis upon enforced conformity to rules and regulations and more emphasis upon employee self-control through knowledge, information, and judgment.
2. Employees share a sense of commitment to the goals of the wider organization beyond their immediate job boundaries. There are shared beliefs about the values and goals of the organization.
3. Authority and power are delegated and dispersed. Specialized knowledge and experience are sources of influence and authority in addition to the authority of organizational position. The system is less autocratic than the bureaucratic system. Executives are *not* viewed as omniscient because they occupy a management position.
4. Communication is horizontal and diagonal (as well as vertical). Communication consists more of advice and information than of direct orders.

[8]The organic system is depicted in Tom Burns and G. M. Stalker, *The Management of Innovation* (Chicago: Quadrangle Books, 1961). Warren Bennis uses the term organic-adaptive. See Warren Bennis, *Changing Organizations* (New York: McGraw-Hill Book Company, 1966).

5. Collaboration and consultation are emphasized. There is a sharing of authority and responsibility.
6. In comparison with the bureaucracy there are often a wider span of control (more employees per supervisor) and fewer levels of management.
7. Organization members take on responsibilities for solving problems. This contrasts with the bureaucratic tendency to avoid individual responsibility and pass it on to the boss or someone else.

It ought to be recognized that the bureaucratic and organic conceptualizations given above are pure or polar types. Many enterprises contain some features of both and they are in between the two forms. Also, certain departments of a company, for example, production, may be operated according to the principles of a bureaucracy. Other departments, for example, research and development, may be operated according to the organic model.

Contingency Approach

The early view of organizational theorists was that there existed universal principles of organization and management. However, empirical research conducted during the past twenty-five years has shown that the optimal design of the organization depends upon many factors, both internal and external to the enterprise.[9] Therefore contemporary thinking advocates the contingency approach to organizational design. This requires an evaluation of the many interacting forces when constructing and operating an organization.

Complex organizations, in which technology is advancing rapidly and market and social forces are also shifting, tend to have large and

[9]See, for example, Burns and Stalker, *Ibid.*; Joan Woodward, *Industrial Organization: Theory and Practice* (London: Oxford University Press, 1965).

influential staff groups. Group decision making is common. There is a high ratio of administrative and technical personnel to production employees. Decision making is based more upon technical knowledge and less upon coercive power. Horizontal and diagonal relationships are just as important in work flow and decision making as vertical relationships. Project, matrix, and task force structures are more common here. There is more of a tendency to fit the job to the employee. Management by objectives is a fairly common management practice.

In contrast, those enterprises operating under standardized, stable conditions—such as the post office, steel industry, textiles, and wearing apparel—tend more toward the mechanistic or bureaucratic system. Thus, there is no *one* right pattern of organization and management. Practicing executives must be both enlightened and adaptable to shape their management systems to the situation and environment.

Questions for Review and Discussion

1. Reflect upon an organization (company, college club or sorority, etc.) with which you have had close association. Describe some organizational problems you have observed there.

2. The bureaucratic form of organization has been widely criticized as being too rigid, cumbersome, and slow in responding to problems. Some people claim that it suppresses employee initiative. In view of these charges how do you account for its continuing widespread use?

3. "The greater the division of labor and specialization in an organization the more there is need for creation of better methods of coordination." Explain this statement.

4. Explain systems concepts as they apply to organization. How does systems theory aid in the understanding of organizational processes?

5. Explain project and matrix forms of organization and their application.

6. What is delegation? What aspects of a manager's job can be delegated? What parts of the job ought to be retained by the manager?

7. Compare and contrast the bureaucratic and organic forms of organization.

8. What conditions give rise to the need for staff? When might a new staff function be created?

CASE PROBLEM

THE ENGINEERING DEPARTMENT

The Engineering Department of the Schoharie Corporation contained several functional engineering sections. Each section was comprised of a manager, ten to fifteen engineers and technicians plus two or three draftspersons. These draftspersons prepared engineering drawings from oral instructions and sketches provided by the engineers within the section. The quality of the work performed by these draftspersons was generally considered to be very good by the engineers throughout the entire department. Each draftsperson had to possess considerable skill because he or she was generally assigned a variety of drawing projects ranging from simple to complex.

As part of its continuing responsibility to cut costs and improve efficiency throughout the company, the Methods and Systems Engineering (M&SE) section

Organization and Jobs

of the corporation made an analysis of all the drafting activities in the engineering department. It found out that some draftspersons were overloaded and others were idle for portions of the work day. The M&SE section prepared a plan to centralize all drafting services within a central service section of the engineering department. It successfully sold the proposal to the director of the engineering department and to the executive vice-president of the corporation. The claimed advantages of the new plan were as follows: (1) Work loads among the draftspersons would be more uniform; (2) Idle time would be eliminated; (3) Greater specialization would be achieved by grouping draftspersons into four job classifications; (4) There would be closer control of each draftsperson's activities; (5) Training of new draftspersons would be more efficient in a central service section.

In accordance with the plan for reorganization, all of the 45 draftspersons were taken away from the functional engineering sections and placed in a newly created Drafting Services section within the engineering department. This new section, headed by a manager, had three coordinators who routed work to the individual draftspersons.

To obtain drafting service after the reorganization the following procedure was used: (1) Engineer filled out work order request which was signed by the group leader and the section manager; (2) Work order with engineering sketch was sent to drafting services section via interoffice mail (rush jobs hand-carried); (3) Coordinator assigned work orders, in order received, to draftspersons according to his or her judgment of their skills and experience; (4) Completed drawings were sent by interoffice mail to section manager of section that requested them. He or she then gave them to group leader who in turn gave them to the engineer who initiated original work order.

In operating under this new system the engineers soon learned that the drawings came back from the drafting services section with many errors. To get errors corrected required a repeat of the entire work order process with signatures, interoffice mail, etc. If the project was urgent, the engineer would make a personal trip to discuss the matter with the coordinator and draftsperson. Often the draftspersons were assigned drawing projects on which they had no previous experience. In these instances the draftsperson had to contact the initiating engineer via telephone or personally to obtain guidance and instructions.

To minimize mistakes and costly delays, the engineers began to prepare much more detailed sketches and written instructions than they formerly had done when the draftspersons worked in the same section with the engineer. The engineers found that sometimes their work orders were not signed by their own managers and sent to the Drafting Services section until several days after they had first initiated their orders. Sometimes sketches and drawings became temporarily lost in the process of passing through several offices and persons. The engineers felt that the productivity of the draftspersons was declining. Apparently, the draftspersons viewed each new drawing to be prepared as just another drawing in an unending series of drawings.

The engineers began to complain openly about the new system for obtaining engineering drawings. Their complaints were heard by the managers of the various engineering sections. These managers understood the problems and frustrations of the engineers but cautioned that more time should be allowed to work the defects out of the system.

Questions
1. Analyze this case from the standpoint of organization principles and human behavior concepts.
2. A work flow analysis and principles of technical efficiency initially indicated that the central drafting services system would be superior to the old organizational arrangement. What factors may have been overlooked in this technical analysis?
3. Analyze this case from the viewpoints of
   a. the engineers
   b. the draftspersons
4. Are problems such as those in this case endemic to all service pool arrangements (e.g. stenographic, maintenance, custodial)? Can pools work successfully?
5. How would you solve the problems brought out in this case?

Suggestions for Further Reading

Blau, Peter M. *The Dynamics of Bureaucracy,* rev. ed. Chicago: University of Chicago Press, 1963.

Davis, Stanley M., and Paul R. Lawrence. "Problems of Matrix Organizations." *Harvard Business Review,* Vol. 56, No. 3 (May–June 1978), pp. 131–142.

Kast, Fremont E., and James E. Rosenzweig. *Organization and Management: A Systems and Contingency Approach,* 3rd ed. New York: McGraw-Hill Book Co., 1979.

Katz, Daniel, Robert L. Kahn, and J. Stacy Adams (eds.). *The Study of Organizations.* San Francisco: Jossey-Bass, Inc., 1980.

Klein, Lisl. *New Forms of Work Organization.* New York: Cambridge University Press, 1976.

Lawrence, Paul R., and Jay W. Lorsch. *Organization and Environment.* Boston: Harvard Business School, 1967.

Mace, Myles L. "The President and the Board of Directors." *Harvard Business Review,* Vol. 50, No. 2 (March–April 1972), pp. 37–49.

Miles, Raymond E., and Charles C. Snow, *Organizational Strategy, Structure, and Process.* New York: McGraw-Hill Book Co., 1978.

Mintzberg, Henry, "Organization Design: Fashion or Fit?" *Harvard Business Review,* Vol. 59, No. 1 (January–February 1981), pp. 103–116.

Nystrom, Paul C., and William H. Starbuck (eds.). *Handbook of Organizational Design,* Volumes I and II. New York: Oxford University Press, 1981.

5

Job Design and Analysis

For a great many years the conventional practice has been for personnel managers to take the content of the jobs in an organization as a given factor. They would analyze these jobs to set proper rates of pay, and they would recruit, select, and train workers to fill these jobs. Engineers and production specialists were responsible for designing job content according to engineering principles and the needs of the production process. This is the way matters are still handled in a great many companies.

However, progressive managers have learned that designing jobs according to engineering and production needs is insufficient. Such a practice often yields jobs, groups of jobs, and work flow that make sense from a purely technical engineering standpoint but which produce poor performance and frustration from a human standpoint. Accordingly, the concepts and frame of reference of the behavioral sciences are now being blended with the engineering-production focus to develop jobs and work roles that are compatible with the technical-human-organizational matrix.

In this chapter we shall examine the changes in thinking that have occurred in regard to job design. Then we shall devote our attention to job analysis—the detailed and systematic study of jobs. Job analysis plays a role in human resource and organization planning, employee recruitment and selection, setting of proper rates of pay, work methods improvement, design of training programs, performance appraisal, accident prevention, and equal employment opportunity.

JOB DESIGN

The design of jobs—their content and structure—affects both productivity and employee motivation and morale. Historically, jobs in work organizations just evolved. It was the supervisor's job to group tasks into jobs and to assign workers to these jobs. With the advent of the industrial revolution and the rise of the factory system of production, factory superintendents began to assign narrow, specialized jobs to each worker.

Adam Smith, in his classic work *An Inquiry into the Nature and the Causes of the Wealth of Nations* (1776), originated the term "division of labor" and explained its advantages. He described in detail the various specialized tasks of producing pins in a factory. This division of labor enhanced individual dexterity and made it

85

unnecessary to consume time in changing from one task to another kind of task.

Despite Adam Smith's analysis and the practices of factory bosses in the 18th and 19th centuries, it was not until the dawn of the 20th century that the design of jobs into narrow, specialized units acquired a systematic, carefully formulated rationale. The two developments that brought this about were the scientific management movement led by Frederick W. Taylor and the Detroit style of mass production introduced by Henry Ford into the automobile industry. Both of these movements have been compatible in their philosophies and together they have heavily influenced the thinking of all who are involved in the creation of production processes and the design of jobs.

Taylor and his followers in the field of scientific management advocated the division of jobs into their smallest units of accomplishment, methods improvement, standardization of work methods, training, and wage incentives. Time and motion study was the principal tool for analyzing jobs and setting time standards. Taylor emphasized that it was management, not the worker, that should determine exactly how the job was to be done and how much time should be required to do it.

The automobile assembly line is the hallmark of Detroit-style mass production. It is the quintessence of minute division of labor, of machine pacing of the workers and of repetitiveness. It is considered to be highly efficient in the engineering sense. Other industries have adopted the assembly line to produce their products.

The philosophies and techniques of scientific management and of Detroit-style mass production have been the predominant influences guiding the thinking of industrial managers, production engineers, and industrial engineers in the laying out of production processes and the design of jobs for the first two thirds of the twentieth century. We shall label this the "engineering approach to job design."

Engineering Approach to Job Design

The principles followed in designing jobs in accordance with the engineering approach are as follows:

1. *Division of Labor and Specialization.* Each job should contain only a few simple tasks.
2. *Low Skill Requirements.* Keep skill needs at a minimum. Learning time should be short.
3. *Repetition.* Do identical, simple tasks over and over again.
4. *Specification and Standardization.* Work motions, methods, and tooling are decided and standardized, in writing, by the industrial engineer.
5. *Minimal Social Interaction.* In laying out work stations the engineers often have an ancillary purpose of minimizing conversation and social contact among workers because they believe this interferes with workers' performance.
6. *Movement of Materials and Parts.* Bring all materials and parts to the operator. Minimize walking. Minimize internal handling of materials and parts at the workstation.
7. *Control Work Pace.* The speed of movement and output at each work station is controlled either by (a) machine pacing and the speed of the assembly line or (b) time standards for each operation.

We might say, then, that the engineering approach to job design has focused upon tooling, equipment, machine controls, materials-handling requirements, and the physiological configurations of the workers in relation to the workplace. It has emphasized workloads, work pace, and the assignment of people who can match the demands of the job.

The principal motive force inducing employees to produce is assumed to be money. The money can either be paid in the form of a wage incentive tied directly to output or in the form of an hourly wage with an hourly or daily quota of units to be produced specified by management.

This traditional or engineering approach to job design and to control of employees' work effort has been moderately successful in achieving good levels of production at reasonable costs, especially for routine kinds of operations.

Difficulties with Engineering Approach

Missing from the conventional engineering formulation has been an appreciation of the psychological nature of people and of the sociological and organizational environment in which they work. A time-study engineer may spend 30 minutes making a time study of a worker and then set a standard rate of, say, 75 pieces per hour. However, this is the microscopic view. It ignores the abilities, attitudes, and aspirations of the individual and the effects upon the employee's performance of the work group, supervision, and organizational practices.

Since the 1950s there has been a change in the nature of the work force. It is better educated and has higher expectations than earlier generations. Years ago workers accepted drudgery and monotony because they had no alternative. But employees who have grown up in an era of affluence and of mass secondary school and college education expect more from work and they have more to contribute. They seek more say-so about affairs in their places of employment.

When people work on narrow, confining jobs of limited scope they cannot develop pride in their work. They know that their operations are only insignificant parts of the whole product or function. They have no chance to develop or apply real skills. Their jobs may require surface attention in that they must continuously pay attention to what they are doing and perhaps watch dials and gauges. But their work is not really interesting or absorbing. No real thinking is required. Jobs that are routine and repetitive are commonly felt by employees to be boring and monotonous. Variety is lacking.

If workplaces are designed so that conversation and social contact are limited or impossible, then employees suffer further frustration. Finally, jobs designed according to conventional engineering principles allow workers practically no control over their work methods or work pace.

A Contemporary Orientation

Managers have often been aware of the disadvantages accompanying the traditional or engineering system of job design. But until relatively recently they have not had sound guidance for alternative approaches.

Commencing in the 1960s and continuing through the present time behavioral scientists and personnel researchers have been constructing theories to guide the process of job design. These theories have been tested and applied in a variety of organizations in the United States and Europe.

A pioneer in the development of job design research has been Frederick Herzberg, a university psychologist. He has conducted extensive research into work and has identified those factors that are motivators (achievement, recognition, work itself, responsibility, advancement, and growth) and those that are merely maintenance or hygienic factors (company policies, working conditions, interpersonal relations, pay, and job security). Herzberg asserts that work becomes more satisfying and the employee more productive as more motivators are introduced into the job content. If hygienic factors are unsatisfactory, people will be discontent. But if these are adequate people will not necessarily be motivated to work harder. The key, according to Herzberg, is to insure that the hygienic factors are adequate in order to minimize frustration and complaints and to generate

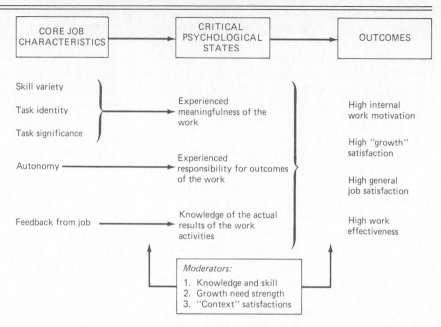

FIGURE 5-1 The Complete Job Characteristic's Model. *Reprinted with permission from J. Richard Hackman and Greg R. Oldham,* **Work Redesign** *(Reading, Mass.: Addison-Wesley Publishing Co.),* © *1980, Figure 4.6.*

a feeling of well being. Then build motivators into employees' jobs.[1]

Building upon the foundations of others Hackman and Oldham have constructed what is called the "job characteristics theory."[2] In designing jobs, Hackman and Oldham state, the objective is to integrate into them those attributes that create conditions for strong employee motivation, satisfaction, and performance. People will work hard on their jobs when they are rewarded for what they do and when their work is satisfying to them.

The Hackman and Oldham theory can be best understood by examining Figure 5-1. The theory postulates that there are three essential psychological states that determine whether

people have high work motivation. The first is knowledge of the results of one's work activities. This means that the individual finds out rather promptly whether his work is well received and whether it meets quality standards. The second is real responsibility for the outcomes of one's work. This means that the employee can control the job and determine results. He has some discretion. The third psychological state is experienced meaningfulness of the work. The person feels that the work being done is important and necessary.

The core job characteristics that contribute toward meaningful work are *skill variety* (various tasks using different skills), *task identity* (doing a whole piece of work with an observable outcome), and *task significance* (important to other people in the organization and beyond). In order to enhance experienced responsibility the job should allow reasonable *autonomy* (discretion and control of work procedures and work schedules). And finally to enhance knowledge of actual results the job should provide for *feedback* to the employee of information on the quantity and quality of his performance.

[1]For further information on Frederick Herzberg's work see his publications: *Work and the Nature of Man* (Cleveland: World Publishingn Co., 1966); "One More Time: How Do You Motivate Employees?" *Harvard Business Review,* Vol. 46, No. 1 (January–February 1968), pp. 53–62; and "The Wise Old Turk," *Harvard Business Review,* Vol. 52, No. 5 (September–October 1974), pp. 70–80.

[2]J. Richard Hackman and Greg R. Oldham, *Work Redesign* (Reading, Mass.: Addison-Wesley Publishing Company, 1980).

If the job contains ample amounts of the core job characteristics, these will satisfy the critical psychological states. These in turn should generate favorable outcomes in terms of high internal motivation, high growth satisfaction, high general job satisfaction, and high work effectiveness. However, the relationships among these dimensions may not always be simple and straightforward. The "moderators" shown in Figure 5-1 must be taken into account. If an employee does not possess adequate knowledge and skill to do the job properly then he will experience frustration and favorable outcomes will not occur. Also some employees have low needs for growth and personal accomplishment. These people will not respond strongly even if all the core job characteristics are present. And lastly, if the job context factors (hygiene factors in Herzberg's terminology) are poor the person is unlikely to be enthusiastic about having the job made more challenging and complex. If such things as pay, job security, or relations with one's supervisor are bad, these conditions must be improved before the individual will respond favorably to job enrichment efforts.

Job Designs for Motivation

Starting with relatively simple methods and moving to more complex designs we shall describe five different ways of designing jobs which will have a greater probability of generating high employee motivation and job satisfaction than the traditional engineering system. Sometimes, but certainly not always, these job designs may yield higher output as well.

Job Rotation. Having an employee on a routine, repetitive job move from one routine job to another, and back again, every few hours or days is a form of job rotation that has been found in some instances to relieve boredom and monotony. Norman Maier has described an industrial application where job rotation improved employee response. There were two jobs, sold-

erers and dusters, in the central office of a telephone company. The dusters had continuously to go over the equipment to keep it clean and the solderers constantly looked for broken connections which they repaired. Morale was low and turnover was serious. By permitting the employees to exchange jobs every two hours, not only did morale improve but productivity increased as well.[3]

If employees rotate to jobs requiring slightly new and different skills, they then become more valuable to the organization. Flexibility in staffing is gained. Per se, job rotation simply adds a little variety and may temporarily add interest to the job.

Griffin states that among the companies that have adopted job rotation are American Cyanamid, Bethlehem Steel, Ford Motor Company, Prudential Insurance, TRW Systems, and Western Electric.[4]

Larger Units of Accomplishment. An inspector, who visually examines objects as they come endlessly off a production line, may indeed find this job to be monotonous. However, by segregating the units into batches, a sense of accomplishment may be achieved when each batch is complete. Most of us have undertaken tasks that seemed endless. However, by establishing subgoals on the road to completion, we gain a sense of making real progress as we do our work. Examples occur in such activities as cutting the lawn, pulling weeds in flower beds, and painting one's house.

Job Enlargement. Job enlargement means adding more and different tasks to a specialized job. Thus it adds variety. When additional simple tasks are added to a job that was initially simple in nature, this process is called horizontal job loading or horizontal job enlargement.

[3]Norman R. F. Maier, *Psychology in Industrial Organizations*, 4th ed. (Boston: Houghton Mifflin Company, 1973), p. 433.

[4]Ricky W. Griffin, *Task Design: An Integrative Approach* (Glenview, Ill.: Scott, Foresman and Company, 1982) p. 25.

Presumably this action adds interest to the work and reduces monotony and boredom.

Griffin reports that successful job enlargement programs were installed at Detroit Edison Company, American Telephone and Telegraph, Colonial Insurance Company, and Maytag, to name only a few of the numerous companies that have used it.[5]

Job enlargement programs conducted in the 1950s and 60s often contained some elements of what we now call *job enrichment.* Not only was more variety added to simple jobs, but also employees were given some discretion in deciding work methods and work pace. They also often had responsibility for checking their own quality.

Job Enrichment. Job enrichment has been characterized as vertical job loading. Enriching a narrow, simple job means adding duties and responsibilities that will provide for skill variety, task identity, task significance, autonomy, and feedback on job performance. An enriched job should provide for high internal work motivation and employee satisfaction. Work output often is high as well.

Specific action steps for designing enriched jobs are as follows:

1. *Natural Work Units.* Create natural or logical work units so employees can experience a sense of ownership of their work and can develop a feeling of responsibility. Natural work units can be based upon such dimensions as type of customer, departmental boundaries, or classes of products.
2. *Larger Modules of Work.* Combine several duties, requiring various skills, into each job. This also enhances task identity.
3. *Client Relationships.* The employee should have direct knowledge of and, if possible, direct contact with the person or group that receives his completed work. Examples of a client relationship are a secretary doing work for a supervisor and a draftsperson preparing drawings for an engineer. In this way the employee can obtain feedback on how well his or her work meets the needs of those who use that work. A client relationship also enhances autonomy because the secretary and the draftsperson, in the examples given, bear personal responsibility for handling relationships with their clients. Conversely if secretaries, draftspersons, and other categories of employees are assigned to a "pool" from which services are requisitioned through a paperwork procedure, they lose all sense of a client relationship.
4. *Vertical Job Loading.* To load a job vertically is to incorporate some "planning" and "controlling" duties into the job. Employees make some of their own decisions regarding work methods—setting up the equipment, scheduling the work, and checking on the quality of the work they produce. When a job is loaded vertically employees exercise personal accountability for their performance. They identify and correct their own errors.
5. *Information and Feedback.* People should be given full information necessary to do their jobs and they should receive direct feedback on the quality and quantity of their performance. In traditional job designs the feedback is given to the employee by the boss. The subordinate often views this as an evaluation of character and it is resented. The feedback should be as objective as possible.

Favorable results with job enrichment in terms of such measures as quality, quantity, attendance, costs, and morale have been found in such diverse applications as chemists and production workers in a chemicals company, janitors in an electronics firm, stockholder correspondents in a telecommunications company, and tax examiners in the Internal Revenue Service.[6]

[5]Griffin, Ibid., p. 21.

[6]Among the many references on job enrichment are Harold M. F. Rush, *Job Design for Motivation* (New York: The

Self-managed Work Teams. Self-managed work teams are also called autonomous work groups or integrated work teams. Typically, work groups of, say, ten to twenty employees plan, coordinate, and control their own activities. They have a team leader who is generally a working supervisor, rather than a member of management.

The teams are given the authority not only to perform direct production operations but also to do certain activities that traditionally are done by service and staff groups. Thus, an assembly group may take on the added tasks of planning work methods, inspecting output, maintaining equipment, and even selecting employees for the team. These groups have the authority to regulate their own work tempo. Key decisions are often made as group decisions.

The objective in setting up self-managed work teams is to create groups around whole units of work wherein the components of the work and the processes are interdependent. Generally several different skills and jobs are combined into each team. The team is accountable for performance of its whole unit of work (e.g. making subassemblies, processing customer claims) and given the personnel and resources necessary to complete the work properly. The reward system (pay, promotion, recognition) is commonly related to both group and individual achievement.

Companies which have used self-managed work teams in at least some of their operations are the Volvo automobile plant at Kalmar, Sweden, the Butler Manufacturing Company plant at Story City, Iowa, Hunsfos Pulp and Paper Mill in Norway, Rade Koncar in Yugoslavia, Syntex Corporation in Mexico and California, and the General Foods pet food plant in Topeka, Kansas.[7]

Perspective on Job Design

A great many experiments and ongoing programs which incorporate those characteristics that comprise meaningful and motivating work have also demonstrated positive benefits in important performance indexes: lower turnover, lower absenteeism, fewer grievances, more favorable responses by employees in attitude surveys, and higher productivity. However, some programs have had only modest success and others have been failures. A great many forces interact simultaneously in any job-employee-organization-management system. Job content and structure are only part of the system. Let us look at some of the factors that favor success in job design efforts.

First and foremost is strong commitment on the part of top management to design jobs and work structures which enhance the quality of work life in the organization.

The employees should have desires to grow, to achieve, and to contribute. They should seek intrinsic satisfaction in the work itself. It should be evident, though, that not all people seek challenging jobs. Additionally the employees involved must possess (or be willing and able to acquire) the requisite knowledge and skills to adequately perform enriched jobs. Lower level managers must be secure and must believe in enrichment strategies. They should not feel threatened by the increased authority and responsibility granted to rank-and-file employees.

The technology should be compatible with enrichment efforts. For example, if an existing

Conference Board, 1971); J. Richard Hackman and Greg R. Oldham, *Work Redesign* op. cit.; Frederick Herzberg, "One More Time: How Do You Motivate Employees?" op. cit.; Robert N. Ford, *Motivation Through the Work Itself* (New York: American Management Association, 1969); and John R. Maher, ed., *New Perspectives in Job Enrichment* (New York: Van Nostrand Reinhold, 1971).

[7]Descriptions of these programs can be found in *Work in America, Report of a Special Task Force to the Secretary of Health, Education, and Welfare* (Cambridge, Mass.: MIT Press, 1973), pp. 188 ff.; Ricky W. Griffin, *Task Design*, op. cit., pp. 192–196; and J. Richard Hackman and Greg R. Oldham, *Work Redesign* op. cit., pp. 165–168.

plant contains a heavy capital investment in equipment that was installed to be operated according to engineering job design principles, then it would be very costly to redesign jobs and work flow. On the other hand, in planning a new manufacturing facility, in service activities, and in salaried office functions, there is often considerable freedom to innovate.

Finally, if enriched jobs require more skill and greater responsibility, then management must be willing to adjust the wages of the people involved to reward them fairly for the higher job demands.

JOB INFORMATION AND PERSONNEL MANAGEMENT

Accurate and up-to-date information is essential to the operation of a sound personnel program. An organization is composed of people who are grouped together into teams (designated as sections, departments, divisions, and so on) to do work in order to achieve agreed-upon goals. These basic elements, people and their assigned jobs—are organized into small units, which in turn are combined into larger units, such as divisions and plants, and these are finally related one to the other into companies, institutions, or governmental units.

Sound management practice requires that each of the entities above be defined and specified. The purpose and objectives of each organizational unit from the top on down to individual jobs should be determined, recorded, and communicated to appropriate parties involved. Likewise, the functions of each organizational unit and the relationship of one to the other must be established and agreed upon. This work is all part and parcel of good organization planning. The determination and recording of the specific content of each job and of the necessary employee skills and abilities to fill the jobs is likewise vital to successful administra-

tion. The method and procedure employed to determine the duties, responsibilities, working conditions, and working relationship of and between jobs and the human qualifications of employees are called *job analysis*.

What Is Job Analysis?

Job analysis is the process of determining, by observation and study, and reporting pertinent information about a specific job. It includes the identification of the tasks performed; the machines and equipment utilized; the materials, products, or services involved; and the training, skills, knowledges, and personal traits required of the worker.

Modern-day usage of the term *job analysis* has tended to restrict it to the type of job study associated with various personnel programs, such as employee selection, job evaluation, wage surveys, training, accident prevention, and the like. However, the term is also sometimes applied to a detailed and quantitative study of jobs and job operations by industrial engineers in connection with time and motion study, methods improvement, and work measurement programs. The industrial engineering approach usually breaks down each job into detailed tasks and often specifies each hand and arm motion to be utilized by the worker. In other words, the work is subdivided into elements, and times are determined for each one. The goal is usually to establish a standard time for each type of operation performed by each worker. Work simplification and methods improvement are generally part and parcel of every analysis.

Because industrial engineering techniques, such as work simplification, methods engineering, time and motion study, and work measurement, are outside the scope of this book, our explanations in this chapter will be confined to job analysis from the personnel management viewpoint.

Simply stated, job analysis is a procedure

for obtaining pertinent job information. This information is recorded, basically on two forms or pieces of paper, to make a permanent record. One is called a job description and the other is called a job specification. The relationship between these is shown in Figure 5-2.

The actual content and format of job descriptions and specifications vary greatly from one organization to another. Indeed there is even some confusion between the two terms in some circles. Some practitioners make no distinction between a job description and a specification. They use them interchangeably. However, the more common practice is to designate the objective listing of job title, summary, and duties as the description and to call the enumeration of employee qualifications the job specification. The determination of the human characteristics needed to fill a job calls for value judgments. The specification is actually derived from the description by translating the job activities and requirements into particular skills and abilities. But to a certain extent the level of ability demanded is dependent upon management policy and standards. For example, some organizations require that their secretaries have a post-

high school business education (one to two years), whereas others accept simply a high school diploma and concentrate upon training from within.

Figure 5-3 shows a job description and specification for an experimental mechanic, a highly skilled hourly paid job. In this case the statement of job content (the job description) and the statement of employee qualifications (the job specification) are contained in one form.

Uses for Job Analysis and Job Information

A comprehensive job analysis program is an essential ingredient of sound personnel management. Job information derived from such a program has many important applications. These are as follows:

Organization and Human Resource Planning. When it is determined that certain types and amounts of work must be done, this work must be divided into specific jobs at all levels in the organization, from unskilled laborer up

FIGURE 5-2 Job Description and Job Specification in Job Analysis.

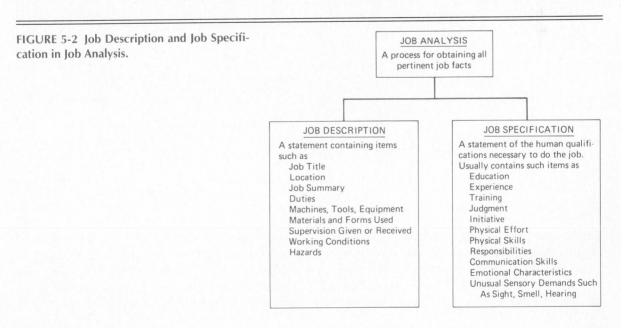

JOB ANALYSIS
A process for obtaining all pertinent job facts

JOB DESCRIPTION
A statement containing items such as
    Job Title
    Location
    Job Summary
    Duties
    Machines, Tools, Equipment
    Materials and Forms Used
    Supervision Given or Received
    Working Conditions
    Hazards

JOB SPECIFICATION
A statement of the human qualifications necessary to do the job. Usually contains such items as
    Education
    Experience
    Training
    Judgment
    Initiative
    Physical Effort
    Physical Skills
    Responsibilities
    Communication Skills
    Emotional Characteristics
    Unusual Sensory Demands Such
        As Sight, Smell, Hearing

FIGURE 5-3 Job Description and Specification: Experimental Mechanic.

JOB DESCRIPTION AND SPECIFICATION

JOB ____Experimental Mechanic_____ JOB NO. ___H 75_____

DATE EFFECTIVE____August 21, 1978_____ GRADE ___12_____

JOB FUNCTION: Perform experimental and developmental work that requires devising, machining, fabricating, assembling, and modifying components of new or special equipment and machinery. Construct and run-in special purpose machinery and equipment.

DUTIES: Working from rough sketches, machine drawings, and verbal instructions, devise, construct, and modify, using various machine tools and assembly equipment, components of generating equipment such as special trays, pumps, and heat exchangers as well as special machinery, equipment, and tools necessary for the manufacture of company products. Analyze requirements of machinery and equipment to be built, develop own work techniques, make alterations and tests as work progresses in coordination with engineers and supervision. Follow through to insure successful functioning of machinery or equipment.

Set up and operate machine tools, solder parts, layout and perform bench work as required.

Read and interpret intricate machine and assembly drawings and sketches.

May be required to machine parts to tolerances of .001 inch.

MACHINES, TOOLS, AND EQUIPMENT: Engine lathe, turret lathe, shaper, planer, milling machine, boring mill, drill press, surface grinder, tool grinder, power saw, hydro and mechanical presses, gages and precision measuring instruments, soldering equipment, common hand tools.

DIRECTION OF OTHERS: Instruct others in the operation of machinery and equipment he has developed and constructed. May supervise the activities of helpers.

WORKING CONDITIONS: General shop and machine tool noise. Dirt, grease, and coolants from operation of machine tools and assembly of machines and equipment.

HAZARDS: Serious cuts, bruises, and burns may occur from operation of machine tools, soldering, and assembly activities.

EDUCATION: High school graduate or equivalent.

VOCATIONAL PREPARATION: Completion of machinist apprenticeship program (4 years) or equivalent.

PREVIOUS EXPERIENCE: 3–4 years as journeyman machinist and mechanic working on variety of machine tools and products.

IN- PLANT TRAINING: One year at company as machinist or mechanic, preferably in experimental work.

MENTAL DEMAND: A high degree of ingenuity and judgment is required to plan and build equipment when working from only rough sketches or verbal instructions. Must exhibit considerable resourcefulness to experiment and make repeated trials and adaptations of equipment where procedures are not well established.

PHYSICAL DEMAND: May lift and carry objects weighing up to 40 pounds occasionally. Normal work position is standing or walking.

Analysis By _____ Approved By _____

through the chief executive officer. In establishing the organization structure, it is necessary to "package" the work to be done into meaningful units. Job analysis aids in determining the number and kinds of jobs and the qualifications needed to fill these jobs. Thus, it is an essential element of effective manpower planning. At managerial levels, accurate job descriptions and specifications are intimately related to the preparation of inventories of executive talent.

Recruitment, Selection, and Placement. To carry out an employment program, it is necessary to have clear statements of the work to be performed and of the skills and knowledge that must be possessed by the employees who will fill these jobs. Basically the goal is to match, as closely as possible, the job requirements with the worker's aptitudes, abilities, and interests. It is not possible to staff varied jobs accurately in an organization by having available job title data only. Full job information is necessary.

Equal Employment Opportunity. Equal employment opportunity laws, regulations, and court orders have made accurate job analysis of extreme importance. The burden of proof is upon the employer to justify an educational requirement of, say, a college degree for a specific job if that employer is charged with discrimination in hiring, placement, or promotion. Furthermore, if a company pays women less than men for performing jobs that on the surface appear the same, the burden of proof must be borne by management to show that in fact there are real differences in the duties and requirements of the work done by the men and women. If selection tests are to be validated by the *content validity* method (as opposed to *criterion-related validity*), then very detailed and specific information on job tasks and worker skills must be obtained. And finally, those employers covered by the Rehabilitation Act of 1973 (those holding government contracts) should study their jobs carefully to ascertain which ones could be performed adequately by persons with certain physical or mental handicaps.

Establishing Proper Rates of Pay. This involves a determination of the relative worth of jobs within the organization by means of the technique called job evaluation and a comparison of wages paid inside the organization with those paid for comparable jobs in other companies via a wage survey. Job evaluation insures internal pay equity of one job to another, whereas surveying the going wages in a labor market insures that the level of wages within an organization is correct in relation to the community or the industry. For job evaluation purposes, job descriptions must be very complete; for conducting a wage survey, condensed descriptions are generally sufficient.

Redesign of the Job. Jobs may be studied in order to improve work methods, reduce errors, eliminate unnecessary handling of materials and duplication of effort, reduce fatigue, increase employee commitment and responsibility, and in general, to improve the performance of the employee–job unit. Quite often the optimum results in this work can be gained by combining the approaches of the industrial engineer, the human factors psychologist, and the organizational behaviorist.

Employee Training and Management Development. Many firms provide new employees with copies of the descriptions and specifications for the jobs to which they have been assigned. This practice aids in orienting them and acquainting them with what they are expected to do. Job information is also very helpful to those who administer training and development programs. It helps them determine the content and subject matter needed in training courses. Selection of trainees is also facilitated by studying job information.

Performance Appraisal. Job analysis data can be adapted to help establish clear-cut standards of performance for every job. Standards of performance are mostly qualitative (they may also contain some quantitative information) statements of what management expects of the employees assigned to each job. In evaluating the performance of each employee (for pay adjustments, employee development, and so on) the supervisor can compare the actual contribution of each worker with the written standard. Performance appraisals can never become fully objective and impartial, but the usage of written standards helps make them more objective.

Safety and Health. The process of conducting a detailed job analysis provides an excellent opportunity to uncover and identify hazardous conditions and unhealthy environmental factors (such as heat, noise, fumes, and dust), so that corrective measures can be taken to minimize and avoid the possibility of human injury.

Job Categories

In analyzing and describing jobs, job analysts and personnel managers find it helpful to classify jobs into groups. All jobs within each category have certain characteristics in common, especially in regard to education and training requirements and in regard to broad skill and knowledge demands. Figure 5-4 shows the generally accepted titles, responsibilities, and training requirements for the principal job groups found in work organizations. Not all establishments employ people in every job category.

For wage and salary administration and related purposes, employees are generally grouped into three very broad divisions. *Nonexempt*, hourly paid personnel, are employed in unskilled, semiskilled, skilled, and technician jobs. Nonexempt office personnel are employed in secretarial and clerical jobs. Administrative, professional, sales, and managerial personnel are classified as *exempt*. The term *exempt* means that the work content of the job is such that the employer is not required to pay job holders time-and-one-half for hours worked over 40 in a week

FIGURE 5-4 The Principal Categories of Jobs in Organizations.

Unskilled. Perform simple work usually requiring much physical effort. Short training period ranges from a few hours to two weeks. *Examples:* laborer, janitor.

Semiskilled. Operate equipment, assemble parts. Manipulative tasks confined to definite work routine. Exercise alertness to avoid damage to product or equipment. Training period ranges from few weeks to few months. *Examples:* assembler, truck driver, machine operator.

Skilled. Perform complex tasks requiring comprehensive knowledge of materials, processes, and equipment. Often must exhibit considerable dexterity. Training period of 3 to 4 years; apprenticeship may be required. *Examples:* electrician, machinist, tool and die maker, lithographer.

Technician. Perform highly skilled work requiring considerable knowledge, judgment, and experience within a limited range. Requires formal education beyond high school in a field of technology (generally a two-year college). *Examples:* computer technician, medical laboratory technician, electronics technician.

Secretarial-Clerical. Perform various office duties including typing, taking dictation, routine computations, compiling simple reports, simple data collection and analysis. Requires high school education; may require specialized training in a business institute. *Examples:* secretary, clerk, accounting clerk.

Administrative. Performs responsible office work directly related to managerial policies. Analyze information and prepare reports. Exercise independent judgment. Commonly requires a college education. *Examples:* executive assistant, budget examiner, financial analyst, personnel specialist.

Professional. Work is intellectual and varied in character. Consistently exercises discretion and independent judgment. Work requires knowledge of an advanced type in a field of science or technology. Requires at least a 4-year college education in a technical field, often plus graduate specialization. *Examples:* engineer, chemist, economist.

Manager. Directs an enterprise or component thereof. Directs the activities of subordinates. Has authority to hire and fire. Has broad discretionary powers. *Examples:* president, general manager, supervisor.

Sales. Typically contacts potential customers away from employer's place of business. Solicits orders and provides certain services. Training requirements vary greatly. *Examples:* sales person, account executive.

in accordance with provisions of the Fair Labor Standards Act. Nonexempt employees, on the other hand, must be paid time-and-one-half for hours in excess of 40.

Job Analysis Terms

Certain terms are widely used in the field of job analysis.

A *task* is an action or related group of actions designed to produce a definite outcome or result. In common parlance a task is the same as a duty. A task may be primarily physical, such as operating a drill press; primarily mental, such as analyzing data; or primarily interpersonal, such as negotiating with someone.

A *position* is a collection of tasks and responsibilities regularly assigned to one person. A *job* is a group of positions that involve generally the same duties, skills, knowledge, and responsibilities. Thus, a position consists of the particular, and often unique, set of duties assigned to an individual. There may be ten people, all of whom are classified under the same job title; yet each may perform slightly different work. Many secretaries may have the same job title. Yet the secretary to the general manager may have slightly different duties from the secretary to the project engineer.

An *occupation* is a composite of many closely related jobs found in many establishments. Basically, when we are within the four walls of an enterprise we use the term *job*. But when we refer to that job as it may be set up in various organizations, the more generalized term *occupation* is used. *The Dictionary of Occupational Titles*[8] is the standard reference work in the occupational information field. It contains the definitions of over 22,000 distinct occupations. It also gives educational, vocational, and worker trait requirements and vocational interests for each major occupation.

[8]U.S. Department of Labor, *Dictionary of Occupational Titles*, 4th ed. (Washington, D.C., U.S. Government Printing Office, 1977).

Methods of Analyzing Jobs

There are seven ways by which job information can be gathered: (1) observation, (2) questionnaire, (3) interview, (4) check list, (5) daily diary, (6) conference of experts, and (7) a combination of two or more of these.

It is generally not possible to use the observation method alone to gather enough information to prepare a job description and a specification. It is true that industrial engineers rely principally upon observation to conduct motion and time studies. However, they deal primarily with repetitive, short-cycle, unskilled, and semiskilled jobs. They do not have to develop a job specification that calls for value judgments on worker qualifications (best obtained by interviewing the supervisor). Actual observation is very desirable to acquaint the job analyst with the materials and equipment used, the working conditions and hazards, and to obtain a sharp, visual impression of just what is involved in the work.

The questionnaire method is popular with management engineering consultants who are hired to install a job evaluation plan and who feel they must accomplish a lot in a minimum of time. Usually, the procedure involves the preparation of a detailed questionnaire, which is then distributed to all employees, who fill it out on company time and who return it to their supervisors for verification. The supervisor is supposed to discuss any errors in the employee's response with him, make corrections, and then transmit it to the group responsible for conducting the job analysis program (generally the personnel department). Figure 5-5 shows an example of a questionnaire for collecting job

FIGURE 5-5 Employee Job Analysis Questionnaire.

INDIVIDUAL JOB ANALYSIS QUESTIONNAIRE

Name_____ Department _____

Payroll Title_____ Name, Immediate Supervisor_____

Instructions: Please read the entire form before making any entries. Answer each question as accurately and carefully as possible. When completed return this form to your supervisor. If you have any questions ask your supervisor.

Your Duties
What duties and tasks do you personally perform daily?

What duties do you perform only at stated intervals such as semi weekly, weekly or monthly? Indicate which period applies to each duty.

What duties do you perform only at irregular intervals?

Supervision of Others
How many employees are directly under your supervision? (List job titles and number of people assigned to each job.)

Do you have full discretionary authority to assign work; correct and discipline; recommend pay increases, transfers, promotions and discharge; and to answer grievances?

Do you only assign work, instruct, and coordinate the activities of your subordinates?

Materials, Tools, and Equipment
What are the principal materials and products that you handle?

List the names of the machines and equipment used in your work.

List the names of the principal hand tools and instruments used in your work.

What is the Source of Your Instructions? (e.g., oral, written, blueprints, specifications, etc.)

What Contacts Are You Required to Make with Persons Other Than Your Immediate Supervisor and Departmental Associates?

     a) Give the job titles and the department or organization of those with whom you deal.

     b) Describe the nature of these contacts.

Decisions
What decisions do you have to make without consulting your supervisor?

Responsibility
     a) Describe the nature of your responsibility for money, machinery, equipment, and reports.

     b) What monetary loss can occur through an honest error?

FIGURE 5-5 (Continued)

Records and Reports
a) What records and reports do you personally prepare?

b) What is the source of the data?

Checking of Your Work
a) How is your work inspected, checked, or verified?

b) Who does this?

Physical Requirements
a) What percentage of the time do you spend in the following working positions?

Standing _____%,   Sitting _____%,   Walking about _____%?

b) What weight in pounds must you personally lift and carry?_____pounds

c) What percentage of the working day do you actually spend lifting and carrying this weight? _____%

d) Are any special physical skills, eye-hand coordination, and manual dexterity skills required on your job?

Working Conditions
Describe any conditions present in the location and nature of your work, such as noise, heat, dust, fumes, etc., which you consider unfavorable or disagreeable.

Hazards
Describe the dangers or accident hazards present in your job.

_____

THIS PORTION IS TO BE FILLED OUT BY YOUR SUPERVISOR.

Education Requirements
What is the lowest grade of grammar school, high school, or college required of a person starting in this job?

Previous Experience
a) What kind of previous work experience is necessary for minimum satisfactory performance for a new employee on this job?

b) Give the length of experience required.

Training
Assuming that a new employee on this job has the necessary education and experience to quality for the work, what training is necessary after the employee is on the job to achieve an acceptable performance level? (Specify training needed and period of time to acquire it.)

_____   _____
Date   Signature of Supervisor

analysis data directly from the employees themselves.

The questionnaire method requires somewhat less staff time than the interview method. In other words the cost of collecting the job data is lower with this technique. All the employees participate and answer questions about their jobs. With the interview method, only one or perhaps two individuals on a job are interviewed. However, the questionnaire approach has serious disadvantages. The accuracy of the information leaves much to be desired. Job analysis work requires specialized knowledge and training. The average employee, although he knows best just what his duties are, is not trained to identify the essential aspects of work and often cannot express the information in a meaningful and clear fashion. Any questionnaire is open to varying interpretations. To depend exclusively upon questionnaires as the source of job information is bound to introduce some errors into the program.

Many organizations employ job analysts who interview employees and/or their supervisors in order to obtain all the pertinent information. When the interview of both the supervisor and the employee is combined with a short observation at the job by a trained analyst, this procedure constitutes a very thorough and sound approach. It is the one most widely used. Analysts essentially ask the same kinds of questions that appear in Figure 5-5. However, they know how to differentiate between essential and nonessential information. They have a consistency of viewpoint and judgment. They can ask probing questions to uncover facts that might be overlooked if employees simply filled out a questionnaire. Because analysts must compose and write job descriptions, they are in the best position to do so if they have actually seen the job being performed and if they have talked to the employees and their immediate superiors. An important byproduct of a job analysis program is that it often creates greater understanding and common agreement between the job holder and

boss on the precise requirements of the job. Often in practice, analysts run into cases in which workers have stated that they perform certain tasks, whereas supervisors state that those tasks are really not a part of the job and belong to someone else. The opposite is common also.

The check list method can be used in large organizations that have a large number of people assigned to the same or similar jobs. The staff group that prepares a check list for each of the various jobs in the enterprise or agency must first collect enough information to prepare a meaningful check list. Such information can be obtained by asking supervisors, methods engineers, and others familiar with the work to record the tasks comprising each job. When a check list has been prepared for a job, say a supply clerk in an Army depot, then it is sent to all supply clerks in all depots. The job holders are asked to check all listed tasks that they perform and to indicate by check mark the amount of time spent on each task as well as the training and experience required to be proficient in each task. They may also be asked to write in additional required tasks not contained on the prepared list. A typical job may contain 200 or 300 task statements. This technique is amenable to tabulation and recording on electronic data-processing equipment. The check list method is rather costly and somewhat impractical for small organizations, however, because of the setup costs involved in developing check lists for every job.[9]

The daily diary method requires the job holders to record in detail their activities throughout each day. If done faithfully this technique is accurate and eliminates the error of memory recall of the questionnaire and check list devices. However, it adds considerably to the

[9]A description of the check list method as applied by the United States Air Force is contained in Joseph E. Morsh, "Job Analysis in the United States Air Force," *Personnel Psychology,,* Vol. 37 (1962), pp. 7–17.

workload of each production employee and for this reason is seldom used in practice.

The conference of experts technique of collecting job information is quite useful for obtaining various viewpoints and an overall perspective of the jobs. However, supervisors, staff specialists, and technicians may be removed enough from the work itself that they lack intimate familiarity with its details and complexities. Thus accuracy suffers.

Content of Information Collected

As indicated previously, the nature of the information collected when analyzing jobs is determined by the use that will be made of the data. If a company simply wishes to prepare brief descriptions so that it can conduct a labor market wage survey, then the analyst will obtain only that information necessary to describe the significant duties and requirements of jobs with special emphasis upon those features that differentiate it from related jobs. Because the most common practice in business and industry is to prepare job descriptions and specifications for purposes of hiring, job evaluation, and for acquainting new people with the exact nature of their jobs and with what management expects of them, the content of information collected will be explained from this standpoint.

The items given below are the principal ones covered when analyzing jobs.

1. *Job Title and Location:* These designate the job and the organizational unit in which it is located. Some standardization of job titling is desirable.
2. *Job Summary:* This is included in most job descriptions to give the reader a quick capsule explanation of the job. It is usually one or two sentences in length.
3. *Job Duties:* A comprehensive listing of duties is included together with an indication of the frequency of occurrence or percentage of time devoted to each major duty. Always includes *what* the job holder does along with some indication of *how* he performs the tasks.
4. *Machines, Tools, and Equipment:* A listing of all the tooling and work aids used in the job.
5. *Materials, Products, Services:* Raw materials used and products made or services performed.
6. *Supervision Given:* For supervisory and group leader jobs, the number of persons supervised and their job titles are given.
7. *Relation to Other Jobs:* Identify jobs from which persons can be promoted into this job. Also state the jobs to which persons in this job can be promoted.
8. *Mental Skills:* Includes various mental skills such as ability to interpret complex data and ideas, resourcefulness, and ability to influence others.
9. *Physical Demand:* Kind and amount of physical exertion. Normal working position such as sitting or standing.
10. *Physical Skills:* Examples are manual dexterity and eye-and-foot coordination.
11. *Responsibilities:* Examples are responsibility for product and equipment and responsibility for preventing monetary loss to organization.
12. *Working Conditions:* Environmental conditions such as cold, heat, dust, noise.
13. *Hazards:* Typical work hazards encountered (e.g., broken bones) and probability of occurrence.
14. *Education:* Identify specific kinds of reasoning, language, and mathematical skills required and amount of schooling needed to provide such skills.
15. *Vocational Preparation:* This includes vocational education, apprenticeship training, prior work experience, and in-plant job training.

FUNCTIONAL JOB ANALYSIS

Functional job analysis is a very detailed method for analyzing jobs and recording the job information collected. It was developed by the U.S. Training and Employment Service of the Department of Labor. The system is explained in the *Handbook for Analyzing Jobs*[10] and is used in the *Dictionary of Occupational Titles*, 4th ed. Functional job analysis is really a comprehensive system for collecting and classifying the various kinds of data which describe the work performed in jobs and the worker traits required to perform these jobs.

According to this approach the categories of information needed to properly analyze any job are as follows:

1. Work performed
   a. Worker functions
   b. Work fields
   c. Materials, products, subject matter, and services
2. Worker traits
   a. Training time
   b. Aptitudes
   c. Temperaments
   d. Interests
   e. Physical demands
   f. Environmental conditions

Worker Functions. All job-worker situations involve a relationship of the employee to *data*, *people*, and *things*. The functional job analysis format gives a standard hierarchical classification of tasks under these three categories. There are six data-handling tasks, "comparing" being the simplest and "synthesizing" the most complex. There are eight people tasks, "taking instructions-helping" being the simplest and "mentoring" the moxt complex. Of the seven

[10]U.S. Department of Labor, *Handbook for Analyzing Jobs* (Washington, D.C.: Government Printing Office, 1972).

thing tasks, "handling" is the simplest and "setting up" the most complex.

Work Fields. All the jobs in the U.S. economy are classified under 100 different work fields. Some examples of work fields are welding, masoning, printing, writing, engineering, and teaching. In describing the content of each work field *methods verbs* are used. For example, for the surveying field methods verbs such as *calculating, measuring,* and *plotting* are used. Certain *machines, tools, equipment and work aids* are used in the various work fields. In the surveying field, no machines are used but tools include drafting tools, levels, pencils, and pens. Equipment includes transits and geodometers. Work aids include blueprints, charts, maps, and rods.

Materials, Products, Subject Matter, and Services. Jobs are characterized according to the items of these types that are involved. Materials mean raw materials being processed such as fabric, metal, or wood. Products are final products made such as furniture, paper, or apparel. Subject matter includes such items as arts, biological sciences, natural sciences, and social science. Services include items such as transportation, communication, sanitation, and personal services.

Worker Traits. The information here specifies the qualifications and temperaments required by the employee to adequately perform the job. It includes the following categories:

Training time. (a) general educational development and (b) specific vocational preparation.
Aptitudes. Eleven aptitudes such as intelligence, motor coordination, and manual dexterity.
Temperaments. These are personal traits required of the employee by the specific job-worker situation. There are ten factors such as adaptability to making generalizations and adaptability to performing under stress.

Interests. Five pairs of bipolar vocational interest factors.

Physical demands. Six main categories such as strength, climbing, and seeing.

Environmental conditions. Seven factors such as heat, cold, noise, and hazards.

By using this detailed job analysis procedure, management can efficiently compare, compile, quantify, classify, and summarize jobs and job information.

ADMINISTRATION OF THE JOB ANALYSIS PROGRAM

The responsibility for analyzing jobs and preparing descriptions and specifications is usually assigned to the personnel department. If the organization is very large, undoubtedly there will be a section within this department that does such work. This may be called the wage and salary section, employee compensation section, or the job analysis group. The reason for placing responsibility for job analysis within the personnel department is that it is intimately concerned with utilizing job information for so many of its other programs—that is, manpower planning, recruitment, selection, placement, training, job evaluation, area wage surveys, and safety.

Sometimes the industrial engineering department prepares the job descriptions and specifications, especially for production and maintenance type of jobs. Many feel this is logical because it is a natural outgrowth of the industrial engineer's activities in methods study and work measurement. Many practitioners feel that this work requires engineering talent, because it is analytical, precise, and detailed in nature.

Procedurally, it is advisable for those charged with the job analysis function to obtain full cooperation and participation from operating supervision. Many companies follow the practice of submitting the completed description and specification to the supervisor of the job involved for approval. This is to insure that the job as described is accurately represented and that the supervisor agrees with the way it has been written up. Some firms also follow the practice of showing the job write-up to the job holder for approval. This is particularly true for professional, executive, and administrative positions. The policy of obtaining approval from operating management reduces the possibility of later complaints and obstruction of the program.

If there is anything certain in our modern complex industrial system, it is the constancy of change. This applies well to jobs and positions. There are many circumstances that can cause changes in the nature, content, and worker requirements of jobs. New machinery and equipment may be introduced. Operating procedures may change. The company may be reorganized. If the firm grows and employment expands, jobs may become more specialized. Changing technology may add new skill requirements to some jobs and take them away from others. Therefore, a job analysis program must be kept up to date. Descriptions cannot be filed away and then forgotten. There are two ways of insuring that the information on file is an accurate representation of current conditions in the organization. One method places major reliance upon the operating supervisors. They must be trained to report any significant changes in the make-up of the jobs in their units. This responsibility is likely to rank quite low in their system of priorities because their superiors will generally emphasize production, costs, quality, and efficiency. The second approach is more positive, more thorough, and also more costly. It requires the job analysis group to conduct periodic audits (usually annually) of the jobs in every department in order to pick up and evaluate any noteworthy changes in the composition and nature of the jobs.

Questions for review and discussion

1. What factors have traditionally governed the design of jobs in industry? What problems have resulted from this approach?
2. What concepts have been applied to job design in more recent years? What considerations determine whether the traditional or the more modern approach will be successful in a given application?
3. Explain the meaning of the following occupational categories:
   a. Semiskilled labor.
   b. Skilled labor.
   c. Executive position.
   d. Administrative position.
   e. Professional position.
4. Explain how equal employment opportunity regulations have added special significance to sound job analysis.
5. What is "functional job analysis" as used by the U.S. Department of Labor?
6. What are the principal methods that can be used to analyze jobs? What method or methods would you use? Why?
7. Distinguish between a job description and a job specification. What information commonly appears on each?
8. If you were a job analyst in a company, would you describe jobs as they actually existed or as some supervisor or manager said they should exist? (Assume there is a difference between actual job content and requirements and proposed content and requirements).

EXERCISE

Make a thorough analysis of a job as it is currently being performed by interviewing an employee of your college or university (or in some other organization where you can obtain good cooperation). Concentrate upon interviewing the employee to obtain the information you desire. You may wish to supplement this with an interview with the person who supervises this employee plus a brief observation of the job and its work environment. Use the job analysis questionnaire in Figure 5-5 as your guide to the questions to ask. (This questionnaire can serve not only as a form for every employee himself to fill out but also as a schedule or guide to assist the job analyst in covering all the necessary points when interviewing an employee.)

After you have collected the necessary data, prepare a job description and a specification. Show these to the employee and/or the supervisor to determine whether they feel your write-up accurately describes the job and the human qualifications.

Suggestions for Further Reading

Aldag, Ramon J., and Arthur P. Brief. *Task Design and Employee Motivation*. Glenview, Ill.: Scott, Foresman and Company, 1979.

Davis, Louis E., and James C. Taylor, Eds. *Design of Jobs*. Baltimore: Penguin Books, Inc., 1972.

Fine, Sidney A., and Wretha W. Wiley. *An Introduction to Functional Job Analysis.* Kalamazoo, Mich.: W. E. Upjohn Institute, 1971.

Griffin, Ricky W. *Task Design: An Integrative Approach.* Glenview, Ill.: Scott, Foresman and Company, 1982.

Hackman, J. Richard, and Greg R. Oldham. *Work Redesign.* Reading, Mass.: Addison-Wesley Publishing Co., 1980.

Herzberg, Frederick. "The Wise Old Turk," *Harvard Business Review,* Vol. 52, No. 5 (September–October 1974), pp. 70–80.

McCormick, Ernest J. "Job and Task Analysis," In M. D. Dunnette, ed. *Handbook of Industrial and Organizational Psychology.* Chicago: Rand McNally, 1976.

U.S. Department of Labor. *Dictionary of Occupational Titles,* 4th ed. Washington, D.C.: Government Printing Office, 1977.

——— . *Handbook for Analyzing Jobs.* Washington, D.C.: Government Printing Office, 1972.

PART III

Employment and Development of People

Human Resource Planning

Why should management conduct human resource planning? Three hypothetical but very realistic examples will demonstrate the need.

The average age of the upper management personnel of the Longworth Corporation is high. Within six years three fourths of all the managers at the levels of the president, vice-presidents, and division heads will reach normal retirement age. The president and the director of personnel have recently met to discuss this situation. At this meeting the director of personnel agreed that he would prepare a plan for dealing with the problem of management succession.

In another company, the Glenmont Corporation, the director of research and development, with her immediate staff, is preparing a proposal for $1,000,000 to be submitted to the U.S. Department of Energy for the development, design, construction, and testing of prototype solar energy cells. As a part of its proposal, Glenmont must provide a comprehensive description of the scientific, engineering, managerial, and technical support personnel who would be assigned to this project.

Our third company, The Exeter Company, has just signed a consent agreement with the Office of Federal Contract Compliance Programs of the U.S. Department of Labor and with the Equal Employment Opportunity Commission. In this agreement the company agrees to increase its employment of women and blacks and to upgrade women and blacks into skilled trades and supervisory positions. Within the next four years the company must increase its employment of these categories of personnel 25 per cent above present levels. The Affirmative Action Coordinator in the personnel department must collect detailed work force data and classify employees by age, sex, race, job title, pay grade, department, and the like in order to monitor progress toward meeting this goal.

Carefully constructed human resource plans, including skills inventories, forecasts of needs, and implementation programs are essential to meeting the needs described in the three foregoing examples.

Human resource planning is also sometimes called manpower planning. Other terms used to designate this function are personnel planning and employment planning. What is human resource planning? It is a *process for determining and assuring that the organization will have an adequate number of qualified persons, available at the proper times, performing jobs which meet the needs of the enterprise and which provide satisfaction for the individuals involved.* Let us examine this definition. Human resource planning is an ongoing process. It is not static. It involves many interrelated activities. The plan must be modified and updated as conditions require. It includes the planning and development of human resource programs, such as recruitment, performance appraisal, and training to assure that people's needs of the organization are met. Strictly speaking, we should call this function "human resource planning and action programming." But for conciseness of language, we shall simply say human resource planning and remember that this term includes action programming. Furthermore, human resource planning requires detailed analysis of the present and the future to ensure that the organization has the right number of people available who possess the right kinds of skills to perform the jobs required by the enterprise when the work is needed. And finally, the definition acknowledges that the entire system should match the organization's needs for productive people with the needs of these people for personal career satisfaction.

REASONS FOR HUMAN RESOURCE PLANNING

The importance of systematic manpower planning has been recognized only in recent years. Traditionally, management assumed that it could always obtain the personnel it required whenever it needed them. For the most part, firms did not engage in formal human resource planning. A company may be able to get by with such a casual approach if it is small, changes little, and the skills it employs are relatively simple. But formal personnel planning is essential for the enterprise that is moderate to large in size, that experiences changes in technology, products, markets, and internal organization, and that utilizes a lot of high-talent personnel.

One survey of 195 large U.S. corporations revealed that over 95 per cent of the firms engaged in strategic business planning and 80 per cent of these firms included human resource

planning as part of their long-range business plans. Seventy per cent of those doing manpower planning concentrated upon managerial and technical personnel. The remainder also included other employee groups in the plans.[1]

Here are some specific reasons why management should carry on systematic human resource planning.

1. *Future Personnel Needs.* Planning is vital for ascertaining personnel needs for the future.
2. *Coping with Change.* Human resource planning enables the enterprise to adapt to changes in competitive forces, markets, technology, products, and government regulations. Such changes often generate changes in job content, skill demands, number and types of personnel.
3. *High-Talent Personnel.* The mix of people employed in many organizations has shifted toward the high-talent occupations—managerial and professional personnel. There is often a scarcity of such talent. The lead time to hire and develop high talent personnel is long. Another facet of the high-talent personnel problem is management succession planning. Who will replace retiring top executives?
4. *Strategic Planning.* The modern competitive enterprise engages in strategic planning. Human resource planning is an essential component of strategic planning.
5. *Equal Employment Opportunity.* The Federal government's equal employment opportunity and affirmative action regulations mandate that employers meet agreed goals for the hiring, placing, training, upgrading, and compensation of protected categories of people.
6. *Foundation for Personnel Functions.* Personnel planning provides essential information for designing and implementing personnel ac-

[1]Alpander, Guvenc G., "Human Resource Planning in U.S. Corporations," *California Management Review*, Vol. XXII, No. 2 (Spring 1980), pp. 24–32.

tivities such as recruitment, selection, transfers, promotions, layoffs, and training.

THE PLANNING PROCESS

Planning for human resources should be tied in with overall enterprise long-range planning. Unfortunately, many enterprises do no formal long-range or strategic planning. For many organizations, the creation and adoption of an annual budget constitutes the sole mechanism of planning for organization needs. Of course, if top management does not undertake strategic business planning and wishes to only go as far as the annual budget-planning process, the personnel director can develop limited manpower plans and programs geared to the one-year cycle. He can also campaign for more comprehensive and longer range planning as a means for strengthening the organization.

Many companies carry out systematic planning only for those categories of personnel which have been in short supply or for those types of skills which require a long development time within the organization. Basically both of these conditions generally apply to highly skilled and technical personnel and to managers. All organizations that conduct extensive yearly recruiting at the colleges and universities must carefully plan their needs and their utilization of management trainees, accountants, engineers, scientists, and sales personnel. Likewise, companies that employ large numbers of craftsmen must carefully plan the input to their apprentice-training program as well as the placement of the graduates.

Because unskilled and semiskilled hourly paid personnel and routine clerical personnel are often abundantly available in most labor markets, many firms only plan for short-term needs regarding these types of employees. However, such an informal approach may not be advisable even for these kinds of workers because some of these employees may eventually be upgraded to better jobs. A careful planning of needs, qualifications, utilization, training needs, and career paths would be worthwhile.

The major components of the human resource-planning process are: (1) goals and plans of the organization, (2) current human resource situation, (3) human resource forecast, (4) implementation programs, and (5) audit and adjustment (see Figure 6-1). Organizations differ substantially in the degree of sophistication they exhibit in doing their manpower planning. Furthermore, this art is still developing, so that we have not yet reached the point at which there is a universally accepted set of procedures for carrying out the mechanics of the process. Although the degree of sophistication varies and the detailed mechanics vary, there is agreement upon the major processes and contents of manpower planning and this is what we shall describe.

Goals and Plans of Organization

Human resource planning is a part of the overall strategic planning for the entire enterprise. A personnel vice-president and his staff cannot make useful plans for periods of, let's say, one, three, and five years hence, unless they have data on possible corporate expansion, new products, new plants, new markets, and so on. Important steps involved in overall planning for the enterprise are listed below:

1. Analyze and evaluate environmental influences.
   a. Political trends and legislation which will have an impact upon the business.
   b. Economic conditions such as competition, inflation, rate of change in gross national product, and unemployment level.
   c. Social trends in leisure time, consumer tastes, work values, and retirement.
   d. Technological advances affecting the enterprise.

2. Identify the values and aspirations of the organization's directors and executives.
3. Identify and evaluate the internal strengths and weaknesses of the enterprise. Consider human, financial, and technical resources and existing facilities.
4. Develop a strategy which relates the strengths of the company and the aspirations of the executives with opportunities perceived in the environment.
5. Create specific enterprise objectives and plans for achieving these objectives.
6. Prepare plans for the functional areas of the business: production, finance, marketing, research and development, engineering, and personnel. Determine strengths, deficiencies, and needs.
7. Communicate with members of the organization and involve them in the planning processes.

FIGURE 6-1 Major Steps in the Human Resource Planning Process.

GOALS AND PLANS OF ORGANIZATION

Strategic planning: public policy, social trends, economic conditions, technology, market conditions, strengths and weaknesses of organization, projected outputs for planning periods.

CURRENT HUMAN RESOURCE SITUATION

Skills inventory: numbers of people grouped by job, department, organizational level, location, age, education, in-service training completed, performance.

HUMAN RESOURCE FORECAST

a. Present workforce: project retirements, layoffs, promotions, and quits for planning periods.
b. Demand for people: Translate plans and forecast for organization into demand for employees for planning periods.
c. Comparison of demand with supply: Net additions or subtractions found by comparing (a) with (b).

IMPLEMENTATION PROGRAMS

Recruitment, selection and placement; performance appraisal; career planning; transfer, promotion, layoff; training and development; motivation and compensation.

AUDIT AND ADJUSTMENT

Measure implementation progress, compare with plan, take corrective action. Change human resource plans if enterprise plans are altered. Periodically update skills inventory, forecast, and implementation programs.

Employment and Development of People

8. Evaluate progress toward implementation of plans and take corrective action where necessary.

The existing human resources within the organization constitute an important input into the development of the overall strategic plans for the enterprise. Furthermore, the output of the planning process described above provides data upon which the human resource plans and projections can be based. Is the corporation going to launch a major new product line? Must technical manpower be augmented in order to bid successfully for government R&D contracts? Shall an obsolete facility be closed down and a new one constructed? Are certain business functions going to be reorganized? All such activities as these impact heavily on manpower needs.

The Planning Period. How far into the future shall we plan human resource needs? Of course, the human resource plan is derived from the overall enterprise strategic plan. Different kinds of businesses plan ahead for different numbers of years. Some businesses, such as electric utilities, oil companies, and telephone companies, plan ten to twenty years ahead. Such long-range planning by businesses is the exception, however. Most plan only for the fairly short run of, say, one to three years.

The extent and rapidity of change in the forces affecting the business determines the utility of forecasts into the future. Some establishments can tie their forecasts directly into population growth trends—public schools, postal service, public utilities—hence, longer range planning is feasible. In other lines of business—women's fashions for example—there is so much uncertainty about the future that planning and forecasting beyond one or two seasons is fraught with risk. Generally speaking however, human resource planning for up to one year is considered short range and is widely practiced. Planning for two to four years is considered intermediate range and planning for five years and beyond is called long range.

Probably all business planning that extends beyond a year or two entails great risk. In the 1970s, electric utilities projected continued high growth rates in power consumption. They constructed multibillion dollar nuclear power plants to meet this predicted demand. This action has nearly bankrupted some utilities because the growth in power consumption did not materialize.

Current Human Resource Situation

The second phase of the planning process is the preparation of an inventory of personnel presently within the organization. This is often called a *skills inventory* or a manpower information system. A skills inventory consists of up-to-date information regarding the qualifications of selected categories of personnel. Normally, skills inventories are prepared only for certain categories of personnel such as all members of management, or all technical and professional personnel, or all craftspersons. A total manpower information system would include data on all employees within the organization. However, such a total information system is very rarely established because of the great cost of preparation and updating and because detailed information for many categories of personnel such as unskilled and semiskilled would seldom be used.

A survey by The Conference Board revealed that 37 per cent of those firms responding used skills inventories for lower-level exempt (supervisory and professional) personnel, 33 per cent used inventories for office and clerical personnel, and 19 per cent used them for production or operations personnel.[2] See Table 6-1.

The skills inventory has several important uses. When the human resource forecast is prepared later, one can compare the number, types,

[2]Harriet Gorlin, *Personnel Practices I: Recruitment, Placement, Training, Communication*, Information Bulletin No. 89 (New York: The Conference Board, 1981), table 18.

TABLE 6-1. Usage of Skills Inventories.[1]

	Total Respondents					
	Nonexempt					
	Production or Operations		Office and Clerical		Lower level Exempt	
Practice	No.	%	No.	%	No.	%
Total Respondents	*335*	*100*	*523*	*100*	*523*	*100*
Respondents maintaining skills inventories	*64*	*19*	*173*	*33*	*191*	*37*
For respondents maintaining skills inventories:	64	100	173	100	191	100
Data included						
Education and training		45		61		63
Work history		44		57		60
Specific work skills		42		54		57
Language proficiency		23		30		34
Avocations and hobbies		20		23		24
Test results		20		28		25
Other[2]		8		6		8
When inventory information is gathered or amended						
At hiring		42		50		50
At job change or promotion		25		30		32
Annually		14		22		26
At request of employee		30		35		36
Other		13		10		9
Skills inventory used as a search tool in filling job openings		31		47		55

Source: Reprinted by permission from Harriet Gorlin, *Personnel Practices I: Recruitment, Placement, Training, Communication* (New York: The Conference Board, 1981), Table 18, excerpted.

[1]Data from 523 companies (335 for production or operations jobs) in manufacturing, gas and electric utility, banking, and insurance industries regarding skills inventory practices.

[2]Includes career aspirations and preferences for work assignments and locations.

and skills specified by the forecast with the present baseline or current position given by the skills inventory to ascertain what skills must be developed from present personnel via training, upgrading, and special development efforts or obtained from external manpower sources.

Another important use of a skills inventory is to find or identify talent within the organization for specific job openings. For example, which employees within the corporation meet the following job specification: masters degree in mechanical engineering, at least six years of responsible professional experience in internal combustion engine design, at least five years engineering supervisory experience, a proven record of innovation such as demonstrated by patents; person to head a team of engineers engaged in the design and development of a new fuel efficient, nonpolluting automotive engine. A skills inventory used in the talent search mode is available for screening a large number of people and for making a first rough cut at selection. It cannot, however, provide for a specific matching of interests, temperament, and ambitions with job parameters. Personalized selection is required after the pool of possible candidates is identified.

An up-to-date skills inventory is valuable for the preparation of rosters of qualified technical and managerial personnel to be submitted on project proposals for government contracts. Furthermore, an inventory can be used in conjunction with an affirmative action program to monitor progress toward meeting employment goals. And finally, the existence of a skills inventory enhances the opportunities for employees to satisfy their career aspirations through development and promotion.

Practice varies as to just how much information is contained in a skills inventory. Some or all of the following may be included:

Personal Data: Name, date of birth, sex.
Education: Degree(s), colleges, dates, curricula.
   Special-training courses.

Employment History: Company—present job, dates, pay grade. Previous employers—jobs, dates, pay.
Performance and Potential: Performance appraisal ratings, assessment center evaluations.
Career Goals: Personal preferences for special training, assignments, jobs, locations.

See Figure 6-2 for an illustrative human resource inventory card. The inventory data for each employee is obtained by having each employee fill out a personal history form. The supervisor should review and discuss this with the employee. If summary performance appraisal data is to be included, it can be obtained from the personnel folder in the personnel office. Such evaluative material must be treated with the utmost confidentiality. There is danger that some persons may view these performance evaluations as fixed and immutable. People could be unfairly labeled and damaged. A performance evaluation is someone's opinion about someone else. Performance can change—opinions differ. Therefore, this information must be used with great discretion.

An example of a comprehensive skills inventory system is that of the North American Rockwell Corporation (now called Rockwell International). Their skills index covers 34,000 technical, salaried employees in seven major aerospace and systems divisions. Each division has a highly trained personnel specialist who manages the index for the division. All skills index information is stored on computer tapes. It is readily available for talent searches and for summary printouts classified in various ways.[3]

Another corporation which has created a computerized human resource inventory system is the Xerox Corporation. The basic document is a personal history form made out by the individ-

[3]Robert H. Murphy, "A Personalized Skills Inventory: The North American Rockwell Story" in Elmer H. Burack and James W. Walker, eds., *Manpower Planning and Programming* (Boston: Allyn & Bacon, Inc., 1972).

FIGURE 6-2 A Sample Human Resource Inventory Card.

HUMAN RESOURCE DATA CARD
Saratoga-Acme Corporation

Name _____Alton T. Farnam_____   Date of Birth _5/17/42_   Hire Date _6/21/67_

Sex _____Male_____   Marital Status ___Married___

Present Position ___Director of Personnel___   Dates ___2/14/77–present___

Prior Positions at Saratoga-Acme: Dates:

   Assistant Director of Personnel   4/11/74–2/13/77

   Employment & Training Manager   11/19/71–4/10/74

   Safety Director   6/21/67–11/18/71

Pre-Saratoga Experience: Dates:

   Production Supervisor, Raynor Corp.   6/2/65–6/20/67

   Management Trainee, Raynor Corp.   6/30/64–6/1/65

Education:

   Rensselaer Polytechnic Institute – B.S. in Management, 9/60–6/64

Special Courses:

   Advanced Management Program – Harvard Univ., 9/77–12/77

   Equal Employment Opportunity Seminar – AMA – Oct. 1976

Career Interests:

   Seeks promotion to senior executive position in general management

Performance in Current Position:

Unsatisfactory	Meets Minimum Requirements	Fully Satisfactory Performance	Consistently Exceeds Requirements	Outstanding
☐	☐	☐	☒	☐

Assessment Center Rating:

   Has potential for top executive position in general management. Needs exposure to other areas of management.

Development Needs:

   Transfer to general management position such as assistant manager or manager of operations.

Employment and Development of People

ual. Together the individual and his manager discuss and record career goals and logical steps to attain the goals. Performance appraisal information is added to the document by the manager. Xerox has prepared lists of appropriate developmental experiences for candidates in various jobs which have a large population base. Xerox uses its system for career development and for manpower planning.[4]

Computerized System. Although the small organization can advantageously collect, store, and retrieve its manpower information manually by means of file folders, card files, and various proprietary filing systems, an electronic data processing or computerized system is practically a must for the larger organization that wishes to handle data for hundreds or even thousands of people. A computerized system is expensive. However, a computer offers great advantages in terms of tremendous data storage and retrieval capabilities. And the computer can supply printouts of manpower information classified in many meaningful ways. If the personnel director and other members of top management are worried about a possible high concentration of upper-level managers only a few years away from retirement and the problem of management succession, the computer can readily provide a printout of the age distribution of all managers by level, job, and department. If the personnel director wishes to know precisely what progress the company is making toward its affirmative action goals, the computer can provide a printout of the number and percentage of women and minority employees classified by pay grade, job title, and department. Walker reports that most large corporations have adopted, or are in the process of installing, computerized personnel information systems.[5]

[4]Douglas M. Reid, "Human Resource Planning: A Tool for People Development," *Personnel*, Vol. 54, No. 2 (March–April 1977), pp. 15–25.

[5]James W. Walker, "The New, More Substantive Approach to Manpower Planning," *Management Review*, Vol. 66, No. 7 (July 1977), pp. 29–30.

Human Resource Forecast

The human resource forecast is a determination of the *demand* for people and of the appropriate types and skills for given periods in the future such as one, three, and five years hence. The forecast also requires the preparation of an estimate of the *supply* of people who will be available for the selected periods. The supply is composed of two parts. The first part is an estimate of the numbers and types of employees presently on the payroll who still will be available by the ends of the chosen periods. The second part of the supply is that portion which must be recruited externally. These figures for the planning periods are obtained by subtracting the internally available manpower from the projected demand. If the figures are positive, people will have to be hired; if negative, people may eventually have to be laid off.

The demand forecast is derived from the information generated in Step 1—Goals and Plans of the Organization of the human-resource-planning process, described earlier. Step 1 should provide the human resource planners with data on such factors as projected dollar volume of sales, units to be produced, number of clients to be serviced, new facilities to be constructed, new functional departments to be created, and so on.

Generally, manpower planners must use a variety of techniques to project future personnel needs. The techniques available range from judgment to rather sophisticated quantitative models. We will describe four major categories of forecasting techniques. These are: (1) judgment and experience, (2) budgetary planning, (3) work standards data, and (4) key predictive factors.

Judgment and Experience. This category includes estimates made by people who are very familiar with the products, processes, and jobs in the business. It is appropriate for relatively short-run forecasts of, say, up to two years. Supervisors and managers of the various units of the business make estimates of future manpower needs by judgmentally converting information on short-term future business activity (units to be produced, clients to be served, projects to be completed) into numbers and types of people needed. *Rules of thumb and decision rules* are also subsets of this category. For example, the production manager may know from past experience that for every 1,000 unit increase in production output he must add a second shift of 15 more machine operators and one foreman.

The *Delphi* technique is a systematic way of obtaining and refining judgments by a group of experts. It was originally developed by the Rand Corporation as a way of doing technological forecasting but it can be applied to manpower planning and forecasting as well. A panel of persons very familiar with the problem at hand is formed. The experts work privately and not in an assembled group. This is to avoid concurrence and conformity induced by face-to-face peer group social pressure. Each expert is asked to make predictions of future events. A moderator or intermediary collects the predictions, summarizes them, and then distributes them to the panel members for another round of forecasts. Eventually, convergence of opinion takes place and an acceptable forecast is obtained.

Budgetary Planning. Most organizations, other than the very small single proprietorship, prepare annual budgets. A budget is a plan expressed in financial and numerical terms. It is both an instrument for planning and for managerial control. Most budgetary planning is done on an annual basis. Often the budget for the whole organization is built up from the individual departmental budgets. After the tentative departmental budgets are prepared, they must be combined and adjusted by upper-level management to properly allocate resources among all units and to bring income and expenditures into balance. For many enterprises, the annual process of budget preparation and review constitutes the only formal planning that is done. In this case it can become the principal vehicle for

planning of manpower needs. Individual departmental managers must translate activity levels (units to be produced, students to be enrolled, clients to be served, etc.) and projects (R&D development programs, new products to be introduced, etc.) into rather detailed needs for personnel, materials, expenses, equipment, and facilities. In creating the budget, the managers must itemize the various categories of personnel in detail and in aggregate. This process forces them to think through their plans and needs for the year and to justify these plans and needs to higher management.

Work Standards Data. By means of industrial engineering work measurement techniques, many companies have established rather comprehensive sets of data for man-hours or unit times to perform a great many tasks. These standards are most prevalent for direct production tasks but some companies have also prepared work standards for maintenance and clerical activities. The forecasting procedure involves the translation of overall enterprise volume of activity into production schedules for all production departments. The projected units of output for each department are converted into man-hours, man-days, and number of employees by applying the established time standards.

The measured work standards technique generally cannot be used for determining professional, administrative, and executive personnel needs. Judgment, past experience, and managerial intent are the major determinants of how many and what kinds of personnel are needed. For example, the size of the corporate research laboratory is determined more by the attitudes of top management than it is by the volume of units produced by the company.

Key Predictive Factors. The essence of the "key predictive factors" technique is to find one (or a very limited number) of business factors or key indicators with which total manpower correlates highly. To identify such a factor, the human resource-planning office must examine several business factors such as dollar sales volume, units produced, or number of clients served to find which factor or factors yield a good historical correlation between number of employees and changes in the business factor.

A considerable amount of quantitative analysis may be necessary to determine the relationships between changes in the various business indicators and changes in manpower. In some kinds of business the total number of employees is not directly proportional to product volume. For example, in a continuous process industry such as an oil refinery, it might require almost as many people to run a plant at 80 per cent of capacity as at full capacity. Another consideration is that many enterprises make a variety of products (or services). Some of these may be quite labor intensive and others may not be. Therefore, the manpower analysis must be conducted separately for each of the product divisions. Charts and formulas can be created to show the aggregate figures for the corporation.

If manpower projections are being made for several years into the future, it is important to incorporate changes (hopefully improvements) in productivity into the calculations. For example, 10 years ago, a total hourly employment of 500 persons may have been necessary to produce 10,000 units of product per year. Five years ago, only 450 persons were needed to produce the same 10,000 units. Now our hypothetical company can produce 10,000 units with just 410 hourly employees. This is an improvement of roughly 2 per cent per year. The future productivity improvement may be greater than or less than this 2 per cent a year average. The manpower planners must investigate likely changes in technology, working hours, and manpower utilization in order to accurately estimate the probable efficiency improvement in the years to come.

Statistical and operations research techniques constitute useful analytic tools for making manpower forecasts. Only in the last few years have organizations begun systematically to apply these techniques for human resource

planning. Among the quantitative techniques available for use in this application are statistical correlation (linear, curvilinear, multiple regression), stochastic analysis-incorporating probabilities, linear programming, network flow methods, and computer simulation.[6]

We have talked about ways of making estimates of human resource needs (demand analysis) for the future. While the planning group is making these projections it must also make a *supply* analysis. First it must determine the personnel presently available within the organization. The planning group must also forecast the probable losses from the current roster due to retirements, resignations, discharges, deaths, and disabilities. Table 6-2 shows such an analysis for managerial and professional personnel in hypothetical Company A. In this figure, we see that at managerial level 5, there is one person (the president) who will reach retirement age before January 1, 1990. The company will have to find a replacement before that date. This chart only projects losses out of the present complement of personnel. Of course the staffing of an organization is dynamic. During the course of the five-year analysis period, some people at lower levels will be promoted to higher ranks. Also new hires will be gradually added to replace the losses. And if Company A were a division of a very large corporation, some personnel would be expected to transfer out to other divisions and some people would transfer in from other divisions. Table 6-2 shows that there will be 337 managerial and professional personnel available on January 1, 1990. By comparing this total with the projected demand for 1990, we can determine how many persons will have to be hired from outside the company. Of course, this is a prediction of what will happen over the course of the next five years. Conditions will change and some of the original as-

[6]For a description of both quantitative and judgmental techniques, see Don R. Bryant, Michael J. Maggard, and Robert P. Taylor, "Manpower Planning Models and Techniques," *Business Horizons*, Vol. XVI, No. 3 (April 1973), pp. 69–77.

TABLE 6-2. Present Managerial and Professional Personnel Projected Five Years Ahead—Company A.

	Current Personnel Jan. 1, 1985	Retirements	Other Losses*	Total Losses	Estimated Personnel Available Jan. 1, 1990
Managerial					
Level 5	1	1	0	1	0
" 4	6	1	0	1	5
" 3	34	6	1	7	27
" 2	97	15	6	21	76
" 1	185	20	34	54	131
Professional					
Level 4	17	2	1	3	14
" 3	27	4	4	8	19
" 2	46	1	9	10	36
" 1	39	0	10	10	29
Totals	452	50	65	115	337

*Other Losses include resignations, discharges, deaths, disabled, and early retirements.

sumption may have to be altered. Therefore, the forecast for both demand and supply should be updated annually or more often as conditions dictate.

Management Succession Planning. A special or particular type of human resource forecasting is management succession planning. This process is also called management progression forecast or management replacement planning.

Many companies follow a practice of filling most managerial vacancies by promotion from within. Some firms, especially for their middle and upper levels of managerial personnel, assign a rating to each individual indicating his or her potential for promotion. This rating is based upon the regular performance appraisal prepared by each person's immediate organizational superior. But in addition, for management succession purposes, each individual is evalu-

ated in depth by a team of higher level managers. Assessment center data may also be utilized to develop the rating. These ratings are treated as highly confidential. Then, for each position, several individuals are identified as highly qualified to replace the incumbent should he leave the organization. By means of management succession planning, delays in filling vacancies can be avoided and people can be trained to take over the vacancies when they occur.

However, there is a real danger in designating certain people as the "crown princes" or "heir apparents." Giving particular managers an option or prior claim upon specific higher positions cuts all others off from a chance for these better jobs. It can destroy morale and give the masses of managers the notion that things have been "fixed" through political connections.

A better approach is to identify a pool of managers, all of whom have good potential for

120

advancement. This pool of people can then be given special training and developmental assignments in accordance with their interests and organizational opportunities. None in the pool is given a claim upon a specific higher level job. But all are given opportunities to qualify for any of a number of jobs should they open up.

Implementation Programs

Implementation requires converting the human resource plan into action. For example, if a shortage of engineering personnel has been forecast and if the plans indicate both stepped up recruitment plus training and upgrading of present engineering talent, then both recruitment and development programs will have to be strengthened and expanded. We shall discuss principal implementation actions only briefly here because each of these matters is covered in depth in separate chapters, or major parts thereof, elsewhere in this book.

Recruitment, Selection, Placement. Often, the analysis of manpower needs reveals a shortage of specific critical skills such as certain specialized engineers, scientists, or middle-level managers. In such cases the personnel executive must identify potentially good sources of supply and then efforts must be made to attract likely candidates to the company.

The selection program should be professionally designed and, among other considerations, special care should be taken to insure compliance with equal employment opportunity regulations in regard to such aspects as selection testing and the setting of qualification standards.

Usually, companies hire for specific job openings. However, some organizations hire a group of qualified individuals for the organization and not for specific jobs. Some examples are the employment of management interns in government and management trainees in pri-

vate industry. In these cases, the group of trainees moves through a variety of assignments over a one- or two-year period. Then the placement function is put into play. An effort is made to match individual job preferences and qualifications with organization needs.

Performance Appraisal. Performance appraisal has two fundamental uses. The first use is concerned with decisions in regard to pay increases, promotions, transfers, and discharges. The second use is concerned with employee development. This includes the identification of needs for self-improvement, training, and special broadening assignments. Management by objectives, which is a principal appraisal method as well as a system for managing, is a major technique used for individual (especially management) development.

Career Development. Formal, integrated career development in organizations is very new. However, certain components of what we now call career management have existed in some organizations for a long time. Some organizations have created channels or pathways of promotion. In the armed forces, for example, years of development have established various career paths for military officers. For unionized blue collar workers, some companies have set up occupational lines of progression. Often these have been built around the technology of manufacturing operations as in the making of steel or paper.

The contemporary concept of career development places much greater emphasis upon individual choice and self-analysis than formerly existed. In place of rather random movements, reassignments, opportunities, and setbacks shaping the individual's occupational pathway through time, today progressive personnel departments are setting up career development systems that focus upon both individual career guidance and self-analysis plus planned opportunities and developmental activities.

Promotion, Transfer, Layoff, Retirement. Organizations are ever changing. Because of the needs of the business and the individuals, there is always some movement of people occurring. In implementing the human resource plans, some people may be promoted to jobs of higher responsibility and others may be transferred to different jobs either to fill definite vacancies or to perform assignments to develop the individual. Some units of the business may be forced to reduce the workforce via layoffs. Administering a layoff program can be quite complicated. The union–employer contract, for example, may spell out job, department, shift, or plantwide seniority units or some combination thereof.

To effectuate certain parts of a manpower plan, some firms have offered inducements for early retirement for certain individuals or classes of personnel. Early retirement is supposed to be voluntary and not coerced; however, some managements place unwanted persons in meaningless or demeaning jobs to induce them to retire.

The 1978 amendments to the Age Discrimination in Employment Act of 1967 raised the protected age limit for employees in private industry and state and local government from 65 to 70, effective January 1, 1979. Thus, employers are no longer allowed to have a mandatory retirement age of 65, as has been traditional. Although the trend in recent years has been toward early retirement, before age 65, this amendment has introduced a new dimension. There will be greater uncertainty in planning by management for replacement needs for retirees. Depending upon individual preferences and pension arrangements, people will be leaving organizations at ages spreading from about 60 up to 70.

Training and Development. As technology changes, as new products or services are introduced, as reorganizations occur, and as people are upgraded, there is a need for well-designed and well-executed training and development programs. This includes formal classroom courses both in-house and at nearby colleges as well as on-the-job learning, coaching, and planned special assignments.

Motivation and Compensation. The entire system of motivation, leadership, compensation, and rewards serves to help accomplish the human resource plan. If the organization is not paying competitive rates, for example, for some of its key job classes, then it will have real trouble recruiting and retaining people. Or if the treatment of employees is perceived to be arbitrary and capricious (a leadership problem), then again the firm will have trouble meeting its manpower needs.

Audit and Adjustment

For any of various reasons, the programs for meeting the human resource targets may be falling short of objectives. A system for measuring progress should be set up. Many measures can be used depending upon the specific program being evaluated.

What percentage of the company's engineers have earned their professional engineer (P.E.) license (if the goal is to upgrade the engineering department personnel)? How many apprentices are being graduated each year from the machinist apprentice program (if the goal is to "grow from within" skilled tradespersons)? What percentages of first-, second-, third-, and fourth-level managerial positions are now occupied by women and blacks (if affirmative action goal accomplishment is being monitored)? Of course, if results fall short of targets, then changes must be made.

Another reason for reviewing progress is to ascertain if changes in the manpower plans are made necessary because of changed conditions or because some of the original planning assumptions have been proven wrong.

CONCLUSION

Just as general strategic planning, financial planning, and market planning are concomitants of the successful business organization, so too is formal human resource planning and development. Some firms drift along for several years without paying adequate attention to human resource programs, but long-term organizational success cannot be achieved without a reasonable effort toward manpower planning and development.

We have discussed in some depth the five main components of human resource planning and implementation. These are: (1) goals and plans of the organization, (2) current human resource situation, (3) human resource forecast, (4) implementation programs, and (5) audit and adjustment. A major point made is that human resource planning should be closely linked to general institutional planning.

Effective personnel management is not the handling of a potpourri of various personnel functions such as hiring, training, compensation, and benefits. It is rather an integrated whole that is designed to enhance both organizational objectives and individual employee satisfactions. Sound human resource planning is a basic instrument for achieving this holistic view of personnel.

Questions for Review and Discussion

1. Give reasons why it is desirable for complex organizations to carry out formal human resource planning.
2. Why should human resource planning be linked to the overall institutional or enterprise planning?
3. List and explain the key components of human resource planning.
4. What is a skills inventory? What does it contain? How is it prepared?
5. What methods can be used to make a forecast of human resource demand?
6. Show how human resource planning for a bank would differ from planning or a high-technology firm that is heavily dependent upon obtaining large commercial and government contracts.
7. Using a club, campus, or community organization with which you are familiar as a case example, prepare a three-year human resource plan for officers and committee chairmen. How would you insure that new officers and committee chairmen possess the skills and attributes needed to fulfill their responsibilities? How would you insure an adequate supply of people to staff the various positions?

CASE PROBLEMS

PROBLEM 1

The ABC Company, a public utility, has an engineering department composed of 200 employees. The major share of the work involves cost estimation, specification writing, and equipment planning and ordering. Some of the work also involves basic engineering analysis and design. Over two thirds of the engineering force is composed of employees who possess only a high school education and who have served a number of years as mechanics, electricians, and other types of craftspersons before being promoted into the engineering department. Quite frequently foremen who had been inept at supervising people but who had good technical knowledge were transferred to the engineering department and classified as engineers. The one third of the engineering force that does possess college degrees in engineering are assigned to the more complex technical phases of the work, involving the application of engineering principles. Most of the supervisory positions in the engineering department are held by graduate engineers.

Over the years the company has placed major emphasis upon the operating phases of the business. Those recruited directly upon graduation from college are placed in a management-training program of twelve months' duration. They are rotated through a number of assignments in various departments of the company including the engineering department. Only a small percentage of these "college hires" are assigned permanently to the engineering department, however. Of the total number of college graduates hired by the company each year, about one half hold engineering degrees and the other half are composed mostly of liberal arts and business administration graduates. Many of the engineers eventually attain managerial positions in the nontechnical phases of the business.

As technology has advanced, the top management of the ABC Company has experienced a real need for more graduate engineers in the engineering department. It feels that in the past it diluted the workforce in this department too thin by assigning too many nonengineers and nondegree holders to this type of work. In many instances the engineering department had become the dumping ground for misfits from operating departments. For these interdepartmental transfers the engineering department had had no practical selection methods. It had pretty much taken whoever was offered.

In recent years there has been a problem of low morale, particularly among those engineering personnel who have had an engineering education. They have noticed that promotions for engineers were few and far between, whereas those college graduates who had gone into other departments rose in the organization quite rapidly. The general attitude has evolved in the minds of higher management that engineers were best utilized as technical specialists—as functional individual contributors. There was also the feeling that engineers as a group are poor at dealing with people, and therefore they would make poor supervisors.

Recently the personnel department made an analysis of the salaries and rate of progress of all those college graduates hired fresh from college during the years 1975–1980. During these years engineers and nonengineers had been hired in about equal proportions. It was found that those persons who were now working in nonengineering departments (regardless of their college preparation) were receiving higher salaries and had attained higher-ranking positions than those who were doing engineering work.

Salary levels for engineering personnel are considered adequate in comparison with rates paid by other companies for the same occupations. The company conducts an annual salary survey and makes a sincere effort to keep its salaries competitive.

Questions
1. Assuming that you have been given the task of recommending a program of action to solve the problems contained in this case study, what would be your proposals for the following critical areas?
   a. Selection policies and procedures for transfers of employees to engineering jobs.
   b. Low morale of graduate engineers within the engineering department.
   c. Inequitable promotion opportunities.
   d. Using former craftspersons and foremen on engineering jobs.
2. Should engineers look to their advancement primarily by going into administrative and executive work or by achieving status and economic advancement within the engineering profession itself?

PROBLEM 2: THE REDMONT CORPORATION[7]

The Redmont Corporation is engaged in both manufacturing and research and development for civilian markets and for Federal government defense projects. Founded in 1947, the firm grew steadily and reached peak employment in 1979 of 2500 with annual sales of 100 million dollars. The years up to 1979 were the good years. Both management and the employees had been optimistic. The company had been successful in selling its products in civilian markets and government contracts had been coming in steadily. Wages and employee morale were good. Employment had increased gradually and rather steadily over the years.

But in 1979 business started turning sour. In 1980, the country began experiencing a general economic recession. Redmont started losing both government contracts and civilian business. Competition became intense. From peak employment of 2500 in 1979, the total workforce declined to 1500 by 1982. The production and maintenance employees were unionized; hence, these people were laid off according to seniority provisions of the union-company agreement. Sales and employment were stable in 1983. By 1984 business had improved substantially and employment had increased to 2100.

The corporation has a machine shop, metal fabrication, and assembly operations employing about 700 people as of 1984. In the peak year of 1979 there were 1200 people employed in these three manufacturing departments. The Planning and Methods Section is a staff unit attached to the manufacturing division (comprising these three departments). The function of this section is to plan the flow of production job orders through all the manufacturing operations. The planner works from the engineering drawings to determine whether the

[7] The author expresses his appreciation to Thomas Schoonmaker for the basic idea for this case.

shop has the capability of producing the parts and assemblies. Infrequently, work must be contracted out because of the lack of manufacturing capability.

If the product can be made within the shop, the planner must prepare a detailed planning sheet for each individual part and assembly to show all manufacturing operations and the sequence in which they are to be performed. This specialist must be able to read and understand complicated engineering drawings and specifications. The planner must possess a good knowledge of manufacturing methods, equipment, and processes. She or he must specify quality checks. After work orders are assigned to the shop, she or he must follow up and devise solutions to manufacturing problems. Corrective action could involve revising the tooling, assigning to a different machine, selecting alternative manufacturing processes, changing sequence of operations, and revising the planning sheet instructions. The planner must be able to deal effectively with engineering, quality assurance, and production personnel.

In 1979 there were twenty planning and methods specialists in this section. By 1982, as a result of heavy layoffs throughout the company, this section had been cut back to only nine specialists. Although these people were not unionized, the company had generally cut back the salaried work force on the basis of seniority. Most of the eleven people lost by this section had been laid off, and the layoffs fell mostly upon the younger personnel. By 1984 eight of the nine planning and methods specialists were over 53 years of age.

The traditional source of planning and methods specialists had been the machine shop apprentice program. This four-year program consisted of on-the-job training in a variety of machine tool processes and fabrication methods plus classroom work and theory at a local community college (tuition paid by the company). At the conclusion of the program, the graduates received a two-year associate degree from the college plus their certificate as a journeyman machinist. The apprentice program was small with about seven or eight people graduating each year. Most took jobs as machinists while a very few went into salaried jobs in planning and methods, production control, and industrial engineering. After an apprentice graduate or a journeyman machinist had been assigned to the Planning and Methods Section, it took about a year and a half of guided on-the-job training and diversified assignments to develop him or her into a qualified planning specialist. In 1980 the company top management abolished the entire apprentice program because of the severe decline in business and of its forecast of continuing hard times in the future.

By 1984 company sales had improved significantly from the depressed level of 1980–1982. The workload in Planning and Methods was getting heavier and with only nine people available considerable overtime work was required.

The dilemma facing the Director of Personnel and top management is how to meet possible future manpower needs in the Planning and Methods Section. The traditional source of new personnel has disappeared with the abandonment of the apprentice program. With a somewhat uncertain business future, top management is very reluctant to make the financial and staffing investment needed to reactivate the program. Inasmuch as the section is staffed primarily with older personnel and the workload is increasing, how should manpower needs be met?

Among the alternatives being considered are:

1. Promote promising individuals from among the current ranks of machinists. However, the heavy layoffs of 1980–1982 have depleted the ranks of young machinists. The available personnel are mostly in their fifties.
2. Recruit technical graduates from two-year community colleges. Set up an on-the-job training program within the Planning and Methods Section.

Questions

Assume it is now 1984. Identify several other possible courses of action in addition to the alternatives given above. What are the advantages and disadvantages of all the possible solutions? Lay out a specific plan of action including techniques of implementation.

Suggestions for Further Reading

Biles, George E., and Stevan R. Holmberg (eds.). *Strategic Human Resources Planning*. Salt Lake City: Brighton Publishing Company, 1980.

Bright, William E. "How One Company Manages Its Human Resources." *Harvard Business Review,* Vol. 54, No. 1 (January–February 1976), pp. 81–93.

Burack, Elmer H., and Nicholas J. Mathys. *Human Resource Planning: A Pragmatic Approach to Manpower Staffing and Development*. Lake Forest, Ill.: Brace-Park Press, 1979.

_____ and Thomas G. Gutteridge. "Institutional Manpower Planning: Rhetoric Versus Reality," *California Management Review.* Vol. XX, No. 3 (Spring 1978), pp. 13–22.

Coleman, Bruce P. "An Integrated System for Manpower Planning," *Business Horizons,* Vol. XIII, No. 5 (October 1970), pp. 89–95.

Foltman, Felician F. *Manpower Information for Effective Management: Part 1: Collecting and Managing Employee Information*. Ithaca: New York State School of Industrial and Labor Relations, Cornell University, 1973.

_____ *Manpower Information for Effective Management: Part 2: Skills Inventories and Manpower Planning*. Ithaca: New York State School of Industrial and Labor Relations, Cornell University, 1973.

Patten, Thomas H., Jr. *Manpower Planning and the Development of Human Resources.* New York: John Wiley & Sons, Inc., 1971.

Vetter, Eric W. *Manpower Planning for High Talent Personnel.* Ann Arbor, Mich.: University of Michigan, Bureau of Industrial Relations, 1967.

Walker, James W. *Human Resource Planning.* New York: McGraw Hill Book Co., 1980.

7 Recruitment and Selection

The human resources of most organizations are properly viewed as their most important asset. The successes and failures of the organization are largely determined by the caliber of its workforce (starting with management) and by the efforts it exerts. Therefore, the policies and programs an enterprise adopts to meet its manpower needs are of vital significance.

The employment function of a personnel program encompasses the areas of human resource planning, recruitment, selection, placement, and changes of employment status such as transfers, promotions, layoffs, and discharges.

In this chapter we shall discuss recruitment and selection issues, policies, and techniques. The chapter following this one is devoted to an in-depth look at the principal selection techniques of testing and interviewing plus the assessment center, which is a comprehensive method of evaluating candidates.

An understanding of the concepts of labor market and labor supply provides a foundation for our examination of recruitment and selection.

LABOR MARKET CONSIDERATIONS

A labor market is a geographic area within which employers recruit workers and workers seek employment. It is the place where the forces of supply and demand interact. It is usually thought to consist of a central city or cities and the surrounding territory in which persons can change their place of employment without changing their place of residence. When management decides to go into the labor market to obtain additional employees, it finds that it operates vastly differently from product or financial markets. A labor market tends to be unstructured for the most part; it is unorganized. The procedures by which a company recruits workers and the methods by which workers go about obtaining jobs are highly variable. The process is not necessarily channeled through a public or a private employment agency. Laws and regulations governing the process are of a very minimal nature. In fact, if one looks at the process from the standpoint of workers seeking jobs, the whole procedure seems rather haphazard and catch-as-catch-can. Some job seekers obtain employment through friends and relatives, others through direct visits to the plant gate, others through their unions, and still others through employment agencies. Pure chance plays a large part in determining whether John Smith gets a job in plant A or in plant B.

A labor market is characterized by a great diversity of wage rates for the same occupations. If one were to examine occupational wage survey statistics compiled by the Bureau of Labor Statistics of the United States Department of Labor for any of a number of major cities in the country, he would find the highest wage paid for an occupation being in the nature of two to two-and-one-half times that of the lowest. This variation in wages for the same kind of work is caused by many factors. Principal ones are differences among the employers in ability to pay, productivity, and management attitude toward wage levels. Certain nonwage factors, such as greater job security, may mean that a firm that pays only modest wages may still attract and hold the labor it requires. For in the labor market (except for very high-level talent) it is the buyer (employer) and not the seller (worker) who establishes the wage level.

Lack of labor mobility is still another characteristic of a labor market. An employee generally will not resign from his job in Company A to take a job in Company B for 15 cents more per hour. Nonwage factors play a large role in determining the attractiveness of jobs. Nonwage factors include such matters as job security, employee benefits, quality of supervision, and the friendliness of co-workers. Employees do not have ready access to information on wages and nonwage factors at the various employers in a labor market. Unless conditions are very bad at one's place of employment or unless the person knows conditions are very good at another company, she will tend to stay put.

From the standpoint of an individual company, the considerations that determine the quantity and quality of labor that it can recruit are quite complex. The supply is influenced by the population in the labor market, the attractiveness of the jobs and the company (for example, wage rate, benefits and services, reputation of company for job security), amount of unemployment in the labor market, commuting patterns (location of the employer with respect to transportation lines), and the particular skills needed in relation to their availability in the local community. First to come to the attention of an organization seeking additional employees, quite logically, would be those who are presently unemployed. Those who are currently drawing state unemployment insurance benefits are registered with the local state employment service office.

The labor force is not fixed and unchanging in size. Annually, young people enter the labor force and older workers leave through retirements and disability. In any given community there may be a net in-migration or out-migration caused by a complex of factors. The principal factor is the availability of decent jobs. Also the pool of people who are available and looking for work expands and contracts over time. In times of high demand for labor, people who would not ordinarily seek employment—retired persons or certain housewives, for example—may be drawn into the work force whereas in times of low demand, many people may withdraw from the labor force. Those who withdraw may include persons with very limited skills and those who have suffered protracted unemployment and who have become discouraged about job prospects.

The personnel policies of an individual employer are a major determinant of its ability to obtain the labor that it requires. What kind of reputation as a place to work has an organization created for itself by its actions and treatment of present employees?

The experience of companies that have built new plants or facilities in towns or small cities where one would ordinarily expect they would find difficulty in obtaining sufficient labor has often revealed that a good reputation as a place to work (that is, good wages, steady employment, and so on) can exercise a powerful pull to draw people from great distances to obtain employment. In-plant training programs for previously untrained people can frequently supply the necessary skills.

RECRUITMENT AND SELECTION POLICY ISSUES

Personnel directors and management, generally, must face several policy issues involved with the conduct of their recruitment and selection programs. We shall here discuss some important topics about which management decisions must be made.

Fill Vacancies from Within or from Outside?

If an opening occurs for a business-machine operator or a buyer, should people be hired from the outside and assigned directly to these jobs? Most companies announce to their employees that they follow a policy of promotion from within as far as possible. There are several advantages to such a policy:

1. Most people expect to advance to positions of higher pay and status during their work careers. Therefore, this policy fosters high morale. One opening in a higher-level position may cause a succession of individual advancements as people each in turn move up.
2. Management can more accurately appraise the skills, knowledge, and personality characteristics of its present employees than it can of job applicants who are interviewed in the employment office. Therefore, there is less risk of error in selection and placement.
3. The recruitment and selection problem is simplified because there are only a few entry jobs, and the formal education, skill, and knowledge requirements for these are relatively modest.

Although there are manifestly beneficial effects from following a policy of filling vacancies from within as much as possible, there are inherent problems and limitations also. In order for a company to fill its job openings from within, it must have in operation training programs by which people in lower-level jobs can learn new skills in order to qualify for upgrading to more demanding work. In a sense this is a strength and an advantage of the "fill vacancies from within" policy. However, small organizations often feel that they cannot afford the expense of comprehensive employee-training programs. A policy of upgrading from within requires that the persons hired have aptitudes and potential for moving ahead. In some cases they may be overqualified for entry jobs. If promotions do not actually materialize, these overqualified persons will be disappointed and frustrated at their lack of progress. An exclusive promotion-from-within policy prevents the infusion of new ideas and knowledge at the upper levels. This in effect might be called organizational inbreeding. Subordinates, having been taught and molded by their bosses, often know no other way of doing things. When promoted to positions of power and influence they tend to perpetuate outdated practices.

As a generalization, the most fruitful policy is probably that of filling the majority of vacancies from within but going to the outside when fully qualified talent is not available inside the organization. It is also probably wise to fill a moderate percentage of the higher-level managerial and professional positions by going to the outside labor market to inject new ideas into the organization.

Equal Employment Opportunity

Employers are required by Federal law not to discriminate against individuals or groups in regard to hiring, testing, pay, benefits, promotion, and other conditions of employment on the basis of race, color, religion, sex, national origin, or age. In practical terms this means that employers must provide job opportunities for black people, Hispanic Americans, other minorities, women, and older persons (up to age 70). If the organization holds a contract to provide goods or services to the Federal government, it must also create and maintain an affirmative action plan to hire and promote members of the various protected groups.

If adverse impact results from the operation of the recruitment and selection program, the employer may then be required to demonstrate that the selection instruments used (such as application blanks, interviews, and tests) are job-related and valid. The term "adverse impact" means that in the employment process a protected group is treated significantly worse than is the majority group of employees in regard to hiring, promotion, and other employment processes.

Selection Standards— Credentials Barriers

Oftentimes companies adopt qualification requirements that lack a proven relationship to success or failure on the job.

Educational attainment is a principal selection hurdle used by most organizations. Thus some companies specify that a high school education is necessary for employment in unskilled and semiskilled factory jobs such as materials handler, laborer, and machine operator. A college degree is usually a prerequisite for admis-

sion into administrative and managerial positions. Some craftsmen and engineers are required to be licensed in order to perform certain tasks. As a screening device education possesses a considerable measure of merit. The process of going through elementary and high school and college is in itself a selection screen. By and large those who possess the greatest perseverance and demonstrated ability under the specified conditions of the educational system are the ones who successfully complete school. These are presumed to have the right talents and acquired skills, both technical and social. But heavy reliance upon a diploma or a college degree as a condition of employment yields some clear disadvantages.

It automatically eliminates from consideration those who have dropped out of school. Largely, these are the poor, the underprivileged, and those who are poorly adapted to the discipline of the school system. Those who have not gone through the formal credentializing process are not necessarily unqualified. Sometimes the barriers are erected by a small elite group that is already in an occupation or profession and that wants to maintain its choice economic and social position by sharply restricting entrance to the field of work. Some craft unions, for example, achieve just such an end by artificially long periods of apprenticeship, high initiation fees, and contractual limits on the number of apprentices who can enter the trade. Certain professional associations act similarly by licensing rules and control of educational and internship programs. "Credentialitis" is another manifestation of the trend toward bureaucratization of modern organizational life. But this not only denies job opportunities to those who might do well if given a chance but it also artificially shrinks the pool of talent available to an industry, firm, or occupation. A number of brilliant people did poorly in school. Winston Churchill is an outstanding example. The educational establishment tends to homogenize its students. The nonconformist is rejected or rejects himself or herself.

If one grants the line of argument above to

be true, what course of action should personnel executives adopt for an employment policy? Clearly they should not ignore educational attainment as a selection guide. It does correlate with probability of occupational success in a generalized way when one is speaking of large numbers of persons. A realistic policy would be to set general educational qualifications for the various jobs in a company based upon a sound job analysis program. But deliberate emphasis can be given to hiring some people, say 5 to 15 per cent of the total in a given category, who lack the formal education desired but who give promise of reasonable success by virtue of appropriate work experience, interest, motivation, and recommendation by qualified observers. Additional training can be obtained after hiring through participation in evening school and in-service training programs.

The Lie Detector

Many organizations experience serious problems with employee theft and embezzlement. To combat this problem a large number of firms have hired polygraph operators to screen their people to identify potential and actual wrong-doers. Although theft and embezzlement constitute the prime problems inducing managements to use polygraph testing, other problem areas are employee lying, giving away trade secrets, drug abuse, and alcoholism.

In actuality there is no such instrument as a true lie detector. The polygraph is surrogate for a lie detector. It is an instrument that is attached at various points on the subject's body. It measures rate of breathing, heart beat, changes in blood pressure, and skin current (galvanic skin response, associated with sweating of the palms of the hands). The theory behind the polygraph technique is that lying causes distinctive physiological reactions in persons who know they are not telling the truth.

Accuracy rates in polygraph testing average about 75 per cent.[1] Although the machine measures physiological states or changes fairly accurately, there is no simple correlation between these conditions and the truthfulness of the subject. There can be great individual differences in the reaction of people to various kinds of stress. Polygraph interpretations can be invalid when subjects show extreme nervousness; have high or low blood pressure, heart disease, and respiratory disorder; have pronounced neuroses or psychoses, or are pathological liars; and when they suffer from emotional and physical fatigue.

From a civil liberties standpoint, there are serious questions about the use of the polygraph. Among these are invasion of privacy, violation of the Fifth Amendment (of the U.S. Constitution) privilege against self-incrimination, the Constitutional presumption of innocence until proven guilty, and violation of the Fourth Amendment's protection against unreasonable searches.

Despite the serious doubts about the advisability of using the polygraph, it is widely used in employment situations. Eighty-one per cent of the firms responding to a survey conducted by the National Association of Chain Drug Stores reported that they use the polygraph. They used it for both pre-employment screening and for checking on current employees.[2] Citing two university researchers, *Business Week* says one fifth of the nation's largest companies in a wide range of business fields use lie detectors.[3]

As of 1981 seventeen states and the District of Columbia had enacted laws that restricted the freedom of employers in some way in using the polygraph in the hiring process and in checking upon present employees.[4]

[1]Lykken, D., "The Right Way to Use a Lie Detector," *Psychology Today*, Vol. 8 (March 1975), p. 56.

[2]"Polygraph Usage in Chain Pharmacies," *Journal of the American Pharmaceutical Association*, Vol. NS16, No. 4 (April 1976), p. 182.

[3]*Business Week*, (February 6, 1978), p. 100.

[4]Kenneth F. Englade, "The Business of the Polygraph," *Across the Board*, Vol. 19, No. 9 (October 1982), pp. 20–27.

Privacy of Employee Records

In direct opposition to the investigative philosophy of users of polygraphs has been the affirmative measures that several big companies such as Bank of America and International Business Machines Corporation have taken in recent years to protect the privacy of job applicants and employees.

For example, IBM job applicants are not asked about the employment of their spouses, about possible relatives at IBM, about possible prior treatment for mental illness, or about arrest records (however, any convictions within the past five years are asked about). IBM does not use polygraph or personality tests but it does use aptitude tests. Line or operating managers are allowed to see relevant information in the personnel files regarding employees' work performance and awards, however they cannot see information of a personal nature such as medical insurance claims, personal finances, or wage garnishments. Only personnel officials can see this information. Information is not given to outside creditors and attorneys without the employee's consent. Generally, employees have full access to their own personnel files.[5]

Other Policy Issues

Relatives of Employees. Should a husband and wife be allowed to work in the same department? Should a son work in a department managed by his father? Most commonly, organizations do not allow a person to be placed in a unit of the enterprise where he or she can be the recipient of special benefits of treatment bestowed by a relative.

Quality of Persons Hired. The quality of people that an enterprise can attract is determined by many factors including pay rates, employee benefits, and reputation of the enterprise. Seldom does the management of a low-wage firm explicitly state that it hires people of inferior qualifications. It just happens. However, some employers that maintain good employment conditions adopt a formal policy of recruiting and selecting the very best people available.

It is advisable for management to forthrightly face the issue of the quality of employees it can attract and retain.

THE EMPLOYMENT PROCESS

The principal elements in the employment process are diagramed in Figure 7-1.

The employment process begins with a perceived need to obtain a person (or persons) to perform some job. Commonly a manager submits a written request to the personnel department stating that he or she wishes to fill a given position. The position should be defined in terms of its job description and job specification. This process should be integrated with the human resource plans of the enterprise. Organizations typically have established procedures governing authorizations to hire new people and to replace those who resign or retire.

Recruitment involves identifying sources of potential employees, informing people of job openings, and attracting applicants who have the requisite qualifications to perform the jobs. People may be recruited either from within or from outside the enterprise. As shown in Figure 7-1, the job requirements as expressed in job descriptions and job specifications identify the kinds of people to be recruited.

The recruitment activity should generate a supply of applicants for each job opening that is greater than the number to be hired so that the employer can be selective and can obtain those who truly meet the job requirements.

[5]"IBM's Guidelines to Employee Privacy," *Harvard Business Review,* Vol. 54, No. 5 (September–October 1976), pp. 82–90; "Private Files," *Wall Street Journal* (April 24, 1978).

FIGURE 7-1 The Principal Components of the Employment Process

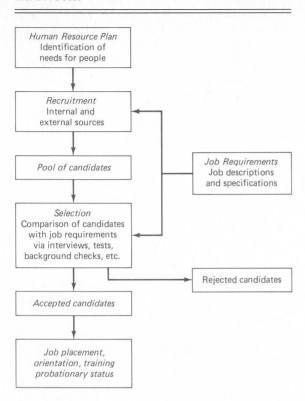

not meet the requirements of the employing organization and (2) those who are hired. It must be noted that some individuals who are rejected may meet the minimal standard set by the employer, yet they are rejected because there are other candidates who possess superior qualifications.

At various stages in the entire employment sequence candidates may voluntarily withdraw. As they learn more about the enterprise and its policies, the manager for whom they will work, the pay rate and benefits, and the details of the job involved, they may decide to withdraw. Because voluntary withdrawals can occur at various points in the employment process they are not shown in Figure 7-1.

Those who are hired are normally given an orientation to the organization, its policies and benefits, to their department and job, and to their immediate supervisor and co-workers. Most often a newly hired employee is assigned to a specific job in a given department and is provided with relevant on-the-job training. However, some newly hired persons may be placed in a special developmental program involving several training and job assignments. This is sometimes done with management trainees hired directly out of college.

The last element in the employment process is probationary status. This is the tryout period on the job. Depending upon managerial policy and the level of the job the probationary period can vary in length from 30 days for unskilled and semiskilled jobs up to a year or more for professional and managerial jobs. During the probationary period employees can be discharged by the supervisor with little or no recourse available to the individual. After completion of the probationary period, normally employees have certain (perhaps minimal) rights to appeal a discharge. Of course, if the employees are represented by a union and covered by a labor agreement they enjoy considerable protection against arbitrary discharge after successfully completing their probationary status.

Selection involves choosing, from among a pool of candidates, the person (or persons) who best match the qualification criteria for the job involved. The selection process can range from a single interview in a very simple procedure to multiple interviews and tests, a weighted application blank, an assessment center, and an intensive background investigation in a more sophisticated hiring procedure.

Figure 7-1 indicates that the job requirements block is closely related to the selection activity. The various selection techniques become content-valid and effective only when they are keyed closely to the job demands and human qualifications detailed in job descriptions and specifications.

The selection process yields two groups of applicants: (1) those rejected because they do

The probationary status of employees is properly viewed as a part of the employment process because the relative success of the hiring activity is partly measured by the percentage of those hired who successfully complete their probationary periods.

SOURCES OF PEOPLE

Recruitment is the development and maintenance of adequate manpower sources. It involves the creation of a pool of available labor from which the organization can draw when it needs additional employees.

One convenient way of classifying the sources of supply is to divide the sources into the two categories: (1) inside sources and (2) outside sources. Thus if a particular job vacancy occurs, it can be filled by transfering or promoting another employee from within the company to that post. If there is to be a net addition to the size of the workforce then, of course, someone will have to be employed from the outside as well. In filling vacancies from within, it is still necessary to match job requirements with worker qualifications. The selection process must still be employed. But it means that present employees are given first chance for any better or more attractive jobs before outsiders are considered.

Inside Sources

If management wishes to fill vacancies by choosing from among present employees it may utilize any of three procedures: (1) informal search, (2) skills inventory, or (3) job posting.

Informal Search. Typically, the manager of the department having the vacancy speaks to the personnel manager and together they give consideration to one or more possible candidates for the position. The manager may interview the employee who is first choice and offer the job to that individual or the manager may interview several employees and then offer the job to the one he favors. Although this informal method is quite commonly used, it tends to keep most employees, who might be interested in the opportunity, ignorant of the vacancy and to deny them the chance to apply.

Skills Inventory. Some organizations maintain a skills inventory which provides in some detail the qualifications of every employee. When a job opening occurs the inventory can be searched to supply a list of employees having qualifications that match or approximate the requirements of the position.

Job Posting. Job posting involves announcing the job openings on bulletin boards and in periodic announcements to office employees. Typically, the bulletins give job title, a brief job description, pay grade, and department. Interested employees can apply for the jobs. Collective-bargaining agreements usually contain a provision for job posting and bidding. The practice has become widespread in nonunion establishments as well. Job posting helps firms meet equal employment opportunity and affirmative action requirements of an "open" recruitment system.

Outside Sources and Recruitment Methods

Depending upon management policy, the type of jobs involved, and the nature of the labor market, management has a number of options available for obtaining people from outside the organization.

Employment Agencies. Every state in the United States operates a *state employment service* which is affiliated with the United States Employment Service. Typically, the states have branch offices in most cities of 10,000 population or more. The service is free to all applicants. Funding for these state employment agencies is primarily provided by the Federal government. Over the years employers have tended to use these public employment agencies to obtain people for blue-collar jobs, for retail store clerks, and for lower-paying service-type jobs.

There are literally thousands of *private employment agencies* in the United States. Job seekers register with the agency. Upon being hired by an employer who has listed job openings with the agency, a fee is paid to the agency. Most commonly the employer pays the fee but in some cases the employee pays.

Another type of employment agency is the *executive recruitment firm.* The clients of these firms are companies seeking managerial and high-level professional talent. Executive recruitment firms maintain files of resumés of people of executive caliber. For a client company they will also seek out currently employed managers who might be induced to quit their present company for a better opportunity.

Unsolicited Applicants. The typical organization receives many applicants who live in the area and simply walk into the employment office to inquire about job openings. Employers often find that this is a satisfactory way of meeting their needs for hourly paid blue-collar workers and clerical personnel.

Oftentimes technical, professional, and administrative-type personnel will apply for jobs by sending their resumés to the personnel offices of well-known firms, even though these firms have not advertised any openings.

Labor Unions. In those occupations and industries where employment is generally of short duration and intermittent, labor unions typically operate hiring halls. These are common in the construction, longshoring, and maritime industries.

Professional Associations. Many professional associations in the engineering, scientific, accounting, health care, and education fields operate placement services for their members. Furthermore, at their annual conventions they typically provide services and facilities that enable job seekers and employers to meet.

Schools and Colleges. Alert employment managers make it a practice to contact school principals and guidance counselors to recruit graduates for office clerical jobs, store clerks, and trainees for a variety of industrial jobs. Business and technical institutes, both public and proprietary, provide training for such occupations as secretaries, junior accountants, computer operators, mechanics, electronic technicians, and medical technicians.

Companies, especially larger firms, obtain a major portion of their managerial, professional, and technical personnel via direct recruitment at colleges and universities. The typical campus interview of one-half hour constitutes rough screening. The employer then invites the most promising candidates to a company facility or headquarters for interviews with several managers. After consultation among these managers formal job offers are made to a subset of those who visited the company premises.

Advertising. Advertising in newspapers, trade magazines, and professional journals is a very widely used method of recruiting. It also usually generates a large pool of applicants. Not only does advertising reach those who are currently unemployed but it also attracts those holding jobs who seek better job opportunities.

Employee Referrals. A significant percentage of jobs are obtained through word-of-mouth and through friends already employed in an organization. Especially for skills that are in short supply, some companies formalize the process of employee referrals by actively soliciting employee nominations, providing information on job requirements, and giving recognition to individuals who successfully recruit new employees.

Prevalence of Methods

A Conference Board survey of firms in the manufacturing, gas and electric utility, banking, and insurance industries reveals that unsolicited applications at company employment offices result in the largest number of new employees in production and clerical occupations, whereas newsaper advertising yields the largest number of new employees in the lower level exempt occupations (professional, technical, and supervisory jobs). See Table 7-1.

THE SELECTION PROCESS

Whereas the goal of recruitment is to create a large pool of persons who are available and willing to work for a particular company, the selection process has as its objective the sorting out or elimination of those judged unqualified to meet job and organization requirements. Thus, in a sense, recruitment tends to be positive in that it seeks to persuade people to apply for work at the company, whereas selection tends to be somewhat negative because it rejects a good portion of those who apply.

The most common approach to the selection problem is to choose individuals who possess the necessary skills, abilities, and personality to successfully fill specific jobs in the organization. Thus, the employment manager typically has in his possession an employment requisition initiated by some operating manager requesting, say, one design draftsperson with five years drafting experience to start work on

April 15 at a certain wage rate. This is essentially a problem of matching a person to the job. But what course of action should the employment manager follow when a bright young person, fresh out of technical school but with no practical experience, applies? The question being raised here is as follows: Does the employment policy of the company permit the hiring of a good candidate because she or he will be a valuable asset to the organization even if she or he does not meet the specific requirements of the present job opening? Let us now go one step further. What action should be taken if the company is not hiring anyone at present, but one or more very promising individuals applies for a job, and the employment manager has every reason to believe that hiring will be resumed within a few weeks or months? Should the good candidates be rejected, or should they be hired and placed in a reserve pool or training program in expectation of future needs? As implied earlier, the prevailing practice in industry is to reject all applicants in these hypothetical situations unless there is a specific job vacancy and the applicant meets the stated qualifications.

But there is another approach to selection that admittedly is more feasible for a large than for a small organization. Under this system certain basic entrance standards are established, such as a minimum amount of education, minimum age, physical requirements, minimum score on a mental ability test, and so on. All those who meet or exceed these requirements of the organization are considered further for specific aptitudes, abilities, and vocational preferences that would fit them for one of a number of possible jobs. The military services, in effect, follow this policy of selecting first for the organization and then differentially placing men and women where they are best fitted.

Fundamentally, then, there can be certain very positive aspects to the selection process. Instead of concentrating simply upon the rejection of applicants, the employment manager can transform his thinking into the task of deciding

TABLE 7-1. Recruiting Sources Resulting in Largest Number of New Hires.[1]

	Total Respondents					
	Nonexempt				Lower level Exempt	
Practice	Production or Operations		Office and Clerical			
	No.	%	No.	%	No.	%
Total Respondents	335	100	523	100	523	100
	Rank[2]	%[3]	Rank[2]	%[3]	Rank[2]	%[3]
Source						
Unsolicited applications at company employment office	1	61	1	52	3	19
Unsolicited letters or resumes received by mail	5	5	6	8	4	16
State employment agencies	3	24	5	14	6	4
Private employment agencies	6	3	3	24	2	34
Union employment services	8	1	—	—	11	*
Community groups	10	*	10	*	11	*
Advertising in general newspapers	2	30	2	43	1	43
Advertising in trade publications	11	*	10	*	7	2
Radio or TV advertising	9	*	—	—	—	—
High schools	8	1	7	2	10	*
Private vocational or trade schools	7	2	8	1	9	*
Colleges	—	—	9	*	3	19
Job or career fairs	10	*	9	*	8	2
Employee referrals	4	22	4	21	5	12

Source: From Harriet Gorlin, *Personnel Practices I: Recruitment, Placement, Training, Communication* (New York: The Conference Board, 1981), Table 2, excepted. Reprinted by permission.

[1]Survey covers firms in manufacturing, gas and electric utility, banking, and insurance industries.

[2]Some sources are equal in rank.

[3]Percent of total respondents mentioning this source

*Less than one percent

where in the organization the applicant would best fit.

Employee selection is a two-way process. Those engaged in designing and implementing a hiring program must always remember that job candidates are making judgments to enable themselves to select the organization and the job just as managers are making judgments to select individuals. Hiring officials have a responsibility to provide job applicants with full and accurate information so that they can make reasonable responses throughout the entire recruitment and selection process.

Considerations in Making the Selection Decision

There are a number of important factors that must be taken into account when attempting to make a decision regarding an applicant or applicants.

Organizational and Social Environment. The selection process necessitates the matching of a person with the job in a particular organizational and social environment. Those charged with operating the hiring program must have available a complete set of job descriptions and specifications for all jobs in the organization so that they can have detailed knowledge of the duties and human qualifications necessary to fill these jobs. A prime objective of the selection process is to find out enough about the applicant's background, training, personality, aptitudes, skills, and interests so that this matching process can be done accurately. But there is more to it than this. Even if a person is eminently qualified to perform the work of, say, a computer operator or a quality control laboratory technician, he or she may fail because of the particular organizational and social environment in that company.

For example, in one company a very attractive and well-qualified young woman, age 21, was hired as a stenographer in an office contain-ing several male engineers and two middle-aged, long-service female secretaries. Although the young woman performed her work well and the men liked her work, she was eventually frozen out and forced to resign because of the antagonism of the two older women, who were very jealous of her charms.

Many factors affect the success or failure of an employee besides his or her basic ability to do the job. Miller and Form have developed a rating scale method for evaluating the social skills required in the performance of jobs. They give consideration to seven social factors: scope of social contacts, status range of contacts, social demands off the job, social leadership, skill intensity, social participation, and direct and indirect personal responsibility for others.[6] In addition to these, many other environmental factors must be taken into account. Among these are social cliques, degree of receptiveness of a work group to newcomers, the personality and idiosyncrasies of the boss, group standards and norms, and organizational pressures. In general, it is not actually possible to measure all these organizational and social influences. The best that can be done is for the employment manager to be perceptive and aware of these environmental factors so that she or he can judge whether a particular applicant will adapt himself successfully to the situation.[7]

Successive Hurdles or Multiple Correlation? The vast majority of employee selection programs are based upon the successive-hurdles technique. This means that to be hired, applicants must successfully pass each and every screening device (that is, application blank, interviews, tests, medical examination, and background check). Some candidates are rejected at

[6]Delbert C. Miller and W. H. Form, *Industrial Sociology* (New York: Harper and Row, 1951), pp. 430–436.

[7]For additional thoughts on the subject of social and organizational environment see Milton M. Mandell, "The Effect of Organizational Environment," in M. J. Dooher and E. Marting, *Selection of Management Personnel* (New York: American Management Association, 1957), pp. 336–341.

each step or hurdle. For a person to go successfully from one hurdle to the next, he or she must meet or exceed the requirements for each hurdle. For example, the job seeker may be rejected as early as the application blank stage because the education and previous work experience may be insufficient to meet the established hiring standard. In designing a selection procedure according to the successive-hurdles method, the selection device that has the highest correlation with job success (validity) is placed first in the sequence, the one with the next highest relationship with on-the-job performance is placed second, and so forth. Those applicants who have little chance of succeeding on the job are eliminated at the first hurdle. Both the candidates' time and the company's time and expense are saved by not having to put grossly unqualified persons through the entire procedure before a decision is made.

The multiple-correlation approach, which is less commonly used, is based upon the assumption that a deficiency in one factor can be counterbalanced by an excess amount of another. For example the education of one candidate as shown on the application form may be below the job requirements, yet the interviewer may decide to carry the individual further along in the selection sequence because of superior related work experience and apparent high motivation (as revealed during the interview). Also, if a battery of selection tests is used, the procedure may entail the compiling of a composite test score index. A low score on one test can then be counterbalanced by a high score on another. In the multiple-correlation technique a person is routed through all the selection steps before a decision is made. The decision criteria may be all reduced to numbers. Thus a scored application blank may be used, the interviewer may assign a numerical rating to the candidates, and of course all tests may be numerically graded. If the combined score on all selection criteria exceeds the level needed to qualify, then the job seeker is hired. If not, he or she is rejected.

Which selection method should be adopted?

If an applicant is grossly unqualified to pass even the preliminary interview because she or he lacks essential abilities, there is no point in sending the applicant through all the remaining hurdles. On the other hand, if a person looks reasonably good on the early hurdles, and is mediocre in one minor factor, there is some logic in giving the person the full treatment before making the final decision.

Certain chance factors may cause a person to fail one hurdle (for example, the interviewer may dislike the person's looks, or the conditions under which a test is administered may be nonstandard); therefore, for borderline cases it makes sense to judge the whole person before rejecting anyone.

SELECTION PROCEDURE

Selection procedures are most properly tailor-made to meet the particular needs of the employing organization. The thoroughness of the procedure depends upon various factors. The consequences of faulty selection must be weighed. This is influenced by the length of the training period, money invested in the new employee, level and complexity of the job, and possible damage to the organization if the incumbent job holder fails.

Another factor influencing the thoroughness of the selection sequence is company policy and top-management attitude. Some organizations deliberately overhire and count upon weeding out poor performers after a few months on the payroll. This simply defers the selection decision until management has had a chance to observe the new employees' behavior closely. However, this procedure is costly for both the organization and the individuals involved. It wastes their time, because they might more profitably be employed elsewhere, where the employer does not overhire.

Employment and Development of People

A Proposed Selection Procedure

Although it is true that the steps in the selection procedure should be varied to meet the special needs of the organization, the following is a model program that will work well in most cases. Adaptations can be made to suit individual situations. For example, the medical examination can be placed quite early in the procedure if physical stamina, agility, strength, and so on are critical to the work and if only a small portion of the general population can be expected to pass the examination. There are ten basic steps:

1. Reception in employment office.
2. Preliminary interview.
3. Application blank.
4. Selection tests.
5. Main employment office interview.
6. Investigation of applicant's background.
7. Final selection interview by manager or supervisor.
8. Medical examination.
9. Induction.
10. Probation.

The decision to add persons to the payroll in particular departments of an organization is not made in the personnel department. This is a function of operating or line management, which then initiates an employment requisition that is sent to the personnel department.

In a large company processing a heavy stream of applicants at all times, the preliminary interview would be conducted by a special interviewer located in the employment office. But in most moderate or smaller-scale operations the preliminary interview and the main employment office interview would be conducted by one and the same person. Thus all candidates might be given a ten-minute screening interview, at which time the interviewer would inform applicants of the nature of the current job openings. He might then elicit data from the candidates pertaining to their education, experi-

ence, skills, job interests, and availability for accepting employment. If the requirements of the company and the interests and qualifications of the job seeker seem to match in this rough initial screening, the individual would be given a much more detailed and comprehensive interview.

Selection tests (often called *psychological* or *personnel tests*) should be administered prior to the main employment office interview so that the interviewer can have the test results before him when he evaluates the candidate.

It is now appropriate to examine the major selection devices.

Application Blank

The application blank is practically a universally used tool to obtain information about applicants that will aid management in evaluating their suitability for employment. It is reviewed by the interviewer(s) to give him or her written information describing the candidates. The typical application blank contains questions that identify the person (name, address, telephone number, sex, etc.), questions about the individual's education and work experience, and questions that may be specific to the particular organization and its needs (special skills, licenses, willingness to relocate, etc.). Many companies use separate forms for hourly jobs, for office jobs, and for professional and managerial jobs.

Traditionally, the items included on application blanks have been chosen judgmentally, on the basis of past experience in the organization and a survey of the forms used by other firms. The interpretation of the responses given by the various applicants commonly is made judgmentally by the interviewer. If a given candidate has changed jobs often, what does this mean? What meaning should be given to specific extracurricular activities while in college or to certain civic organizations? The skilled interviewer gains information from the application form that enables him or her to draw tentative inferences about the applicant's suitability for the job for which he is being considered. Further investigation through interviews, tests, and background investigation may support or refute these inferences. It is essential that interviewers systematically compare their evaluations of responses to questions on the applications to the actual performance of people after they have been hired. In this way erroneous conclusions and interviewer biases can be minimized.

Weighted Application Blank. An application blank can be designed so that there is an empirical relationship between subsequent job performance and the answers the applicants have given on the application form at the time of hiring. An application form that has been designed through statistical correlations is called a *weighted application blank*. The scorings or weights assigned to the questions are specific for each job group and are determined in accordance with the predictive power of each question. In order for candidates to pass this selection hurdle a total cut-off or passing score may be required. The technique is most appropriate where there are a large number of employees in given jobs and where less sophisticated methods of selection have not yielded good results. If there is a long or costly training period, if turnover has been high, or if the rate of failures of new employees has been excessive, then the time and expense to design a weighted application blank may be justified.

In developing a weighted blank, it is necessary to identify those items of personal history of present employees that differentiate between groups of successful and unsuccessful employees. Thus, if it is found that an insurance company's successful life insurance salesmen tend to be married, have high living expenses, and belong to a large number of clubs and organizations, whereas their unsuccessful ones are single, have low living expenses, and belong to few organizations, these factors can be given a definite statistical scoring when evaluating a person's application. For picking store man-

agement trainees, a large retailing chain has found definite correlations with job performance and the following: location of last permanent residence, marital status, father's occupation, health, previous experience in retailing, rank in high school or college class, and compensation of last previous job compared with starting salary of this job.

Reliance upon the statistical formula of a weighted application can result in false predictions in individual cases. However, it improves predictive probabilities. Or stated another way, it increases the employment office's batting average in the long run when hiring and rejecting large numbers of people.

A *biographical information blank* (or questionnaire) is very similar to a weighted application blank. But it usually contains more questions than a weighted application blank and includes items that probe deeper into the individual's life history, socio-economic level, family background, attitudes, interests, education, and work experience. The questions utilize the multiple-choice answer format. A specific score is attached to each choice, but, of course, the scoring is unknown to the applicants.

Schneider reports that biographical information blanks have demonstrated greater predictive power (i.e., higher validity coefficients) than both intelligence and personality tests. He states that validity coefficients for biographical information are consistently superior to those obtained with other selection techniques when all techniques are developed with equal care. He says that biographical questionnaires work well because people's behavior over time is consistent and because people are more likely to succeed in environments where they have a previously established compatible response pattern.[8]

[8]Benjamin Schneider, *Staffing Organizations* (Pacific Palisades, Cal.: Goodyear Publishing Co., Inc. 1976), p. 203. For information on constructing weighted application blanks see J. J. Asher, "The Biographical Item: Can It Be Improved?" *Personnel Psychology*, Vol. 25 (1972), pp. 251–269; George W. England, *Development and Use of Weighted Application Blanks*,

It ought to be noted, however, that the weighted application procedure may unjustly discriminate against people who have never had the opportunity to engage in the "right" personal history experiences that would give them a high score on the weighted application form.

Equal Employment Considerations. An application blank should be thoughtfully designed so that it conforms to the standards of the Federal Equal Employment Opportunity Commission and of the Human Rights Commission in the state where it is used. By and large the questions asked should relate to the kinds of jobs for which candidates are being hired. If the Commission investigates a charge of discrimination regarding pre-employment inquiries, the burden of proof is placed upon the employer if there has been adverse impact upon members of protected groups such as minorities, women, and older workers. Employers are generally on safe ground if they have based their questions upon information derived from job analysis or if they use a professionally developed, weighted application blank.

Selection Tests

In recent years selection tests, which are usually constructed by industrial psychologists, have become a well-accepted part of the selection procedure for the majority of medium- and large-sized companies. They may not utilize them for all of the jobs for which they hire, but certainly for some. Widespread use of tests commenced with World War I, when the Army Alpha Test was used to aid in the selection and placement of soldiers. The testing movement picked up momentum between the two wars,

and has certainly come into its own since the 1940s.

The installation of a sound testing program in an organization is time consuming and costly. Just because a test has been found useful for selecting clerks in company A is no reason to assert that it will be useful for picking clerks in company B. Each test adopted must be proven out (validated) in one's own organization before reliance can be placed upon it. The proper way to look at tests is to ask this question: To what extent will a given test or test battery improve the accuracy of selection predictions over that obtained without tests? Will the organization obtain a higher percentage of successful employees through the use of tests? The theory and application of selection testing, because it is such a complex and important topic, will be treated at length in Chapter 8, "Testing, Interviewing, and Assessment Centers."

Interview

Despite the impressive development of the testing process as an aid to selection, the interview remains the single most important tool in the hiring program. The interviewer is in the unique position of being able to evaluate information obtained from the application blank, a preceding interview (such as the preliminary employment office interview), tests, and background investigation. He can integrate these data with personal impressions and observations to reach a decision regarding the suitability of the applicant for employment.

Interviewing is primarily an art, not a science. It is subjective. Untrained interviewers will make many erroneous judgments. They will often decide to accept or reject a person upon totally insufficient evidence. However, research studies have shown that adequately trained interviewers using sound procedures can and do achieve good results.

Interviewing, like selection testing, will be comprehensively treated in Chapter 8.

rev. ed., (Minneapolis: Industrial Relations Center, University of Minneosota, 1971); Daniel G. Lawrence et al., "Design and Use of Weighted Application Blanks," *Personnel Administrator,* Vol. 27, No. 3 (March 1982) pp. 47–53.

Medical Examination

The pre-employment medical (or physical) examination plays an important part in the screening process. It serves four major purposes:

1. To reject those whose physical qualifications are insufficient to meet the requirements of the work they are being considered for.
2. To obtain a record of the physical condition at the time of hiring in the event of a workers' compensation claim for an injury that occurs later.
3. To prevent the employment of those with contagious diseases.
4. To place properly those who are otherwise employable but whose physically handicapped condition requires assignment to specified jobs only.

The first three purposes of the medical examination are generally well understood. The fourth is not. The examination should be used as a positive aid to selective placement and not as a device to eliminate all but the perfect physical specimen. Those with physical handicaps must live and seek to support themselves by gainful employment if at all possible. There is no need for their plight to be intensified by an arbitrary denial of employment opportunities. Fundamentally, physical standards should be geared to job requirements. They must be realistic and justified. The physical demands of all jobs are clearly not the same. Some require great physical stamina, others demand accurate color perception, and still others call for manual dexterity. The job analysis program should identify and record the specific physical demands of the various jobs and job families. Thus it can be determined to what jobs persons with specified physical handicaps may be safely assigned.

Background Investigation

An investigation into a promising candidate's background is too often overlooked by the employing organization. It requires a little time and money, but the trouble is generally well worth the effort. Previous employers and school officials can often provide valuable insights into the applicant's personality and behavior. Because—as stated previously—the best guide to what a person will do in the future is what he has done in the past, it behooves the careful employment manager to examine this past.

What are the sources for obtaining this background information? There exist four categories of sources. These are (1) school and college officials, (2) previous employers, (3) character references supplied by the applicant, and (4) other sources, such as neighbors of the applicant, the retail credit bureau, police records, and so on.

Category (3) is generally unreliable and can be eliminated for all practical purposes. It is a rare person who will list on an application persons who would supply anything but a most favorable recommendation. In addition, personal friends of the applicant have usually not been in a position actually to observe the work habits of the individual. They know him as a "nice guy," not necessarily as a worker in the work environment.

Previous employers are in a position to supply information regarding quantity and quality of work produced, cooperativeness, dependability, initiative, and relations with associates and supervisor. This is a good opportunity to verify the accuracy of information the applicant has given, such as jobs held, wage rate, wage increases, and reason for leaving. Previous employers can be asked if they would be willing to rehire the person and why.

If the person has graduated from high school within the last five to six years, it is advisable to contact the school principal or guidance counselor to obtain information on attendance record, grade point average, rank in graduating class, extracurricular activities, level of aspiration, motivation, emotional adjustment, and other impressions. Similar data can be elicited from college professors and department chairmen.

144

If the employment manager is doing the checking, a most fruitful approach is to do it by telephone or actual personal visit to the source of information. Previous employers and school officials will seldom be as frank and specific if they are called upon to write a formal reference letter. Conversation over the phone or in person permits a much deeper probing than can be obtained by letter.

Because other employers, supervisors, personnel people, and school officials have their biases, just like anyone else, it is very important to evaluate the source of each piece of information. Is a particularly negative appraisal due primarily to a clash of personalities between a former boss and the applicant? How well do the informants know the person?

Responsibilities of Line Management

Line or operating management plays a key role in an employee-hiring program. Not only does the line manager or supervisor make the initial decision to add someone to the payroll, but he or she also conducts the final selection interview, at which point the candidate who has been sent to him from the personnel department can be accepted or rejected.

Because personnel departments in industry were originally established many years ago to relieve operating managers of certain personnel responsibilities and to take advantage of specialized competence by means of centralization, the question may reasonably be asked as to why line managers should be involved in the selection process. Could they not trust the personnel department to do a competent job? The answer is that organizationally line or operating department managers are being held responsible for the successful and efficient operation of their units. Accordingly, they must be given a say-so in the selection and placement of workers in their departments. The caliber of their work force vitally affects the success of their efforts. The personnel department performs very valu-

able services for line management by recruiting, testing, and interviewing job applicants. Normally it will choose the individual it feels is best qualified to fit the particular work situation. This person will then be sent to the department manager or supervisor for a final selection interview and decision. In most cases the line manager will concur with the choice of the personnel department. However, he or she should be granted the right of rejection.

There is still another reason for involving the prospective supervisor in this hiring process. Employment is a two-way street. Not only does the company have a right to reject applicants, but also candidates have the right to interview a future boss to decide whether they would like to work for that person.

Rejecting Applicants

Interviewers, being no different from most other people in this respect, frequently find it awkward to inform an applicant, directly to his or her face, that he or she does not measure up to the company's standards—that he or she is unsuitable. There is thus an urge to let the rejected applicant off lightly with such statements as "Perhaps at another time we will be able to hire you," or "We will keep your application on file and call you if we need you."

If those responsible for making the employment decision are sure in their own minds that the applicant should not be hired, there is no justification for holding out vague hopes. If he or she is a well-qualified individual but there are no openings at present for one of his or her talents but it is expected that there will be openings in the near future, then it makes sense to so inform him or her. But if he or she is definitely not suitable he or she should not be kept dangling.

The interviewer has the threefold objectives of maintaining the person's ego and self-concept, maintaining goodwill toward the organization, and definitely letting the applicant know that he or she is rejected. There are a number of ways of communicating to the person the fact that he or she is being rejected. If the applicant can clearly see that his or her vocational interests and aptitudes or his or her wage level needs are totally incompatible with the situation, he or she may gracefully withdraw. If the individual possesses certain skills and abilities that might be very appropriate in another job situation (other than that which is open in the company), he or she may be informed that while the pattern of his or her skills, interests, and abilities is good, they do not match the particular job for which the company is now hiring.

If the person possesses all the required technical abilities but is being rejected because of personality, this presents a difficult challenge to the interviewer. Since personality traits cannot be measured objectively, there is danger of creating the feeling that the applicant is being rejected capriciously or discriminated against if he is told his personality is unsuitable. This situation demands real skill on the part of the interviewer to diplomatically convey the impression that the interviewee is being rejected. At times it is best to just imply that the company is going to pick just one or a very few out of a number of good candidates. The competitive situation will cause just the top few to be hired.

AUDITING THE RECRUITMENT AND SELECTION EFFORT

In order to insure that the entire hiring program is effective—that it accomplishes the results expected—and that it is carried on in the soundest way, a comprehensive periodic audit should be conducted. Below is a list of some of the important areas to be examined in such an audit.

- Have well-defined recruitment and selection policies and procedures been developed?

- Do wage rates, employee benefits, and level of employee satisfaction have a positive effect upon the ability to attract qualified people?
- Does the program meet equal employment opportunity and affirmative action standards?
- Is there a sufficient pool of applicants from which to draw?
- Is there a delay in filling job openings?
- Is the recruitment effort selective? Do those who apply possess the necessary skills?
- Which sources provide the most qualified people?
- What percentage of those who apply are hired?
- What percentage of those hired resign or are discharged during the probationary period?
- What is the cost of recruitment and selection per person hired?
- How well do the predictions derived from each of the selection techniques correlate with job performance? How well do those hired perform on the job?
- Has feedback been obtained from applicants regarding treatment received throughout the employment process?

Questions for Review and Discussion
1. If you were president of your own company, what considerations would guide your judgment on the following employment issues:
   a. Hiring relatives of employees.
   b. Promotion from within as opposed to finding the best person available for the job, regardless of whether she is now a company employee or must be recruited from the outside.
   c. Hiring physically handicapped persons.
   d. Hiring college students for the summer.
   e. Hiring disadvantaged persons.
2. In what ways may the social and organizational environment affect the performance and adjustment of an otherwise fully qualified new employee?
3. Explain ways in which a company's employment practices and procedures may change

in accordance with changes in the supply-demand situation for labor.

4. Explain in some detail how you would go about analyzing and evaluating the effectiveness and efficiency of an employee selection program.

5. What is your opinion regarding the use of the polygraph (lie detector) to screen job applicants and present employees? Are there other methods to prevent or minimize employee theft and embezzlement?

6. Why does the properly developed, weighted application blank have such high predictive power? Why do you think it is not used more widely?

7. The recruitment and selection process typically focuses upon obtaining candidates who meet the needs of the organization. But it is also important for the job seeker to evaluate the organization and the persons with whom he will work. Give ways in which this can be done.

Suggestions for Further Reading

Bureau of National Affairs, Inc. *Selection Procedures and Personnel Forms.* Rockville, Md.: Bureau of National Affairs, Inc., 1976.

Finkle, Robert, and William Jones. *Assessing Corporate Talent: A Key to Managerial Manpower Planning.* New York: John Wiley & Sons, Inc., 1970.

Hawk, R. H. *The Recruitment Function,* New York: American Management Association, 1967.

Kessler, Clemm C. III, and George J. Gibbs. "Getting the Most from Application Blanks and References," *Personnel,* Vol. 52, No. 1 (January–February 1975), pp. 53–62.

"Recruitment Strategies," *Personnel Administrator,* Vol. 28, No. 3 (March 1983), pp. 25–58; a series of five articles on recruitment.

Robb, Warren D. "How's Your College Relations Program?" *Personnel Administrator,* Vol. 25, (June 1980), pp. 101–106.

Schneider, Benjamin. *Staffing Organizations.* Pacific Palisades, Cal.: Goodyear Publishing Co., Inc., 1976.

Wanous, John P. *Organizational Entry: Recruitment, Selection, and Socialization of Newcomers,* Reading, Mass.: Addison-Wesley, 1980.

Yoder, Dale, and Herbert G. Heneman, Jr. *Staffing Policies and Strategies.* Rockville, Md.: Bureau of National Affairs, Inc., 1974.

Testing, Interviewing, and Assessment Centers

The preceding chapter was concerned with recruitment and selection policies and procedures. The two employment techniques upon which greatest reliance is usually placed when making hiring decisions are selection testing and interviews. The interview is the primary selection tool in nearly all employment programs. Because they are objective and hold the promise of increasing the accuracy of applicant evaluation, tests have gained a prominent place in the hiring programs of countless organizations. Assessment centers, which utilize multiple evaluation techniques, have been used successfully by many prominent corporations, primarily to identify men and women possessing potential for moving into management (or higher management) positions.

SELECTION TESTING

In our society psychological tests are used for a variety of purposes. They are used in public and private schools and colleges for guidance and counseling students, for vocational guidance for adults seeking help in their careers, for assessment and counseling of patients in mental hospitals, for research into human behavior and personality, for choosing students for college admission, and for selection of employees in business and other organizations. We are interested, in our discussion, in the value and usage of tests in the employment process.

Not only are tests used as an aid for selecting new employees for the organization (their most common purpose in industry), but they are also used for differential placement or assignment to the most suitable job after a person has been hired. They are frequently used to select employees for promotion and transfer within the organization, to select candidates for assignment to a company training program, and to act as an aid for diagnosis when counseling individual problem employees.

A test (the term *psychological test* is commonly used because psychologists have done the most work in developing tests, and the field has tended to become their special province) has been defined in a number of ways. A broad definition is that given by Cronbach, who states that a test is a systematic procedure for observing a person's behavior and describing it with the aid of a numerical scale or a category-system.[1] Blum states that a test is a sample of an aspect of an individual's behavior, performance, or attitude.[2] We may define a psychological test as *a systematic procedure for sampling human behavior.* Usually, in employment situations a test is given under standardized and controlled conditions.

A survey of company practices regarding the use of selection tests that was conducted by The Conference Board revealed that 37 per cent of the firms used tests for lower-level exempt employees (supervisors and professionals), 36 per cent of the firms used tests for office and clerical employees, and 21 per cent of the firms used them for production or operations employees.[3] See Table 8-1.

Contributions of Tests to Selection

Most tests are objective. The score received by the person taking the test is not influenced by the opinions of those evaluating the test results. If tests are looked upon as a part of the total selection process (not as a substitute for other devices), they can add significantly to the accuracy of prediction of job success for applicants. In other words the utilization of valid tests can result in the hiring of better-qualified employees. This in turn may mean less turnover of newly hired employees, lower training costs, and higher output and quality of work. It may also mean better adjustment to the job and working environment. Insofar as tests aid in the evaluation of people, fewer errors will be made in placement of employees on particular jobs. If a costly and lengthy training course is necessary for certain types of work, more accurate appraisal of candidates through testing would reduce the number of failures in the course.

[1] Lee J. Cronbach, *Essentials of Psychological Testing*, 3rd ed. (New York: Harper and Row, 1970), p. 26.
[2] Milton L. Blum, *Industrial Psychology and Its Social Foundations*, rev. ed. (New York: Harper and Row, 1956), p. 267.
[3] Harriet Gorlin, *Personnel Practices I: Recruitment, Placement, Training, Communication*, Information Bulletin No. 89 (New York: The Conference Board, 1981), Table 20.

FUNDAMENTAL GUIDES TO TESTING

Because the field of selection testing is an involved subject, it is important at the outset to examine some of the necessary requirements governing the use of tests.

1. Tests should be used as a supplement to other selection devices, not as a substitute for them. Even a full battery of tests can provide only a sample of a person's total pattern of behavior. Therefore, it is necessary to give credence to information derived from other sources such as interviews, application form, and background investigation to obtain a reasonably complete picture of the candidate.
2. Tests are more accurate at predicting failures than successes. If we divide the characteristics that make for employee success on the job into the "can do" factors (skills, knowledge, general abilities) and the "will do" factors (personality, motivation, interests), we find that tests in their present stage of development are more accurate at measuring the "can do" characteristics. Therefore, if a person fails tests of ability, we can reasonably conclude that he is unable to perform the work satisfactorily. However, if he does pass these tests, he may still fail because of poor adjustment to the supervisor and work associates, lack of motivation, lack of interest in the work, family difficulties, and other factors that are very difficult to predict at the time a person is hired.
3. Tests are most useful in picking a select group of people who are most likely to succeed on the job from among a much larger group. A test, or group of tests, cannot reveal with certainty that a particular individual will succeed on the job. But professionally designed and installed tests can predict rather well that a particular group, from among a much larger group who took the test, will succeed on the job.

TABLE 8-1. Usage of Tests.[1]

	Total Respondents					
	Nonexempt					
Practice	Production or Operations		Office and Clerical		Lower level Exempt	
	No.	%	No.	%	No.	%
Total Respondents	335	100	523	100	523	100
Respondents with programs	72	21	188	36	192	37
For respondents with programs:	72	100	188	100	192	100
Types of tests used						
Intelligence (mental ability)		22		14		23
Mechanical aptitude		44		10		11
Clerical aptitude		11		54		18
Particular skill measurement		31		42		23
Personality		11		7		17
Polygraph or voice stress analysis		—		3		2
How tests are developed						
By a commercial test publisher		33		40		26
Internally, by the company		22		19		8
By an outside consultant for the company		14		11		17
By a trade or professional association		8		17		9
Studies are conducted to ensure that tests are job-related and valid		47		48		35
When tests are conducted						
Preemployment		53		75		44
During evaluation for promotion or transfer		32		31		23
During employee counseling		6		4		5
Immediately after hiring		3		2[2]		2

Source: Reprinted by permission from Harriet Gorlin, *Personnel Practices I: Recruitment, Placement, Training, Communication* (New York: The Conference Board, 1981), Table 20, excerpted.

[1] Data from 523 companies (335 for production or operations jobs) in manufacturing, gas and electric utility, banking, and insurance industries regarding testing practices.

[2] Less than one per cent.

4. A test should be validated in one's own organization to be of any value. It is always necessary to test the test itself before any degree of confidence can be placed in its ability to predict performance on the job. A valid test is one that measures what it is supposed to measure. It will, with reasonable accuracy, predict success or failure on the job.

5. Tests can make their greatest contribution in those situations where it has been difficult to obtain satisfactory employees by using other selection methods. Conversely, if it has been relatively easy to find good employees by other selection devices, there may be no need to resort to the expense of testing. Thus an employer picking common laborers probably has no need to test them, because there are many in the labor force who can do this work and their suitability can generally be identified by physical examination and interview.

6. Those who administer tests and make decisions whether to hire or reject are cautioned not to consider the numerical score on a test to be an exact measure of the characteristic being evaluated. Psychological tests are not so accurate that we can say that a person earning a score of 92 is definitely better qualified than another having a score of 90. Likewise, it is possible for an applicant to score a few points below the cutoff score and still be successful on the job.

TESTING CONCEPTS

It is pertinent at this point in our discussion of selection testing to examine those significant testing concepts and methods that are essential to a sound understanding of how to use tests in a practical situation.

The reliability of a test is the consistency with which it yields the same score throughout a series of measurements. If a test is to be of any value, the person being tested should receive the same score (or nearly the same), or one's relative standing in the group should show little change if one takes the test on April 15 or on May 12.

A considerable number of factors can cause a test to have low reliability. If the test is not administered under standardized conditions, the reliability will tend to be low. Thus, in a shorthand test for stenographers if the material is not dictated with the same degree of clarity and at the same speed every time, we cannot expect the test to be reliable. In addition people vary from time to time in their emotional state, their degree of attention, attitude, health, fatigue, and so on. If a particular test has few test questions and is short, chance may determine whether an individual does or does not know a particular fact. Also luck in selection of answers by guessing may introduce variance into the scores.

There exist four different ways in which the reliability of a test can be determined. More precisely there are four distinct types of test reliability. These are (1) equivalent- (alternate-) form; (2) test-retest; (3) split-half; and (4) odd-even item split.

The equivalent- or alternate-form type of reliability requires the creation of two essentially equivalent forms of the same test. These should be made up by a systematic selection of test items from the same universe or population of possible questions. The scores of a group of people on Form A of the test can then be compared statistically with their scores on Form B.

The test-retest method involves administering the test to a group of persons today and then having them take the same test at a later date. This is generally a good way of measuring reliability. However, the individuals may remember some of their answers from the first time and score slightly higher the second time, especially if it is a speed test.

The split-half form of reliability is found by dividing a test in half and relating scores obtained on the first half to scores on the second half of the same test.

The odd-even item split is simply another way of cutting a test in half. The scores on odd-numbered test items and those on the even-numbered items are correlated. Both the split-half and the odd-even methods are used to ascertain the internal consistency of a test.

The reliability can readily be determined by the test designer and is commonly reported in the manual that accompanies a test. Reliability is expressed by a coefficient of correlation, which will be explained later. Generally the reliability coefficient should exceed .85.

Validity

The validity of a test is the degree to which it measures what it is intended to measure. Or expressed slightly differently, validity shows the extent to which a test does the job for which it is used. In an employment situation a valid test is one that accurately predicts the criterion of job success. A criterion is a measurement of how satisfactory an employee is on the job or in the total employment situation. Actually there are five distinct kinds of validity:

1. Concurrent validity (present-employee method).
2. Predictive validity (follow-up method).
3. Content validity.
4. Construct validity.
5. Face validity.

Concurrent validity refers to the degree to which test scores relate to the performance of employees presently on the payroll. This is often referred to as the present-employee method of validating a test. The procedure involves giving the test to a group of present employees who are working on the job for which the selection test is to be used. Then the scores that they receive are correlated with some measure of their performance on the job. Commonly used gauges of job performance are quantity and quality of work, attendance, accident frequency, dollar volume of sales (for sales personnel), and supervisors' ratings. If those who receive high scores on the test are also the best workers, then the test is valid.

Predictive validity (follow-up method) is determined by giving the test in question to all who apply for the job. Since we are testing the test to see whether it is valid, acceptances or rejections are not made on the basis of test scores at this time. Rather the hiring decision is made on the basis of the other selection instruments, such as the application form and the interview. After those who have been hired have been on the job for a long enough time to obtain a true measure of their work performance (several months to a year or more), a statistical correlation is computed between the criterion of performance and test scores for the group of people involved. If those who made the highest scores at the time of hiring later turned out to be the most proficient workers and those who made the lowest scores turned out to be the poorest, then the test is valid.

In comparing the concurrent with the predictive method we find that the concurrent approach permits an immediate determination of the usefulness of a test. The predictive technique requires a long wait before one knows whether the test is going to be useful. Hence the concurrent validation is most commonly used in business and industry. However, this present-employee method possesses inherent weaknesses. With it we are dealing with a group of very select people, namely those who have remained on the job for a period of time. They have passed their probationary period, and presumably most of the unsatisfactory employees either have been already discharged or have quit. Few supervisors will endure incompetent workers for an extended period of time. Thus, present employees are not a representative sample of future job applicants. If one is trying to validate an aptitude test he will find that the experience that present workers have had in that type of activity will cause them to score higher than untrained applicants. In addition, the validity coefficient obtained by using the narrow range of test scores and performance scores for this select group of people will tend to be lower than if the range of performance were very wide.

Content validity shows how well the subject matter or behaviors required in a test are representative of important aspects of performance on the job. Content validity is *not* measured by statistical correlation between test scores and job performance measures. Rather it is determined judgmentally and logically. The foundation for content validation is a thorough and detailed job analysis. Once the job analysis is completed, a test (or tests) is selected which includes significant portions of behavior actually required on the job. Content validity is most appropriate for achievement tests. Thus, a typing test for a typist would contain a representative sample of the kind of material that was actually required on the job. A skilled machinist must be able to read drawings of machine parts and assemblies. Thus, a test of this skill would logically contain mechanical drawing symbols, terminology, sketches, and conventional modes of representation.

Content validity is not appropriate for selection procedures which seek to measure intelligence, aptitudes, and personality. Generally, criterion-related or statistical validity is preferred when trying to establish that a test is valid for selection purposes. However, content validity may be used in those situations where criterion-related validity is infeasible, as in the case of small organizations that hire too few persons to obtain a reasonable sample size.

Construct validity is a concept employed by psychologists to explain just what a particular test is measuring. Does the test measure and correlate with the theoretical construct or hy-

pothesis? Thus, the concept of anxiety may be hypothesized to be measured by certain test items derived from the meaning and description of anxiety in its technical or scientific sense. Construct validity is most commonly used in clinical psychology, projective-personality techniques, and counseling with personality inventories. It is important in test development and research. The use of construct validity in the employment field is quite new. The effort involved in establishing construct validity involves much research including criterion-related (statistical correlation) studies and possibly also content validity studies.

Face validity simply refers to whether the test questions seem to relate to the job or subject in question. People are more willing to accept tests that seem logically valid. A test for hiring mechanics should, many people feel, contain questions relating to tools, gears, levers, cams, machinery, and so forth. However, face validity cannot be measured statistically. Also a test may appear logically valid on the surface, but a careful validation study may yield a very poor statistical correlation with the criterion.

In summary then, the most important types of validity for personnel management purposes are concurrent, predictive, and content.

Coefficient of Correlation

Correlation is a statistical concept that indicates the degree of closeness of relationship between two series of numbers. In selection testing it is applied to both reliability and to validity. However, it should be noted that a high degree of correlation between one factor and another does not necessarily mean that the first causes the second. All it means is that the first measure relates closely to the second. It may actually be that the first factor causes the second, or it may be that both factors are influenced by some other common factor that has not been determined.

A correlation coefficient can range from

zero up to +1.00. A zero coefficient indicates absolutely no relationship between the two series of numbers, whereas a coefficient of +1.00 indicates a perfect positive relationship. Negative correlation is also possible. Thus a coefficient of −1.00 indicates a perfect inverse relationship between the two measures. For validation work it is impossible to obtain a correlation coefficient of +1.00. Commonly the validity coefficient for a useful single test ranges between .25 and .40. By using a number of tests and entering into a rather involved statistical process called multiple regression analysis, it is possible to develop a combined predictive equation from those several tests that often give a significantly higher validity coefficient.

If the correlation between test scores and job performance scores is .50, this means that the test is measuring or accounting for $(.50)^2 = .25$, or 25 per cent of the variability. Other factors that are often unknown or at least not measurable account for the rest of the variation. Thus, tests generally cannot account for future problems that an employee may encounter, such as financial, health, or domestic difficulties, changes in the demands of the job, or unusual and unexpected job pressures.

There are a number of procedures for computing the coefficient of correlation. If there are only a few numbers involved, the rank-difference method can be effectively used. For a large number of individual cases the Pearsonian product-moment method is most appropriate. This technique requires that both test scores and criterion scores be quantitative and continuously distributed.

If it is not possible to obtain continuous data for job performance, as in certain cases in which supervisory ratings are employed, then the biserial correlation method may be appropriate. This is true if the data are divided into two groups, such as acceptable and unacceptable performance.[4]

[4]Information on statistical analysis of tests and matters of test validation can be obtained from Marvin D. Dunnette, *Personnel Selection and Placement* (Belmont, Calif.: Wadsworth

DEVELOPING A TESTING PROGRAM

There are over one thousand tests on the market and literally scores of tests that purport to measure such attributes as intelligence or clerical aptitude. For a particular application one test is certainly not as good as another. It requires a great deal of planning, analysis, and experimenting to develop a useful battery of tests for a particular selection situation.

Because a great deal of technical knowledge is necessary to establish a new testing program, the services of a qualified person are required to guide the effort. Who is qualified to do this work? The individual in charge should be either a fully qualified industrial psychologist or else a personnel management specialist who has taken a number of college courses in psychology, psychometrics, and statistics. For the administration of the ordinary testing program, the services of a professional psychologist are not required; however, the individual in charge must have had adequate training and experience in the theory and practice of testing and in statistics. If, on the other hand, a company wishes to conduct a full-scale testing program, including projective tests of personality, then only a professionally qualified psychologist who has had intensive graduate training in the psychology of personality can properly interpret such tests.

Steps to Install a Program

The steps that must be carried out to create a new testing program are as follows:

1. Decide the objectives of the testing program.
2. Analyze jobs to identify those characteristics that appear necessary for job success.

Publishing Company, Inc., 1966); Benjamin Schneider, *Staffing Organizations* (Pacific Palisades, Calif.: Goodyear Publishing Co., Inc., 1976).

3. Make a tentative choice of tests for a tryout.
4. Administer these tests to an experimental group of people.
5. Establish criteria of job success.
6. Analyze results and make decisions regarding test application.

Decide Program Objective. A wide range of choices is available as far as testing objectives and policy is concerned. Shall tests be utilized only for hiring new employees, or shall they also be used for picking present employees for upgrading, transfer, and promotion? Shall all the present employees be tested (executives as well) in order to make a comprehensive assessment of present manpower capabilities? If the testing program is to be developed only for the selection of new employees, shall it be for all types of work in the organization or only for certain jobs? Initially should the testing effort be directed only toward improving the accuracy of selection for a particular group of jobs? If this last approach is adopted, it is logical to start with those jobs for which it has been difficult to find satisfactory employees in the past. Let us assume, in the discussion that follows, that a testing program is being set up for certain jobs. From this initial installation, it may be reasonable, then, to expand the program to cover all types of work in the organization.

Analyze Jobs. Although a great many companies have on file job descriptions and specifications that were prepared for job evaluation and recruitment and selection purposes, it is unlikely that the jobs were analyzed from the standpoint of identifying detailed human characteristics that may be revealed in selection tests. Job analysis of this type must be very specific and detailed. Generalities will not do, because they cover too wide a range of skills and aptitudes. Among the items the analyst will seek to uncover are the need for such things as motor habits, eye-hand coordination, finger and arm dexterity, perceptual and sensory abilities, and specific personality characteristics. One useful frame of reference for making this job analysis is to seek those attributes that differentiate good from poor workers.

Choose Tests for Tryout. Once the list of attributes deemed essential for success on the job has been uncovered, it is then possible to choose tests to measure these characteristics. Usually the test program designer will choose from among commercially available tests rather than undergo the time and expense of creating his own test to apply to this one job. This latter approach, though necessary at times, is quite costly. Generally the program designer will select an individual test to measure each of the essential job characteristics. Therefore he will, in essence, be constructing a trial test battery. In picking commercially available tests he will give weight to such factors as reliability, face validity, proper level of difficulty, ease of administration, and cost.

Administer Tests to an Experimental Group. It is now necessary to try out these tests by administering them to an experimental group. The best group upon whom to try out the tests consists of, as was discussed previously under the topic of *validity*, applicants for the job under consideration. It is absolutely essential none of these applicants be rejected on the basis of his test score during this trial period because it is not known as yet whether there is any relationship between test scores and future work performance. We are testing the test at this point. Because this follow-up method of ascertaining test validity is a very lengthy process, many organizations will find it advisable to administer the test battery to those presently on the job as well. There is no reason why concurrent and predictive (follow-up) validity cannot be computed in the same test tryout.

Establish Criteria of Employee Success. Establishing criteria of success is one of the more difficult parts of the test installation program. It is difficult, not because of a lack of criteria, but because it is extremely hard to find criteria that accurately, fully, and fairly measure job success. Most of the criteria available measure only one small aspect of the job. The one that is all-inclusive—supervisor's ratings—is often inaccurate because it is so terribly personal and subjective. Where possible, it is most fruitful to obtain several measures of work behavior and performance and correlate test scores with each of these. The following is a list of commonly used criteria:

1. Quantity of output.
2. Quality of output.
3. Grades in training courses.
4. Accident frequency.
5. Attendance.
6. Rate of promotion in the organization.
7. Professional achievements, such as patents, published writings, and formal awards.
8. Performance ratings made by supervisor.

Analysis and Decision Making. Let us assume, for the present, that we are concerned with only one test and that we are relating scores on this test to a measure of job performance that is continuously distributed, such as

units produced or dollar volume of sales. The most useful way of working with these data is to plot a graph of the criterion scores for the ordinate and the test scores for the abscissa. Figure 8-1 represents a hypothetical case of monthly dollar sales for thirty-one salespersons plotted against their test scores at the time of hiring. The product-moment coefficient of correlation between the criterion and test scores can be computed to find the validity coefficient.

Assuming that we have obtained a representative sample of the population of applicants in this validation study, it appears by inspection that this test will be a useful instrument for selecting salespersons. The dispersion of scores from the hypothetical trend line is not great. Those who score high on the test turn out to be good at sales and vice versa.

The next question is where shall we place the passing or cutting score on the test. Before this can be done intelligently, it is necessary to establish the level of acceptable sales performance. Line *Q-Q* has been set at $16,000. Now we can evaluate the alternatives related to placing the passing score far to the right (high) against placing it far to the left (low). The *selec-*

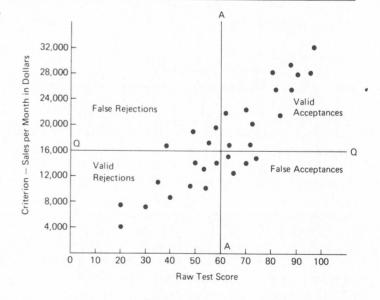

FIGURE 8-1 Scatter Diagram of Average Monthly Sales Versus Test Scores.

tion ratio is the number placed on the job or hired divided by the total number tested. If the cutting score (line *A-A*) is moved to the right, say to 80 or 90, we are almost certain not to have any failures. However, the supply of labor available to a particular organization may not permit it to be so "choosy." If the cutting score, line *A-A*, is placed at 60, it is clear that some employees who passed the test sold less than $16,000 per month. These are called "false acceptances." Likewise some who scored below 60 were successful, because they sold over $16,000. So a few future applicants scoring under 60 (false rejections) would be successful if they were not rejected at that figure. This is the risk inherent in all selection instruments that have a validity coefficient less than 1.00. They will always reject some potential successes and accept some future failures.

The decision of where to place the cutting score is determined by the level of acceptable performance expected, the supply of labor available to the organization in relation to its needs for labor, the cost involved in screening many applicants just to hire a few, and the seriousness of hiring a failure (cost of training, and so on). Over a period of time some companies find it necessary to lower their standards if they cannot obtain people of the caliber they desire.

Combining Several Tests into a Battery. Because no single test can be expected to measure all the capacities and abilities necessary to perform a job satisfactorily, personnel specialists often find it advantageous to use a number of tests. A series of tests developed for a particular purpose is called a *battery.*

If, for example, a particular test has a validity coefficient with job performance of .29, it is often possible to utilize additional tests that measure different characteristics and thereby obtain a higher combined validity coefficient. The statistical procedure by which tests can be selected and combined in this fashion is called multiple correlation. Initially it is necessary to have a number of tests for which the validity coefficients are known. Presumably each test measures a different aptitude or ability. Those tests are used that have a high correlation with the criterion and a low correlation with each other. If they had a high correlation with each other, they would be measuring the same characteristic. The multiple correlation technique, which is explained in most standard statistics textbooks, selects the most appropriate tests and develops weighting factors so that a prediction equation is constructed. With this prediction equation it is possible for a particular candidate to overcome a low score on one test with a high score on another and still obtain a passing composite score.

When a battery of tests is used, it is possible, instead of computing a composite score, to simply plot a profile of the scores that an applicant has obtained on the various tests. By means of this approach the profile can be compared with a normal or standard profile typical of successful workers in that occupation in the organization.

TYPES OF TESTS

Tests can be classified according to the type of human behavior measured as follows:

1. Aptitude.
   a. General mental ability or intelligence.
   b. Special aptitudes, such as mechanical aptitude, dexterity, manipulative capacity, clerical, sales, vision, and perception.
2. Achievement.
3. Vocational interest.
4. Situation.
5. Personality.

Aptitude tests measure the latent or potential ability to do something, provide the individual is given proper training. Achievement tests, also called proficiency tests, measure an acquired skill or acquired knowledge. Ordinarily this acquired skill is obtained as a result of a training program and on-the-job experience. With both aptitude and achievement tests, measures of maximum performance are ordinarily obtained, because it is expected that those being tested will exert their utmost while taking the tests.

If a company trains most of its employees for the work they have to do and if it hires inexperienced help and develops it within the organization, aptitude tests are most necessary to measure what new employees will ultimately be able to do. On the other hand if a company, as a matter of employment policy, hires only experienced stenographers and machinists, for example, then achievement tests are most appropriate for measuring the level of skills and abilities they already possess.

In addition to basic capacity to do a given kind of work, the success or failure of people at work is strongly determined by their personalities and how they interact with other people. Personality tests seek to evaluate such characteristics as emotional maturity, sociability, ascendancy, responsibility, conformity, nervous symptoms, and objectivity.

Situation tests are really combination tests representing elements of achievement, of aptitude, and of personality. Because they are quite different from standard objective, pencil and paper, tests they are properly classified as a distinct type of test.

General Mental-Ability Tests

Psychological testing really began with mental ability (also called intelligence) testing around 1900. More work has been done in creating, developing, experimenting, and refining general mental-ability tests than any other major type of test. The original work on mental-ability testing was done by Alfred Binet, a French physician, who created a test to classify school children according to their ability to learn and succeed at schoolwork.

Just what is meant by the term *intelligence?* Although a variety of sometimes conflicting definitions have been proposed, and thus there is no general agreement as to a precise definition, Thurstone has isolated the specific types of mental abilities that most of these tests measure. These are verbal comprehension, word fluency, memory, inductive reasoning, number facility, speed of perception, and spatial visualization.[5]

Some of the more widely used mental ability tests for employee selection are the Thurstone Test of Mental Alertness, the Adaptability Test, and the SRA Verbal Form (published by Science Research Associates, Inc.); the Wesman Personnel Classification Test (published by The Psychological Corporation); and the Wonderlic Personnel Test (published by E. F. Wonderlic).

Special Aptitude Tests

A great number and variety of tests have been created to measure capacity to learn a particular kind of work.

Mechanical aptitude tests, for example, measure the capacities of spatial visualization, perceptual speed, knowledge of mechanical matter, and sometimes shop arithmetic. They do not measure manual dexterity and manipulative skill. Typical occupations for which such tests have proven useful are machinists, mechanics, maintenance workers, and mechanical technicians. Some widely used tests of this general type are the Bennett Tests of Mechanical Comprehension and the Revised Minnesota Paper Form Board Test (published by The Psychological Corporation); the SRA Mechanical Aptitudes Test and the SRA Test of Mechanical Concepts (published by Science Research Associates, Inc.). Figure 8-2 contains sample items from the SRA Test of Mechanical Concepts.

Psychomotor tests measure such abilities as

[5]L. L. Thurstone, *Primary Mental Abilities*, The Psychometric Laboratory, the University of Chicago, No. 50 (September 1948).

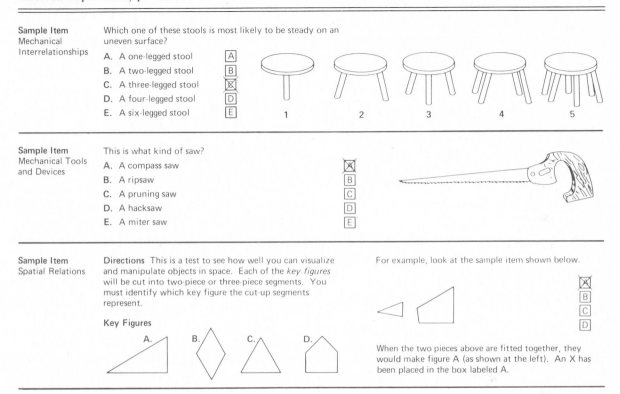

Sample Item
Mechanical
Interrelationships

Which one of these stools is most likely to be steady on an uneven surface?

A. A one-legged stool
B. A two-legged stool
C. A three-legged stool
D. A four-legged stool
E. A six-legged stool

Sample Item
Mechanical Tools
and Devices

This is what kind of saw?

A. A compass saw
B. A ripsaw
C. A pruning saw
D. A hacksaw
E. A miter saw

Sample Item
Spatial Relations

Directions This is a test to see how well you can visualize and manipulate objects in space. Each of the *key figures* will be cut into two-piece or three-piece segments. You must identify which key figure the cut-up segments represent.

Key Figures

A.   B.   C.   D.

For example, look at the sample item shown below.

When the two pieces above are fitted together, they would make figure A (as shown at the left). An X has been placed in the box labeled A.

manual dexterity, motor ability, and eye-hand coordination. Tests of this type are important for selecting workers to do semiskilled, repetitive operations such as bench assembly work, packing, certain testing and inspection, watch assembly, and the like. Commonly used psychomotor tests are the Purdue Pegboard (distributed by Science Research Associates, Inc.), the Hand-Tool Dexterity Test (distributed by The Psychological Corporation), and the Minnesota Rate of Manipulation Test (distributed by the Educational Test Bureau).

Clerical aptitude tests have been created to measure specific capacities involved in office work. Such tests typically contain test items on spelling, computation, comparisons, copying, vocabulary, and grammar. Examples of clerical tests are Office Skills Tests and Short Tests of Clerical Ability (published by Science Research Associates, Inc.); General Clerical Test and Short Employment Tests (published by The Psychological Corporation). Figure 8-3 shows sample items from Office Skills Tests.

Achievement Tests

If a company wishes to hire experienced employees who already possess the requisite skills and knowledge, it would do well to investigate the value of specific achievement or proficiency tests to evaluate these candidates. Achievement tests can be classified into two categories. One measures job knowledge and may be either of

Testing, Interviewing, and Assessment Centers

159

Sample Item Filing

You are to look at the item in the "To Be Filed" column and find the number of the item in the "Existing File" that this new item should *follow*. Mark an "X" on *that* number in the row of circled numbers on the right. If there is no number given for your choice, put an "X" in the *blank* circle.

	Existing File	To Be Filed	
1.	Philip Jenkins	A. B. Reynolds	① ② ③ ⊗ ○
2.	J. C. Kile		
3.	Thomas Morris Company		
4.	Paulson Company, Inc.	John Jones	② ③ ④ ⑤ ⊗

Sample Item Numerical Skills

Examples:

1. 61
   + 24

○ 70
○ 74
○ 75
○ 84
⊗ 85

2. $\frac{3}{4}$
  $- \frac{1}{4}$

○ 2
○ 1
○ $\frac{1}{2}$
○ $\frac{1}{4}$
○ $\frac{3}{16}$

3. A special return envelope is purchased by a city agency for $79.00 per thousand. How much would 10,000 envelopes cost?

○ $ .79
○ $ 7.90
○ $ 79.00
○ $790.00
○ $7900.00

Sample Item Coding

In this test you will be given code lists similar to these.

34 male
21 female

M adult
U teenager
Z child

Below the code lists you will find a list of items. Each item is followed by circles containing five possible codes. Your task is to find the correct code combination for the item and mark an "X" in the appropriate circle. Look at the following examples. An "X" has been placed on the answer for example 1. What would you mark for example 2?

Examples:

1. female adult ⟨34U⟩ ⟨34M⟩ ⟨86Z⟩ ⟨24M⊗⟩ ⟨21U⟩

2. male child ⟨21Z⟩ ⟨34Z⟩ ⟨34U⟩ ⟨21U⟩ ⟨34M⟩

Sample Item Grammar

Albert ____?____ the letters that you dictated.

○ typing
○ having typed
○ is typed
⊗ typed
○ type

the oral or the written type. The other category is a *work sample,* in which a typical portion of the actual job is administered as a test. Thus, a stenographer may have to listen to a recording, take down the words in shorthand, transcribe these, and type them.

Quite logically many companies have developed their own achievement tests to select people for specific jobs. Because the work carried on in many organizations is peculiar to these businesses only, it is understandable that these tests are not distributed commercially. Many work sample tests have content validity only. Personnel specialists and operating supervisors have taken portions of real jobs and asked job candidates to do the work. If a man claims to have had experience as a truck driver or a mailing-machine operator, there is probably no better way to find out if he can do the work than to try him out on it.

Vocational Interest Tests

Vocational interest tests are inventories of the likes and dislikes of people in relation to occupations, hobbies, and recreational activities. The basic assumption behind these tests is that there exists a definite pattern of interests for those who are successful in an occupation and that if one likes the same kind of things that practitioners in an occupation like, then the person being examined will like that kind of work.

One of the most widely used interest tests is the Strong Vocational Interest Blank, first published in 1927. It contains 400 questions of the "like-indifferent-dislike" variety. The blank for men is scored for forty-seven occupations; the one for women is scored for twenty-seven occupations. Strong developed the scoring system for his test by administering it to successful members of each of the various occupations. If an examinee answers the 400 items in a pattern similar to the way in which, say, successful personnel managers have answered it, he or she is given a high score opposite the words *personnel*

manager on the report form. In the late 1970s the Strong-Campbell Interest Inventory, which is a combined test for both men and women, was developed.[6]

The Kuder Preference Record is another commonly used interest test.[7] It scores for ten broad interest areas or clusters. These are outdoor, mechanical, computational, scientific, persuasive, artistic, literary, musical, social service, and clerical. Profiles for a considerable number of occupations have been developed empirically in terms of these ten interest areas.

Because it is possible for a job-seeking person definitely to fake or slant answers in a certain direction in order to be hired, interest tests are much more useful for individual vocational guidance than they are for employee selection.

Situational Tests

A situational test evaluates individuals in a real-like situation by asking them to cope with or solve critical elements of a real job. An illustration of this type of test is the leaderless group discussion. In this test a group of candidates for a job (usually of a supervisory or executive type) are placed in a room, given a practical problem to discuss and solve, and are observed by others. No one is appointed leader. The observers note how they interact with one another. Who had the most useful ideas? Who emerged as a leader? Who conciliated opposing views? Who was most convincing in oral expression? These and many other qualities are noted by the observers. The group oral performance test makes it possible to evaluate effectiveness and skill in interpersonal relations.

Another type of situational test is the "in-basket" test. This simulates key aspects of the job of an administrator. It consists of realistic letters, telephone messages, memoranda, and reports that have supposedly collected in the

---

[6] Published by The Psychological Corporation.
[7] Published by Science Research Associates.

"in-basket" on the desk of a manager. Each person taking this test is provided with adequate background information about the particular organization and its line of business. He is told that he is a new incumbent in the position and must take action on the various items in the in-basket. The candidate is asked to handle these materials in the most appropriate way. This may involve writing letters, notes, or self-reminders, delegating a matter to a subordinate, setting up a meeting with another person, deciding to make a phone call, and the like. Scoring of the subjects' performance is carried out by a group of raters or assessors who consider both content and style of responses. The assessors may interview the candidates to learn their reasoning for each of their actions or nonactions on the items in the exercise.[8]

Both the leaderless group discussion and the in-basket test are widely used in industry to aid in the selection of managers, especially as components of assessment centers.

Personality Tests

There are two types of personality tests:

1. Objective pencil-and-paper tests (personality inventories).
2. Projective tests.

Because they are suitable for group testing and can be scored objectively, most personality tests are of the objective type. Objective personality tests in common usage are the Personal Audit, Survey of Values, and Thurstone Temperament Schedule (published by Science Research Associates); and the Edwards Personal Preference Schedule and the Work Environment

[8] Further information on the in-basket test is contained in Norman Frederiksen, "Factors in In-Basket Performance," *Psychological Monographs: General and Applied*, Vol. 76 (1962), pp. 1–6; and Felix M. Lopez, Jr., *Evaluating Executive Decision Making: The In-Basket Technique* (New York: American Management Association, Research Study No. 75, 1966).

Preference Schedule (published by The Psychological Corporation).

Personality tests of this type have the disadvantages of interest inventories. They can be faked by sophisticated candidates. There is a strong motivation always to give socially acceptable answers. In addition, self-report devices such as these reveal how a person thinks she would behave in a certain situation. This does not necessarily mean she would actually act that way in a real-life problem. In other words many persons do not really know themselves. Personality inventories have had rather limited success in predicting employee performance on the job. They are more useful for individual counseling.

A projective personality test is one in which the subject is asked to project his own interpretation into certain standard stimulus situations. The meaning he attaches to the stimulus depends upon personal values, motives, and personality. Theoretically the number of responses that various people can give to a single stimulus is infinite. Two well-known projective tests are the Rorschach and the Thematic Apperception Test.

The Rorschach test, developed in 1921 by Hermann Rorschach, consists of ten cards, each containing a different inkblot. These inkblots are of various colors. The person is asked to explain what he sees in each blot. The explanations provide clues to personality. A full evaluation can be made only when the analyst knows about the subject's family background, education, past experiences, and has evaluations obtained from others who know the individual.

The Thematic Apperception Test, developed in 1938, consists of a series of twenty pictures, there being a different set for men and women. The person tested must interpret each picture by telling a story about it in terms of what that person believes is happening and what will be the outcome.

All projective tests must be administered individually. Interpretation of the results is a job only for a qualified clinical psychologist or a psychiatrist. The interpretation is highly subjective and unstandardized. In a sense it is impressionistic. Quantitative scores are not developed.

Personality Testing in Perspective. If one were to ask a representative sample of personnel managers the most common reason for employee failure on the job, they would undoubtedly say that temperament, personality, and adjustment to the job environment, not ability, are the main causes. Yet the measuring instruments now available—objective and projective tests—are not sufficiently advanced in their stage of development to obtain really accurate predictions of employee behavior.

Two psychologists, Guion and Gottier, have made a comprehensive analysis of published validation studies of the most commonly used personality inventories and projective tests. The record is poor. They state that the conventional personality tests have not demonstrated general usefulness as selection tools in the employment process.[9]

Some critics charge that the personality-testing process is not scientific because the value judgments of the test designers determine the interpretations of the individual's personality. Furthermore, those being tested must answer the questions in a pattern that matches the way current successful managers have answered the questions on the same tests. But this process involves circular reasoning. How could different types of individuals ever be hired so that they themselves could be included in a criterion group for a validation study if they had the wrong pattern of personality traits in the first place?

It is difficult to state with confidence that particular jobs require a defined personality configuration in order for the job incumbents to be successful. For example, American history has demonstrated that successful U.S. presidents have had quite different personalities.

[9] Robert M. Guion and Richard F. Gottier, "Validity of Personality Measures in Personnel Selection," *Personnel Psychology*, Vol. 18, No. 2 (Summer 1965), pp. 135–164.

Sports fans also know that successful managers of professional baseball and football teams can have very different personalities.

Testing and Equal Employment Opportunity

Selection tests have the potential for inadvertantly discriminating against racial and ethnic minorities, women, and older workers. If certain minority groups score lower on tests, does this mean they have less capability of adequately performing the jobs they are seeking than mainstream whites?

If the use of selection instruments such as tests results in an "adverse impact" upon protected groups, the burden of proof is placed upon the employer to show that the tests used are job-related or predictive of performance on the jobs. This means the selection instruments must be validated. Standards and procedures for the proper use of selection instruments in the context of equal employment opportunity have been developed by the Equal Employment Opportunity Commission in cooperation with other Federal agencies under authority granted to these agencies by Title VII-Equal Employment Opportunity (as amended) of the Civil Rights Act of 1964 and various other statutes.

THE SELECTION INTERVIEW

The interview is the most universally used selection method. Although many employers do not use tests to aid in reaching an employment decision, there are hardly any who do not interview the applicant in order to help make a definite assessment. In fact, multiple interviews are commonly employed. In the proposed selection procedure outlined in Chapter 7, provision is made for three: the preliminary, the main employment office interview, and the final decision-making interview by the prospective supervisor. For high-level positions in many organizations, several operating executives interview the candidate and compare impressions before a definite decision is made.

The interviewer is in the unique position of being able to integrate all the information and impressions obtained about the applicant from all sources: application form, preliminary interviews, test scores, and background checks. The interviewer can assess the applicant on such attributes as personal appearance, mannerisms, emotional stability, maturity, attitudes, motivation, and interests. He can gauge how well the candidate will adjust to the social situation in the organization. The interview permits deep probing into the person's home and family background, education, previous work experience, avocations, and other pertinent areas.

Interview Defined. *An interview is a conversation or verbal interaction, normally between two people, for a particular purpose.* The intention is to explore certain subject areas. Extraneous topics are ordinarily minimized. There are a great many types of interviews that occur in an organization, such as appraisal interview between supervisor and subordinate, a salesperson dealing with a purchasing agent, a counseling interview, a grievance interview, a data-gathering interview in connection with a research project, and a job analysis interview. The basic principles of interviewing apply alike to all of these; however, the specific techniques employed will differ.

Objectives of the Selection Interview. The goals of selection interviews can be grouped into three broad categories. First, the interviewer seeks to obtain enough knowledge about candidates to determine whether they are suitable for employment in the organization and for the particular job under consideration. Many will believe that this is the only purpose of an employment interview. But this is not so. Employment is a two-way proposition. Not only is the employer choosing an employee, but also the job seeker is choosing an employer. He or she may reject many as being unsuitable for his or her needs. Therefore, the interview has as a second purpose the giving of sufficient information about the organization, the job, and the people such that the applicant is able to make an intelligent decision on acceptance or rejection of the job if it should be offered. The third goal of an interviewing situation is to deal with the candidate in such a manner as to maintain and create good will toward the company and its management.

Limitations of the Interview. The author once met an industrial executive who claimed he could determine five minutes after a job seeker entered the office door whether he was suitable for hiring. Nonsense! Anyone planning to engage in employment interviewing must understand the inherent weaknesses of this technique. Fundamentally, the major defect of the interview is its subjectivity. The decisions made by the interviewer are based upon his or her opinion, and that opinion is subject to bias and prejudice. Two interviewers may interview the same candidate and come up with different evaluations.

The applicant, trying to create a favorable impression in the eyes of the interviewer, may behave in an unnatural fashion. The behavior and responses of the applicant are considerably affected by the interviewer's own personality. Interviews are not standardized, and it is difficult to quantify the results.

Many attributes cannot be measured by an interview. Intelligence, motor abilities, manual skills, creativity, strength, health, and many other factors can be measured more appropriately by other devices.

However, numerous research studies have shown that when combined with other selection techniques, interviews that are conducted by properly trained personnel under the proper conditions do have a very positive and significant predictive value.

Some Research Findings. In a comprehensive review of published research on the employment interview, starting with Walter D. Scott's pioneering investigations in 1915 through to the work of recent researchers, Eugene C. Mayfield has uncovered a number of important findings: (1) Interviewers are quite consistent in the way they rate the same interviewee. When re-interviewing the same person or listening to a tape recording of the original interview at a later date, they make about the same ratings as originally. (2) If different interviewers conduct an unstructured interview and have no prior information on the candidates, they generally come up with quite different ratings of the same interviewees. In other words, the interrater reliability is low. (3) Structured interviews, for instance, the patterned interview, yield fairly consistent ratings of the same persons by different interviewers. The interrater reliability tends to be high. However, if the interviewers used quite different structured forms, their ratings of the same candidates differed substantially. (4) Many investigators report rather low validity (predictions of job success) with the interview. However, very encouraging results are obtained when a team approach is used. The team method can be applied through the "board" technique in which three or four interviewers sit as a panel to interview applicants. The team method can also be used when applicants are interviewed separately by a number of persons who then compare judgments to arrive at a final group decision. (5) The attitudes and biases of interviewers heavily influence their ratings. (6) Interviewers tend to be influenced in their judgments more by unfavorable than by favorable information. They tend to search for negative data. Experiments have shown that it is easier to induce shifts in ratings toward rejection than toward acceptance. (7) Interviewers tend to arrive at their decisions to accept or reject fairly early in the course of an unstructured interview.[10]

A more recent review of research investigations on the employment interview prepared by Richard D. Arvey and James E. Campion adds further support to Eugene Mayfield's conclusion that the use of board or panel interviews is a promising way of improving the reliability and validity of the interview. Arvey and Campion also state that the use of directly related job analysis and other job information as a basis for interview questions is a valuable method for improving the accuracy of the interview. In discussing why the interview is so widely used, Arvey and Campion point out that it serves important functions that cannot be performed accurately by available psychometric technology. The interviewer can note the applicant's verbal fluency, sociability, job interests, career plans, mannerisms, and likes and dislikes.[11]

PSYCHOLOGICAL FOUNDATIONS FOR INTERVIEWS

A working knowledge of the psychological basis for interviewing is desirable for those who engage in this activity.

Motivation of Interviewees

The desire of interviewees to explain themselves fully and to reveal freely their experiences, goals, and attitudes is strongly influenced by the

[10] Eugene C. Mayfield, "The Selection Interview: A Reevaluation of Published Research," *Personnel Psychology,* Vol. 17 (1964), pp. 239–260.

[11] Richard D. Arvey and James E. Campion, "The Employment Interview: A Summary and Review of Recent Research," *Personnel Psychology,* Vol. 35, No. 2 (Summer 1982), pp. 281–322.

personality and behavior of the interviewers. Applicants are most likely to speak freely and honestly if they perceive that interviewers understand them and accept what they have to say. Interviewers must be empathic. They must understand the applicant's point of view and refrain from criticizing, directly or by implication, what has been said. Job seekers are most likely to be motivated to communicate freely and fully when they receive satisfaction from the interviewing process and when their personal relationships with the interviewer are healthy and need-satisfying.

It is important to recognize that people are often unaware of the reasons for their own actions and attitudes. If called upon to explain why they behaved in a certain way, they may honestly not know their own motives.

Human beings exhibit both rational and nonrational or emotional behavior. An engineer may take pride on being coldly objective and analytical in work at the office, yet may be guided almost entirely by feelings and emotions in choosing a political party, buying a new suit, or choosing friends. There is a great tendency for people to "think with their hearts" and not their minds. In an interviewing situation the interviewer should be perceptive of emotional responses to such questions as "How did you get along with your boss?" or "Tell me about your childhood."

Barriers to Communication

If the person being interviewed feels there is a basic clash between her values and goals and those of the interviewer, she will tend to be inhibited. If she feels that the inteviewer is not "with her," that he will reject, as being socially unacceptable, certain of her statements, then she will present only that information that will reveal herself favorably. Should the candidate feel that her statements and opinions might at any time be used to harm her, she will also be reluctant to speak freely. A vast gulf between the inteviewer and the applicant in social status, language, and education can cause a breakdown in communication if the inteviewer gives evidence of being snobbish, aloof, or indifferent toward the candidate.

Interviewer Bias

Countless research experiments have demonstrated that the opinions and biases of the interviewer have a powerful influence upon the decisions reached. An early and classic experiment in the field was conducted in 1914, when the New York Commissioner of Public Charities organized a study of the physical, mental, and social characteristics of 2,000 destitute men. Twelve men did the interviewing. One of the areas under investigation was the cause of the men's poverty. One of the interviewers, who happened to be a prohibitionist, attributed the men's destitution primarily to the excessive use of liquor, whereas another interviewer, who was a socialist, reported that their difficulty was due mainly to depressed economic conditions and factory layoffs. A more recent study by Ferber and Wales, in connection with the public's attitude toward prefabricated housing, showed that the responses were definitely influenced by the interviewer's own bias toward such housing.[12]

In view of the foregoing, it is vital that all interviewers be made aware of the effects of bias upon evaluations. All interviewers must seek to know fully their own prejudices so that they can discount these biases when appraising people in the interview.

Past Is Clue to Future

The most accurate guide to how a person will perform in the future can be obtained by reviewing what he or she has done in the past. Most

[12]Robert Ferber and Hugh Wales, "Detection and Correction of Interview Bias," *Public Opinion Quarterly,* Vol. 16 (1952), pp. 107–127.

people's fundamental personalities, attitudes, and ways of behaving are developed early in life. In analyzing backgrounds, it is necessary to explore childhood environments, school and college experiences, previous job experiences, social lives and recreations, present family lives, health, and financial pictures. It is unsound for the interviewer to draw categorical and dogmatic conclusions from a single incident. If the applicant failed on one job, it does not necessarily follow that he or she will fail on all future jobs. If grades in high school were only mediocre, it does not prove that the person has only a mediocre mentality. It is the whole pattern that counts. The inteviewer must make tentative inferences from certain disclosures and then look for evidence in other facets of the person's life to substantiate the impression. If the inference cannot be verified by other facts, it should be rejected.

TYPES OF INTERVIEWS

Interviews can be classified according to the techniques and structure utilized. Such a method of categorizing interviews would be (1) planned, (2) patterned, (3) stress, and (4) panel.

The *planned* interview has also been referred to as the depth interview or the action interview. Basically, in this approach, the inteviewer has outlined in advance the subject areas to be explored. For the beginning interviewer this would be recorded in writing, although it would be unwise to refer to notes frequently. The practiced interviewer knows from experience all the areas that must be explored. Subjects to be probed include home life, present domestic situation, education, previous work experience, social adjustment, attitudes, and recreational interests. The object is to get the individual to talk freely and expansively on these topics. The interviewer probes in depth for clues that would indicate potential success or failure on the job.

In this inteview it is also necessary to provide information about the organization, nature of the work, pay, opportunities for advancement, and demands made on the employee. The applicant must be given sufficient information to decide whether the employment opportunity is suitable to his or her needs and interests.

The *patterned* interview, sometimes called the standardized interview, uses as its basis an extremely comprehensive questionnaire. It is therefore highly structured. Two of the best-known patterned interview procedures are the McMurry Patterned Interview Form[13] and the Diagnostic Interviewer's Guide developed by E. F. Wonderlic. McMurry has prepared different interview forms for office and factory jobs, for sales positions, and for executive positions. Since patterned interview forms ask so many detailed questions, no stone is left unturned in exploring the background, knowledge, attitudes, and motivation of the job seeker. Validation studies have revealed good results with this method. These favorable results are probably due as much to careful training of interviewers and sound selection procedures as they are to the form itself. Experienced interviewers generally do not like to be constrained by a rigid schedule of questions.

The *stress* interview was devised during World War II by the United States Government for selecting undercover agents for the Office of Strategic Services. In these interviews the interviewers assume roles of hostility toward the subjects. They become interrogators. They put interviewees on the defensive and deliberately try to annoy, embarrass, and frustrate them. They try to cause the candidate to lose control of his or her emotions. Sometimes the candidate is assigned a problem of unusual difficulty and with considerable annoyances thrown into the situation.

The object of the stress interview is to find those persons who are able to maintain control over their behavior when they are highly

---

[13]Published by the Dartnell Corporation, Chicago.

aroused emotionally. They must be able to act poised and well adjusted. They must be resourceful and have their wits about them in this situation.

The stress interview should be used only by a very well-trained person and only for those types of occupations in which action under stress is an essential ingredient of the job, for example, police work, spying, or secret agents. For the typical industrial or business situation this technique is generally inappropriate. It tends to inhibit open and complete response. When interviewers deliberately adopt hostile attitudes toward applicants, they find that the latter, being on the defensive, will tend to guard their every response and give only socially acceptable answers.

In the *panel* inteview there are three or more interviewers, often called an examining board, and a job candidate or interviewee. The panel technique is often used in various governmental jurisdictions (along with tests and other techniques) to select employees in professional and administrative classifications. It is alleged that the panel technique permits more comprehensive investigation of applicants because there are several questioners and that the panel members, after candidates have left the room, can discuss their individual interpretations of performance. Presumably the impressions and biases of the interviewers can be brought out into the open and a consensus evaluation developed.

PREPARING FOR THE INTERVIEW

A number of actions should be taken prior to the actual interview itself. Privacy is of utmost importance. The conversation between the interviewer and the interviewee must not be overheard. This is to insure unrestrained responses from the applicant.

Enough time should be allowed to permit a complete exposition of all the facts necessary for a fair assessment of the job seeker. For a main employment office selection interview (not a preliminary interview), this would mean a time period of 25 to 30 minutes for candidates for unskilled and semiskilled work. On the other hand for higher-level jobs, such as technical, managerial, and sales, where personality and motivation are critically important, an allowance of one hour per interview is not excessive.

Immediately prior to the actual interview, the interviewer should study all available data pertaining to the applicant. This may include the application form, preliminary interviewer's comments, test scores, and so on. Certain facts may thus stand out and indicate the need for intensive investigation. Also, from past experience, the employment interviewer will know those areas that are critical to job success.

In order to insure that all of the vital areas have been explored, a guide sheet may be utilized. This is especially useful for beginning interviewers. The topics and items in Table 8-2 can serve as a good check list.

CONDUCTING THE INTERVIEW

In commencing the interview, the employer representative must take the lead. The immediate objective is to establish a feeling of confidence and trust, to develop a favorable emotional feeling or a feeling of harmony between the job-seeker and the interviewer. This is called rapport. Generally this can be accomplished by showing that one is interested and going to be helpful and supportive in manner. The conversation should be opened with items that do not have sharp emotional overtones. Because the job-seeker is almost always under tension and apprehension, at least initially, the interviewer

TABLE 8-2. Interviewer's Guide.

A. *Appearance and Mannerisms*
   Dress

   Poise and bearing

   Speech and voice

   Facial expression

   Neatness and cleanliness

   Nervousness

B. *Education*
   Did person actually
      graduate from high
      school, college?

   Courses taken, major area
      of concentration

   Reasons for choice of
      major course area

   Rank in class

   Courses liked best and
      least and why

   Extra curricular activities

   Method of financing
      higher education

   Special recognition and
      honors received

C. *Work History*
   Nature of jobs held

   How did you obtain jobs?

   Type of work liked best,
      least

   Relations and attitude
      toward superiors on
      previous jobs

Reasons for changing jobs

Career goals, short term
   and long term

Progress (pay increases,
   promotions) made

Any unexplained gaps in
   job history?

D. *Personality, Attitudes, and
      Social Adjustment*
   Present interests and
      spare-time activities

   Offices held in
      organizations
      (exclude religious
      and ethnic
      organizations)

   Personal goals in life; level
      of aspiration

   Attitudes toward work
      associates; toward
      authority

   Strength of interest in job
      applied for; in
      organization

   Emotional maturity

   What is your strongest
      achievement?

E. *Health*
   Past and present health
      problems

   Any physical limitations
      that might affect
      ability to do job

must create a relaxed atmosphere so that the individual will be able to express himself spontaneously.

Because a prime objective is to learn as much about the candidate as is necessary to make a reliable assessment, the interviewer must make skillful use of questions. He should use broad questions in order to encourage a thorough response. Thus, it is sound to say "Tell me about the duties, responsibilities and relationiships of your last job." This is better than "Did you have to write reports? Did you take readings of the meters on the chemical equipment? How did you coordinate with other departments?" By opening up a general area for discussion in an interested but very broadly structured fashion, interviewers will elicit those ideas that are most important in applicants' minds. They will tend to speak about those things that are most critical. This will provide clues to values and personalities. If interviewees wander off the subject and waste time, interviewers can gently channel the conversation by another question.

For the person who seems reluctant to speak, often a deliberate pause on the part of the interviewer can be stimulating. By looking at the individual in a warm but expectant manner, the interviewer can convey the idea that he is receptive and would like the person to amplify more fully.

Leading questions—those that signal a desired response—should be avoided because the applicant may then refrain from expressing true feelings. Examples of leading questions are "Did you get along well with your supervisor?" "You would not object to shift work, would you?" Instead it would be better to say "Tell me about your last supervisor" or "How do you feel about shift work?"

By refraining from criticizing or acting shocked at the individual's responses, one thereby encourages a person to reveal his or her true self. The individual will tend to talk about failures as well as successes if the interviewer does not show anger (by facial expression, voice, or nature of comments) at the revelations. The interviewer might indicate that others have had similar difficulties.

Immediately after the interview is completed and the candidate has left the room, the interviewer should record his or her impressions on a rating form. If several other interviews intervene, much will be forgotten. On the other hand it is generally unwise to engage in extensive note taking and impression recording during the course of the inteview. Not knowing what is being recorded, in such a situation, the interviewee may become apprehensive and speak in a more guarded fashion henceforth. Occasional note taking of objective data is acceptable. However, recording of the subjective conclusions of the interviewer during the conversation should be avoided.

COMMON PITFALLS IN INTERVIEWING

It is pertinent to discuss some of the frequent errors made in selection interviewing. By being aware of these problems, a practicing interviewer can seek to minimize their occurrence.

In judging people, probably all of us are, initially at least, prone to the condition called the halo effect. The halo effect is a situation in which a single prominent characteristic of the individual may dominate one's judgment of all other traits. This can work in both a positive and negative fashion. Thus, if a person is neat, clean-cut, and alert, the interviewer might jump to the conclusion that the person is also intelligent, ambitious, and dependable. Conversely if a person is sloppy and slovenly, the interviewer might conclude that he or she is also ignorant and lacking in essential skills and job knowledge. But these conclusions are not necessarily so. In rating an individual on each of a number of traits, interviewers should have definite substantive evidence. If this has not been obtained, they must note that they cannot fairly judge certain attributes.

Previously, in discussing the psychological foundations of interviewing, the subject of interviewer bias was explained. Because people are not entirely rational beings, emotion, bias, and subjectivity cannot be eliminated. But it is essential that the interviewer be fully aware of his or her own attitudes and prejudices in order to discount them. Certain mannerisms or expressions of the applicant may evoke strong emotional overtones for the interviewer. These may be either positive or negative. But the key question is whether the matter has any real bearing on future job performance. Some interviewers subconsciously conclude that those who have interests and values similar to their own are therefore good prospects. In fact many organizations acquire a distinct "personality" because employers tend to think that those who are just like themselves are good people and those who have opposing attitudes, motivations, and values are not.

Finally, failure to listen is a common weakness, especially for untrained interviewers, who in their enthusiasm might tend to do most of the talking. But a talking interviewer can learn but little while vocalizing.

ASSESSMENT CENTERS

Assessment centers have come into wide prominence since the early 1970s for selecting men and women for promotion into management from nonsupervisory positions, for selecting individuals for promotion into higher management positions from supervisory levels, and for hiring college graduates (including MBAs) for management trainee positions. Many of America's leading corporations, including AT&T, Sears, General Electric, and IBM, have experienced considerable success with the assessment center technique.

An assessment center is a method or process for evaluating people. It uses multiple measurement techniques such as simulation exercises, tests, biographical questionnaires, interviews, and observation of assessee behavior by trained assessors. The dimensions and qualities that are evaluated are determined by comprehensive analysis of the demands and human behaviors required for the jobs involved. After the group of candidates have performed the various assigned exercises and tests, the assessors (observers) meet to develop a pooled evaluation of each individual. The typical assessment center processess candidates in groups of ten to twelve people who perform the various exercises and other activities over a two- to three-day period. The discussions and evaluations of the candidates by the assessors generally require an additional two days.

The assessment center technique was first used by the German Army prior to World War II. The British used the procedure for selecting officers during that war. At that time also the United States Office of Strategic Services used assessment centers to pick undercover agents. The first application in American industry was by the American Telephone and Telegraph Company, which launched its Management Progress Study in 1956.

Bell System's Management Progress Study was a longitudinal research investigation into selection techniques and the careers of managers. The purpose of the project was to determine whether measurements and ratings made in the early phases of a person's career at an assessment center are predictive of his subsequent accomplishments five, ten, and twenty years later. In this study small groups of young men were brought to the center for three and a half days of intensive measurement, observation, and evaluation. A total of 422 men were assessed. Two thirds of these were college graduates who were assessed soon after being hired. The other third were former hourly paid craftsmen who had advanced to the lowest (foreman) level of management. They were not college graduates except for a handful who had earned degrees via evening school.

The techniques used for collecting information on the people included (1) a two-hour interview; (2) an in-basket exercise; (3) a business game involving a manufacturing problem; (4) a leaderless group situational exercise that involved the evaluation of foremen for promotion; (5) projective personality tests such as the Thematic Apperception Test; (6) pencil-and-paper intelligence, aptitude, and personality tests; (7) a personal history questionnaire and an autobiographical essay. In addition it should be pointed out that trained staff members observed each group problem and recorded impressions of each individual. In 1965 correlations were made between predictions at the assessment center and criteria of performance in subsequent years. Specifically these criteria were management level achieved and current salary. In two of the groups who had the longest service in management from the date of original assessment, the assessors made accurate assessments of management level to be achieved in 78 per cent of the cases. Of those people whom the raters judged would not reach middle management within nine to ten years, the raters were correct in their predictions in 95 per cent of the cases.

Of the specific techniques used, the situational exercises and the aptitude tests exhibited the highest correlations with subsequent job performance. Among the aptitude tests the intelligence test, particularly the verbal portion, showed the highest correlation. The personality questionnaires showed the lowest correlations with performance.

It should be pointed out that the Management Progress Study was strictly a research endeavor. The information collected on each person and the predictions made were kept under strict control. They were not made available to line managers because this might influence their judgments on promotion of the people who had been assessed. The results of the Management Progress Study were so favorable that the Bell System established in the mid-1960s over fifty assessment centers throughout the country. The measurement techniques were essentially the same as those employed in the research project. But since the method had been proven, the results of the ratings and measurements *were* transmitted to operating management for actual use in making personnel decisions regarding those who had gone through the centers. The staffs of these centers were experienced Bell System managers of proven competence.

Another corporation to adopt the assessment center method is Exxon. Their project is called Early Identification of Management Potential. It has included all ranks of management from the first-line supervisor up to the chairman of the board. Measuring instruments have included both published and custom-made pencil-and-paper tests, a personal interview, and a biographical questionnaire. Situational exercises were not employed. The best predictors in the Exxon project turned out to be the biographical data and the mental ability data.

An important component of a majority of assessment centers is the group discussion, often leaderless and with assigned roles. In such a simulation the group is given a problem to solve and is instructed to arrive at a group decision. Typical problems assigned to a group of candidates are a promotion decision, bonus allocation, discipline, or a production expansion plan.

Because the assessment center method is costly and requires a fairly advanced degree of sophistication of personnel and psychological knowledge, so far it has been used primarily by large companies. But those using it have clearly indicated satisfaction with the results. And if one considers the cost of faulty selection of managers with its consequent effect upon performance, turnover, and morale, the cost benefit effectiveness becomes evident.[14]

Questions for Review and Discussion

1. Because tests are objective and factual, could they be used in place of interviews for selection?
2. A personnel manager has stated that a certain test battery has been very accurate in predicting success for sales personnel in a company. What reliance could one place in this same test battery for picking sales persons in another company?
3. The making of hiring decisions is a probability process. It is not possible to say with certainty that a given individual will be successful in a given job after hiring. Why is this so? Give sources of error in the hiring decision-making process. What factors could

[14]Further information on assessment centers can be found in Douglas W. Bray and Donald L. Grant, "The As-

impede an outstanding individual's performance after hiring?

4. Describe your own experience as an interviewee applying for a job. Was the interview conducted well? What could have been done better?

5. Distinguish among the following kinds of validity:
   a. Content.

b. Concurrent.

c. Predictive.

6. Distinguish between an aptitude and an achievement test.

7. Discuss the problems involved in the use of personality tests for selection purposes.

8. Describe the purposes and operation of an assessment center. What are the advantages of an assessment center over traditional techniques of evaluating people?

CASE PROBLEMS

PROBLEM 1

The XYZ Company manufactures a wide diversity of industrial and consumer products. Each year it hires approximately twenty-five college graduates (engineering, business administration, and liberal arts) by sending its college-relations manager to about fifteen college campuses to recruit graduating seniors. In a conversation with a college professor, the college-relations manager made the following statement:

"I have been doing nearly all of the college recruiting for my company for the past ten years. I have full authority to hire these new graduates. My company does not think it is necessary to invite the best prospects to the home plant for further inteviews by other managers (as many other companies do). I allow one half hour for each interview. In that length of time I am able to make a pretty accurate evaluation of the prospect. Although I have full authority to hire on the spot, I generally wait until I return to my office. At that time I review my written notes on all the better persons whom I interviewed and then send out letters containing offers of employment. I have been quite happy with this method of hiring. My company has found it to be an economical and practical procedure."

Question
Evaluate this approach to the hiring of college graduates.

sessment Center in the Measurement of Potential for Business Management," *Psychological Monographs: General and Applied*, No. 625, Vol. 80, No. 17 (1966); Allen I. Kraut, "New Frontiers for Assessment Centers," *Personnel*, Vol. 54, No. 4 (July–August 1976), pp. 30–38; William C. Byham, "Starting an Assessment Center the Correct Way," *The Personnel Administrator*, Vol. 25, No. 2 (February 1980), pp. 27–32.

PROBLEM 2

The Ventnor Corporation is a growing firm that owns and operates three department stores in an urban area of 400,000 population in the East. It was established fifteen years ago by the current president.

The second person in the past year to hold the position of director of merchandising has just quit. In fact both of these individuals would have been asked to resign if they had not seen the handwriting on the wall and left voluntarily.

The occasion of the resignation of the second director of merchandising has prompted the president to call a meeting of the executive vice-president, the director of personnel, and himself to diagnose the problem of high turnover of managers hired from the outside and to come up with a course of corrective action. In the past two years nine middle- and top-level managers have either quit voluntarily or been asked to leave.

When the meeting convenes the director of personnel reviews the process of recruitment and selection. Candidates have been obtained both from a private employment agency and from responses to advertisements in newspapers and trade journals. Selection instruments consist of an application form, three tests (a mental ability test plus two personality tests), limited reference checking, and interviews with the executives concerned with the position involved.

The executive vice-president feels that they have made some errors of judgment in hiring certain individuals. Their resumes looked good and they talked as if they knew their work but a few weeks on the job often revealed their inability to get results. He says that the assistant store manager of the downtown store, hired last year, talked a good line but accomplished little on the job.

The president wonders if insufficient attention has been given to matching up the person with the job requirements. "At least on the surface it seems that all those hired had a record of accomplishment in their careers but when dealing with other managers here they just didn't seem to fit into the organization. The controller hired in January lasted only five months. He came here and immediately started firing and demoting many persons on his staff. Some of these changes perhaps were necessary but he destroyed both morale and performance in the accounting department."

The director of personnel offers the view that they have placed too much emphasis on surface personality traits at the time of hiring and not enough on a proven record of performance in retail merchandising. Three out of the nine managers came from unrelated industries.

The executive vice-president points out that most of those hired had certain characteristics in common. They were all in their thirties and had moved around a great deal from job to job within a firm and from company to company. Many appeared to have moved up in terms of enlarged job responsibilities but some had simply made a number of lateral moves. All were ambitious and restless men. They tended to step on others in their drive to get ahead. Upon joining Ventnor most proved to be upsetting to the personnel with whom they had to work, especially so with their immediate subordinates.

In closing the meeting the president asks the director of personnel to investigate the desirability of engaging the services of a consulting industrial psychologist to review the managerial selection program and to help screen future candidates.

Questions

1. What is the problem here? Has the top management group decided what they want and how to achieve it?
2. Just how much risk is involved in hiring a major executive?
3. Offer possible reasons for the apparent failure of this management hiring program.
4. What responsibilities do the existing top management group have toward a newly hired manager? How can they influence his likelihood of success or failure?
5. What recommendations would you make to the president of this company?

Suggestions for Further Reading

Ability Testing: Uses, Consequences, and Controversies. Washington, D.C.: National Academy Press, 1982.

Arvey, Richard D. *Fairness in Selecting Employees.* Reading, Mass.: Addison-Wesley, 1979.

Cascio, Wayne F. *Applied Psychology in Personnel Management,* 2nd ed. Reston, Va.: Reston Publishing Company, Inc., 1982, Part IV.

Cronbach, Lee J. *Essentials of Psychological Testing,* 3rd ed. New York: Harper and Row, Publishers, 1970.

Goodale, James G. *The Fine Art of Interviewing.* Englewood Cliffs, N.J.: Prentice-Hall, Inc., 1982.

Keil, E. C. *Assessment Centers: A Guide for Human Resource Management.* Reading, Mass.: Addison-Wesley Publishing, 1981.

Lopez, Felix M. *Personnel Interviewing: Theory and Practice,* 2nd ed. New York: McGraw-Hill Book Company, 1975.

Miner, Mary G., and John B. Miner. *Employee Selection Within the Law.* Washington, D.C.: Bureau of National Affairs, 1978.

Morgan, Henry H., and John W. Cogger. *The Interviewer's Manual,* New York: Drake-Beam & Associates, 1982.

Thornton, George C. III, and William C. Byham. *Assessment Centers and Managerial Performance,* New York: Academic Press, 1982.

Equal Employment Opportunity

This chapter deals with the special employment problems of nonwhites (predominantly blacks but also including some other groups)— Hispanic Americans, women, older workers, and handicapped persons.

Black Americans have experienced and do continue to experience lower earnings and much higher unemployment than whites. Although a few of the states had enacted laws in the 1940s banning discrimination on the basis of race, color, or national origin in regard to employment, housing, and places of public accommodation, it was the U.S. Supreme Court ruling in *Brown* v. *Board of Education*, in 1954, that launched the great efforts throughout the nation in subsequent years to rectify decades of neglect and discrimination. While *Brown* v. *Board of Education* dealt with public school segregation, it marked a great shift in the historic attitude of the Supreme Court and it also paved the way for a change in the public consciousness and for the civil rights legislation of the 1960s. Public demonstrations and civil rights campaigns in the 1960s, most notably those led by Martin Luther King, Jr., awakened the nation to the plight of black Americans and spurred the institutions of government to take action to help them gain equality of treatment in employment as well as in education, housing, public accommodation, and in voting rights.

Although women were granted wage parity with men by the Equal Pay Act of 1963 and granted equal employment opportunity by Title VII of the Civil Rights Act of 1964, it was not until the 1970s that they began to make substantial advances in the labor force. Each succeeding decade in the twentieth century has seen increased labor force participation by women of working age; however, they have been confined by custom and the forces of discrimination to the lower-paying occupations until very recently. Only in the 1970s have women moved into the better-paying managerial, sales, and professional occupations in any substantial numbers. As in the case of blacks, laws on the books are insufficient to achieve economic progress and employment parity. People must help themselves and campaign for improvement in their condition. For females, the women's liberation movement has been the mechanism for focusing public attention upon the need for change.

Quiet recently the special employment problems of older Americans have received greater national concern. Historically America has been a youth-oriented culture. With an increasing percentage of the population comprised of older people, and with the formation of more organizations to represent them, we now witness greater awareness of the problems confronting older citizens in the labor force.

Among these problems are difficulty in obtaining jobs, forced retirements at an arbitrarily set age, and persistent employer preferences for hiring and promoting younger workers. Younger workers are presumed to be more vigorous, less rigid in their ways, and more physically attractive.

Traditionally, physically and mentally handicapped persons who could adequately perform certain jobs have been largely confined to their homes, to state-run institutions, and to sheltered workshops. But the Rehabilitation Act of 1973 requires those firms holding Federal government contracts to take affirmative action to employ qualified physically and mentally handicapped persons.

Under the American free enterprise system with its theoretically open and free labor markets, employers were historically able to hire, promote, and fire whomever and whenever they wished. If the typical individualistic employer of say, 1935 or 1945, were to be transplanted to the 1980s, he would be surprised and even shocked to learn that racial and ethnic minorities, women, older workers, and handicapped persons have acquired substantial employment rights by law. Today even benign neglect of protected groups is not allowed (passive discrimination is outlawed). Employers must take affirmative action to make job opportunities available.

A profound change has been occurring in the workplaces of America because of the pressures for equal employment opportunity and affirmative action. The actors in this ongoing drama are employers, unions, employees, Congress and the President, the courts, government regulatory agencies, organized minorities and women's groups, and even the general public.

In this chapter we shall examine the special problems confronting nonwhites (especially blacks), Hispanics, women, older employees, and handicapped workers. We shall study the principal equal employment opportunity laws and the interpretations that give meaning to them. Then we will explore the impact of equal

employment opportunity laws and regulations upon personnel programs in the areas of recruitment, selection, testing, performance appraisal, promotions, and seniority. The important contemporary issues of sexual harassment and comparable worth will be analyzed. Finally, we shall discuss the concerns expressed by many people of possible reverse discrimination resulting from vigorous enforcement of affirmative action mandates.

THE SITUATION OF NONWHITES AND HISPANIC AMERICANS

In population and employment statistics published by the government, the nonwhite category includes blacks, Asian Americans, and American Indians. Blacks comprise nine-tenths of this classification. To a considerable extent both the economic progress and the economic problems facing blacks have been derived from their massive migration from the rural South to the big cities of the North and West. This mass movement began during World War II with the opening up of thousands of jobs in defense industries. The migration continued from the 1940s through the 1960s. Lacking the education and skills necessary to qualify for good jobs in an industrialized economy, many blacks obtained only laboring jobs or else filled the ranks of the unemployed. Even though many northern states had enacted antidiscrimination laws in the late 1940s and early 1950s, blacks in the North encountered pervasive discrimination in job and housing markets. Even if qualified, they were often denied decent jobs. Even if financially able, they were denied housing in good neighborhoods. Their homes and life patterns were confined more and more to the big city slums.

For a good many years the unemployment rates for blacks have averaged about twice those for whites. Table 9-1 shows, for example, that in

TABLE 9-1. Unemployment Rates of Black and Other Races Compared with Whites, 1956–1981.

	Race	
Year	White (Per Cent)	Black and Other (Per Cent)
1956	3.6	8.3
1961	6.0	12.4
1966	3.3	7.3
1971	5.4	9.9
1976	7.0	13.1
1981	6.7	14.2

Source: U.S. Department of Labor, *Employment and Training Report of the President, 1982* (Washington, D.C.; 1983), Table A-28, p. 190

1956 the white unemployment rate was 3.6 per cent while the rate for blacks (and other races) was 8.3 per cent. In 1981 the rate for whites was 6.7 per cent and for blacks (and other races) it was 14.2 per cent.

The median weekly earnings of black (and other races) workers in the economy as a whole have averaged about 80 per cent of earnings of white workers.[1] The primary reason for this disparity is that blacks have been concentrated in the lower-paying occupations.

Poverty in America is not confined to any one race or ethnic group. However, in relation to their numbers in the population, blacks are much more likely to be poor than are whites. In 1981, for example, 34.2 per cent of all blacks had annual incomes below the poverty level, as officially designated by the U.S. Department of Labor. In contrast only 11.1 per cent of all whites had incomes below the poverty line.[2]

[1]U.S. Department of Labor, *Handbook of Labor Statistics,* Bulletin 2070 (Washington, D.C.; The Department, 1980), Tble 60, p.118.

[2]U.S. Department of Labor, *Employment and Training Report of the President, 1982* (Washington, D.C.; The Department, 1983), Table G-8, p. 336.

Hispanic Americans are persons of Mexican, Puerto Rican, Cuban, and Central or South American family origin. According to the U.S. Census Bureau the 1980 population of Hispanic Americans was 14.6 million (6.4 per cent of total population). Hispanics are the fastest growing segment of the U.S. population. This is caused by a very high birth rate and large-scale immigration from Latin America. Average earnings of Hispanic Americans are higher than those of blacks, but significantly lower than the earnings of whites.

THE SITUATION OF WOMEN

Although not a minority group in society, women traditionally have received minority-like treatment. But in recent years this undesirable condition has been changing for the better.

In the nineteenth century the majority of people lived on farms. Women in the family engaged not only in domestic activities—cooking, sewing, housecleaning, raising children—but also participated in numerous chores on the farm. Our agricultural society had become transformed into an industrialized society by 1900. Families flocked to the cities and women's roles changed somewhat.

The proper place for the housewife and mother was believed to be in the home. The role of the husband and father was to work away from home in shops and offices during the daytime. Young, single women typically obtained employment as seamstresses, domestic servants, clerks, stenographers, or, if educated, as schoolteachers. Gainful employment, for most young women, was viewed as a temporary interlude between school and marriage. Marriage was most preferred and it conferred a beneficial social position in the neighborhood. To be a single woman well into one's 30s was considered most unfortunate. The modern concept of a career woman, whether single or married, was practically unheard of. College education for young women was reserved mainly for the daughters of wealthy families. Families with more modest incomes, if college was considered at all for their children, usually emphasized higher education for the young men who would follow professional careers. A college degree was not considered to be important for daughters, whose career was expected to be marriage and a family.

Up until very recent years the prevailing practice has been to employ women in a limited number of occupations that were considered appropriate for females. People think that the vast majority of schoolteachers have always been women. Yet during the nineteenth century teaching was predominantly a male occupation. Secretaries are considered almost universally to be women. Yet prior to the World War I period stenographers and secretaries were generally males. Since World War II bank tellers have mostly been female. Yet before then it was a male occupation. There is nothing inherent in the content of these occupations that requires them to be performed by one sex and not the other. Stereotyped roles tend to become sanctified and tend not to be challenged by society.

The traditional, limited role of women in the economic life of our nation has been changing rapidly in recent decades. Women's labor-force participation rate has been steadily increasing for many years. In 1955 the female labor force participation rate was 35.7 per cent. By 1982 it had climbed to 52.1 per cent.[3] Forces that have brought about this greater tendency for women to be in the labor force are later age at marriage, lower birth rates, labor-saving devices in the home, greater prevalence of divorce, and better educational opportunities. Another factor that has become significant since the late 1960s

has been the persistence of inflation. Inflation eroded the real earnings of male family breadwinners and forced wives into the labor market to maintain family living standards.

The weekly earnings of women in the economy as a whole have hovered around 60 per cent of the earnings of men for a great number of years. There are many reasons for this condition. Discrimination is only one factor. We shall examine this matter later in the chapter in the section "Comparable Worth."

Special Problems of Married Women

Working women who are married and who are raising children face special problems. Because it is only relatively recently that vast numbers of married careerwomen have been in the labor force, institutional arrangements to help meet their special problems have been developed only during the past few years.

The typical pattern for most young, single women has been to work only two to four years after graduation from school, get married, leave the labor force for several years while bearing and raising children, and then perhaps to return to the labor force in their mid- or late 30s. But a growing recent trend has been for thousands of women to look upon their jobs as long-term careers. If they are married and have children, they take relatively brief maternity leaves and then return to their jobs. The working mother must make arrangements for someone to take care of her children while she is at work. This can be a relative, friend, daycare center, or nursery school.

Some progressive companies have created programs to accommodate working mothers. Among these are liberal maternity leaves, part-time work, flexible hours of work, and subsidies toward childcare arrangements.

When a woman as well as her husband are career-oriented, strains may emerge. Should the woman place the demands of her job ahead of her family? What should she do if her boss asks

[3]The labor force participation rate is the percentage of persons of working age (16 years and over) in the noninstitutional population who are in the labor force, either employed or unemployed (but looking for work). Data are from *Employment and Training Report of the President, 1982,* op. cit., Table A-5, p. 155.

her to work overtime in the evening and her child's sitter goes home at 5:30? A more serious dilemma occurs when a corporation offers the husband (or wife) a promotion to a job in a distant city and the spouse holds a very desirable job in a different firm. Which person should sacrifice his (her) career?

Pregnancy Disability

Prior to 1978 most employers had very restrictive policies regarding paid maternity leave, the right of women to return to their jobs after the maternity leave had expired, and payment of medical expenses arising from childbirth. The Supreme Court, in its case decisions, generally upheld such restrictive policies. But the situation changed in 1978 when Congress enacted the Pregnancy Disability Amendment to Title VII of the Civil Rights Act of 1964. This amendment states that pregnant women cannot be forced to leave their jobs at an arbitrarily set time in their pregnancy. Rather the date must be based upon her inability to work as determined by a physician. The employer cannot deny paid sick leave for pregnancy if it has a paid sick leave plan for other types of disabilities. Further, if the employer pays medical and hospital costs for illnesses it must do so for pregnancy and childbirth.

EEO LAWS AND REGULATIONS

The first serious national effort to ban discrimination in employment was launched in 1941 when President Franklin D. Roosevelt by executive order created a Fair Employment Practices Committee, which was active throughout World War II. The executive order stated that employers and unions had a duty "to provide for the full and equitable participation of all workers in defense industries, without discrimination be-

cause of race, creed, color, or national origin." The committee lacked statutory authority to require compliance with its orders, but it did settle thousands of cases by conciliation. Since 1945 every president has had a similar committee whose jurisdiction was confined to establishments doing business with the Federal government. Under President Kennedy the committee was given the power to apply sanctions and to cancel government contracts.

With regard to legislation, the states preceded the Federal government by nearly twenty years. New York State pioneered by adopting a general antidiscrimination law in 1945. By 1960 sixteen states had laws with positive enforcement powers. By 1967 the number had grown to thirty-two states. These included practically all the states excluding the South.

Beginning in 1963 and extending over the next ten years, Congress enacted a number of significant laws that clearly demonstrate a national commitment to prohibit discrimination in employment. Concurrent with this legislative initiative has been activity by the President of the United States and the executive branch of the government to eliminate employment discrimination by organizations holding government contracts and effectively to enforce the antidiscrimination laws passed by Congress.

Chronologically in the order of their enactment are the following principal equal employment opportunity laws and orders:

1. Equal Pay Act of 1963.
2. Title VII—Equal Employment Opportunity of Civil Rights Act of 1964, as amended by Equal Employment Opportunity Act of 1972.
3. Executive Order 11246 (1965) as amended by Executive Order 11375 (1967).
4. Age Discrimination in Employment Act of 1967, as amended.
5. Rehabilitation Act of 1973.

The key features of these laws are given in Table 9-2.

TABLE 9-2. Principal Federal Laws and Orders Against Discrimination in Employment.

Act or Order	Equal Pay Act of 1963	Title VII of Civil Rights Act of 1964 as Amended by Equal Employment Opportunity Act of 1972	Executive Order 11246 (1965) as Amended by 11375 (1967)	Age Discrimination in Employment Act of 1967 as Amended	Rehabilitation Act of 1973
Coverage	Private employers covered by Fair Labor Standards Act; also includes federal, state, and local governments.	All private employers of 15 or more persons, unions with 15 or more members, employment agencies, educational institutions, state and local governments.	All organizations with federal contracts or subcontracts over $10,000, federal government employment.	All private employers of 20 or more persons, unions with 25 or more members, employment agencies, state and local governments, federal government employment.	All private employers having federal contracts or subcontracts over $2500.
Principal Mandate of Act	Prohibits discrimination on the basis of sex by paying employees of one sex at a rate less than the wages paid employees of the opposite sex for jobs of substantially equal content.	Prohibits discrimination in employment, including hiring, testing, upgrading, pay, benefits, training, and other conditions of employment on the basis of race, color, religion, sex, or national origin.		Prohibits discrimination against employees 40 through 69 years of age in regard to hiring, discharge, retirement, pay, conditions, and privileges of employment.	Employer must take affirmative action to employ and advance handicapped persons as defined in Act.

Employment and Development of People

Administered by	Equal Employment Opportunity Commission	Equal Employment Opportunity Commission	Office of Federal Contract Compliance Programs of U.S. Dept. of Labor; Office of Personnel Management for federal employment.	Equal Employment Opportunity Commission.	Office of Federal Contract Compliance Programs, Department of Labor
Enforcement and Sanctions	EEOC attempts conciliation. If no settlement EEOC may sue in U.S. District Court.	First, EEOC attmepts conciliation. If no settlement, EEOC may sue in U.S. District Court. Aggrieved individual may also file suit. Court may enjoin the unlawful employment practice and order appropriate affirmative action including reinstatement or hiring, back pay or other relief.	Federal government may revoke present contract or disqualify organization from future government contracts.	First, EEOC tries conciliation. If no settlement, EEOC may sue in U.S. District Court. Aggrieved individual may also file suit. Court may compel employment, reinstatement, promotion, back pay	U.S. Labor Department tries conciliation, firm may be disqualified from government contracts. Labor Dept. may file suit in court.
Affirmative Action Plan Requirements	Affirmative action plan not required.	Not specifically required by law but affirmative action may be required by court order.	Each contractor with 250 or more employees and holding a federal contract for more than $1,000,000 must maintain affirmative action plan. Goals and timetables required.	Affirmative action not required.	Each contractor with 100 or more employees and holding a federal contract for more than $100,000 must maintain affirmative action plan. Goals and timetables not required.

The entire field of equal employment opportunity is very dynamic. It is not an area of settled law with hard and fast regulations and legal precedents. Rather as regulatory agency rulings and U.S. court decisions are issued, the area is evolving and changing. It is important that personnel executives, corporate officials, and their legal counsels keep abreast of changes in this evolving field of law and practice.

Equal Pay Act of 1963

The Equal Pay Act of 1963 was, in form, an amendment to the Fair Labor Standards Act (Wage and Hour Law). This law is administered by the Equal Employment Opportunity Commission. It provides that it is illegal to pay women less than men for doing substantially the same work on jobs requiring equivalent skill, effort, responsibility, and under similar working conditions. Of course, the law makes it illegal to pay men less than women as well. But the purpose of the law was to eliminate the rather widespread practice in industry of having separate men's and women's wage scales with women's being lower. Exceptions to the equal pay rule are permitted where a differential payment is based upon a seniority, merit, or piece-rate pay system.

Title VII—Equal Employment Opportunity

Title VII of the Civil Rights Act of 1964 is labeled "Equal Employment Opportunity." Title VII was strengthened by the Equal Employment Opportunity Act of 1972. Before delving into this law, a quotation of the Supreme Court of the United States in its landmark *Griggs* v. *Duke Power Company* decision is in order because it describes so well the tone and purpose of Title VII.

The objective of Congress in the enactment of Title VII is plain from the language of the statute. It is to achieve equality of employment opportunity and remove barriers that have operated in the past to favor an identifiable group of white employees over other employees. Under the Act, practices, procedures, or tests neutral on their face, or even neutral in terms of intent, cannot be maintained if they operate to "freeze" the status quo of prior discriminatory practices.

. . . Congress did not intend by Title VII, however, to guarantee to every person a job regardless of qualifications. In short, the Act does not command that any person be hired simply because he was formerly the subject of discrimination, or because he is a member of a minority group. Discriminatory preference for any group, minority or majority, is precisely and only what Congress has proscribed. What is required by Congress is the removal of artificial, arbitrary, and unnecessary barriers to employment when the barriers operate invidiously to discriminate on the basis of racial or other impermissible classification.[4]

Title VII, as amended, covers all private employers of 15 or more persons, unions having 15 or more members, employment agencies, educational institutions both public and private, and state and local governments. This law prohibits discrimination because of race, color, religion, sex, or national origin in all employment practices including hiring, firing, promotion, compensation, and other privileges and conditions of employment.

Title VII is administered by the Equal Employment Opportunity Commission (EEOC) which is a five-member independent agency appointed by the President with the consent of the Senate.

An individual who feels she has been the victim of discrimination must file a complaint with the EEOC within 180 days of the date on

[4]From decision of Supreme Court of the United States, *Griggs* v. *Duke Power Co.*, 401 U.S. 424 (1971). Reported in *Employment Practices* (Chicago: Commerce Clearing House, March 18, 1971).

which the claimed unlawful employment practice occurred. In those states having a state law against discrimination that has positive enforcement powers, the aggrieved person must first file a charge with the appropriate state agency. After allowing 60 days for the state to act, the individual may then file the charge with the EEOC and at this point the Commission may assume jurisdiction. The Commission makes agreements with state agencies whereby the latter will cooperate in carrying out the purposes of the federal law. Upon taking jurisdiction over a case the EEOC conducts an investigation and attempts to settle the matter by conciliation. If conciliation is not successful, the EEOC may bring a civil action in a U.S. District Court in order to obtain restitution for the claimed violation. Also, a complainant may, if she chooses, personally file a complaint in a District Court to seek redress.

Executive Order 11246 and Affirmative Action

Executive Order 11246 was issued by President Lyndon Johnson in 1965 and was amended in 1967 by Executive Order 11375. The Order as amended bans discrimination in employment because of race, color, religion, sex, or national origin for organizations holding federal government contracts. The Order also bans discrimination in Federal government employment but our discussion will concentrate upon the application of the Order to government contractors.

The Order covers all organizations holding government contracts or subcontracts of $10,000 or more. Each organization with 250 or more employees and a prime contract or a subcontract for more than $1,000,000 is required to maintain a written affirmative action program for each of its establishments. The concept of a "written affirmative action program" was first articulated in 1968 by the Office of Federal Contract Compliance Programs (OFCCP) of the Department of Labor, which administers the Order. Subsequent orders issued by the Secretary of Labor and the OFCCP have explicitly spelled out the requirements of affirmative action programs. Each agency of the goverment which grants contracts to companies is responsible for obtaining compliance with the rules and regulations. A noncomplying company may be denied a government contract initially or it may lose its contract.

The government has placed a great amount of force behind its efforts to get organizations to design and implement affirmative action programs. While such programs are mandated for government contractors (private companies, universities, indeed all organizations holding government contracts), other employers would do well to meet the overall standards because under Title VII of the Civil Rights Act an affirmative action program may be required as part of a conciliated settlement with the EEOC or it may be ordered by a federal court in settlement of a case.

The key features of an affirmative action program are as follows:

1. *Policy statement*
   The chief executive must issue a written statement declaring that the organization will not discriminate because of race, color, religion, national origin, sex, or physical handicap[5] in recruitment, hiring, training, compensation, and promotion.
2. *Communication of Policy*
   The commitment to EEO policy must be disseminated to recruitment sources, subcontractors, relevant unions, and all employees.
3. *Assignment of Responsibility*
   A major executive should be given responsibility to plan, coordinate, and evaluate the ongoing program.

---

[5]Affirmative action for the handicapped is required by the Rehabilitation Act of 1973.

4. *Workforce Analysis*

Analyze the present workforce to determine the number of each minority type, women, and handicapped in each job classification, pay grade, and department. Analyze the relevant labor market for the kinds of skills utilized in the company to determine possible underutilization of particular minorities, women, or the handicapped.

5. *Goals and Timetables*

This is a crucial part of an affirmative action plan and the feature that has caused controversy. For each major job classification, management must set a numerical goal for the employment of minority, women, and handicapped employees in reasonable relation to their representation in the relevant labor force. Dates for achieving these goals must be established.

6. *Implementation*

Actions must be carried out in the areas of recruitment, selection (qualifications requirements, applications, interviewing, testing), upward mobility system, wage and salary program, benefits, maternity leaves, and lay-off and recall policy.

7. *Internal Audit and Reporting System*

Gather data and evaluate progress toward meeting goals on a quarterly basis. Take corrective action where needed.

8. *Support of Company and Community Programs*

Train supervisors in affirmative action requirements and their implementation. Provide job and career counseling to employees. Cooperate with community institutions in regard to such matters as day-care centers for children, transportation, and housing.

Enforcement Guidelines and Remedies

Because the standards used in Title VII and Executive Order 11246 cases are very similar, we shall discuss together (as one) the criteria used by the administrative agencies and the courts for deciding cases under these two regulations.

Top management's good intentions are not sufficient to avoid prosecution for discrimination. The results of a company's actions and *not* its intentions are what determine whether it is discriminating. It is illegal to continue company policies and practices that have an adverse impact upon protected groups unless the firm can demonstrate that a practice is necessary for the safe and efficient operation of the business. Once a plaintiff (the aggrieved individual or group) shows a prima facie case of discrimination by demonstrating adverse impact upon a protected group (blacks, women, etc.), the burden of proof shifts to the company to justify its employment practice.

What is adverse impact? It is a concept which relates to the entire employment process in the organization wherein the protected group is treated significantly worse than the majority group in the organization in regard to hiring, job assignment, promotion, and other employment conditions. For example, the plaintiff may demonstrate that the firm has a disparate rejection rate for blacks compared with whites. Or the firm may be using a restricted policy to exclude members of a minority group. Or in a private, nonclass action case the aggrieved person must show that she or he was qualified for the job but was rejected by the firm that is still seeking other applicants whose qualifications are comparable to the complainant's.

Language in Title VII and court decisions allows companies charged with discrimination to offer four kinds of defenses. These are:

1. *Bona fide occupational qualification reasonably necessary to the normal operation of the enterprise.* This exception to the proscription against discrimination has been very narrowly construed by the EEOC and the courts.
2. *Bona fide merit or seniority system.* For example, it may be legal to promote men ahead of women if men rank higher in seniority under a union-employer agreement.
3. *Business Necessity.* Here the company must establish, via overriding evidence, that the dis-

criminatory practice is necessary for the safe and efficient operation of the business.

4. *No adverse impact.* The company may demonstrate with data that it has not rejected minorities or women at a significantly greater rate than nonminorities or men.

Remedies. When courts have found that discrimination has existed in an organization, they have ordered that the employer must "make whole" and restore the rightful economic status to the individuals involved. A firm may be ordered to hire individuals or reinstate them with back pay and seniority, and to promote people. If pervasive discrimination has been found in an organization, the courts may order that the employer "make whole" *all* persons in the affected class, not only those who filed charges. The court may also require the installation of a comprehensive affirmative action program.

OLDER WORKERS AND AGE DISCRIMINATION

There were 32 million persons, ages 45 and over, who were in the labor force in 1981. In comparison with the great public attention that has been focused upon the employment problems of women and minorities since the mid-1960s, only modest efforts have been directed toward the problems of older persons in the labor force. But this situation has been changing rapidly. With an aging population the interest groups representing older Americans have become stronger, more vocal, and more politically active.

Executives have traditionally preferred to hire and promote younger workers. Rosen and Jerdee devised a unique research design to uncover the biases and stereotyped views that managers hold of older employees. They presented *identical* case incidents to a large national sample of *Harvard Business Review* subscribers. The only difference in the incidents is that the central individual was labeled as a young person in the version sent to half the respondents and an older person in the version sent to the other half. The results of this survey study showed that the respondents perceived older employees to be inflexible and resistant to change. They were less likely to make efforts to retrain older employees. Also there was a tendency to deny promotions to older employees compared with identically qualified younger persons. Rosen and Jerdee concluded that some of the discriminatory bias was subconscious because a questionnaire filled out by the same respondents revealed rather supportive attitudes toward older employees in regard to management policies, affirmative action, and mandatory retirement.[6]

In his summary of research studies comparing older with younger workers on several dimensions, Fjerstad reports that older workers had fewer work injuries but they take longer to recover when injured. Productivity comparisons from various studies showed essentially no differences between younger and older office workers but they showed that among production workers, those under 25 and those over 55 produced slightly less than the 25–54 age group. Absenteeism and turnover were lower for the over 45 age group.[7]

Older persons, typically those over age 45, commonly face special problems that are not experienced by younger persons. If unemployed they find difficulty in obtaining new jobs because employers often prefer younger personnel. Sometimes companies pressure older employees to retire early or blatantly fire them to lower their payroll costs in times of business adversity or to create openings for younger em-

[6]Benson Rosen and Thomas H. Jerdee, "Too Old or Not Too Old," *Harvard Business Review,* Vol. 55, No. 6 (November-December 1977), pp. 97–106.

[7]Robert L. Fjerstad, "Is It Economical to Hire the Over-Forty-five Worker?" *Personnel Administration,* Vol. 28, No. 2 (March-April 1965).

ployees whom the management prefers. Also, sometimes older employees are passed over for promotion in favor of younger candidates.

Management also faces some problems in the employment of older workers. What should it do with individual older employees whose performance has truly declined but not sufficiently to substantiate discharge? Under what circumstances can management exclude older workers from jobs where quick reflexes and safety may be a relevant job factor, as for bus drivers and airline pilots? If the average age of a workforce is high, employers generally must pay higher premiums for group life insurance, pensions, and health insurance.

Age Discrimination in Employment Act, as Amended

The Age Discrimination in Employment Act of 1967, as amended, covers workers and managers in any private business firm that employs 20 or more persons. It also covers actions taken by an employment agency and those taken by labor unions having at least 25 members. Also protected by the law are employees of state and local governments and those in the federal civil service. This law prohibits discrimination because of age against persons at least 40 but less than 70 years of age in regard to hiring, discharge, retirement, pay, and conditions and privileges of employment. The law is administered by the Equal Employment Opportunity Commission.

In the first few years after initial enactment of this law, there was relatively little litigation over age discrimination. However, in the severe economic recessions of 1974–1975 and 1981–1983, companies laid off and discharged thousands of salaried employees to cut payroll costs. Hourly paid workers were laid off, too, but union contracts required the process to be carried out according to seniority rules. Salaried employees often invoked the procedures of the

law to try to regain their jobs. In 1980 the Equal Employment Opportunity Commission received 8,779 complaints of discharge due to age discrimination.[8] In one widely publicized court case a U.S. Court of Appeals in San Francisco upheld a $1.9 million jury award to three executives of the I. Magnin subsidiary of Federated Department Stores whom the court determined had been fired because of age discrimination. All three executives were in their early 50s at the time of their discharges.[9]

Until the 1978 Amendments were enacted, the 1967 law protected people in the 40-to-65 age bracket. The major purpose of the 1978 Amendments was to raise from 65 to 70 the age at which employees can be forced to retire. Excluded from the higher age limit for mandatory retirement are high-level executives who are entitled to annual pensions of $27,000 or more. For a great many years the mandatory retirement age for federal civil service employees was 70. The 1978 amendments eliminated the age limit entirely. Compulsory early retirement is allowed under the amended law, just as under the original 1967 Act, for bona fide occupational reasons. These exceptions are interpreted narrowly. Early retirements for air-traffic controllers, airline pilots, and agents of the FBI have been approved.

Nearly all of private industry has used 65 as the normal and mandatory retirement age since the 1930s and geared its pension plans to retiremen at that age. In doing so, it followed the example of the Social Security system which was enacted into law in 1935.

Arguments in favor of raising the retirement age to 70 are that it is discriminatory to force people to give up their jobs if they are still ready and able to work and that if people tend to work beyond 65 they will collect old age benefits under the Social Security system at a later age and thus reduce the heavy financial drain on the system. Also many persons employed in the

[8]*Wall Street Journal*, October 8, 1981.
[9]*Wall Street Journal*, April 2, 1982.

private sector are not covered by a pension plan through their employer. Thus they must work beyond age 65.

On the other hand, if senior employees continue to work longer years in their organizations, promotion opportunities for younger personnel are restricted. Furthermore, if some older employees' performance has declined materially with advancing age, the burden is placed upon management to utilize an objective performance appraisal method to substantiate a discharge for just cause.

THE HANDICAPPED

It is estimated that there are 12 million handicapped persons in the United States who are "employable." However, a large percentage of these are unemployed. The Rehabilitation Act of 1973 requires all private employers with federal contracts over $2500 to take affirmative action to recruit, hire, and advance "qualified" handicapped persons. Companies with 100 or more employees and holding a federal contract for more than $100,000 must maintain affirmative action plans for the handicapped. However, goals and timetables are not required.

Enforcement action by the Department of Labor in the first three or four years after enactment was slow. There has been confusion in the minds of employers as to just who is a handicapped person and how far they must go in accommodating their workplaces for such individuals. Questions such as these arise. What kind of jobs can an epileptic safely perform? Can a blind person do data-processing work? How about an individual afflicted with cerebral palsy? What about mentally retarded persons?

With this law prodding them, companies have found that they can successfully utilize many handicapped persons that previously would have been turned away at the employ-

ment office door. Union Carbide Corporation is advertising sales-representative jobs in handicapped groups' newspapers and U.S. Steel Corporation has started recruiting at the National Technical Institute for the Deaf at Rochester Institute of Technology.[10]

IMPACT OF EEO UPON PERSONNEL ACTIVITIES

Equal Employment Opportunity laws and regulations have had a profound effect upon the way companies, educational institutions, and public employers carry out their personnel functions. For the most part the standards for performance of such activities as recruitment, selection, and upgrading have been raised significantly. Many executives have resented the intrusion of the government into their human resource programs. However, EEO is firmly established as public policy and companies have found that raising the quality of their personnel programs to meet equal employment opportunity requirements has had generally beneficial effects in other areas as well.

To insure that EEO is really integrated into the fabric of an organization special efforts are required. The commitment of top management and the requisite policies, programs, and procedures must be communicated fully to all operating and staff managers. Training seminars should be given to familiarize key personnel with the laws, regulations, and important court decisions. Definite goals regarding hiring, placing, training, and promoting minorities and women can be set for each department of the organization. Audits should be conducted to ascertain progress toward meeting the agreed-upon goals. Then managers can be rewarded in relation to their achievement of these goals.

[10]*Wall Street Journal* (January 27, 1976), pp. 1 & 11.

Recruitment

Many state antidiscrimination laws, with their enforcement regulations, are very explicit in prohibiting certain kinds of recruitment advertising and preemployment specifications. Title VII does not expressly prohibit specific kinds of specifications and inquiries; however, the EEOC and the courts look upon certain practices with extreme disfavor and their use may constitute evidence of intent to discriminate.

Help-wanted advertising and specifications given to employment agencies or used internally in a company cannot indicate a preference or a limitation based on sex, age, race, color, religion, or national origin. An advertisement for "laborers under age 40" would be illegal. An airline cannot specify that it seeks only women for flight attendants. Likewise a company cannot advertise for women or female stenographers and thereby exclude males.

Companies should participate in career days and job fairs sponsored by schools and community agencies. To recruit blacks employers often find it advantageous to make special "outreach" efforts to attract inner city blacks. They can also make contacts with local chapters of the NAACP and the Urban League. Handicapped workers can be recruited through such establishments as sheltered workshops and aid-to-blind agencies. Word-of-mouth recruitment through present employees would not widen the employment base but it rather tends to perpetuate the current racial and ethnic pattern.

Selection

Personnel specialists must be careful, in designing an employment application form, that they do not include illegal questions. Likewise they and other managers must avoid unlawful inquiries in interviews. Among the inquiries ruled illegal by New York State's Division for Human Rights, for example, are the following:

- To inquire of a woman's ability to reproduce, and attitudes toward family planning.
- To require a photograph of applicant at any time before hiring.
- To inquire about religious affiliation.
- To ask age or date of birth, but it is legal to ask if the person is between the age of 18 and 70.[11]

It is of course reasonable to establish education and training requirements for jobs. But several court decisions and EEOC rulings have stated, loud and clear, that such requirements must have a manifest relationship to the jobs for which people are being hired. Subjective, unsupported judgments will not suffice. For example, an employer was found guilty of racial job bias by reason of a requirement that applicants for a sales representative position must have a college degree. Business necessity was not demonstrated.[12]

The federal Equal Employment Opportunity Commission considers the questions listed below, used in application blanks or in interviews, to be evidence of discrimination unless the employer can clearly establish that they are job relevant or there is a business necessity for the information.

- Arrest and conviction record
- Garnishment record
- Credit references
- Marital status
- Provisions for childcare
- Pregnancy and future childbearing plans
- Physical or mental handicaps
- Height and weight[13]

[11]*Rulings on Inquiries Relating to Race, Creed, Color, National Origin, Sex, Age, Disability, Marital Status, or Arrest Record* (Albany: State of New York, Division of Human Rights, 1975).

[12]EEOC Decision, No. 70-402, January 19, 1970 as reported in *Labor Law Reports, Employment Practices Guide*, Vol. 1 (Chicago: Commerce Clearing House), paragraph 437.25.

[13]*Conducting the Lawful Employment Interview*, 2nd ed., New York: Executive Enterprises Publications Co., Inc. 1979, p. 7.

Guidelines for Selection. In 1978 the Equal Employment Opportunity Commission, Civil Service Commission, Department of Justice, and Office of Federal Contract Compliance Programs together issued their *Uniform Guidelines on Employee Selection Procedures.*[14] These guidelines are complex. They provide standards for the use of selection techniques, including tests, interviews, application forms, training programs, and probationary programs. The *Guidelines* specify a rule of thumb that can be used to ascertain whether adverse impact in selection exists. This is commonly called the "80 per cent or four-fifths rule." This rule states that if the selection rate for a protected group (blacks, Hispanics, women, etc.) is less than 80 per cent of the selection rate for the majority group, then adverse impact is presumed to exist. Thus if 50 per cent of all blacks who apply are hired compared with 60 per cent of all whites hired, the relationship of these selection ratios would be 83 per cent and no adverse impact would be presumed to exist.

Testing

Except for the more progressive and professionally managed organizations, a great many firms have accepted and rejected job candidates on the basis of arbitrarily set passing score cutoff points on tests when in fact management has not known whether those scoring above the cutoffs would be any more successful on the job than those scoring below. In short they have not bothered to validate the tests they were using. They have exhibited implicit and unfounded faith in their tests.

Title VII, Equal Employment Opportunity does permit employers "to give and to act upon the results of any professionally developed abil-

ity test provided that such test, its administration, or action upon the results is not designed, intended, or used to discriminate because of race, color, religion, sex, or national origin."[15]

In order to provide guidance to employers the Equal Employment Opportunity Commission has issued guidelines for the use of testing. These provide that the use of a test that adversely affects hiring, promotion, transfer, or any other employment opportunity for those classes protected by the law constitutes discrimination unless the test has been properly validated and evidences a high degree of utility. The guidelines recognize three different kinds of validity (1) criterion-related validity; (2) content validity; and (3) construct validity. Criterion-related validity is the most widely used method of establishing the utility of selection tests. It requires the collection of job performance data and the correlation of such data statistically with test scores for a representative sample of people. The guidelines define the concept of "unfairness" and specify procedures to be followed to alleviate such a condition. "Unfairness" occurs whem members of one race, sex, or ethnic group characteristically obtain lower scores on a selection procedure than members of another group and the differences in scores are not reflected in differences in a measure of job performance. When such a condition occurs, the selection procedure may unfairly deny job opportunities to members of the group obtaining the lower score. If there are job progression structures for advancement, tests may be used at the entry-level grade to predict ability to perform at higher-level positions. But such testing is allowed only if there is a high probability that persons employed will in fact attain the higher-level job within a reasonable period of time.

In 1971 the U.S. Supreme Court issued a landmark decision in the *Griggs* v. *Duke Power Company* case. In 1965 the company had established a policy that to qualify for placement in

---

[14]*Federal Register,* 43, August 25, 1978; also published in *Employment Practices Guide* (Commerce Clearing House, Chicago, Ill.)

[15]*Guidelines,* Ibid.

any but the labor department an employee had to obtain satisfactory scores on both the Wonderlic Personnel Test (a mental ability test) and the Bennett Mechanical Comprehension Test, as well as have a high school education. The required scores were set at the national median for high school graduates on these two tests. A group of black employees challenged these requirements in federal courts on the basis that they were denied promotion opportunities because of these selection devices.

The Supreme Court ruled unanimously that the company had unlawfully discriminated against these persons. The court said that "if an employment practice which operates to exclude blacks cannot be shown to be related to job performance, the practice is prohibited." It further held that neither the school completion requirement nor the intelligence test was shown to bear a demonstrable relationship to successful job performance.[16]

In 1975 in *Albermarle Paper Co.* v. *Moody*, the Supreme Court handed down another important decision on testing that sharpens and strengthens the requirements. Albermarle Paper Company in North Carolina had been using for several years the Wonderlic Personnel Test and the Revised Beta (a nonverbal intelligence test) to select employees for admission into various skilled lines of progression from the unskilled labor pool. Four black employees had challenged the use of these tests in a class action suit. The Court specifically endorsed the EEOC Guidelines on testing and said that Albermarle's validation study was defective in four respects:

1. Use of a test in jobs for which it had not been validated. Each test had shown significant correlation for only a few of the eight lines of progression. But both tests were required for all jobs. A test may be used in jobs other than those for which it has been validated only if there are no significant differences between the studied and unstudied jobs. However, Albermarle had conducted no job analysis.

[16]*Griggs* v. *Duke Power Company,* op cit.

2. Using subjective supervisory ratings as criteria for test validation. Supervisory ratings can legitimately be used, but they must be used with far more care than was shown by Albermarle.
3. Usings tests for entry-level jobs that were validated only for upper-level jobs.
4. Validating tests on a group of job-experienced white workers whereas the tests were given to new job seekers, who were younger, inexperienced, and often nonwhite.[17]

It will be recalled from our discussion in Chapter 8, "Testing, Interviewing, and Assessment Centers," that there are four kinds of validity. They are (1) concurrent, (2) predictive, (3) content, and (4) construct. Concurrent and predictive validation techniques together are called "criterion-related" methods because they statistically correlate test scores with measures of job performance. No correlation studies are used for content and construct validity. The EEOC guidelines on testing express a decided preference for criterion-related studies and allow use of content and construct validity methods only when use of the criterion method is not feasible.

A criterion-related study must include (1) graphs and statistics showing relationship between tests and job criteria; (2) average test scores and criteria for all relevant subgroups, including minority and nonminority groups where differential validity is required; and (3) for each test a minimum passing score that is reasonable and consistent with normal expectations for the group being studied. In addition, where supervisory ratings are used for a criterion they must be founded upon careful job analysis information.

While criterion-related validity is preferred, content validity might be acceptable to the EEOC and the courts in those cases where there is too small a number of job holders, especially

[17]*Albermarle Paper Co.* v. *Moody* 422 US 407, Reported in *Labor Law Reports: Employment Practices,* No. 86, (Chicago: Commerce Clearing House, June 30, 1975).

of different races and sexes, to obtain proper statistical data. Also, content validation is proper for an achievement or proficiency test. In this case the courts require a comprehensive assessment of duties and responsibilities of the job and an assessment of the required knowledges, skills, and other abilities required of the job incumbents. It must be demonstrated by systematic job analysis that the items on the test are actually derived from the job.

Accommodating for the Handicapped. With the impetus given to companies by the Rehabilitation Act of 1973 to increase their hiring of physically and mentally handicapped persons, personnel officers need to re-examine existing hiring specifications to see if they can all be supported by accurate job analysis data or whether, in fact, deaf persons, persons with a missing limb, mentally retarded individuals, and persons with other handicaps could effectively do certain jobs. Would the modern bureaucratic organization have hired any of the following people?

• Tom was a young deaf man who liked to tinker with gadgets and who claimed he could invent new and wonderful things.
• Frank, a college graduate, could walk with leg braces only with great difficulty, but for the most part was confined to a wheelchair. Yet he had aspiration for executive leadership.
• Max lost both legs and one hand in a war, but he had a good education and a desire for a major executive job.

Because of arbitrarily established hiring standards, most firms probably would not hire any of these three individuals. Yet all were outstanding in their chosen fields of work.[18]

---

[18]The three individuals referred to are Thomas A. Edison, Franklin D. Roosevelt, and Max Cleland, Director of U.S. Veterans Administration in the administration of President Jimmy Carter.

Performance Appraisal

Performance appraisal is really a systematic, organized way for making and recording judgments about the performance of employees. For those jobs in which the work is quantifiable and measurable, appraisals can be objective to a degree. Other jobs are difficult to measure, and the resultant evaluations of the job holders tend to be subjective. When it is used to select people for promotion or for layoff, companies can run afoul of the law if minorities and women are involved and they suffer an "adverse impact." The Zia Corporation, a contractor with the U.S. Atomic Energy Commission at Los Alamos, New Mexico, was found by the court to have violated the law when it used supervisory ratings to decide whom to lay off and there was a disparate impact upon Spanish-surnamed employees. The Court of Appeals held that Zia had violated the regulations because the ratings were not based on any definite identifiable criteria based on quality or quantity of work or specific performances that were based upon some kind of record. The ratings were faulted for being too subjective.[19]

The responsibility then rests with all organizations to insure that their employee appraisal systems are soundly designed and executed in order to satisfy EEOC requirements. Companies that have won their cases before the EEOC and the courts have had the following features in their appraisal systems.

1. Written job analysis was used as a basis for appraisals.
2. Raters (supervisors) were provided with written instructions.
3. Employees were evaluated on observable behavior or on job results.
4. The appraisals were discussed with the employees.

---

[19]U.S. Court of Appeals, 10th Circuit, *Brito* v. *Zia Company*, 478F. 2nd 1200 (1973).

Promotions

Affirmative Action regulations require companies to keep adequate records to monitor upward mobility of "affected class" employees (those who suffer and continue to suffer effects of discrimination). Barriers to upward mobility must be identified and overcome. The selection standards and procedures for promotion should conform to EEOC guidelines. This means that there must be objective job descriptions and the standards required for promotion must be written and validated. The EEOC and the OFCCP have tended to hold that women and minorities should be given a chance at the better jobs if "minimally" qualified, even though they may not be "best" qualified (when competing with white males, for example).

Seniority

Seniority systems used for upgrading and promotion and for order of layoff have come under much attack for women and minorities in EEO litigation. Because these protected groups have moved into industry in large numbers only in recent years, it is obvious that they rank low on seniority lists when it comes time to promote and lay off. Therefore, they will be adversely affected if employers abide strictly by seniority rules as spelled out in union-employer contracts.

Section 803 (h) of Title VII of the 1964 Civil Right Act provides that

> It shall not be an unlawful employment practice for an employer to apply different standards of compensation, or different terms, conditions, or privileges of employment pursuant to a bona fide seniority or merit system . . . provided that such differences are not the results of an intention to discriminate because of race, color, religion, sex, or national origin.

For a good number of years the Federal district courts and courts of appeals issued inconsistent decisions on cases challenging the way companies applied their seniority rules.

However in recent years the U.S. Supreme Court has ruled, in three important cases, that bona fide seniority systems, whether adopted before or after the enactment of Title VII in 1964, are valid unless it can be proven that adoption or maintenance of these systems resulted from intent to discriminate.[20] Unless intent to discriminate can be proven, the EEOC and the courts cannot invalidate bona fide seniority plans that lay off minority individuals or women before whites or males if the protected classes possess lower seniority.

SEXUAL HARASSMENT

A female factory worker in a predominantly male plant is subjected to frequent unwanted touching, verbal sexual propositions, and lewd jokes by co-workers. She complains to her foreman and to the personnel department but the practices continue.

A male manager invites his secretary to dinner at a restaurant in a neighboring city. At the dinner he urges her to spend the night with him at a hotel. She declines. He offers her a large salary increase if she agrees. She still declines. He then warns that her job will be in jeopardy if she continues to decline.

The foregoing are two examples of sexual harassment situations that occur in work organizations. This is a very old problem that has only recently been given formal attention by management, government officials, and the

---

[20]See for example Thomas R. Bagly, "The Supreme Court Reaffirms Broad Immunity for Seniority Systems," *Labor Law Journal*, Vol. 33, No. 7 (July 1982), pp. 409–416. This article discusses the cases of *International Brotherhood of Teamsters* v. *United States*, 431 U.S. 324 (U.S. SCt, 1977); *American Tobacco Company* v. *Patterson*, 50 USLW 4364 (U.S. SCt, 1982); and *Pullman-Standard* v. *Swint*, 50 USLW 4425 (U.S. SCt, 1982).

courts. Only in recent years have legal remedies been available to victims of sexual harassment.

Sexual harassment may take the form of verbal abuse; unwanted touching, petting, and pinching; sexist remarks about clothing, body, or sexual activities; leering at a person's body; and demanding sexual favors accompanied by threats regarding one's job, performance appraisal, promotion, or salary.

When faced with unwanted sexual advances a woman confronts a dilemma. She most certainly will be embarrassed. Regardless of her response she may worry about ostracism by fellow employees. Oftentimes sexual harassment is perpetrated by a woman's own supervisor. It is very risky to enter a complaint against the very person who controls job tenure and employment opportunities. The aggrieved woman may fear punishment in the form of denial of an earned pay raise, bad performance appraisal, denial of a promised promotion, or outright discharge.

Surveys of sexual harassment in the workplace show that it is prevalent. For example, a study of Federal government employees revealed that 42 per cent of 694,000 women and 15 per cent of 1,168,000 men said that they had experienced some form of sexual harassment.[21]

The vast majority of reported cases involve men harassing women. This is a result of our culture and traditions. Men typically occupy positions of power in work organizations, whereas women hold lower-ranking jobs and are subordinate to men. Thus they have been vulnerable to such pressures. Additionally some males believe that sexual overtures to women will enhance their macho self-image. But when such advances are unwanted, persistent, and power-based they consitute harassment.

As more and more women move into the ranks of management, we can expect to see an increase in the number of cases of female bosses pressuring male subordinates for sexual favors.

What Constitutes Sexual Harassment?

In 1980 the Equal Employment Opportunity Commission issued its "Guidelines on Discrimination on the Basis of Sex." The guidelines provide that:

> Unwelcome sexual advances, requests for sexual favors, and other verbal or physical conduct of a sexual nature constitute sexual harassment when (1) submission to such conduct is made either explicitly or implicitly a term or condition of an individual's employment, (2) submission to or rejection of such conduct by an individual is used as the basis for employment decisions affecting such individual, or (3) such conduct has the purpose or effect of unreasonably interfering with an individual's work performance or creating an intimidating, hostile, or offensive working environment.

The crucial element in most sexual harassment cases is the *power* which the alleged offender holds over the target person. Thus supervisors and managers are in a position where they can use the authority of their positions to sexually harass subordinates. On the other hand, if the individual making the sexual advances is simply a co-worker, then the person who is the target of the unwelcome advances can often rebuff the overtures without fear of retaliation. Nevertheless, co-worker harassment can also be serious if it is persistent, threatening, or embarrassing.

Remedies and Legal Considerations

The victim of unwanted sexual advances can pursue any of three possible courses of action in an effort to correct the situation.

First, she (because the victim is most often a female we shall use "she" throughout our dis-

[21]*Merit Systems Protection Board Report on Sexual Harassment in the Federal Workplace,* given before the Subcommittee on Investigations, Committee on the Post Office and Civil Service, U.S. House of Representatives, September 1980.

cussion) can appeal to management either informally or by submitting a formal complaint. The efficacy of this recourse depends upon the inclinations of management and whether the organization has, in place, a policy covering sexual harassment.

Second, she can appeal to the Equal Employment Opportunity Commission. The Commission has ruled that sexual harassment constitutes a violation of Title VII of the Civil Rights Act of 1964. The guidelines, referenced earlier, impose a liability upon employers for the acts of their supervisors for any sexual harassment of employees, regardless of whether the conduct of the supervisors was known to the employer. Although employer liability for the acts of co-workers is less stringent, the employer is still accountable for such acts of harassment if the employer knew, or should have known, of the conduct in question unless the employer can show that it took prompt and appropriate action to correct the problem upon learning of it.

If an individual is successful in her case before the Equal Employment Opportunity Commission, she can be reinstated to her job and be awarded back pay (if indeed she had been discharged for resisting sexual advances).

A third avenue of potential recourse for a victim of sexual harassment is to file suit in a state court under that state's law of intentional torts and under common law. The victim may claim that a supervisor has committed assault and battery against her. Assault involves fear of imminent physical injury, whereas battery consists of an unpermitted contact ranging from a mild physical contact to a severe injury. The victim may be able to recover damages not only from the supervisor who committed the act or acts but also from the employer under the tort law doctrine of *respondeat superior*. This doctrine holds that the company is responsible for the acts of an employee (supervisor in this case) for all acts committed within the scope of employment.

A brief review of two court decisions can serve to illustrate the application of the law in sexual harassment cases.

In *Tomkins* v. *Public Service Electric & Gas Co.*,[22] Adrienne Tomkins, an office worker, was eligible for promotion to a secretarial position when her supervisor took her to lunch away from the company premises. She charged in her court suit that he made sexual advances toward her at that time. He also detained her against her will by means of economic threats and physical force. Ms. Tomkins later complained to higher management. As a result of her complaint she suffered a disciplinary layoff and threats of demotion and salary reduction. Eventually the company fired her. The Court of Appeals for the Third Circuit found in favor of Ms. Tomkins. It said that Title VII is violated when a supervisor, with the actual or constructive knowledge of the employer, makes sexual advances toward a subordinate employee and conditions the employee's job status—evaluation, continued employment, promotion, or other aspects of career development—on a favorable response to those advances, and the employer does not take prompt remedial action after acquiring such knowledge.

In *Heelan* v. *Johns-Manville Corporation*,[23] Mary Heelan claimed that her refusal to have sexual relations with her supervisor resulted in her being fired. She complained to several members of management including an assistant to the president and the executive vice-president. They did nothing. The court ruled that the sexual advances occurred, were unwanted, and were refused. It also found the company liable for damages because Ms. Heelan had informed members of management and they had not conducted an adequate inquiry nor had they attempted to make restitution. The courts awarded Ms. Heelan back pay, lost employment benefits, and attorney's fees.

[22]422 F. Supp. 553 (DC N.J., 1976). 12 EPD paragraph 11,267, CA-3, 1977, 15 EPD paragraph 7954.
[23]451 F. Supp. (DC Colo., 1978), 16 EPD paragraph 8330.

Implications for Personnel Management

Because sexual harassment by itself is wrong, and because employers can be held legally liable for the actions of their supervisors and managers who are found guilty of harassment (and liable, in some circumstances, for harassment by co-workers), it is important that companies adopt policies and procedures to control this problem.

At the outset a company should establish a policy condemning sexual harassment. It should announce that sanctions will be applied against proven offenders. The policy statement should contain a definition of sexual harassment and it should give examples of proscribed behavior. Additionally it should be made clear that retaliation against the aggrieved person for filing charges will not be tolerated.

The policy should be communicated in writing to all employees. This announcement should inform the employees of management's genuine concern about the issue and state that management will listen to and act upon allegations that are well founded.

The company should establish procedures for the implementation of the policy. An employee who feels that she has been the victim of harassment should have the right to discuss the matter with a designated member of the personnel department. This person should provide supportive counsel and offer to mediate the dispute between the aggrieved person and the alleged perpetrator. Mary P. Rowe, who has mediated hundreds of harassment cases, states that from her experience it is often helpful for the aggrieved person to write a letter to the alleged harasser explaining her position and what she would like to see happen.[24]

A formal grievance procedure should be created to handle harassment cases. If the organization already has an operating grievance procedure, it can be utilized. It ought to be emphasized that not all allegations of harassment are true. Male employees and supervisors may be unjustly accused. Their rights must be protected.

Management must carefully document every aspect of its investigations and actions taken. This is important should litigation occur later.

The company should present in-house seminars for all members of management. These should explain fully the organizations policies and procedures. Managers should be taught how to process harassment cases.

Finally, the company should assign responsibility for implementation of the policy to a high-level manager such as an equal employment opportunity compliance officer or the human resource (personnel) manager.

COMPARABLE WORTH

The median annual earnings of all women workers in the economy as a whole stood at 63.3 per cent of the median annual earnings of men in 1956 and at only 58.8 per cent in 1975.[25] The situation has not improved much since 1975. If we compare men's and women's earnings within the same occupation, the gap is significant but smaller. For example, in 1981 the median weekly earnings of women computer programmers were 73.6 per cent of the earnings of men programmers. Women lawyers earned 71.0 per cent of the amount earned by men lawyers. Women food service workers earned 79.7 per cent of the amount earned by men.[26]

Because the disparity between women's

[24]Mary P. Rowe, "Dealing with Sexual Harassment," *Harvard Business Review*, Vol. 59, No. 3 (May–June 1981), pp. 42–45.

[25]U.S. Department of Commerce, Bureau of the Census, *Current Population Reports*, Series P 60.

[26]Nancy F. Rytina, "Earnings of Men and Women: A

and men's earnings is so large, persistent, and pervasive, unions, women workers in industry, and women's rights advocates have, in recent years, advanced claims for "comparable worth." Although the concept of comparable worth has not been defined by authorities in any precise way, a great deal has been written about the topic in the last few years.

Concepts of social justice and of distributive justice hold that individuals and groups should be treated equitably in comparison with one another along recognized dimensions. Thus the *rewards* going to a person (or group) divided by that person's (group's) *contributions* should be proportional to the *rewards* going to another person (group) divided by the second person's (group's) contributions. For example, if a job populated predominantly by women, such as a librarian, requires a college degree and five years of related experience, the librarians should be paid the same salary as mechanical engineers (populated mainly by men) if the mechanical-engineering job requires comparable (but not the same) education and work experience.[27]

In 1981 the U.S. Supreme Court offered as a definition of comparable worth the claims by women for "increased compensation on the basis of a comparison of the intrinsic worth or difficulty of their job with that of other jobs in the same organization or community."[28]

Why Women's Earnings Are Lower

Many factors account for the generally lower annual or weekly earnings of women in comparison with the earnings of men. Let us review the principal causal factors.

1. *Outright Discrimination.* Traditional practice was to pay women lower wages than men even when they were employed in the same jobs within the same organization. Companies could do this because women did not have sufficient bargaining power to gain parity with men. Since enactment of the Equal Pay Act of 1963 this practice has been illegal. However, violations of the intent of the law still occur.

2. *Fewer Years in the Labor Force.* Women typically enter the labor force, work a few years, marry, bear children, leave the labor force for several years, and then re-enter the labor force. All in all they work fewer years than their male counterparts in the same occupation. Hence they receive fewer increases in pay under seniority and merit pay plans.

3. *Concentration in Lower Paying Occupations.* Certain occupations which have traditionally paid relatively low wages are populated largely by women. Principal among these "women's" occupations are clerical jobs in offices, sales clerks in stores, and nurses' aides in hospitals. Conversely, few women are employed in high-paying engineering occupations and in the skilled trades.

4. *Concentration in Lower Paying Industries.* Large numbers of women are employed in low-paying industries such as banking, primary and secondary education, retailing, textile manufacturing, and wearing apparel manufacturing.

5. *Job Evaluation and Market Wage Comparisons.* Companies with some degree of management sophistication set wage rates for jobs by means of job evaluation which, on the surface at least, is sexless. Job evaluation creates a hierarchy of jobs from those low in skill, effort, responsibility, and working conditions to those ranking high on these factors. But actual pay rates are assigned to jobs by conducting labor market wage surveys for key (or benchmark) jobs. The job evaluation ratings of jobs are blended with the market pay rates to set the wage rates in the company. If the market undervalues the worth of women,

Look at Specific Occupations," *Monthly Labor Review,* Vol. 105, No. 4 (April 1982), pp. 25–31.

[27]Distributive justice is developed by George Homans in his *Social Behavior: Its Elementary Forms* (New York: Harcourt, Brace & World, 1961).

[28]*County of Washington* v. *Gunther,* 452 US 161 (US Sct, 1981), 26 EPD paragraph 31,877.

then even employers who intend to treat women fairly will perpetuate their inequitable treatment, if they emphasize market rates and if women in their companies are concentrated in certain "women's" jobs.

Legal Considerations

The Equal Pay Act outlaws the payment of a wage rate to employees of one sex which is less than that paid to employees of the opposite sex on jobs that require equal skill, effort, and responsibility and that are performed under similar working conditions. Inequalities in pay to individuals are allowed if they are caused by a seniority system, a merit system, a system that measures earnings by quality or quantity of production, or by a factor other than sex.

Title VII of the Civil Rights Act, which is broader in scope than the Equal Pay Act, also specifically forbids discrimination in compensation.

In the *County of Washington v. Gunther*,[29] an important legal case, the U.S. Supreme Court ruled that Title VII prohibits an employer from intentionally paying women less than men because of their sex. In this case the county conducted a labor market wage survey of male jail guards and female matrons. The two jobs were somewhat different in content. The county evaluated the female matrons' jobs at a value of 95 per cent of the male jail guards' jobs, but paid the matrons 70 per cent of the male rate. The court did not rule on the specific merits of the case but stated that the case could properly be brought to court under Title VII even where the jobs were not substantially equal. (The case was remanded to a lower court for disposition.)

Reducing the Wage Disparities

The comparable worth doctrine is somewhat vague in its meaning and hence difficult to operationalize. Nevertheless, the objective of

[29]Ibid.

achieving approximate parity between men's and women's earnings is desirable on the basis of social justice.

Several measures can be followed to accomplish this goal within individual organizations. Companies can refine their job evaluation systems so that jobs populated heavily by women are evaluated accurately in comparison with jobs staffed largely by men. Management can also develop single job evaluation plans that encompass all the jobs within the organization. Typically companies use three distinct plans, one for hourly paid workers, one for nonexempt office employees, and one for exempt professional and managerial personnel. Finally, and perhaps most importantly, management can take steps to eliminate job segregation by sex. If men and women are represented in jobs in roughly equal percentages, then employers are less likely to pay women less than men. Women must be able to move into the generally higher-paying jobs now occupied mainly by men.

To reduce the earnings gap between men and women among different organizations in a labor market or in the economy as a whole is a very tall order. Economic factors, supply and demand, bargaining power, extent of unionization, and the like exert a strong impact.

There is no universally accepted system for evaluating the dollar worth of jobs throughout the economy as a whole. It is unlikely that there will be one in the foreseeable future.

The best hope for reducing the earnings disparity is through vigorous enforcement of the Equal Pay Act and Title VII and by a rapid reduction in segregation of women into women's jobs and men into men's jobs.

REVERSE DISCRIMINATION

A few years ago a young man (an acquaintance of the author) applied to the telephone company for employment as an installer-repairman. He was turned down for this job but was offered a job as an office clerk—a job paying substantially less money than the installer-repairman position. He was told that the company had to increase substantially the number of women and blacks in its craft jobs, and hence was not hiring white males in the foreseeable future for these jobs, but he could have a clerical job because there were few white males in this job category. Because of examples like this, and countless comparable ones, many people have complained bitterly that companies are forced by government affirmative action rules to favor the hiring, job assignment, or promotion of blacks over whites and of women over men.

Yet Section 703j of Title VII of the Civil Rights Act contains express language that seems to prevent preferential treatment for any individual or group on account of an imbalance which may exist in regard to the total number or percentage of persons of any race, color, religion, sex, or national origin in an organization in comparison with the number or percentage of such persons in the community or in the available work force. Despite this stated Congressional intent, the U.S. Department of Labor and the EEOC have required thousands of companies to hire and promote many more blacks and women in order to meet affirmative action goals and timetables. With scarce job opportunities this has meant that often whites and males were turned down in favor of blacks and females.

Advocates of affirmative action have asserted that "goals" are different from fixed, numerical "quotas" and hence are perfectly proper and legal. Laurence H. Silberman, who was Under Secretary of Labor from 1970 to 1973 and who helped devise minority employment goals for government contractors at that time, has had second thoughts about the value of affirmative action goals. He writes that the distinction between goals and quotas is more metaphysical than real. He claims that the elimination of goals or quotas would not wipe out the gains minorities have made over the years.[30]

[30]Laurence H. Silberman, "The Road to Racial Quotas," *Wall Street Journal* (August 11, 1977).

If pressure from the government to increase the employment opportunities of women and minorities since the mid-1960s had not taken place, it is extremely doubtful whether any real change would have occurred. On the other hand, should a white person who is better qualified than a protected minority person be denied a job or a promotion simply because the company needs to meet a numerical quota or goal in order to retain its government contract? The problem of apparent reverse discrimination is very difficult to resolve. It is unlikely ever to be resolved to the full satisfaction of all contesting parties. The law says that employment decisions must not be made in favor of or against people on the basis of race, color, age, sex, or national origin. This still leaves employers considerable latitude to use other criteria in selecting people for hire or promotion. In the future when the various protected groups have achieved greater parity with nonminorities in employment status, there will be less pressure to give the minorities special preference to correct alleged imbalances.

In June 1979, the United States Supreme Court ruled in favor of a racial quota in a case involving admission to a craft-training program. Brian Weber, a white employee at the Kaiser Aluminum and Chemical Corporation plant in Louisiana, had sued both the company and his union, the United Steelworkers, after he was denied admission to a craft-training program. In 1974 the union and the company had signed a collective bargaining agreement that provided for creation of a craft-training program and selection for the program on the basis of seniority. The agreement also provided that at least 50 per cent of the trainees were to be black until the percentage of black skilled craft workers in the plant approximated the percentage of blacks in the community.

In reversing two lower Federal courts, the Supreme Court upheld the plan adopted at the Kaiser plant. Noting the narrowness of its inquiry, the Court held that Title VII does not forbid private employees and unions from

200

voluntarily agreeing upon affirmative action plans that accord racial preferences in the manner used at Kaiser.

Questions for Review and Discussion

1. What reasons account for the generally lower earnings of black workers compared with white workers? Of women compared with men?
2. How can one ascertain whether adverse impact or a pattern of discrimination exists within an organization?
3. What steps must a company take to comply with governmental affirmative action requirements?
4. Some people argue that to change deep-seated beliefs such as racial prejudice or discriminatory attitudes toward women, it is better to re-educate the public and leaders of business rather than to force change by legal mandates and compulsion from government regulatory agencies. Discuss this issue of achieving change by education versus compulsion.
5. Are there any differences between the requirements of Title VII of the Civil Rights Act and Executive Order 11246, as amended? If so, explain.
6. How have equal employment opportunity regulations and court decisions changed the way employers carry out selection testing?
7. What is sexual harassment in the workplace? Why has it only recently come to public attention? What can a female victim do to protect her situation? What can management do to minimize sexual harassment within its organization?
8. What is meant by the term "comparable worth"? In order for women to achieve parity with men in weekly pay, what active steps need to be taken within an organization? In the economy as a whole?
9. How can management protect itself against charges of discrimination when making promotion and merit pay decisions?

CASE PROBLEM

THE ALTAMONT DIVISION

Most of the business of the Altamont Division of the Chittenden Corporation consists of contracts from the United States Department of Defense. The Division is located in a small Eastern city of 40,000 population. Of this population, about 12 per cent are blacks and 3 per cent are Hispanic Americans. Altamont has total employment of about 1100. Only thirty-five of these are black, eleven are Hispanics, and one is physically handicapped. All of these are employed in lower-level jobs. The total employment at Altamont has declined gradually over the past five years from a peak of 1400 to its present level because of cutbacks in government business. About 25 per cent of the total employment is in scientific and technical jobs. There are no blacks or Hispanics and only fifteen women in these scientific and technical positions. The division employs many women but they fill primarily the clerical and blue collar assembly jobs.

Because it is a government contractor, Altamont is required to maintain an affirmative action program. On paper the program appears to commit the Altamont management to many activities to hire and improve the status of minorities, women, and the handicapped. Among the actions stated in the plan are:

1. Hire more blacks and Hispanic Americans.
2. Provide minorities, women, and the handicapped equal opportunity to improve their qualifications for advancement and to participate in training and development for supervision. Likewise they will participate on an equal basis in training programs, reassignments, and temporary promotions.
3. There shall be no disparity in compensation received by minorities, women, and the handicapped in comparison with nonminorities for equivalent duties and responsibilities.
4. Sufficient resources will be provided to administer an effective EEO program.
5. There will be an EEO Committee whose function is to monitor and suggest changes in the program as required. Also an EEO Manager shall be appointed to coordinate the entire program. An important responsibility of the Manager is to process employee grievances regarding equal employment opportunity. The EEO Manager reports to the Director of Personnel.

There is a pervasive feeling among many employees and managers in the Division that the affirmative action program exists only on paper and that little has been done to implement it. Privately the EEO Manager, who is black, says that top management has only given lip service to the program and doesn't really believe in EEO. He notes that no blacks have been hired in the past year. Only one black and one woman were permitted to be enrolled in the last supervisory training program and to date, neither has been appointed to a permanent supervisory position. (Both are being continued as acting-supervisors.)

The Director of Personnel retired two months ago. You have recently been hired as the new Director of Personnel and have been promised full support in your activities by the Division general manager. You find that the EEO program suffers because of budget limitations, a gradually declining level of employment in the Division, and a lack of understanding of EEO concepts throughout the organization generally. You have also determined that much of the EEO annual budget is spent by the EEO Committee (composed of the EEO Manager and five other management personnel) in attendance at training seminars and conferences given at resort hotels in Florida and California. You believe in managerial training but you wonder how much good has been accomplished from attendance at these conferences. Also, you have learned that women and minority employees have rarely filed discrimination complaints and grievances out of fear of being labeled troublemakers and thereby made more vulnerable to layoff.

Question

What actions would you, as the new Director of Personnel, take to improve the affirmative action program in order to have it meet its stated objectives?

Suggestions for Further Reading

Anderson, Howard J., and Michael D. Levin-Epstein. *Primer of Equal Employment Opportunity*, 2nd ed. Washington, D.C.: Bureau of National Affairs, 1982.

Collins, Eliza G. C., and Timothy B. Blodgett. "Sexual Harassment: Some See It . . . Some Won't," *Harvard Business Review*, Vol. 59, No. 2 (March–April 1981), pp. 76–95.

Gold, Michael E. *A Dialogue on Comparable Worth*. Ithaca: New York State School of Industrial and Labor Relations, Cornell University, 1983.

Hennig, Margaret, and Ann Jardim. *The Managerial Women*. Garden City, N.Y.: Anchor Press/Doubleday, 1977.

Pati, Gopal C., and Glenn Morrison. "Enabling the Disabled," *Harvard Business Review*, Vol. 60, No. 4 (July–August 1981), pp. 152–168.

Rowe, Mary P. "Dealing with Sexual Harassment," *Harvard Business Review*, Vol. 59, No. 3 (May–June 1981), pp. 42–45.

Shaeffer, Ruth G. *Nondiscrimination in Employment—and Beyond*, Report 782. New York: The Conference Board, 1980.

Thomas, Clarence. "Pay Equity and Comparable Worth," *Labor Law Journal*, Vol. 34, No. 1 (January 1983), pp. 3–12.

Treisman, Donald J., and Heidi I. Hartmann, eds. *Women, Work, and Wages: Equal Pay for Jobs of Equal Value*. Washington, D.C.: National Academy Press, 1981.

Wallace, Phyllis A., ed. *Women in the Workplace*. Boston: Auburn House Publishing Company, 1982.

10

Performance Appraisal and Management by Objectives

In our daily lives we continually size up and form opinions of the people with whom we come in contact. In social relations this is done quite casually, often subconsciously, and rarely systematically. If one wishes to select a barber, dentist, physician, or a home builder, he may be somewhat more thorough in the manner in which he forms judgments. When we move into the area of cooperative group endeavors—in short, organizations—we find that supervisors must continually judge the contributions and abilities of their subordinates. Certain individuals are more adept at doing one type of work than another, certain ones cannot be depended upon to carry through an assignment to completion, others show great initiative and reliability and can take on projects with a minimum of supervision. The supervisor must frequently make decisions pertaining to the pay treatment of her or his employees, as well as employee placement, transfer, promotion, and individual development. Shall these personnel actions be based upon spur-of-the-moment decisions, or shall they be based upon carefully thought-out judgments made by a supervisor in collaboration with others and formulated in a systematic manner?

Because managers must make judgments of their employees almost constantly and for many reasons, the question naturally arises as to

whether this should be formalized into a systematic performance appraisal program or whether it should be a haphazard, disorganized affair. Because evaluation goes on all of the time, the question is not whether to appraise employees. Rather it is *how* to evaluate people. The overwhelming weight of argument is in favor of the formalized performance appraisal approach.

Under a formalized appraisal system supervisors and managers are encouraged to observe the behavior of their people. They tend to be interested in their training and development. Judgments, often from many raters, are recorded on paper and placed in the individual's personnel folder. Decisions on personnel changes of status are not left to the vagaries of recollections of busy supervisors. Human memory is often unreliable. Hidden talents are sometimes uncovered, especially if a number of raters appraise the same individual. A formal rating procedure minimizes the likelihood of capable people being overlooked for training opportunities, pay raises, promotions, and new assignments. It is difficult to operate a large organization without some form of written appraisal plan. When comparing candidates for promotion from different organizational units, management must have written records of ratings so that sound decisions can be made. Sometimes the ultimate decision maker is high

204

in the organizational hierarchy, and she or he does not personally know the individuals being considered for the post. Reliance must be placed on ratings, records, and written recommendations.

To what extent do companies actually use formal performance appraisal plans? In a survey of several hundred companies in manufacturing, gas and electric utility, banking, and insurance industries, The Conference Board found that 75 per cent of the responding firms used performance appraisal for their production or operations employees, 94 per cent appraised their office and clerical personnel, and 93 per cent appraised their lower level exempt personnel (supervisory and technical).[1]

In this chapter we shall examine the meaning and applications of appraisals, basic considerations in appraisal, appraisal techniques, problems in rating, appraisal and personal development, and the special problems involved in postappraisal interviews. We shall also explore management by objectives which is both a process for managing and an appraisal technique.

Appraisal Defined

Performance appraisal is the systematic evaluation of individuals with respect to their performance on the job and their potential for development. Ordinarily the evaluation is made by each person's immediate superior in the organization, and this rating is reviewed in turn by his superior. Thus, all people in the organization who appraise others are also evaluated by their own superior. As we shall see later there are some variations of this boss-rates-subordinate practice, but it is by far

the most common arrangement. It is considered good practice for managers to do more than simply rate their subordinates. They should also work out, jointly with each of their subordinates, a plan for correcting deficiencies, building upon strengths, and developing the individual. This appraisal and employee development go hand in hand.

Management by objectives has become very popular in recent years. The philosophy underlying this system is different from that of conventional appraisal. Management by objectives emphasizes the setting of performance goals on a mutually agreeable basis by discussion between the individual and the immediate manager. The superior plays more of a supportive and coaching role than a judgmental one. This appraisal system is most commonly used for managerial, professional, and sales personnel. In its broadest sense management by objectives is really a process of managing. It embodies the heart of the managerial art.

Although performance appraisal is the most commonly used designation, other labels are sometimes employed. The following terms are all generally synonymous: *personnel appraisal, personnel review, progress report, merit rating, and performance evaluation.*

Applications of Appraisals

Employee appraisal is an essential part of effective personnel management. Its purpose and uses are as follows:

Employee Performance. Appraisals are an aid to creating and maintaining a satisfactory level of performance by employees on their present jobs. When the actual evaluation process is followed up with an appraisal interview with each employee, it may contribute toward more effective or improved performance on the part of many individuals.

Employee Development. The appraisal may highlight needs and opportunities for growth

<hr>

[1]The total number of companies, for all four industries combined, responding to the survey for production or operations employees was 335. For the office and clerical group and for the lower-level exempt group 523 firms responded. Harriet Gorlin, *Personnel Practices I: Recruitment, Placement, Training, Communication* (New York: The Conference Board, 1981).

and development of the person. Growth may be accomplished by self-study, formal training courses, or job-related activities, such as special broadening assignments and job rotation. It should be clear that training and development of employees and managers strengthen the organization as well as aid the individuals.

Supervisory Understanding. A formal and periodic appraisal encourages supervisors to observe the behavior of their subordinates. Encouraged by the proper top-management attitude, they can be motivated to take an interest in each person and to offer help. If carried out properly the entire appraisal process can facilitate mutual understanding between the supervisor and subordinates.

Guide to Job Changes. An appraisal aids decision making for promotions, transfers, layoffs (where seniority may not be the controlling factor), and discharges (for inadequate performance). Systematic assessments of an individual by a number of raters, made over a period of time and recorded in writing, help to make this process reasonable and sound. It should give due consideration to the needs of both the organization and the individual.

Wage and Salary Treatment. Many organizations relate the size and frequency of pay increases to the rating assigned to the employee in the performance appraisal.

Validate Personnel Programs. The accuracy of predictions made in the employee selection process is often determined by comparing or correlating performance ratings with test scores, interviewers' evaluations, and so on. An indication of the worth of a training program can sometimes be determined by an analysis of employee performance after completion of a particular course of instruction.

In summary, the various uses for performance appraisal can be classified into two broad categories. One category concerns the obtaining of evaluation data on employees for decision making for various personnel actions such as pay increases, promotions, transfers, discharges, and for selection test validation. The other main use is for employee development including performance improvement, training, coaching, and counseling.

BASIC CONSIDERATIONS IN APPRAISAL

When raters evaluate someone, they tend to think in terms of what kind of a person he or she is and what he or she has done. Thus, appraisal plans require raters to rate or score employees on personal traits and characteristics and on contributions. Determination of the former is rather subjective, since different raters may appraise the same individual differently. Ann Smith's attitude toward the company may seem acceptable to one supervisor, but another boss may feel that Smith is a little too critical of company policies and scores her lower on that account. Employee contributions—what a person actually accomplishes on the job—can be more objectively ascertained. For many jobs the quantity of work produced is readily measurable, and it serves as an excellent gauge of the employee's performance. Such measures are available for a high proportion of direct labor jobs in industry. On the other hand, it is very difficult to measure the output of a receptionist, an engineer, a maintenance person, or a public relations director.

It might be readily conceded that an employer is primarily interested in assessing employees' performance (that is, contributions), and therefore these factors should be counted most heavily. However, it is also apparent that such personal traits as cooperativeness, dependability, attitude, initiative, and ability to get along with others also have a bearing upon the employee's value to the organization. These characteristics affect relations with the boss and with co-workers, and they influence effectiveness on the job.

In recent years management has tended to place the greatest weight in appraisal upon the actual results people achieve on their jobs. It is recognized that two people can have quite different personalities and yet be equally effective in their work. This can be true even on the same job or occupation.

Standards of Performance

In order to evaluate employees, it is necessary to have something against which to compare them. Thus, it is possible simply to compare one person with another. This in essence is the ranking method of rating. However, an approach that is likely to be more fruitful is to establish, in writing, definite standards of accomplishment employees can reasonably be expected to meet. Such a method makes it possible for both the supervisor and subordinate to reach agreement on just what is expected in terms of performance.

A useful starting point for developing written standards is the job description. For professional and managerial personnel much can be gained by having the individual and boss jointly develop the standard. For lower level employees, whose jobs tend to be very precisely defined and limited, the supervisor quite generally will inform subordinates of expectations in terms of quantity and quality of work, attendance, punctuality, job knowledge, and thoroughness.

The following are some examples of performance standards for management personnel. It will be noted that they are of necessity expressed in somewhat general terms. Judgment on the part of the rater is required to determine how well the individual meets these expectations.

1. *For a controller:* effectiveness of and improvement in accounting procedures; promptness with which management is informed of operating and financial results; soundness of policies and procedures recommended; quality, quantity, and timeliness of suggestions given to corporate office executives; quality, quantity, timeliness of suggestions and guidance given to plant management.

2. *For a manufacturing manager:* production schedules for the division are met; product meets established quality standards; injury frequency is less than 10.0 per hundred full-time workers; manufacturing overhead maintained within expense budget limits for level of operations; equipment down-time does not exceed 8 per cent; efficiency of direct labor utilization is at least 90 per cent of established standards; manager creates and maintains satisfactory level of morale within his division; manager provides adequate cross-training assignments for his personnel.

It should be pointed out that performance standards are relative to the group and to the organization. Not only are the needs of each organization different, but from one company to another the caliber of the manpower will vary. The expectations of management are higher in some companies than others.

Performance and Potential

Depending upon the purposes of the employee appraisal program, the evaluation may be directed toward either the actual performance of the individual on the present job or the potential for promotion to a higher-level position. Quite often the raters are asked to make judgments in both areas.

To determine a person's potential for taking on greater job responsibilities and for advancement requires a great deal of knowledge and skill on the part of the appraiser. The demands of the individual's present job may not give the opportunity to demonstrate his other full abilities. The question of potential for growth can be answered fairly only when one considers "growth for what?" If an engineer is being considered for promotion to a supervisory position in the engineering department, he or she must possess a certain cluster of aptitudes and abilities. On the other hand, if that same person is being considered for a high-level staff position, he or she will need quite different qualifications. Thus, it would be folly to design an appraisal-rating form that simply asked the question "Potential for Promotion?"

Quite generally supervisors can more accurately appraise the potential of a subordinate if they deliberately plan new and varied job assignments that will confront the person with a variety of problems and require a number of his abilities.

Of course, the issue of employees' performance on their present jobs is often more urgent than that of advancement to higher level ones. In this case the appraisal program will give major emphasis to contributions in comparison with established standards, to quantity and quality of work, to attendance, dependability, job knowledge, and to cooperation with others. Where present day-to-day job performance is more vital than the potential for future advancement, the appraisal program is more likely to be geared to improving performance on one's present job, wage and salary treatment, and training needs for the individual.

Who Does the Appraising?

The prevailing practice in nearly all private and public organizations is to have the supervisors and managers of each department evaluate the performance of each of their subordinates. Most commonly these ratings are reviewed by their immediate superiors. The presumption for such a procedure is that the person charged with responsibility for managing a department has the proper understanding of organizational objectives, needs, and influences. Being held accountable for the successful operation of the department or unit, he or she must, presumably, have control over personnel-administration decisions affecting people in the department.

However, there is another aspect to this picture. The view that a supervisor receives of his subordinates is not complete. Certain features of their behavior are unknown or only partially known to him. If given the opportunity, a person's work associates could supply considerable information and insight. The military services of the United States use peer ratings in the service academies and in officer candidate schools. Peer ratings do not supplant ratings by superior officers; rather they supplement the customary type of rating in order to make decisions on promotions, job assignments, and selection for special-training schools. In reviewing the many research studies conducted in connection with peer ratings in the military services, Hollander found that in some of the studies peer ratings were a more valid predictor of leadership performance than were ratings by superior officers. In summary he found that peer ratings yielded good reliability and validity and were a very useful appraisal method.[2]

Roadman reported on a research investigation in a large industrial corporation where peer ratings of managers, who participated in a 4-week middle-manager-training program, were highly predictive of promotions two years hence. At the conclusion of the course the managers rated one another. The ratings were not available to the participants' operating divisions and hence could not have influenced the promotion decisions.[3]

Lewin and Zwany have reviewed the research on peer ratings. They state:

[2]E. P. Hollander, "Buddy Ratings: Military Research and Industrial Implications," *Personnel Psychology*, Vol. 7, No. 3 (Autumn 1954), pp. 385–393.

[3]Harry E. Roadman, "An Industrial Use of Peer Ratings," *Journal of Applied Psychology*, Vol. 48, No. 4 (1964), pp. 211–214.

In summary; peer evaluations are valid tools for predicting future success and are superior to all other measures available at the time of rating. The simplicity in administering and scoring peer ratings also results in a highly practical procedure.[4]

In summarizing fifteen selected studies of the predictive validity of peer evaluations, they determined that both the mean and median correlation coefficients were .41.

Peer ratings are widely used by professors in colleges and universities for promotion and tenure decisions. They are also used by physicians in clinics. However, peer ratings are rare in business and industry.

The group appraisal method, wherein each supervisor evaluates not only her or his own subordinates but also those working for other supervisors, can be very effective. This is especially true where the supervisors have interaction with one anothers' subordinates and have a chance to observe their behavior. Multiple judges can modify or cancel out a bias by the immediate supervisor (who makes the sole determination in most appraisal systems.)

Approaches to Appraisal

Over the years quite a variety of techniques have been created to appraise employees. These techniques can be classified according to the concept underlying each method. These approaches are as follows:

1. *Comparison against standards*
   The standards can consist of descriptions of various levels of behavior or the standards can consist of numerical scales. Examples are the various types of rating scales and check lists.

[4]Arie Y. Lewin and Abram Zwany, "Peer Nominations: A Model, Literature Critique, and a Paradigm for Research," *Personnel Psychology*, Vol. 29, No. 3 (Autumn 1976), p. 430.

2. *Interpersonal comparisons*
   The ratee is ranked against others in the same job or department on a global or overall basis. No written standards of performance are used.
3. *Setting of goals*
   Each individual's performance is compared against his or her agreed-upon objectives. This is the management-by-objectives method.
4. *Free-form essay*
   Performance is described and compared against generalized standards existing in the mind of the rater.
5. *Direct performance measures*
   Direct counts of output, quality, attendance, sales dollars, etc. are used. This approach tends to be combined with some of the other approaches such as comparison against standards and management by objectives. Direct performance measures account for only part of the total performance of most employees in most jobs. Qualitative gauges of performance are needed to evaluate the remainder.

APPRAISAL METHODS

We shall now examine the principal kinds of appraisal techniques that are in use.

1. Rating scales
   a. Personal traits and behavior scales
   b. Job dimension scales
   c. Behaviorally anchored rating scales
2. Management by objectives
3. Interpersonal comparisons
   a. Ranking
   b. Forced distribution
4. Check list
5. Essay
6. Critical incident

Rating Scales

Personal Traits and Behavior Scales. The personal traits and behavior scale technique is the oldest and most widely used of all appraisal methods. It is sometimes referred to as the conventional rating scale technique. Most commonly the rater, who is usually the ratee's direct supervisor, is supplied with a printed form, one for each person to be rated. This form contains a number of qualities and characteristics to be rated. For nonsupervisory workers typical qualities rated are quantity and quality of work, job knowledge, cooperativeness, dependability, initiative, industriousness, and attitude. For managerial personnel typical factors are analytical ability, judgment, leadership, creative ability, initiative, knowledge of work, and emotional stability.

Ratings scales can be continuous wherein the rater places a mark somewhere along a numbered line or they can have discrete steps, such as five steps ranging from poor to excellent. Figure 10-1 is an example of a conventional rating scale form that uses five discrete steps for each factor being rated.

One means of insuring that the rater has based scoring upon substantial evidence is to leave space on the form after each factor and require an explanation for each rating. In effect the rater is asked to give examples of the subject's behavior that justify the assigned rating. Also, sometimes certain direct measures of performance are asked for on the form such as number of absences or units produced.

One major advantage that all rating scale techniques have in common is that they require an evaluation of employee performance on several dimensions or factors. Research has demonstrated that one overall rating of work performance is not as effective in evaluating people as are several specific performance factors. Seashore et al. found a low degree of relationship among four individual job measures and overall job performance for 975 nonsupervisory employees working for a delivery service firm out of 27 locations throughout the country.[5]

The rating scale technique using personal traits and behaviors is relatively easy to construct and each rating form can apply to a wide range of job categories. Typically, a company will construct one form for managerial personnel, another for nonsupervisory office employees, and another for hourly workers. Rating scales are easy to use and understand. Various statistical summaries can be prepared from the rating sheets.

There are also serious disadvantages. The evaluation of the kinds of personal traits that are so commonly used—cooperativeness, personality, attitude, judgment, etc.—is a subjective process. Also, management is really concerned about job performance. This is the "bottom line," to use the financial analyst's term. People with different personalities may be equally effective in job performance. Numerical scoring gives an illusion of precision that is really unfounded. The rating scale technique is also subject to the well-known errors of *halo effect, leniency or strictness, central tendency,* and *interpersonal bias.* These are described later under "Problems in Rating."

Job Dimension Scales. The job dimension technique requires that a different set of scales be constructed for each job or job family. The dimensions or factors used are taken from the job description. Each factor is a major job duty or responsibility. Thus, for a secretary, job dimensions might be: take dictation and transcribe, type letters and reports, schedule appointments and meetings, receive visitors, maintain petty cash fund, arrange hotel and travel reservations. Figure 10-2 is a job dimension rating form for an industrial nurse. Dimensional scales share many of the same strengths and weaknesses of trait and behavior scales. However, they do get away from the trait rating

[5]Stanley E. Seashore, B. P. Indik, and B. S. Georgopoulos, "Relationships Among Criteria of Job Performance," *Journal of Applied Psychology,* Vol. 44, No. 3 (June 1960), pp. 195–202.

FIGURE 10-1 A Conventional Rating Scale Form Using Five Discrete Steps for Each Factor Being Rated.

Job Knowledge

1	2	3	4	5
Serious gaps in his knowledge of essentials of job	Satisfactory knowledge of routine aspects of job	Adequately informed on most phases of job	Good knowledge of all phases of job	Excellent understanding of his job. Extremely well informed

Judgment

1	2	3	4	5
Decisions often wrong or ineffective	Judgment often sound but makes some errors	Good decisions resulting from sound analysis of factors	Sound, logical thinker	Consistently makes sound decisions, even on complex issues

Oral and Written Communication

1	2	3	4	5
Unable to express ideas clearly. Often misunderstood	Expresses ideas satisfactorily on routine topics	Generally expresses thoughts adequately	Consistently expresses thoughts clearly	Outstanding in written and oral expression

Attitude

1	2	3	4	5
Uncooperative, resents suggestions, no enthusiasm	Often cooperates, often accepts suggestions	Satisfactory cooperation, accepts new ideas	Responsive, cooperates well, helpful to others	Excellent in cooperation, welcomes new ideas, very helpful and enthusiastic

Quantity of Work

1	2	3	4	5
Falls below minimum requirements	Usually meets minimum requirements	Satisfactory quantity	Usually well exceeds minimum	Consistently produces superior quantity

Quality of Work

1	2	3	4	5
Poor quality, many errors or rejects	Quality usually o.k. Some errors or rejects	Satisfactory quality	Quality exceeds normal standards	Consistent high quality work

Overall Evaluation

1	2	3	4	5
Poor	Fair	Satisfactory	Good	Excellent

problem because they focus directly upon job duties. The rater is not asked to judge personality factors. Because a separate form must be created for each job it is more practical to use this technique in those organizations that have many employees in a very few job titles. Municipal police and fire departments would fit this criterion as would a district sales office or a restaurant.

Behaviorally Anchored Rating Scales. The behaviorally anchored rating scale technique (BARS) is quite new. Development work by psychologists has been going on since the 1960s.

Performance Appraisal and Management by Objectives

FIGURE 10-2 Dimensionalized Rating Scale for Industrial Nurse.

JOB DIMENSION	Excellent	Good	Satisfactory	Fair	Poor
Render first aid and treat job injuries and illnesses.					
Operate therapy equipment.					
Provide medication for minor ailments such as colds and headaches.					
Teach first-aid classes.					
Dispense safety glasses.					
Maintain inventory of medical supplies and safety glasses.					
Keep records of treatment rendered.					
Drive automobile to transport employees to hospital.					

The technique has considerable promise. It appears to overcome some of the problems inherent in regular or conventional rating scales. Because it is new and because considerable time and effort are required to construct a BARS, the technique has not been used much in industry as yet.[6]

A separate rating form must be developed for each job or job family. The rating form contains job factors or dimensions that are specific for each different job. Each job dimension contains seven or nine anchors which are specific statements that illustrate actual job performance.

---

[6]For explanations of development work and research into this method see: P. C. Smith and L. M. Kendall, "Retranslation of Expectations: An Approach to the Construction of Unambiguous Anchors for Rating Scales," *Journal of Applied Psychology*, Vol. 47 (1963), pp. 149–155; L. Fogli, C. L. Hulin, and M. R. Blood, "Development of First-Level Behavioral Job Criteria," *Journal of Applied Psychology*, Vol. 55 (1971), pp. 3–8.

To develop a BARS the active participation of the job holders and their supervisors is most desirable. First, the key job dimensions or areas of responsibility must be identified. Second, the job holders and their supervisors are asked to describe a great many examples of actual job behavior that pertain to various degrees of job performance. Third, these examples or incidents are classified under the various job dimensions or areas of responsibility. Fourth, these knowledgeable people are asked to rate each item of job behavior by assigning it a number on a scale from 1 to 7 or 1 to 9. A "1" would indicate the lowest level of job performance and a "7" or "9" would show the highest level. Then the average scale value for each incident of behavior is computed. If there is little agreement among raters on the scoring of particular items, then these are eliminated. The final seven or nine items of behavior (with their scores) become the anchors for each job dimension.

Figure 10-3 is the BARS for the job dimension "supervising sales personnel" for rating department managers in a retail store. In this situation comparable behaviorally anchored scales were prepared for the other eight job dimensions which were: handling customer complaints, meeting deadlines, merchandise ordering, developing special promotions, assessing sales trends, using company systems, communicating relevant information, and diagnosing problems.

An advantage of BARS is that the scales with anchor points are directly applicable to the jobs being evaluated. This aids feedback to the job holders for performance improvement and reinforcement for appropriate behavior. Because of employee participation in development they are better able to accept the feedback. Also the procedure for constructing the scales yields anchors that are very job specific and concrete. This contrasts with the often vague traits used in conventional rating scales.

On the other hand it is costly and time consuming to create BARS. It has been claimed that interrater reliability (that is, the degree to which

FIGURE 10-3 A Behaviorally Anchored Rating Scale for the Job Dimension "Supervising Sales Personnel" for a Department Manager of a Store. *From: J. P. Campbell, R. Arvey, M. D. Dunnette, and L. V. Hellervik, "The Development and Evaluation of Behaviorally Based Rating Scales." Journal of Applied Psychology, Vol. 57, No. 1 (1973), p. 17. Copyright 1973 by the American Psychological Association. Reprinted by permission.*

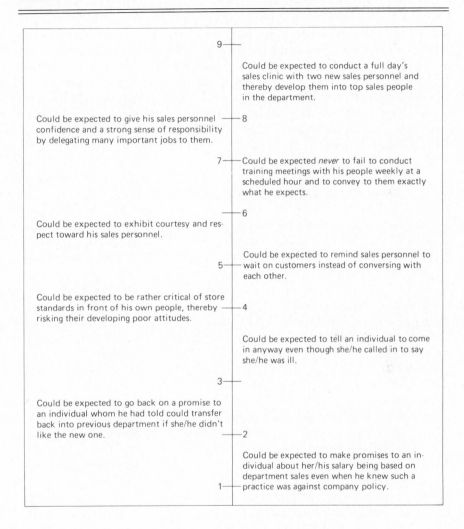

different raters agree upon the proper assessment for a given set of appraisees) for BARS is better than for conventional rating scales. However, a review of several research studies has yielded mixed results in this regard. Likewise the results of leniency error investigations for BARS compared with conventional rating scales have been mixed.[7] Thus we can say that BARS

[7] D. P. Schwab, H. G. Heneman III, and T. A. De Cotiis, "Behaviorally Anchored Rating Scales: A Review of the Literature," *Journal of Applied Psychology*, Vol. 28, No. 4 (Winter 1975), pp. 549–562.

holds promise but more development work needs to be done.

Management by Objectives

Management by objectives (MBO) has enjoyed wide acceptance in recent years. In fact, it has emerged as the most frequently used method for the appraisal of managers at all levels.[8] Because MBO is so very different in concept from the other evaluation methods we will discuss it later in the chapter after we have had an opportunity to explore problems that seem to be inherent in these other techniques.

Interpersonal Comparisons

Ranking. The ranking method requires the rater, who is usually the supervisor, to rank subordinates on an overall or global basis according to their job performance and value to the organization. Thus, someone must end up as low person on the totem pole and someone must be high person. One aid to this ranking process is to have raters choose the best and poorest performers first. Then they can select the best and poorest of the remaining employees and so on until all of the group has been evaluated. This is called *alternative ranking.*

Another ranking plan is to have raters group ratees into, say, the lowest third, the middle third (average performance), and the highest third.

The *paired-comparison* technique is basically a very organized way of obtaining a rank-order listing of employees. It necessitates the comparison of each employee with every other employee, one at a time.

[8]Robert I. Lazer and Walter S. Wikstrom, *Appraising Managerial Performance: Current Practices and Future Directions* (Report No. 723), (New York: The Conference Board, 1977), p. 22. In this survey the essay method was second in frequency of usage and rating scales third.

An employee's standing in the final rank-order list is based upon the number of times he or she is chosen over the other individual in all the paired comparisons. If there are N employees to be rated, then $N(N-1)/2$ separate comparisons must be made.

A major weakness of the ranking method is that it does not reveal the amount of difference between persons in adjacent ranks. Also, the technique does not consider specific components of behavior. Only the whole person is judged. There are not standards of performance. In addition it is difficult to integrate the rankings across several departments.

Forced Distribution. The forced distribution procedure has been designed to prevent supervisors from clustering their employees at the high end of the scale. Clustering at the high end has been a persistent problem, for example, in performance rating of military officers in the U.S. armed forces. Forced distribution also avoids clustering around the midpoint, as occurs in some organizations.

The rater is required to distribute ratings in a pattern to conform to a normal frequency distribution (or some other arbitrary distribution). Typically each supervisor must allocate 10 per cent to the highest category, 20 per cent to the next, 40 per cent to the middle bracket, 20 per cent to the below-average bracket, and 10 per cent to the bottom grouping.

The forced distribution technique is based upon questionable reasoning. It would be a coincidence indeed if the *actual* distribution of performances in any given department conformed to a normal curve or any other arbitrarily set distribution. This technique brings to mind the college statistics professor who was teaching a graduate class of only four students. At the beginning of the semester she announced that there would be one A granted, two C's, and one F, and this is exactly how she assigned the grades at the completion of the course!

Check List

Although a check list could be either *unweighted* (no score assigned to each statement) or *weighted*, the weighted technique is the more useful of the two methods.

A weighted check list contains a large number of statements which describe various aspects of behavior that can occur in the job for which it has been designed. Each statement has a weight or score attached to it. In appraising an individual's performance, the rater checks those statements which accurately portray the behavior of the employee. Generally the check list given to the rater does not show the item weights. The scoring is done in the personnel office.

The weighted check list makes the supervisor think in terms of very specific aspects of behavior. However, the method is costly to install because a separate list must be constructed for every job or job family.

Essay

In the essay method the rater describes the performance, traits, and behavior of the employee. The essay can be completely free flowing but more commonly the personnel office devises a form which asks each supervisor to answer in his own words such general questions as the strengths and weaknesses of the employee, leadership ability, technical effectiveness, promotion potential, and development needs. Very often the essay method is combined with the conventional rating scale form.

To do a sound job of appraisal, the supervisor must devote considerable time and thought to writing the analysis. This is both a virtue and a defect of the essay method. On the other hand it induces the rater to be observant in order to obtain sufficient information to write essay descriptions. However, the technique demands more time than the average supervisor can (or will) spend. Also, the employee may receive a weak rating in comparison with others simply because the supervisor is a poor writer.

Critical Incident

In developing the critical incident system in a company, the major performance factors that are important for each broad grouping of jobs (e.g. sales, supervision, technician jobs) are first identified by persons who have close knowledge of the work. Then the supervisor is given a notebook containing these performance categories. Frequently throughout the year the supervisor must directly observe and record examples of behavior under the categories that indicate effective or successful action and those that show ineffective or poor performance.

This technique is a variant of the essay method. The rater obtains a great many specific examples of behavior so that written evaluations for each factor can be factually documented. Vague generalities are avoided. This procedure can provide a sound basis for feedback to the individual and is thus valuable for developmental purposes.

A danger of this method is the very real possibility that it can lead to overly close supervision, with the boss "breathing down the necks" of people. It may give the employees the impression that everything they do will be recorded in the boss's "little black book."

PROBLEMS IN RATING

Being conducted by humans, performance appraisal is frequently subject to a number of errors and weaknesses. Certain of these errors are more common in some appraisal methods than others, as will be revealed by the discussion to follow.

Halo Effect

The halo effect is the tendency of most raters to let the rating they assign to one characteristic excessively influence their rating on all subsequent traits. Many supervisors tend to give an employee approximately the same rating on all factors. The rating-scale technique is particularly susceptible to the halo effect. One way of minimizing its influence is to have the supervisor judge all of his subordinates on a single factor or trait before going on to the next factor. In this way he can consider all of the employees relative to a standard or to each other on each trait.

Leniency or Strictness

Some supervisors have a tendency to be liberal in their ratings; that is, they assign consistently high values or scores to their people. This is a very common error in rating programs. Somewhat less common, but equally damaging to the usefulness of appraisals, is the tendency of some supervisors to give consistently low ratings. Both of these trends can arise from varying standards of performance among supervisors and from different interpretations of what they observe in employee performance. It is due to the subjectiveness of mankind. It can be partially overcome by holding meetings or training sessions for the raters so that they can reach common agreement on just what they expect. Of course, if the employees in Department A are consistently judged higher than those in Department B, it is difficult to determine whether this reflects true differences in their abilities and contributions or whether it simply reveals leniency on the part of one manager and strictness on the part of another.

Central Tendency

Some raters are reluctant to rate people at the outer ends of the scale. Quite frequently this central tendency is caused by lack of knowledge of the behavior of the persons being rated. The rater knows that management policy dictates that employees be appraised at periodic intervals. But if the rater is unfamiliar with some of the individuals, she or he may play it safe by neither condemning nor praising. The rater would be hard-pressed to substantiate such judgments. As we shall see shortly, under the heading "Organizational Influences," the way in which the appraisal information is handled by higher management sometimes induces supervisors to rate down the middle.

Interpersonal Relations—Bias

How a supervisor feels about each of the individuals working for her or him—personal likes or dislikes—has a tremendous effect upon ratings of their performance. This is especially operative in those situations where objective measures of performance are either not available or difficult to develop.

> In one working group consisting of professional employees in the government, there was a change of directors in charge of the force. A new director was brought in from a distant location when the previous head was promoted to another branch. Within the space of a few months, the new man had completely inverted the ratings of his people. Those who had been rated high by the previous director were rated unsatisfactory by the new man, and vice versa. One man who had been classified lowest in the group because the previous head had considered him unsatisfactory, was promoted to be second in command within the space of eighteen months. Although all the men were sincere, conscientious people, there was a difference in point of view and of personalities between the new director and most of them.

Experimental evidence to demonstrate the powerful force of interpersonal relations has been developed by Kallejian, Brown, and Weschler. In this experiment, which concerned a research and development laboratory, a clinically skilled interviewer interviewed 32 employees regarding their relations with their co-workers and superiors. On the basis of these interviews, the interviewer formulated an evaluation of the personality of the superiors who rated each group of employees. The interviewer then predicted how the superiors actually had rated these people. He did it on the basis of his knowledge of interpersonal relations because he was not familiar with the technical work of the laboratory. When the ratings were correlated with the supervisors' ratings on overall effectiveness the results were accurate at the 3 per cent level of significance. When correlated for 17 specific characteristics of performance, the ratings were accurate at the 5 per cent level of significance.[9]

Organizational Influences

Nowhere is the subjectivity of performance evaluation more glaring than when ratings change according to the way they are going to be used by management. Fundamentally raters tend to take into consideration the end use of the appraisal data when they rate their subordinates. Perhaps this is only natural.

If they know that promotions and pay increases hinge on the ratings, they tend to rate on the high side (they are lenient). Effective supervisors tend to go to bat for their employees. Besides it would look bad for a boss (and relations with subordinates would suffer) if other departments received higher pay increases.

On the other hand, when appraisals are made principally for the development of the employees, supervisors tend to emphasize weaknesses. The whole focus is upon what is wrong with these people and what they have to do to improve.

Actual experience with rating plans has demonstrated that supervisors will rate their

[9]Verne Kallejian, Paula Brown, and I. R. Weschler, "The Impact of Interpersonal Relations on Ratings of Performance," *Public Personnel Review* (October 1953), pp. 166–170.

people near the middle of the spectrum (average) if their bosses put pressure on them to correct the subpar performers (or get rid of them) and if they are called upon to justify a rating of outstanding. In other words they will follow the path of least resistance, because they know that the "big boss" will be demanding of them in relation to those rated low or very high.

Experience has also shown that ratings tend to be higher when supervisors and managers know that they must explain their judgments to their subordinates.

APPRAISAL AND PERSONAL DEVELOPMENT

The appraisal process is quite properly viewed as an integral part of the development of people in the organization. Such development leads to improved job performance and the acquiring of new skills and knowledge by the individual. This can qualify the employee for broader responsibilities, more rewarding assignments, and promotion. A development plan should be tailor-made for each employee (whether he or she be an hourly worker, an engineer, or a manager).

A development plan generally includes the following steps:

1. Analyze job duties and responsibilities. Supervisor and employee discuss these to reach agreement upon these job requirements.
2. Establish standards of job performance. Supervisor discusses these with the employee so that there is common understanding and agreement.
3. Supervisor observes employee performance over a period of time.
4. Appraise the employee. Judge potential for growth and advancement. Compare performance with preestablished standards. Supervisor prepares appraisal report.

5. Supervisor conducts discussion of performance with the employee and shows the employee the appraisal report. Employee expresses his or her viewpoints. Often coaching is carried out informally on a day-to-day basis as supervisor and subordinate interact on the job.
6. Establish a plan for employee development. This may include special assignments and participation in formal training courses. Supervisors can stimulate growth by providing appropriate financial and nonfinancial incentives. Development plans should emphasize strengths upon which the person can build rather than trying to overcome idiosyncrasies of personality.
7. Periodically review progress with employee. Grant proper recognition for accomplishments.

The foregoing process may be conducted with either little employee participation or with substantial involvement. For example, does the subordinate have any say-so in setting the standards of performance or in creating a plan for development? Not only from the standpoint of respect for the dignity of the individual but also to gain commitment, the supervisor ought to involve the subordinates in the decision process.

A keystone of this entire process is the communication between the supervisor and each individual. In the next section we examine the special problems of postappraisal interviews.

Problems with Postappraisal Interviews

Operating supervisors and managers tend to resist postappraisal interviews because of the experiences they have had with them, both with their subordinates and with their superiors when they themselves have been appraised. Let us now look at the typical interview conducted according to the rules laid down in many company manuals.

Usually on an annual basis the boss calls employees into the office one at a time for the appraisal interview. Both parties tend to build up emotionally for this. The boss plans what she is going to say, and the subordinate tends to be apprehensive about what he is going to hear. When the actual interview commences, the supervisor tries to put the individual at ease by talking about the weather, the latest big league ball game, golf, or family. The employee knows this is just an interlude before getting down to serious business. Then the supervisor explains her overall evaluation in broad terms. She initially mentions some good aspects of the employee's performance and may then give the employee a chance to express his views. Next the supervisor speaks of weaknesses and past failures. She allows the employee to explain himself. Then the supervisor explains what steps must be taken to improve performance. She may, at this point, ask for the employee's ideas on improvement. One variation of the procedure above provides an opportunity, before the boss announces her evaluation, for the person to tell how he would rate himself.

Let us now examine the sources of trouble with this approach. In the first place the employee is put on the defensive. He is on the "hot seat" and knows it. When the boss, who is in a position of authority, criticizes him, it is a threat to the employee's self-esteem and integrity. His personal security may even be threatened by the process.

According to Douglas McGregor this conventional approach to the appraisal interview comes very close to a violation of the integrity of the individual. The boss is placed in the position of playing God. He is judging and at times criticizing the personal worth of the employee.[10]

[10]Douglas McGregor, "An Uneasy Look at Performance Appraisal," *Harvard Business Review*, Vol. 35, No. 3 (May–June 1957), pp. 89–94.

There is a tendency for supervisors to criticize those personality traits that annoy them. There is the case of the well-qualified and competent engineer whose boss picked on him in the interview because he did not smile more often. This trait did not affect work performance, and being forty years old he would find it difficult to change anyway. The question may be further explored by asking what right the supervisor had to try to remake this engineer's personality. It is possible that in a few months' time a new supervisor might have been put in charge of this man, and he or she would be perfectly content with his mannerisms.

The subordinate may disagree with the boss's rating and may fight back at the criticism. But knowing the power the superior has over job tenure, he or she will be at a disadvantage in doing so. In any case the interview will become unpleasant for both parties. If the employee is submissive, he or she may simply take the criticism with little visible reaction. The boss may misinterpret this passive behavior and assume the employee fully agrees.

Employees and managers alike often say that they want to know where they stand in the eyes of their superiors. But what they really want is reassurance, approval, and support.

That a postappraisal interview is an emotionally charged experience and even a traumatic one for some is revealed by the following example:

> John, a man of 48, was clearly exhausted emotionally when we met at the restaurant. He had taught at this junior college for two years and had just, this morning, gone through his second appraisal interview with the director. John had been called on the carpet the previous year for the way he organized his courses. This time to prepare himself for the experience he had gone to his minister for words of advice on how to stand up to the criticism. Despite this encouragement and help John was clearly beat when I talked with him. His whole conversation was devoted to the way he had again been raked over the coals by the director.

Most personnel specialists would agree that the purposes of postappraisal interviews are to let subordinates know where they stand in the eyes of the boss, to point out weaknesses so that the person can correct them, to point out strengths, and to show the person how to improve performance. But research evidence shows that things often do not work out as planned. Based upon an investigation in a large industrial corporation that had prided itself for having a sound traditional performance appraisal system, Meyer, Kay, and French found that criticism has a negative effect on achievement of goals and that defensiveness on the part of the subordinate in the face of criticism causes deteriorated performance. In comparing actual interviews containing many criticisms with those having few criticisms it was found that goal achievement was poorer ten to twelve weeks hence for those receiving an above average number of criticisms. High criticism constitutes a threat to one's self-esteem and it prevents a meaningful, constructive relationship between superior and subordinate from emerging.[11]

Approaches and Solutions to Appraisal Interview Problems

Nearly everyone agrees that there should be feedback from supervisors to employees. One of the very important responsibilities of a supervisor is to coach and counsel subordinates. The most fruitful approach to the interview is dependent on the situation, the job, the person, and the goals to be accomplished.

For the New Employee. If an employee is new to the company and relatively inexperi-

[11]H. H. Meyer, E. Kay, and J. R. P. French, Jr., "Split Roles in Performance Appraisal," *Harvard Business Review*, Vol. 43, No. 1 (January–February 1965), pp. 123–129.

enced and untrained, he or she expects to have to learn a great deal before becoming fully qualified and accepted. Most organizations designate the initial learning time as a probationary period. Employees know they are on trial and so do supervisors. If the probationary term is six months in length, the supervisor does not wait until the very end to talk to the person about performance. On the contrary, from the very start a concerted effort has been made to orient the person to the new environment and to train that person properly. In day-to-day contacts the supervisor will coach the employees, give help on methods, techniques, and the details of the job. He or she will guide and mold behavior to conform to the standards of the organization. If all of the foregoing is carried out with proper regard for the rights and feelings of the newcomer, the guidance and correction will be readily accepted. The new employee will be eager to be accepted. So this type of appraisal discussion should in ordinary circumstances pose no great obstacles.

For Other Employees. For trained and experienced employees, for those who have worked for the organization for some time at whatever level they may be (worker or manager), certain general principles can be followed.

The success of the appraisal discussion depends to a large extent upon the climate that management in general and the supervisor in particular have established ahead of time. There must be an atmosphere of confidence and trust. The subordinate must know that the boss is supportive and approving. In this kind of atmosphere, the individual knows that criticism and suggestions for improvement are meant to assist rather than damage.

Prior to the discussion the supervisor must have done a very thorough job of evaluating the person's performance, so that he or she feels confident.

The supervisor must concentrate upon results rather than personality traits. People can readily accept discussion of the objective facts of work schedules, outputs, accomplishments, reports completed, sales made, scrap losses, budgets, profits, and the like. Criticism and discussion of personality traits, mannerisms, and so on are seldom fruitful. Such discussion usually causes resentment. Managers must recognize that a number of employees, each having different personalities, can all achieve satisfactory results. Suggestions for improvement should be directed toward the objective facts of the job. Develop with the individual joint plans for the future. Do not criticize the individual as a person.

The supervisor should try to capitalize upon a person's strengths. This may mean giving full range to a person's assets and skills. If a person is poor at doing detail work but good at assignments where breadth and vision are demanded, then it makes little sense to try to force him to be effective at detail work.

Finally the supervisor must recognize that he or she may have biases, idiosyncrasies, and faulty impressions. His or her concept of how people and things shape up is just one view. His or her concept is not the only one possible. There may be a number of ways of performing work and of reaching job and unit goals.

Frequent Coaching and Guidance. The alert and effective supervisor does not wait until the end of the year to talk to employees about their work and progress. As the needs of the situation dictate, he or she makes it a practice to praise Sarah, who has done a fine job on her assigned project, to find out what help Henry needs because he has fallen behind, and to redirect Joe's seemingly scatter-shot efforts. On these occasions, if he or she deems it desirable, the supervisor may expand the discussion somewhat into other areas of the person's work, interests, and aspirations. Although not labeled as formal appraisal interviews, these conversations serve to regulate the work, motivate the individual, let him or her know where he or she stands, and provide an opportunity for the boss to coach the team members.

MANAGEMENT BY OBJECTIVES

Management by objectives has been designed to overcome certain of the inherent problems of traditional appraisal systems. It really constitutes a new way of managing. A major goal is to enhance the superior-subordinate relationship, strengthen the motivational climate, and improve performance.

The key features of management by objectives are as follows:

1. Superior and subordinate get together and jointly agree upon and list the principal duties and areas of responsibility of the individual's job.
2. The person sets his own short-term performance goals or targets in cooperation with the superior. The superior guides the goal-setting process to insure that it relates to the realities and needs of the organization.
3. They agree upon criteria for measuring and evaluating performance.
4. From time to time, more often than once per year, the superior and subordinate get together to evaluate progress toward the agreed-upon goals. At these meetings new or modified goals are set for the ensuing period.
5. The superior plays a supportive role. He tries, on a day-to-day basis, to help the person reach the agreed-upon goals. He counsels and coaches.
6. In the appraisal process the superior plays less the role of a judge and more the role of one who helps the person attain the goals or targets.
7. The process focuses upon results accomplished and not upon personal traits.

As it is applied in practice, certain variations from the methods, here described, occur. The procedure given here is closest to that formulated by Douglas McGregor.[12] It is also very similar to the work-planning-and-review method developed by a team of behavioral researchers at the General Electric Company.[13] Some writers emphasize that top executives meet with their immediate subordinates in groups to set goals for the company and for the major divisions. This process is carried on down the various echelons of the organization. Also the executives meet privately with their subordinates to establish individual goals.

Targets set can be both quantitative and qualitative. Thus, a manager of manufacturing for the ensuing year might set personal and divisional targets of a reduction in direct costs of 4 per cent, reduction of spoiled product by 2 per cent, and increase of return on investment to 14 per cent. Qualitative goals may be to improve work flow, to institute better on-the-job training, and to improve shop housekeeping.

Figure 10-4 is an example of an MBO worksheet that has been made out jointly by a store manager for a tire and rubber company and his immediate superior. The left-hand column shows six major areas of the store manager's responsibilities. The present levels of performance are shown for each of these six areas. Next are listed the targeted objectives for each area. In this example the time period to reach each goal is one year. Finally, the worksheet shows some plans that have been discussed as possible ways of achieving these agreed-upon goals. In this particular illustration quantitative measures are available for each of the performance areas.

Management by objectives that involves mutual goal setting is most appropriate for tech-

[12]McGregor, op. cit., pp. 89–94. See also Douglas McGregor, *The Human Side of Enterprise* (New York: McGraw-Hill Book Company, 1960), ch. 5.

[13]Meyer, Kay, and French, op. cit., pp. 127–129.

FIGURE 10-4 A Management by Objectives Worksheet for a Tire and Rubber Company Store Manager.

HIGH-PERFORMANCE TIRE & RUBBER COMPANY

Name: _T. M. ROBBINS_   Position: _STORE MANAGER_

Area of Responsibility	Type of Measure	Levels of Performance		Time Period	Plans for Meeting Objectives	Results Achieved
		Present Level	Objective			
1. Retail sales	Units Dollars	350/mo. $25,000/mo.	450/mo. $32,000/mo.	1 year	Increase advertising flyers and newspaper ads. More customer safety checks in shop (tread wear, shocks).	
2. Operating Costs	Dollars	$7,000/mo.	$6,600/mo.	1 year	Control overtime and use of part time help; consolidate merchandise orders; reduce bad debts.	
3. Service Sales (Brakes, exhaust systems, shock absorbers, etc.)	Dollars	$5,500/mo.	$6,500/mo.	1 year	Increase advertising; use discount coupons for state inspections.	
4. Wholesale sales	# of tires	95/mo.	110/mo.	1 year	More contacts with dealers; discount and promotional allowances.	
5. Quality of Service	# of written customer complaints	7/year	3/year	1 year	Better training of mechanics; better scheduling of appointments; handle complaints more promptly.	
6. Safety	# of lost workday injuries	4/year	0/year	1 year	Safety training; maintain equipment better.	

_____   _____
Employee's Signature   _Supervisor's Signature_

_____   _____
Date   _Date_

nical, professional, supervisory, and executive personnel. In these positions there is generally enough latitude and room for discretion to make it possible for the person to participate in setting work goals, tackle new projects, and invent new ways to solve problems. This method is generally not applicable for hourly workers because their jobs are usually too restricted in scope. There is little discretionary opportunity for them to shape their jobs. Their duties, responsibilities, and performance targets are imposed upon them by industrial engineers and supervision.

Management by objectives possesses a number of advantages. By participating in the setting of the goals, the individual acquires a stake or a vested interest in trying to meet them. The General Electric Company research referred to earlier revealed definitely greater accomplishment for those persons who set defined goals than for those who did not.[14] Both the superior and subordinate are on the same team working for a better-functioning group. A person is not rated against a fixed rating scale. Targets and responsibilities are set and evaluated in terms of

[14]Meyer, Kay, and French, op. cit., p. 127.

the particular situation and abilities. Defensive feelings are minimized because the superior is not a judge but a helper. Emphasis is on performance and not personality traits. The emphasis is also upon the present and the future, which can be controlled. In conventional appraisal the focus is upon the past, which cannot be altered.

However, it must be made clear that management by objectives is not a panacea. A highly directive, authoritarian manager may find it difficult if not impossible to lead people in this participative, human-being-centered, supportive style. The subordinate may try to set easily attainable goals in order to look good when meeting with a superior to review progress. If too much weight is placed upon quantifiable goals such as profits, costs, and efficiency, qualitative goals such as investment in human resources (training, health, and morale builders) may be downgraded.

Management by objectives has certain disadvantages when used for allocating salary increases and for promotions. Because goal setting and goal attainment are so individualized it is difficult to compare the performance of one person with another or to a standard to which everybody is held. Remember that in MBO performance standards are personal, not uniform throughout a department. Likewise MBO focuses upon short run goals and their attainment. It does not concentrate upon identification of traits that would qualify one for a new and different job.

Carroll and Tosi have summarized the conclusions of many research investigations into the MBO process. They report that the goal-setting process is highly instrumental in gaining improved subsequent performance. The degree to which performance improves depends upon whether the goals are at the proper level of difficulty for the individual, whether proper time limits are set, and whether the goals are specific. Feedback information on performance is useful when it is timely, specific, and task-relevant. Participation yields greater subordinate acceptance of decisions and with proper leadership

can generate high-quality decisions. Participation must be genuine not manipulative. Legitimate participation tends to yield higher satisfaction and performance.[15]

ISSUES AND PERSPECTIVES

There is widespread acknowledgment among personnel specialists and upper level managers that sound performance appraisal programs can be beneficial to both the organization and the individual. However, there is also general recognition that many appraisal programs contain serious weaknesses. Principal weaknesses are resistance by supervisors to the devoting of adequate time and attention to appraisals, bias and favoritism in making evaluations, lack of reliability and validity in ratings, problems between supervisors and subordinates in discussing and acting upon the appraisals, and the tying of appraisals to the reward system.

Industrial psychologists and personnel specialists have strived mightily over the years to design appraisal systems that would yield good reliability and validity and that could be effectively used by managers. Progress has been made but the ideal system has not been found. The most appropriate system to use is governed by the specific objectives to be achieved. For development of the individual and performance improvement management by objectives has come to be recognized as the best system. MBO is very widely used especially for managerial and professional positions. This system, however, is less useful as an evaluation technique to allocate rewards such as salary increases and promotions where interpersonal comparisons and comparisons against standards must be made.

[15]Stephen J. Carroll, Jr., and Henry L. Tosi, Jr., *Management by Objectives: Applications and Research* (New York: Macmillan Publishing Co., Inc., 1973), ch. 1.

If all categories of employees are considered, the conventional rating scale technique remains most popular. Its weaknesses can be alleviated by careful definition of the factors being rated, concentrating more on performance contributions and less on personality traits, including factors that can be objectively measured where possible, requiring written substantiations of the ratings, and using multiple raters.

Weighted check lists, forced choice, and behaviorally anchored rating scales all have considerable merit; however their acceptance by organizations is impeded greatly by their fairly high cost for development.

The interaction between the supervisor-rater and the subordinate-ratee is a critical part of the appraisal process. The discussion of the subordinate's performance is most effective when the supervisor is supportive, when the parties focus upon job results not personalities, and when there is openness and joint problem solving.

Should subordinates rate their supervisors? This is hardly ever done. In fact the issue itself is ignored in bureaucratic organizations. Yet very positive benefits could be obtained if management would work out procedures by which employees could fill out evaluation forms to rate their supervisors on those aspects of the work that can be directly observed by the subordinates. A prerequisite to success with such a program would be trust and honesty among management and the employees. Because subordinates view their supervisors from a particular perspective and because they may not appreciate all the demands placed upon their supervisors, rating by subordinates should be properly viewed as only part of the input that makes up the total appraisal of the supervisors. Nevertheless it can be a valuable input that is totally ignored in most organizations.

Another issue for consideration is the relation of the annual salary interview and the developmental discussion. Current thinking suggests that appraisal discussions between the manager and his subordinate that are focused upon performance, development, and career goals should be conducted at entirely different times during the year from the discussion concerned with the individual's salary treatment for the ensuing period. The purposes of the two interviews are quite different. For salary administration a manager is normally provided a budgeted amount of money that he or she can allocate among the people in the department. He or she may use various criteria for assigning the different amounts of money. A significant factor is the performance of the employees compared with each other or compared with a standard. When the manager invites each individual into his or her office for the salary discussion, the salary decision has already been made. It has been approved by the manager's boss. If there is disagreement between the manager and and the manager's subordinate as to the amount of salary increase, the manager tends to sell the decision. If the manager were to admit a mistake, he or she would have to go to the boss, acknowledge the error, and ask approval for an upward adjustment.

The atmosphere of the developmental interview should be totally different. Here the manager should be very supportive. There should be a free interchange of plans, suggestions, and goals. Neither party should be put on the defensive. Nor should bargaining for salary occur in a developmental interview.

Questions for Review and Discussion

1. What objective measures can be used to evaluate performance in the following occupations: computer salesperson, development engineer, factory foremen, president of a department store, stenographer?
2. Research studies have rather consistently shown that performance evaluation by one's peers yields good reliability and validity. Yet this appraisal method is rarely used in business or in government. Why do you think this is so?
3. Explain the following:
   a. Halo effect.

b. Central tendency.

c. Leniency or strictness.

How can these problems be overcome?

4. In some organizations the initial wave of enthusiasm upon the installation of a new appraisal program soon subsides. Appraisal forms are filled out by supervisors, filed in personnel folders, and then forgotten. Supervisors rarely conduct appraisal interviews unless a person is doing very poor work. Supervisors look upon appraisal as an extra chore done somehow to satisfy the personnel department. What actions can you suggest to solve these problems?

5. Explain how the interaction and relations between the supervisor and the employee affect the appraisal process and the performance of the employee.

6. For years industrial psychologists have tried to devise new appraisal techniques that will eliminate or reduce rater bias and error. Do you think such a goal can be fully attained? Identify other major problems besides rater bias and error.

7. A long-service professional employee has received good or excellent overall evaluations from all his supervisors. Recently she has been given a poor overall rating by a relatively new supervisor. Give possible explanations for this.

8. Describe management by objectives. How does it differ from traditional appraisal methods? What are its advantages and possible limitations?

CASE PROBLEMS

PROBLEM 1

You are the director of employee relations for the McDavitt Manufacturing Company, which has annual sales of $25 million and total employment of 600. A little, over a year ago you played a prominent role in the installation of a management-by-objectives program in the company. Among the main features of the program are setting of objectives, delineation of areas of accountability, adoption of performance measurement criteria, and appraisal discussions between superior and subordinate. You feel that your own department ought to be a model of the successful application of the program.

About a year ago objectives and plans were developed jointly by yourself and each of your subordinates. You are especially concerned at this time about the performance of the safety director, Henry Phillips. He has responsibility for organizing and directing the safety and health program. In carrying out his responsibilities he must work in close cooperation with the managers of the operating departments. Among the key components of the safety and health program are policies and procedures, engineering and hazard elimination, industrial hygiene, safety education and training, accident investigation and analysis, rules enforcement, and first-aid treatment.

Henry Phillips had been appointed safety director about a year and a half ago. At that time the accident frequency and severity rates were 60 per cent above the industry average and an inspector from the Occupational Safety and Health Administration had cited the company for several serious violations of federal standards. When you held your first objectives-setting discussion with Phillips nearly a year ago, he had already made substantial progress toward improving the safety and health performance of the company. However, a great deal remained to be accomplished. At that time sound safety and health attitudes and behavior had not yet permeated all segments of management.

Shown below are the jointly established objectives set one year ago and the actual results achieved as of last month:

Objectives	Results
1. Reduce number of lost workday cases incidence rate per 100 workers from 4.7 to 3.5.	Reduction to 4.2
2. Reduce the lost workdays rate (severity) per 100 workers from 85 to 65.	Reduction to 75.
3. Personally conduct monthly safety meetings with plant supervision.	Goal has been met.
4. Insure that plant supervisors conduct short biweekly safety meetings with their people.	Only about 50 per cent of meetings have been held.
5. Reduce health and safety grievances from 2 per month to 1 in 3 months.	Grievances average 1 per month.
6. Revise and update policy and procedure manual.	Completed.
7. Work with engineering department to correct noxious fumes in processing department.	Project initiated and one quarter completed.

You feel that Henry Phillips has the requisite job knowledge for his responsibilities. He performs well in developing plans, programs, and procedures, and in diagnosing problems. However, you feel that he should be more aggressive in selling his ideas to operating managers and in getting them to improve the safety performance of their units.

Henry Phillips will be coming to your office in about a half hour for an appraisal discussion.

Questions
1. How would you conduct the interview? What would you say? Work out a plan for this interview.
2. Role play this interview. Henry Phillips's viewpoint upon commencing the interview is that he has worked very hard during the past year to achieve the goals agreed upon and has made good progress. However, his efforts have suffered from a lack of full cooperation from many of the mangers and supervisors in the operating departments. Safety and health of workers are usually given a low priority in competition with production and cost reduction goals.

PROBLEM 2

Ralph V., age 39, mill manager for The Pulp and Paper Company, arrived at his office on Friday morning as usual. Shortly after his arrival he received a telephone call from Mr. Jenkins, the executive vice-president of the company, asking him to come immediately to his office. Once in Mr. Jenkins' office, he was informed that he was being discharged effective as of the end of that day. Mr. Jenkins stated that he had been dissatisfied with Ralph V.'s performance for a long time and had been contemplating this move for many months. Ralph V. was stunned and visibly shaken. He protested that he did not believe his work had been unsatisfactory and that he had worked many long hours over the past five years to meet the multitude of problems encountered in running the mill. Mr. Jenkins stated that his decision was final. In fact a new mill manager had recently been hired to take Ralph V.'s place. The new man was going to report on the following Monday. Acknowledging the abruptness of this termination, Mr. Jenkins offered the mill manager six weeks' pay as a separation allowance.

Ralph had originally been hired five years previous as assistant mill manager. He was promoted to mill manager after one year when the old manager retired. The mill manager was in charge of all paper-manufacturing operations in a mill employing 500 people. The functions of operations, maintenance, production control, and quality control were under his jurisdiction. Organizationally, the mill manager reported to the vice-president of the fine paper division, who in turn reported to the executive vice-president of the corporation. Ralph V. had originally been hired from the outside by Mr. Jenkins. He came well recommended.

A few days later in discussing Ralph V. and his termination the personnel manager said privately:

> He was a very affable guy. Very talkative and outgoing. He was popular with his foremen. Whenever I visited his office on business I found it difficult to get away because he had so many stories to tell that did not really relate to the job. Ralph also took pride in counseling and coaching foremen, group leaders, and hourly workers. There was many a man who probably should have been discharged for poor work or violation of plant rules whom Ralph reformed and saved for the company. Ralph "cooked his own goose," however, when he got into a serious argument with his immediate boss, Jake Richards, the vice-president of the division, about a year ago. Ralph was hired originally by the executive vice-president and he reported to him before Richards was employed. The new vice-president of the fine paper division was hired a little over a year ago to give the division more managerial attention and improve its profit picture. He became Ralph's immediate boss.

The director of engineering in commenting upon the situation made the following remarks:

> Ralph was just not on top of things. He tended to have a continuous stream of people in his office to get decisions on production problems and also to talk about social matters and trivia. He was active in various fraternal and civic organizations

in town and spent a great deal of time on the telephone handling these matters. In fact he also lost some normal job time handling these outside affairs.

He was lax about planning, anticipating problems, and knowing what was going on in his own mill. Oftentimes the foremen would run the production lines at only half or three-quarter speed because of troubles with the equipment or the product. Yet this could go on for a whole day or two and he would be unable to diagnose the cause of the trouble. Again, quality of the paper coming off the machines might be low, and Ralph would not take prompt corrective action. Also there were recurring problems with maintenance and housekeeping.

However, I do say that many of the problems in the mill were not fully Ralph's fault. He was not given the essential services he required to run a tight ship. He should have had more support from higher management.

One of the long-service superintendents in the mill made these remarks about two months later:

Things aren't noticeably different under the new mill manager than they were under Ralph. The new man has many good ideas, but we still have frequent breakdowns of equipment, bottlenecks, and quality problems. I think Ralph was the "fall guy" for all that's wrong around here. Many of us have been wondering who is going to be fired next. I understand Jake Richards was determined to get rid of Ralph and never made an effort to help him.

The discharged mill manager, Ralph, was interviewed privately at lunch about two weeks later. He made these remarks:

I'm somewhat bitter about this whole thing. I was never given any real signals that this was coming. I had been in Mr. Jenkins's office just a few days before that Friday morning talking about various production matters. He did not act unusual at that time. As a matter of fact I always got along fine with Jenkins. I will agree that on a couple of occasions in the past he told me that he was displeased with production levels in the mill. But I did not take that to mean any strong criticism because he knew (or I thought he knew) that I was trying to run the operation with some equipment that was old and subject to serious breakdowns. Besides he didn't always let me hire the people I needed. I had very few foremen who were fully qualified.

I understand they hired my replacement behind my back and had been negotiating for months to get him.

I think Jake Richards was working on Jenkins for a long time to have him fire me—that is ever since he and I had the squabble about my refusing to fire one of the group leaders about a year ago.

Questions
1. Evaluate the way in which Ralph was discharged.
2. Would you antitipate that the new mill manager would have any special problems upon commencing his new job? Discuss.
3. What do you think of the method top management adopted to assure continuity of operations, namely, timing the hiring of the new manager to coincide with the discharge of the old one?

4. If an executive is performing unsatisfactorily, what action should his immediate superior take?
5. Should a manager have due process appeal rights? Why? How?

MBO EXERCISE

A purpose of this exercise is to provide students an opportunity to learn how to develop performance objectives jointly by working with an individual job holder (student). Other purposes are to learn ways of measuring or evaluating job performance and to learn how to design an MBO worksheet that could be used in a real organizational situation.

Divide the class into groups of about 5–6 persons each. After each group is formed the members describe to one another a job that they have held or now hold. Then the group selects one person's job to be used for this MBO exercise. The group will interview the job holder and prepare an MBO worksheet.

The group should explore with the job holder the major responsibility areas of the job. A method for measuring or evaluating performance in each area should be identified. To enhance objectivity in performance evaluation it is advantageous to use quantitative measures of performance wherever possible. However some job components cannot be measured quantitatively so qualitative gauges to performance must be used.

Next, the current level of performance in each area of responsibility should be recorded. The reasonable performance targets or objectives for the future should be jointly decided with the job holder. A time period (6 months, 9 months, one year, etc.) for achieving each objective should be agreed upon. There should be some discussion of possible ways of achieving each objective.

Each group should design and hand into the instructor an MBO worksheet. Figure 10-4 may be used as a guide.

Suggestions for Further Reading

Beer, Michael. "Performance Appraisal: Dilemmas and Possibilities," *Organizational Dynamics,* Vol. 9, No. 3 (Winter 1981), pp. 24–36.

Carroll, Stephen J. Jr., and Craig E. Schneier. *Performance Appraisal and Review Systems.* Glenview, Ill.: Scott, Foresman, and Co., 1983.

Cascio, Wayne F., and H. John Bernardin. "Implications of Performance Appraisal Litigation for Personnel Decisions," *Personnel Psychology,* Vol. 34, No. 2 (Summer 1981), pp. 221–226.

Cederblom, Douglas. "The Performance Appraisal Interview: A Review, Implications, and Suggestions," *Academy of Management Review,* Vol. 7, No. 2 (April 1982), pp. 219–227.

Cummings, L. L., and Donald P. Schwab. *Performance in Organizations*. Glenview, Ill.: Scott, Foresman and Co., 1973.

Giglioni, G. B., J. B. Giglioni, and J. A. Bryant. "Performance Appraisal: Here Comes the Judge," *California Management Review*, Vol. XXIV, No. 2 (Winter 1981), pp. 14–23.

Kleiman, Lawrence S., and Richard L. Durham. "Performance Appraisal, Promotion, and the Courts: A Critical Review," *Personnel Psychology*, Vol. 34, No. 1, (Spring 1981), pp. 103–121.

Latham, Gary P., and Kenneth N. Wexley. *Increasing Productivity Through Performance Appraisal*, Reading, Mass: Addison-Wesley Publishing Co., 1981.

Patten, Thomas H., Jr. *A Manager's Guide to Performance Appraisal: Pride, Prejudice, and the Law of Equal Opportunity*. New York: The Free Press, 1982.

11 Career Development

Traditionally employing organizations did little or nothing to help employees plan and develop their careers. The personnel management program focused primarily upon the needs of the organization in hiring, placing, transferring, promoting, and laying off people. This state of affairs has been changing in recent years.

Starting in the 1970s there has been concern by managers, employees, scholars, and public policy makers with improving the quality of working life. Working men and women, especially those who are young and those who possess postsecondary education, have expressed desires for meaningful jobs, increased personal freedom, better opportunities, and more say-so in matters affecting them in the workplace. Public policy in the area of equal employment opportunity has been causing companies to give greater attention to training and promotion opportunities for ethnic minorities and women.

In very recent years leading professionals in the field of human resource management have been creating career development designs and programs. There is a growing body of solid literature in the field of careers, career planning, and career management. Some of our leading corporations have set up career development programs. Among these are General Electric,

Xerox, TRW, 3M Company, and Travelers Insurance Company.

Some organizations have concentrated their career development efforts upon management personnel only. But they would do well to broaden their activities to include nonmanagement employees. These comprise 80 to 90 per cent of the total people in the typical organization. These people have development needs and aspirations, they experience transfers and promotions, and they often need to acquire new skills. They are essential to the success of any organization and they ought not to be neglected.

Why Have a Career Development Program?

There are several cogent reasons which explain why employers ought to establish career development programs. Whereas only the well-financed and larger organizations may have the resources and expertise to operate full-blown programs, even smaller companies can carry out simplified but effective programs. We shall address the situation of the smaller company later. The following are important reasons for adopting career development programs:

1. *Equal Employment Opportunity.* In order to provide better opportunities for minorities and women to move up in their organizations from entry level jobs, the Equal Employment Opportunity Commission and the Office of Federal Contract Compliance Programs of the Department of Labor have been requiring organizations to identify career paths and eliminate barriers to upgrading for minorities and women.

2. *Quality of Working Life.* Employees, especially younger ones, express desires to obtain greater control over their own careers. They are less willing than earlier generations of employees to simply accept the roles and assignments given them at the convenience of management. They want greater job satisfaction and more career options.

3. *Competition for High-Talent Personnel.* Highly educated professionals and managers often give preference in selecting a company for which to work to those that are supportive of their career aspirations and have career development programs.

4. *Avoid Obsolescence, New Skills.* Rapid changes in technology, demographic changes, ups and downs in the economy, and changes in consumer demand can render obsolete the skills that employees in various occupations have acquired, often through years of training. Career development programs can assist individuals in anticipating changes and can help them gain new skills for which there is a real demand.

5. *Retention of Personnel.* By instituting career development programs in their organizations, management may reduce turnover of employees caused by frustration of individual career ambitions.

6. *Improved Utilization of Personnel.* Too often people are kept in jobs which they have outgrown or which are dead-end assignments. Performance is better when people are placed in jobs they like and which fit their ambitions.

CAREER DEVELOPMENT PROCESSES AND CONCEPTS

A career is a lifelong sequence of jobs integrated with the attitudes and motives of the person as he or she engages in these work roles. It is important to understand that a career is more than a group of jobs held by a person during his lifetime. It also consists of the training the individual follows in preparation for work roles and the aims, hopes, ambitions, and feelings in regard to these work roles. In this book we are primarily concerned with paid jobs in a company, nonprofit organization, or governmental agency. However, a career, broadly speaking, can also comprise unpaid work such as homemaking or volunteer activities in the community.

One's career has importance for several reasons. It helps to establish the individual's identity and status. A career provides meaning and focus for one's life. Because most jobs are performed in proximity to others, work takes on a social meaning as well. Work can provide an opportunity for satisfying the employee's desire for recognition and achievement. Of course, one's job is also instrumental in providing money to obtain the necessities and luxuries for living.

Career Stages

Van Maanen and Schein have described the major stages of a typical persons's career.[1] Their stages are expressed in broad terms.

1. *Exploration stage*

[1]John Van Maanen and Edgar H. Schein, "Career Development," appearing as Chapter 2 in J. Richard Hackman and J. Lloyd Suttle, *Improving Life at Work* (Santa Monica, Cal.: Goodyear Publishing Co., Inc., 1977), pp. 54–57.

Occupational images are obtained from mass media, books, and movies. Advice and example are provided by parents and teachers. The individual makes self-assessment of his or her strengths and weaknesses. Each person makes a choice of educational path through school and college (or many do). The individual tests his or her ability to work and accomplish real vocational tasks.

2. *Establishment stage (early career)*
   a. Job seeking, getting hired
   b. Induction and orientation
   c. First job assignment

   Often the new employee experiences reality shock at substages (b) and (c). She or he faces unfulfilled expectations, anxiety, and disillusionment in early job experiences. The employee must demonstrate performance. Often early assignments are hard, dirty, or unpleasant.

   d. Leveling off, transfer, and/or promotion

   Supervisor tells employee he or she is succeeding or failing. If succeeding the person acquires feeling of competence and commitment to organization. If failing, he or she experiences insecurity and anxiety. May have to look for another job.

   e. Granting of tenure

   If tenure is granted the person feels happy. He or she has "made it."

3. *Maintenance stage*
   a. Mid-career

   Person is given more important work assignments. This is a period of maximum productivity and value to the organization. Individual feels sense of personal growth and feels secure in his role.

   b. Late career

   Job assignments utilize individual's wisdom, perspective, and judgment. May teach younger employees. Person may face threats to his or her position from younger, better-trained, and more aggressive employees. In late portion of mid-career stage or early part of late-career

stage the person must work out his or her "midlife crisis." The person adjusts ambitions and goals to be realistic with what can be accomplished in the years remaining.

4. *Decline stage*

   Planning for retirement. Learning to accept a reduced role. New accommodations to family, friends, and community.

Career Success

Traditionally career success has been defined by people as having a job paying a good salary, having high occupational status, and moving upward to positions of greater responsibility, pay, influence, and prestige. The employee and manager alike have been expected to be committed to the organization. It has been assumed that if employees did a good job and were loyal, then management would reward them with job security, benefits, promotions, and respect. This traditional "organization man" orientation has been very widespread.

However, Hall and other authorities on career development have observed that many people nowadays—employees, professionals, and managers—have adopted a somewhat different orientation for themselves. The essence of this newer mode of thinking about one's career is personal freedom, self-determination, and a personal view of success. We will call this the *personal fulfillment* career orientation. Here are the main features of this newer pattern of thinking about career satisfaction:

1. The individual tries to control his or her own career development. The person, decides whether to acquire additional training, to seek particular jobs, and perhaps, to move out of the organization.
2. Freedom, growth, and self-determination are important personal values.

3. The person seeks a healthy balance among job, organization, family, friends, and recreation. He is not a "workaholic."
4. Success is personally defined. This may include the traditional goals of money, advancement, and prestige but it also may include self-fulfillment, self-respect, strong friendship ties, and happiness gained through off-the-job activities.
5. The person is not passive and compliant. He or she plots his or her own course through life. He or she is not a conforming, organization man. Rather, he or she is mobile and assumes full responsibility for his or her own destiny.[2]

Career Development

We shall now examine the meaning of the term *career development* along with its two components, which are career planning and career management.

Career development is the planning of one's career and the implementation of career plans by means of education, training, job search and acquisition, and work experiences. If we look at the process more from the perspective of the organization, then career development is the process of guiding the placement, movement, and growth of employees through assessment, planned training activities, and planned job assignments.

Career planning is a subset of career development. It is the personal process of planning one's work-life. This includes evaluating one's abilities and interests, examining career opportunities, setting career goals, and planning appropriate developmental activities. Although career planning is mainly an individual process,

the employing organization can assist through career counseling offered by the personnel staff and the supervisors, through workshops to assist the people in evaluating themselves and in deciding upon developmental programs, through career-planning workbooks made available to interested employees, and through the dissemination of information about jobs within the organization and outside the organization.

Career management is the other subset of career development. Whereas career planning is primarily a personal process, career management focuses more upon plans and activities done by the organization. In career management the management of the organization matches individual employee career plans with organizational needs and implements programs to accomplish these joint objectives. The personnel department plays a central role in orchestrating this entire process. Individual career plans are related to the organization's human resource inventory and needs forecast. Management designs career paths. It provides information about job openings and makes career counseling available to the employees. Employee performance and potential are assessed. Management supports education and training programs. It provides for employee development on the job.

Figure 11-1 is a chart showing the content of career planning and career management and showing these as the two components of career development. The arrow connecting the two blocks signifies that career planning and career management are interrelated processes.

CAREER PLANNING

The steps in the career-planning process are: (1) Appraise one's self; (2) Identify opportunities; (3) Set goals; (4) Prepare plans; (5) Implement plans. Let us examine each of these steps.

---

[2]Hall calls this mode the Protean career (after Proteus in Greek mythology). See Douglas T. Hall. *Careers in Organizations* (Pacific Palisades, Cal.: Goodyear Publishing Co., Inc. 1976), pp. 200–203.

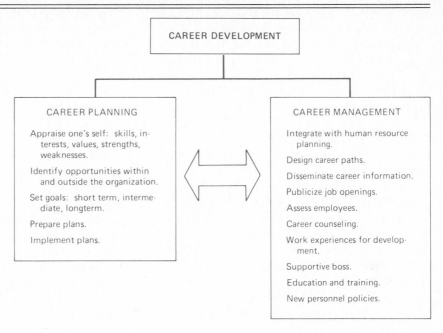

FIGURE 11-1 The Contents of Career Planning and Career Management as Components of Career Development.

CAREER DEVELOPMENT

CAREER PLANNING

Appraise one's self: skills, interests, values, strengths, weaknesses.

Identify opportunities within and outside the organization.

Set goals: short term, intermediate, longterm.

Prepare plans.

Implement plans.

CAREER MANAGEMENT

Integrate with human resource planning.

Design career paths.

Disseminate career information.

Publicize job openings.

Assess employees.

Career counseling.

Work experiences for development.

Supportive boss.

Education and training.

New personnel policies.

Self-appraisal

The starting point of career planning is get to know oneself. What kind of a person am I? What skills do I possess? What are my values and interests? What do I like to do? What do I dislike? What are my strengths and limitations?

Various self-directed career-planning workbooks are available to help people assess themselves.[3] These contain text material plus exercises. A good introductory exercise is to ask the individual to write his own obituary as he would like it to appear x years hence upon death. The individual is asked to write down what he would like others to remember him by? What did he always want to do but never found time or opportunity to do? What are his life and career concerns?

[3]Examples are: Walter D. Storey, *Career Dimensions I and Career Dimensions II* (Crotonville, N.Y.: General Electric Company, 1976); Bernard Haldane, *Career Satisfaction and Success* (New York: AMACOM, 1974); A. G. Kirn, *Lifework Planning* (Hartford: Arthur G. Kirn & Associates, 1974).

Another exercise to assist in self-analysis requires the person to identify his or her strengths and weaknesses in regard to technical, interpersonal, communications, administrative, and personal skills. He is then asked to indicate the degree of importance he attaches to such job characteristics as autonomy, security, affiliation with others, financial rewards, and influence over others. Next is asked to describe jobs he has held that are most and least rewarding. Finally, he is asked to describe his ideal next job.

Another means of finding out information about oneself is to take aptitude and vocational interest tests. These are administered by career counseling centers at schools and colleges.

Identify Opportunities

One's skills, interests, and values should be related to career opportunities. Although some would argue that there is always room for one more good person in a declining occupation,

Career Development

235

those choosing this course of action ought to recognize they will have a "tough row to hoe." This course is like trying to swim upstream. It is a good idea to study trends in the economy, population demographics, technology, and public policy because these shape the future job market. The aerospace program of the 1960s, for example, caused a high demand for physicists. A change in public policy in the 1970s caused a drastic decline in demand for persons trained in this profession.

In the society at large an excellent source of occupational information is the *Occupational Outlook Handbook*, prepared by the U.S. Department of Labor. A new edition is published biennially. Also many technical and professional societies publish information about careers in their specialties.

The personnel office should publish information regarding jobs within the organization. This can take the form of organization charts, lists of titles and actual description of jobs classifed according to pay level, department, and location. The personnel office also should publish the requisite qualifications for each of these jobs. Job openings, as they occur, can be announced through bulletin board notices and interoffice announcements.

Opportunities within one's organization are influenced by the growth or contraction of the business, company policy regarding employee development and promotion from within, and internal office politics. Are people promoted on the basis of performance or on the basis of interpersonal politics and influence maneuvering?

Set Goals

After the individual has appraised personal strengths, weaknesses, interests, and values and after obtaining knowledge of job trends and opportunities, career goals can be properly established. This will require the setting of short-term, intermediate, and long-term goals. Goals that lead to growth should be challenging so that the individual gains new skills and outlooks. The goals should be consistent with one's capabilities and compatible with one's self-image.

Prepare Plans

In thinking through the measures one will need to take to meet one's goals it is advisable to consult with one's supervisor and with the responsible member of the personnel department. Plans may be made for any of various actions designed to achieve the career goals. Reasonably one ought to start with feasible short-term on-the-job learning experiences and useful off-the-job training activities. As success is achieved on the early activities, bigger and longer run developmental projects can be tackled. The planning should take into account the special needs of the person such as skills and experiences required to reach the various goals.

Implement Plans

For implementation of one's plans it is most desirable that the organizational climate be supportive. This means that top-level management must encourage all echelons of management to help their subordinates develop their careers. Actions to implement the plans may include special project assignments, temporary job transfers, filling in for the boss during the boss's vacation, in-service training classes, self-study reading assignments, assignment to a special task force, and evening classes in an area college.

Career-Planning Workshops

The career-planning elements explained above can be integrated into a training program or series of workshops. An example of this is a 14-session personal career management course offered to employees of the Colorado Springs Division of the Hewlett-Packard Company.[4] This course consists of two principal components: (a) self-appraisal and (b) preparation of a formal career development plan. Included in the self-appraisal portion of the course are the following: a structured written self-interview, the Strong-Campbell Interest Test, the Allport-Vernon-Lindzey Study of Values, a log of one's activities throughout one 24-hour period, interviews with two significant others about oneself, and a representation of one's life style graphically. In the second portion of the course—preparing a formal career development plan—the participants learn about jobs and career opportunities at the company, study the stages of development in adulthood, prepare a recipe for success at the company, learn how to select a new job and interview for it, complete a life projection exercise to envision their lives in ten years, and, finally, they discuss the use of power to enhance one's career.

CAREER MANAGEMENT

Now we shall identify and explain the features of a rather complete career management system. The organization having limited resources may not be able to implement all of these features. It probably would have to do without an assessment center and may be able to offer only modest education and training programs.

The key ingredients of an effective career-management program are as follows: (1) Integrate with human resource planning; (2) Design career paths, (3) Disseminate career information, (4) Publicize job openings, (5) Assess employees, (6) Career counseling, (7) Work experiences for development, (8) Role of the boss, (9) Education and training, (10) New personnel policies and practices.

Integrate with Human Resource Planning

The proper starting point for career management is human resource planning. This is the foundation for most of a company's personnel programs. The human resource plan contains an inventory of current manpower (numbers of people, sex, age distribution, skills, location, etc.), a forecast of manpower needs for various time points in the future, an analysis of the gap between needs (demand) and projected supply of manpower, and a set of implementation programs to meet human resource needs. The supply and demand portions of human resource planning deal with people in the aggregate. At the implementation stage individuals are hired, placed, trained, appraised, transferred and promoted, and supervised. It is at this implementation stage that career management intersects with human resource planning.

There must be a system of matching job openings with the skills and talents of present employees. What percentage of job openings are going to be filled by hiring from the outside and what percentage are going to be filled by transfers and promotions of present employees? What kinds of developmental experiences through work assignments will be offered to employees? What education and training programs will be offered?

The personnel staff must work with operating managers and with front-line supervisors to translate the human resource plans into employee development activities to meet present and projected manpower needs.

Design Career Paths

Lines of job progression to successively higher level jobs have evolved in a great many organizations over the years. Thus, lines of promotion

---

[4] Warren R. Wilhelm, "Helping Workers to Self-manage Their Careers," *Personnel Administrator,* Vol. 28, No. 8 (August 1983), pp. 83–89.

for skilled craftsmen have been commonly regularized. An employee goes from apprentice or from helper to mechanic second class and then mechanic first class. In production departments of companies in heavy industries such as paper, chemical, and steel many lines of progression have been formalized.

Despite the tradition among skilled crafts and in some heavy industries, most organizations have not systematically designed career paths for employee development. But they should do so. The starting point is the collection of job descriptions for all the jobs in the organization. Equipped with these, a committee of managers representing the various departments can be formed to design rational career paths. Career paths can be created for growth within various broad occupational groupings such as clerical-office, data processing, research laboratory, sales, personnel, engineering, crafts, and manufacturing. Each successive job in the path should contain at least one new skill requirement that was not present in the previous job. Furthermore, the jobs in each career path should bear a rational relationship to one another. Thus Job A, the first or lowest job in a career path, should contain many skill elements that are also present in Job B, the second job in the progression. Therefore, when an employee moves from Job A to Job B he or she does not have to learn an entirely new set of skills. Rather, he or she takes on more responsibility and adds one or two new skills. Career paths for the development of managers and high-level staff personnel should include jobs in several different functional departments to provide broad knowledge and perspectives of the business.

Figure 11-2 is an example of career paths or ladders that have been developed for a manufacturing plant. This chart shows four main channels for advancement. These are production operations, maintenance crafts, storeroom, and quality control and technical services. A unique feature of this chart is that it shows many entry points or positions into which people can be hired from outside the organization.

Many companies that employ large numbers of technical and professional personnel have designed career paths for these people that parallel the ranks in the management hierarchy up through the upper middle management level. This is desirable. Such professional career paths provide opportunities for progressively greater responsibility and also reward the individuals with more money and prestige. The BDM Corporation, which provides diversified technical and professional services, has five career ladders for their exempt personnel covering pay grades 21 through 32. These ladders are designed as follows: technical ladder, technical with leadership option, management ladder, administrative ladder, and administrative with leadership option. Qualified technical professionals can move up the various ranks in the technical ladder to grade level 31 and need not seek transfer or promotion into line management in order to advance. Likewise people can move up the staff administrative ladder to grade level 30. Individuals can tranfer from one ladder to another. However parallel promotion steps are provided so that technical and professional personnel can advance very high in the rank and compensation system.[5]

Disseminate Career Information

The personnel department should prepare a written description, often in simple brochure form, of job and career opportunities in the organization. Many companies prepare such literature for use in their college recruiting programs. But such information ought to be prepared for other jobs and careers in addition to those for college graduates.

[5] John P. Riceman, "How to Operate a Successful Career Development Program," *Management Review*, Vol. 71, No. 5, pp. 21–24.

FIGURE 11-2 Career Paths or Ladders in a Manufacturing Unit. *From: Elmer H. Burack and Nicholas Mathys, "Career Ladders, Pathing and Planning: Some Neglected Basics,"* **Human Resource Management,** *Vol. 18, No. 2 (Summer 1979), pp. 2–8. Reprinted by permission.*

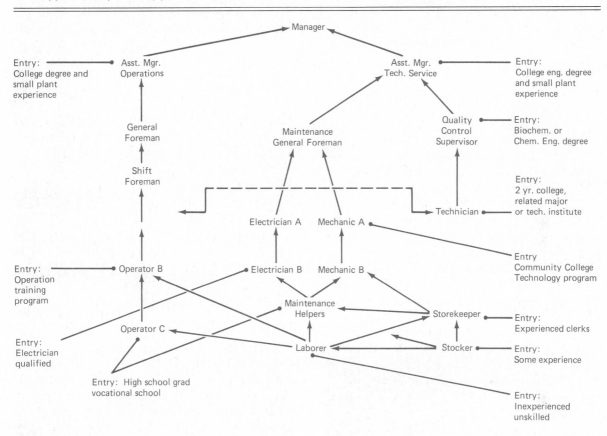

In designing career brochures it is important to be realistic. If there is no growth in some segments of the business, then the literature should point out forthrightly that job opportunities are scarce in those segments.

Publicize Job Openings

In far too many organizations information about the creation of new jobs and the opening up of existing jobs because of transfers, promotions, or terminations is kept secret among a small group of managers. Such a practice is unsound because too often qualified candidates are overlooked.

All job openings should be publicized by means of bulletin board announcements and interoffice news media. These announcements should give a condensed statement of job duties, indicate the qualifications needed, and indicate the pay grade and job location.

Assess Employees

For the benefit of both the employing organization and the individual, employee performance and potential must be assessed. A well-designed and implemented performance appraisal system can yield much valuable information for career development. Most performance appraisal reports are written by the employee's immediate supervisor. He should know each employee well. But his report is prepared from the perspective of just one person. It can be incomplete and biased. A more thorough, in-depth, and balanced evaluation of people can be obtained through use of an assessment center.

An assessment center is a system for evaluating a small group of persons by using several evaluation techniques such as simulation exercises, tests, biographical questionnaires, interviews, and observation by trained assessors. The assessment center method has shown good predictive validity for identifying potentially successful managers. It is, however, a costly method. For this reason its usage tends to be restricted to the selection of managerial personnel. It has been used successfully not only for selection but also for employee development. When used for employee development each participant is offered a counseling session at which he can see and discuss the evaluations made of his performance in all the exercises and tests.

Career Counseling

Career counseling can be conducted in three modes. In one mode it is conducted (it is hoped) by each supervisor and manager during a performance appraisal interview with each subordinate. In this interview the two parties can discuss opportunities for career development such as special projects, new responsibilities, and training opportunities.

Often a wider view of career opportunities can be provided by a career counseling resource person in the personnel department. This individual can help employees plan their careers and inform them of possible avenues for training and development.

A third mode for career counseling is that offered in a career workshop. A career workshop takes the participants through a series of planned exercises to help them plan their careers. It also can offer individualized counseling.

Work Experiences for Development

Probably the most powerful vehicle for employee development consists of planned work experiences to help the individual learn and master relevant knowledge and skills. These planned experiences can take many forms: challenging jobs, job rotation, temporary project assignments, assignment to a temporary task force, promotions, temporary lateral transfers, and even an occasional downward transfer to learn specific skills.

Role of the Boss

Unfortunately, most organizations do not train their managers to be developers of talent and they do not reward them for doing a good job in this area. For any career development program to work, this negative state of affairs has got to change. If managers are held accountable only for production and profits, these are the things they will emphasize. If top management really believes in "people development" it will reward those managers who do this well by granting pay increases, verbal recognition, and promotions.

Some managers hoard their good talent. They have spent much time and effort in developing good employees and they are reluctant to let them move on to bigger and better jobs. Top management, again, sets the policy and the climate in this regard. Lower level managers should not be allowed to block the progress of their people. If these managers are rewarded for developing strong contributors, they need not fear having them move on.

Education and Training

Many kinds of learning cannot be gained adequately on the job; hence employees must be enrolled in various educational and training programs. These programs can range from short in-service courses to teach a specific skill to week-long seminars at a training institute to regular college courses for academic credit. Contemporary thinking is that education and training opportunities ought to be made available to all levels and categories of personnel and not just to a few favored ones.

New Personnel Policies and Practices

The operation of a career development program brings out issues that some organizations may not have faced before. It may be desirable to involve the employee's family in certain career decisions such as new career directions, relocations, and promotions. If the employee's spouse has a job, a contemplated relocation can generate severe intrafamily stress.

Not every individual who is promoted or transferred will succeed in a new position. The personnel department must work out a policy to take care of these people. Normally, they should have the right to move back to a job equivalent in rank and similar in nature to the one they gave up before taking the promotion.

Closely related to the foregoing is the desirability of granting tenure to those who are offered opportunities for various job rotation assignments, transfers, promotions, and training. Because the individuals involved in these experiences are moved about fairly frequently, they are required to make many adjustments in their patterns of behavior and may therefore experience some anxiety. To counter this problem management should announce to these people that they have been granted tenure or reasonable job security with the company. The individuals ought not be worried that one work failure will cause them to be discharged.

A career development system works best when there is a genuinely open internal labor market. This means that employees are adequately informed about careers, jobs, job qualifications, career paths, and job openings. They can apply for job openings and be judged on their merits. Selection of individuals for promotion and transfer opportunities is made on the basis of matching qualifications with job requirements and not on the basis of favoritism and political connections.

THE SMALLER ORGANIZATION

The typical smaller work organization ordinarily does not have the resources in talent, time, and money to plan and operate a complete career development program. What can the smaller organization realistically expect to do?

The smaller organization can adopt a policy of being supportive of its employees' career development. It can design rational career paths. Hopefully it already has job analysis information to aid this process. But if such data are lacking, meetings of managers can be convened to discuss and identify career progression sequences. Condensed descriptions of jobs and career possibilities within the organization can be prepared and distributed to all employees. Job openings can and should be posted on bulletin boards throughout the establishment.

Supervisors can be encouraged to adopt a supportive, developmental stance when they hold performance appraisal meetings with their people. Employees can learn new knowledge and skills by being given additional responsibilities and special projects while performing their present jobs. Transfers and promotions should be carefully thought out not only to meet the needs of the company but also to determine whether a contemplated move will really help the individual develop.

Normally the smaller enterprise does not

spend much money and time providing formal education and training courses for its people. But the personnel director of the smaller firm can at least publicize the course offerings of area two- and four-year colleges and of technical schools. She or he may also be able to work with continuing education specialists from these institutions to offer occasional special courses for personnel within the firm to meet particular needs.

In summary, the management of the smaller enterprise can be sensitive to employee aspirations and can assist them in enhancing their careers. It can work to insure that it maintains an open internal labor market as we have defined the concept previously.

Questions for Review and Discussion

1. Explain the contemporary interest in the establishment of a career development capability by work organizations.
2. Define the following concepts: career, career development, career planning, and career management.
3. Describe the principal stages of a person's work-life.
4. Compare and contrast the traditional "organization-man" career with the newer "personal fulfillment" career orientation.
5. Give the principal components of career planning; of career management.
6. What kind of a career development program is feasible for the smaller enterprise?

Suggestions for Further Reading

Hall, Douglas T. *Careers in Organizations*. Pacific Palisades, Cal.: Goodyear Publishing Co., Inc., 1976.

Kotter, John P., Victor A. Faux, and Charles C. McArthur. *Self-assessment and Career Development*. Englewood Cliffs, N.J.: Prentice-Hall, 1978.

London, Manuel, and Stephen A. Stumpf. *Managing Careers*. Reading, Mass.: Addison-Wesley Co., 1982.

Riceman, John P. "How to Operate a Successful Career Development Program," *Management Review,* Vol. 71, No. 5 (May 1982), pp. 21–24.

Roth, Laurie M. *A Critical Examination of the Dual Ladder Approach to Career Advancement*. New York: Columbia University, Graduate School of Business, 1982.

Schein, Edgar, *Career Dynamics: Matching Individual and Organizational Needs*. Reading, Mass.: Addison-Wesley Co., Inc., 1978.

Wilhelm, Warren R. "Helping Workers to Self-manage Their Careers," *Personnel Administrator*, Vol. 28, No. 8 (August 1983), pp. 83–89.

Employment and Development of People

12

Training

To operate organizations, large or small, requires staffing with competent personnel. Our public educational system is primarily oriented toward teaching broad knowledge and skills to enable people to cope successfully with their environment, to support themselves, and to help advance the society as a whole. Generally speaking, it is not designed to teach specific job skills for positions in particular companies or organizations.

About a million and a half young people enter the labor force each year. Because the vast majority of these are not prepared to perform jobs in work organizations, they must be trained by their employers. Even those who have studied a technical or professional field of work at college must receive some initial training in the form of orientation to the policies, practices, and ways of their specific employing organization. Moreover, because the technology of our productive processes is developing at such a rapid pace, there is also a need for continual retraining of experienced workers to perform new and changed jobs. The automation of recent years is but an advanced stage of the technological developments that have been taking place at an increased pace in recent decades.

Fifty years ago new workers were expected to pick up necessary job skills and knowledge from experienced fellow employees. The new-comers were typically called learners or helpers. Although it cannot be denied that this method of learning worked, it certainly did not work well. It was quite haphazard and caused the learning process to be very slow. Many incorrect procedures were often acquired. Frequently old-timers would deliberately seek to protect their positions and status by hazing the new men and by confining the learners' activities to the menial part of the work.

Large-scale systematic training activities in industry got their start during the periods of war production during World Wars I and II. Especially noteworthy were the Training-Within-Industry (TWI) and the Engineering, Science, and Management War Training (ESMWT) programs of World War II. The TWI program trained people in industry in procedures for teaching job skills to others (Job Instruction Training), in developing better work methods (Job Methods Training), and in industrial relations (Job Relations Training). The ESMWT program consisted largely of specialized technical courses offered by colleges and technical schools to employees in defense industries.

This chapter will explore the nature of training, objectives to be accomplished, organizational considerations in training, the learning process and learning principles, training methods, and training programs. Means of evaluating the effectiveness of training will also be discussed.

Training Defined

Training is the organized procedure by which people learn knowledge and/or skills for a definite purpose. The objective of training is to achieve a change in the behavior of those trained. In the industrial situation this means that the trainees shall acquire new manipulative skills, technical knowledge, problem-solving ability, or attitudes. It is expected that the employees apply their newly acquired knowledge and skills on the job in such a way as to aid in the achievement of organizational goals.

Training is often distinguished from education. Education is thought of as being broader in scope. Its purpose is to develop the individual. Commonly, education is considered to be formal education in a school, college, or university, whereas training is vocationally oriented and occurs in a work organization. Training usually has a more immediate utilitarian purpose than education. In practice, training and education frequently occur at the same time. This is to say that the distinction is not always necessary or appropriate. Some formal vocational school programs are quite immediately practical and job-oriented, whereas some executive development programs in industry cover fundamental principles and philosophy, are broad in scope, and certainly should be designated as education.

TRAINING IN THE ORGANIZATION

Tangible Benefits of Training

Training is a vital and necessary activity in all organizations. It plays a large part in determining the effectiveness and efficiency of the estab-

lishment. Let us now examine some of the major contributions that training can make:

1. *Reduced learning time to reach acceptable performance.* By having qualified instructors and carefully controlled learning situations, management in countless cases has been able to obtain shortened learning periods and higher productivity from new employees.

2. *Improved performance on present job.* Training applies not only to new employees but to experienced people as well. It can help employees increase their level of performance on their present job assignments.

3. *Attitude formation.* A common objective of company training programs is the molding of employee attitudes to achieve support for company activities and to obtain better cooperation and greater loyalty.

4. *Aid in solving operational problems.* Training of both supervisory and hourly paid employees can help reduce turnover, absenteeism, accidents, and grievance rates. For example, inept supervision is often a cause of employee dissatisfaction and grievances. Supervisory training in such areas as labor relations, leadership, human relations, and administration may improve supervisor-subordinate relationships. Other operational problems that training can help solve are low morale, poor customer service, excessive waste and scrap loss, and poor work methods.

5. *Fill manpower needs.* One manufacturing company found it impossible to recruit sufficient skilled machinists and toolmakers. Hence it concluded that the best way to solve this manpower problem, in the long run, was to establish its own apprentice-training program. A number of small manufacturers in the wearing apparel industry in an Eastern city continually find difficulty in hiring adequate numbers of skilled sewing-machine operators. None of these firms has any type of organized training program. Yet a large company in the same city seldom is short of labor, because it operates a complete training

school for sewing-machine operators. Consequently, it is able to recruit green labor and train these people to become experienced stitchers.

6. *Benefits to employees themselves.* As employees acquire new knowledge and job skills they increase their market value and earning power. The possession of useful skills enhances their value to their employer and thereby increases their job security. Training may also qualify them for promotion to more responsible jobs.

Organization for Training

In small companies training is, to a great extent, of the on-the-job variety, and it is done by line supervision. If personnel departments exist in these companies, the planning and coordination of training activities is typically one of the many responsibilities of the personnel manager. It is rare to find specialization carried to the point of having a separate training section within the personnel department.

On the other hand, the vast majority of larger companies have a separate training section within the personnel or industrial relations department. Organizationally the training and management development functions may be combined within one section.

The training activity is a staff function. It performs in the areas of policy formulation, advice, service, and control for organizationwide training activities. More specifically the training director and her or his assistants must commonly perform the following functions: (1) determination of training needs: (2) development of overall plans, objectives, and assignment of responsibilities; (3) development of training programs in consultation with line executives; (4) collection and preparation of training materials, outlines, curricula, textbooks, and audiovisual aids; (5) instruction of certain courses (often orientation and supervisory development courses) and selection of qualified instructors for others;

(6) training of certain operating personnel who are designated as instructors to develop teaching skills; (7) administration and coordination of all training programs; and (8) evaluation of effectiveness of training effort.

Line Training Responsibilities

Top line executive management (this may be the president or executive vice-president or a top division manager in a decentralized company) has the responsibility for authorizing basic training policies. Likewise it must review and approve the broad outlines of training plans and programs without, of course, concerning itself with details. It must approve the training budget. If, for example, the training director thinks it would be desirable to inaugurate a comprehensive executive development program, the wholehearted support of the chief executive officer of the organization must be secured before such an activity can be undertaken. It would be the training director who would formulate complete plans for carrying out an executive development program. However, these plans would have to be approved by top line management. A training director might feel that certain managers should be sent to one of the extended on-campus executive development courses given by a number of major universities. The actual selection of a person and the decision to release that person from a present job for the duration of the course is a line management responsibility.

What are the training duties and responsibilities of lower line management? Foremen, general foremen, and office supervisors must be alert to recognize training problems that exist in their departments. They may participate in the creation of special tailor-made training programs to help solve specific problems in their units. They must bear direct responsibility for the successful conduct of an on-the-job training activity in their departments. If certain employees are to perform in the role of on-the-job instructors, the supervisor must insure that these employees have themselves been adequately trained in the principles of teaching. The supervisor must coach and counsel subordinates in order to obtain adequate performance. In effect a supervisor is a trainer, often personally responsible for the orientation of new employees. He or she may conduct safety-training meetings with personnel. The supervisor selects, from among subordinates, those who should participate in formal training programs. He or she is responsible not only for meeting production goals but also for developing people.

Discovering Training Needs

Sometimes a manager decides to set up a training program becuse it is the popular thing to do and because other companies are doing it. However a company can literally pour thousands of dollars down the drain unless it attacks its training problems on a more systematic basis.

Training programs should be established only when it is felt that they can aid in solving specific operational problems. Therefore, the rational way of deciding what kind of training activity to undertake is to make an analysis of the entire organization (people, jobs, technology, and so on) to identify trouble spots where training may help.

It should be pointed out at this time that training is not a cure-all. If employee output is low, this may be corrected by better skill training. On the other hand, the problem may not be one of inadequate training at all. It might be due to faulty material, process equipment, or engineering design. If it appears that the general caliber of the work force is low, this condition might be corrected by training. However, it could be that the general wage level is so low that the company cannot recruit good employees.

The identification of specific problem areas in the organization can suggest ways in which training may help toward a solution. The following are ways of discovering training needs:

1. Identify organizational and production problems
   a. Low productivity
   b. High costs
   c. Poor material control
   d. Poor quality, excessive scrap and waste
   e. Excessive labor-management strife
   f. Excessive grievances
   g. Excessive violation of rules of conduct, poor discipline
   h. High employee turnover
   i. Excessive absenteeism
   j. Delayed production, schedules not met
2. Analyze jobs and employees
   a. Job analysis
   b. Employee appraisal
   c. Testing
3. Collect employee and managerial opinions
   Interviews and questionnaires to obtain views regarding perceived problem areas and deficiencies which would indicate desirable training programs
4. Anticipate impending and future problems
   a. Expansion of business
   b. New products, new services
   c. New designs
   d. New plants
   e. New technology
   f. Organizational changes
   g. Human resource inventory—compare present human resources with forecasted needs

THE LEARNING PROCESS

Learning is really the core of the training process. When management installs a new training activity, it reasonably expects that through participation in this training employees will exhibit new or changed behavior. Indeed, *learning can be defined as that human process by which skills, knowledge, habits, and attitudes are acquired and utilized in such a way that behavior is modified.*

Employment and Development of People

We know that a person has learned when he demonstrates it by performance. If John is studying German, he shows that he has learned by translating a passage in a book. A mathematics student, by solving written homework problems, has demonstrated that she has learned the assigned lesson. Likewise, a welding trainee reveals that she has learned to make a pipe weld by actually doing it.

Principles of Learning

Psychologists, primarily through experimentation, have developed a number of important principles of learning. These are equally pertinent for application by training directors who administer programs, for classroom instructors who teach employees, and for supervisors who train employees on the job.

Motivation. If trainees are not receptive to instruction, if they can see no reason to learn, then a training effort can hardly get off the ground. Adequate motivation is essential to the success of any learning situation. People are goal-oriented in their behavior. They will exert themselves to fulfill a felt need. Learning is effective when the trainees perceive that they can satisfy some goal through participation in a training program.

There are two kinds of motives: intrinsic and extrinsic. In intrinsic motivation the work itself is satisfying to the individual, who takes pleasure in the work or schooling and derives a feeling of accomplishment upon successful completion. Extrinsic motivation refers to the holding out of incentives or external rewards for the successful completion of a task. Such incentives may be praise from the boss or the instructor, higher pay, a bonus, prestige, better working conditions, and the like. Both types of motivation are important to the learning process. However, learning is quite difficult if the external incentives are available but intrinsic motivation is lacking. This situation can be illustrated by a college student who has chosen to enroll in an engineering curriculum because the salaries paid to graduate engineers are very good. However, this long-range goal is unlikely to motivate Eloise to learn mathematics, physics, electronics, solid mechanics, and fluid mechanics if she dislikes these subjects. She may grit her teeth and force herself to get through these courses, but the learning will be quite painful. Conversely, learning engineering is easy for the student who has the aptitude plus the intrinsic interest in the subject matter.

Both rewards and punishment play a powerful role in motivation to learn. A reward for a desired response serves to stimulate a repetition of that behavior. Thus, students may receive praise from their parents for doing well in school, and this will motivate them to continue to do well. Punishment tends to inhibit a certain response, but it does not necessarily eliminate it. Mild punishment is effective if it is immediate and if the learner understands the reason for it. Supervisors and trainers must be very judicious in the way they administer punishment. If a learner has been doing poorly, threatening her with a discharge or reprimanding her may cause her to alter her behavior, but most generally such action will affect many other aspects of her behavior in addition to the learning situation. It may cause her to fear or resent her instructor or boss so much that she cannot concentrate upon learning the work at hand. Employees may learn to follow company rules of conduct because those who do not are clearly punished. But often an emphasis on punishment by management is only effective as long as there is repeated punishment or the threat of it. Employees will concentrate on avoiding punishment rather than doing the right thing. In the long run, people will learn to behave in a desired way if they understand the reasons for such prescribed conduct and if they are rewarded for such behavior.

Knowledge of Results. Somewhat related to motivation is knowledge of the learner's progress. Research experiments have demonstrated that people learn faster when they are informed of their accomplishments. After analyzing numerous research experiments concerning such diverse activities as line drawing, use of gunsights, dot-dash code receiving, and typing, Wolfe has concluded that it is essential that trainees be given knowledge of their efforts. He states that such knowledge should be automatic, immediate, and meaningfully related to the task at hand.[1] Thus in a training classroom students' examinations should be graded and returned to them so that they can know where they have erred and what they have done correctly. In on-the-job training the supervisor should inform the employees of their successes and failures so that employees can adjust their efforts if necessary. People like to experience a feeling of progress. They want to know where they stand. If an instructor returns examination papers to a class of students with only the raw scores recorded, this knowledge will be meaningless until they are told how all the grades were distributed and how they stand in relation to expected performance. Learning is facilitated when the trainee has some criterion with which to judge progress.

Learn by Doing. It is extremely difficult for a learner simply to listen to a teacher explain how to do something and then be able to do it solely from the explanation. It is by actually performing the task that a student really learns. The greater the number of human senses involved, the more complete is the learning. If one is teaching a physical task, such as operating a machine or sharpening a tool, it is easy to see how practice can be provided. But what if one is teaching theories and concepts? Actually a variety of techniques are possible. Laboratory experiments can be devised. Written problems can be assigned. Case studies and role playing can be

utilized. Although not constituting full learning by doing, oral discussion and debate help to strengthen the learning of ideas.

When learning a task by practice, is it better to combine the total time devoted to practice into one concentrated session, or should the practice be subdivided into small time periods? The available research evidence seems to favor spaced practice sessions. Experiments with massed as opposed to spaced practice for simple motor skills and memorizing show that learning is superior for that type of practice that has a series of short rest periods.[2]

Is Theory Desirable? Does the chemistry laboratory technician need to understand why chemical reactions occur as they do? Does the process operator in an oil refinery need to know why she must turn valves and adjust temperatures and pressures? Do workers perform better if they understand the principles underlying the work they do?

The prevailing weight of evidence shows that learning is faster and can be applied better to new situations if the trainees understand the principles involved. This was found to be true for boys shooting at targets that were underwater: a knowledge of refraction increased the accuracy of shooting. It was also true for college students who had to solve simple reasoning problems. Those who were told the principles upon which the problems were based did better than those who were simply given sample solutions to a few problems. Those who were given a series of problems in such a manner that they could derive their own principles did still better in future problems.[3]

From the foregoing it is clear that a person who understands the theory behind the work is

[1]Dael Wolfle, "Training" in S. S. Stevens, ed., *Handbook of Experimental Psychology* (New York: John Wiley & Sons, Inc., 1951), pp. 1267–1286.

[2]See E. R. Hilgard, *Theories of Learning,* 2nd ed. (New York: Appleton-Century-Crofts, Inc., 1956), p. 487. Also William McGehee and Paul W. Thayer, *Training in Business and Industry* (New York: John Wiley & Sons, Inc., 1961), pp. 151–153.

[3]Dael Wolfle in S. S. Stevens, op. cit., pp. 1277–1278.

in a good position to readily adapt to new problem situations as they arise. The person, however, who has simply been trained to perform as an automaton will be hopelessly lost when confronted with situations out of the ordinary. This principle of teaching theory as well as practice does not mean that we need a graduate electrical engineer to repair a television set. But it does mean that the TV repairman, for example, should possess a practical, working knowledge of electronics as it applies to television receivers.

In summary, employees should be taught sufficient theory to understand the principles and reasons underlying their work and to cope successfully with the general run of problems they may encounter.

Learning Motor Skills. In motor-skill work, muscular movement is prominent, but it is under sensory control. Examples of motor skills are skiing, skating, swimming, carpentry, setting up and operating machine tools, welding, glass blowing, using hand tools, and operating a sewing machine. The instructor must show and explain the materials, tools, and equipment that he will use. He should then demonstrate how to perform the activity. If the activity is complicated, the instructor should break the operation down into logical components, explain the steps involved, and then demonstrate. Next the learner should start practicing the operation. He should understand what he is doing and be able to explain the activity. The instructor should provide guidance and feedback. The learner must know if his performance is progressing properly or improperly. Generally after practicing for a period of time, a rest pause should be provided. Distributed practice periods are generally more fruitful than prolonged and concentrated practice.

Learning Concepts and Attitudes. Learning concepts and attitudes is much more complex than learning motor skills. At one extreme is rote learning, where a person may have to memorize a poem, learn the names of the parts of a machine, or learn a computer language. At the other extreme one may learn for depth of understanding. There may be all sorts of interconnections and associations among the ideas learned—the reasons why as well as beliefs, attitudes, and philosophies. One may search for general theorems, truths, and laws.

There are many ways to learn ideas and attitudes. We can learn by trail and error and personal experience. We can read and observe. We can learn by listening and talking with others.

The learning of ideas is enhanced when students participate actively in the process. They may work on problems and exercises and ask and answer questions. This may be both written work and oral discussion in class. It is especially valuable to encourage students to explore problems and issues in some depth so that they discover relationships and principles for themselves. It may save time if the instructor organizes all the subject matter and explains it logically and clearly to the trainees. But, at least part of the time, opportunity should be provided for them to work on exercises, problems, and concepts and discover truths for themselves.

Indeed, a fundamental question in designing a classroom learning experience is whether to depend heavily upon the lecture method of instruction or to foster a high degree of group discussion and interaction. The answer to this question depends somewhat upon the objectives of the program of training or education. If the purpose is solely to provide information of a factual nature to the group, the lecture method, which is highly leader-centered, is quite satisfactory. However, if the material to be learned is subject to varied interpretation and is not precise or explicit, then group discussion, with a group-centered method of conducting the class, is clearly superior. There is also evidence that retention of factual knowledge is greater in classes having a high degree of group-member interaction. This result appears to be caused by the learning reinforcement that comes from the testing of one's ideas with others and from the intellectual stimulation this generates.

Courses whose purposes are to modify attitudes, facilitate behavioral adjustments, aid interpersonal relations, and promote self-insight are clearly superior when the trainer adopts a democratic, participative leadership style. High member interaction is most conducive to these goals. A very authoritarian trainer tends to be ineffective in changing group attitudes, but a leader who generates high member involvement can more effectively modify opinions, prejudices, and emotions.[4]

TRAINING METHODS

Those who administer training programs have a great choice of methods for imparting learning in trainees. The particular method selected is determined by considerations of cost, time available, number of persons to be trained, depth of knowledge required, background of the trainees, and many other factors. The following is a listing of the major training methods:

1. On-the-job
2. Vestibule
3. Classroom methods
   a. Lecture
   b. Conference
   c. Case study
   d. Role playing
   e. Programmed instruction
   f. Computer-assisted instruction
   g. Learner-controlled instruction
   h. Simulation and games

[4] A discussion of when to use leader-centered and group-centered training styles, based upon an extensive review of available research, is contained in Alan C. Filley and Franklin C. Jesse, "Training Leadership Style: A Survey of Research," *Personnel Administration*, Vol. 28, No. 3 (May–June 1965), pp. 14–21.

On-the-Job Training

The vast majority of all training carried on is of the on-the-job variety. Much of what passes for on-the-job training is extremely haphazard. For example, a young engineer fresh out of college took a position in a large corporation. He was immediately assigned to an application engineering job. For training he was told to read a stack of books describing company standard procedures and specifications. His boss assumed that by studying these he would learn his job. As another example, Bill was hired as a machine operator in a government arsenal. He was expected to turn out precision parts on milling machines and boring mills for military weapons. He had had machine experience in another company but had never worked on this specific product under these conditions. He was given no instruction by the foremen. What he learned he had to gain informally by asking help from experienced work associates.

How should on-the-job training programs be conducted? Primary responsibility rests with each departmental supervisor. If he or she understands training principles and methods and if he or she takes an interest in proper training of new employees, chances are that it will be done properly. The training may be done either by the supervisor himself or by a designated experienced nonsupervisory employee. The person doing the training must be given recognition for the work. He or she must not consider training to be an unpleasant chore that interferes with production. The instructor must first receive training in the principles and techniques of instruction. It is the responsibility of the training department to teach all on-the-job instructors how to instruct.

The instructor must assemble all necessary equipment, procedure sheets, working materials, and training aids. He or she must break down the material to be learned into meaningful packages and present it to the employee in a manner appropriate to the job to be learned. In many instances he or she will actually demonstrate how the work is to be performed. He or she will carefully guide and observe the trainee as he or she performs the work. Correction will be given as required.

A variety of training aids and techniques can be used in conjunction with on-the-job training. Among these are procedure charts, pictures, manuals, sample problems, demonstrations, oral and written explanations, and tape recordings.

On-the-job training is most appropriate for teaching knowledge and skills that can be learned in a relatively short time (a few days to several weeks) and when only one or at most a very few employees must be trained at the same time for the same job. If a great depth of theory must be acquired, then this can be accomplished more efficiently in a classroom. On-the-job training is useful for learning unskilled and semiskilled manual jobs, clerical jobs, and sales work. For skilled, technical, professional, and supervisory jobs, the underlying educational background must be obtained by other means; however, the applied aspects of these jobs are quite generally learned right on the job.

On-the-job training has the advantage of permitting the trainee to learn on the actual equipment and in the environment of the job. He can actually experience a feeling of accomplishment as he produces useful products. If only a few are to be trained at one time, it is cheaper for the employer to resort to on-the-job training rather than to invest in a vestibule school or classroom setup. Quite often expensive manufacturing equipment cannot be duplicated in the classroom.

Vestibule Training

Vestibule training is the term used to designate training in a classroom for semiskilled production and clerical jobs. It is particularly appropriate when a large number of employees must be trained at the same time for the same kind of work. Where it is used, there is a greater likelihood that management will have well-qualified instructors in charge. The emphasis tends to be upon learning rather than production. It has been used to train clerks, bank tellers, inspectors, machine operators, testers, typists, and the like.

In vestibule training an attempt is made to duplicate, as nearly as possible, the actual material, equipment, and conditions found in a real workplace. Typically the learning time ranges from a few days to a few weeks. Theory can more easily be presented in a vestibule school than on-the-job. The learning conditions are carefully controlled.

Classroom Methods

Classroom instruction is most useful when philosophy, concepts, attitudes, theories, and problem-solving abilities must be learned. This means that a considerable depth of knowledge must be acquired. There are certain aspects of nearly all jobs that can be learned better in the classroom than on the job. Certain portions of company orientation and safety training can be accomplished most effectively in the classroom. Most commonly, however, we think of the various classroom methods being used for technical, professional, and managerial personnel, where a considerable grounding in theories, principles, and concepts is necessary. Let us now examine some of the principal classroom instruction techniques.

Lecture. The standard instructional method in colleges and universities—the lecture—is a formal, organized talk by the instructor to a group of students. The lecturer is presumed to possess a considerable depth of knowledge of the subject at hand. He or she seeks to communicate thoughts in such a manner as to interest the class and cause them to retain what has been said. Quite often the students will take notes as aids to learning.

The principal virtue of the lecture method

is that it can be used for very large groups, and thus the cost per trainee is low. It can be organized rigorously so that ideas and principles relate properly one to the other.

However, the limitations of this method may outweigh its advantages. The learners are passive. It violates the principle of learning by doing. It constitutes one-way communication. There is no feedback from the audience. The presentation must be geared to a particular level of knowledge and may bore the advanced student and be beyond the capabilities of the slow learner. It tends to emphasize the accumulation of facts and figures; however, this does not mean that the learners will be able to apply their knowledge. Because it is difficult to hold the full attention of listeners for a sustained period, lecturers are tempted to resort to anecdotes, jokes, and other attention-getters. This activity may eventually overshadow the real purpose of the instruction.

The most fruitful way to use the lecture is to combine it with other techniques. Thus, a teacher may conduct a class by the combined lecture-discussion method, and may then lecture only to add new information that the group does not possess, and may give formal reading assignments, present demonstrations, and show films.

Conference. A conference is a small group meeting, conducted according to an organized plan, in which the leader seeks to develop knowledge and understanding by obtaining a considerable amount of oral participation from the trainees or students. It overcomes certain of the disadvantages of the lecture, because here students play very active roles. They are not passive. In fact, the very success of any conference is dependent upon contributions from the students. Learning is facilitated through building upon the ideas contributed by the conferees. The people, to an extent, learn from one another.

There are three basic kinds of conferences:

(1) the directed conference (also called the guided or instructional conference); (2) the consultative conference; and (3) the problem-solving conference. The directed conference is most commonly used for training purposes, because the instructor has certain concepts for the class to absorb and guides the group carefully to insure that they cover these ideas. Conferences are not limited to training purposes, however. They are frequently used in all sorts of organizations to attack operating problems by bringing to bear the pooled thinking of a number of people. For solving business problems, either the consultative or the problem-solving method may be used.

Let us examine some of the features of a directed conference used for training purposes. Because it depends for its success upon the active participation of the conferees, the size of the group must be limited to fifteen to twenty persons. The people should sit facing one another around a conference table rather than theater-style, as in an ordinary classroom. The students should have some knowledge of the subject to be discussed before coming to the conference. This can be obtained from assigned readings or previous experience or both. The instructor introduces the topic and invites viewpoints from the group on problem areas related to this topic. The instructor must, by the skillful use of questions, make sure that the class analyzes the topic thoroughly. Often he will record student responses on the blackboard. He will summarize progress made at pertinent points throughout the session. Points of disagreement will also be highlighted. In the directed conference the instructor or leader may introduce new material by occasional brief periods of lecturing.

In contrast to the lecture, the students play a very active part in determining the progress of the conference. They are not forced to submit passively to the instructor's viewpoints. They are expected to make assertive statements and to ask questions. They learn not only from the instructor but also from one another. It is rare for a trainee to become bored or to fall asleep in a conference, whereas this condition is common in the lecture. Interest tends to be high. The conference is ideally suited to tearing apart problems and issues and examining them from different viewpoints. It is an excellent procedure for reducing dogmatism and modifying attitudes. Because they have had a part in developing solutions and reaching conclusions, the conferees are often willing to accept these conclusions.

Case Study. In the teaching of mathematics, it is almost universal practice for the instructor to assign problems for the students to work out to illustrate the principles previously taught. This method gives the student an opportunity to apply his knowledge to the solution of realistic problems. Likewise, this principle can be applied to the teaching of those subjects concerned with human affairs. Case studies are extensively used in teaching law, personnel management, labor relations, marketing, production management, and business policy.

Cases can be used in either of two ways. First, as stated above, they can be used subsequent to the exposition of formal theory. In this way students must apply their theory and knowledge to specific situations. Second, they may be assigned to students for written analysis and/or oral class discussion without any prior explanation of pertinent concepts and theory. The students are expected to derive useful generalizations and principles themselves. This second approach places heavy demands on the student. It requires that the students have a good deal of maturity and some background in the subject area.

The case study method is very popular in graduate professional schools of law and business administration. It is also frequently used in supervisory and executive training in industry.

Case discussions in class are usually conducted in a conference atmosphere. Students soon learn that there is no single answer to a particular problem. Engineers who are used to a right and wrong dichotomy are often initially frustrated in case discussions because the instructor does not tell them what is the right solution.

The case study method of instruction provides for learning by doing. Good cases are usually based upon real experiences and problem situations; therefore, student interest tends to be high. They are excellent for developing analytical thinking and fostering problem-solving ability. Narrowmindedness is reduced because the trainees soon learn that others have studied the identical problem and come up with different patterns of analysis and solution. Students must often defend their proposals in the face of keen criticism from others. The case method is an excellent means for integrating the knowledge obtained from a number of foundation disciplines.

Role Playing. Role playing is actually a technique that should be used in conjunction with some other instructional method such as the lecture or the conference. Originally developed by J. L. Moreno for group therapy for mentally disturbed people, it has been widely used for human relations and leadership training. It is primarily used to give trainees an opportunity to learn human relations skills through practice and to develop insight into their own behavior and its effect upon others.[5]

In role playing two or more trainees are assigned parts to play before the rest of the class. There are no lines to memorize and no rehearsals. The role players are provided with either written or oral descriptions of a situation and the

[5]References on role playing are Norman R. F. Maier, A. R. Solem, and A. A. Maier, *The Role-Play Technique: A Handbook for Management and Leadership Practice* (LaJolla, Cal.: University Associates, 1975); and Wallace Wohlking, "Role Playing," Chapter 36 in Robert L. Craig (ed.), *Training and Development Handbook,* 2nd ed. (New York: McGraw-Hill Book Co., 1976).

role they are to play. After being allowed sufficient time to plan their actions, they must then act out their parts spontaneously before the group. Typical role-playing situations are a supervisor discussing a grievance with an employee, a supervisor conducting a postappraisal interview with an employee, an employment interviewer conducting a hiring interview, and a salesperson making a presentation to a purchasing agent.

Role playing for developing human relations understanding and skills has a number of advantages. It provides an opportunity for students actually to put into practice the knowledge they have absorbed from textbooks, lectures, and discussions. It is learning by doing. They become sensitive to the way their behavior affects others. It helps people to appreciate other points of view as when roles are switched (that is, the boss plays the part of the worker). Knowledge of results is immediate, because the role players themselves as well as the class analyze and criticize the behavior of the players. Interest and involvement tend to be high.

Programmed Instruction.
Programmed instruction (sometimes packaged in a device called a teaching machine) was developed in the late 1950s for both school and industrial applications.

The key features of programmed learning are (1) students learn at their own pace; (2) instructors are not a key part of the learning; (3) the material to be learned is broken down into very small units or stages; (4) each step logically builds upon those that have preceded it; (5) the student is given immediate knowledge of results for each answer given; and (6) there is active participation by the learner at each step in the program.

Some types of programs take into account individual differences in background. If a student is unable to give the right answer to a question or a series of questions, the student will be directed along a different branch of the program to be provided with the fundamentals missed.

To date, programmed instruction has been used primarily for teaching factual knowledge, such as mathematics, a foreign language, and job routines. It has not been used to develop philosophical concepts, attitudes, or clinical problem-solving skills. The cost of creating a single program is very great.

Computer-Assisted Instruction.
Computer-assisted instruction is grounded in some of the learning principles employed in programmed instruction. It is often used to provide drill and practice to help students learn material that is well structured such as grammar, basic mathematics, and reading. It can also be used as an adjunct to other educational methods to develop problem-solving skills. Computer-assisted instruction is costly. It has been used mostly to teach basic skills in schools. Its adaptation to teaching job skills in industry has been slow.

Learner-Controlled Instruction.
Learner-controlled instruction (LCI) is a relatively new method of training in which the trainees are given considerable choice in determining for themselves the pace at which they learn, the sequencing of the learning steps, the methods used in the process, and the evaluation of their own learning.

A large variety of learning methods and media are made available to the trainees. These can include books, films, games, case studies, simulations, group discussions, and role playing. The learners may also be given the opportunity to interview key individuals in the organization.

The instructor plays the role of a facilitator, offering assistance to the students. He does not use a rigid set of lesson plans nor does he use standard examinations. The students work substantially on their own with general guidance by the instructor.

Learning objectives are set by the trainer with some participation by the students. They are expected to feel accountable for meeting their agreed-upon objectives.

In a complete training program learner-controlled instruction is but a part of the total learning design. It generally is not the only learning approach utilized.

Among the corporations that have used LCI in their training programs are Allied Supermarkets, Giant Foods, Interstate Motor Freight Systems, and the Marriott Corporation.[6]

Simulation and Games. A simulator is any kind of equipment or technique that duplicates as nearly as possible the actual conditions encountered on the job. Certain portions of the training of military and commercial aircraft pilots are conducted in flight simulators. Astronauts receive part of their training in simulators. Business games are a form of simulation. Student participants make various business decisions in a competitive market situation. They learn the consequences of their actions after their decision-data is fed into a computer which has been programmed with a model which is supposed to be a realistic representation of the economic market situation.

Trainee interest and motivation are normally high in simulation exercises because the actions taken closely duplicate real job conditions. Simulation is very useful (and even necessary) where on-the-job practice could result in a serious injury, a costly error, or the destruction of valuable material.

[6]References on learner-controlled instruction are Robert L. Craig (ed.) *Training and Development Handbook,* 2nd ed. (New York: McGraw-Hill Book Co., 1976), Chapter 42; John H. Cox, "A New Look at Learner-Controlled Instruction," *Training and Development Journal,* Vol. 36, No. 3, (March 1982), pp. 90–94; David R. MacDonald and Michael R. Stewart, "Industrial Applications of Learner-controlled Instruction," *Personnel Journal,* Vol. 62, No. 10, (October 1983), pp. 820–825.

TRAINING PROGRAMS

Principles of learning and training methods are useful only insofar as they contribute to effective training in a specific program. We shall now examine the more important kinds of training programs found in work organizations.

Orientation

Although proper orientation is easily and often neglected, it is essential for insuring that new employees get off to the right start. Although other terms, such as *induction* and *indoctrination* are also used, *orientation* is most accurately reflective of the real meaning of the process. *Orientation is the guided adjustment of the employee to the organization and work environment.*

The objectives of orientation are multifold. In carrying out such a program management seeks to create favorable attitudes toward the company, its policies, and its personnel. It can instill a feeling of belonging and acceptance. It can generate enthusiasm and high morale. Quite frankly many employers seek to mold employees' attitudes and behavior so that they fit in well with the organization and accept management policies and ethos. A well-run orientation program may minimize the likelihood of rules violations, discharges, quits, grievances and misunderstandings.

After an employee is hired, both the personnel department and the supervisor play key roles in the orientation process. The relative part played by each depends upon management intention and the resources of the personnel department. In small companies either having no personnel department or else having only a skeleton one, the major responsibility for new employee orientation falls upon the operating supervisor. Even in large companies with extensive personnel departments, there are certain orientation tasks that essentially belong to the employee's own department.

What is the role of the supervisors in orientation? They are responsible for making the newcomer feel wanted and needed. They should pave the way ahead of time by informing present employees that a new employee is going to work in their midst. They should give reasons for adding a new employee, so that any suspicion or resentment is allayed. The supervisors should review, with the new employee, the nature of his or her duties, introduce him or her to each person with whom he or she will come in contact, and show him or her the department or work area and its facilities. In introducing him or her to other employees with whom he or she will deal, the supervisor should make it a point to explain the function of these individuals, so that the new employee can properly deal with them in the future. Thus, a factory production worker should become acquainted with the group leader, inspector, maintenance people, setup people, union steward, timekeeper, and the like. The employee should be told what is expected in terms of performance and conduct. He must know what he can expect from the company regarding pay, pay increases, promotion opportunities, holidays, vacations, and benefit plans.

The personnel department is responsible for seeing that the orientation program is initiated in the first place and that it is carried out according to plan. It should train line supervisors in the performance of their orientation responsibilities. In some companies it exerts staff control over these line supervisors by requiring them to fill out a check list form that shows they have done specific orientation tasks for each new employee.

The following is a listing of important content information and actions that may be included in an orientation program. It includes fundamental things that should be done with each new employee. However, the list is not conclusive, since every organization will make adaptations to fit its needs.

EMPLOYEE ORIENTATION CONTENT

1. Company history, policies, practices.
2. Company products and/or services.
3. Company plants and facilities.
4. Organization structure (in general).
5. Employee responsibilities to company.
6. Company responsibilities to employee.
7. Pay treatment.
8. Rules of conduct.
9. Tour of department.
10. Work schedules.
11. Collective bargaining agreement.
12. Benefit plans—life insurance, medical, hospitalization, pension, unemployment.
13. Safety program.
14. Training opportunities.
15. Promotion policy.
16. Introduction to fellow employees.
17. Establishment of a feeling of belonging and acceptance, showing genuine interest in new employee.
18. Employee appraisal system.
19. Work assignment.

Experimental evidence of the value of proper orientation of new workers is reported by Myers and Gomersall, who conducted the research at the Texas Instruments Company. Interviews with about 400 factory operators who had been on the job only about a month disclosed that (1) they felt very anxious the first few days on the job; (2) hazing by older workers intensified their anxiety; (3) turnover of new people was caused primarily by anxiety; (4) they were reluctant to discuss problems with their supervisors. As a result of this background information, Myers and Gomersall devised an experiment with a control group and an experimental group. The control group was given the conventional two-hour orientation consisting of a briefing on hours of work, insurance, parking, work rules, and the need to conform to company expectations. The experimental group of new workers was given a full day's orientation. This included the same two-hour orientation provided the control group. But in addition they spent the remainder of their first day in a conference room with the trainers. There was no work the first day. Emphasis was placed upon getting acquainted with one another and the company. They were encouraged to relax. Four key points were emphasized: (1) their likelihood of success in the job was very good; (2) they should disregard hazing by older employees; (3) they were encouraged to take the initiative in asking questions of their supervisors; (4) they were told about their new supervisor and how he would behave. Then they were introduced to the supervisor and training operators. What were the results of this experiment? For the experimental group job-learning time was reduced, output was higher, and attendance was better. Waste and rejects were also lower for the experimental group. The researchers attributed this gain to lowered anxiety through better orientation. Supervisors were also aided in improving their role in the orientation process.[7]

Job Skills and Knowledge

When we speak of training for job skills and knowledge, we are not talking about any specific program. Rather we are referring to the variety of training programs, methods, and aids that have been established to answer particular training needs. Either on-the-job or classroom techniques may be employed. The subject matter will vary according to the training problem encountered. Although many who are unsophisticated regarding training tend to look upon it as primarily for new employees, in actuality a vast amount of training effort must be continuously expended on further education and re-

[7]Earl R. Gomersall and M. Scott Myers, "Breakthrough in On-the-Job Training," *Harvard Business Review*, Vol. 44, No. 4 (July–August 1966), pp. 62–72.

training of old employees. The content and demands of jobs change with time, the expectations of management change, and above all the technological revolution that is going on in our civilization means that old ways become obsolete and new skills must continuously be introduced. Quite frequently the best answer to a shortage of labor for particular kinds of work is to grow skilled workers from within.

Perhaps an illustration of a job-skill program may be appropriate. In the cutting and packing department of a paper mill, the foreman was plagued by low output, poor quality, and failure to meet schedules. He wanted to get rid of several of his workers. The assistant personnel manager asked him one day if he had ever actually taken the time to really train his people. The foreman said that no, he hadn't. Because they had been on the job when he took charge, he assumed they knew how to do their work. Working together, the foreman and the personnel man, developed an on-the-job training plan that drew heavily upon Job Instruction Training procedures of the Training-Within-Industry program of the World War II era. This training effort, when combined with improved work methods, was largely instrumental in raising the productivity level of the department to an acceptable level.

Apprentice Training

The apprenticeship system, which is a way of developing skilled craftsmen, is a descendant of the craft guild system of the Middle Ages. The apprentices in America before the Industrial Revolution generally lived in the homes of the master craftsmen to whom they were indentured and received no wages but simply were given room, board, and clothing. Boys became apprentices at an early age—typically at the age of 14. Apprenticeships commonly lasted for seven years. The training was entirely of the on-the-job variety. Much of the work was menial and routine.

In 1937 Congress passed a national apprenticeship law, popularly known as the Fitzgerald Act. Its purpose is to promote the furtherance of apprentice training and to extend apprenticeship standards on a voluntary basis throughout the United States. A Bureau of Apprenticeship was established within the United States Department of Labor. The act also reorganized and enlarged the Federal Committee on Apprenticeship. This committee has recommended certain essentials of an effective apprenticeship program. There should be a minimum starting age of 16, an approved schedule of work experience supplemented by at least 144 hours per year of related classroom instruction in subjects related to the trade, a progressively increasing schedule of wages, proper supervision of on-the-job training, and periodic evaluation of the apprentice's work.

Apprenticeable trades are those requiring at least 4,000 hours (two years) of training experience through employment. Recognized apprenticeable trades exist in approximately 300 skilled occupations grouped by the United States Department of Labor under 90 general trade classifications. Typical occupations and their term of apprenticeship in years are airplane mechanic—four years, carpenter—four years, photoengraver—five–six years, and rigger—two years.

The apprenticeship system in this country is very loosely organized. Each employer is free to run his program as he sees fit (union participation especially in the building trades is often necessary). But there is no requirement to conform to state or Federal standards for the various trades. Thus an apprentice graduate from Company X may have received vastly inferior training to that of a graduate from Company Y. Some employers still look upon apprentices as a source of cheap labor, and their time is often occupied with menial tasks. Yet properly run according to state and Federal standards, countless apprentice programs are turning out well-qualified journeymen. For these companies skilled-labor needs are being adequately met.

The advantages of apprentice training to the trainees are that they receive decent wages while learning and that they acquire a valuable skill that commands a high wage in the labor market. Skilled craftsmen in many industries earn as much or more than technicians, subprofessionals, and beginning professional employees, such as engineers and scientists.

Training the Disadvantaged

Commencing in the mid-1960s the Federal government enacted a series of programs to help disadvantaged people learn useful job skills and to obtain regular jobs. Most of these programs were administered in Washington and they included a good deal of experimentation to determine what methods would be effective. Disadvantaged persons are those who are undereducated for today's job market, lack useful job skills, have a record of family welfare dependency, are chronically unemployed, and have a very low annual income.

In 1973 Congress enacted the Comprehensive Employment and Training Act. This law phased out most of the programs administered by the Federal government and assigned the primary responsibility for program planning and administration to state and local governments. Funding still came from Washington. In practice CETA funds were largely used to provide jobs for disadvantaged persons in public service jobs such as deputy sheriffs, police matrons, firefighters, office clerks, and custodians.

In 1982 Congress switched strategies again because the problem of high unemployment among the disadvantaged seemed intractable. It replaced the CETA program with the Job Training Partnership Act. This new law prohibits public service employment. The thrust of this law is to create a partnership between private business and local governments to provide remedial education, training, and employment assistance to low income and unemployed youths and adults.

The program operates through Service Delivery Areas (SDAs) authorized by state governors. In each SDA there must be a Private Industry Council (PIC), the majority of whose members come from local business and industry. PICs and local government officials jointly develop training plans. Training activities may include remedial education, skills training, on-the-job training, advanced career training, work experience, pre-apprenticeship programs, and job search assistance.

EVALUATION OF THE TRAINING EFFORT

If management invests in training programs for employees, it understandably expects to see some tangible benefits derived therefrom. When a staff training director approaches top management for approval to establish a new training activity, the question reasonably can be asked as to what good the course will do and why the company should invest such and such a sum of money in it. In short, the question is, "How can we determine the value of a training program?"

Training directors use a number of techniques to evaluate the effectiveness of training programs. Generally speaking, the usefulness of these methods is inversely proportional to the ease with which the evaluation can be done. One approach is to pass out a questionnaire to the trainees at the completion of the program to obtain their opinions as to its worth. Their opinions could also be elicited by means of interviews. Another approach is to measure the knowledge and/or skill that employees possess at the beginning of training and again at the completion of training. This is accomplished by administering the same examination (or an alternate form of a single examination) before and after.

The real purpose of training is to cause a change in employee behavior on the job and ultimately to improve the effectiveness of the organization. The aforementioned evaluation techniques do not measure employee behavior on the job. Thus, if employees say they liked a course of instruction, this is not the real payoff. A comparison of before-and-after test scores does not really get to the point either. People may show that they have learned a lot on classroom examinations, yet they may not transfer this learning to the job.

A better way of measuring the worth of training is to use various indexes of work performance and compare them after the course with measures before the course. In this manner the output and quality of work of production workers, salespersons, stenographers, and other workers can be used for evaluation purposes. Though at first glance this seems to be a fruitful approach to the problem of evaluation, there is a basic flaw in the method. We have no way of knowing whether the training activity caused an improvement in the performance index or whether it was achieved as a result of a combination of other factors. An improvement might have been caused by better production planning, better supervision, new work methods, and improved materials, as well as training.

The most refined method for evaluating training (and one that avoids the errors of other techniques) is to measure performance before and after training for both a control group and an experimental group. This procedure can be accomplished by selecting two groups of employees that are approximately equivalent in education, experience, skill, job conditions, and performance. Subject one group to the training program and give no training to the other (control) group. Some time after training is completed, choose relevant performance measures and compare results for the two groups. This method is somewhat cumbersome from the administrative standpoint; however, it is one of the most fruitful methods available. Unfortunately, such a rigorous experimental approach to training evaluation is seldom carried out in practice.

Questions for Review and Discussion

1. Often top executives are unwilling to devote funds for adequate employee and manager training. They believe that such expenditures are an unwarranted drain on resources. Should training be viewed as an expense or as an investment? Discuss.
2. How can one determine what kinds of training programs to offer?
3. Discuss the following concepts as they affect learning:
   a. Motivation.
   b. Knowledge of results.
   c. Learn by doing.
   d. Teaching the theory underlying the activity.
4. Why is orientation training important for new employees? Why do you think companies often fail to conduct such programs?
5. What factors should be evaluated when deciding whether to train employees on the job or in a classroom?
6. A company is going to set up formal training for selected groups of its employees in the categories listed below. Of the various instructional methods available, which would be most suitable for each category?
   a. Word-processing equipment for secretaries.
   b. An attitude-building course for employees and supervisors on the issue of sexual harassment on the job.
   c. Training of sales personnel who call on potential corporate customers.
   d. Industrial safety.
7. Quite commonly education and training courses are evaluated by means of brief questionnaires given to participants at the end of a course. How valid and useful is this method of evaluation? Are there better methods? Discuss.

CASE PROBLEM

The Ajax Manufacturing Company is in a very competitive metal products business. It employs 4,000 people. Because the designs and prices for its products are quite similar to those of its competitors, it maintains its sales by emphasizing quality and service. About a year ago it lost two of its major customers, who had been dissatisfied with excessive manufacturing defects. The Ajax Company, upon studying the problem, decided that its basic engineering was sound but that carelessness and lack of quality consciousness on the part of production workers, inspectors, and manufacturing supervision were a prime cause of the trouble. Accordingly, it established a quality control course to solve the problem.

The course was given after working hours, from 7:00 to 9:00 P.M. each Thursday for ten weeks. Employees were not paid to attend. Technically, attendance was voluntary; however, management intimated that employees who attended faithfully would have the fact recorded in their personnel records. This fact would be considered in future pay raises and promotions.

The course was taught by a staff engineer from the Quality Control Department. Consisting mainly of lectures, the course was varied at times to include movies on quality control and some discussions. The course covered such topics as the need for high quality, "quality can't be inspected into a product, it must be built in," conditions affecting quality, costs of poor quality, inspection standards, inspection procedures and methods, statistical quality control, sampling inspection, and control chart procedures. The course was open to all interested employees in the plant, including supervisors. Attendance at the early sessions averaged around fifty. Toward the end of the course it had declined to about twenty-five.

The training director made the following comment at the conclusion of the course. "Frank Smith (the instructor) did a good job of lecturing. He was interesting, informative, and spiced his talks with humor at appropriate times. It was not his fault that attendance fell off."

Questions
1. Do you think this training program was organized and administered properly?
2. Are there other training methods that could properly have been used?
3. Evaluate this approach to improving product quality.

Suggestions for Further Reading

Craig, Robert L., ed. *Training and Development Handbook,* 2nd ed. New York: McGraw-Hill Book Company, 1976.

Gardner, James E. *Helping Employees Develop Job Skill: A Casebook of Training Approaches.* Washington, D.C.: Bureau of National Affairs, Inc., 1976.

Laird, Dugan. *Approaches to Training and Development.* Reading, Mass.: Addison-Wesley Publishing Co. 1978.

MacDonald, David R., and Michael R. Stewart. "Industrial Applications of Learner-Controlled Instruction," *Personnel Journal,* Vol. 62, No. 10 (October 1983), pp. 820–825.

"Measuring Training Effectiveness." *Personnel Administrator,* Vol. 28, No. 11 (November 1983), a series of six articles on training effectiveness.

Rehder, Robert R. "Education and Training: Have the Japanese Beaten Us Again?" *Personnel Journal,* Vol. 62, No. 1 (January 1983), pp. 42–47.

Wexley, Kenneth N., and Gary P. Latham. *Developing and Training Human Resources in Organizations.* Glenview, Ill.: Scott, Foresman and Company, 1981.

Yoder, Dale, and Herbert G. Heneman, Jr., eds. *Training and Development.* Washington, D.C.: Bureau of National Affairs, Inc., 1977.

13

Management and Organization Development

Successful enterprises devote significant and continuing efforts to training and developing their management personnel. Qualified managers of the caliber and quantity needed throughout our society do not just emerge from the labor force without consciously planned programs on the part of work organizations, large and small. When undertaking to create a management development program, top management must fully understand just what it is trying to accomplish. What is management? What do managers do? What knowledge and skills must they possess? How can these best be acquired? What are the merits of on-the-job development compared with classroom training?

In this chapter we shall also study the nature of organization development. Whereas management development tends to focus upon developing managers as individuals, organization development seeks to improve the overall functioning of groups and departments. Organization development tries to facilitate problem solving, foster collaboration, and increase commitment to organization objectives. Organization development activities may involve a broader spectrum of the enterprise than just managers. In addition to managers it may include professionals, technicians, administrators, and staff support personnel.

NATURE OF MANAGEMENT DEVELOPMENT

What Is Management Development?

Management development is a systematic process of training and growth by which individuals gain and apply knowledge, skills, insights, and attitudes to manage work organizations effectively. As explained in the previous chapter on training, training and the learning process really involve the implication that there will be changed behavior on the part of the individual. Managers develop not only by participation in formal courses of instruction but also through actual job experiences in a work environment. The role of the company is to establish the program and the developmental opportunities for its managers and potential managers. But it must be recognized that simply exposing employees to lectures, case studies, readings, job rotation assignments, and the like does not guarantee that they will learn. An equal, and perhaps more important, counterpart to the efforts of the organization are those of the individual. There has been increasing recognition that the company can set the proper climate, but that the major effort must be made by the individuals themselves. Thus, self-development is an important concept in the whole program for management development. The participants must have the motivation and the capacity to learn and develop. They must make the requisite efforts to grow.

What Is a Manager?

Before one can obtain an adequate understanding of the principles and procedures of management training and development, one must know what a manager is and what he does.

Management is a process of utilizing material and human resources to accomplish designated objectives. It involves the organization, direction, coordination, and evaluation of people to achieve these goals.

The word *manager* has been used in a variety of ways by industrialists and theorists. To some the term *manager* means top executive. To others a manager is any person who supervises other employees. In fact, one large manufacturing company uses the term without any status connotations. In this firm a manager may supervise a number of managers, and in turn may report to a manager. Thus, the organization structure contains a number of echelons, each level possessing the designation of manager.

The most commonly accepted view is to consider as members of management all those who coordinate and direct the activities of others plus all those administrative and staff people who deal with others outside their own group and who have a decided impact upon the organization. Thus, all supervisors from a foreman up through a corporation president are decidedly managers. Administrative personnel such as planners, coordinators, executive assistants, and the like are also members of management even though they do not supervise other employees. They are members of the management team because their work is related to or affects management policies, practices, and actions.

Usually, engineers and scientists are considered to be professionals but not managers.

Another way of understanding what managing is and what managers do is to examine the functions of management. The process of management consists of planning, organizing, staffing, leading, and controlling. Planning encompasses looking ahead to the future, setting goals, and figuring out policies, procedures, and methods for accomplishing these goals. The cognitive and decision-making processes are heavily involved in planning. Organizing involves the breaking down of the total work to be done into jobs, groups, and departments and the establishment of workable relationships between these units. It includes such elements as grouping activities both by level and by type, setting up jobs, determining authority and responsibility relationships, setting up patterns of communication, delegating, and using staff. Staffing refers to the process of recruiting and selecting people to run the enterprise. Leading is the motivation and direction of people to achieve a desired goal. It integrates the personal goals of the employees with the objectives of the enterprise. Finally, the control function of management includes measurement of work performed, comparison of actual performance with a predetermined standard, and then the taking of corrective action, when necessary, to insure that performance meets standard.

Knowledge and Skills of the Manager

Although a foreman is just as much a manager as a top executive officer, the nature of his or her work and the skills he or she must utilize to do this work are different from those of a major executive. A foreman must devote a majority of his or her time to leadership activities. He or she must be an expert at applied human relations. He or she must motivate, communicate, direct, correct, discipline, coordinate, teach, and reward his or her subordinates. He or she must also be able to teach people the technical aspects of the products and processes with which they must work. He or she must effectively solve routine technical problems of the work processes. A foreman primarily carries out directions from above. The scope of his or her discretionary power is quite limited.

Top executives need very little technical skill pertaining to the products and processes of the business they manage. To be sure, they must have an appreciation or general knowledge of the capabilities and limitations of these technical processes, but these are executives who hire others to design, install, operate, and maintain the facilities. Major executives devote much of their time to forecasting, policy formulation, and planning. They deal, to a considerable extent, with forces and people outside their own organizations. They are concerned with the economic, social, and political environment. They must be adept at integrating the various functional branches of an organization, such as production, sales, finance, and industrial relations. Top managers spend a high percentage of their time interacting with other people in group conferences and two-person face-to-face dealings. Executives not only exert their authority and power to get things done through their subordinates, but also they frequently seek to persuade and influence others outside their own hierarchical sphere.

In analyzing the skills needed by an administrator (manager, according to our terminology), Katz speaks of three types: technical, human, and conceptual skills. Technical skill refers to proficiency in handling methods, processes, and techniques of a particular kind of business or activity. Human skill refers to the ability to work effectively with others and build cooperative group relations to achieve goals. Conceptual skill, as Katz describes it, is the ability to see the organization as a whole, to recognize interrelationships among functions of a business and external forces, and to be able to guide effectively the organization in considera-

tion of the multitudinous forces affecting it. Coordination depends upon conceptual skill. Conceptual skills are concerned with the realm of ideas and creativeness. Technical skill is an essential ingredient of lower-level management, human skill is important at all levels of management, and conceptual skill is especially critical in top executive positions.[1]

Evolution of Management Development

Formal management development programs began to appear in large corporations in the 1950s. Since then there has been growing sophistication in the organization and content of such endeavors. They have spread to smaller corporations and to governmental agencies at the Federal and state level. Several forces have operated to cause the expansion of management development activities.

There has been a pronounced shift from owner-managed to professionally managed enterprises. Management has been recognized as a distinct kind of occupation consisting of teachable skills and a unified body of knowledge. Management can be described as an emerging profession. Professions consist of two kinds: the learned (law, medicine, teaching, and so on) and the artistic (acting, music, and so on). We are here concerned with the learned professions. A profession has the following characteristics:

1. It requires advanced, specialized formal education and training.
2. It requires the consistent exercise of discretion and independent judgment.
3. It is based on a deep and organized body of

[1]Robert L. Katz, "Skills of an Effective Administrator," *Harvard Business Review,* Vol. 33, No. 1 (January–February 1955), pp. 33–41.

knowledge. Efforts are continually made to expand the knowledge through research.

4. The members of the profession have a keenly developed sense of ethics and public responsibility.
5. The members of the profession have a sense of common identity and purpose. There is a professional organization that seeks to advance the field and uphold professional standards.
6. It demands certain recognized standards of competence in terms of education, training, experience, and human performance.

It must be recognized that management is still an emerging profession. It is not full-fledged, because of the lack of recognized standards of competence, and because the members have not created or adhered to any generally accepted code of ethics. There exists great variation in the routes people take to become managers and in performance after they acquire their positions. But the point being made is that management has been acquiring more and more of the characteristics of a profession even though it has still not arrived there.

Within the past few decades there has been an ever-increasing amount of research-generated knowledge of the principles and techniques of administration. This applies both to general management and to its various functional fields, such as personnel and industrial relations, production, finance, marketing, and accounting. The universities through their schools of business, public administration, industrial management, and social science have carried on much of this research effort under both government and industry sponsorship. Generally the business community has looked favorably upon knowledge and has tried to apply it in those situations where it is appropriate.

The rapid rate of technological and social change has made it imperative to have managers who are trained to cope with these developments. Among the manifestations of this change

are expansion into overseas markets and the rise of the multinational corporation, intense competition in the United States from foreign firms, and new products of greater technical complexity.

There has been increased recognition by business and industrial leaders of the social and public responsibilities of the corporation. Companies must now acknowledge their responsibility for minimizing environmental pollution and meeting the costs thereof. Organized consumer groups are demanding better products and services. Minority groups are demanding more and better job opportunities. And, as the representative of the public interest, government is regulating private business more closely. These public and social responsibilities require that managers in business have broader vision and a greater understanding of the interdependence of the institutions of our society. The older and narrower focus upon the firm as simply a profit-maximizing instrument is insufficient for present-day realities.

Start at the Top

Management training and development can succeed best when it pervades the entire organization and when it begins with top management. This is a fundamental necessity for any program of this type to be successful. However, in actual practice this simple idea has not been grasped by top business and industrial leaders. Many thousands of dollars are spent annually on foremen's training conferences throughout this country, yet much of this effort is fruitless. A management development program can succeed only in a climate of sound management from the top to the bottom of the organization.

The author has been personally involved in teaching numerous supervisory courses where top management has said in effect, "We think that the company could be improved if we could make better leaders of our supervisors and improve their management knowledge and skills." However, the realities of the situation are such that supervisors may learn the latest and soundest principles and techniques of management in the classroom but not be allowed to apply the knowledge to the job because, so often, higher management does not practice this pattern of management itself. The realities of the authority structure in industry are such that a supervisor must conform to the demands of his superiors. If this pattern of leadership is in conflict with the principles that the supervisor learned in his management course, he may experience serious frustration and impaired performance.

In a significant and pioneering research project aimed at evaluating the effectiveness of foreman-leadership training at the International Harvester Company, Fleishman, Harris, and Burtt found that foremen performed back on the job in a manner that conformed to the attitudes and behavior of their bosses. If their superiors rated high on what the researchers labeled a "consideration score," then the foremen also rated high on a "consideration score," and vice versa. Their ratings were irrespective of knowledge and attitudes developed during participation in the leadership course. The researchers concluded that foremen are more responsive to their day-to-day climate on the job than to any special course of training they may have taken.[2]

From this study and the evidence of other researchers, consultants, and management training specialists, it is clear that management training and development, to be effective, must begin with top executive officers of a firm. As they acquire new insights and skills and as they begin to practice these in their work, they are in a sound position to launch formal development activities for members of middle and lower management.

[2]Edwin A. Fleishman, Edwin F. Harris, and Harold E. Burtt, *Leadership and Supervision in Industry: An Evaluation of a Supervisory Training Program* (Columbus, Ohio: Bureau of Educational Research, The Ohio State University, 1955).

PLANNING AND ADMINISTERING THE PROGRAM

The inauguration of a management development program must be authorized by the chief executive officer of an organization, because it involves fundamental policy decisions, important actions by executives all down the line, and the expenditure, in some cases, of considerable sums of money. Ordinarily the planning and guiding of an executive development program is carried out by a committee composed of major executives, whereas the day-to-day administration is performed by the personnel or human resource department.

Let us now examine the essential ingredients of a management development program. The key elements are

1. Analysis of organization needs.
2. Appraisal of present management talent.
3. Management human resource inventory.
4. Planning of individual development programs.
5. Establishment of training and development programs.
6. Program evaluation.

Analysis of Organization Needs

After the key decision to launch a management-development program has been made, the first thing to do is organization planning. The organization structure must be studied to ascertain whether activities and functions are grouped properly. Forecasts must be made of the growth of the business. Projected new products and services must be identified. What will the organization consist of five or ten years hence in terms of functions, departments, and executive positions? Will any portions of the organization have to be reduced in size?

The next step is to prepare descriptions and specifications for all management jobs. The purpose is to obtain a record of the kinds of management work performed and the kinds of executives and administrators needed in the organization. It is necessary at this stage to highlight the kind of education, experience, training, special knowledge, skills, and personal traits required for each job. If the company already has in operation a comprehensive job-analysis program (as it should have), then it will be necessary at this point only to collect the job descriptions and job specifications for all management activities, review them, and make desired summarizations.

Top management must make a policy decision as to whether it wishes to fill contemplated vacancies in management ranks from within the organization or whether it wants to hire from the outside. This decision will depend to some extent upon the caliber and number of present personnel in comparison with projected needs. Most commonly companies hire on the outside to fill their lowest-level positions and then promote from within. In effect they grow their own executives except where they have a critical shortage of specialized high-level talent.

Appraisal of Present Management Talent

The purpose of this part of the program is to determine qualitatively what the organization has in terms of management talent. Existing performance appraisal data should be examined to determine if they properly identify the developmental needs of individuals and if they contain estimates of their potential for moving ahead. If the existing appraisal information is inadequate, then the appraisal system must be revised to meet the needs of the management development program. It is also appropriate to utilize data from an assessment center.

Management Human Resource Inventory

At this stage it is necessary to prepare an inventory of present management personnel. For each member of the management team, a card is prepared, listing such data as name, age, length of service, education, work experience previous to company employment, company experience, training courses completed, health record, psychological test results, and performance appraisal data. This information is often summarized and stored in a computer. If the data have been judiciously classified into categories, it then becomes possible to select via the computer all those individuals possessing a desired kind of background. For example, the computer may be set up to select all those who are college graduates, who have had at least 5 years' experience in the supervision of research and development projects, and who are rated above average by their bosses.

Some organizations go one step further than the preparation of a management inventory. They set up *replacement tables or charts* that show each individual's background and rating, and projected promotions and transfers. Quite often this is prepared in organization-chart form with certain coding used to portray a person's rating and planned movement. For example, Mr. A, the plant manager may be 67 years of age and three years from retirement. Ms. B, the manager of manufacturing, may be 47, a college graduate, have 18 years of diversified plant experience, be rated outstanding in ability and potential, and be picked to fill the plant manager's position when Mr. A retires. The replacement chart may also show that there are several capable executives who will be given serious consideration for the plant manager's post at the time Mr. A actually retires.

Although the replacement chart is certainly a systematic way of mapping out plans for the utilization of management manpower, it must be recognized that conditions may change rapidly, so that the earmarking of individuals for particular jobs several years hence is highly speculative.

Planning of Individual Development Programs

This activity must be performed by each executive working cooperatively with each of his or her subordinates. The executive should be guided heavily by the results of the performance appraisal, which will indicate strengths and weaknesses for each person. A development plan should be tailor-made for each individual. In setting up this development plan, each executive should give consideration to the expressed interests and goals of subordinates as well as the training and developmental opportunities that exist within the organization.

Establishment of Training and Development Programs

This step of the broad management development effort involves the setting up of well-conceived training and development opportunities on a companywide basis. The personnel department or its training section will establish certain training programs—such as leadership courses, management games, strategic planning seminars, courses with local universities, and so on—as needs, time, and costs dictate. Top management may wish to send certain individuals to executive development courses at universities. It may establish a companywide system of job rotation or of multiple management.

The personnel department executives must take an active part in keeping abreast of new developments in the field of management education and development. They must carefully study training needs and recommend to top management that certain specific programs be set up as conditions dictate. These staff officers must continually work with line managers to insure that they are developing their subordinates and that they are not denying qualified candidates the opportunity to participate in formal courses. The staff training executives should keep adequate records to audit and control the management development activities throughout the entire organization.

Program Evaluation

Because management development entails the expenditure of large amounts of time and money, top management quite reasonably needs to have evidence of the benefits derived from the activity. Have the training and development improved individual and organizational performance?

As discussed in the chapter on training, it is extremely difficult to obtain definitive proof that a given course has had a real impact. However, a variety of evaluation techniques are available to give evidence and an indication of the value of management development efforts. These can range from questionnaires filled out by participants at the end of each course (a measure of attitudes and feelings) to careful measures of individual managers' job performance six months or one year later to a comparison of the performance of those who attended the course with those who did not. But because an organization is an interacting system and there are many forces affecting the performance of individuals it is hard to isolate the changes induced by participation in the training activity.

What is industry practice in regard to program evaluation? A survey of training directors and personnel executives revealed that only 15 per cent of the companies conducted some kind of limited cost/benefit analysis of their programs and another 10 per cent examined such factors as improved sales results or increased longevity of productive employment for the individuals involved. Most survey respondents claimed benefits could only be measured in subjective terms and not in dollars and cents.[3]

DEVELOPMENT THROUGH WORK EXPERIENCE

There are two principal methods by which people can acquire the knowledge, skills, and attitudes to become competent managers. One is through formal training and education courses; the other is through on-the-job experiences. Fifty years ago in the United States, almost all management development occurred on the job. (Most of the learning was unorganized and haphazard.) In the 1950s when the management development movement in industry was working up a full head of steam, the major emphasis was upon taking managers away from their jobs for a period of time so they could attend executive development and supervisory training classes.

Now it is recognized that both classroom and on-the-job training are important. Formal course work is invaluable for learning new knowledge, new techniques, and broader concepts. Yet real learning can occur only when the learner has an opportunity to practice and apply his ideas. This must be done on the job. It must be further recognized that a manager, by the very nature of his position, serves as a teacher for his subordinates. The authority structure of the organization and the responsibilities of a manager cause him continually to guide and mold the behavior of his subordinates so that they conform to his expectations.

Of the two influences, formal training courses and on-the-job development guided by

[3]William H. Wagel, "Consensus: Evaluating Management Development and Training Programs," *Personnel*, Vol. 54, No. 4 (July–August 1977). pp. 4–10.

the boss, the latter is the most powerful. Yet it is totally unsound to place sole reliance upon on-the-job development because many executives and managers are themselves unqualified to carry out this important task. They may lack the skill, the interest, or the patience. They may possess wholly faulty notions of administration, and for them to impose such ideas upon all their subordinates would be tantamount to deliberately weakening the organization. Yet when on-the-job development is properly balanced with classroom training, and when both are carried out in an atmosphere of sound management emanating from the very top of the company, then we have a workable formula for management development.

We shall now examine some of the important techniques of management development.

Understudies

An understudy is a person who is in training to assume, at a future time, the full duties and responsibilities of the position currently held by his or her superior. It is a means of insuring that a fully trained individual is available to take over the job of a manager when he or she leaves his or her post because of promotion, retirement, or transfer.

There are several ways of arranging for understudies. A department manager may pick one individual within the unit to become an understudy. He or she will then teach him or her his or her own job and let him or her grapple with the problems that confront the manager daily. Or the department manager may choose several subordinates who will act as understudies. They may take turns at filling their boss's job when he or she is absent because of vacation, a business trip, or illness. Or the manager may designate one subordinate to be an administrative assistant. This assistant will handle a great variety of administrative matters that the superior may choose to delegate. Quite often the choice of an understudy is not made by a department head alone; he or she must consult with superiors.

An understudy can gain the requisite experience to take over the boss's job in a number of ways. When the manager is handling daily operating problems, he or she may discuss these with the helper to get ideas and provide experience at decision making. The boss may assign the understudy to investigate and make written recommendations regarding long-term problems. There may arise occasions when the understudy can be assigned direct supervision of a two- or three-person task force. This will give an opportunity to try out leadership skills. The understudy may also be sent to important executive meetings in place of or in attendance with the superior. He or she may be called upon to make presentations and proposals before higher executives.

The understudy method is a practical and fairly quick way of training designated persons for greater management responsibilities. It emphasizes learning by doing. Motivation of the learner tends to be high.

On the other hand, this technique has serious disadvantages. It insures that things will be done pretty much as they always have been. It does not infuse any new ideas into the unit. The understudy will have been picked in the first place because his way of thinking and acting is similar to that of the boss. The other major disadvantage of the understudy approach is that it destroys the incentive to get ahead for all the other employees in the unit who have not been made the understudy.

Job Rotation

The transferring of executives from job to job and from plant to plant on a coordinated, planned basis is a popular practice among industrial concerns. Under the typical arrangement a top-management committee oversees the operation of the program and makes the final decisions on the reassignment of managers. When a manager takes a new post on such a program, it is no mere orientation assignment. He or she is placed in an important line or staff position in which he or she must assume full charge and make regular management decisions. Quite often this executive on the rotational program will be backstopped at each location by experienced, permanent personnel who will exercise a steadying influence and keep things running if the individual has difficulty. Job assignments under a rational scheme typically last from six months to two years. Sometimes the new job assignment will represent a promotion for the individual. The executives to whom these rotating managers report evaluate their performance and funnel appraisal reports back to the central coordinating committee.

In the modern corporation a high proportion of the entry jobs for junior executives and engineers demands a considerable degree of technical knowledge and specialization. As a person increases in stature with time, he or she can never acquire the broad perspective and diversified skills needed for promotion unless he or she is deliberately taken out of his or her specialty and placed in different types of situations. To obtain the generalists who are ultimately needed at upper-management levels, the enterprise must take action to provide a variety of job experiences for those judged to have the potential for major executive ranks. Job rotation answers this need. It also serves to break down departmental provincialism—the feeling that only my department is important and others' problems are not worthy of my concern. When a number of managers have served in one another's units, they can all understand the reasons why a certain function must be done in a particular way. Interdepartmental cooperation is enhanced.

Job rotation injects new ideas into the different departments of an organization. Under this system of management development, a manager is not destined to end up in just one spot. He is equipped to step into any one of several executive posts in any of various functional divisions. Thus, the organization gains management strength in depth.

Coaching

It is quite common for consultants and researchers to find, upon interviewing employees and managers alike, that they are rarely told by their superiors how they are doing. Their supervisors have not taken the time to sit down with them to discuss their performance on specific assignments or on their last few months' work. Yet, if properly done, coaching is something every supervisor can do. It costs little money, and it contributes toward improved performance by the individual and ultimately by the whole work group.

A manager should recognize an obligation to take a decided interest in the training and advancement of those who work for him. His coaching responsibility can be implemented by doing a number of things. He can delegate more. He can assign not only the routine chores, but he can invite his people to tackle some of the more complex problems, which he may have felt could be properly handled only by himself. An executive can give his subordinates an opportunity to participate in making important decisions affecting the department. This can be done either on an individual basis or else by a group conference of all management members in the department.

The effective coach avoids criticizing his subordinate's personality. He concentrates upon the work and the job. What constitutes a good or bad personality is a matter of opinion. Besides, it is extremely difficult to change another's personality. To do so would appear high-handed to many persons.

As a management development technique, coaching requires the least centralized staff coordination. Every executive can coach his people regardless of whether top management has set up any formal management development pro-

gram. It can yield immediate benefits to the organization, the coach, and the individual. It constitutes learning by doing. The learner can experience a feeling of progress. He can see the fruits of his efforts.

Multiple Management

Multiple management is the designation given to the system whereby permanent advisory committees of managers study problems of the company and make recommendations to higher management. The concept of multiple management, or the junior-board-of-executives system, as it is sometimes called, was pioneered by Charles P. McCormick in 1932 when he established his Junior Board of Executives at McCormick & Company in Baltimore. McCormick went on to set up a Factory Board, a Sales Board, and the Junior Sales Associates. Although originally appointed by the president of the company, the Junior Board itself now rates its own members and sets up a membership committee to appoint new ones. For each succeeding term of office, some of the old members must be dropped and new people added to the Board. At McCormick & Company the various boards are granted wide latitude to investigate problems in different facets of the business. When a board has arrived at a solution to a problem, the members must agree unanimously before the proposal can be submitted to the Senior Board of Directors (which is the regular stockholder-elected board). This insures that problems are thoroughly worked out. The latter board is under no compulsion to adopt proposals of the subordinate boards. Junior boards serve in an advisory capacity only. However, the vast majority of recommendations are adopted by the Senior Board. The junior-board-of-executives system has been used successfully by a number of companies in addition to McCormick & Company. A junior board is different from the ordinary committee found in all businesses. Junior boards are formally organized under a set of by-laws. The members rate one another to decide which ones deserve to retain membership after their term of office expires and which should be dropped. Often board members are paid extra compensation for their services. Most importantly the boards do far more than merely discuss topics. Committees within the board are assigned definite projects by the chairperson. They must conduct thorough investigations and submit written reports to the entire board. The junior boards ordinarily have broad authority to study nearly any phase of a company's business.

As a management development technique, multiple management has several advantages: (1) it gives board members an opportunity to gain knowledge and experience in aspects of the business other than their own specialty; (2) it helps identify those who have good executive talent; (3) the members gain practical experience in group decision making and in teamwork. In addition, junior boards can make significant contributions to organizational performance.

Action Learning

Action learning was created by Professor Reginald W. Revans of Great Britain in the 1960s and has been used in many corporations throughout Europe. In action learning the participants work on real problems, most commonly from within their own companies but also sometimes from outside organizations. They do not tackle problems from their own job assignments. The learners or participants must formulate their own descriptions of actual, on-going problems. They must diagnose the problems and take action to implement their proposed solutions. Each participant belongs to a group called a "project set," which consists of four or five other trainees of diverse backgrounds plus two advisors, one from inside the company and one from outside. Typically, a project set (group) meets for one full day every week. The group reviews each mem-

ber's progress on the project, discusses the member's diagnosis of the problem, and offers constructive criticism. Ordinarily the trainees work on their projects over a period of many weeks (or months). Each participant, in addition to the consultations within his or her own project set, works with a client-executive in whose department or company the participant's problem exists. This client-executive must be committed to working in a supportive way with the trainee on the project and to seeing it through to full implementation. The completion of a project is not the preparation of a technical report but rather the actual implementation of the recommendations.

When an action-learning program is first set up, the participants are brought together for initial orientation to play business games to develop a sense of working in teams, and to meet with the sponsoring executives who pay for the program and with the client-executives with whom they will work on projects.[4]

FORMAL TRAINING COURSES

Formal training courses for managers can be conducted in a number of ways and under a variety of conditions. Several of the training techniques discussed in Chapter 12, "Training," find important applications in supervisory and executive training. The conference method is probably used more than any other single technique. Role playing and written case studies are ideally suited for use within the conference type of classes. Extensive reading assignments in company literature, college textbooks, and journal articles are frequently given to middle- and top-management trainees. At the foreman level, reading assignments tend to be light. Professional training specialists tend to feel that fore-

[4]Nancy Foy, "Action Learning Comes to Industry," *Harvard Business Review*, Vol. 55, No. 5 (September–October 1977), pp. 158–168.

men, because the majority lack a college education and because they are not required to read extensively on the job, would be frustrated by long required-reading assignments.

The lecture method is employed in courses for all levels of management. However, it is rare to find any training course that consists entirely of lectures. Lectures are usually interspersed with discussions, films, case studies, role playing, and demonstrations.

Who does the teaching in management training courses? The answer is that practice varies considerably. Subjects dealing with the company, its policies, and organization are often taught by either a major line executive or a member of the training staff. Quite often a business organization will engage professors from schools of business administration and engineering to teach courses in statistics, operations research, production planning, and management information systems. Or these management techniques may be taught by specialists within the company who are professionally qualified in these topics. Those courses concerned with the particular processes and technology of the industry, for example, metalworking in the metal fabrication industry and food processing in the canning industry, are most generally taught by qualified engineers and technicians within the organization. College professors and consultants are often hired by companies to teach courses in organization theory, industrial relations, report writing, public speaking, reading improvement, and strategic planning.

Subject Matter and Course Content

The essential subject matter appropriate for management training is as follows:

1. The company or organization
   a. Objectives and philosophy
   b. Policies and procedures
   c. Products and services
   d. Organization structure and organization dynamics
   e. Plant facilities
   f. Financial picture
   g. The labor agreement and union-management relations
2. Management principles and techniques
   a. Organization principles
   b. Financial planning and management
   c. Management information systems
   d. Production planning and control
   e. Strategic planning
   f. Personnel management (human resource management)
   g. Wage and salary administration
   h. Cost analysis and control
   i. Statistics and probability
   j. Operations research
   k. Data processing and computers
   l. Marketing
   m. Risk management
3. Human relations
   a. Fundamentals of human behavior
   b. Motivation
   c. Group dynamics
   d. Attitudes
   e. Conflict resolution
   f. Managing change
   g. Patterns of management
   h. Concepts of leadership
   i. Power, authority, influence
   j. Communication
   k. Personnel management responsibilities of supervision in such areas as selection, training, pay administration, counseling, appraisal, discipline, and grievance handling.
4. Technical knowledge and skills
   These are peculiar to every type of business and to every type of work. Managers, of course, must have an adequate understanding of the technology, products, processes, and methods of their line of business.
5. Economic, social, and political environment
   a. Business ethics
   b. Economic system

c. Relations with local, state, and Federal governments
d. Community relations
e. Social responsibilities
f. Legal framework for business
g. Business operations in foreign countries
h. Environmental issues such as land use and pollution control
i. Consumerism
6. Personal skills
a. Speaking
b. Report writing
c. Conducting meetings
d. Reading improvement
e. Interpersonal skills, listening, feedback, communication

Any of these individual topics might constitute an entire twenty to thirty (or more) classroom hour course. Because resources in any company are limited, the training department staff must decide in what subject areas the greatest needs lie. It can then establish courses to tackle these problems first.

The training needs of a newly appointed manager are somewhat different from those of experienced ones. The experienced person will need only a very light coverage of subject area 1 above, "The Company or Organization," whereas this is a logical starting point, and one that demands great emphasis, for the newcomer.

Emphasis Varies with Management Level. Although foremen, department heads, plant managers, and vice-presidents are all members of management, the nature of their duties and responsibilities differ rather substantially. The six main subject areas listed above are necessary for all levels of management. However, certain topics are more appropriate for one level than another. For example, foremen are not directly involved in the economic, social, and political environment of a corporation, whereas vice-presidents are. Not only the content but also the depth of knowledge and skill vary according to the level and nature of the personnel involved.

Courses for top management will emphasize such subjects as economics, finance, organization theory, human relations, policy formulation, administrative controls, business operations overseas, the business person in politics, labor relations, and public relations. Because top executives, to a large extent, control their organizations' relations with the outside world, there is usually considerabl. time devoted to topics concerned with the economic, social, and political environment. Courses for members of middle management tend to contain elements of both top- and lower-level management programs. They, of course, devote considerable time to human relations and personnel management principles because these are essential at all levels of management. Middle-level executives must often possess a solid grounding in such management techniques as cost analysis and control, data processing, production planning and control, and wage and salary administration.

Courses for first-level supervisors concentrate upon technical processes of the business, human relations, and personal skills. They tend to be immediately practical. They are closely related to the supervisor's day-to-day job.

University Nondegree Programs

Approximately forty colleges and universities offer residential programs in management for executives employed in industry. These programs are given on the college campus, and in most cases the participants are sent by their companies. The employer pays full tuition and living expenses plus the individual's salary. In addition to these broad-coverage management programs—they are often called advanced management or executive-development programs—there are literally scores of special-purpose programs given by universities. In the discussion that follows, we shall confine ourselves to the broad, residential executive-development programs.

The first university executive-development program was started in 1931 at the Massachusetts Institute of Technology. This was the Sloan Fellowship program, which provided financial support for a few young industrial executives each year to spend a year of study in industrial management. The next program—and the first really large-scale one—was started in 1943 by the Harvard Business School at the request of the United States Office of Education to train executives in war industries. Terminated at the end of World War II, this program was soon reactivated and modified by Harvard because of strong requests from private industry. The Harvard Advanced Management Program is 13 weeks in length and is for top-level executives. The program is designed to handle two groups of about 160 people each year, one group starting in September and the other in February. Largely using the case method of teaching, the faculty offers the following courses in the program: business policy, marketing management, accounting and financial policy, finance, business policy, marketing management, accounting and financial policy, finance, business history, problems in labor relations, business and world society, human behavior in organizations, mathematical concepts for decision making, and simulation.

University Short Courses. In addition to comprehensive management development programs, many universities offer a variety of short courses, typically from one day to one week in length. For example, the Graduate School of Business Administration of the University of Michigan offered during the 1983–1984 year courses as follows: corporate financial management, managing the accounting function, basic management for the newly appointed manager, meeting the Japanese challenge, management by objectives, organization development, strategies in industrial marketing, career planning in organizations, and human resource planning. This is but a partial listing of the program offerings.[5]

Corporate Institutes

A few of the very large American corporations have set up their own educational institutions to provide short programs of study for their management personnel. Among the firms having such institutes are General Electric, IBM, American Telephone and Telegraph, International Harvester, Johnson and Johnson, and Westinghouse.

Illustrative of these is the General Electric Management Research and Development Institute, established at Crotonville, New York, in 1955. This Institute offers a thirteen-week program called the Advanced Management Course, which is designed primarily for the top four levels of management. The program content includes management theory, business policies, general management, and economic, social, and political issues. It also includes job-related material designed to help in the management of a GE product department. A variety of instructional methods is used, including case studies. Instruction is given by both GE executives and professors from leading universities.

The content of a two-week course in managerial skills development (for beginning managers) offered by a prominent American corporation contains sessions on the following topics: company organization, communications, time management, decision making, managerial styles, conducting performance appraisals, conducting meetings, managing conflict, and a business game via computer simulation.

[5]Graduate School of Business Administration, *Management Programs, July 1983–June 1984* (Ann Arbor: The University of Michigan, 1984).

Management Games

A management game—also called a business game— is a classroom simulation exercise in which teams of students compete against each other or against an environment to achieve given objectives. The game is intended to be a close representation of real-life conditions. Often the controlling features of a game are expressed in the form of a mathematical model.

A typical top-management type game consists of three teams—each representing a company—that compete in producing and selling the same product in the same marketing area. Each company tries to achieve a good financial position, to increase its assets, to make a good return on investment, and to place itself in a strong position for the future. Each team or company makes quarterly decisions in regard to product price, advertising, production volume and cost, research and development expenditure, and investment in additional plant manufacturing capacity. These decisions are fed into a computer that has been programmed with a mathematical model that simulates a typical economic situation in the market. The computer then feeds back to each team its own performance data derived from the interaction with the other competing teams. Teams can change their strategies as the game progresses and determine the impact upon performance of such changes.

A game contains many, but not all, the variables present in real-life business. Student-managers can learn the consequences of their decisions in a classroom situation, which is a low-risk environment. Student enthusiasm tends to be high when playing management games. Students play different roles in their teams and they learn how to work together cooperatively. A game takes the learning situation a step farther than can be done in a case study. In addition to diagnosing a problem and deciding upon a course of action, the students can learn what happens when they implement their decisions.

A limitation of management games is that the mathematical model, practically of necessity, has to be a simplified representation of real life. Because it is simplified (or if it is inaccurate) it may generate erroneous learning for the students.

Transactional Analysis

Transactional analysis (TA) is a technique used to help people better understand their own and others' behavior, especially in interpersonal relationships. Courses in TA are given to managers, salespersons, and professionals to help them improve interpersonal communications and effectiveness.

Dr. Eric Berne is generally credited with developing the basic concepts and theory of transactional analysis. It is based upon concepts of psychotherapy; however TA concepts and formulations are expressed in lay language so that it has become very popular in recent years. Besides Berne, others who have done important work in developing transactional analysis and in disseminating information about it are Thomas A. Harris, Muriel James, and Dorothy Jongeward.[6]

The primary concepts in transactional analysis are ego states, transactions, strokes, and ways people spend their time.

There are three ego states: parent, adult, and child. The *parent* ego state of a person comprises the judgmental, value-laden, rule-making, and moralizing component of personality. It is expressed by advice, admonitions, and "do's and don'ts." The *adult* ego state is authentic, direct, and reality-based. It is rational, fact seeking, thinking, and problem solving. The *child* ego state constitutes the emotional, crea-

[6]Eric Berne, *Transactional Analysis in Psychotherapy* New York: Grove Press, 1961); Eric Berne, *Games People Play* (New York: Grove Press, 1964); Thomas A. Harris, *I'm O.K.— You're O.K.* (New York: Harper & Row, 1967); Muriel James and Dorothy Jongeward, *Born to Win* (Reading, Mass.: Addison-Wesley, 1971).

tive, spontaneous, impulsive component of personality. It must be noted that ego states are not tied to one's chronological age. In the course of daily interactions adults are likely to display all three ego states, however, one state may predominate.

A *transaction* is a basic unit of social interaction. It consists of an exchange of words and behavior between two people. The heart of transactional analysis is the study and diagraming of the exchanges between two people. In this analysis the learner identifies the ego state that both the initiator and the respondent exhibit in the transaction.

A *stroke* is a unit of recognition, which can be positive or negative. People, generally, have a pervasive need for recognition and approval. Examples of positive strokes are: "You did a great job, Henry,"; "Would you like to join us for lunch, Mary?"; "I admire you." Examples of negative strokes are: "You failed again."; "Why are you here?"; "You did that job wrong."

The ways in which people *spend their time* are classified into six categories: withdrawal, rituals, activities, pastimes, psychological games, and authentic encounters or intimacy.

Courses in transactional analysis have become quite popular and widely used in American industry. By exposing their managerial personnel to these courses, top management hopes to improve their self-understanding, interpersonal effectiveness, communication, and leadership skills. The goals of TA are very similar to the goals of sensitivity training which is discussed later in this chapter. Transactional analysis generates much less tension in the learner and it is less threatening to him than is sensitivity training.

Management Development in Perspective. Management training and development are intimately related to the entire system of management practice in an organization. If administration is disorganized, haphazard, and faulty, then sound management development will be extremely difficult to accomplish. Executives and supervisors learn, to a great extent, by precept and example while on the job.

Management development activities must be undertaken on behalf of and by all members of management, not just a chosen few. An organization stands or falls on the basis of the total efforts of the entire team. An effective, going concern cannot afford to neglect a large segment of its leadership in favor of an elite corps.

Those in charge of guiding the whole program can appropriately adopt an eclectic view toward the process. They must not place all of their eggs in one basket of, say, job rotation or coaching or management games; rather they must establish a multidimensional program that reaches to every manager and educates in a variety of ways for a variety of specific purposes.

ORGANIZATION DEVELOPMENT

A host of problems that occur daily in the typical company tend to be ignored by the conventional improvement efforts of management development specialists, personnel managers, and management consultants. These are some common examples:

Professional staff members of the research and development department of a manufacturing firm feel that project teams do not communicate with one another effectively, laboratory leadership is too loose and sporadic, project funding procedures are inconsistent, and many scientists are underutilized in relation to their talents.

Administrators and staff specialists in Government Bureau A have learned that it is advisable for them to always record in writing their conversations and commitments made with other administrators, on a daily basis, as a defensive measure to protect their own positions. Many claim to have learned from bitter experience that higher-echelon administrators often look for scapegoats when programs are under criticism. They place the blame on lower-level functionaries.

Manager *A* vigorously opposes a proposal concerning new product development advanced by Manager *B*. Manager *A* advances numerous arguments that have the aura of rationality but the underlying reason for the opposition is a personal animosity and suspicion of Manager *B*. The culture of the organization does not permit such feelings to be recognized openly, hence they surface indirectly.

Specifically, what is organization development (often called, simply, OD)? *OD is a planned process designed to improve organizational effectiveness and health through modifications in individual and group behavior, culture, and systems of the organization using knowledge and technology of applied behavioral science.* Frequently, a consultant (called a change agent) is used to assist in diagnosing the situation and in helping the client develop action programs to improve the organizational effectiveness. The change agent may come from outside the organization or may be a full-time member of the organization but external to the particular client group being helped. An important component of OD is the systematic assessment of the needs of the organization and the problem areas to be worked on. The client group normally plays an important role in carrying out the assessment.

OD is a developing and evolving field of activity. It does not consist of a fixed methodology. The professional practitioners, including researchers, writers, and consultants, have created and applied a variety of approaches and techniques for organizational improvement. However there are certain commonalities. Most practitioners in this field have been trained in the behavioral sciences. Most tend to emphasize the people dimensions of organizational effectiveness, such as attitudes, norms, values, interpersonal skills, and behavior patterns. However, they do not ignore such elements as organization structure, reward systems, managerial con-

trol, and technology. Most lean philosophically toward a supportive, collaborative, and participative system of management.

Values of OD Movement

It is imperative that corporate executives who are considering whether to launch an OD effort in their establishments gain a full understanding of its underlying values, because these values differ somewhat from those prevailing in work organizations. In many respects the OD values strike a responsive chord in managers who believe these values represent what *ought* to be, even though day-to-day experience typifies an opposed set of values. Let us now review the dominant values of the OD movement.

People Are Basically Good. If one considers that mankind is fundamentally evil, lazy, irresponsible, and selfish, then she or he copes with this situation by installing all sorts of controls and punishments that force people to behave according to the will of the owner, master, or boss. On the other hand, if people are viewed as potentially good, responsible, helpful, and trustworthy, then one leads by being supportive and creating opportunities for growth, self-control, and personal responsibility.

Need for Confirmation and Support. Often organization members are conditioned to believe that "no news is good news." Supervisors pay attention to their people only when they make a job assignment or when they want to find fault for an alleged failure. Yet we all have a human need to be confirmed as a person and to know that the boss really does care about us.

Accept Differences Among People. The health of an organization can be enhanced if the managers and employees accept differences in personality and viewpoints. The conventional rule that subordinates ought not disagree with the boss is challenged by organization development precepts. It is legitimate to raise opposing views in staff meetings. It is legitimate to take an unpopular stand and disagree with the group. The organization is strengthened when employees have a variety of backgrounds and orientations.

Express Feelings and Emotions. In the business world the prevailing view is that people must exhibit only their rational side to others. Many believe that to exhibit sentiment, emotion, anger, or tenderness is to show weakness.

Yet high levels of motivation, commitment, and creativity depend, not upon detachment, but upon giving full range to one's expression and feelings. We expect people in the performing arts to express their emotions because this is required in order to reach the peak of their talents. If members of the business organization are to apply themselves to the fullest of their abilities, we should also expect them to exhibit anger, joy, and exhilaration.

Be Authentic, Open, and Direct. Duplicity is exhibited widely in work establishments. In the game of influence maneuvering that seems to go on continually, many managers feel that they must manipulate others, tell half-truths, and mask their true motives.

But is such behavior truly productive? Organization development practitioners think not. Honesty and directness enable people to put their energy into the real problems of the job rather than force them to spend their efforts in fending off the machinations of others.

Foster Cooperation. Some executives know of no other way to manage their people than to generate win-lose competition for salary increases, choice work assignments, and for the bestowal of their favors. They view life as a raw struggle where only the fittest survive. Yet work roles in modern organizations are highly interdependent. People must learn that teamwork and collaboration generate a greater volume of production than does destructive interpersonal competition.

Confront Conflict. Rather than suppress conflict (interpersonal conflict, not violence), gloss it over, or ignore it, it ought to be brought out into the open in order to identify root causes and to work out a satisfactory resolution.

Objectives

When top management decides to establish an organization development program it commonly has a number of objectives in mind. One goal may be to increase the openness of communication among people, levels in the structure, and departments, and to build into the system a process of feedback of performance and attitudes to aid in making adjustments. Managers and employees can be expected to increase their commitment, self-direction, and self-control. They will acquire a greater sense of ownership of the objectives of the organization.

Another aim of OD may be to have decisions made on the basis of information and knowledge by people who are close to the point of the actual action, rather than follow the bureaucratic practice of "bucking" decisions up to the top of the hierarchy. As a result of OD, collaborative effort, rather than destructive energy-wasting competition, can be expected to increase. Underlying hostilities and conflict will be brought out into the open, and constructive efforts made toward their resolution. And finally, organization development can help facilitate the kind of change in the enterprise which is viewed as necessary by getting the organization members involved in the process of analysis and implementation.

The OD Process

Organization development starts with the perception by some responsible executive (or group of executives) that there are inadequacies within the organization that can probably be corrected by the introduction of organization development activities. If the requisite professional competence for OD is not available within the enterprise, then management will engage the services of a qualified outside consultant— sometimes also called a facilitator or change agent—to help diagnose the organizational situation and to develop OD activities, called interventions, to solve the problems identified. In recent years many larger corporations have acquired OD competence within their own personnel (or human resource) departments. Specifically these resource people are usually located within the management training or OD group of the personnel department.

The OD consultant, whether from within or from outside the organization, works closely with the management team in information gathering, joint diagnosis, and selection of the particular interventions or activities to be utilized to improve the functioning of the organization. The change agent is a skilled advisor who helps the whole management team recognize its problems, learn the skills to resolve them, and then work out solutions on the job. The consultant does not serve as a master mind who imposes his own solutions. Rather he or she is a *process* specialist who helps managers solve their organizational problems.

Elements of the OD Process

The OD process comprises the following five components:

1. Diagnosis.
2. Selection and design of interventions.
3. Implementation of intervention.
4. Evaluation.
5. Adjustment and maintenance of system.

The *diagnosis* phase of organization development assesses the health (or illness) of the organization. It identifies problems and clues to the causes of these problems. The particular target unit may be the whole organization, a major division, a plant, a department, or a group of people within a department. The diagnosis typically focuses upon such organizational processes as communication patterns, goal setting, planning and decision making, conflict resolution, relations among different departments and groups, and superior-subordinate relations.

The tools that can be used for diagnosis are questionnaires, interviews, direct observation, and analysis of documents and reports. A questionnaire administered to all the personnel of a given department or establishment might ask such questions as:

1. To what extent do you feel free to talk to your superior about problems of your job?
2. How well are you kept informed of relevant matters in your department?
3. To what extent are promotions awarded to those who have performed well?
4. To what degree do the members of your department cooperate and help one another?

Whereas a questionnaire can be administered to large numbers of people, respondents can be anonymous, and it can be designed for objective scoring, an interview is a personalized face-to-face contact. It is useful for an in-depth exploration of information uncovered via the questionnaire.

Direct observation generally involves the observation of a group of people and the recording of their behavior on observation data sheets which list the various elements of behavior to be collected. A variant, which is really a combination of the questionnaire and observation, asks all those people within an organization who deal with a given department, say production, to record the experiences and impressions they have acquired in dealing with that department.

The final source of information about an organization's problems consists of documents and reports that may already be available. A study of existing reports may reveal those departments having excessive scrap, costs, turn-over, absences, or grievances.

After the diagnosis phase of OD has been carried out, one turns next to *selection and design of interventions*. Indeed this step is intimately related to diagnosis. If it has been determined that the relations between Department *A* and Department *B* have been stormy and nonproductive, then the consultant and the client managers may design an intergroup workshop involving members of both departments. If the diagnosis phase uncovers the fact that there is insufficient openness, trust, and cooperation within a department, then a laboratory training program may be designed.

Implementation of intervention is the third phase of the OD process. Implementation involves working with the people in the target organizational units. The intervention may take the form of workshops, feedback of data to participants, group discussions, written exercises, on-the-job activities, redesign of control systems, redesign of jobs and numerous other activities. It is important to recognize that OD is not a "one-shot, quick cure" for an organization's ills. Achieving real, lasting change in the attitudes and behavior of organizational members takes a great deal of effort and much time.

The fourth stage is *evaluation*. The OD efforts must be evaluated to determine what results are being achieved and to determine if these efforts must be redirected. Depending upon the nature of the problems to be corrected, the evaluation effort may be simple or complex. In some cases simple observation of or interviews with the participants may be sufficient. In other instances more sophisticated evaluation designs may be needed. For example the same survey instrument may be administered before the OD intervention and six months after the intervention to detect changes. Or, experimental and control groups may be compared.

The fifth and final step is *adjustment and maintenance of the system*. This step is often omitted, but it should not be. As evaluation information is received from step four, the change agent and the management clients should determine what changes, if any, should be made in the OD interventions. Are the intended results being realized? If not, why not? Have there been unintended results? Have other parts of the organization been changed by the OD efforts? Organization development is properly viewed as an on-going process. Adjustments are to be expected as the process proceeds.

INTERVENTIONS

The interventions of organization development are the planned activities that are introduced into the system to accomplish the desired changes and improvements. Interventions are the methods and techniques that have been created by OD professionals and others to achieve improvements in the functioning of organizations. The major kinds of interventions are as follows: survey feedback, process consultation, sensitivity (laboratory) training, managerial grid, goal setting and planning, and team building. In addition, there are other kinds of interventions used by OD consultants which have been developed from somewhat different intellectual roots. Among these are changes in the organization structure, job enrichment, compensation systems, work flow, and participative management systems.

It ought to be clear that no single company and no single consultant would utilize all these techniques. The choice of a particular intervention strategy depends upon the diagnosis of needs and upon the particular orientations of the management of the client firm and of the consultant.

Survey Feedback

Attitude surveys have been used by progressive companies for many years to ascertain the viewpoints of the employees about such matters as wages, hours, working conditions, and the treatment they get from their supervisors. However, with the traditional attitude survey the analysis of the results and the development of action plans to correct the deficiencies is the exclusive province of the personnel department and upper management. Except for receiving a summary of the tabulated responses in the company newspaper, the employees have no involvement.

The OD way of handling attitude surveys is to feed back the results to all the people who filled out the questionnaires. The data is first provided to the top executive team. Then each executive holds a meeting with the people reporting directly to her or him to analyze and evaluate the survey results in a workshop setting. In these workshops plans are formulated to take actions to correct the problems identified by the survey. This workshop process proceeds downward throughout the entire hierarchy. Even rank and file workers are involved in discussing the survey results that apply to their own work unit. They can suggest solutions to problems. The workshop is conducted by the relevant manager or supervisor. Often the OD consultant participates in the workshops as a resource person.

Process Consultation

Although used by many practitioners the leading innovator and spokesman for process consultation is Edgar Schein.[7] The process consultant helps the organization members with whom she or he is dealing learn to develop the skills needed to diagnose and solve the on-going problems of their organization. The consultant does not mastermind matters for them, but instead helps the people diagnose a number of important human processes such as communi-

[7]See Edgar H. Schein, *Process Consultation: Its Role in Organization Development* (Reading, Mass.: Addison-Wesley Publishing Co., 1969).

cation, member roles and functions in groups, group problem solving and decision-making, group norms, leadership and authority, intergroup cooperation and competition, and conflict.

The process consultant meets with the department members in work teams, observes their interactions and problem-solving procedures, and feeds back to the teams observations along the human dimensions mentioned above. She or he helps the team members understand the interaction, influence, and decision-making processes that have gone on in their work team meetings. She or he coaches and counsels individuals and groups to help them understand their behavior and help them work out more effective behavior. But the consultant does not impose prescriptions.

Sensitivity Training

Sensitivity training (often called T-group or laboratory training) is an experiential method using relatively unstructured face-to-face groups as the principal learning vehicle.

The objectives of sensitivity training are to help people understand themselves better, to create better understanding of others, to gain insight into the group process, and to develop specific behavioral skills. Many people go through life never really understanding why they feel and act as they do. They do not really know how others feel about them. They are insensitive to the effects of their behavior upon others.

Employees give great deference to their bosses. Supervisors may, year after year, issue orders to subordinates and criticize them without ever fully realizing that many of them may fear or hate them. If such bosses have an opportunity to participate in a sensitivity-training course, they can be expected to gain important insights into themselves and their effect upon others. Quite often trainees are upset about what they learn.

T-group programs also seek to improve communication skills. They help the trainee become an active listener—to really learn through listening. When engaged in conversation, many of us concentrate upon what we are going to say rather than upon what the other fellow is saying.

Additional goals are to aid participants to work more effectively as group or team members and to perform leadership roles at times. Also one can see how informal groups coalesce, how people come to play different roles, how informal leadership may emerge, and how an organization actually takes structure and form. They can observe and experience interpersonal influence.

How is sensitivity training carried on? Although methods vary somewhat depending upon the specific orientation of the program, the core of most programs is the face-to-face, largely unstructured T-group. This group typically consists of from eight to about sixteen persons. At times there may be no leader, no agenda, and no stated goal for this small group. The group is left to its own devices to develop interaction and on-going experiences that serve as the real substance of the learning process. At other times the designated "trainer" introduces certain planned activities involving interaction between paired individuals and subgroups. The participants are encouraged to give feedback to each other on their personal feelings and reactions to what is happening in the group and on their reactions to one another's behavior. The emphasis is on the "here and now," not on the participants' experiences before they come to the program.

One or two professional trainers sit in with each T-group. However, the trainer tends to remain in the background. He does not lecture to them, does not rule certain conduct right and other conduct wrong, and does not pass out rewards and penalties (grades) as in conventional training courses. The role of the trainer sometimes seems ambiguous to the T-group members. At times the trainer plays the role of a detached observer, at other times acts as a group member, and at others clearly introduces planned exercises for the group to engage in. The trainer's true role is to help the individuals and the group to learn from their own experiences in the group.

The emphasis in T-group work is not upon learning specific objective facts but rather upon gaining understanding of feelings, gestures, attitudes, and emotions—in short, sensitivity to oneself and others. There is a high degree of participation, feeling, and involvement in the typical session.

In addition to the T-groups, laboratory training also may include role playing, intergroup competitive exercises, self-insight questionnaires, theory sessions with lectures, background readings, panel discussions, and training films.

The major criticisms of sensitivity training have been that it generates too much emotional stress for the participants, that the process takes one's psychological defenses away (and thus constitutes an invasion of privacy), and that it is very difficult for the participants to carry over the openness, trust, and equalitarianism from the T-group to their ordinary job environments. Because of these problems, sensitivity training which emphasizes primarily introspection and interpersonal relations has declined drastically in usage over the past decade or so. Nowadays a sensitivity-training group is generally composed of people from the same organization or department who are brought together to improve their understanding, attitudes, and interpersonal relationships to solve real work problems. Sometimes the intervention may be called something other than sensitivity training. It might be called such things as team building or *managerial grid* (phases 1 and 2).

The Managerial Grid

The managerial grid, created by Robert R. Blake and Jane S. Mouton, utilizes small face-to-face groups as the basic learning mechanism.

The theoretical formulation underlying a grid seminar is the "managerial grid." This is a graphic way of expressing underlying assumptions and theories about ways of managing people in work organizations. Blake and Mouton have synthesized and summarized the salient features of current theory in organizational behavior. They postulate that managers may evidence a concern for production or a concern for people (or a combination of these) in their styles of management. The graphic representation in grid form displays concern for production along the abscissa or X-axis on a scale from 1 through 9. The ordinate or Y-axis expresses concern for people and is also on a scale of 1 through 9. See Figure 13-1. A management theory that exhibits a maximum concern for production and a minimal interest in people (9, 1) is characterized by a high-pressure, authoritarian style. The converse of 9, 1 management is 1, 9, which shows a low concern for production and a high concern for people. This has been labeled "country-club" management. Leadership that evidences a high concern for both people and production is labeled 9, 9. This is held to be a most desirable pattern of management from the standpoint of conflict resolution, creativity, commitment, morale, and productivity. In addition to these three positions on the grid, there is the 1, 1 theory of management wherein management basically abdicates its responsibilities for both people and productivity and the 5, 5 theory wherein management compromises and adopts an "organization-man" strategy. These five basic theories of management can be supplemented by eight other positions or combinations on the grid to make a total of thirteen formulations.

There are six steps or phases in grid organization development. Phase 1 consists of studying the managerial grid as a theoretical framework for understanding human behavior in the organization. The participants are pointed toward a full comprehension of 9, 9 management as a basis of organizational excellence.

The grid seminar, typically of one week's duration, is composed of a number of study

FIGURE 13-1 The Managerial Grid.

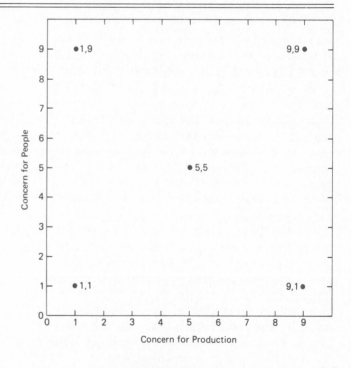

teams of five to nine members each. Participants come from various organizations. The objectives of the one-week seminar include helping each person to recognize his own grid style, developing team action skills, facilitating interpersonal communication within a team, strengthening the use of the critique for problem solving and learning, and helping the members analyze their own corporate work culture.

Phase 2, called teamwork development, is a seminar of one week's duration consisting of the members of the management of a single company grouped into family teams. Thus, a plant manager and his immediate subordinates could constitute one seminar team. Each member's perception of the team's culture is developed and discussed in the context of the actual problems faced on the job, whether they be financial, market strategy, quality control, union relations, or the like. The teams also work on objective-setting and problem-solving projects related to their area of corporate responsibilities. Participants learn the benefits of openness and directness in introducing problems and working them through to solutions.

Phase 3, designated intergroup development, focuses upon the relationships between different divisions, departments, and units. Frequently marketing, production, and engineering departments exemplify contrasting orientations to the solutions of common problems. A major goal of Phase 3 is to develop improved ways of resolving differences.

Phase 4 involves the creation of an ideal strategic model for the organization. The participants are primarily the chief executive and his or her immediate subordinates, although there is input from many other managers. These top executives study books and articles written by successful business leaders who have described their corporate strategy problems and how they met them. When reading this resource literature the executives are provided with study guides that help them analyze the material according to six areas: financial objectives, nature of the business, nature of the markets, organization struc-

ture, policy, and development requirements. After completion of the above work, the team meets for essentially a full week of activity to relate the knowledge gained from the written sources to the formulation of an idealized corporate strategy plan.

Phase 5 is implementation of the strategic model. This is carried out by working through the natural components of the corporation, whether they be divisions, profit centers, or product lines. For each component a planning team is established whose function is to examine all the essential elements of its operations.

The sixth and last phase is a systematic critique of progress achieved using as a guide generalized criteria that Blake and Mouton have devised and presented under the designation *Corporate Excellence Rubric*.[8]

Goal Setting and Planning

Logically, many would claim that goal setting and planning ought to be an essential part of any organization improvement program. Indeed it should come near the beginning.

One method for accomplishing this is for top management to establish corporate and divisional goals for such items as return on investment, share of the market, new products, human resources, and community relations. Then each organizational unit, working down through the structure, sets its own goals, somewhat independently of top-management goals, but with knowledge of them. The statements of these goals are sent to the top management

[8]This account of grid organization development is derived from Robert R. Blake and Jane S. Mouton, *Building a Dynamic Corporation Through Grid Organization Development* (Reading, Mass.: Addison-Wesley Publishing Co., 1969). The reader may also wish to consult Robert R. Blake and Jane S. Mouton, *Corporate Excellence Through Grid Organization Development* (Houston, Texas: Gulf Publishing Company, 1968). The theoretical formulation of the managerial grid is presented in Robert R. Blake and Jane S. Mouton, *The Managerial Grid* (Houston, Texas: Gulf Publishing Company, 1964).

group. Analysis is made. If there are discrepancies top management may adjust its goals in the light of information from the various units. Also the discrepancies may be identified by top management and sent back to the various units for modification. With successive interactions an agreed-upon set of organization-wide goals can emerge. A high level of commitment to the goals can emerge from this process.

Team Building

Team building is one of the most frequently used OD interventions. The heart of team building is a series of off-site problem-solving sessions of two to five days duration. They are usually for family groups, that is, a manager and all those reporting directly to her or him. Sometimes they are also carried out for two or three interacting departments. These sessions are normally conducted by a third party, either the external OD consultant or the internal staff consultant.

Important purposes of team building are to set goals and priorities, clarify roles and responsibilities, identify problems and conflicts, improve communication and understanding, and to diagnose the ways in which the department is functioning.

Part and parcel of team-building programs is feedback of diagnostic information collected by the OD consultant. Before the team-building meetings she or he may have discovered such dysfunctional aspects as employee alienation, overlap of responsibilities, missed deadlines, and destructive interpersonal competition.

In the team-building meetings the consultant helps the group frame an agenda, encouraging the people to be open and direct. They are encouraged to take risks in what they say and do. Trust and full expression of opinions are also encouraged. Actually, the behavior of the manager of the department tends to set the tone for the level of candor and trust the members will exhibit.

Other Interventions

The methodologies described above are the major techniques or interventions utilized by organization development practitioners. However, there are other important techniques that are used for organizational improvement and change. These other techniques have generally been created previous to the emergence of the OD movement or independent from it. They constitute worthwhile strategies and are often incorporated into OD programs. These other interventions, explained in other chapters of this book, are the following:

1. *Job enrichment:* the adding of decision-making, responsibility, challenge, and larger units of accomplishment to routine jobs.
2. *Management by objectives:* collaboration between manager and each subordinate in setting the subordinate's work goals, evaluating progress, and setting new goals.
3. *Changes in organization structure:* introducing different organization designs such as project and matrix organization or decentralization.
4. *Participative management:* participative problem-solving meetings, Scanlon plans, union-management cooperation.

CONCLUDING OBSERVATIONS

Organization development is most successful when there is a deep commitment to it on the part of top management. Further, since changing the culture of an organization to one of collaboration, openness, and trust is an integral part of OD, the OD effort must infuse the whole organization.

Because of the orientation and training of its leading proponents, organization development tends to focus upon changing attitudes, and values, and enhancing interpersonal skills.

However, OD professionals do recognize that structural changes in the system such as job redesign, organization redesign, and new compensation plans are also very important for achieving lasting improvement in the performance of an organization.

Finally OD should be viewed as a long-term, continuing process rather than a short-term "shot-in-the-arm" for the organization.

Questions for Review and Discussion

1. What is a manager and what does a manager do?
2. Why is it necessary that management training and development activities be started with top executives first?
3. What are the essential components of a comprehensive management development program?
4. Which techniques, of those discussed in Chapters 12 and 13, are most effective for accomplishing the following objectives?
   a. Impart factual knowledge.
   b. Induce atittude change.
   c. Develop awareness of one's self and one's effect upon others.
   d. Enhance cooperation among members of a department.
5. What do you think of the philosophical values of the organization development movement? Do you think these values are widely supported by American managers?
6. Think of some organization where you have worked or where you now are a member. How might it benefit from OD? What specific interventions would you recommend?
7. If an OD effort is successful in a given organization, how would you know it? What measure or gauges could be used? Is it likely that the culture of that organization will have been changed?

CASE PROBLEM

A SUPERVISORY TRAINING COURSE

James Westmore was contacted on the telephone by the Extension Director of State University Labor—Management Center. Westmore was a professor at a private university in a nearby city. The director invited Westmore to teach a ten-session supervisory training course to the shop foremen at the Peerless Machine and Foundry Works. He suggested that Professor Westmore visit the personnel manager at Peerless to become oriented to the company and its problems.

The Peerless company employed 300 people and produced heavy iron and steel products. The personnel manager told Professor Westmore that he liked to take advantage of State University's services by having it give one course for the foremen every year on some aspects of supervision and industrial relations. The full cost of these courses were paid by State University as part of its extension program for industrial, labor, and public organizations.

Inasmuch as the company could not spare the foremen during the working day, the course was given one afternoon each week for ten weeks from 4 to 6 P.M. The foremen came directly to the course from their jobs. They received time and one half overtime for these extra hours. Because the company lacked training class facilities, the personnel manager arranged that it be held in the quarters of a fraternal club a few blocks from the plant.

This fraternal club was situated in an old house in a declining section of the town. A makeshift classroom was set up in the former dining room of the house. Old card tables were placed back to back to make a conference-type layout. The blackboard consisted of an old slate supported by a card table and leaned against the wall. Light was provided by an old-fashioned chandelier from which several bulbs were missing.

On the Monday afternoon of the first class Professor Westmore found that he had to introduce himself to the class of sixteen foremen. The personnel manager had left word with one of the men to say that he was busy and could not make it. Because there was no chalk for the slate board, one of the foremen volunteered to go to the store to buy some.

Professor Westmore had prepared a course outline that contained the following topics: (1) nature of a foreman's job, (2) what foremen expect from management, (3) what workers expect from their foremen, (4) elementary aspects of organization, (5) motivation, (6) making work assignments, (7) coaching, (8) complaints and grievances, (9) leadership, and (10) discipline. He made weekly assignments of about 25 to 30 pages in a textbook on supervision. The classes were conducted on a lecture-discussion basis with some case studies used.

Professor Westmore noticed that the men were always late for the class although they seemed to be in and about the building. Finally at 4:00 P.M. on the the third week he decided to explore the building. To his surprise he found most of the men drinking beer at a bar located on the second floor. In class the foremen were courteously attentive on the surface but basically seemed unenthusiastic. In many of the discussions they stated that they had learned about various aspects of human relations and supervision in courses given to them by other instructors in previous years. Professor Westmore began to wonder if he had been hired to repeat instruction that had been given previously. The men said on more than one occasion that the ideas about leadership and human relations contained in the book and in Professor Westmore's talks were O.K. in theory, but they wouldn't work at the Peerless plant because of MacGregor, the factory manager. They claimed that MacGregor knew nothing about human relations and was tough to deal with, that the union always went directly to the personnel manager with the grievances, and that they, as foremen, had no authority. All discipline was handled by the personnel manager.

Westmore observed to himself that these foremen felt more like workers than members of management. They even dressed in the blue jeans and shop work clothes. The pattern-shop foreman made the following statement to him one day: "I have worked here for twenty-five years and have been a foreman for fifteen. But maybe I should have taken a job somewhere else. One day I was standing on the street corner when a truck from the Acme Steel Company went by. The truckdriver must have just gotten his paycheck, because he threw his checkstub out the window and I picked it up. He gets $300 a week, and that is lots more than I get as a foreman."

Questions

1. Was this training course launched properly?
2. What could foremen training accomplish in this company?
3. What do you think of the course content and method of instruction?
4. How do you account for the behavior of the foremen in this training program?
5. If you had free rein to make needed changes, what actions and what kind of management development program would you establish for this company? How would you carry out your program?

Suggestions for Further Reading

Burke, W. Warner. *Organization Development: Principles and Practices.* Boston: Little, Brown and Co., 1982.

Digman, Lester A. "Management Development: Needs and Practices," *Personnel,* Vol. 57, No. 4 (July–August 1980), pp. 45–57.

Levinson, Harry. "Executive Development: What You Need to Know," *Training and Development Journal,* Vol. 35, No. 9 (September 1981), pp. 84–95.

Lippitt, Gordon L. *Organizational Renewal,* 2nd ed., Englewood Cliffs, N.J.: Prentice-Hall, 1982.

Livingston, J. Sterling. "New Trends in Applied Management Development," *Training and Development Journal,* Vol. 37, (January 1983), pp. 14–16+.

MacDonald, Charles R. *Performance-Based Supervisory Development.* Amherst, Mass.: Human Resource Development Press, 1982.

Robey, Daniel, and Steven Altman. *Organizational Development,* New York: Macmillan Publishing Co., Inc., 1982.

Watson, Charles E. *Management Development Through Training.* Reading, Mass.: Addison-Wesley Publishing Co., Inc., 1980.

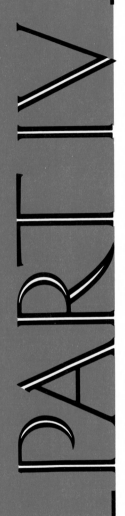

PART IV

Understanding and Managing People

14 People and Motivation

Human beings, as individuals, are very complex in their psychological makeup. When they interact with one another in groups and in large organizations, the complexities are multiplied. Scientists still have much to learn about the nature of mankind. However, as a result of systematic experimentation, observation, and clinical studies, behavioral scientists have developed insights into the nature and conditions of human behavior.

This chapter is essentially concerned with an analysis of the reasons people behave as they do, and with an explanation of various means by which management can stimulate and guide the conduct and actions of members of its organization. We shall explore the subject of human motivation and look into some important theories of motivation. Why do people act as they do? What do they seek out of life? Do most human drives and wants form a consistent pattern? We shall delve into the subject of human adjustment and the concepts of adaptive and maladaptive behavior. What are the characteristics of behavior induced by frustration? How can one's job induce frustrations?

Finally, and most importantly, we shall discuss ways in which motivational principles can be applied by management in the work situation. The concept of integration of goals—the joining together of the drives and wants of employees with those of the organization for which they work—will be examined.

HUMAN BEHAVIOR FUNDAMENTALS

In efforts to guide and direct others, the manager must first of all acquire an understanding of the nature of human behavior and why people act as they do.

Self-concept and Personality

To understand other people, we must be aware of how they think and feel about themselves. This image of self that individuals hold may not be fully accurate. Nevertheless, they will tend to behave in accordance with their own self-image. Their actions are a function of how they view themselves. Their behavior will be logical from their point of view although it may not appear logical from our own perspective. Even though people's knowledge of themselves may be a little vague, they will strive at all times to be true to their own views of themselves.

How does a person acquire his self-concept? The strongest influence is that in the home during one's formative years as a child. If a child is raised in a family where people are demonstrative, he will learn that this is approved behavior. If high but attainable standards of achievement are expected by his parents, he will tend to hold to such standards throughout life. Children in the family are rewarded or punished for all sorts of behavior. They learn to avoid physical and emotional pain and to repeat that behavior which gains approval and reward. In addition to the influences of the parents, brothers, and sisters, are those of friends, associates, teachers, and other authority figures. As a child matures he gains a view of his personal worth on the basis of the way others respond to him and on the basis of his achievements. Thus, a person's sense of personal worth is conferred on him as well as derived in relation to his accomplishments. Gradually as maturation takes place, the individual acquires rather definite beliefs about what his behavior, values, and goals ought to be. These become internalized.

In addition to self-concept everyone also acquires a personal view of his world. He perceives and responds to other people, places, things, and events. His personal frame of reference is an amalgam of his self-image, behavior, and his perception of the world about him. His perceptions and preconceived notions of his environment help determine whether he will be bold or meek, optimistic or pessimistic, trusting or suspicious.

Based upon his self-concept and his view of the world about him, each individual develops an accommodation and a characteristic way of acting. He will always behave in such a way as to protect and improve his adequacy in his world as he sees it. His behavior is internally logical and consistent as he sees it.

In talking about *self*, we have in a sense also been talking about personality. Personality is the sum total of the physical, mental, emotional, and social characteristics of a person. It is the integrating process by which all the physiological and psychological components of man are combined into the whole. Psychologists, in their research investigations, have devised many ways of quantifying bodily sensations, perceptions, intelligence, attitudes, and motives. However, these do not act singly. They are all contained within the unified whole of the person. Elsie Edwards is the personnel director. It is not simply her intelligence alone nor her emotional state alone that is Elsie Edwards. All of her attributes operate together to reveal her characteristic responses. The *self* and *personality* are one and the same. Personality is more than the sum of all the various attributes of a person; it is the organization of these parts.

When a human being is internally consistent, we speak of him or her as having a well-adjusted personality. When he or she is externally adapted to his or her environment, we say he or she is well-adapted. When one is both adjusted and adapted, we say that he or she has an integrated personality.

As a person matures, he gains more needs and abilities, and he also deepens many of those he already possesses. As new ideas, traits, and outlooks are gained, these are incorporated into the person so as not to upset his equilibrium. With maturation his private world expands. His perception of the world about him is always colored by his frame of reference and his self-image. Actually everyone, in a sense, lives in his own private world. The personality becomes complete and integrated only when it interacts with other people, things, and groups. We can understand ourselves only as we can understand others; conversely we can understand others only if we also understand ourselves.

Human Behavior Is Caused

Initially it is important to know that all human behavior has a cause (or causes). There is a reason for a person's behaving as she does. A stimulus is present to initiate behavior on the part of the individual. For example, physiological changes in the body accompanying the passage of time since a person has had her last meal will give rise to a feeling of emptiness and discomfort in her stomach. There will be a feeling of hunger. We call this a need or a feeling of tension inside the person. The person will normally then seek food to alleviate her hunger so that she can again experience a feeling of well-being. To generalize, we can say that one or more stimuli may interact with an individual. The person will then experience a state of tension such that she seeks to fulfill her need and reduce the level of tension and discomfort. She adopts a type of behavior that will satisfy her need.

The cause for human behavior constitutes an interaction between a stimulus (noise, light, a threat) and the person's own internal interpretation of that stimulus. Thus, to one person a sound may be annoying, whereas another may consider it like soothing music. If one employee smiles at another, the second may view the smile as a leering smirk. On the other hand, someone else may consider it a smile of approbation. One's perception is determined by background, personality, and the circumstances surrounding the event.

The actions of rational human beings are goal-directed. Our behavior is aimed toward the fulfillment of basic wants, drives, and needs. The politician who does favors for constituents hopes thereby to gain their votes at election time so that he can retain his office. The piece-rate worker in the clothing factory may work very hard to increase her earnings because she desires to buy a new coat or a car. It is important to understand that behavior is purposeful and that it is caused. People are not uncooperative just for the sake of being perverse. There are causes for such behavior. The successful leader is the one who can uncover these causes and take steps to correct them. Bawling out an uncooperative worker does not get at the cause. This constitutes treating the symptom only.

Motives are the mainspring of action in people. The leader who wishes to incite his followers to reach an objective must hold out the promise of reward once the objective is attained. What rewards do people seek in life? The answer is that they seek to fulfill their wants, drives, and needs.

The term *motive* implies action to satisfy a need. The terms *need, want, drive,* and *motive* are often used interchangeably by psychologists. Motivation can be defined as a willingness to expend energy to achieve a goal or a reward. Let us look at the chart below in order better to understand motivation.

Need	Behavior	Reward
Respect from others	Outstanding work on the job	Praise, pay increase, status symbols

Assume that an engineer in industry seeks to win the admiration and esteem not only of his boss but also of his fellow engineers. This feeling is called a need or a motive. Although there are perhaps a number of ways of achieving this, let us assume that our engineer chooses to work unusually diligently on a particular design project so that it becomes evident to his supervisor that he has made a major contribution. The supervisor may then choose to reward the engineer for his performance with oral praise, with a pay increase at salary review time, with certain formal recognition in the company newspaper, or by means of a letter of commendation to higher management. Depending upon how the individual perceives these forms of reward, the original need may be wholly or partially satisfied.

The psychology of learning tells us about the *law of effect, which states that behavior that is perceived to be rewarding will tend to be repeated, whereas behavior that goes unrewarded or is punished will tend to be extinguished.* This has great import for trainers, personnel directors, and managers. Over the long run they can induce desired behavior such as high-quality workmanship, good attendance, loyalty, or initiative by their choice of rewards and the way they are administered. Unrewarded behavior tends to disappear, as evidenced by the example of a high-level engineer in the department of public works of a state government who worked out a plan for saving $250,000 for the government. He installed the plan on his own authority and then proudly informed his boss about his cost saving. His boss showed not the slightest interest in this accomplishment. What his boss was interested in was new and bigger projects to expand the prestige of his department, not ways to reduce expenses. The engineer got the message and did not repeat his cost-cutting venture.

Classification of Needs

To understand human needs adequately, it is useful to classify them as to type. Thus we have innate or primary needs, such as food, shelter, water, rest to overcome fatigue, and so on. These are inborn needs. Generally speaking, they are not conditioned by experience. The innate needs are primarily physiological in nature. Gratification of these needs is vital to the survival of a human being as an organism.

The other major type of need is called an acquired or secondary need. These needs are dependent upon our experience. They are learned. They vary greatly from person to person and from one group to another. The need for a lady to wear white gloves and a hat at certain social gatherings in warm weather is certainly not inborn. It is culturally determined. It is acquired from her parents and friends. It is largely a manifestation of the desire to belong

and be accepted by others. In the home the child feels a need to be wanted and loved. We are all familiar with the serious emotional problems that occur in children who are rejected by their parents. The same motives to be needed, to be wanted, and to belong are present in adults. An employee can readily sense when the boss disapproves of her. If a supervisor or manager, by attitude and actions, makes it apparent that he or she dislikes an employee, this usually causes anxiety, tension, and frustration in the subordinate. If the supervisor's attitude is readily apparent to the other employees, his or her attitude often has an effect upon their relations with the rejected employee. Figure 14.1 presents a classification and listing of basic human needs.

The drive to obtain safety and security has several ramifications. Partly it is related to the innate physiological need for self-preservation. The aim is to avoid bodily harm, to avoid suffering, to continue to exist. The need for security is also social in context. The fact that one knows that others like him, respect him, and want him to continue to be a part of the group or organization, enhances his feeling of security. We can call it a feeling of emotional security. The struggle to achieve a measure of security is fundamental for most people. Some achieve financial security by means of hard work, superior ability, and fortuitous circumstances. Others turn to collective security from their group. Thus, we have various health and welfare programs to provide a measure of security for eligible members. These may take the form of a pension plan operated by a private employer for its employees, a group insurance program paid for by union members' dues, or a comprehensive social security program provided by a national government for its citizens.

The egoistic needs are concerned primarily with a person's view or conception of self. Satisfaction of these needs tends to enhance one's ego. Some writers refer to the egoistic needs as *personal* drives. They are often called the higher needs, because a person is seldom motivated to fulfill them until after he or she has first met his

FIGURE 14-1 A Classification of Basic Human Needs.

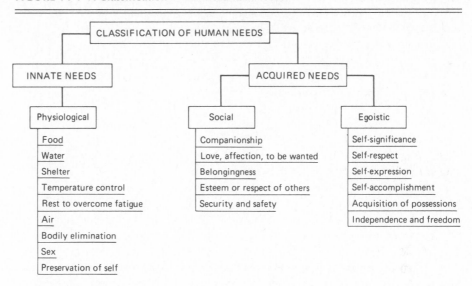

or her physiological and social wants. Business executives and political leaders tend to be strongly motivated to meet their egoistic needs. They have a drive for power, prestige, and status. They seek to make their mark in the world. They want to accomplish and achieve. They want others to hear their words. But persons of lesser fame also desire satisfaction of their personal needs. The bookkeeper with forty years' service who has labored long and hard in the back room of a merchandising establishment feels a warm glow when someone praises him, and he feels very important if his boss asks him for his advice on an involved accounting problem.

Hierarchy of Needs—Maslow

The psychologist A. H. Maslow has developed a widely acclaimed theory of human motivation in which he postulates that there is a definite rank-order priority of human needs. Until the more basic wants are fulfilled, a person will not strive to meet his higher needs. Maslow classifies needs into five categories:

1. Physiological.
2. Safety, stability, and security.
3. Belongingness and love.
4. Self-esteem and the esteem of others.
5. Self-actualization, self-realization, and self-accomplishment.[1]

The implications of the hierarchical nature of human motivation are important for an understanding of why people behave as they do. If a person has barely enough food, water, and shelter to survive, her entire energies are devoted to eking out an existence. She is not interested in status, prestige, or making her ideas known to others. She cannot afford the luxury of engaging in ego-enhancing activities. Once the basic physiological and safety wants are met, then people strive for companionship, belongingness, love, affection, and the esteem of others. When she has a superabundance of food, clothing, and shelter, the fulfillment of these needs no longer motivates our hypothetical person. She turns to her higher needs. The higher

[1]A. H. Maslow, *Motivation and Personality* (New York: Harper and Row, 1954). See especially ch. 5.

needs are social and psychological in nature. They are less concrete and more nebulous than the survival needs. Particularly when we concern ourselves with the egoistic drives, we find that full satisfaction seldom occurs. People can always take more recognition, more praise, more status, and more adulation.

Characteristics of Acquired Needs

The strength and pattern of the acquired needs vary considerably from one person to another. The boy who is raised on a farm in Iowa will tend to seek somewhat different satisfactions in life from the boy whose father is a corporation executive and who lives in the suburbs of New York City. The former may cherish the values of family, neighbors, the soil, and the open air, whereas the latter may struggle hard to climb the corporate ladder and thereby achieve power and wealth. Therefore, we can say that when people exist in different environments and when their experiences are different, the pattern and intensity of their motives will vary. Anthropologists have observed that among some peoples on earth the great urge to acquire more goods and possessions that is so characteristic of Americans is totally absent. Likewise competition serves successfully as a motivator for company salesmen and for college athletes, but it is far less successful as a stimulus to higher production for blue-collar workers in the factory.

Acquired needs vary over time for the same individual. A young breadwinner raising a family has an urgent need for a higher income, whereas the same person, after his children have reached adulthood, finds a lesser need for material rewards but may seek more leisure time or pursue cultural activities.

Learned needs do not operate upon a person singly. They occur in groups. The desire to achieve a higher income may be based upon one's desire for greater status and respect in the company and the community at large as well as the desire to obtain more of the material comforts of life. Very frequently people are not fully aware of why they behave as they do. They are not able to say "I do this because I seek security." Their motives are often hidden from conscious recognition.

HUMAN ADJUSTMENT

Human adjustment is concerned with the way people react in the process of seeking to satisfy their needs. Some, whom we call well-adjusted individuals, are relatively successful in meeting and solving the myriad problems that the average person faces. We speak of them as possessing a mature personality. These persons are goal-centered and adopt a flexible, resourceful, problem-solving form of behavior.

If an obstacle or barrier presents itself on the path to attainment of their goals, they are adaptive. They try other ways of relieving tension and satisfying their needs. They may intensify their efforts, they may reorganize their perception of the problem, and they may adopt substitute goals. Others, who are not so fortunate, may be poorly adjusted to meet the problems of life. They may exhibit what we call maladjusted or maladaptive behavior. They may be disorganized and unproductive in relieving tension and fulfilling their needs. Their actions take on the characteristics of frustrated behavior.

Now all persons cannot be conveniently classified into the two categories of well-adjusted or maladjusted. People fall along a continuum. The terms are relative. Many persons whom we would ordinarily consider to be well adjusted may in a particular situation lose their tempers, swear, or develop a tension headache. When goal-directed behavior is successful it leads to a reduction of internal tension and a satisfaction of needs. However, all of us experience situations that irritate, annoy, and vex us. Sally may have missed her usual train on the way to work in the morning causing her to miss an important business contact. Or if the boss is in a grumpy mood, the entire office force may become apprehensive.

Defense Mechanisms

When motivated behavior encounters an apparently insurmountable barrier, and when a problem-solving approach fails to achieve the goal, then frustration occurs. All of us encounter situations in which our self-integrity is threatened and we must find an outlet. We speak of the various forms of behavior that people may adopt in the face of frustration as *defense mechanisms*. Occasional resort to a defense mechanism as an outlet does not mean that a person is maladjusted. It is when frustration-directed behavior dominates one's whole life that we can say that a person is abnormal and needs expert help.

Now the barriers to the fulfillment of needs and wants can be both external and internal. If a boy who is sent to the store by his mother to buy a bottle of milk finds his way blocked by two neighborhood bullies, then the obstacle to the attainment of his goal is clearly external. If a salesperson continually repels potential customers because of his own antagonistic personality, then this barrier is internal to the salesperson. To a considerable extent the most difficult obstacles to surmount are those arising within the person himself. Likewise some barriers are "thing-type" obstacles; for example, it is too cold or the car has a flat tire. Others are "people-type" barriers. The most vexing type is that involving people. Executives whose jobs require that they try to persuade others to act know that this can be a very challenging assignment.

The defense mechanisms that people may adopt as an outlet from frustration can be classified into four broad categories:

1. Aggression.
2. Withdrawal.
3. Fixation.
4. Compromise.

Within each category are a number of subcategories. The particular form of reaction a person adopts depends upon his personality, the situation, and how he perceives the barrier. The frustration tolerance of people varies considerably. Some are much more susceptible to frustration than others. Different people will react differently under the same circumstances.

Let us now examine the various forms of frustrated behavior. One of the most common forms is *aggression*. This is primarily an attack response designed to inflict injury or damage. We see aggression nearly every day in one form or other. It is readily apparent in children, where it usually takes the form of a physical attack (for example, hitting another child because he has taken a toy). With adults, physical violence as an outlet for frustration certainly occurs too (for example, violence on union picket lines to prevent strike-breakers from going to work). However, education and training have taught most adults in most situations to channel their aggressive impulses into nonviolent forms. Thus we find a person spreading rumors about another whom he dislikes or uttering vituperative remarks against the source of a frustration. In labor-management relations examples of aggression are the firing of a worker because he is active in organizing a union, or, on the employee's part, a deliberate slowdown in protest against the actions of the company.

There are a number of kinds of *withdrawal* reactions that occur. Basically when a person withdraws, he seeks either physically or mentally to avoid the obstacle or situation. Thus, we find flights into *fantasy* and daydreaming. By so doing a person can obtain satisfaction through a temporary escape from reality. Physical *escape* or absence from the situation is another type of defense mechanism. The worker who continually changes jobs because of dissatisfaction with what he is doing at the time may simply be avoiding a sound appraisal of himself and a mature approach to his problems. *Regression* consists of adopting less mature, more childish behavior. Sometimes it signifies an attempt to return to the security and comfort of one's childhood. Symptoms of regressive behavior in adults are crying, pouting, horseplay, loss of emotional control, and homesickness. A continual longing for the good old days may be a reaction to frustration. Those who live in the past do so because the present is unhappy for them.

Still another form of withdrawal is *resignation*. This involves giving up the struggle. After repeated failure the individual may cease trying. The downtrodden worker who has lost all hope of better things from a job may have simply became resigned to an unsatisfactory existence.

Fixation, the third major type of frustrated behavior, consists of a compulsion to continue repeatedly a type of behavior that does not result in the attainment of a goal. It does not reduce tension. The person is figuratively hitting his head against a stone wall. Persisting in the old way of doing things, even when unsuccessful, may be the only recourse that some people know. They are afraid or do not know how to try something else.

Compromise reactions, the fourth major category, consist of *sublimation, rationalization,* and *projection.* Compromise involves altering one's objectives either actually or symbolically. Thus in *sublimation* an individual will adopt a substitute goal, or behavior, generally one that is on a higher ethical plane and socially more acceptable. *Rationalization* involves protecting one's ego by claiming that he really didn't want something anyway. It may take the form of giving false reasons for one's conduct. Alibiing is a form of rationalization. Sometimes a person finds his or her own thoughts or actions so intolerable that he or she ascribes them to another individual. Such an action constitutes *projection.* Examples of this can be found in the unfaithful

husband who accuses his wife of infidelity or in the irritable person who accuses others of being irritable. The person who adopts this form of defense machanism often believes his accusations to be true.

SIGNIFICANT MOTIVATION THEORIES

So far in this chapter we have studied motivation by examining basic human needs and wants and by discussing Maslow's hierarchy of needs. Let us now turn to four other important theories of motivation. The first has been formulated by psychologist Frederick Herzberg. It is a theory of motivation in the context of a work organization. That is, it is a theory of work motivation rather than a more general theory of human motivation. The second, by Harvard psychologist David McClelland, is concerned with achievement motivation, not only in the context of individuals but also in the context of achievement drives in entire societies. The third theory is behavior modification. Although relatively new to managers and to work organizations it is supported by over thirty years of experimental work by Harvard psychologist B. F. Skinner. The fourth is the expectancy model of motivation formulated by Victor Vroom.

Motivation–Hygiene Theory

In the late 1950s Professor Herzberg and his research associates conducted careful interviews

[2]The original motivator-hygienic factor theory is presented in Frederick Herzberg, Bernard Mausner, and Barbara B. Snyderman, *The Motivation to Work,* 2nd ed. (New York: John Wiley & Sons, Inc., 1959). A more complete formulation and further research investigations are contained in Frederick Herzberg, *Work and the Nature of Man* (Cleveland: The World Publishing Company, 1966).

with two hundred engineers and accountants who worked for eleven different companies in the Pittsburgh area.[2] This research endeavor was designed to test the concept that man has two sets of needs: (1) his lower-order needs to avoid loss of life, hunger, pain, and other deprivations and (2) his needs to grow psychologically. Included under his psychological growth needs are those of knowing more, seeing more relationships in what one knows, creativity, being effective in vague situations, maintaining individuality in the face of group pressures, and real growth through self-achievement.

The interviewers asked these men to tell about events in the course of their employment that caused them to feel a marked improvement in job satisfaction and also about those situations that caused a substantial reduction in job satisfaction. A great many probing questions were asked in each interview to pinpoint just how and why the people felt as they did and how their feelings affected their job performance and personal relationships.

When the results of the research were analyzed, the researchers found that one group of factors accounted for high levels of job satisfaction. These were labeled *motivators* because they seemed to be effective in motivating the individual to superior performance and effort. These factors were *achievement, recognition, work itself, responsibility*, and *advancement*. All of these satisfiers related to the job content.

Another group of factors, labeled *hygienic* or *maintenance* factors seemed to focus on discontent with their work situation. However, these factors were seldom mentioned by the respondents as causing positive job satisfaction. These factors pertained primarily to the job context or environment. These factors were *company policy and administration, supervision, salary, interpersonal relations*, and *working conditions*.

What are the practical implications of the research? The hygienic or maintenance factors provide an essential base on which to build. If employees' wages, fringe benefits, working conditions, eating facilities, job rights, and status systems are inadequate, they will feel uneasy and discontent. They may complain openly about job conditions and company policies. They may even become very antagonistic toward the company. However, if all these maintenance needs are taken care of adequately, the people will not necessarily work any harder. But these factors do serve as a base upon which to add the motivators to improve job performance.

It is true that certain people, in these studies, reported that they received job satisfaction solely from maintenance factors. Herzberg has asserted that such individuals show only a temporary satisfaction when hygiene factors are improved, they show little interest in the kind and quality of their work, they experience little satisfaction from accomplishments, and they tend to show a chronic dissatisfaction with various aspects of job context (such as pay, status, and job security).[3]

How can top management apply Herzberg's motivators—achievement, recognition, the work itself, responsibility, and advancement—in a practical way to create a high level of job performance? It must create a climate where employees and managers can reach satisfactions for their higher-order needs. Some of the specific leadership practices that it can institute are delegation of responsibility and authority, job enrichment, full utilization of employees' skills and training, establishment of an atmosphere of approval toward subordinates, granting of earned pay increases, and granting promotions when deserved.

Herzberg holds that motivation-seekers are motivated by the nature of the work itself, have a higher tolerance for poor hygienic factors, and show capacity to enjoy their work.

Although numerous researchers have independently replicated Herzberg's two-dimensional theory of work motivation, the theory

[3]Herzberg, *Work and the Nature of man*, op. cit., p. 90.

does have its critics. Some scholars and researchers have commented that this two-factor explanation of job satisfaction is a great oversimplification of the whole motivational complex of the world of work. Also the Herzberg research technique does not include any statistical correlations between the *motivators* and actual job performance. Vroom has asserted that employees who are interviewed may attribute the causes of their satisfaction to their own achievements on the job while they ascribe their dissatisfactions not to their own inadequacies, but to factors in the work environment (hygienic factors).[4] Some studies also show that hourly paid blue-collar workers place more emphasis upon maintenance factors (such as pay and job security) than do higher-level employees. In effect maintenance or hygienic factors may be considered as motivators by blue-collar people.[5] Regardless of the criticisms, however, the motivator-hygienic factor theory of Herzberg has received considerable support from independent investigators. Although not all employees are motivated primarily by job content (we already know that humans are very complex and variable), the theory does provide a very useful way of analyzing work motivation and of predicting the probable employee responses to managerial leadership practices.

Intrinsic and Extrinsic Motivation

Intrinsic motivation is that which occurs while a person is performing an activity in which he

[4]Victor H. Vroom, *Work and Motivation* (New York: John Wiley & Sons, Inc., 1964), p. 129.

[5]Critiques of the motivator-hygienic two-factor theory are contained in Victor H. Vroom, op. cit., pp. 127–129; Lyman W. Porter, "Personnel Management," *Annual Review of Psychology,* Vol. 17 (1966), p. 411; A. Kornhauser, *Mental Health of the Industrial Worker* (New York: John Wiley & Sons, Inc., 1965); and Orlando Behling, George Labovitz, and Richard Kosmo, "The Herzberg Controversy: A Critical Reappraisal," *Academy of Management Journal,* Vol. 11, No. 1 (March 1968), pp. 99–108.

gains satisfaction from engaging in that activity itself. This is called internal reward and it is directly part of the job content. Extrinsic motivators are the incentives or rewards that a person can enjoy after finishing work. This is related to the job environment or an external reward.

Traditionally work has been viewed as necessary drudgery. Rewards came in the form of pay, which was enjoyed off the job; holidays and vacations, which were enjoyed off the job; cafeterias and lounges, which were enjoyed away from the job; and pensions, which were received after retirement from work.

Modern behavioral research has tended to emphasize that work itself can be satisfying. This has been postulated in the writings of Herzberg, just discussed, and of other behavioral scientists such as Rensis Likert, Chris Argyris, and Douglas McGregor.

Managers in some of our more enlightened corporations have been applying this concept by placing people on jobs for which they are trained and are interested, by new concepts of job design and work flow, and by gearing recognition directly to the job.

Although there are those enthusiasts for intrinsic motivation who would substantially downgrade all efforts toward extrinsic motivation, in reality both are necessary. If working conditions, wages, job security, and fringe benefits are inadequate, a company will find it difficult to recruit and retain good people. Turnover, absenteeism, and grievances tend to be high where management ignores external forms of reward. Large bureaucracies, in both government and industry, tend to do quite well in meeting people's maintenance needs. What they so often lack is emphasis upon challenging assignments, an encouragement of innovation, and large rewards for achievement. By emphasizing job tenure, loyalty, and conformity, bureaucracies tend to repel those with an enterprising spirit and drive.

A sound motivational climate must provide both extrinsic and intrinsic motivators.

Achievement Motivation

Beginning in the 1940s, a group of researchers led by Harvard psychologist David C. Mc-Clelland began investigating the achievement motive in people. For a measuring instrument they used a projective test of personality, the Thematic Apperception Test. In this research, subjects were shown a series of pictures and then asked to tell a story about each picture. This technique reveals the inner dynamics of a person's personality. What does a man think about and what does he daydream about when he is not required to think about anything in particular? If a man spends his time thinking about doing things better—about building, creating, and doing—then psychologists say he has an achievement orientation. On the other hand if one spends his time thinking about his family and friends, he has an affiliation orientation. Of course, the reader will recognize that most people are not entirely achievement-oriented or entirely affiliation-oriented. They possess some of each. But there are people who lean much more in one direction than the other.[6]

McClelland's research, which has now been carried on for many years, has uncovered some important things about achievement-oriented people. They actually tend to translate their thinking into action. They are not idle dreamers. They place great demands upon themselves. They are persistent and they are realists. They are not romantics.

For the achiever accomplishment is often an end in itself. This is comparable to the mountain climber who was asked why he continually tried to scale Mount Everest. His answer, "Because it is there," has become classic.[7]

The achievement-oriented individual believes in moderate risk taking. He or she is not a reckless adventurer. Rather he or she takes calculated risks. He or she also tends to be very sanguine about the likelihood of success and persists for the long-term pull. Such individuals also seek concrete feedback on how they are doing.

How do high-achievement-oriented people get that way? Parental influence is paramount. The parents set high standards of accomplishment. They show warmth and encouragement. The father is not domineering or authoritarian. Discipline is consistent and specific, but it is neither harsh nor all-pervasive. Over-disciplined children tend to be overregulated and docile. McClelland found that middle-class parents—managers, professionals, and entrepreneurs—tend to impart a decidedly stronger achievement drive than do lower-class parents.

People also acquire their achievement drive (or lack of it) from the culture and predominant values of the society in which they live. Mc-Clelland has charted the tendencies of many societies throughout the world and for different periods in history. He did this by coding the contents of the literature of a people. Schoolbooks were especially useful. The values imparted to the youth are instrumental in shaping that nation's future. The United States scores high in achievement. Business careers offer abundant opportunities for realization of this motive. The Protestant Ethic helped shape this orientation in the population. In recent years the Soviet Union has also scored high in the achievement motive. McClelland has found a positive coefficient of correlation of .53 between achievement scores derived from the literature of twenty-two nations and their subsequent economic growth rate.[8]

After people are on the payroll, management bears the responsibility of establishing a leadership climate that encourages the achievement motive to thrive in the organization.

[6]David C. McClelland, *The Achieving Society* (Princeton, N.J.: D. Van Nostrand Company, 1961).

[7]This statement was made by the British mountaineer George Leigh Mallory, who tried to scale Everest repeatedly in the early 1920s. He tragically perished in 1924 when very near the top.

[8]David C. McClelland, "Business Drive and National Achievement," *Harvard Business Review,* Vol. 40 (July–August 1962).

Behavior Modification

In very recent years the work of Harvard psychologist B. F. Skinner has come to the attention of human resource specialists and managers in industry. Skinner's early experiments in the 1940s dealt with conditioning the behavior of pigeons. Later he investigated the shaping of human behavior in countless experiments. Until recently most of the applications of Skinner's principles had been in psychotherapy, in handling disturbed and retarded children, in schools, and in programmed instruction. Nowadays, business firms are learning how behavioral modification can be used in their establishments to motivate performance.

Skinner is a leading proponent of the behaviorist school of psychology, which holds that behavior is caused primarily by externally induced stimuli. He asserts that behavioral scientists should give up their emphasis upon the inner life of man and upon free will. Rather they should concentrate upon relations between man and environment.

Let us look at the basic concepts of behavior modification. Skinner and his disciples say that all behavior is shaped and maintained by its consequences. A man does something because of the reinforcement he received from similar behavior in the past. If the outcome of his action is pleasing to him, the likelihood of his repeating that same action is high. A reinforcer is something that increases the probability of a behavior occurring again. We can look upon a reinforcer as a reward or incentive to behave in a certain way. Reinforcers may be tangible like food or money and they can be intangible like praise and approval.

There can be four distinct strategies or methods for inducing desire behavior: (1) positive reinforcement; (2) negative reinforcement; (3) extinction or no reinforcement; (4) punishment.

Positive reinforcement is most recommended by Skinner. It is a reward or stimulus given after a response which increases the likelihood of a desired response. Favorable emotions are aroused. The individual tends to develop favorable attitudes toward the person who applies the positive reinforcement. Figure 14-2 gives a variety of positive reinforcers or rewards that can be used in organizational life. Remember that the responses of individual employees to a given reward may vary somewhat.

Negative reinforcement (not the same as punishment) increases the frequency of a response by the removal or termination of some unfavorable condition. It a supervisor criticizes a subordinate who has done sloppy work, this action is negative reinforcement. But the criticism ceases as soon as the employee does careful, neat work. The removal of the aversive criticism by

FIGURE 14-2 Possible Positive Reinforcers That Can Be Used to Motivate or Guide Behavior.

Pay increase

Bonus

Suggestion plan award

Praise, support, confirmation of performance

A caring attitude by supervisor

Approval of action

Help with work

Choice of job assignments

Choice of desk, office, workplace

Request for ideas

Feedback of information about one's performance

Freedom from close control

Promotion

Opportunity to enroll in training program

Friendship with supervisor and co-workers

Status symbols

Prestige

Interesting work

Job security

Favorable performance evaluation

Understanding and Managing People

the boss results in an increase in desired behavior.

With *extinction* nothing happens after the employee exhibits his or her behavior. The behavior is not rewarded or punished. Because the behavior is not reinforced one way or another, such behavior will decrease in frequency. If we neither laugh nor criticize the boisterous show-off person in a group, he will soon lose his tendency to show off in that particular gathering.

Punishment is an aversive event that follows behavior and is designed to decrease the frequency of the particular behavior. It is a widely used technique in our society. It can be applied in two ways. The first is by inflicting physical or emotional pain and the second is by withdrawal of a desired stimulus such as food or water. Punishment has many undesirable features. When the punishing agent is absent, the individual may again exhibit the undesired response. Punishment tells someone what not to do but it does not shape behavior in the desired direction. The person being punished may retaliate against the punisher. And finally, punishment can cause psychological and physical damage to the individual.

Reinforcement can be applied according to three different schedules: (1) continuous; (2) fixed ratio but not continuous; and (3) variable ratio. A continuous schedule rewards a person every time the desired behavior is exhibited. Piece-rate wage incentive and salespersons' commission plans work this way. A fixed-ratio schedule might reward the person, say, every second time he exhibits the sought-after behavior. With a variable ratio, behavior is reinforced randomly.

Another variable is the amount of time that elapses between the behavior and its reinforcement. Skinner says that reinforcement should be very prompt or immediate.

Behavior modification can be applied to such activities as employee training, job design, wage payment, supervision of workers, control of quantity and quality of output, and attendance control. Let us consider the supervision of workers and the regulation of their quantity and quality of work. It is desirable to set goals for individual and group output and quality. If possible these should be set in quantifiable terms. Measurement of performance and feedback of that data to the employees should be done on a daily or weekly basis as is appropriate according to work operation cycles of their jobs. The very process of informing employees how they are doing is a form of reinforcement. The supervisor should provide praise, recognition, approval, and personal interest in various ways to indicate reinforcement for what the individual is doing right. This positive reinforcement may consist of a smile, a nod of approval, a specific statement that the person met a quota, and an offer to buy her or him a cup of coffee. Initially the reinforcement should come as soon as possible after the behavior and regularly. But as time goes on the reinforcement can be less often and of unpredictable frequency. In certain situations it may be practical to reward workers with free time. Thus, if they meet an agreed-upon daily output quota before the end of the shift, they can go home.

Behavior modification is not a panacea. Several motivational forces often affect an individual at the same time and these may conflict with one another. A direct piece-work wage incentive plan is a prime example. The worker is supposedly reinforced by management to maximize output up to the limits of skill and energy. However, the work group often pressures the worker to restrict output because of fear of a rate cut by management and because of a fear that very fast workers will "show up" the ordinary and slower workers. The work organization situation often is much more complex than the school or laboratory situation in which conflicting influences can be minimized.

Skinner's theory has also been criticized by some writers because it denies the existence of free will and the autonomous, inner-motivated man. These latter concepts are central to the constructs of Abraham Maslow and Douglas McGregor.

Expectancy Model

Formulated by Victor Vroom, the expectancy model of motivation is useful for analyzing and explaining the motivation of individuals in an organizational setting.[9] The model does not explain the factors or content of what motivates people to work as do the theories of Maslow and Herzberg. Rather it helps one understand the thought processes (which may be conscious and organized but which also can be subconscious or disorganized) that an individual goes through in deciding whether or not to exert the effort to try to achieve any of various possible goals. It is a useful tool for analysis and research. But the expectancy model does not offer specific substantive answers for managers who are trying to improve the motivational climate for their work units.

To understand the expectancy model, one must first learn the meaning of three concepts used in expressing the model. These are valence, expectancy, and instrumentality.

Valence is the degree or extent to which a person desires a particular outcome. It can be measured by asking an individual to state how important any of various outcomes or goals are to her or him. Other terms that can be used to represent the concept of valence are *preference*, *expected utility*, or *affective orientation* toward a particular outcome.

Expectancy is the perceived probability that effort or behavior by the person will yield a particular outcome or result. This probability is subjectively determined by the individual.

Instrumentality is the degree or extent to

[9]Victor H. Vroom, *Work and Motivation* (New York: John Wiley & Sons, Inc. 1964).

which the person believes the attainment of the first-level outcome will yield a second-level outcome (which is the ultimate goal of the person). A second-level outcome is a human need such as companionship, security, respect of others, or accomplishment.

Figure 14-3 shows how the elements in the expectancy model are tied together. Let us trace through the flow from element to element and relate the model to real behavior. Let us assume the case of a production engineer in a manufacturing plant who is responsible for the efficient and reliable operation of the production machinery. He feels a strong need for a substantial pay increase so that he can accumulate funds to make a down payment on a house for himself and his growing family. The engineer knows that his manager wants to increase the number of units per hour produced by production process number one. The engineer knows also that to increase productivity would require much ingenuity and effort on his part. He is not fully sure whether he can succeed in re-engineering the line to raise productivity. He thinks, but is not really sure, that if he can successfully raise productivity, his manager will reward him with a handsome pay raise. Applying these facts to the expectancy model we note that the engineer has a strong *valence* or desire for a higher income so he can buy a house. He thinks the probability of achieving the action (expectancy number 1) of reworking the process equipment and raising productivity is reasonably good. Multiplying the valence times expectancy number 1 gives us the strength of his motivational force to engage in the *action*. The engineer must also determine the probability (expectancy number 2) that his successful action will cause his boss to raise his pay (*organizational reward* or

---

FIGURE 14-3 Expectancy Model of Motivation.

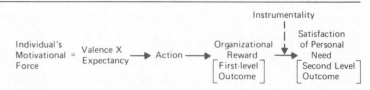

Understanding and Managing People

first-level outcome).[10] The instrumentality is the closeness of the relationship between the pay increase and the purchase of the house (satisfaction of personal need).

Vroom's expectancy model of motivation has been tested empirically by a great many scholars and researchers. The results of these investigations have generally been supportive of its theoretical constructs and formulation. Researchers generally determine the valences and expectancies by directly asking employees questions about their goals and perceptions of likelihoods of achieving them.

The practical value of the expectancy model for managers is that it demonstrates that motivation is highly individualized from person to person. The manager must know the special concerns and strengths of his people. If he desires to obtain particular kinds of performance from them, he must inform them of the connections between performance and reward. He must learn of their expectancies and valences and perhaps he can increase the motivational force of individuals through supportive performance appraisal discussions.

MORALE AND PRODUCTIVITY

For a great number of years, it has been assumed that a work force that possesses high morale is also likely to exhibit high productivity. It has seemed logical to managers that happy workers are also productive workers. However, research investigators have demonstrated that there is no simple relationship between morale and productivity. Enough instances of high productivity and low morale and of high morale

[10]In general, organizational rewards could consist of many items such as a promotion, pay raise, assignment to more interesting work, and a news item about the employee in the company newspaper.

and low productivity have been observed to cast doubt upon the once-assumed direct relationship. The heart of the matter is that morale is a complex concept. It includes many facets.

Some writers have emphasized the satisfaction of needs as a dimension of morale. Others have stressed the social approach by concentrating upon group bonds and friendships. Still others have emphasized attitudes toward supervision, the work, and the organization. And finally other writers have concentrated on the interaction of personality with the work situation. Recognizing that morale is multidimensional, let us define it as the *total satisfactions a person derives from job, work group, boss, the organization, and environment. It is also affected by one's personality structure. Morale pertains to the general feeling of well-being, satisfaction, and happiness of people.*

Productivity is output divided by input. Commonly, the productivity of an industry or of an establishment is measured by the total physical or dollar volume of output divided by the man-hours of input for a given time span. The productivity of a work group or of individuals is generally expressed in terms of the units produced during a given period, say, a day, week, or month. Productivity of routine repetitive work is easy to measure. But the output of creative and intellectual efforts is very difficult to measure. Thus, professional and executive work accomplishments may have a long time span before completion and considerable judgment may be required to determine the real value of work done.

Vroom has tabulated the results of twenty investigations into the relationship between morale (job satisfaction in Vroom's terms) and job performance. These studies were made by many researchers working independently. They pertained to such diverse occupational groups as insurance agents, bus drivers, female office employees, sales clerks, farmers, and supervisors in a package delivery company. Statistical correlations between satisfaction and performance ranged from $+.86$ to $-.31$, with a median of

+ .14 for all studies.[11] Thus, there seems to be a low but positive relationship between overall morale or job satisfaction and productivity of various work groups in general. Yet there are enough instances of negative correlations to alert us to the fact that intervening factors may be present.

For various reasons, productivity can be reasonably good while morale is low. Many industrial plants are highly engineered. Output may be high under machine-paced and assembly-line conditions. Jobs may have been carefully analyzed, improved, and subdivided by industrial engineers. Materials and parts may flow smoothly from work station to work station. In-process inventory may be kept at a minimum. Measured daywork standards may have been established for each worker's job. Under such conditions productivity of shop departments may be good even though employees dislike their jobs and their conditions of work.

Rensis Likert claims that the relationship between morale and productivity for complex and varied work such as research, engineering, and life insurance selling tends to be moderately high.[12] It seems that when the performance depends solely upon the man or the team and when the job cannot be engineered, then those employees who feel favorably disposed toward their job situation are also more likely to be motivated to produce.

Situations in which morale is high but performance is poor also occur with some frequency. This discrepancy can occur when a pleasant, social, country-club atmosphere is encouraged or permitted by supervision. The people may gain considerable pleasure from coming to the office each day to meet their friends and socialize. But the motivation to produce may be minimal.

Actually, job attitudes and morale can be quite positive for two reasons. The first has just been given above. Employees gain social satisfaction from interactions at the workplace. Working conditions and supervision may be good. Second, high morale may result from high motivation to produce. Much recent behavioral research has demonstrated that when a leadership and work-group climate is structured to generate high work motivation, then employee satisfactions and attitudes are often positive. In other words, management should put its eggs in the basket that creates a highly motivated work force. Good morale and job satisfaction are likely to follow. But if top management spends its efforts on morale-building programs *only*—for instance, wages, working conditions, recreation programs, and financial benefits—it will become disillusioned when work performance remains low. It should not be assumed, however, that money spent on morale-building programs is necessarily wasted. Numerous investigations have demonstrated that there is a positive correlation between high morale and low turnover and low absenteeism. Worker loyalty and stability are important.

APPLYING MOTIVATIONAL CONCEPTS

We have, so far, discussed a number of basic concepts and theoretical foundations for understanding individual behavior, motivation, and reactions to blocking of motives. The executive must be able to apply knowledge of human behavior dynamics to real work situations in order to elicit acceptable performance from the work force. There is no simple formula to tell the manager how to lead and motivate people. The executive must be perceptive with regard to the character of people and the demands of the situation. She or he must be adaptable and flexible in applying motivational principles. Responses of employees are a function of the reward sys-

---

[11]Victor H. Vroom, op. cit., pp. 183–185.
[12]Rensis Likert, *New Patterns of Management* (New York: McGraw-Hill Book Company, 1961), ch. 6.

tem and how they perceive the rewards as satisfying their needs.

Power and Force

The traditional method of motivating people to work in private business has been to apply the "carrot and the stick" from a strong power base. The manager who is unschooled in the fundamentals of human behavior feels this is the best way to move people. The carrot has been the weekly paycheck, or direct wage incentives, or bonuses for managers. The stick has been the threat of demotion, transfer to an undesirable assignment, or discharge. Even though discharges may be invoked infrequently in a given organization, they occur just often enough to cause employees generally to be apprehensive about their job security. Another form of the carrot and the stick is to deny pay raises to individual employees or even to cut their pay at a time when the cost of living rises yearly.

The use of pay increments that are tied to performance is sound from the point of view of motivation theory. However, pay is seldom administered in a manner fully consistent with motivation theory. Hence, it does not commonly generate the kind of strong performance that it could. Also those managers who are philosophically addicted to the "carrot and the stick" do not understand the rich array of other positive reinforcers available to motivate people.

The use of threats or the "stick" suffers from all the disadvantages of punishment that we discussed previously under behavior modification. In addition, when employees are protected against arbitrary treatment by their union they are unlikely to jump whenever the supervisor says jump. Our high standard of living, such that basic physical wants are met for most people, means that nowadays they are motivated more by social and egoistic drives than formerly. In addition the relatively high educational attainment of the labor force generates a desire on employees' part to participate in deci-

sions at the workplace and to have some measure of autonomy. Hence, autocratic leadership is less effective now than it was a generation or two ago.

Money as a Motivator

Money should be looked upon as one instrument among many for managing motivation. Managers in industry often tend to place major reliance upon pay, bonuses, and money incentives because they are easiest to manipulate. But the results do not always justify the efforts to use money as a motivator. There is abundant evidence that many blue-collar workers will deliberately restrict output even when working on a direct wage-incentive plan.

Yes, pay is important for providing the material necessities of life. But it is most important for what it symbolizes to the recipient. To use pay effectively as a motivational tool the manager must study people, the conditions under which they work, and the tasks they perform. Many jobs require close team cooperation. For such jobs an individual pay-incentive plan can be destructive of group cooperation. On the other hand, a wage-incentive plan that rewards all members of the group for increased team output can be effective.

The value of money is determined by what people have learned to associate it with. For the young female secretary, a good salary symbolizes stylish clothes in abundance. For the young married father it represents a down payment on a home. For the executive who has just been promoted, a substantial pay boost tells him that his company superiors think highly of him. It is an index of progress.

McClelland points out that several research studies have revealed that persons who score high in achievement motivation on psychological tests do not work harder for the prospect of making more money alone. They are motivated by the love of accomplishment, interest in their work, and by success itself. The money comes afterward and of course is appreciated. On the other hand, people with a low achievement drive quite often will work for more money when it symbolizes something that they dearly want.[13] Such people tend to have no intrinsic interest in their work. But they will strive for the things money can buy, such as a new automobile, a new television set, or a vacation cruise in the Caribbean.

Competition

Competition as a form of motivation is widely used in our society. Examples that first come to mind for most of us are, perhaps, the competition that occurs in sporting events (both amateur and professional) and in games among friends, for example, a game of cards. In business, competition is most commonly used in sales departments. It is practically standard practice to have salesmen compete against one another for various awards and prizes. Another form of competition is that which takes place among members of the management hierarchy in most organizations for the prize of a promotion. Because there are fewer positions as one approaches the top of the organizational pyramid, the competition can get very intense and at times even vicious. If a number of people are striving for the same goal, and if that goal is attainable by only the one who wins, we know that such competition can motivate many people to give their maximum efforts.

However, competition has serious limitations when used within an organization. If, for example, all the members of one department are competing for a single promotion, considerable jealousy and hostility are bound to develop among the employees. Mutual cooperation will be poor. So in this case individualistic competition will, as in most cases, cause a destruction

---

[13]David C. McClelland, "Money as a Motivator: Some Research Insights," *The McKinsey Quarterly* (Fall 1967), pp. 10–21.

of teamwork. In this situation where people are competing for a promotion that can go to only one, the standards for selection of the winner can seldom be completely objective. Therefore, the losers may justifiably consider that bias and favoritism entered into the selection.

Another serious disadvantage of competition as a motivator is the frustration experienced by the losers. Any of the various forms of behavior induced by frustration may occur: aggression, regression, resignation, fixation, sublimation, and so on.

If the stakes are high, if the penalty for losing is great, then we find destruction of teamwork, lower morale, and frustration to be common consequences.

Job Design and Work Flow

The nature of work itself strongly influences whether employees show interest and zest or whether they experience boredom and monotony. Actually the matter is determined by the nature of the worker himself (many seek challenging work; others accept routine, repetitive work), the nature of the job, and the leadership and social environment in which the employee performs. We examine the matter of job design and its effect upon worker performance in Chapter 5, "Job Design and Analysis," and Chapter 15, "Quality of Working Life."

Integration of Goals

A desirable and somewhat idealized system of work motivation is to provide opportunities for need-satisfaction through doing the job itself. The object of this pattern of motivation is to develop employee commitment to the objectives of the organization. Management sets up a system of rewards that causes high levels of job satisfaction at the same time that the employees are working productively to meet the objectives of their job, department, and plant.

Such a system of motivation is the essence of what Douglas McGregor called Theory Y management.[14] Rensis Likert has called it System 4 management.[15] This approach holds that people will exercise self-direction and self-control in working for objectives to which they are committed. They will become committed to working for organization goals to the extent that they gain real satisfaction from doing so. This style of leadership has sometimes been called "management by integration and self-control."

It emphasizes openness and trust, supportive supervision, and participation in decision making. It activates all motives—economic, social, and egoistic. To a considerable extent employees can gratify many of their drives for security, belongingness, status, self-expression, self-significance, and achievement right on the job.

This system of motivation works best in situations where people have some freedom to exercise their own initiative, where they can see a direct connection between their efforts and the performance of their organizational unit, and where their work careers constitute a dominant focus in their lives. These conditions fit many executives. They are dedicated to their work and their organizations. They enjoy their jobs so much that the jobs do not seem like work to them. They adopt a proprietary interest in their companies. Not only is intrinsic motivation maximized but so is extrinsic motivation. These people exercise considerable influence and power. They can make things happen. They may command vast human and material resources. Their opinions mean much both in their organizations and in their communities. They enjoy prestige, high status, and high pay. They are operating at the high end of Maslow's hierarchy of needs.

Many other types of people in our society tend to enjoy this highly satisfactory motivational situation. This is true for many professionals such as college professors, attorneys, economists, engineers, and scientists. This integration of goals also tends to hold true for the self-employed and the small businessperson.

However, it must be admitted that it is very difficult for workers on low-level, repetitive jobs to experience this form of motivation. They may have been conditioned by past experience to expect no real satisfaction from their work. They may stay on their jobs and perform solely for their pay. Their jobs may have been so highly engineered or regimented that there is no opportunity for growth, recognition, and achievement.

Participation

Participation means the physical and mental involvement of people in an activity. Specifically, in the field of personnel management, the term has come to mean the involvement of employees in decision making. In this sense it means primarily mental involvement and ego involvement. Many managers speak loosely of developing participation in their employees. They exhort employees to "put their shoulders to the wheel," to help management cut costs, to attend company social functions, and to give generously to the Community Chest drive. These activities do not constitute true participation. Genuine participation includes those situations in which management actively encourages employees and lower-echelon managers to help make decisions regarding the business and the work. Although it is top management's job to set policy and establish overall goals, there is plenty of opportunity for subordinate members of the organization to participate in decision making in such areas as production methods, materials handling, cost reduction, safety, employee relations problems, and working conditions.

Participation in decision making can take many forms: consultative supervision, quality

[14]Douglas McGregor, *The Human Side of Enterprise* (New York: McGraw-Hill Book Company, 1960).
[15]Rensis Likert, *The Human Organization* (New York: McGraw-Hill Book Company, 1967).

circles, multiple management, labor-management cooperation, suggestion programs, and others.

Questions for Review and Discussion

1. Explain the meaning of the following concepts:
   a. Self-concept.
   b. Personality.
   c. Motive.
   d. Defense mechanism.
2. Explain Maslow's hierarchy of needs.
3. Explain Herzberg's motivation-hygiene theory.
4. What are the characteristics of high-achievement-oriented persons?
5. Do you think B. F. Skinner's behavior modification theory is compatible with Maslow's and Herzberg's theories?
6. Distinguish between morale and motivation. If workers have high morale, is their productivity also likely to be high?
7. How can individual motives and organizational goals be integrated?
8. Discuss the importance of money as a motivator.
9. Analyze the satisfactions you have obtained from the various jobs you have held. What differences do you note?
10. Explain the expectancy model of motivation.

CASE PROBLEMS

PROBLEM 1

A college senior related the following story to his professor:[16]

Part I

Last summer I was hired by the Department of Public Works of my home city in Ohio (a city of about 25,000 population) to work as a combined crew leader-truck driver. I had worked the previous two summers as a laborer in the department.

The functions of the department were to collect garbage and trash from households and commercial establishments, to repair and resurface streets, and to maintain public buildings and parks. The department personnel consisted of a superintendent, two foremen, an office clerk, twenty-two regular employees, and eight to ten temporary summer help composed of both college and high-school students.

[16]The author expresses his appreciation to Mark H. Baranello, a former student, for providing the essential features of this case.

At the beginning of the summer I was assigned as a crew leader-truck driver to collect brush, tree limbs, and garden trimmings set out at the street by residents of the city. I had a crew of four high school boys ranging in age from 16 to 18. The boys only worked four hours a day. Thus, I had two of them in the morning and two in the afternoon. Brush collection was regarded as a nuisance by the regular personnel in the department and they preferred to avoid this task. Therefore it was assigned to the summer workers.

From the start I had trouble getting the boys to really produce. The morning crew consisted of Edward and Thomas. Edward, age 17, was the son of one of the foremen in the department and was a high school football star. He did as little work as possible. Thomas, age 16, was a friend of Edward's and modeled his behavior after him. I spent considerable effort coaxing and prodding these boys to work harder. They were slow workers and took frequent rest breaks. The afternoon crew of Red and Alex was slightly more ambitious and output was somewhat better. In dealing with the morning crew I often pointed out that the afternoon boys had a better attitude and got more work done. This was supposed to improve their efforts but mainly it caused resentment and no more work output. In actuality I felt that neither the morning nor the afternoon crew was doing a good job. The boys were fully aware of my disappointment in their performance.

This was my first surpervisory assignment and I was unsure of myself in how to handle the leadership role. I appealed to Edward's father, the foreman, to speak to his son. The father said he did this but it yielded no change in Edward's attitude and performance. I became worried that the superintendent would find out about the weak performance of my crews. My major leadership efforts were directed toward shaming the boys for shirking their responsibilities. However, because their pay rate was quite low it did not seem fair to baldly tell them they were not even earning their pay.

Midway through the summer a change took place. We were taken off the residential brush collection and given the job of working along the sides and beds of various creeks to remove debris and to cut down weeds and brush. At this time of year the stream beds were mostly dry. The debris had to be carried to the truck, which I parked at the nearest bridge. The four high-school boys were hired full time and given a raise from $3.35 to $3.50 per hour. Also two regular year-round workers were assigned to this project. These regular employees had reputations of being mediocre to average workers. Both had very limited educations.

Knowing that work attitudes had not been good in the first half of the summer and that I was having difficulty in supervising the boys, I consulted the superintendent and one of the foremen on how to organize and direct this new assignment.

Questions
1. Why do you think the crew leader was having difficulty in obtaining good productive effort from his crew members?

2. What plan would you recommend for organizing and directing the creek clean-up work in order to increase motivation and output?

Part II

We decided to group the six persons into two crews, each being assigned to a different section of a creek. A typical day consisted of entering a creek bed at a bridge and working down to the next bridge. Along the way the banks would be mowed with hand scythes. Any debris lying in the bed, on the banks, and under bridges would be picked up and carried to the dump truck parked at the next bridge.

Each crew consisted of two high school boys and a regular adult employee. Those who seemed to be compatible with one another were put together in a crew.

I altered my style of supervision from that used in the residential brush collection. I explained the work groupings and outlined generally how the work was to be done. I set only rough boundary conditions on work methods and scheduling and left the specifics to each crew. Each crew set its own work pace and decided when to take rest periods and coffe breaks. I did, however, tell them approximately how much of a creek ought to be completed in a day.

As truck driver, I dropped off each crew at different job sites along a creek. I spent much of my time shuttling back and forth between crews, loading the truck, and answering questions. I personally did not do any weed cutting and debris collecting. I tried to understand each person as an individual and to take an interest in him. I talked to Edward about his high school athletics and this pleased him. When someone handled a task well, I praised him. I no longer stood over them like a drill sergeant. In general, I changed from my previous style of frequent criticism to support, encouragement, and praise.

In some cases where the terrain was suitable I started the two groups at one bridge working on opposite sides of a creek. Their goal was to finish at the next bridge. Thus, we had some friendly competition. The boys seemed to look upon this as fun.

Within a few days after starting this new activity, work effort, cooperation, and output rose appreciably. They stayed at a fully satisfactory level throughout the remaining weeks of the summer. Instead of the resentment shown toward me in the first part of the summer the boys showed an attitude of friendliness and co-operation.

Questions
1. How do the organization and supervision of the work that was actually used compare with your proposed plan?
2. Relate motivational principles to the methods used in Part II of this case.

PROBLEM 2: FRANK DENBY

Frank Denby, age 53, has had 33 years of service with the Zenco Corporation. He now holds the rank of Engineer in the Manufacturing Engineering Department, which is part of the Consumer Products Division (3200 employees) of the Corporation. Upon earning his Associate Degree in Mechanical Technology from a nearby community college (a two-year program), Frank started work with the company in the machine shop. Following this he spent several years as an engineering technician. A few years later he was promoted to the position of supervisor of one of the manufacturing departments. Twelve years ago he transferred to the Manufacturing Engineering Department at the rank of Associate Engineer.

The Zenco Corporation is a fairly large, multidivision, multiproduct manufacturing firm which makes a variety of products in both the consumer- and producer-goods fields.

The Manufacturing Engineering Department employs 15 engineers and is headed by Joe Kincaid, Manager. Its functions are to keep the manufacturing lines running, minimize down time, devise improvements to existing equipment, and improve output and reliability of the equipment. If a new product is introduced it must determine the production process and equipment to be used. Additionally it keeps process instructions and specifications used by manufacturing, supervision, and operations up to date.

Four years ago Frank was assigned to work as a manufacturing engineer on Production Process B. The machinery in place had been designed and installed in the mid-1960s. It broke down frequently and output was considered low by the standards of the 1980s.

After becoming thoroughly familiar with the existing machinery and the components (of a product) processed on that machinery, Denby determined that he could design and build an entirely new machine, based upon a different engineering concept, to process the components. He then went to the machine tool department and personally built a small prototype of a new machine. He tried out the prototype by running the components through it. It was successful.

Encouraged by the success of his model Frank then made some rough sketches of a full-size production machine. He supervised machinists, electricians, and mechanics in the building of this machine. Next he had it installed in Production Process B in place of an old machine. The output per hour was four times as much as that obtained from the old, 1960-era equipment. Furthermore Frank's machine was more reliable, down time was less, and the output was of a uniformly higher quality.

Throughout the eight months that Frank devoted to this project, he kept his direct supervisor, Joe Kincaid, informed of his activities. Kincaid approved of his efforts but did not directly involve himself in the project. The new production machine was built without the benefit of a formal capital budget appropriation. Rather it was constructed from materials available in the plant, purchase of certain parts within the regular budget authorizations, and by using skilled tradespersons from the tool room.

After Denby's new machine had been in operation for about four months, Kincaid, in consultation with other managers, decided that it should be duplicated and manufactured by an outside vendor. The additional machines could then be installed in other production lines. At this point the project was turned over to the Design Engineering Department which engaged the services of a vendor to produce additional machines incorporating the same engineering concepts as in Frank's machine.

The work that Frank had accomplished was "above and beyond the call of duty." He had basically performed the functions of a design engineer, manufacturing engineer, and machine shop and project manager in designing, building, installing, and proving his new machine. Based upon the volume of components produced by his machine, Frank calculated that he had saved the Zenco Corporation $1.2 million in its first year of operation. He had worked very hard on this activity for many months and had put in many hours of overtime as well. He felt he deserved substantial recognition for his accomplishment.

Frank's regularly scheduled performance appraisal meeting with Joe Kincaid occured after the machine had been in operation for several months. Kincaid rated his performance, overall, as excellent. He granted Frank a merit salary increase of 9 per cent for the ensuing year. This was 2 per cent above the average increase in the department. Frank told Kincaid that he felt he deserved a much larger salary increase and a promotion to the rank of Engineer. Joe Kincaid replied that he could not grant him a larger salary increase (the amount had previously been approved by Kincaid's superior). Also he could not recommend him for promotion to Engineer because it was company policy that those holding the rank of Engineer and above must possess at least a bachelor's degree in engineering. Frank was severely disappointed.[1]

A few weeks later the first two of the machines ordered from the vendor were installed and placed into operation. Although based upon Frank's engineering concept these were supposed to incorporate certain improvements and refinements. However they were subject to frequent breakdowns. Quality and quantity were inferior to that of Frank's machine. Technical personnel from both the vendor and Zenco's Design Engineering Department worked on these machines but were unable to overcome the deficiencies after several months of effort.

Finally Joe Kincaid assigned Frank to the job of correcting the problems in these two machines. Supervising machinists and mechanics, Frank made several basic modifications to the machines and achieved acceptable performance over a period of three months.

Frank observed that Kincaid, in his conversations, was taking much of the credit for the innovations he had made in his original machine and in overcoming the defects in the vendor-supplied machines. A few months later Kincaid was promoted and moved into another division.

Denby was getting increasingly irritated that he had not been granted some

---

[1]Engineering grades from the lowest to highest were as follows: Assistant Engineer, Associate Engineer, Engineer, Senior Engineer, and Project Engineer.

significant recognition for his very considerable accomplishments. He knew that under the company's suggestion plan an employee whose suggestion for improvements resulted in dollar savings was entitled to 20 per cent of the first year's net savings. Hourly paid and nonexempt office employees were eligible for awards under the suggestion plan whether or not their suggestions dealt with their own jobs or other areas of the business. Engineers were not entitled to monetary awards for suggestions directly connected with their own jobs, but they were eligible for awards for ideas outside their own field of work. However, the company did have a policy of making substantial monetary awards occasionally to scientists and engineers who made extrordinary contributions (such as inventions) of benefit to the firm.

After Joe Kincaid left, Frank asked his new manager, Ed Henry, for a merit salary increase and a promotion to the rank of Engineer. Henry said he would look into the matter but time elapsed and nothing was done.

Then Denby wrote a letter to the Division General Manager explaining in detail the significant work he had done. He even included photographs of his machine. He asked for and was granted a private interview with the General Manager. This appeal was entirely legitimate in accordance with the company's "open door" appeal policy. One month later Frank was promoted to the rank of Engineer. Ed Henry also handed him a check for $1,500 signed by the corporation president. This was in recognition of his excellent work.

Frank refused to accept the $1,500. He told Ed Henry he felt he deserved much more than that amount. He said that his machine had saved the company $1.2 million in the first year of operation. His design had been copied in the other machines made by the vendor. Henry replied that he had no authority to grant Denby a larger sum.

Denby received his promotion and the offer of $1,500 with some bitterness. Over a year and a half had elapsed since he had installed his machine. It was evident that no recognition whatever would have been accorded him if he had not gone to the Division General Manager to plead his case.

Frank had begun to do just what was absolutely required in his job and nothing more. He openly complained to his colleagues that the company had mistreated him. Occasionally he left work early and arrived late in the morning. As the weeks and months passed his attitude toward the company became more negative. He spent more and more of his time conversing with fellow engineers and taking extended coffee breaks. When given a direct assignment by his manager he performed acceptably but rather slowly, and without his former enthusiasm.

Frank Denby is very friendly with his colleagues. They respect his talents. However they think he has let his bitterness against the company seriously affect his performance and outlook.

Questions
1. Retracing the series of events in the case, at what points in time and how should management have handled Frank Denby differently? How should he have been recognized for his accomplishments? When? What should Joe Kin-

caid have done? What should Ed Henry have done? What should higher management have done, if anything?

2. Does the Zenco Corporation appear to have adequate policies and procedures to handle a case like Frank Denby's? Discuss.

3. Assume that you have recently been appointed Manager of Manufacturing Engineering to succeed Ed Henry. What, if anything, could you do to regenerate Frank Denby's former level of motivation and performance?

Suggestions for Further Reading

Dowling, William F. Jr., and Leonard R. Sayles. *How Managers Motivate: The Imperatives of Supervision*, 2nd. ed. New York: McGraw-Hill Book Company, 1978.

Franken, Robert E. *Human Motivation.* Monterey, Cal.: Brooks/Cole, 1982.

Frederiksen, Lee W. (ed.) *Handbook of Organizational Behavior Modification.* Somerset, N.J.: John Wiley & Sons, Inc., 1982.

Garin, Robert H., and John F. Cooper, "The Morale-Productivity Relationship: How Close?" *Personnel,* Vol. 58, No. 1 (January–February 1981), pp. 57–62.

Hackman, J. Richard, and Greg R. Oldham. *Work Redesign.* Reading, Mass.: Addison-Wesley Publishing Co., 1980.

Herzberg, Frederick. *The Managerial Choice: To Be Efficient and to Be Human.* Homewood, Ill.: Dow-Jones Irwin, 1976.

Locke, Edwin A. "The Myths of Behavioral Mod in Organizations," *Academy of Management Review,* Vol. 2, No. 4 (October 1977), pp. 543–553.

Maslow, A. H. *Motivation and Personality,* 2nd ed. New York: Harper and Row, Publishers, 1970.

Skinner, B. F. *Beyond Freedom and Dignity.* New York: Alfred A. Knopf, Inc., 1971.

Ullrich, Robert A. *Motivation Methods that Work: How to Increase the Productivity of Every Employee.* Englewood Cliffs, N.J.: Prentice-Hall, 1981.

15 Quality of Working Life

Commencing in the early 1970s there has been a rising interest in the quality of working life for both blue- and white-collar workers. Managements of many leading corporations have been concerned to the point that they have launched comprehensive projects to improve work force productivity, organizational effectiveness, and the quality of working life. Although various leaders in management, labor, government, and the universities had in past years intermittently expressed concern about such matters as decent wages, hours, working conditions, and the problems of boredom, monotony, and fatigue, the issue of quality of working life did not become focused into a coherent thesis until the 1970s.

Some evidence of the rising tide of interest in quality of working life issues is the fact that the second international conference on quality of work life held in Toronto in 1981 attracted 1,500 participants. The 200 unionists and 750 management people combined outnumbered the academicians, consultants, and government officials in attendance.[1]

The single event that sparked public attention to this important issue was the strike in March 1972 of approximately 8,000 workers at

the new General Motors's Lordstown, Ohio, plant. Both workers and their union leaders charged, with considerable justification, that General Motors's management had cut the workforce and speeded up the pace of work on the assembly line. The national news media began to issue reports about the problems at this plant and in other companies throughout the country. These reports asserted that many American workers, especially young ones in the mass production industries, were experiencing a sense of frustration and alienation over their conditions of employment.

Leaders in many organizations have been studying the matter of quality of working life and how to improve it. Quite generally productivity improvement has been studied in concert with quality of working life. Among the concerned agencies and organizations have been the National Center for Productivity and Quality of Working Life (a Federal agency) and private organizations such as the Work in America Institute and the American Quality of Work Center. Scores of American and European corporations have on-going projects in this field. Among these are General Foods, Corning Glass Works, General Motors, and Texas Instruments in the United States and Volvo, Saab-Scandia, Norsk Hydro, and Olivetti in Europe. Also university scholars and researchers have been

---

[1]"Quality of Work Life: Catching On," *Business Week,* September 21, 1981, pp. 72–80.

doing considerable work in the area of quality of working life.

In this chapter we shall investigate the meaning of work, conditions of working life facing many employees, the meaning of the concept "quality of working life," strategies for improving both quality of working life and productivity, examples of successful industrial programs, and issues involved in implementation.

THE NATURE OF WORK

Historically, cultural values about work have shifted greatly over the years. In ancient times work was performed mostly by slaves. The Renaissance and Reformation brought great changes in prevailing attitudes toward work. Work acquired a moral dignity of its own. Hard work and frugality were a way of pleasing God and were the road to salvation. Max Weber, the German sociologist and historical scholar, explained that the rise of capitalism in the eighteenth century was related to the earlier glorification of the values of hard work, saving, and the accumulation of material wealth by the originators of Protestantism—Martin Luther and John Calvin. He labeled these values the Protestant ethic. The idea that work was virtuous was brought to North America from Europe.

Work is an activity that produces something of value for other people. It includes paid employment plus unpaid work in the household and on the farm by family members.[2]

Work serves many purposes. The economic function of work for producing goods and services is its most obvious value. In return for production the worker is paid wages that enable the purchase of food, clothing, shelter, plus other needs and luxuries of life. But work serves other values as well.

Part of the social needs of people are supplied at the workplace where they meet, converse, and share experiences. One's job connotes a certain social status both for the worker and his or her family. Work also contributes to an employee's self-esteem by reflecting a contribution to the work group, department, and company. If a person is competent and meets his own personal and the boss's expectations, this contributes to a sense of personal worth. Also, an individual's occupation helps shape a sense of identity. He or she will often identify himself or herself, when meeting strangers, by stating occupation and the name of employer. Thus, we learn that Frank is a technician at Tyler General Hospital, Maxine is a machinist at U.S. Steel, and Edward is a professor at Cornell.

Let us now look at those features of work in modern industrialized society that tend to be common to a great many enterprises. Of course there are variations in the degree to which these factors are present from one establishment to the next. First we note that the work role is separate from the family role. Contrary to the situation in agrarian societies, work in an industrialized society is sharply separated from family life in orientation, content, time, and location.

Employees at all organizational levels are expected to be compliant and obedient to autocratic authority. The prevailing organizational ethic is that the boss knows best or, at least, that he has the right to impose his will upon subordinates on the job. Especially in larger organizations employees are subjected to strict discipline and regimentation. These organizations enforce a complex system of rules and require employees to perform (and rest) according to strict work pace and time controls.

Typically jobs are defined narrowly. This means that each job demands only a narrow

<hr>

[2]*Work in America,* Report of a Special Task Force to the Secretary of Health, Education, and Welfare (Cambridge, Mass.: The MIT Press, 1973), p.3.

range of skills. The conventional wisdom of industrial managers is that minute division of labor increases efficiency and output.

Another feature of work in modern society is the underlying threat of layoff. This has long been characteristic of employment in private enterprises because of fluctuations in market demand and layoffs due to technological changes. In recent years public sector employees have also had to face the problem of lack of job security. For example, declining student enrollments in many communities have caused teacher layoffs in public schools. Managers have become subject to layoffs as well.

CONTEMPORARY PROBLEMS OF AMERICAN WORKERS

In this section we shall examine two contradictory viewpoints about the state of American workers' attitudes and satisfaction (or dissatisfaction) concerning their jobs. Each viewpoint has plenty of vocal and articulate proponents.

Workers-Are-Dissatisfied Thesis

We have seen that work manifests significance over and above its strict economic function by providing meaning, social relationships, self-esteem, sense of personal worth, respect from others, and a sense of identity.

Behavioral science investigators have detected substantial differences in the degree of satisfaction people in various occupations say they obtain from their jobs. When asked the question, "What type of work would you try to get into if you could start all over again?" a high percentage of those in professional occupations stated they would choose the same type of work again. On the other hand, few of the blue-collar workers said they would choose the same work.

The percentages of professionals who would choose similar work again were as follows: urban university professors, 93 per cent; mathematicians, 91 per cent; biologists, 89 per cent; lawyers, 83 per cent; journalists (Washington correspondents), 82 per cent. For white-collar workers (a cross-section), 43 per cent would select similar work again. For blue-collar workers some of the results were as follows: skilled printers, 52 per cent; paperworkers, 42 per cent; skilled autoworkers, 41 per cent; skilled steelworkers, 41 per cent; unskilled steelworkers, 21 per cent; unskilled autoworkers, 16 per cent. A cross-section of blue-collar workers (all occupations surveyed) was 24 per cent.[3]

The reader can see from the foregoing that job satisfaction (as evidenced by the survey question) corresponds rather closely with the social status and prestige ranking of occupations. There is also a rather close correlation between the educational level required for an occupation and job satisfaction. People in the higher-ranking jobs have more autonomy at work, have greater influence over what they do and what happens to them at work, more commonly experience a sense of work accomplishment, and can feel they are making their "mark" in what they do.

Discontent is concentrated more among blue-collar workers and white-collar workers (white-collar as distinct from professional and managerial personnel). The causes of discontent are many and varied but can generally be related to the features of work in modern industrialized society discussed earlier.

Alienation. The term *alienation* is used by social scientists to designate the constellation of attitudes, frustrations, and behaviors of people existing under the conditions we are talking about. Alienation contains the following ingredients: (1) powerlessness, (2) meaningless, (3)

[3]Ibid., pp. 15–16. This survey is taken from a report by Robert Kahn, "The Work Module," (1972).

isolation, and (4) self-estrangement.[4] *Powerlessness* means that the individual feels he has no capacity to affect management policies and rules, job conditions, and immediate work processes. *Meaninglessness* refers to the condition in which the employee derives no sense of meaning or accomplishment from the product or service he works on. *Isolation* designates the feeling of being socially isolated from others in one's place of employment. There may be little social contact and lack of membership in social groups. *Self-estrangement* consists of boredom and lack of ego-involvement in one's job.

Conditions of Work. Let us look at the conditions of work life of many workers. We shall start with the blue-collar worker. Blue-collar workers (often called hourly paid workers) are those who work in factories, construction, transportation, and service industries in unskilled, semiskilled, or skilled capacities. They generally must punch a time clock at the beginning and end of their daily shifts. Typical jobs are machine tender, janitor, assembler, sewing machine operator, laborer, and production welder.

There are many sources for discontent and alienation with variation, of course, from one situation to the next. In their quest for efficiency industrial engineers have driven toward machine pacing of the worker in many factories. This is true of assembly lines along a moving conveyer belt and of production processes in which workers load and unload one or more machines in controlled sequence.

The automobile assembly line is the epitome of the fast-paced, short-cycle, repetitive production process in industry. The assembly line does yield high productivity but this is achieved at a large human cost in terms of monotony, fatigue, and alienation.

The discipline of the industrial plant tends to be strict. In many plants an employee must get permission from the boss to leave the work station to go to the rest room. He or she must start and stop work by the plant whistle, cannot clean up at the end of the shift before a designated time, and cannot argue with the foreman. The pressure for production is often relentless.

Contrary to popular belief many people must still work amid conditions of dirt, noise, and danger in American industry. A *Wall Street Journal* article entitled "Brutal, Mindless Labor Remains a Daily Reality for Millions in the U.S." portrays striking examples of the adversities many must face daily. From midnight until 10 A.M. a foundry worker in Ohio works in an inferno of heat, filth, and noise. He shovels thousands of pounds of red-hot slag from beneath a furnace into large bins on wheels. He must, at times, crawl inside a cooled furnace to chip hardened slag with a hammer and chisel. Then he lines the furnace with blobs of thick, sticky mud before the furnace is fired again. The article also describes a coke-oven worker in Pennsylvania who ranges back and forth over the hot brick top of a battery of ovens wearing wooden pallets under his shoes and a rubber mask. His task is to pull off thick steel lids on the oven tops with an iron bar so he can dump in coal from "lorry cars" that move along the oven roofs on rails. The job is filthy, hot, monotonous, and dangerous. The man is surrounded by thick acrid smoke.[5]

Although many people think sweatshops are a relic of the past, this is not so. Thousands of people—mostly immigrants and illegal aliens—work in dirty, dingy lofts at wages below the legal minimum making men's and women's clothing. These sweatshops employ Haitians, Mexicans, Dominicans, Columbians, Puerto Ricans, Jamaicans, and Asian-Americans. The employees work on piece rates that generally are so low that they cannot earn the legal minimum of $3.35 per hour even if they work very hard. Many of these sweatshops are concentrated in the New York City area. It is

___

[4]Robert Blauner, *Alienation and Freedom: The Factory Worker and His Industry* (Chicago: University of Chicago Press, 1964).

[5]*Wall Street Journal* (July 16, 1971).

difficult for state and federal labor department inspectors to effectively enforce the labor laws in these ubiquitous sweatshops.[6]

Lack of task variety is a source of discontent for many. The extreme task specialization of modern production processes has contributed to boredom and monotony. Sometimes workers are less conscious of the repetitive nature of their jobs if they have opportunities for social interaction while they work. However, factory noise and physical separation of work stations frequently minimize the possibility of conversing, exchanging stories and experiences, and joking.

For unskilled and semiskilled jobs, especially, there is little if any opportunity for the worker to express ideas and ingenuity. The planning of work methods and tooling is done by the engineer and the supervisor. The worker is simply a "hired hand." Many behavioral scientists contend that workers have a desire for autonomy and some degree of control over their jobs but that this desire is frustrated by ever-present bureaucratic controls.

What is the situation for white-collar workers? By white-collar personnel we mean such occupations as clerks, typists, stenographers, secretaries, record keepers, sales clerks in stores, and key punch operators. The proportion of these types in the labor force has been increasing. The routinization and regimentation of the factory have now invaded the office. There is little to distinguish the long rows of desk workers from the long rows of factory bench hands except for cleaner working conditions in the office. There is often extreme task specialization in the office. Many companies time study their white-collar workers and set time standards for their tasks just as they do for the factory jobs. A great array of business machines, copiers, and computers are in use. Many white-collar personnel are simply office machine tenders.

Job Pressures and Health. Evidence is being accumulated that job satisfaction or its opposite, job frustration, has a substantial effect upon health. A scientific investigation of aging revealed that the strongest predictor of longevity was work satisfaction. The second-ranking factor was general happiness. These two factors were better predictors of longevity than a rating by an examining physician, a measure of smoking, or of genetic inheritance.[7]

Although it is well known that many factors such as smoking and excess body weight contribute to heart disease, scientists have also determined that certain factors in the work situation contribute to the risk of acquiring heart disease. These are job dissatisfaction (tedious work, lack of recognition, poor relations with co-workers, and poor working conditions), low self-esteem related to the job, and occupational stress (work overload and time pressures). Other factors contributing to heart disease are lack of stability, security, and support in the job environment. Peptic ulcers, arthritis, and stroke also have been correlated with job stress.[8]

Workers-Are-Satisfied Thesis

Several writers and investigators have disputed the claim that a large segment of American workers are alienated and derive little satisfaction from their jobs. To support their contentions, these critics cite data from both job satisfaction surveys and from statistical indicators of labor turnover, absenteeism, strikes, and productivity.

In a review of 2,000 surveys of job satisfaction of many groups in many industries conducted over many years, Robert Kahn reported that there is a consistency in response patterns. Few people were extremely satisfied, but fewer still were extremely dissatisfied. The modal re-

[6]Rinker Buck, "The New Sweatshops: A Penny for Your Collar," *New York*, January 29, 1979, pp. 40–45.

[7]Erdman Palmore, "Predicting Longevity: A Follow-up Controlling for Age," *Gerontologist* (Winter 1969).
[8]*Work in America*, op. cit., pp. 77–81.

sponse was on the positive side of neutrality—"pretty satisfied." The portion dissatisfied was in the 10–21 per cent range.[9] Measures of labor turnover, absenteeism, strikes, and productivity do show definite fluctuations from year to year but these fluctuations are more closely correlated with changes in other factors such as economic cycles, supply and demand for labor, and inflationary trends than with shifts in worker satisfaction.[10]

The critics also refer to periodic public opinion polls such as Gallup and Roper which have, for a good number of years, revealed that the majority of persons questioned say they are satisfied with their jobs.[11]

Analysis and Explanation

What are we to make of the contradictory views and evidence? It is inaccurate to make a sweeping statement that workers are or are not satisfied with their jobs. There is really considerable variation from individual to individual and group to group. University of Michigan survey data reveal that those most dissatisfied tend to be young (under 30 years of age), blacks, those earning low wages, and operators and nonfarm laborers. Blue-collar workers are more dissatisfied than white-collar personnel.[12]

Self-employed persons express greatest job satisfaction. They are their own bosses and have great autonomy. However, with each passing decade there have been fewer opportunities to be self-employed. In the mid-nineteenth century more than half of all employed persons were self-employed. By 1970 the percentage of self-employed had dropped below 10 per cent.

Managerial, technical, and professional employees are more satisfied with their jobs than are lower-ranking personnel. Information published by the Opinion Research Corporation demonstrates that discontent among hourly paid and clerical employees has been growing in recent years. This conclusion is based upon questionnaire responses of 175,000 employees in 159 companies that have been surveyed many times since 1950. There is a "hierarchy gap" in the levels of job satisfaction between managers and those of hourly and clerical personnel.[13]

Job discontent and frustration can be caused by (a) jobs of limited scope and those having tasks of short cycle, jobs with no opportunity to exercise discretion and initiative, excessive bureaucratic controls, and oppressive supervision; or by (b) low wages, bad working conditions, and job insecurity. The key to the question of how working people view their jobs is simply this—What are their expectations from work? Do they primarily want decent wages so they have adequate money to obtain their life satisfactions off the job? Or do they expect not only decent wages and working conditions but also a high quality of working life? Do they want interesting work, variety, challenge, and autonomy? People bring to the workplace quite different value systems. These different value systems are culturally determined—family upbringing, education, peer group relations, and early job experiences.

Some persons have high aspirations, are career-oriented, and seek intrinsic satisfaction from their jobs. However, they may find themselves in stifling bureaucratic job situations. The

[9]As quoted in Harold Wool, "What's Wrong with Work in America?—A Review Essay," *Monthly Labor Review,* Vol. 96, No. 3 (March 1973), pp. 38–44.

[10]Ibid., pp. 41–42.

[11]For further information see Mitchell Fein, "The Real Needs and Goals for Blue-Collar Workers," *The Conference Board Record,* Vol. X, No. 2 (February 1973), pp. 26–33; H. Roy Kaplan, "How Do Workers View Their Work in America?," *Monthly Labor Review,* Vol. 96, No. 6 (June 1973), pp. 46–47.

[12]R. P. Quinn, T. W. Mangione, M. S. Baldi De Mandilovitch, "Evaluating Working Conditions in America," *Monthly Labor Review,* Vol. 96, No. 11 (November 1973), pp. 32–42.

[13]Michael R. Cooper, B. S. Morgan, P. M. Foley, and L. B. Kaplan, "Changing Employee Values: Deepening Discontent?" *Harvard Business Review,* Vol. 57, No. 1 (January–February 1979), pp. 117–125.

boss may not care to hear their ideas. Their jobs may be limited in scope and promotion opportunities could be rare. Such people tend to seek expression for their abilities and ambitions in off-the-job activities—social activities, professional societies, or part-time businesses.

Regardless of the contrasting theses on job satisfaction and conditions of work in America, there is widespread recognition that both productivity and quality of working life can and should be improved.

Productivity in an enterprise and in the economy as a whole is based upon a combination of human, organizational, technological, and capital investment factors. Over the past three decades in the United States there has been a pronounced shift toward labor-intensive service industries in which technology plays a lesser role than does the labor of the human being. Examples of these sectors of the economy are education, health care, and government. Certainly in these industries innovative programs to raise human productivity can have a substantial payoff. Also, in manufacturing industries where machines and technology loom large, experiments have demonstrated that new designs for work systems and "people management" can yield substantial and lasting gains in productivity.

The percentage of the labor force which is college-educated has been increasing rather steadily since the late 1940s. The big boom in college enrollments occurred in the 1960s. Ordinarily a college degree has served as a key to the door of opportunity and the good life in America. However, by the 1980s, we now have a glut of college-educated people in the job market. The college graduates are moving downward to lower-income and lower-status jobs. This condition is generating high frustration among college-educated young people. Employers can help alleviate this problem by establishing career development, job enrichment, and other innovative quality-of-working-life programs.

Even those workers of lesser education and aspiration, who look upon their jobs simply as a way of making a living, can cultivate a taste for a high level of involvement in their work. Many experiments have shown that once given the opportunity, ordinary hourly paid workers can make real contributions toward solving job problems and improving productivity.

QUALITY OF WORKING LIFE

The most widely quoted definition of quality of working life is that formulated by Richard E. Walton. Professor Walton expains it in terms of eight broad conditions of employment that constitute a good or desirable quality of working life. Walton's features or conditions are as follows:

1. Adequate and fair compensation.
2. Safe and healthy working conditions.
3. Immediate opportunity to use and develop human capacities. This includes autonomy, work requiring multiple skills, information and perspective, whole tasks, and involvement in planning.
4. Future opportunity for continued growth and security. This includes expanding one's capabilities, opportunity to use new knowledge and skills, promotion opportunities, plus job and income security.
5. Social integration in the work organization. This includes freedom from prejudice, egalitarianism, supportive primary work groups, a sense of community, and interpersonal openness.
6. Constitutionalism in the work organization. This included rights to privacy and free speech. It also includes equitable treatment of employees and "due process" procedures in handling employees and in appeal procedures.
7. Work and total life space. Walton argues for

a balanced relationship among work and nonwork and family aspects of life.

8. Social relevance of work. The employing organization should perform in a socially beneficial manner.[14]

Clearly, of course, many employers do provide a work life climate that meets several of Walton's criteria such as adequate compensation and safe working conditions. Some companies also have interesting, challenging jobs and offer many opportunities for training and advancement. However, it is rare to find work-life situations that satisfy all eight of Walton's criteria. We can view these eight features as goals to aim for.

Because of individual differences among people and because of differences in the opportunities for need-satisfaction from one department of a company to another, we should expect considerable variation in the satisfactions experienced by different employees in the same organization.

STRATEGIES FOR IMPROVEMENT

As stated earlier many employing organizations, both in the United States and abroad, have programs to enhance both the quality of working life and productivity. Especially in the private, competitive sector management is nearly always looking for ways to cut costs and increase output. Productivity could be improved in ways that reduce the quality of working life. Thus management could raise work loads, reduce the number of personnel, and fractionate jobs further. This might increase productivity in the short run but it would most certainly increase employee tensions. We are concerned here pri-

marily with programs that have as their objective both work-life improvement and improvement in performance.

A variety of strategies or approaches have been devised by experimenters. We shall here describe the principal strategies that have been employed. Typically an organization uses one or possibly two strategies as its main theme and supplements this with one or more subsidiary approaches.

Participative Management

By *participative management* we mean a system of management in which employees participate in making management decisions that affect them and their jobs. This process increases employee motivation, generates ideas that may not have occurred to management alone, and reduces resistance to new methods and processes. It helps meet the human needs for autonomy, achievement, and self-expression. Although participative management can be structured in a number of ways, typically it involves a departmental supervisor conducting meetings with his immediate subordinates to make plans and decisions regarding such matters as tooling, equipment, methods, safety, distribution of tasks, and working conditions. Generally the supervisor retains final decision-making authority but works closely with people in getting ideas, testing their reactions, and shaping solutions. Because participative management is so different in concept from the traditional "boss-knows-it all" style of leadership, front line supervisors require specific training in the theory and methods of participative management.

In addition to consultation by supervisors with their subordinates, participative management can occur by means of quality circles, union–management cooperation, Scanlon plans, and suggestion plans.

One innovative form of participative management is "Face-to-Face" at Pacific Northwest Bell, formerly a unit of AT&T. Face-to-face is a

---

[14]Richard E. Walton, "Quality of Working Life: What Is It?" *Sloan Management Review,* Vol. 15, No. 1 (Fall 1973), pp. 11–21.

formal system in which employees define problems, needs, and priorities for improvement. Employees at all levels in the organization become involved in the process. Continuing feedback and evaluation of progress is built into the program. The process is guided in each organizational unit by a coordinating committee and a coordinator. This committee interviews employees to identify problems and needs. Questionnaires are administered to employees to obtain data on the breadth and depth of concern about key issues. Results from the interviews and questionnaires are fed back to the employee groups as a basis for discussion. The employee teams prepare plans giving objectives, proposed actions, assignment of accountability, and completion dates.

The "Face-to-Face" program was initiated by the company management in 1977. In 1980 the entire Bell System negotiated an agreement with its unions to work toward the improvement of the quality of work life jointly. The "Face-to-Face" process was continued and accepted into the quality of work life system.[15]

Self-Managed Work Teams

Self-managed work teams are also called *autonomous work groups* or *integrated work teams.* In this method work groups of say, ten to twenty employees, plan, coordinate, and control their own activities. They have a team leader who is often a worker, not a member of management.

Groups of employees are given the authority not only to perform direct production operations but also to do certain activities that traditionally are done by service and staff groups. Thus, an assembly group may take on the added tasks of planning work methods, inspecting output, maintaining equipment, and

even selecting employees for the team. These groups have authority to regulate their own work tempo. Key decisions are often made as group decisions.

The objective in setting up self-managed work teams is to create teams around whole units of work wherein the components of the work and the processes are interdependent. Generally several different skills and jobs are combined into each team. The team is accountable for performance of its whole unit of work (e.g., making subassemblies, processing customer claims) and given the personnel and resources necessary to complete the work properly. The reward system (pay, recognition, promotion) is related to both group and individual achievement.

A major American corporation that has had ongoing quality-of-working-life programs since the mid-1970s is General Motors. Among these has been the self-managed work-team concept established at G. M.'s Delco-Remy battery plant in Fitzgerald, Ga., in 1975. The organization structure at Fitzgerald consists of four major components: (1) 25 plant-operating teams (workers and team leaders); (2) a support team consisting of such entities as plant manager, superintendent of quality control, superintendent of production control, product engineer, and general supervisor of manufacturing; (3) technical service teams comprising such units as engineering, shipping and receiving, purchasing and scheduling, and accounting, and (4) area coordinators. As experience with the teams developed the operating teams were even given significant responsibilities for budget preparation. In the operating teams employees were able to increase their wages as they learned additional jobs within their teams.

Results of the program at the Fitzgerald plant have generally been positive. The indexes of employee attitudes measured by questionnaires have been more favorable than the average for General Motors as a whole. The product quality index has risen over the years. Employee absenteeism and turnover have been substan-

[15]Robert Zager and Michael P. Rosow (eds.) *The Innovation Organization: Productivity Programs in Action.* Elmsford, N.Y.: Pergamon Press, Inc., 1982, ch. 2.

tially lower than at comparable G.M. battery plants.[16]

Job Redesign and Enrichment

The content of jobs can be changed to enrich them and make them more meaningful to the job holders. Narrow tasks can be combined into larger units of accomplishment. Client relationships can be established so that employees have a sense of doing their work for someone whom they know, such as in the case of a secretary doing work for a supervisor. Jobs can be loaded vertically by adding planning and controlling tasks. Additionally, direct feedback of information on performance can be given to the employees so they can judge the quality of their own work in relation to expected standards.

Effective Leadership and Supervisory Behavior

Although there is no formula that teaches one how to be an effective supervisor, research evidence accumulated over many years has uncovered many useful insights. Employees like to work for supervisors who show consideration for them, who are supportive, and who are fair and just in their treatment. The supervisor should create and atmosphere of approval in relations with subordinates. Employees' perception of their quality of working life is affected heavily by the treatment they receive from their supervisors.

The effective supervisor also must take actions to help get the work out. This dimension has been variously labeled "facilitation and goal emphasis," "initiating structure," and "production-centered" leadership. The supervisor must be able to organize and direct people who will produce work. She or he must possess technical knowledge in order to diagnose production

[16]Ibid, ch. 7.

difficulties. She or he must set challenging but attainable performance standards. In certain circumstances the employees themselves may participate in setting output standards. The supervisor must help people solve work and equipment problems and must also provide job instruction. In implementing this facilitation dimension of the job the supervisor should not be overbearing nor pressure people around.

Another important dimension of effective leadership and supervision is the development of teamwork among employees. The supervisor should generate an appropriate degree of participation in day-to-day decisions. Employees should care about their work and about the department. They should be highly involved and not apathetic.

Career Development

To more fully utilize the talents of their people, to help employees realize their career ambitions, and to enhance their feelings of achievement and recognition, many of the more progressive corporations are nowadays carrying on systematic career planning and development activities. The principal components of a comprehensive career program within an organization are (1) human resource planning; (2) communication of job opportunities and career path information to employees; (3) career counseling both by the supervisor as part of performance appraisal and by the personnel department; (4) provision for education and training of employees both within and outside the organization; and (5) special broadening job assignments and job rotation. In addition to these basic components some organizations have formal assessment centers to analyze and evaluate the capacities and potential of their personnel.

"Second careers" is a concept that is gaining acceptance in recent years. Because of pronounced changes in the demand for occupations (for example, the demand for teachers is down now whereas the demand for health-care personnel is up) and because of the emergence of new occupations, working people should have opportunities to reassess themselves in mature life and make a start on a new and different career. To effectuate this our labor market and educational institutions should provide assistance to those seeking new careers. Personnel managers should also see that the career development programs in their organizations provide opportunities for employees to change their career paths, where feasible.

Alternative Work Schedules

Alternative work schedules are becoming increasingly common in both the private and public sectors. Such schedules appear in three different forms: (1) flexitime or flexible hours, (2) part-time employment and job sharing, and (3) compressed workweek.

Flexitime has been applied in various modes. In the most common mode employees must be on the job for a certain core period each day, say 9.30 A.M. to 3:30 P.M. They can select a definite starting and quitting time, say 7:00 A.M. to 3:30 P.M. (including one-half hour for lunch), that will provide eight hours of work per day. With flexitime employees gain a sense of freedom and of controlling their own time. They gain the opportunity of conducting limited personal business during the work day. Potential benefits for the organization are higher morale and less absenteeism.

Part-time employment and job sharing are especially attractive to working mothers with young children at home. Often retirees would like the daily stimulation and earnings provided by a job but do not wish to work a full eight-hour day, day in and day out.

In a compressed workweek a full week of work is accomplished in less than five days. Commonly, employees work four days of 10-hour shifts or they may work three days of 12-hour shifts. Compressed workweeks give all employees longer weekends which are often de-

sired. Companies may benefit if they have heavy investment in capital equipment that ought to be operated as many hours per day as possible to yield a good return on investment.

Job Security

American executives have traditionally attached little importance to job security for their employees. As soon as there was a downturn of business for their firms they would lay off workers and salaried personnel to cut costs.

Job security has always ranked high on the employees' list of priorities. Spurred by the very deep recession and mass layoffs of the 1980–1983 periods, workers and unions have pressed hard for protection against layoffs. And now enlightened managers have come to realize that there are heavy costs to the firm of frequent layoffs and real benefits from a program of employment stability.

Layoffs are expensive. They entail severance pay, higher unemployment insurance tax rates, and the extra cost of training workers when demand picks up. Fear of layoffs can drive good employees to seek jobs elsewhere. Fear of layoffs depresses productivity because employees resist technological innovation and cost-reduction measures.

Some of the most successful firms in the United States have policies of employment security and no layoffs. Among these are IBM, Lincoln Electric, Bell Laboratories, Mallinckrodt, 3M Company, Polaroid, Texaco, and Wyeth Laboratories.[17]

In 1982 both General Motors and Ford set up programs with the United Automobile Workers Union to seek ways of avoiding layoffs, to retain workers for new technologies, and to transfer employees to other jobs when their jobs must be eliminated. Both corporations have es-

[17]James F. Bolt, "Job Security: Its Time Has Come," *Harvard Business Review,* Vol. 61, No. 6 (November–December 1983), pp. 115–123.

tablished extensive retraining programs at many of their plants.[18]

Administrative Justice

Administrative or organizational justice insures that disciplinary and grievance handling proceedings are carried out according to recognized principles of due process. For example, in administering discipline and discharge the affected employee is given a written statement of the charges against him, he has the right to defend himself, he has the right of counsel or representation, and final appeal is before an impartial party such as an arbitrator.

CONCLUDING COMMENTS

Most quality-of-working-life programs constitute an attempt to increase employee satisfaction and performance through increased intrinsic motivation. These programs seek to involve employees more thoroughly in decisions and activities of their jobs, work groups, department, and to some extent of the whole organization. These endeavors try to enhance the motivators as defined by psychologist Frederick Herzberg—achievement, recognition, work itself, responsibility, advancement, and growth.

These programs do not, by and large, try to improve all components of quality of working life. For example, largely missing from such programs is attention to employee privacy, due process and just cause, freedom of expression, and equitable treatment. Also absent from most programs is a mechanism to provide for job security.

[18]"New Blueprints in the Drive for Job Security," *Business Week*, January 9, 1984, p. 91.

Despite the foregoing omissions this author thinks that the quality-of-working-life movement is generally on the right track. Much of the work is based upon sound theory and research of the behavioral sciences. It should be a continuing movement for many years.

Success in any program to enhance performance and the quality of working life requires a deep understanding of the entire process by top management of the organization. Likewise top officials must be thoroughly committed to the activity and must understand the investment required and the possible problems to be encountered along the way.

Questions for Review and Discussion
1. Based upon the working people whom you know well, would you say that most persons are quite oriented toward their work? Are their jobs a central focus of their lives? What differences do you note among people?
2. What values does one's job provide the individual over and above the purely utilitarian one of earning a living?
3. What features of work in our modern organizations can cause frustration and alienation?
4. Why is the level of job satisfaction generally higher for managers, professionals, and self-employed individuals than for blue-collar workers?
5. Educational attainment of the workforce has risen steadily over the years. Also the percentage of college graduates in the workforce has increased substantially. How do these factors affect satisfaction with work?
6. What features comprise a high quality of working life?
7. Explain the following: self-managed work teams, job enrichment, participative management, career development.

Suggestions for Further Reading

Barbash, Jack, R. J. Lampman, S. A. Levitan, and G. Taylor (eds.) *The Work Ethic—A Critical Analysis.* Madison, Wis.: Industrial Relations Research Association, 1983.

Davis, Louis E., and Albert B. Cherns (eds) *The Quality of Working Life,* Vols. I and II. New York: The Free Press, 1975.

Glaser, Edward M. "Productivity Gains Through Work-Life Improvement," *Personnel,* Vol. 57, No. 1 (Jan.–Feb. 1982), pp. 71–77.

Greenberg, Paul D., and Edward M. Glaser. *Some Issues in Joint Union–Management Quality of Work-Life Improvement Efforts.* Kalamazoo, Mich.: W. E. Upjohn Institute for Employment Research, 1980.

Hackman, J. Richard, and J. Lloyd Suttle (eds.). *Improving Life at Work.* Santa Monica, Cal.: Goodyear Publishing Co., Inc., 1977.

"The New Industrial Relations," *Business Week* (May 11, 1981), pp. 84–98.

Rosow, Jerome M., "Quality of Work-Life Issues for the 1980s," *Training and Development Journal,* Vol. 35, No. 3 (March 1981), pp. 33–52.

Runcie, John F. "By Days I Make the Cars," *Harvard Business Review,* Vol. 58, No. 3 (May–June 1980), pp. 106–115.

Work in America. Report of a Special Task Force to the Secretary of Health, Education, and Welfare. Cambridge, Mass.: The MIT Press, 1973.

Zager, Robert, and Michael P. Rosow (eds.) *The Innovative Organization: Productivity Programs in Action.* New York: Pergamon Press, 1982.

16 Leadership, Supervision, and Management Systems

A supervisor persuades a team of engineers that they must revise their procedures drastically in order to meet the scheduled delivery date in the space technology program. A young lady stenographer takes the initiative in making arrangements and getting the other young women to help in giving an office party for an associate who is moving to the West Coast with her husband. An engineer who senses strong discontent among fellow engineers because they must constantly put in long hours of overtime discusses the matter with the others and agrees to act as their spokesperson before the boss. A telephone lineman takes charge when his gang experiences difficulty running cable while the foreman is temporarily away from the job.

All of the foregoing acts are examples of leadership behavior. In the first situation the supervisor's leadership behavior was an integral part of a formal position of authority and command in the organization. In the other three instances the leadership acts were initiated by employees who volunteered their services. They exhibited actions of an informal leader. They were not endowed with formal authority by the organization.

Leading is the element of management that impels others to action. It is one of the essential functions that must be performed by all supervisors and executives—that is, by all who direct the work of other people. Leading, of all the key functions of management—planning, organizing, staffing, leading, and controlling—is one of the most difficult to understand, acquire, and evaluate. For centuries scholars have been speculating on the nature of leadership. Yet only in recent years have researchers conducted systematic investigations that have yielded useful insights into the dimensions of leadership.

Supervision is front-line management. The supervisor directs and controls the activities of nonsupervisory personnel. We shall explore the nature of the supervisor's job and also look at those supervisory behaviors that have been found effective in achieving employee satisfaction and high unit performance.

Because the overall style of management and organizational climate are so influential in determining the performance of individual departments within an establishment, we shall examine, also in this chapter, different systems of management.

NATURE OF LEADERSHIP

Leading is the process of influencing others to act to accomplish specified objectives. A precise and comprehensive definition of leadership is that formulated by Tannenbaum, Weschler, and

Massarik, who state that it consists of interpersonal influence, exercised in a situation and directed, by means of the communication process, toward the attainment of a specified goal or goals. They point out that leadership always involves attempts by a person (leader) to affect or influence the behavior of a follower (or followers) in a situation.[1]

The effective leader gets others (followers) to act. He or she may impel them to action by any of numerous devices: persuasion, influence, power, threat of force, and appeal to legitimate right.

The person who occupies a leadership position must transmit feelings and exhortations to followers by the process we call communication. Communication involves both the sending of messages and understanding by the receiver. The successful leader is the one who can appeal to constituents in a meaningful way. He or she talks their language.

Among the objectives the leader seeks to have the group accomplish may be those of the larger organization, as when a foreman exhorts workers to increase production to meet the schedule set by top management. The leader also is an agent of the led. He or she seeks to satisfy the needs of followers. Thus, a foreman may go to bat for workers to obtain higher pay classifications for them because both he and they honestly believe the higher pay rates are justified. It should be emphasized that the leader of a group in a formal organization has the dual objectives of representing the interests of the group to higher management and of getting subordinates to work for the goals of the enterprise as a whole. The problem of leadership is further complicated by the fact that individuals within a group of followers may (and usually do) possess varied and conflicting goals. These may not always be compatible with the objectives of the total organization or of the immediate group.

Followership is intimately related to leadership. A person's attempted leadership is only effective insofar as he is able to cause others to respond favorably to initiation of action. In fact, the way a subordinate reacts to a boss's directives affects the latter's manner of leading. A supervisor may learn from experience that it is unwise to assign Joan and Henry to work as partners on a maintenance repair job because Joan has previously said that she will not work with Henry. Of course, the supervisor could threaten to discharge Joan unless she works with Henry. But the supervisor knows that forcing the two to work together is folly because their incompatibility prevents effective work cooperation.

FOUNDATIONS OF LEADERSHIP

For centuries writers, historians, and the public in general held to the notion that leadership was primarily exercised by great men, that they were "born" and not "made" (by education and training), and that real progress and change in civilization awaited the coming of such individuals.

Indeed even in the late nineteenth and early twentieth centuries in America, writers depicting the successes of great industrial giants asserted that their position of authority and power derived mainly from their superior birth, superior ability, and superior personal magnetism. These powers were possessed only by a fortunate few. But such theories have been largely discredited as a result of the scientific investigation of leadership by modern researchers.

Traits, Situation, and Group

In selecting supervisors from within the ranks of a company, can management identify those employees who will be good leaders by the per-

[1] Robert Tannenbaum, Irving R. Weschler, and Fred Massarik, *Leadership and Organization: A Behavioral Science Approach* (New York: McGraw-Hill Book Company, 1961), p. 24.

sonality traits they exhibit? Is there a distinct leadership type? Do leaders as a whole possess traits that distinguish them from nonleaders?

Over the years innumerable investigators have sought to answer such questions as these. They have employed such methods as observation of behavior in group situations, analysis of biographical data, psychological testing of persons occupying leadership positions, and ratings by observers. It has been asserted that a commanding voice, vigorous health, tall stature, a striking appearance, and dominance are common characteristics of leaders. However, the fact of the matter is that to a considerable extent these studies have yielded a confusing and often contradictory array of characteristics allegedly possessed by leaders. It has been found that the traits claimed to be possessed by leaders are also widely exhibited by followers as well.

As a result of a comprehensive investigation of leadership, Stogdill concluded that the pattern of leadership traits differs with the situation. There is no single personality configuration that typifies a leader. He observed that the evidence strongly suggests that leadership is a relationship that exists among people in a social situation and that a person who becomes a leader in one situation may not do so in a different situation.[2]

There are three main variables to be weighed when one analyzes the leadership process: (1) a *leader* operating in a (2) *situation* in relation to the (3) *personalities, attitudes, and abilities* of the followers. The present state of knowledge is such that it is not now possible to define with precision the specific leader qualities and behaviors required for effective performance in defined situations with particular types of followers. However, the general dimensions of the problem are known.

Different types of followers—the group that is led—respond to different kinds of leadership. Some have great initiative and self-confidence; they respond best when they can assert themselves and work on their own. Other subordinates by reason of their background and personality development must have everything structured for them. Otherwise they feel lost. They require close guidance. Some employees like to take on new and important responsibilities; others simply are willing to "put their time in" and are content to obtain all their satisfactions off the job. Some persons exhibit little identification with the goals of the organization. Again we find that some employee groups possess a high level of education. They accordingly will respond to a particular style of leadership that would be quite inappropriate for a group having little formal education.

There are innumerable situations in which leadership must operate. Variations exist in the nature of the tasks, organizational environment, time dimensions, and social and cultural environment. The relationship that a leader or supervisor has with the boss affects the way he or she deals with subordinates. On the one hand, there may be mutual confidence and trust between them; on the other, the supervisor may feel insecure in respect to the boss. The insecure position of a supervisor is bound to transmit itself into dealings with subordinates.

Different jobs within the work organization require different abilities. The assertive, exuberant, outgoing, people-centered sales manager would be ill at ease and ill-equipped to supervise a design engineering department. Likewise it should be apparent that the skills and behavior required by our industrial giants in the early twentieth century—the Rockefellers, Fords, and Carnegies—to found industrial empires were quite different from the coordinative and administrative skills needed by the present-day executive to guide a modern enterprise.

[2]Ralph M. Stogdill, "Personal Factors Associated with Leadership: A Survey of the Literature," *The Journal of Psychology*, Vol. 25 (January 1948), pp. 35–71. Added evidence of the view that leadership is specific to the situation can be found in an experimental investigation by Launor F. Carter and Mary Nixon, "An Investigation of the Relationship Between Four Criteria of Leadership Ability for Three Different Tasks," *The Journal of Psychology*, Vol. 27 (January 1949), pp. 245–261.

A business leader operating in a Latin-American cultural climate must behave differently from one operating the same kind of enterprise in New York State. Variations between these two environments exist in the customs and expectations of the people both within and outside the work organization.

Any Common Traits?

We have emphasized that there is no such thing as the "leader type." Different situations and different groups require different leadership abilities. Generally speaking there are considerable variations in the personality, ability, capabilities, and skills of successful leaders. Yet with all the research that has been done into this problem, it can reasonably be asked whether there are not a few characteristics of successful leaders that the practical executive can give attention to when selecting subordinate leaders. The answer is that yes, there are some traits that appear in a majority of the investigations of leadership. But it should be remembered that although the statistical correlations between these traits and leadership ability are positive, the correlations are often low. The correlations also do not prove a cause-and-effect relationship. It may actually require one set of traits to achieve a position of leadership and another, but related, set of abilities to maintain that position.

Intelligence. Countless research studies have shown that a leader has somewhat greater intelligence than his or her followers. However, a leader will not usually have a great excess of intelligence over the average of the followers.[3] A manager of scientists would have, on the average, somewhat higher intelligence than followers. But a person possessing the level of intelligence of a typical Ph.D. in physics would

have far too much to supervise successfully a gang of laborers.

Social Skills. Leaders score fairly high on various measures of social skills, sociability, and friendliness toward others. They score high on interpersonal skills including tactfulness.[4]

Activity and Social Participation. A person is unlikely to rise to a position of leadership and is unlikely to maintain that position if he is passive, apathetic, or aloof. The successful leader tends to initiate action for others. He proposes, suggests, and coordinates. Leaders tend to participate actively in group functions. They are able to obtain cooperation from others.[5]

Need for Achievement. Leaders exhibit a strong need to achieve and to excel. They show persistence in overcoming obstacles. They are vigorous in pursuing their objectives and completing tasks. They are creative in problem solving.[6]

AUTHORITY AND POWER

In the formal organization—whether it be industrial, commercial, governmental, military, or philanthropic—leadership takes place in conjunction with authority and power. In fact, these are to a substantial degree necessary concomitants of leadership.

Authority is defined as the legitimate right to direct or influence the behavior of others. The legitimacy component of authority implies that which is morally or legally proper. This legitimacy may derive from the laws of the state, from the charter of the organization, and from rule and custom of the society.

---

[3]Ralph M. Stogdill, *Handbook of Leadership: A Survey of Theory and Research.* (New York: The Free Press, 1974), pp. 43–45, 78.

[4]Ibid., pp. 57–58, 80.
[5]Ibid., pp. 56, 75, 80–82.
[6]Ibid., pp. 75, 80–82.

In our economic institutions—factories, offices, stores, banks—authority is customarily viewed as flowing from the top of the organization structure downward through the hierarchy—from the board of directors to the president, to the various echelons of managers, to the front-line supervisors, and finally to the workers. Of course in the broad sense, authority in both public and private organizations emanates from the society as a whole. Our organizations exist and operate at the sufferance of the public.

As children are reared and as they mature, they are conditioned to accept the authority and directives of their parents, of their schoolteachers, and of various authority figures in the community. Indeed the school—beginning with the one-room schoolhouse—has served as both a seat of learning and as an institution in which children are trained to accept the kind of authority and discipline that will be imposed upon them when they participate as adults in an industrialized society.

Now it should be apparent that authority and obedience to it are not absolute. People may reject an order given by the leader, whether a corporate manager or the mayor of a city. In the ordinary course of events employees (and citizens) will follow most orders. However, they may reject—passively or overtly—some orders because they believe them to be unfair, unreasonable, or impossible. The followers may individually or as a group reject the person who issues the orders. Conflict, peaceful or violent, may follow. To preclude rejection and subsequent conflict the leader may consult, beforehand, subordinates or certain trusted advisors to ascertain the attitudes of the followers. The leader may then modify plans to try to gain a meeting of the minds and cooperation. Additionally the leader often has available for use, if need be, various elements of power that can be brought to bear to induce the followers to comply with orders and policies. We shall discuss power shortly.

In membership organizations, such as unions, professional and civic organizations, and in democratic governments, the members elect their leaders for fixed terms of office. Thus, the authority of the leaders flows directly from the members. These elected leaders recognize the source of their legitimacy and authority. But there is a general consensus, often bolstered by constitutions, laws, and bylaws, that the members will accept the authority and leadership of these officials during their terms of office.

Power and Leadership

For leadership to be effective, it often must be supported by some measure of power. This is true for both the formal work organization and the informal social group. A leader tries to influence the behavior of other people, giving them instructions, coordinating activities of specialists, seeking to reconcile conflicting views, and seeking to impel them to greater efforts to achieve higher productivity.

What is power? Power is the ability to achieve dominance of one's objectives and methods. It often involves the capacity to employ force if necessary.

French and Raven have postulated that there are five bases or sources of power. Although an understanding of the nature of power is facilitated by this categorization, it should be pointed out that more than one power element is often at work in any given situation. Their bases of power are (1) reward, (2) coercion, (3) legitimacy, (4) identification with the power figure, and (5) expertise.[7]

The arsenal of rewards the executive in industry can dispense to get his employees to work to achieve designated goals is well known. Positive leadership through rewards tends to develop a considerable amount of loyalty and devotion of subordinates toward their leaders.

[7]John R. P. French, Jr., and Bertram Raven, "The Bases of Social Power," in Dorwin Cartwright, ed., *Studies in Social Power* (Ann Arbor, Mich.: Institute for Social Research, 1959).

Understanding and Managing People

Coercion is the application of actual force to secure one's way. In private industry, physical coercion is almost never used by management. But coercion is also punishment. And the business leader often obtains compliance simply by the threat (often implied) of demotion, transfer, layoff, or discharge. The supervisor who shuns and ignores a subordinate is also punishing him or her. So is the supervisor who berates his or her employees.

Legitimate power is analogous to authority in the organization wherein employees ordinarily accept orders from their supervisors because they accept the authority system when they decide to work for that company. Cultural values also provide a basis for legitimate power. Thus, a father in most societies throughout the world is looked upon as the head of the family. So that order and stability may be maintained, the members of an organization know they must abide by the reasonable directives of their officially designated superiors in the hierarchy. Repeated failure to follow legitimate authority would invite chaos.

Sometimes a follower develops a strong emotional attachment to a leader. There is a feeling of oneness between the two. Thus, the leader is able to influence and modify the behavior of the subordinate because the latter identifies strongly with the leader. This is called referent power or identification with a power figure. This type of power is less common in business and industry than any of the other four classifications.

Persons who possess a vast fund of knowledge and technical skill often have power over others who are less well informed. Thus, when the respected physician suggests that people should get vaccinations against flu, his advice is usually heeded by the majority. When the lawyer formulates a procedure for handling litigation, the company president tends to adopt the advice. Power based on expertise is usually limited to a specialized area of activity—that of the expert's specialty, for example, law, engineering, physics, or medicine. The technical expert usually cannot extend his power to other spheres of activity.

LEADERSHIP STYLE

When psychologists began to accept the fact that no single configuration of leader traits is predictive of successful performance, they turned their attention to investigations of leadership style. By style we mean the behaviors of the leader —what he or she does, what he or she emphasizes, and how he or she deals with subordinates.

An early significant experiment was that conducted by White and Lippitt under the direction of Kurt Lewin in 1938 at the University of Iowa.[8] Four groups of ten-year-old boys were each exposed to three different styles of adult leadership—autocratic, democratic, and laissez-faire. The four adult leaders were given training so that each was proficient in the three different leadership styles. The groups of boys were organized into clubs to carry on various craft activities such as carpentry, mural painting, wood carving, soap carving, and the making of plaster of Paris masks. In setting up these groups, the researchers tried to equate them in terms of scholarship and such interpersonal relationships as sociometric attraction or rejection, leadership, quarrelsomeness, obedience, and social activity.

In describing the experiment, we shall concentrate upon the autocratic and democratic leadership patterns, because the laissez-faire style proved to be quite ineffective, as might be expected. In the autocratic situation all determination of policy was made by the leader; he dictated the activity steps one at a time; he dictated the particular work tasks and work companions

[8]Ralph K. White and Ronald Lippitt, *Autocracy and Democracy: An Experimental Inquiry* (New York: Harper and Row, 1960).

of each member; he was personal in his praise or criticism; and he was aloof from active group participation. On the other hand, in the democratically led groups, policies were developed by group discussion. Activity perspective was gained during these discussions, and the leader gave alternatives when suggesting procedures. The boys were free to choose their own partners. The leader was fact-minded in his praise and criticism and tended to be a group member in spirit.

In the autocratic-leadership pattern the leaders spent a high portion of their time giving orders, making disruptive commands, and giving nonobjective praise and criticism. Conversely, the democratic leaders spent much of their time making guiding suggestions, giving information, and encouraging the boys to make their own decisions democratically.

What were the results of this experiment? As far as achieving work goals, the democratic and autocratic groups were about equally efficient. The autocracy created much hostility, aggression, and scapegoating among the boys. Several boys dropped out during the periods of autocratic leadership. There was more dependence and less individuality in the autocracy. In contrast there was more group-mindedness and more friendliness in the democracy. There was more mutual praise, friendly playfulness, and readiness to share group property in the democracy.

During the late 1940s and early 1950s investigators at Ohio State University, studying leadership in many different kinds of organizations found that the many kinds of behavior exhibited by leaders could be conveniently classified into two categories. One category or dimension which they labeled "consideration" covered leader behavior in which there was a high degree of two-way communication, mutual trust, rapport, and friendship between the leader and the group of followers. The other dimension which they called "initiating structure" included such leader behaviors as assigning tasks, emphasizing production goals, and defining the structure and ways of getting jobs done. Some leaders may be more oriented toward "consideration" whereas others may be more oriented toward "initiating structure." And of course, some may give a balanced emphasis to both dimensions.

Starting in the late 1940s and continuing through the 1950s the Institute for Social Research of the University of Michigan carried out many field investigations in a large variety of industrial, commercial, governmental, and other types of organizations. These researchers classified leader behavior into the two categories of "employee-centered" and "production-centered." These are basically synonymous with the Ohio State terms "consideration" and "initiating structure." Publications from the Michigan researchers in that era stated that supervisors or managers of high-producing departments were found to be employee-centered in their behavior toward subordinates and they practiced general (instead of close) supervision.[9]

Later work at Michigan resulted in the formulation by Bowers and Seashore that effective leadership is composed of the following four categories of leader behaviors: (1) support of subordinates, (2) facilitation of interaction among members of the group, (3) emphasis upon meeting goals, and (4) facilitation of the work (planning, coordinating, and providing resources).[10] In testing their model in 40 agencies of a life insurance company, they found that these four categories of leader behavior were significantly correlated with several measures of employee satisfaction and insurance agency performance. There was a somewhat greater relationship between leadership behavior and employee satisfaction than between leadership behavior and

[9]See, for example, Daniel Katz, Nathan Maccoby, and Nancy C. Morse, *Productivity, Supervision, and Morale in an Office Situation* (Ann Arbor, Mich.: University of Michigan, Institute for Social Research, 1950).

[10]David G. Bowers and Stanley E. Seashore, "Predicting Organizational Effectiveness with a Four-Factor Theory of Leadership, *Administrative Science Quarterly*, Vol. II, No. 2 (1966), pp. 238–263.

agency performance. They also found that the behavior of the employees towards each other was significant in determining the level of employee satisfaction and of performances. Further, the managerial leadership was primarily instrumental in shaping the degree to which the peer group was supportive toward its members and helped with the work. Although leadership style plays a major part in controlling work group satisfaction and performance, Bowers and Seashore pointed out that other elements such as power, work patterns, and personal and motivational factors are also significant in determining effectiveness.

SITUATIONAL FACTORS

Contemporary work into leadership has demonstrated that situational factors are very important in moderating the degree to which particular leadership styles are effective. As more and more research investigations have been made, we have learned that the analysis, explanation, and prediction of leadership are very complex. Current research is generally characterized, as "contingency approaches to leadership." Let us now look at the more important situational factors.

Characteristics of Followers. Studies have shown that subordinates who have strong needs for independence, who have confidence in their own abilities, and who believe that what happens to them occurs because of their own behavior, are more productive and more satisfied under participative leadership. Participative leadership is a style of leadership in which subordinates have a real say in decisions affecting them and their work. On the other hand, those who have dependent personalities, who have a low confidence in their own abilities to perform assigned tasks, and believe themselves to be

controlled by chance factors are more receptive to authoritarian leadership.[11]

Task. Some jobs and departments are highly structured and others are not. Much of the work performed by blue-collar workers in factories is quite structured and engineered. The work routines are carefully planned and laid out by industrial engineers. Vast numbers of workers in industry perform machine-tending and parts-assembly operations where the routines have been carefully spelled out. The army of clerks in the offices of the nation are also mainly engaged in specialized, structured tasks.

On the other hand, many jobs are and can be only loosely defined. The work is variable. Job procedures cannot be specified in advance. Such is the work of managers, engineers, scientists, doctors, salespersons, professors, staff specialists, and many skilled craftspersons and technicians.

The leadership style that is most fruitful for unstructured work tends to be different from that for structured jobs. House and Mitchell report on one research study of 325 employees in a manufacturing concern. Regardless of differences in personality, those who were engaged in nonrepetitive, ego-involving tasks were more satisfied under a participative leadership style than under a nonparticipative style. In repetitive tasks, subordinates who scored low on authoritarianism were more satisfied under a participative style.[12]

Organizational Climate. The overall organizational climate is a powerful determinant of both productivity and employee satisfaction, irrespective of the style of leadership practiced by front-line supervisors. Organizational climate

[11]Victor H. Vroom, "Some Personality Determinants of the Effects of Participation," *Journal of Abnormal and Social Psychology,* Vol. 59 (November 1959), pp. 322–327. Robert J. House and Terence R. Mitchell, "Path-Goal Theory of Leadership," *Journal of Contemporary Business,* Vol. 3, No. 4 (Autumn 1974), pp. 81–97.

[12]House and Mitchell, ibid., p. 94.

is a composite of the system of management practiced by the top executives (for example, autocratic, paternalistic, or participative), the culture of the organization, peer group relationships, communication patterns, and motivational forces.

Power of Leader. The extent to which a leader has available for use the various elements of power (reward, coercion, legitimacy, identification, and expertise) frequently determines the degree to which he or she can obtain compliance from the followers. A manager in a company is endowed with many elements of power that help him or her to get performance from his or her people. He or she can hire, fire, promote, and transfer (or effectively recommend these), and can evaluate the performance of people and grant or withhold pay raises. He or she possesses legitimate authority and the symbols of office (desk, title, high status).

At the other end of the spectrum is the informal leader who possesses fewer elements of power over followers. He must gain cooperation by personal persuasion. He holds his position as long as the members feel that he effectively represents their interests.

Leader–Group Relations. One of the most critical aspects of leadership effectiveness is the relationship between the group members and their leader. Is the leader accepted by his or her followers? Do they like and trust him? Is he able to obtain their compliance without exerting a great deal of time and effort for each transaction? How readily do they respond to leader attempts to initiate action?

The effectiveness of the leader and his group is poor if they get along badly. Friction, hostility, and resentment can make accomplishing results difficult. Where the leader knows that his people resent him, he may still get compliance. However, he may resort to the use of threats to induce performance and under such conditions group performance tends to be minimal.

Relationship Among Key Dimensions

It is apparent from the preceding discussion that the effectiveness of a given leadership style is materially affected by situational factors. Production- (task-) oriented leadership may be effective under some conditions and employee-oriented direction may work better under other conditions. Behavioral scientists have been trying to determine, for about 25 years now, the true relationships among the major situational dimensions. A great deal of empirical and theoretical research addressing this matter has been carried on by Fred Fiedler and his associates.[13]

His investigations have sought to explain how certain situational factors interact with leadership style. These factors are (1) leader–member relations, (2) task structure, and (3) leader's power position. He and his associates have systematically investigated the performance of work groups under various combinations of leader's style (production-oriented or employee-oriented) and the three situational factors. Among the groups studied have been athletic teams, church groups, consumer-sales cooperatives, factories, aviation cadets, open-hearth steel crews, supermarket departments, and hospital nursing.

Fiedler has constructed a contingency model of leadership effectiveness based upon the degree of favorableness of the group-task situation. The favorableness of the situation is the degree to which the situation enables the leader to exert influence over the group. According to Fiedler, the most crucial element in leadership is the leader–member relationship, that is, the extent to which they trust him or her and will respond to him or her. Eight situational combinations have been studied and classified. These range from a situation most favorable to the leader (good leader–member relations, structured task, and strong power position) all the way to the most unfavorable situation (poor

[13]Fred E. Fiedler, *A Theory of Leadership Effectiveness* (New York: McGraw-Hill Book Company, 1967).

leader–member relations, unstructured task, and weak power position).

His theory predicts that production-oriented leadership works best under conditions that are either very favorable to the leader or conditions very unfavorable as defined above. The human relations or employee-oriented leadership style is most effective when the conditions are only moderately favorable or moderately unfavorable to the leader (the intermediate range on his 8 combinations of situational factors).

Although there has been some criticism by other psychologists of Fiedler's research constructs and methodology, his work represents a major step forward in our understanding of the relationship of the various situational factors involved in leadership.

Path-Goal Theory. Another contingency theory that has attracted considerable attention in recent years is the path-goal theory of leadership formulated by Evans, House, Mitchell, and others.[14] It is based upon the expectancy model of motivation. This theory recognizes four kinds of leader style or leader behavior. These are (1) directive leadership, (2) supportive leadership, (3) participative leadership, an (4) achievement-oriented leadership.

The central propositions of the theory are (1) that the leader's behavior is acceptable and satisfying to followers to the degree they see such behavior as either an immediate source of satisfaction or as instrumental to future satisfaction, and (2) that the leader's behavior will generate performance by the followers to the extent that satisfaction of their needs is contingent upon effective work performance by them.

The path-goal theory recognizes two categories of situational variables. The first category which is labeled "personal characteristics of the subordinates" is composed of three subfactors:

(1) authoritarianism of followers, (2) belief in locus-of-control of one's life (controlled by one's self internally or subject to external events), and (3) subordinates' perception of own ability (high or low ability). The other situational variable is the "environment." This, too, is comprised of three subfactors as follows: (1) the nature of the task; (2) formal authority system; and (3) the character of the primary work group. Both sets of contingent factors must be assessed in order to predict the results on satisfaction and productivity of specific leader behaviors.

The theory postulates that directive leadership (authoritarian) has a positive correlation with satisfaction of subordinates who are engaged in ambiguous tasks and has a negative correlation with satisfaction for subordinates involved in clear tasks. Supportive leadership has its most positive effect on subordinate satisfaction for those engaged in stressful, frustrating or dissatisfying tasks. Achievement-oriented leadership is most effective in generating subordinate confidence that their efforts will pay off in effective performance where the tasks are ambiguous and nonrepetitive. The theory also postulates several other relationships.[15]

To date, independent empirical investigations of the path-goal theory have been generally supportive of its concepts, formulation, and predictive capacity. But much more research needs to be done.

SUPERVISION

Supervision is the function of leading, coordinating, and directing the work of others to accomplish designated objectives. A supervisor guides his or her subordinates so that they produce the desired quantity and quality of work within the desired time. He must also see that their needs are satisfied and that the group

---

[14]M. G. Evans, "The Effects of Supervisory Behavior on the Path-Goal Relationship," *Organizational Behavior and Human Performance*, 55 (1970), pp. 277–298; House and Mitchell, op. cit.

[15]House and Mitchell, ibid., pp. 90–91.

achieves its objectives with a minimum of friction and a maximum of harmony. In short, a supervisor seeks to have the group accomplish the required work and likewise seeks to promote need satisfactions and high morale among the employees.

A supervisor performs a leadership role. His or her behavior helps motivate employees to work toward approved goals. Without leadership, whether it be of the formal or the informal type, a mass of people are uncoordinated and can accomplish nothing. Supervision is crucial to all organized endeavor. The behavior of a supervisor is vital for determining the level of productivity and morale of the work group. In one research investigation of the attitudes and motivation of 200 accountants and engineers employed in nine companies, supervision was found to be one of the chief causes for dissatisfaction. The dissatisfaction related to such aspects of supervision as incompetency, poor scheduling of work, lack of teaching ability, unfriendly relations, lack of support, and unwillingness to listen to suggestions.[16]

Nature of Supervisor's Job

A very useful definition of a supervisor is that contained in the Labor-Management Relations Act of 1947 (Taft-Hartley Act). Section 101, Subsection 2 (11) defines a supervisor as "any individual having authority, in the interest of the employer, to hire, transfer, suspend, lay off, recall, promote, discharge, assign, reward or discipline other employees, or responsibility to direct them, or to adjust their grievances, or effectively to recommend such action, if in connection with the foregoing the exercise of such authority is not of a merely routine or clerical nature, but requires the use of independent judgment." In formulating this labor relations law the United States Congress decided that foremen and supervisors should be considered, in effect, as members of management and that they should not be entitled to representation elections and bargaining unit certifications conducted by the National Labor Relations Board, as are nonsupervisory employees. Because foremen are direct representatives of the employer in dealings with the rank-and-file worker, Congress evidently felt that it would be inappropriate for foremen and office supervisors to be union members as well.

Common parlance has tended to restrict the use of the term *supervisor* to those individuals who direct the activities of others and who are also in the lower ranks of the management hierarchy. If we divide the organization structure of a typical company into three levels of management—top, middle, and lower—then the word *supervisor* would apply to those at the lower level. In a very large corporation this lowest level would typically consist of two organization levels. Common job titles are foreman, assistant foreman, general foreman, and superintendent. For office and white-collar work the title *supervisor* is used, never foreman. The generic term is *supervisor,* and this can be properly used to apply to persons in charge of production workers as well as those in charge of office workers.

A front line supervisor must have very good understanding of the technology of his department. We are using the term technology in a broad sense to cover both machines and processes technology as well as the technology of "knowledge workers" or professionals which includes scientific and technical concepts and skills. The supervisor is not expected to be skilled in performing the various jobs under his or her direction but he or she is expected to understand the jobs in order to diagnose and solve work problems. In contrast to front-line supervisors, upper level managers do not need intimate knowledge of the multitudes of technologies of their organization. They need planning, administrative, and conceptual skills.

[16]Frederick Herzberg, Bernard Mausner, and Barbara B. Snyderman, *The Motivation to Work,* 2nd ed. (New York: John Wiley & Sons, Inc., 1959), chs. 8 and 13.

The supervisor also must be skilled in the various leadership and human relations functions. Among these are motivation, face-to-face communication, training, and coaching.

Duties and Responsibilities of a Supervisor

If we were to make an on-the-spot analysis of the activities of a supervisor during a typical work week, what would we find? Although we would find some variation from department to department and from company to company in the degree of emphasis devoted to the various supervisory tasks, we would find rather surprising agreement in the list of functions which a supervisor must perform and for which he or she is responsible. In a very hazardous industry, safety would require a great deal of attention from a foreman, whereas in a nonhazardous one this would be a minor part of the job. However, the maintenance of safe working conditions and adherence to rules of safety is definitely a requirement of the latter's job, just as it is with the foreman in the hazardous factory.

Let us now examine the particular duties and responsibilities of a supervisor. You will note that these items are classified as "duties and responsibilities." There would not be enough hours in the day for a supervisor to perform personally all of these items. Therefore, in many instances he or she is responsible for seeing that these tasks are carried out by one or more subordinates. Thus, he or she may delegate to one employee the task of requisitioning materials and supplies or of instructing a new employee in the details of the job. Certain essential leadership functions, such as appraising, counseling, and disciplining, should not be delegated.

The order of appearance of the following duties and responsibilities does not indicate relative importance. They are all essential. For purposes of classification, certain responsibilities are listed under the heading "Personnel Management and Human Relations." However, it must be emphasized that in carrying out practically all the other responsibilities such as production, quality, and costs, the supervisor must deal with people and exercise human relations skills. It is really not possible, in the day-to-day activities of a supervisor, to make a strict line of demarcation between those duties involved in getting out the production and those involved in personnel management.

Production
Requisition materials and supplies.
Expedite the flow of materials and supplies.
Plan utilization of machines and equipment.
Schedule flow of work through the department.
Assign employees to operations and jobs.
Check progress of employees.
Help employees clear production problems.
Maintain records of production.
Meet production schedules.
Maintenance
Check equipment for correct operation.
Order repairs to equipment.
Maintain clean and orderly working environment.
Methods improvement
Devise new and improved work methods.
Cooperate with staff groups such as industrial engineering in developing and installing better methods and procedures.
Quality
Insure that quality standards are met.
Analyze quality reports and take corrective action on defective work.
Inspect incoming materials.
Act on changes in quality standards.
Cooperate and coordinate with quality assurance, engineering, and inspection personnel.
Costs
Control and reduce costs.
Analyze budget.
Determine causes for variances from standard

costs and budgeted costs and take corrective action.

Personnel management and human relations

Request additional employees as needed.

Make final employee-selection decision.

Orient new employees to their environment, the requirements of the organization, and their rights and privileges.

Train employees.

Provide face-to-face leadership.

Appraise performance.

Coach and correct.

Counsel employees.

Recommend pay increases, promotions, transfers, layoffs, and discharges.

Enforce rules and maintain discipline.

Settle complaints and grievances.

Interpret and communicate management policies and directives to subordinates.

Interpret and communicate employee suggestions and criticisms to higher management.

Motivate subordinates; provide rewards for good performance and behavior.

Eliminate hazards and insure safe working practices.

Develop own skills and abilities through self-development activities and participation in company training programs.

Cooperate and coordinate with personnel department in administering the company personnel program within own department.

PATTERN OF EFFECTIVE SUPERVISION

The front-line supervisor plays a significant part in influencing the performance of his work unit. He or she also exerts a major influence upon the job satisfaction and morale of the employees. The questions of what kinds of supervisory practices generate high work group performance and what practices contribute to high employee satisfaction have been the subject of numerous research investigations over many years. Certain general principles and concepts have emerged from these studies. It ought to be pointed out before discussing these principles that they are generalizations. Particular circumstances in individual situations may call for exceptions and deviation from these general guidelines.

Supportive Behavior

Extensive investigations performed by researchers at the Institute for Social Research of the University of Michigan and others have established the importance of supportive behavior by the effective supervisor.[17] What is supportive behavior? The supervisor who is supportive displays confidence and trust in subordinates. He or she shows concern for each employee as a person. He keeps the employees properly informed of events in the department and the organization. He or she solicits ideas from the employees. He or she gives help in solving work problems and gives credit for good work. The supportive supervisor creates an atmosphere of approval toward people. And finally, the supervisor treats employees fairly and equitably.

Supportive supervisory behavior has quite consistently correlated positively and highly with the satisfaction of subordinates.[18] Supportive supervisory behavior, of and by itself, does not consistently generate high performance from a work group. However, when supportive behavior is combined with supervision that acts to facilitate the work and acts to set challenging

---

[17]See, for example, Rensis Likert, *The Human Organization: Its Management and Value* (New York: McGraw-Hill Book Company, 1967), ch. 4.

[18]Gary Yukl, "Toward a Behavioral Theory of Leadership," *Organizational Behavior and Human Performance*, Vol. 6, No. 4 (July 1971), pp. 414–440.

In his writing the author uses the term "consideration" to designate supportive behavior.

Understanding and Managing People

performance goals, as discussed below, then productivity tends to be high.

In his highly acclaimed multivolume work *Lee's Lieutenants: A Study in Command*, Douglas Southall Freeman made perceptive observations about those officers (colonels and generals) who served under General Robert E. Lee in the Confederate Army during the Civil War. Freeman noted that those commanders who were most effective in prolonged field operations (and not in just one battle) *looked out for their men*. They maintained proper discipline and looked out for the well-being of their soldiers in terms of sanitation, food, clothing, and shelter.[19] Although the specific concerns facing the modern industrial supervisor are somewhat different from those of a military leader, the message is the same. A successful supervisor is concerned about the well-being of his or her people.

Facilitation of Work

The effective supervisor provides adequate tools, equipment, and materials so that the employees can do their jobs properly. He or she also provides proper job information, production plans, and schedules. The supervisor gives help in diagnosing technical problems when requested. He or she insures adequate liaison with other departments so that the work flows smoothly and so that necessary cooperation is obtained from other supervisors.

In providing technical help and job instruction the supervisor must exercise care not to supervise the employees too closely. Inexperienced workers and those unsure of themselves do need close guidance, but for experienced and trained personnel, general, rather than close, supervision is advisable.

[19]Douglas Southall Freeman, *Lee's Lieutenants: A Study in Command*, Vol. 3, (New York: Charles Scribner's Sons, 1944), pp xxi–xxii.

Performance Goals

Performance goals which are challenging but attainable contribute to high work-unit productivity. Employees need to know what is expected of them in terms of units to be produced, due dates, reports to be completed, sales to be made, and the like.

Traditionally goals and standards are established by the boss and by upper management. However, goals may also be set jointly by discussion between the boss and his or her subordinates. Thus, in "management by objectives" performance targets for several months ahead are commonly determined mutually. Also, in some organizations participative management techniques are used to set short term production targets.

Livingston has argued persuasively and has offered evidence to show that those managers who display confidence in their subordinates and who communicate an expectation of high performance, tend to manage work units that consistently outperform units run by managers who show little confidence in their employees' capacity to produce.[20]

Influence in Hierarchy

Several research investigations have demonstrated that the really effective supervisor is able to exercise considerable upward influence in dealings with his or her boss.[21] This upward influence impacts upon both productivity and employee satisfaction. To obtain sufficient resources for his or her department and in order

[20]J. Sterling Livingston, "Pygmalion in Management," *Harvard Business Review*, Vol. 47, No. 4 (July–August 1969), pp. 81–89.

[21]Donald Pelz, "Influence: A Key to Effective Leadership in the First-Line Supervisor," *Personnel*, Vol. 29 (1952), pp. 209–217; K. M. Rowland and W. E. Scott, "Psychological Attributes of Effective Leadership in a Formal Organization," *Personnel Psychology*, Vol. 21 (Autumn 1968), pp. 365–377.

for the higher-level manager to come to really understand the problems of his or her department, the supervisor must have influence with that manager. Sometimes, upper-level managers issue orders without having a full understanding of the likely effect upon each and every department. If a given department may have special problems implementing an order from above, the effective supervisor who has upward influence will work out an accommodation with his or her immediate organizational superior. The ineffective supervisor who has little upward influence may do little to make an accommodation or, if he or she tries, he or she may be unsuccessful.

Closely tied to upward influence is the willingness and ability of the supervisor to go to bat for his or her people. The successful supervisor recommends pay raises, promotions, training opportunities, needed improvements in working conditions and the like for his or her people and he or she is effective in gaining these items for them. Such positive and successful behavior not only strengthens employee morale, but also improves employee motivation and effort.

Group Relationships and Participation

Some supervisors feel that they are directing primarily a collection of very separate individuals. They tend to deal with each of their subordinates as individuals and to downplay the relations of the people with one another. They seek to build strong lines of communication and loyalty between themselves and each individual worker, but discourage bonds among the people in the group. Such supervisors foster competition among the men and women for the rewards that they can dispense. This competition, although it may increase individual performance temporarily, tends to generate mistrust, conflict, and lack of cooperation among the employees.

In direct opposition to this foregoing pattern of supervision, the research evidence shows that the best supervisors build up group pride and loyalty. They involve the group as a whole in the problems of the department. They encourage the men and women to interact and help one another. The effective supervisor also engenders a feeling of group responsibility for the success of the whole section or department. Supervisors should be careful not to play favorites or to discriminate against any persons in the work unit.

Closely related to the development of teamwork is group participation in decision making. Participative management is anathema to the authoritarian boss. However, very considerable research evidence supports the view that, under proper conditions, employee participation in departmental decisions (i.e. those under the control of the departmental supervisor) contributes to high unit performance as well as group satisfaction.[22]

Concentration Upon Management Functions

Some supervisors, especially new ones, believe that they can increase the total volume of output of their sections by pitching in and doing direct production work. This may be appropriate for emergency situations, but for day-in and day-out behavior it is counterproductive. The most successful supervisors are those who devote their attention to their management responsibilities of planning, organizing, leading, and controlling. They see to it that the direct production work gets done, but they themselves do not do it. They devote their time to planning, anticipating and preventing crises, coordinating, motivating, coaching, training, deciding, organizing, measuring performance, and taking corrective action where necessary.

[22]See for example, Likert, op. cit., ch. 4; Alfred J. Marrow, David G. Bowers, and Stanley R. Seashore, *Management by Participation* (New York: Harper and Row, Publishers, 1967); and J. B. Ritchie, "Supervision," ch. 3 in *Organizational Behavior: Research and Issues* (Madison, Wis.: Industrial Relations Research Association, 1974).

Organizational Climate

We said earlier, in our discussion of leadership, that organizational climate is a powerful determinant of both productivity and employee satisfaction. Its influence is so strong that it can outweigh the impact of the quality of frontline leadership. The climate of an organization is created by the overall system of management that is practiced. Let us now turn to a discussion of differing systems of management.

MANAGEMENT SYSTEMS

Although several writers have created classification schemes to depict different kinds of management systems, the one formulation that has been built upon years of careful empirical research is that developed by Rensis Likert. His Systems 1, 2, 3, and 4 are based upon work at the Institute for Social Research (which he headed for many years) of the University of Michigan.

When we speak of a system of management, we mean something broader than leadership style. Leadership style is a characteristic of an individual leader, whereas a management system is a style of management composed of a complex of practices and actions that pervades an entire organization. The system of management practiced by the top officials really establishes the organizational climate. The climate of organization A may be distinctly different from organization B. One who works in A and then in B can sense the differences.

In assessing organizational climate, it is desirable to administer questionnaires to both managers and employees. Sometimes there is a distinct difference between the managerial system that the upper level managers *think* they are using and the one that employees *perceive* them to be using. Organizational climate is a composite of the organizational structure, system of mo-

tivation, leadership style, communication patterns, quality of interpersonal relationships, peer-group relationships, quality of discipline, and general treatment of employees. The system of management determines the character of the organization and determines, ultimately, the outcomes such as profits, output, costs, and employee satisfaction.

Likert's Systems

Let us now look at the four systems of management articulated by Rensis Likert.[23]

System 1. System 1 is an exploitive authoritarian system of management. Management endeavors, mainly by tight discipline and force, to extract production from workers with little or no regard for their well-being. The employees fear the bosses and are subservient. The bosses want it this way in order to keep the subordinates "in line." The bosses are aloof from the workers. Employees are competitive and often hostile toward each other. Practically all decisions are made at the top. Punishment for mistakes is emphasized rather than corrective discipline.

This is basically a harsh organizational climate. Employees are used in a bad way.

System 2. System 2 is really benevolent autocracy or paternalism. The employees are expected to be subservient, compliant, and reasonably productive. They are also expected to be loyal. In return management treats them decently—perhaps even kindly. But decision making is centralized at the top. The social atmosphere is harmonious but employees are not involved in plans and decisions. Not only employees but also lower-level managers are expected to do as they are told, to be loyal and dependent.

[23]Likert, op. cit., ch. 3 and Appendix II; and Rensis Likert and Jane G. Likert, *New Ways of Managing Conflict* (New York: McGraw-Hill Book Company, 1976), ch. 5 and Appendix.

Managers are oriented toward human relations but are not disposed toward such practices as job enrichment or genuine consultation.

System 3. System 3 is consultative management. Management sometimes solicits ideas from employees to help solve problems. But management itself makes all the decisions. Suggestion plans may be used for upward communication. The motivational system provides rewards, occasional punishments, and some ego involvement. There is a moderate amount of cooperative teamwork. Performance goals are usually accepted by the employees but there is occasional resistance. Control is primarily performed by upper management but with some shared responsibility at the middle and lower levels.

System 4. With System 4 or participative management, supervision exhibits supportive behavior toward employees quite consistently. There is extensive friendly interaction among supervisors and employees and a high degree of trust. A great deal of the decision-making is by group participation. There is a full flow of information upward, downward, and horizontally in the organization. All human motives are activated and members of the organization are strongly motivated to achieve the organization's goals. Performance data is given directly to the lower levels so that these people can control and adjust their own performance.

Likert argues that the more effective organizations operate more closely toward the System 4 side of the spectrum. He states that three kinds of factors or variables describe an organization. These are causal, intervening, and end-result variables. *Causal variables*, which are responsible for much of the variation in performance from organization to organization, include managerial leadership and policies, information processes, performance goals, technological adequacy, decision-making processes, and extent of utilization of organizational principles. *Intervening variables*, which are shaped by

the causal variables, include peer group leadership, influence, and coordination; group processes such as planning together and sharing information; and confidence in others. The *end-result variables* or outcomes are such things as profits, output, costs, and efficiency.

Based upon research Likert has found that a System 1 style of management may yield favorable end results in the short run but at the expense of a deterioration in the intervening variables. Over a longer time span, the decline of the intervening variables will cause a falloff of the outcomes. If a System 4 style is then introduced into this establishment, it will take a great many months to turn around the intervening variables. Eventually, System 4 will impact pervasively and organizational performance will improve.

Actual organizations in America, of course, are distributed across the entire spectrum of these four systems. There are some small businesses in which the owner-manager works to maximize gains, to squeeze employees, and to discard them when they are no longer useful. The owner is exploitative and predatory. Probably, the majority of organizations in both the private and public sectors operate around System 2 with a moderate percentage possessing some of the characteristics of System 3. True System 4 organizations are quite rare.

JAPANESE SYSTEM OF MANAGEMENT

Commencing in the late 1960s and early 1970s Americans began to notice more and more Japanese-made products in stores and showrooms—televisions, radios, watches, cameras, motorcycles, photocopy machines, and automobiles. American manufacturing executives also noticed the stiff competition they began to face. Consumers liked the very high quality and reasonable prices of Japanese-made goods. As more and more Japanese products flowed into the United States and as the Japanese began to open manufacturing plants in this country, managers, journalists, scholars, and government officials became concerned about the Japanese challenge to American industry. At the producer-goods level, American firms found it increasingly difficult to compete with the Japanese in such products as steel and machine tools.

Productivity in the Japanese economy as a whole rose an average of 8 per cent per year, in the decade of the 1970s, whereas productivity in the United States increased less than 2 per cent per year during the same period.

What are the reasons for the phenomenal success of Japanese industry? Although there are additional factors involved, a principal explanation lies in the nature of Japanese management, Japanese organization, and the culture of the people. Let us now examine the principal dimensions of the Japanese system.[24]

Long-Term Employment. Japanese workers enjoy long-term job security. This is especially true in large companies. Layoffs are rare or nonexistent. Instead of hiring extra people to meet peak production demands, these firms subcontract some of their work and they hire temporary employees. When companies face economic hardships, they may reduce salaries or cut hours of work. The no-layoff policy builds employee trust and loyalty. Workers readily accept labor-saving technologies because they do not have to fear for their jobs.

[24]Some references on Japanese management are Kae H. Chung and Margaret Ann Gray, "Can We Adopt the Japanese Methods of Human Resources Management?" *Personnel Administrator*, Vol. 27, No. 5 (May 1982), pp. 41–46, 80; Nina Hatvany and Vladimir Pucik, "An Integrated Management System: Lessons from the Japanese Experience," *Academy of Management Review*, Vol. 6, No. 3 (1981), pp. 469–480; William Ouchi, *Theory Z: How American Business Can Meet the Japanese Challenge* (Reading, Mass.: Addison-Wesley Publishing Company, 1981).

Promotions and Pay Increases. Seniority is a major factor governing pay increases and promotions. All those persons hired at the same time will receive the same salary increases, especially during their first ten years of employment with a given company. Performance appraisals attach considerable weight to loyalty, enthusiasm, and cooperation. There is no incentive for individuals to try to get ahead of one another or to gain at someone else's expense. It is only after many years with a company that real differentiation in rank will occur among those hired at the same time.

Nonspecialized Careers. For much of their careers Japanese employees move from job to job within their companies. The goal is to develop employees having a variety of skills and to develop an appreciation of the problems of the many functional departments of the business.

Continuing Education. Closely allied to the job rotation concept is the heavy emphasis placed upon participation in the in-service training courses within the company and in evening courses. Workers are expected to upgrade their knowledge and job skills.

Consensual Decision Making. Participative management is ingrained in Japanese organizations. This is true at all levels of the organization structure. In managerial ranks important decisions evolve after many meetings with all interested parties over a considerable period of time. A primary advantage of this widespread participation is that the many people involved in making decisions become committed to their implementation.

Quality circles are the mode of participative decision making at the level of shop-floor workers and factory foremen. These groups, composed of volunteers and consisting of nine employees on average, work on a large variety of problems including product quality, safety procedures, cost reduction, and employee morale matters.

Group Consciousness. The culture of the Japanese company emphasizes teamwork, co-operation, loyalty, and a sense of family. The group, the department, and the company are more important than the individual.

Implicit, Informal Controls. Standards of performance, targets, and objectives are derived from a common sharing of company philosophies and values. Control mechanisms are subtle and implicit and are developed through indoctrination. Group norms exert implicit control over individual employee behavior.

Wholistic Concern for People. The Japanese employer tends to be interested in the entire behavior and welfare of the employees both on and off the job. In this sense the organization has similarities to a religious order or a military unit. Whereas home and community life are often distinctly separated from occupational life in the United States, in Japan these various aspects are closely integrated. Additionally the company provides extensive educational, recreational, housing, health, and insurance benefits for all employees.

Paternalistic Employers. The Japanese employer—that is, the upper-level management as a group—is paternalistic in policies and actions toward employees. There is heavy emphasis upon indoctrinating employees with the company spirit and getting employees to conform to company and group values. In return for acceptance of the company way of doing things, the company takes care of a great many of the employees' needs as described above under "Wholistic Concern for People."

Top Management Facilitators. Although Japanese executives do possess considerable power, they use it carefully and indirectly. They do not give many direct orders. When dealing with subordinates they tactfully ask questions, make suggestions, and provide encouragement. Decisions on actions to take evolve on the basis of information collected and discussions held over a period of time.

Contrasts with American Management

In the United States there is greater emphasis upon individualism and interpersonal competition within the organization. Individual managers are held personally responsible for the performance of their units. Individual employees are held responsible for their own performance. Employees, especially in nonunion establishments, are evaluated on job performance and granted pay raises and promotions in accordance with individual merit (not seniority).

Although there has been much discussion and experimentation with forms of participative management in the United States, in reality most American business firms are run autocratically.

The attachment of employees to individual companies tends to be for only a few years in America. In times of economic difficulty American executives are very prone to lay off employees in order to cut costs. Additionally, American workers and managers alike are likely to seek better jobs elsewhere if they are somewhat dissatisfied with conditions at their current place of employment. Loyalty to one's company tends to be lower in America than in Japan.

Except for management trainees who are being groomed to move into middle and upper level management positions, employees in American firms generally are confined to one narrow job specialty. They are not rotated into a variety of jobs to provide them with multiple skills and a broad perspective of the business.

Applicability to America

To what extent could Japanese management practices be applied in the United States? Individualism and interpersonal competition are deeply rooted in American culture. It is unlikely that this will change and indeed some authorities see this condition as an asset rather than a deficiency in the American ethos.

Participative management has its roots in America and much work has been done. The research, experimentation, and writings of Douglas McGregor, Rensis Likert, and Alfred Marrow are typical of this stream of thought. One form of participative management—quality circles—is spreading rapidly throughout American industry. Quality circles were first introduced into the United States in 1974 by the Lockheed Missiles and Space Company. Among other companies using quality circles successfully are General Electric, IBM, General Motors, and Hewlett-Packard.

Long-term employment and job security could be applied more widely in this country. Indeed, three of our most successful firms—IBM, Hewlett-Packard, and Eli Lilly—have a no-layoff policy. However, it probably would take a revolution in management thinking for most executives to change their practices and engage in the fundamental long-range planning necessary to make employment security a reality.

CONCLUDING OBSERVATIONS

Both students and practitioners of management know that the quality of leadership powerfully shapes organizational effectiveness. Variations in organizational performance and employee satisfaction from one organization to another are primarily caused by the quality of the management, especially top management.

The critical importance of leadership is illustrated by an experience which General Omar N. Bradley relates in his book, *A Soldier's Story.* His book describes the campaigns of the Allied military forces in Europe during World War II to defeat the German forces and liberate the European people. The 90th Infantry Division had performed badly during the early weeks of the invasion of France. When his staff recommended the breakup of this division and the dispersal of the men to other divisions as replacements, Bradley resisted. He asserted that man for man, one division is just as good as another. Divisions varied only in the skill and leadership of their commanders. Bradley replaced the commanding general of the division and gave the new general authority to remove ineffective officers. The new commander replaced only 16 out of a total of 781 officers. Within three months, this division had been transformed into one of the finest divisions on the Allied front.[25]

Leader effectiveness is conditioned by the unique interaction of leader, followers, and the situation. Important situational variables which influence the effectiveness of a given leadership style are characteristics of the followers and of the task, organizational climate, power available to leader, and leader-follower relationships. Significant research by Fiedler, Evans, House and others has helped to uncover and clarify the specific relationships among leaders' style and the situational variables.

We have explored the role and responsibilities of the frontline supervisor and the pressures upon this individual. Then important generalizations about the pattern of effective supervision were discussed. We noted that effective supervisors are supportive towards their subordinates, facilitate the work, set challenging performance goals, exhibit upward influence in the hierarchy, develop strong peer group relations and participation, and concentrate upon management functions.

We examined Rensis Likert's typology of management systems and noted the critical influence of the overall management system upon organizational performance. Finally, we explored the Japanese system of management, the reasons for its success, and possible applications in the U.S.A.

[25]Omar N. Bradley, *A Soldier's Story* (New York: Henry Holt and Company, 1951), pp. 297–298.

1. "A successful leader is an unusually talented individual who is endowed through birth and otherwise with those traits that induce others to follow him. He is born to command." Discuss and evaluate this statement.

2. Give and briefly explain important situational factors which influence leadership effectiveness.

3. Think of situations in which you have observed leaders who fail and situations in which leaders succeed. What factors seem to account for failure and success?

4. Give and explain the principal kinds of supervisory behaviors that tend to generate favorable employee satisfaction and good work-unit performance.

5. Why is a first-line supervisor unique in his position as a member of management? What are the pressures and forces impinging upon the foreman in a typical industrial plant?

6. Explain how the system of management utilized by upper management can substantially influence the ability of supervisors to be effective in achieving good unit performance and employee satisfaction.

7. Contrast Likert's System 1 with System 4 management. Explain causal, intervening, and end-result variables.

8. Describe the Japanese system of management. To what extent could American business apply Japanese practices successfully in the United States?

CASE PROBLEMS

PROBLEM 1[26]

Mr. Johnston, a new man from another department of the company, was appointed supervisor of the instrumentation repair and calibration section. This section was part of a large development-engineering and manufacturing laboratory.

The people in the section consisted of three engineers and nine highly skilled technicians. Their job was to repair and calibrate all electronic laboratory equipment and special manufacturing test equipment, most of which was originally designed by the development engineering group.

Mr. Johnston was introduced to the group by Mr. Foster, his predecessor, during the last two days of the latter's stay on the job. Mr. Foster emphasized the difficult nature of repairing the highly complex electronic equipment. He also noted that in his opinion the human relations aspects of the supervisory job were the most important ones. He felt that letting people work independently and at their own pace would result in their learning from their own mistakes.

During his first few weeks on the job Mr. Johnston made no changes in established procedures but concentrated on getting acquainted with the people, watching them work, and sometimes working with a technician or engineer to find the cause of a difficult instrument repair problem.

[26]The author expresses his appreciation to Carl H. Rosner for the essential features of this case.

He soon realized that the total amount of work performed was rather low. There constantly remained a huge backlog of repair and calibration work to be done. Yet relations with other departments requesting the work were fairly good. In fact, people from these departments did not hesitate to bring in personal television or radio repair work.

Mr. Johnston found that through his working together with someone in his group, the trouble in a piece of equipment was usually located more quickly. He concluded that the men were not working very efficiently or exerting their highest efforts.

Rather than telling them this opinion, he decided to require individual rather than group reports on a weekly basis. These reports were to include the number of instruments repaired, causes of trouble, and the time spent on each piece of equipment, as well as a detailed explanation of the calibration activities of the individual.

Mr. Johnston was pleased to notice an immediate increase in the total number of instruments repaired with a resulting reduction in the backlog of work.

However, there seemed to develop a more strained and formal atmosphere between the supervisor and the group.

Two months later, two competent technicians who had been in the section five and eight years respectively, requested a transfer to another department in the company. They cited the pressure of work as a reason for the request.

Mr. Johnston realized that the request might be due to his increased demands on his people.

Questions

1. Diagnose the situation in this case.
2. What steps should Mr. Johnston take to retain the new, higher level of performance and also restore the friendly atmosphere and high morale previously present in the section?

PROBLEM 2: THE LABORATORY TECHNICIAN[27]

The story that follows was related by a young woman, a college graduate in biochemistry, who had been employed as a laboratory technician, first at Dansville Chemicals, Inc. and second at the Wheeler Chemical Company.

Part I. Dansville Chemicals, Inc.

My first job after graduation from college was that of a laboratory technician at Dansville Chemicals, Inc., a manufacturer of industrial chemicals and certain consumer products. My job involved the analysis of various random samples of

[27]The author expresses his appreciation to Joanne Chin for providing the essential features of this case.

products in the quality control laboratory. The technicians worked in individual cubicles which were located in a large room. The quality control laboratory was under the direction of a manager. Under him were two supervisors who directed the work of the technicians.

The manager prided himself on running a "tight ship." He pressured the supervisors to control the work pace and they constantly pressured the technicians to work at a faster pace. He did not like to see the technicians chew gum on the job, engage in social conversation, or ever look idle (even though the technician might be waiting for a chemical reaction to be completed). He rarely talked informally with the technicians and in fact did not know or bother to learn their names. Likewise, the immediate supervisors seldom initiated any conversations on a personal basis. Interaction among the technicians was made difficult because of the physical arrangement of the cubicles. The partitions made it impossible for the technicians to see one another.

Despite the fact that the analytical work was somewhat varied, I felt that it was boring and tedious.

Employees were allowed to take a combined rest and coffee break twice per day, at 10 A.M. and 2:30 P.M. The starting and ending times were announced by the ringing of a bell. Free coffee was provided by the company. Often, the testing activities of the technicians would not permit stopping precisely at 10 A.M. and 2:30 P.M. However, they lost their break time if they did not stop at these times. Management did not allow breaks at other times. During the breaks, the technicians congregated in one area and the supervisors clustered in another. There was practically no socializing between the technicians and the supervisors.

Employees and supervisors ate lunch in the company cafeteria. The social and physical separation of the different employee groups was very noticeable here. The hourly paid production workers ate apart from the clerical and secretarial personnel. The quality control technicians sat apart from the research technicians. And separated from all of these people were the managerial and professional personnel. Lunchtime for the technicians was over at 12:45 P.M. and their supervisors always insisted that they be back at their work stations promptly.

There was practically no chance for the technicians to be promoted to better-paying and higher-ranking jobs. During the two years I was employed at Dansville, I never knew a technician to be promoted. Although most of us possessed four-year college degrees (a few had two-year associate degrees), we were treated as decidedly inferior by the supervisors and by management generally. There was no program for employees to obtain training to qualify for higher rated jobs. The jobs were rigidly defined and there was no opportunity for us to take on more responsibilities in the laboratory.

Absenteeism tended to be fairly high. Supervisors expressed open annoyance about time missed from work. When some of the employees were absent, the supervisors demanded that those who were there proceed at a faster pace to make up the work lost due to absenteeism. We technicians resented both the aloofness and the constant pressure of the supervisors.

I found that I was often very tired after a day's work. Because I came to dislike conditions on my job, I welcomed any excuse to take time off. After two years I quit my job.

Questions

1. Why do you think management treated the laboratory employees the way it did? What assumptions about human behavior and the conditions of human performance did management appear to hold?
2. Is there anything that employees, individually or as a group, could do to change the way in which management treated them in this company?
3. We are given very little information about job performance and productivity in this case. Do you think it was high, average, or low? Explain.

Part II. Wheeler Chemical Company

After quitting my job at Dansville Chemicals, Inc. I obtained a job at the Wheeler Chemical Company. This job was in the research laboratory but its content was similar to what I had done at Dansville.

Soon after starting work I noticed a very friendly and communicative relationship among the employees. Everyone was on a first-name basis including the supervisor, the department head, and the director of the laboratory. Many times the department head as well as the director stopped to chat with us. Each technician had his or her own desk. Technicians did not have assigned laboratory stations. Rather, they worked at various stations as required by their particular projects. The supervisors, who had glass-enclosed offices out in the laboratory, were easily accessible to their people. The department head's office was centrally located. He maintained an open door policy such that we were welcome to discuss our problems with him without a formal appointment.

The company did not have a cafeteria. Some employees brought their lunches and ate at their desks. Others ate together at nearby restaurants. During lunchtime, certain games such as bridge were played. When the weather was good some employees played volleyball on the lawn outside. Supervisors and employees often mingled in these activities. The company sponsored an annual Christmas party and a summer picnic. These events were well attended by all levels of personnel.

The supervisors often called group meetings to inform the people of progress toward work-unit goals, to find out if there were problems, and to solicit suggestions for solving these problems. We were encouraged, on the job, to develop a team effort to accomplish the work and to figure out the most efficient way of doing it. Because we shared a social closeness, we did not hesitate to voice both suggestions and criticisms.

The research department scheduled many informal seminars during working hours as well as formal seminars in the evening to keep the employees abreast of new developments in their technical fields. Although technicians were encouraged to attend, attendance was not compulsory.

My supervisor encouraged me to take additional college courses in the evening. In accordance with policy, my tuition costs were reimbursed by the company.

There were no time clocks. Work hours were flexible. Sometimes, people came to the laboratory in the evening to work on important projects.

Even though the work tasks were sometimes routine, my job did not seem tedious or boring. I found the teamwork and social activities stimulating. While I had felt very tired at the end of the work day at Dansville, here at Wheeler Chemical Co., I felt physically and mentally better at the end of the day.

Questions

1. Contrast the managerial styles and organizational climates at Dansville Chemicals, Inc. and Wheeler Chemical Company. What assumptions about people and performance seem to guide the thinking of management at Wheeler Chemical Company.

2. Do you think the management system at Wheeler Chemical could be applied successfully at Dansville? How could this system be introduced at Dansville? What could induce management at Dansville to change its style of management?

Suggestions for Further Reading

Argyris, Chris. *Increasing Leadership Effectiveness.* New York: John Wiley & Sons, 1976.

Bass, Bernard M. *Stogdill's Handbook of Leadership: A Survey of Theory and Research,* rev. ed. New York: The Free Press, 1981.

Bittel, Lester R., and Jackson E. Ramsey, "The Limited, Traditional World of Supervisors," *Harvard Business Review,* Vol. 60, No. 4 (July–August 1982), pp. 26–31, 36.

Imundo, Louis V. *The Effective Supervisor's Handbook.* New York: American Management Association, 1981.

Maccoby, Michael. *The Leader: A New Face for American Management.* New York: Simon and Schuster, 1981.

Ouchi, William. *Theory Z: How American Business Can Meet the Japanese Challenge.* Reading, Mass.: Addison-Wesley Publishing Company, 1981.

Sartain, Aaron Q., and Alton W. Baker. *The Supervisor and the Job,* 3rd ed. New York: McGraw-Hill Book Company, 1978.

Sayles, Leonard R. *Leadership: What Effective Managers Really Do . . . and How They Do it.* New York: McGraw-Hill Book Company, 1979.

Strauss, George. "Managerial Practices," Ch. 6 in J. Richard Hackman and J. Lloyd Suttle (eds.), *Improving Life at Work.* Santa Monica, Cal.: Goodyear Publishing Company, 1977.

Yukl, Gary A. *Leadership in Organizations.* Englewood Cliffs, N.J.: Prentice-Hall, 1981.

17 Participative Management

The maintenance superintendent in a steel mill calls a foreman into his office to obtain his suggestions on the most efficient and safest way to dismantle an obsolete overhead crane. A service-engineering manager in the home office of a computer manufacturer calls a meeting of the engineering staff to discuss ways and means of improving service for installations of equipment on customers' premises. Ideas are freely submitted by the engineers. A standing committee composed of both union and management representatives in a machine tool manufacturing company reviews cost reduction and methods improvement suggestions submitted by rank-and-file employees. These three examples illustrate some of the kinds of participation activities that occur in industrial enterprises.

Participation is the term used to designate the process by which people contribute ideas toward the solution of problems affecting the organization and their jobs. The people exercise some degree of influence in the decision-making process. Participation is ego- and task-involvement of an individual or group. It includes not only the physical contribution of the person but also intellectual and emotional involvement in the affairs of the organization.

When managers establish means, on either an informal or a formal basis, for obtaining help from subordinates in the making of plans and decisions, they are tapping the knowledge and creativity of others. Because managers can't possibly know all the answers to all the problems and issues connected with the work of their departments, they can often obtain valuable advice and assistance from their subordinates. The process of participation brings into play the higher drives and motives of man: the drives for self-expression, accomplishment, autonomy, and self-assertion. It lets the employees know that their contributions are sought and appreciated. Great benefits to the company and its members can derive from such leadership; however, participation is not a cure-all or necessarily the most appropriate style of management for all circumstances.

Some writers have proposed that participatory management has positive values over and above its effects upon productivity and morale. In a society such as that in the United States, where the concepts of political democracy and the rights and duties of individuals to take an active part in the affairs of their country are cherished, it is held that the environment at one's place of employment should be fully compatible with these democratic ideals. To put the matter more directly, democracy should be practiced in the factory and office as well as in the outside civic and social life of American citizens. In point of fact, most business and industrial organizations tend to be authoritarian in the internal relations between superiors and subordinates. The system is rather autocratic. Yet this is a basic contradiction, because the executive who practices autocratic leadership at the office preaches the need for maintaining individual freedom in American society as a whole. To that executive it is self-evident that citizens should have a say-so in the shaping of laws and policies that affect them. But often this executive does not know how to apply this democratic value system to a company. Therefore, many spokesmen maintain that participation programs in work organizations derive positive support from the cultural heritage prevailing in the United States of America.

ROLE OF PARTICIPATION IN THE ORGANIZATION

Participation is appropriate for all levels in the organizational hierarchy. In practice in industry it takes place only rarely at the level of the blue-collar and white-collar nonsupervisory employee. Many executives have the notion that these people would have nothing worthwhile to contribute. Participation activities via committees and meetings occur more often at middle and upper levels of management and with professional and technical groups of employees.

A program of management in which employees are invited to contribute ideas and suggestions concerning the running of the business must be distinguished from a system of democratic government. In a democracy the citizens—the people—set up their own governing body and make their own laws through elected representatives. The people have the power at stated times to elect, re-elect, or reject their representatives and executive leaders. However, in a work organization the employees do not select their leaders. Supervisors and managers are appointed from the top of the organization. Only

in a very broad sense do these managers rule with the consent of the governed. If a manager is totally ineffective as a leader, he may be removed by superiors in the organization because they observe that this manager cannot win the support and cooperation of subordinates. But the subordinates do not directly exert control over their supervisors and managers.

Now when a manager consults subordinates and shares some decision-making authority with them, he or she does this voluntarily. The manager still retains the final authority and most of the power to make and implement these decisions; sharing of decision making can be rescinded at any time.

Most of the participation methods and programs that exist in private enterprises in the United States are discretionary on management's part. Management can create the program and it can also abandon it. Exceptions to this primacy of management control are collective bargaining, in which management and union jointly bargain wages and conditions of employment, and union–management cooperation which is established under a collective bargaining framework.

Workers' participation in Europe, often called industrial democracy, has developed over the years from philosophical roots different from participative management in America. European-style participation is based upon Socialist political ideologies and is commonly woven into the laws of the various European countries.

RESEARCH INTO PARTICIPATION

Most of the research investigations into participative management have focused upon those situations in which a leader develops a collaborative relationship with his or her subordinates, consults them from time to time on matters of concern to the work group, shows genuine interest in the people and their suggestions, and allows them discretion in carrying out their duties. Most studies also have dealt with situations in which the group members directly participated in the decision-making process rather than through representatives.

The pioneering research experiment into the effects of democratic methods of leadership was conducted by Lewin, White, and Lippitt at the University of Iowa in 1938. In this study, the effects of autocratic, democratic, and laissez-faire leadership climates upon groups of boys were contrasted. This research was discussed in Chapter 16, "Leadership, Supervision, and Management Systems."

Cummings and Molloy have reviewed the findings of seven different rigorously designed experiments into participative management. These involved a variety of work activities such as laundry, garment making, footwear assembly, clerical work, and maintenance. Generally in these experiments (but with some exceptions), both productivity and employee satisfaction increased under participatory leadership. The authors noted that management's willingness to allow employees to participate in important work decisions lets them know that they are considered competent and valued partners in the organization. This satisfies their needs for recognition, independence, and appreciation by others. Also when employees plan and put into effect their own decisions, satisfaction of the needs and values tied to those decisions is dependent upon effective execution of those decisions.[1]

In reviewing six research experiments that examined the relationship between participation in decision making and member satisfaction, Yukl found that in all studies there was a positive correlation between participation and subordinate satisfaction. In examining seventeen projects that had investigated the relationship between participation and group productivity, he found that eleven had shown a positive correlation between participation and productivity, three found no correlation, two found a negative correlation, and one had mixed relationships for two groups.[2]

The Harwood Manufacturing Company, which makes clothing, has long been famous for its continuing commitment to participative management as a basic strategy for operation of its plants. Starting in the late 1930s the owner-president, Alfred J. Marrow, brought in consulting psychologists to develop ways of improving productivity, reducing labor turnover, and overcoming resistance to changed work methods through use of group problem-solving meetings with the employees. The early activities were controlled experiments. But these were so successful in solving the given problems that top management adopted participative management as a day-to-day way of life.[3]

Evaluation

The weight of evidence supports the conclusion that group participation in decision making often increases group performance and member satisfaction or morale.

Participation also facilitates acceptance of change. People tend to resent change that is forced upon them. How are they to know whether their interests have been adequately considered? In a conference discussion where the people work out the nature and mechanics of a proposed new system, they can analyze all the possible objections and ramifications and decide for themselves whether it is feasible.

Employee development is also enhanced by

[1]Thomas G. Cummings and Edmond S. Molloy, *Improving Productivity and the Quality of Work Life* (New York: Praeger Publishers, 1977), Part III.

[2]Gary Yukl, "Toward a Behavioral Theory of Leadership," *Organizational Behavior and Human Performance*, Vol. 6, No. 4 (July 1971), pp. 414–440.

[3]Alfred J. Marrow, *The Failure of Success* (New York: American Management Association, 1976) and Alfred J. Marrow, David G. Bowers, and Stanley E. Seashore, *Management by Participation* (New York: Harper & Row, 1967).

participative management. Employees, professional personnel, and lower-level administrators get an opportunity to learn about and solve a variety of problems that they would never encounter under conventional authoritarian management, until *after* they might be promoted to higher positions.

However, participation is definitely not a panacea. Participation works best where there is a firm commitment to it on the part of top management and where employees and supervisors have been taught how to participate. Also, it should be noted that there are some situations in which unilateral decisions by the boss are quite appropriate. The manager can not call a meeting every time a decision must be made. In the next section we shall talk about conditions required for effective participation.

CONDITIONS FOR EFFECTIVE PARTICIPATION

Participation is not a magic solution to all the problems encountered in managing a business. Procedures for utilizing participation have their time and their place. Let us examine the principal factors that determine when and where participation can be effectively employed.

Research has demonstrated that subordinates who have strong needs for independence react more favorably toward the opportunity to participate in decision making than do those who have low independence needs and who score high on the authoritarianism-measuring scale. *Need for independence* means that the employees have strong drives to express themselves in their work, to exercise their own judgment, to assert themselves, and to figure things out for themselves.[4]

[4]Victor H. Vroom, "Some Personality Determinants of the Effects of Participation," *Journal of Abnormal and Social Psychology*, Vol. 59 (November 1959), pp. 322–327.

Subordinates must possess a certain minimum amount of intelligence and knowledge for any participation program to succeed. They must have something worthwhile to contribute.

The organizational climate must be supportive of participation. This means that top management must believe in it, encourage it, and practice it in day-to-day relations with subordinate executives. It would be very difficult for low-ranking managers to conduct their departments in a participatory mode if their superiors operated in an authoritarian style.

An indecisive supervisor who cannot make decisions on routine administrative matters should not waste the time of his subordinates by calling meetings to get advice on run-of-the-mill problems. Participation should be utilized for those situations and problems that are important and that have a material impact upon the people involved and the organization.

Managers, supervisors, and employees need to receive training in participatory methods of management. Managers and supervisors must learn how to conduct problem-solving meetings, how to encourage employees to offer suggestions, and how to develop consensus in meetings. They need to learn the basics of group dynamics. Subordinates must be taught just what is expected of them in problem-solving discussions. They must learn to respect the opinions of others and to have the self-confidence to express their own views.

Managers should generally invite participation from their subordinates only on issues that are within their scope of authority and responsibility. It would generate frustration for a low-ranking supervisor in a shop department to gather his or her people to arrive at decisions regarding company wage or vacation policy because this is clearly beyond his or her power to control.

Emergency situations may preclude consultation with subordinates. A decision on a rush shipment of goods or a pressing action to meet a short deadline may clearly call for authoritarian behavior.

TYPES OF PARTICIPATION

As an aid to understanding the various kinds of participation programs and activities that can be utilized, it is helpful to classify them into two broad categories: (1) informal and semiformal methods and (2) formal programs.

1. *Informal and semiformal methods*
   a. Individual.
   b. Manager with group of subordinates.
2. *Formal programs*
   a. Committees.
   b. Quality circles
   c. Junior boards of executives.
   d. Collective bargaining.
   e. Union-management cooperation
   f. Suggestion plans.
   g. Workers' participation—European style.

Informal and Semiformal Methods

The informal and semiformal methods essentially involve relations between a supervisor (or manager) and his or her subordinates. These participation activities tend to take place at irregular intervals. When a specific issue arises, the manager may discuss the matter with one or more direct subordinates. In some departments the manager may schedule regular weekly or biweekly meetings with his or her staff. These meetings may be partially for the purpose of passing on information to the people and partially to involve them in group discussion and decision making.

Individual Participation. Individual participation can occur in a variety of ways. A manager may invite one of his subordinates to his office to obtain his thoughts regarding a contemplated job assignment. The manager may walk through a production department and stop to chat with one of the employees about different ways of performing the work. An employee may seek out his supervisor to exchange views on a new project. In some relationships a subordinate may initiate actions and issues for his supervisor and they may jointly discuss operating problems almost as equals.

Individual participation occurs in an atmosphere of mutual respect and trust. Both the manager and the subordinates feel that they and the work unit have something to gain by a frank exchange of viewpoints regarding operating problems.

The manager who delegates a considerable amount of responsibility to subordinates and who practices general and supportive supervision is, in effect, establishing a climate in which employees feel free to make important decisions regarding their work. This is a form of individual participation.

Individual participation can be very effective, but it has its limitations when compared with group participation. In group discussion the process of free association can take place. A thought contributed by one person sparks an idea in another, and so on in a chain-reaction fashion. Because there are more minds involved in a group discussion, because the people may have specialized knowledge to contribute, and because the people may represent varied backgrounds and interests, the likelihood of developing a group solution that takes into account various special concerns is much higher than with individual one-on-one discussion.

Manager with Group of Subordinates. Group participation can occur at any level in an organization. A foreman may convene a meeting of hourly paid production workers to discuss safety problems. A personnel director may call his or her staff together to lay plans to implement a newly developed affirmative action program. The president of a corporation may call a meeting of all the executives reporting to him or her to work out strategy to deal with an impending strike of the unionized workforce.

In group meetings the manager may allow different degrees of influence by the subordinates. In one case he or she may have already arrived at a tentative decision. He or she presents it to the assembled group for analysis and discussion and indicates that his or her decision is subject to change based upon ideas developed in the meeting. A somewhat greater degree of subordinate influence occurs when the manager has not made a decision beforehand. He presents a problem to the group, invites suggestions and analysis, and then makes a final decision. In both of these forms the group may be able to propose a greater number of alternatives and trace through more consequences than could the manager working alone. Both of the foregoing degrees of participation are commonly called *consultative management*. The manager reserves final decision-making authority. In practical operation of consultative management, the leader will tend to adopt, in a great majority of cases, the decision that has evolved in the group deliberations. Because he or she is consulting his or her subordinates, he or she must value their collective wisdom. But on rare occasions he or she may consider it necessary to render a final decision that is in opposition to the consensus of the group.

Some managers, on some occasions, may choose to allow their subordinates to execise even greater influence in the decision-making process. They may outline the dimensions of a problem (or group of problems), explain the general limits of authority they and the group possess such as funds available or time constraints, and then ask the group to develop a course of action to solve the problem. With this form of subordinate involvement, the manager serves as a conference leader and perhaps also as a resource person to provide information not already possessed by the group. But he lets it be known that he is seeking a solution developed by the group as a whole. He also indicates that he will support the solution worked out by the group. The manager plays a role in the discussions but does not dominate them. Some writers call this more advanced form of subordinate influence *democratic management*.

This form of participatory management does not stop at the exit door of the conference room. The leader, on a day-to-day basis, is receptive to suggestions from his people. He encourages them to take the initiative to plan and control their own work. He also developes a collaborative team relationship within the department. Employees trade ideas and help one another.

Formal Programs

Formal participation programs require the creation of organization structures and formal procedures to carry them out. There tends to be a degree of continuity and permanence to these programs. Certain participants acquire formal positions and titles over and above their regular jobs as employees or managers.

Committees. Committees are ubiquitous. They exist in all kinds of organizations and serve many different purposes. A committee is a group of persons, either elected or appointed, created to perform some function or mission. A group of people called together for one meeting does not constitute a committee. A committee has an existence of its own, a chairperson, designated members, a defined purpose, and often an agreed-upon set of operating procedures. It may be a temporary or ad hoc committee formed to accomplish a specific mission and when its goal has been accomplished, it goes out of existence. Or a committee may be permanent. An example of a temporary committee is one formed to investigate sites for the building of a new facility. When the property is finally selected and purchased, the committee goes out of existence. An example of a permanent committee is a corporate board of directors.

Although the committee system is subject to faults and although the potential weaknesses of committees have been highly publicized, they can serve a very useful purpose. Many authorities feel that complex organizations cannot be managed successfully without the use of some committees which can be used to tap the expertise of people from varied backgrounds in such activities as planning, policy making, and solving of difficult problems. Good staff units can do a lot of investigative, analytical, and evaluative work, but they cannot fully substitute for the interactive deliberation and testing of ideas among people that goes on in committees.

In addition to the problem-solving contributions that committee members may make to the organization, their involvement in committee work can also provide valuable training and self-development. The members acquire specific knowledge about organizational matters, they gain perspective and understanding, and they may improve their skills at the give and take of group interaction.

Quality Circles. The quality circle movement, which originated in Japan, was first introduced into the United States in 1974 by the Lockheed Missiles and Space Company. By 1982 more than 1,000 organizations were using quality circles.[5]

Quality circles were first developed in Japan in the early 1960s by the Union of Japanese Scientists and Engineers. This organization combined the statistical quality control techniques introduced into Japan by two eminent American consultants, W. Edwards Deming and J. M. Juran, in the 1950s with the motivational concepts of Abraham Maslow and Douglas McGregor. By the end of 1979 there were over 100,000 quality circles in operation in Japan. There typically are several circles within each company. The average circle consists of nine people.

What, exactly, is a quality circle? It is a study group of volunteers (containing from five to fifteen people) who meet on a regular basis and work on a large variety of operational and employee problems. The group generally consists of rank-and-file employees plus their immediate supervisor, who usually serves as the circle leader. Although originally created in Japan to focus on improvement of product quality, quality circles both in the U.S. and Japan work on a variety of problems in addition to quality such as cost reduction, production-processing methods, facilities, employee morale issues, and workplace safety.

Organization within a company for quality circles requires four components: A steering committee (one per organization); facilitators (one for every 5–8 quality circles); the leader (one per quality circle); and the members (5–15 per quality circle). The steering committee makes policy and oversees the entire program. It is staffed by a cross-section of the managers at the upper levels of the plant or establishment. The facilitator serves as a guide and a process resource to the various quality circles. He also reports on the effectiveness of the circles to the steering committee. The leader, who is usually the unit supervisor, serves as a stimulator and conference leader for his or her circle but does not attempt to dominate it. Leaders must be given thorough training in group dynamics processes and problem-solving techniques. Circle members are also given thorough training in group processes and problem-solving techniques.

Quality circles do not just generate "wish lists" of what ought to be done. Instead, they analyze problems in depth, create proposed solutions, and make presentations to management on recommended courses of action. Oftentimes the circle will test out its proposal in the plant and follow up to insure success.

The typical circle meets about one hour per week on company time. Some of the problem-solving techniques used are brainstorming, cause-and-effect diagrams, bar graphs showing the frequency of specific problems, randomized sampling of product units produced, and Pareto charts to identify the most serious problems.

What motivates individual employees to become members of a quality circle? Possible mo-

[5]Roy G. Foltz, "QWL's Effect On Productivity," *Personnel Administrator*, Vol. 27, No. 5 (May 1982), p. 20.

tivators are opportunity for learning more about plant operations, improved communication with the supervisor, chance to improve working conditions, close interaction with fellow employees, and opportunity to learn new skills.

American firms use a variety of incentives and rewards to foster the quality circle programs in their establishments. Some offer cash awards to circle members for cost-saving and production-improvement solutions. All companies provide various nonmonetary forms of recognition such as praise, write-ups in the company newsletter, plaques, medals, certificates, and recognition dinners.

Junior Boards of Executives. The junior board of executives system, by which standing committees of managers carry out studies and make recommendations to top management, is also known as *multiple management.* The idea of junior boards of executives was first installed in American industry by Charles P. McCormick in 1932 at McCormick & Company in Baltimore, Md. This system of management has since spread to a number of other companies. Most commonly these boards are composed of members of middle management, with some system existing by which members are rotated into and out of the board.

Generally these junior boards of executives have wide latitude to undertake the study of practically any type of problem area affecting the company's business. Within the board itself there will be committees that carry out investigations in project areas. Typical topics for investigation are company organization, executive compensation, automation, foreign markets, personnel policies, warehousing operations, and use of wage incentives. When the board has reached a decision, a recommendation is sent to top company management, which can accept or reject the proposal.

In addition to McCormick & Company, some other firms using junior boards of executives are Inland Division of General Motors, Kemper Insurance, Motorola, Fox Grocery, Bar-ber-Greene, Cincinati Enquirer division of Combined Communications, and Memphis Publishing. The president of McCormick & Company believes that the junior boards system has substantially contributed to the company's ability to maintain a 16 per cent growth in profits. The general manager of GM's Inland Division has stated that its middle management team system has been an unqualified success.[6]

Collective Bargaining. Collective bargaining, which occurs when a union represents the employees, is a type of participation program distinctly different from all the other participation methods. Collective bargaining is not instituted by management (except in special circumstances), whereas all of the other programs of participation are discretionary on management's part. Bargaining relationships usually commence as a result of a union organizing campaign and an election conducted by the National Labor Relations Board to determine whether the employees wish to have a union represent them in negotiations with the employer over such matters as wages, hours, and other conditions of employment. Although it must be admitted that in some instances a union and an employer may sign an initial labor agreement over the heads of the employees (that is, without a National Labor Relations Board election to determine employee sentiments regarding unionization), and it must be further agreed that a few unions are not democratically run, in the vast majority of cases unions do solicit member opinions at regular meetings regarding bargaining demands to be made of the employer and regarding the handling of day-to-day problems in the shop. The Labor–Management Reporting and Disclosure Act of 1959 (Landrum–Griffin Act) contains strong provisions to ensure union democracy.

Thus, it can be accurately said that employees through their elected leaders do participate

---

[6]"More Power for the Middle Manager," *Dun's Review,* Vol. 111, No. 6 (June 1978).

on an equal basis with company representatives in negotiating labor agreements, in administering the agreement, and in processing grievances. The local union leaders, who are usually company employees as well, help make decisions regarding pay rates, seniority rules, pension plans, order of layoff, vacations, holidays, grievance procedures, benefit plans, and hours of work.

Union–Management Cooperation. The term *union–management cooperation* (sometimes called labor–management cooperation) means a formal program of cooperation and consultation between management and union to solve common problems jointly. At the level of the company there are two broad categories of programs: Those aimed at improvements in plant efficiency and productivity and those aimed at improvements in worker satisfaction and well-being in such areas as health and safety, morale, job training, drug addiction and alcoholism, and preretirement counseling. Those programs that seek to improve plant efficiency and productivity can be of two types. One type provides monetary rewards as in Scanlon Plans (see below) and profit-sharing plans. In the other type teamwork, cooperation, and nonfinancial recognition are emphasized.

Generally, the proposals that are generated in joint labor–management committees are looked upon as suggestions to top management. Management can accept, reject, or modify the proposals, and therefore it retains its traditional prerogatives.

A very early program was that begun in the 1920s by the Baltimore and Ohio Railroad and the Machinists Union to develop ways of improving efficiency. Several thousand joint labor–management committees were established in defense industries in World War II to work on ways of increasing production and employee morale. Practically all these committees were abandoned at the close of the war. Commencing in the 1940s the Tennessee Valley Authority created a labor–management cooperation program that was very successful. This program was initiated at the suggestion of local union leaders.

In recent years the Federal Mediation and Conciliation Service has taken a lead position in encouraging unions and employers to establish joint labor–management committees. In fiscal 1979, the Service was involved in the establishment or administration of 375 labor–management committees. Ongoing, contemporary cooperation programs exist in such organizations as the Minneapolis Star and Tribune Company, a paperboard plant in Marinette, Wis., the Mead Corporation plant in Escanaba, Mich., and many companies in the basic steel industry. In the mid-1970s both General Motors and Ford set up joint quality of worklife programs with the United Automobile Workers Union.

At the industry level cooperation programs have been operating in the construction, retail food, men's clothing, and railroad industries for a good number of years. For example, apprenticeship and training programs have long been managed jointly at the local level in the construction industry. In the late 1970s the Amalgamated Clothing and Textile Workers and the Clothing Manufacturers Association established a program to improve the competitive position of the men's tailored-clothing industry.[7]

An unusual form of labor–management cooperation is that established in Jamestown, N.Y. in 1972. This program is unusual because it is a community-wide effort. Prior to the establishment of this program, many manufacturing firms had moved out of Jamestown and the unemployment rate was high. In 1972 a community-wide labor–management committee was formed. Eighteen companies and eleven unions are affiliated with the central committee. Each participating company has an in-plant committee. Committees have worked to raise plant efficiency, train workers, improve labor–management relations, and improve the quality

[7]Irwing H. Siegel and Edgar Weinberg, *Labor–Management Cooperation: The American Experience*. Kalamazoo, Mich.: W. E. Upjohn Institute for Employment Research, 1982, ch. 6.

of worklife. The community committee has also worked to attract new industry to Jamestown. To date, the efforts in Jamestown have been quite successful.

Another form of union–management cooperation is the Scanlon Plan. The Scanlon Plan (named after Joseph Scanlon, who originated the plan in the late 1930s) contains an incentive feature whereby any reduction in plant payroll costs below an agreed-upon standard or norm is passed on to the employees (or shared with them) in the form of a bonus. The standard is expressed as total payroll cost divided by the sales value of the product. Each department has a two-person committee composed of one management and one union representative (usually the foreman and the shop steward). It reviews suggestions obtained from the employees of that department. A larger plantwide screening committee acts upon the suggestions from all the departmental committees. Where it has been installed, the Scanlon Plan has generally worked well. It depends upon a genuine spirit of cooperation for its success. Experience has shown that with such a program the workers are more willing to accept technological change than in the typical company. There is a greater interest by the workers in the problems of management, the employees tend to help one another to a considerable extent, and foremen actively seek (instead of resent) suggestions for improvement from the workers.

Although the idea of union–management cooperation is very appealing, it has not achieved wide acceptance in American industry. Workers often fear that cooperation on cost-cutting campaigns will endanger their own jobs. Union officials sometimes feel that cooperation programs may weaken their bargaining position to press for economic gains. Some executives fear that union–management cooperation will open the door to union invasion of traditional management prerogatives. Cooperation works best when all parties are secure in their relationships with one another.[8]

[8]Sources on union–management cooperation are Wil-

Suggestion Plans. A suggestion plan is a formalized system established by an employer to encourage employees to submit ideas that will result in improvement for the business and the organization. The payment of monetary awards for accepted suggestions is a fundamental feature of these plans.

A well-run suggestion program can achieve a number of real benefits for the organization. It provides an additional avenue of upward communication. It provides a means by which employees can achieve some measure of participation in the affairs of the business. A suggestion system is looked upon by some people as a technique for improving employee relations and morale. A primary gain from a properly conducted program is the significant reduction in production and operating costs that can accrue. In addition, employees receive money awards and recognition from management.

Although there is considerable variation from organization to organization as far as the mechanics of their suggestion plans are concerned, the essential features of most plans have much in common. Typically, companies will recognize those ideas that will achieve measurable dollar savings in labor and/or material costs through new methods, procedures, materials, and equipment. They also welcome ideas proposing improvements in safety, housekeeping, employee relations, public relations, and those that aid the organization in general. For these latter types it is usually not possible to calculate a definite dollar benefit that will accrue to the organization from adoption of the suggestion. In this case, token awards are granted.

Suggestions are put in writing on special blanks supplied at convenient locations throughout the working area. These are then dropped into suggestion boxes. They are

liam L. Batt, Jr., and Edgar Weinberg, "Labor–Management Cooperation Today," *Harvard Business Review,* Vol. 56, No. 1 (January–February 1978), pp. 96–104; and Charlotte Gold, *Employer-Employee Committees and Worker Participation,* Key Issues No. 20 (Ithaca: New York State School of Industrial and Labor Relations, Cornell University, 1976).

processed by a suggestion secretary, who may be a member of the personnel or industrial engineering departments. Many companies utilize the services of suggestion investigators, who collect all the facts needed to evaluate the ideas adequately. Final decisions on whether to accept, reject, or defer judgment until later are generally made by a suggestion committee, which is usually composed of middle-management individuals. Cash awards are computed on the basis of net annual savings in material and labor costs. Commonly an employee will receive an award equal to a percentage (often 10 or 15 per cent) of the first year's net savings.

The National Association of Suggestion Systems (NASS) estimates that there are about 3,000 formal suggestion systems operating in the United States. Well-run plans can be very cost-effective. In 1982, 225 member companies of NASS reported that they saved a cumulative $600 million from the 323,530 suggestions that they accepted. After subtracting the $78.8 million paid in awards and the expenses of administering the systems, the 225 companies gained a return of $5 to $6 for each $1 invested.[9]

WORKERS' PARTICIPATION— EUROPEAN STYLE

The movement toward participation by employees in organizational decision making has progressed farther in European countries than in the United States. In Europe this process is designated by such labels as industrial democracy, self-management, workers' participation, or the works council system. Whereas participative management in the United States tends to be rather informal and dependent upon the inclinations of managers in their particular organizational units, the process in European

[9]Gail Gregg, "The Power of Suggestion," *Across the Board*, Vol. XX, No. 1 (December 1983), pp. 27–31.

countries is much more highly structured. In many countries it is mandated by law.

The central core of the various systems consists of the works council, which is comprised of worker representatives elected by the employees in each plant or by the union. Large multiunit companies also have central councils composed of representatives of the various plant councils. These councils articulate employee interests in discussions with management.

Although the organizational arrangements for workers' participation vary from country to country, a brief look at the mechanisms in two countries—West Germany and Yugoslavia—will be illustrative.

The works council system in Germany evolved over a period of about a hundred years but it did not achieve fully functioning status until after World War II. The West German Codetermination Law of 1951 established substantial employee influence in the direction of companies in the coal, iron, and steel industries. Under German corporation law most companies have two directing boards. The upper board is called a supervisory board and the lower board is called the management board. The Codetermination Law stipulates that in the coal, iron, and steel industries shareholders shall appoint five members of the supervisory board, the employees shall select five members (two appointed by the works council and three by the trade union), and one member shall be chosen by the board itself as a neutral. This eleven-member supervisory board then selects a three-member managing board, consisting of a commercial director, a technical director, and a labor director. In actual day-to-day practice the employee representatives on the two boards tend to concern themselves with employee-relations matters and do not try actually to manage the companies. This is left to the management representatives. But the labor representatives do possess considerable power, which is brought into play upon occasion. Although judgments on the values of codetermination vary depending on their source and the particular feature under scrutiny, the overall evaluation is positive. Rank-and-file workers strongly approve of it. The harsh authority relationships in the mines and steel firms that existed through World War II have disappeared. A 1968 survey of employee attitudes reported better social services as the primary benefit, followed, in descending order, by higher pay, improved working conditions, increased influence in personnel and business policies, and job security.[10]

The Works Constitution Act of 1952 extended workers' participation to all other private companies having 500 or more employees. Under this law employees in each enterprise elect one third of the members of the supervisory board while the shareholders choose two thirds. This board then selects the three-person managing board which runs the company.

Demands by German labor unions for parity membership in supervisory boards throughout industry led to the enactment of the Codetermination Act of 1976 which became fully effective on July 1, 1978. This law represented a compromise between the position of the unions and the position of businesses which feared that true equality of representation would cripple the decision-making process in companies. This new law partially supercedes the 1952 law in that all companies having 2,000 or more employees have approximate (but not full) parity between worker and stockholder representatives on the supervisory boards.[11]

Under the 1976 law the number of supervisory board members is determined by the total number of employees in the corporation. For companies which regularly employ up to 10,000 people, there must be twelve board members and those with up to 20,000 employees must have sixteen members. Companies larger than this must have twenty-member boards. In a sixteen-member board there are eight shareholder representatives and eight employee representatives. The law provides that two of the employee representatives must be selected by the union. The remaining six employee members are composed of both blue-collar and white-collar representatives in the same ratio of these two categories as they exist in the total employment of the company. The chairman and vice-chairman are chosen by a two-thirds majority. If such a majority cannot be obtained, a second balloting within the board is conducted. In this case the chairman is chosen by the stockholder members and the vice-chairman is chosen by the employee members. In conducting its business, decisions of the board are made by a simple majority vote. In the event of a tie, the chairperson has the power to cast one additional vote to break it. So we can see that the stockholder voice has a slight power advantage. The actual day-to-day management of a company is handled by the management board, which is appointed by the supervisory board.[12]

Although it is too early to tell the full impact of the 1976 law, the system of codetermination that has existed in West Germany since 1951 has met with general approval. Some experts have credited the workers' participation system with contributing toward the peaceful labor–management relations that occurred in West Germany for many years.[13]

The Yugoslavian system is called self-management. It was set up in 1950 after Marshall Tito broke away from the Soviet Union's style of central control of the economy and moved to

[10]Heinz Hartmann, "Codetermination in West Germany," *Industrial Relations*, Vol. 9, No. 2 (February 1970), pp. 137–147.

[11]Full parity continues to exist in the coal and steel industries provided by the 1951 Codetermination Law. Workers in other industries continue to have one-third representation on supervisory boards in companies having from 600 to 2000 employees.

[12]Klaus E. Agthe, "Mitbestimmung: Report on a Social Experiment," *Business Horizons,* Vol. 20, No. 1 (February 1977) pp. 5–14.

[13]Time lost and workers involved in strikes are very low in West Germany compared with other industrial countries in Europe and with the United States and Canada. See Burton Teague, "Can Workers Participate in Management Successfully?" *The Conference Board Record,* Vol. 8, No. 7 (July 1971), pp. 48–52.

decentralize decision making to the level of the enterprise. In this country most of the nonagricultural labor force works in enterprises whose policies are set by worker-elected councils. In every firm the workers elect a workers' council that consists of from 15 to 120 members, depending upon the size of the enterprise. This council selects a managing board whose membership includes the managing director. It is his job really to manage the business. His term of office is four years but he can be removed from office during that period by action of the council. To make the system work effectively, the Yugoslavs have found it necessary over the years officially to endow the managing director with considerable authority. Thus, the charters of most enterprises now state that the managing director has the power to coordinate all the affiliates of a firm in the interests of the whole organization, to ask the councils to annul acts by their management boards if he or she considers them unsound, and to choose his or her own advisory body composed of his or her top executives and technical specialists.[14] Most observers feel that the Yugoslavian system of self-management has been reasonably successful from both the economic and worker satisfaction standpoints.

Strauss and Rosenstein have classified the European (and Israeli) participation systems into three types according to their decision-making processes. First is the joint consultation model, in which management makes the final decisions but employee representatives are heard. This system is used in Sweden, Great Britain, and France. The second model is the joint decision-making model, in which worker representatives and management are jointly represented on a decision-making body (with the employee representatives often in the minority). Illustrative of this pattern is codetermination in West Germany and the Histadrut's joint management plan in

Israel.[15] The third model is the workers control model, where final decision-making authority resides in the elected representatives of the workforce. This is the system used in Yugoslavia.[16]

For the present there seems to be no attempt to import European-style participation into the United States. In a sense the works council system fills a void in Europe that is met by the local union in the United States. Trade unions in Europe commonly bargain only at the level of the whole industry, where the broad structure of wages and terms of employment are settled. They do not participate in day-to-day labor affairs at the shop level as do American unions. However, European workers do have an advantage over their American counterparts in that their works councils are integral parts of their enterprises and that their structure for participation in enterprise decisions is written into law in most instances.

Questions for Review and Discussion

1. What is a quality circle? How are quality circles organized and how do they work? Explain the current interest in quality circles in the United States.
2. What are the advantages of participation to the organization? To the individual employee?
3. Give some examples of situations in which it would be inadvisable to invite participation from subordinates.
4. "The position of a leader is weakened if he or she consults subordinates. They tend to acquire doubts as to the leader's command of the situation, and this causes him or her to lose control." Discuss this viewpoint.
5. Why has the committee method of deliberation and decision making been subject to so much criticism? Despite their shortcomings, committees are widely used in both the pri-

[14]Gilbert Burck, "A Socialist Enterprise That Acts Like a Fierce Capitalistic Competitor," *Fortune*, Vol. 85, No. 1 (January 1972), pp. 82–91, 126.

[15]Histadrut is both a very powerful trade union and the operator of major economic enterprises in Israel.

[16]George Strauss and Eliezer Rosenstein, "Workers Participation: A Critical View," *Industrial Relations*, Vol. 9, No. 2 (February 1970), pp. 197–214.

vate and public sectors. Why do you think this is so?

6. In what ways does collective bargaining differ from the other kinds of participation activities and programs discussed in this chapter?

7. What is meant by the term *union–management cooperation?* What forces have impeded the adoption of these programs throughout industry?

8. Compare and contrast systems of participation in management in Europe and the United States. How would you account for the differences?

9. Explain the system of codetermination used in West Germany. Do you think such a system would work in the United States? Why or why not?

Suggestions for Further Reading

Dewar, Donald. *The Quality Circle Guide to Participation Management.* Englewood Cliffs, N.J.: Spectrum Books, 1982.

Levitan, Sar A., and Clifford M. Johnson. "Labor and Management: The Illusion of Cooperation," *Harvard Business Review* Vol. 61, No. 5 (September–October 1983), pp. 8–16.

Pejovich, Svetozar (ed.). *The Codetermination Movement in the West.* Lexington, Mass.: D. C. Heath and Co., 1978.

Poole, Michael, "Industrial Democracy: A Comparative Analysis," *Industrial Relations,* Vol. 18, No. 3 (Fall 1979), pp. 262–272.

Ramquist, Judith, "Labor–Management Cooperation—The Scanlon Plan at Work," *Sloan Management Review,* Vol. 23 (Spring 1982), pp. 49–55.

Siegel, Irving H., and Edgar Weinberg. *Labor–Management Cooperation: The American Experience.* Kalamazoo, Mich.: W. E. Upjohn Institute for Employment Research, 1982.

Simmons, John, and William Mares, *Working Together.* New York: Alfred A. Knopf, 1983.

Sweeny, Kevin M., et al., "Can Workplace Democracy Boost Productivity?" *Business and Society Review* (Fall 1982), pp. 10–15.

Thompson, Walt. "Is the Organization Ready for Quality Circles?" *Training and Development Journal.* Vol. 36, No. 12 (December 1982), pp. 115 ff.

18

Discipline

Discipline is essential to all organized group action. The members must control their individual urges and cooperate for the common good. In other words they must reasonably conform to the code of behavior established by the leadership of the organization so that the agreed-upon goals can be accomplished.

If the membership of any organization, whether a club, company, union, or nation, will not abide by some code of rules or laws, then that organization faces imminent collapse. Anarchy and chaos ensue. Repeatedly the world has witnessed the tragic spectacle of anarchy, mutiny, terrorism, and social disintegration in such countries as Zaire (formerly the Belgian Congo) in the early 1960s and Lebanon, Northern Ireland, and Cambodia in the 1970s.

In the work organization, skill in achieving a healthy state of discipline is an important qualification for the supervisor. Some supervisors have the knack of developing a willing conformance with the rules of the plant among their people. The employees cooperate, conform, and regulate themselves almost without their noticing any ostensible imposition of authority by the supervisor. On the other hand, other supervisors can rule only, it seems, by frequent resorts to threats and punishment. And with still other supervisors, the people do as they please and violate rules apparently with impunity.

The Meaning of Discipline

Webster's Dictionary gives three basic meanings to the word *discipline*. First it states that it is training that corrects, molds, or perfects. The second meaning is that it is control gained by enforcing obedience. The third meaning is punishment.[1] If we combine meanings one and two we can say that discipline involves the conditioning or molding of behavior by applying rewards or penalties. The third meaning is more narrow in that it pertains only to the act of punishing wrongdoers.

The first dictionary meaning will be treated in this chapter under the heading "Positive Approach." This is the kind of discipline that all managements should seek to create. Positive discipline is actually broader and more fundamental than the dictionary phrase *training that molds, corrects, or perfects* implies. Positive discipline involves the creation of an attitude and an organizational climate wherein the employees willingly conform to established rules and regulations. It is achieved when management applies the principles of positive motivation, when sound leadership is exercised by supervision, and when the entire organization is managed efficiently.

[1]*Webster's Ninth New Collegiate Dictionary* (Springfield, Mass.: Merriam–Webster, Inc., 1983), p. 360.

The second meaning of discipline encompasses the use of penalties or the threat of penalties to cause people to obey orders and to live up to the rules of the game. Often force is employed. This is the kind of discipline exercised by sea captains over sailors since the earliest days of civilization and the kind used in military forces the world over. This form of discipline is explained in this chapter under the heading "Negative Approach."

In all organizations, regardless of whether positive or negative discipline is utilized, some individuals will, upon occasion, break the rules. They are then brought to see the error of their ways and the need for improving performance by applying some form of punishment. This is the third dictionary meaning described above. Under the concept of positive discipline the punishment is administered to correct and rehabilitate, not to injure. Under the concept of negative discipline the punishment is for retribution and to scare others so they will not commit the same crime. Administering the program, handling violators, and assigning penalties are covered in this chapter under the heading "Administering the Disciplinary Program."

APPROACHES TO DISCIPLINE

Because the objective in any organized group endeavor is to develop in the participants such an attitude and behavior that they conform to established norms of conduct, the question is how this can be achieved. On the one hand, those in charge can rule with an iron hand, punish rule violators severely, and, in general, force the members to obey and conform. This mode of leadership has variously been called negative discipline, punitive discipline, autocratic discipline, or rule through fear. The other approach is to develop in people a willingness to obey and abide by the rules and regulations. They do so because they want to, not because they are afraid of the consequences of disobedience. This form of discipline has been called positive or constructive discipline. Let us now examine the methods and implications of each type of discipline.

Negative Approach

This is basically the "big stick" approach to leadership. In industry this brand of disciplinary control was prevalent in the handling of hourly workers prior to the widespread growth of unions in the late 1930s. The union movement has been very successful in providing a considerable measure of security for the workers by granting them protection against arbitrary treatment by management. Disciplinary penalties are often appealed through the grievance procedure. If necessary these may be taken to arbitration for impartial review.

Of course, unions represent only a minority, albeit a large minority, of the employed persons in this country. The threat of punishment is employed by many managements to keep people in line. Although it may be infrequent that a person is suspended or discharged, the power of the boss to impose such penalties is kept ever present in the employees' minds. Written warnings may be handed out extensively to those who fail to meet the established standards of production or to those who are absent from work. The foreman may threaten individuals who do not respond as he or she expects. And of course during periods of business recession, the likelihood of being weeded out is prominent in employees' minds (especially in those companies in which management has considerable discretion as to whom it terminates).

The basic fallacy in negative discipline is that it achieves only the minimum performance necessary to avoid punishment. The people are not given a say-so in formulating the rules, and they are not taught the reason why. They are taught only that they will be punished if they break a rule. The rule-through-fear approach puts the emphasis upon avoidance of punishment, not upon enthusiastic, wholehearted cooperation.

Those who base their leadership upon rule through fear count upon making an example of violators. Public knowledge of the punishment (usually severe) is expected to serve as a deterrent to others. Yet in the whole history of crime, punishment has never been demonstrated to be a truly effective deterrent. The person who breaks the rules does not plan that far ahead. He or she is not thinking of the consequences. He or she is thinking only of immediate wants.

As a philosophy of management for the long run and for the vast majority of followers, the practice of rule through fear can have only limited success. But this does not deny that for certain subordinates at certain times power and force may be the only answers. Some employees, as a consequence of their background and personality development, may respond only to the supervisor who uses a policy of "be tough."

Positive Approach

Positive discipline, often called *constructive discipline*, consists of that type of supervisory leadership that develops a willing adherence to the necessary rules and regulations of the organization. The employees, both as individuals and as a group adhere to the desired standards of behavior because they understand, believe in, and support them.

Discipline must take the form of positive support and reinforcement for approved actions. This is fundamental to all learning. Punishment may be applied for improper behavior, but this is carried out in a supportive, corrective manner. There is no vindictiveness. The aim is to help, not harm, the individual. The supervisor lets it be known that he approves of the violator as a person but that he is training the employee in regard to a specific action.

A necessary prerequisite for the positive approach to discipline is communicating the requirements of the job and the rules and regulations to the employees. Every person must know, when hired and henceforth, just what management and the immediate supervisor expect. The performance standards (that is, workloads) must be fair, attainable with reasonable effort, and consistent from job to job. The rules likewise must be reasonable and few in number. Supervision must communicate the kind of positive behavior expected of employees rather than dwell upon an exhaustive list of detailed prohibitions.

In creating a climate of positive discipline, the supervisor seeks to build a sense of personal responsibility and self-discipline. He or she applies principles of positive motivation and enlightened leadership, recognizing individual differences among subordinates and varying methods and appeals as necessary.

When people are well trained so that they know how far they can go and what the limits of tolerated conduct are, they acquire a sense of security. They know the rules of the game, and they know where they stand.

In orienting a new person to the job and the company, the supervisor should explain what work performance is expected and what help is available to achieve it. He or she should then discuss the principal standards of behavior expected. This will ordinarily include such items as good attendance, notification when justifiably absent, punctuality, cooperation with the supervisor and fellow employees, standards of morality and honesty, and wakefulness throughout the work shift (no sleeping on the job). Particular circumstances in certain shops may require special no-smoking and other safety regulations.

To achieve constructive discipline, a supervisor must set a good example. For example, if he or she expects employees to arrive at work every day on time, he or she must also arrive on time.

Group Responsibility. If a supervisor takes the proper steps to build a cohesive, loyal work group, he or she will find that the group members will generally act to support and augment disciplinary efforts. To do this he or she must first recognize the existence of the informal group and consult with subordinates as a group in departmental meetings. He or she can lead discussions covering the plant rules and regulations as well as the need for them. The people can discuss how these apply to them in their own work situation. If the group understands and believes in the rules, it will often exert social pressure upon its members to insure that they live up to the rules. The group in an informal way may supplement the supervisor's efforts in such areas as prevention of horseplay, achieving good attendance, doing one's fair share of any team work, and controlling the length of coffee breaks.

In formal work organizations employee acceptance of rules and regulations could be greater if they were given a voice in their formulation. This could be accomplished in group meetings where the supervisor encouraged the people to agree upon those minimum norms of conduct which they felt were necessary for effective functioning of the group. Presumably these norms would be those of particular relevance to that group. They would be but a part of the overall regulations of the total organization.

In actual industrial practice management rarely involves the employees in either the formulation or the enforcement of plant rules and regulations. Management almost universally considers discipline to be a management prerogative and responsibility. It is reluctant to share this responsibility with employees or with the union.

ADMINISTERING THE DISCIPLINARY PROGRAM

Even under the best conditions and with excellent supervisory leadership and employee training, somebody is bound to step over the traces now and then. When this happens what action should management take? Are there any generally accepted principles to guide management? Will certain measures be more effective in correcting the errant employee? Will certain actions have harmful repercussions upon future discipline in the organization?

Administrative Justice

Well-established principles and procedures for the handling and adjudicating of civil and criminal offenses against society have evolved in our legal system over a great many years via both common and statute law. Although administrative justice within private organizations has not developed to as advanced a state as in the public law field, certain powerful forces have been operating to create a body of fairly well-accepted principles and procedural requirements.

Probably foremost as a positive force in this direction has been the impact of unionization upon employers and the work force. The presence of a union in a company means, almost invariably, the installation of a formal grievance procedure and generally arbitration as the final step in settling unresolved grievances. It is now about forty years since unions have become widespread in industry. We have accumulated forty years of arbitration experience that has hammered out certain guidelines for the administration of employee justice within the organization. One might say that we have developed an industrial code of common-law principles and precedents. The essence of the matter is that establishments should follow "due process" procedures. Due process means that management must provide the individual with a written statement of the charges against him together with the reasons for the penalty. The individual must have full opportunity for self-defense and for utilization of the formal grievance procedure. Grievance and arbitration procedures have developed over the years to the point that management must bear the burden of proof to show both the fact of wrongdoing and the need for punishment.

It is important to note that disciplinary procedures and grievance procedures interact. Discipline administered by the first-line supervisor is one principal cause for later grievance appeal by the employee and the union. The disciplinary penalty may have been applied for a variety of alleged infractions such as tardiness, absenteeism, low output, excessive defective work, intoxication on the job, insubordination, horseplay, or violation of safety rules. If management takes proper care to administer its discipline fairly and with due concern for procedural safeguards that are designed to protect the rights of the parties, then there is less likelihood of subsequent charges by the employee or union of injustice or discrimination.

It is paradoxical to note that although collective bargaining has had a powerful influence upon the handling of discipline in industry, labor-management agreements contain very little on the subject. It is very rare to find the company rules and regulations with their accompanying penalties shown in the labor agreement. Traditionally management initiates the disciplinary policy and administers the program. The employees and the union have the right to submit a grievance if they do not like the way the case has been handled.

As far as contract language is concerned, most labor contracts merely state that management has the right to discipline, suspend, or discharge for *just cause* and that employees have the right to submit grievances if they consider an action unfair. Just cause means "for good and sufficient reason." Among the factors to be considered in ascertaining whether *due process procedures* were followed and whether there is *just cause* for applying a disciplinary penalty are the following:

- Did the employee have prior knowledge that a particular conduct could be subject to disciplinary action?
- Was the rule that the individual violated reasonably related to the efficient and safe conduct of the business?
- Did management conduct a fair and thorough investigation of the incident?
- Did management determine accurately whether, in fact, the employee had violated the rule?
- Was management's action consistent, one employee compared with another?
- Was the penalty assessed reasonably related to the seriousness of the offense?

Principles for Administration of Disciplinary Action

In administering discipline and penalizing employees, management must constantly be aware of the dual objectives of preserving the interests of the organization as a whole and protecting the rights of the individual. Unless sound policies are adopted and orderly procedures followed, there is a danger that management will look at a case solely in terms of its own needs at the moment rather than in terms of the needs of the employee as well as the organization. Short-run expediency might prevail over long-run considerations. Let us now examine the principal ingredients of a sound disciplinary system.

Definite Policy and Procedure

It is the responsibility of top management to give serious consideration to the need for achieving a healthy state of discipline throughout the organization. It must decide what kind of behavior it expects from its employees and how it hopes to achieve this. Presumably the objective is to create a positive, constructive form of discipline through sound leadership and adequate training of all employees.

Top management must carefully think out the issue of the role of the first-line supervisor in the disciplinary system. Because of the need for consistency of action throughout the company and because the union will generally appeal the penalty over the foreman's head if it is dissatisfied, most industrial concerns have tended to centralize a considerable amount of authority in the hands of the industrial relations (or personnel) director. This can be carried too far, however.

> The personnel manager of a small manufacturer proudly displayed his book of rules and penalties and announced (to the author in an interview), "I handle all disciplinary problems in my plant. The foremen bring the violators to my office, I listen to both their stories, collect further evidence where necessary, and then announce my decision. The foremen in this plant are not able to make proper judgments regarding these cases. Therefore, I handle the whole thing."

With such a policy as followed in that company, the foremen are bound to lose respect and control of their employees.

The need to maintain consistency of action throughout the organization is not incompatible with the need to preserve the authority and position of the foreman. How can this be done? The foreman must be fully instructed regarding the rules and regulations, behavior expected from employees, progressive disciplinary penalties, and the rights of all parties—management, employees, and union. The foreman should be given the authority to issue oral and written warnings on his own. For cases that he thinks are serious enough to warrant suspension and discharge, he should consult his line superior or the industrial relations director before taking action. This not only insures consistency of action throughout the company but also prevents a worker from being fired because of capricious or ill-considered action by the supervisor. In these more serious cases, after all the pertinent facts have been brought out and a decision agreed upon, the first-line supervisor should announce the action to the affected employee.

To insure that the discipline policies and procedure are carefully formulated, that no essential elements are overlooked, and that members of management will support the program, there is considerable merit to involving representatives of middle and lower management in the process of developing the system.

Communication of Rules

Employees must have knowledge of the rule before they can be held accountable. Arbitrators have rescinded penalties when such was not the case.

The most commonly used method of informing employees about company rules is to include a list of the rules, penalties, and explanations thereof in the employee handbook. This is usually handed to a person at the time he is hired. This can be followed up with oral explanations of the more important rules during the initial orientation program. Usually this explanation is given in the department by the employee's supervisor. The reasons behind the rules should also be explained.

In addition to the statement in the handbook and the explanation by the supervisor, the list of rules and penalties may be posted on the bulletin board.

Burden of Proof

The principle of law underlying the English and United States legal systems, that an individual is presumed innocent until proven guilty, applies to industrial discipline cases as well. The burden of proof is upon the employer to show that the worker is guilty of the alleged offense. The degree of proof tends to vary with the seriousness of the charge. If there is serious doubt, arbitrators tend to give the employee the benefit of the doubt.

Consistency of Treatment

Consistency of treatment is one of the most important principles and one that is too easily ignored. Management must not punish one person for an offense and ignore the same offense committed by another (often, more favored) employee. This kind of inconsistency can happen because supervisors in different departments have different standards of what they expect and have different tolerance limits when employees deviate somewhat from the standard. Thus, one supervisor may overlook the occasional taking of a few pencils by an office employee, whereas another considers such action to be stealing and grounds for discharge. In addition to this, a supervisor may have a grudge against one of his people and seize upon any plausible pretext to punish that person, whereas a more favored employee may be granted wide latitude.

The best way to achieve consistency of treatment and application of the rules is through supervisory-training courses and by consistent action by higher management on a day-to-day basis as cases are brought up.

Consider Circumstances of the Case

The need for consistency does not mean that two persons committing an identical offense must always receive identical penalties. The background and circumstances of each case may call for different treatment. But consistency does require that both employees know that they have violated a rule. Management must not condone an infraction by one and not the other. Both must be handled with equal gravity. But it is in deciding the severity of the penalty, or indeed whether there should be any punishment at all, that management must grant due consideration to the full circumstances surrounding each case.

Company policy may specify that any employee who is absent for five consecutive days without notifying the company as to the reason is automatically terminated. Such discharge may actually be invoked in the case of a worker who has had a bad record of unjustified absences. However, a long-service employee with a good employment record may suffer no penalty at all when it is demonstrated that he was absent and did not call in only because he had gone to his hunting camp on an island in the north woods for the weekend and had become bound in by severe storms and a breakdown of his motor launch.

Therefore, extenuating circumstances can modify or dismiss a penalty in a particular case.

Progressive Discipline

Industrial disciplinary penalties have become fairly well standardized as a result of custom and practice. In ascending order of severity these are as follows:

1. Simple oral warning.
2. Oral warning that is noted in the person's employment record.
3. Written warning noted in employment record.
4. Suspension from the job, usually varying in length from one day to two weeks.
5. Discharge.

Sometimes demotion is used as a penalty as is, also, the withholding of a scheduled pay increase. In industrial employment a monetary fine is almost never employed, although this practice is very common in professional team sports, such as baseball, football, and hockey.

In accordance with the concept of positive, corrective discipline, only oral or written warnings are assigned for minor offenses. For the average person such knowledge is sufficient to prevent a repetition. If minor offenses occur again and again, the penalty becomes more severe. A very serious first offense (such as stealing a substantial amount from the employer) usually brings immediate discharge.

The slate is normally wiped clean at the end of one or two years. This makes sense. There is no justification for holding against a person, in perpetuity, indiscretions of past years if he or she has reformed in the meantime.

Reasonable Rules and Standards

The rules and standards of conduct should be reasonable. The plant conditions and management climate must be such that they are capable of attainment. Thus, if a supervisor plans to penalize an employee who does not produce up to standard, he or she must first of all determine whether the standard of output is attainable by the average employee and whether the individual is capable of producing to standard.

> One plant has rather poor working conditions. The employees consistently break a company rule against littering the stairways with trash and bottles; yet the rule is difficult to enforce because there are no lunchroom or locker room facilities. Hence, the employees have no other place to eat lunch or to take their rest breaks.

Right of Representation

In recent years the United States Supreme Court has ruled that an employee in a unionized establishment has the right to demand that a union representative be present at an investigatory interview conducted by a supervisor if the employee believes the interview may result in disciplinary action.[2] What many managers do not know is that the Supreme Court has extended this same right to nonunion employees.

[2]NLRB v. J. Weingarten, Inc., 420 U.S. 251, 95 s.ct. 959 (1974); Paul N. Erickson and Clifford E. Smith, "The Right of Union Representation During Investigatory Interviews," Arbitration Journal, Vol. 33, No. 1, (June 1978), pp. 29–35.

In the Materials Research Corporation case in 1982 the Supreme Court ruled that unrepresented or nonunion employees have the right to demand that a co-worker of their choice be present at an investigatory interview that could lead to discipline. In rendering both the Weingarten and Materials Research decisions, the Court noted that Section 7 of the National Labor Relations Act guarantees all employees, union and nonunion alike, the right to act in concert for mutual aid and protection.[3]

Right of Appeal

Whether a person has actually committed an infraction of the rules may be a matter of opinion in certain instances and depend on the frame of reference of the person making the accusation. For example, if a person disagrees with the boss vigorously on how to carry out an assignment, does this constitute insubordination? For this reason the accused employee should always have the right to appeal to higher authority. Even if the person is truly guilty as charged, it may be best to hold a full hearing before higher authorities to satisfy all parties to the case that the employee has been justly treated.

Now it is a well-established principle of law that a person must not be judged by an accuser. The prosecution and judicial functions must be separated. The judge should not be a party to the dispute or issue. But in work organizations this principle is not fully adhered to. Line managers usually determine whether a violation has occurred, decide its severity, and invoke a penalty against the involved employee. If the employees are represented by a union, a worker who feels that he or she has been disciplined unjustly can appeal the case through the successive steps of the grievance procedure. He or she may, if the union officials think he or she has a

[3]David Israel, "The Weingarten Case Sets Precedent for Co-employee Representation," Personnel Administrator, Vol. 28, No. 2 (February 1983), pp. 23–26.

strong case, have the full backing of the union. Presumably as the case is appealed to successively higher levels of managers, these will take a more detached and broad view than would the person's immediate supervisor. The first genuinely neutral review of a discharge case comes if the union takes it all the way to arbitration. The arbitrator serves as a judge or impartial umpire. Of course, the mere fact that a case can be appealed to arbitration causes both the union and company to sit back and examine a case from all sides to judge in advance how an arbitrator *would* decide such an issue if it were actually brought to him or her.

Nonunion companies can also set up a formal appeals procedure. However, arbitration is practically never used as a final step. The chief executive officer serves as the final appeal step. His objectivity and impartiality will largely depend upon his philosophy of management, his personality, and the circumstances in the particular situation. A distinct separation of the judicial review from the executive function would require wholly different organizational arrangements than exist in most business firms.

RULES AND PENALTIES

Sound management requires that a reasonably comprehensive list of rules and regulations be adopted and reduced to writing. This should be done initially when management formulates its disciplinary policy. The very existence of a carefully developed schedule of rules signifies that management has given reasonable consideration to its disciplinary program. If a company has never thought out its disciplinary code, it can some day find itself in the very awkward spot of creating a rule after someone has done something that displeases management. In civil affairs a person cannot be prosecuted for a law that was legislated only after he committed an act.

Below is a listing of most of the common rules adopted in work organizations. They are grouped into two broad categories: (1) minor or moderate offenses, and (2) serious offenses. Of course, the specific situation in a particular establishment may cause an offense listed as "minor or moderate" to be so serious as to justify discharge. Thus, this listing should be viewed as illustrative only. It should also be noted that circumstances in a department or plant may require the adoption of many special rules. Safety rules are a good example of items that must be tailor-made to the situation:

I *Minor or Moderate Offenses*
Oral or written warning may be assigned for first offense; penalties will become progressively stiffer with repeated violation. Eventual discharge can result.
   a. Habitual tardiness
   b. Unexcused absence on one or more scheduled work days
   c. Failure to report accidental injury
   d. Leaving job or work area without authorization
   e. Loafing
   f. Individual gambling on company property
   g. Fighting
   h. Horseplay
   i. Unauthorized selling or canvassing on company property
   j. Sleeping on the job
   k. Smoking in a prohibited area
   l. Failure to obey safety rules
   m. Reporting for work or being on duty while intoxicated
   n. Clock punching of another's time card
   o. Concealing one's defective work
   p. Work output below standard
   q. Excessive defective work due to employee's own errors
II *Serious Offenses*
   First offense can bring suspension or discharge
   a. Malicious damage or destruction of company property
   b. Gross insubordination

c. Gross immoral, indecent, or disgraceful conduct
d. Stealing
e. Carrying concealed weapons
f. Promotion of gambling on company property
g. Attacking another with intent seriously to injure or maim
h. Deliberate falsification of company records

A Uniform, Published Scale of Penalties?

Opinion differs as to the desirability of fixing in advance a uniform scale of penalties for the various offenses. Those who oppose such a practice claim that the circumstances of each case are different, and it is impossible to decide ahead of time an appropriate penalty that would fit every instance of a particular offense. In some cases extenuating circumstances would justify a lighter penalty, whereas in others a harsher penalty might be called for. Is it as serious for a file clerk to sleep on the job as it is for a plant guard or watchman? If stealing is grounds for discharge, would it be fair to fire an office worker who takes a few wooden lead pencils?

There are some powerful arguments in favor of adopting a schedule of penalties for each offense. It insures consistency of treatment throughout all divisions of a company. Consistency is also achieved over time. An offense today is treated the same as the same offense a year ago. Employees have memories and equitable treatment appeals to them. Employees know where they stand and what to expect if they kick over the traces. A published list of penalties adds an aura of legitimacy to management enforcement action. Excessive or unusual penalties cannot be put into effect by ill-tempered or vindictive supervisors.

A written scale of penalties can be wholly compatible with the logical need for giving full consideration to the severity and circumstances of each offense. Consider the following example:

Penalties and Occurrences

Offense	First		Second		Third	
	Min.	Max.	Min.	Max.	Min.	Max.
Loafing on job	oral warning	1-day suspension	1-day suspension	3-day suspension	3-day suspension	discharge

With each occurrence of the act of loafing, management has reasonable latitude in choosing a penalty. If a person were caught loafing when the work demands were very light, he or she might be given a simple oral warning by the supervisor. On the other hand, if products are coming off a production line and an operator is making no effort to handle his or her assigned items and this causes damage or serious delay, he or she might be suspended without pay for a full day for the first occurrence.

Discharge as a Penalty

Discharge is the supreme punishment in industrial discipline. Some writers have called it industrial capital punishment. Where progressive penalties are assigned for repeated minor offenses, the threat of discharge often serves to "sober up" errant workers. Discharge may be the only feasible course of action in the case of employees whose behavior is so bad as to make their presence in the plant a threat to other employees or to the effective operation of the business.

Arbitrators are reluctant to order discharge unless the evidence is incontrovertible and unless efforts at correction have been tried and have proven unsuccessful. Discharge is particularly grave for a worker with considerable length of service, for he loses his accumulated pension and group insurance benefits plus extended vacation rights. With rigorous employee selection procedures and a careful weeding out of undesirable workers during the initial probationary period, management can almost eliminate the need for discharges of permanent employees.

Questions for Review and Discussion

1. Why is discipline necessary to any organized group activity?
2. Distinguish among the various meanings of the term *discipline*.
3. Evaluate the implications and consequences of maintaining discipline by force or the threat of force.
4. What is positive or constructive discipline? What are the goals of the supervisor in institution a pattern of positive discipline? How can positive discipline be achieved in a workforce?
5. Do you think the local union leadership can or should play an active part in the disciplinary process in a company?
6. Describe the impact of collective bargaining and arbitration upon the handling of disciplinary problems in industry.
7. What should be the role of the first-line supervisor in handling employees who break the rules?
8. Do you think the dual goals of maintaining consistent treatment of all employees and adjusting the penalty to fit the circumstances of the particular case are compatible? Discuss.
9. Why are penalties often of the progressive type?
10. What should be the rights of an employee who has been charged by a supervisor with a rules violation?
11. Do you think a company should adopt a uniform scale of penalties for all offenses? Should these be announced to the employees?
12. Under what circumstances should discharge be used as a penalty?

CASE PROBLEMS

PROBLEM 1

Frank is an operator in a textile mill. Recently his foreman told him that the company was starting a regular program of monitoring the static-eliminator bars mounted on all carding machines.[4] The operation was to be performed monthly and would require about eight hours time each month. The work involved an inspection and cleaning of the bars plus wiping of each bar with special paper that was then sent away to a laboratory for measurements of any radiation leaking from the unit.

Frank refused to do this new work. He stated that he had been hired as a

[4]A static-eliminator bar is an aluminum bar containing a strip of foil that is composed of a radioactive substance. The emission of certain rays from the foil prevents the fibers in the product from clogging the machine.

machine operator, not as a maintenance mechanic or radiation technician. He said that the maintenance mechanic job paid twenty cents more per hour and that such work was outside his job classification. Further, he had heard via the grapevine that it was hazardous to touch the static-eliminator bars.

His foreman told him that he must either perform the duties assigned to him or face immediate discharge. The work was not of a higher skill than his regular job, and it occurred only once per month. The foreman further explained that handling these bars was not hazardous, because they had been used in the mill for two years and no one had been injured from the radiation yet.

Frank still refused to do the work and said he was going to see his union steward. With that the exchange between the foreman and the worker terminated.

That afternoon the foreman went to see his superior, the superintendent, about the matter. The superintendent viewed it as a clear case of insubordination, for which immediate discharge was provided in the rules. He advised the foreman to send Frank to his office, at which time he, the superintendent, would give the man one last chance to comply or be discharged.

Questions

1. Do you think this case involves a straightforward issue of insubordination? Are there any other important issues involved?
2. Can a person ever justifiably refuse to carry out a direct order from a supervisor? Discuss.
3. How would you handle this case if you were the superintendent?
4. What course is open to an employee who feels his boss has given him an order that he cannot or should not carry out?

PROBLEM 2

The ZYZ Company employs a large force of draftspersons of various classifications. The draftspersons are represented by an independent draftsmen's union at this company. The job title of Detailer 3 is an entry classification ordinarily assigned to new, relatively inexperienced detail draftspersons. Normally at the end of one year a Detailer 3 is upgraded to Detailer 2 if work is satisfactory and if he or she demonstrates that he or she can do the slightly higher-level work of a Detailer 2.

On March 11, 1983, Mrs. Mary M., a Detailer 3 hired on January 8, 1982, submitted the following grievance to her superior:

> I request that my rating be changed from Detailer 3 to Detailer 2. I have been doing Detailer 2 work for about six months. I have always turned in jobs on time and in cases of rush work I have always had them in before they were promised. The designer that I work for and my drafting representative (union representative) both agree I am doing Detailer 2 work.

In discussing the grievance in the industrial relations office her supervisor made several assertions. He stated that he hired Mrs. Mary M. with the understanding that her job would involve a lot of short-promise work. A person doing such work must have a good attendance record. He said that she told him that her home problems would not interfere with her job.

The supervisor went on to say that he had spoken to her three times for talking too much and about her habitual tardiness. On February 25 he gave her a written warning notice because of excessive lateness, excessive absenteeism, and too much social conversation on the job.

The supervisor further stated that she was capable of doing Detailer 2 work. In fact, she has been doing some of it for the past six months. When she is on the job, the quality of her work is entirely satisfactory. The problem is that she is late and absent entirely too much. When she is here she talks too much with the other employees.

The absence record for Mrs. Mary M. is shown below:

5/7/82	½ day	Son sick
5/21/82	1 day	Out of town
6/14–15/82	2 days	Personal business
7/16/82	1 day	Illness in family
8/20/82	½ day	Alleged personal illness
8/30/82	½ day	Alleged personal illness
9/20/82	1 day	Personal illness
10/29/82	½ day	Car trouble
11/19/82	1 day	Car trouble
12/9–10/82	2 days	Illness in family
1/3/83	1 day	Personal business
2/18/83	1 day	Illness in family
2/24/83	1 day	Personal business

The supervisor said he would not promote a person with such a record.

Questions
1. Since Mrs. Mary M. has already demonstrated that she has done Detailer 2 work, do you think she should be upgraded?
2. If you were her supervisor, how would you handle this employee?
3. If one's actual work performance is of a higher grade level, does this justify a promotion regardless of excessive tardiness, absences, and talking on the job?
4. How appropriate is a denial of a promotion as a means of discipline?
5. If you were the manager in charge of the drafting department, how would you resolve this problem?
6. Is this primarily a discipline or a promotion case?

Suggestions for Further Reading

Baer, Walter E. *Discipline and Discharge Under the Labor Agreement.* New York: American Management Association, 1972.

Behohlav, James A., and Paul O. Popp. "Making Employee Discipline Work," *Personnel Administrator,* Vol. 23, (March 1978), pp. 22–24.

Harrison, Edward L. "Legal Restrictions on the Employer's Authority to Discipline," *Personnel Journal,* Vol. 61, No. 2 (February 1982), pp. 136–141.

Heshizer, Brian P., and Harry Graham. "Discipline in the Nonunion Company: Protecting Employer and Employee Rights," *Personnel,* Vol. 59, No. 2 (March–April 1982), pp. 71–78.

Malinowski, Arthur A. "An Empirical Analysis of Discharge Cases and the Work History of Employees Reinstated by Labor Arbitrators," *The Arbitration Journal,* Vol. 36, No. 1 (March 1981), pp. 31–46.

Redeker, James R. *Discipline: Policies and Procedures.* Washington, D.C.: Bureau of National Affairs, 1983.

Wheeler, Hoyt. "Punishment Theory and Industrial Discipline," *Industrial Relations,* Vol. 15, No. 2 (May 1976), pp. 235–243.

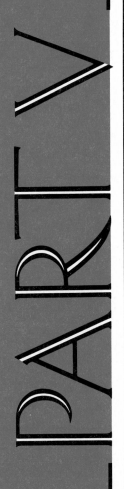

PART V

Labor–Management Relations

Unions and Management

Organized labor exerts a strong influence upon the individual organization and upon the economic, social, and political climate of the United States. When the employees of an establishment are represented by a union, policies and practices affecting the employment relationship that were formerly decided by management alone become subject to joint determination. Wages, hours, and other terms of employment are bargained jointly between union representatives and employer representatives. The decisions reached in contract negotiations on economic matters often impact upon the pricing of company products and services. This in turn may influence the competitive position of the firm in the market place. When management contemplates taking certain personnel actions, it must give consideration to the attitude and position of the union on such matters. Certain actions that had been conducted between managers and employees (as individuals) before the entrance of the union are now carried on through union officials and stewards. The attitudes of the union leaders and the members affect management programs of technological innovation, productivity improvement, job evaluation, and setting of work-load standards.

In the broader social, economic, and political sphere, we find that organized labor plays a significant role. Unions adopt positions on such public issues as unemployment, the state of the economy, inflation, tariffs, health care, the Social Security system, public housing, and minimum wage legislation. They try to influence the decisions of state legislatures and the United States Congress on a variety of legislative issues affecting not only union members but also working people generally and the public at large. Of course, corporations make their voices heard through membership in such organizations as the Business Roundtable and the National Association of Manufacturers. Economically the wage (including fringe benefits) settlements reached in major industries through collective bargaining often affect the volume of employment, the competitive position of the given industry, and the rate of introduction of technological improvements.

Because of the prominent role that unions play in many establishments and in our society as a whole, it is important to develop an adequate understanding of why employees join unions, why some people reject unionization, and attitudes of working people toward unions. We shall also trace the historical development of unions, examine union organization and functions, and note the character of the American labor movement. Finally we shall discuss the impact of a union upon management of an organization and note elements determinative of the climate between a union and management.

MOTIVATION TO JOIN UNIONS

Why do employees join a union? Since human behavior is goal-directed, what drives and wants can be fulfilled by membership in a union? Let us now examine the objectives that employees expect to satisfy through union membership.

Greater Bargaining Power

The individual worker possesses very little bargaining power in comparison with that of the employer. Very few employees are indispensable. A company can generally get along without a particular worker. The employer is in a position to say to the individual employee, "Take or leave the wage and conditions of work I offer you." A worker's bargaining strength lies in the ability to quit if dissatisfied with wage rate and other conditions of employment. However, the worker soon learns that it is inadvisable to continually resign from one job after another. This imposes a great financial and emotional burden. Therefore, employees have found that although their bargaining power as individuals is very limited, they can frequently equal that of the employer by organizing a union and taking concerted action. The threat or actuality of a strike by the union represents the economic and social power that often causes the company to increase its wages to a point where they are acceptable to the union.

The only situation in which an individual employee possesses considerable bargaining power occurs when the worker has a rare and valuable skill or talent. Thus, we find that in artistic and athletic professions, certain exceptionally gifted stars are able to bargain on equal terms with their employers. Likewise, certain executive and professional people in industry are able to command very high salaries because they possess an exceptional talent. But the vast majority of the wage and salary earners are in no such fortunate position. They are replaceable and must take pretty much what is offered them.

Make Their Voices Heard

The desire for self-expression is a fundamental human drive for most people. They wish to communicate their aims, feelings, complaints, and ideas to others. Most employees wish to be more than cogs in a large machine. They want management to listen to them. The union provides a mechanism through which these feelings and thoughts can be transmitted to management.

The entry of a union into an organization brings with it the establishment of a formalized grievance procedure. This provides a means by which employee complaints and problems are brought to the attention of management. The union stewards and officers represent the interests of the employees in presenting these problems to supervision and to higher management.

Minimize Favoritism and Discrimination

Supervisors must make a great many decisions that affect the pay, status, position, and work of their subordinates. Many of these decisions are highly subjective in nature. They are influenced by the personal relationships existing between the supervisor and each employee. Sometimes when one person is granted a larger wage increase than others, they feel that favoritism may have had a part in the decision. Unions press for equality of treatment. For example, one of their maxims is "One job, one rate." This means that all persons doing the same kind of work should receive the same wage rate. As an alternative to this, we may find that the union accepts the concept of a range of wages for each job, but that it insists that all in-grade wage increases be made strictly according to seniority. So it is with other personnel actions, such as promotions, transfers, layoffs, and vacation preference. Unions advocate that the major (but not necessarily the only) criterion for decision making be seniority.

Social Factors

People are commonly influenced in their actions by the behavior of their associates. Many employees are persuaded to join a union by their fellow workers. Often the individual is motivated to go along with the crowd—to be one of the gang. He seeks group acceptance and a feeling of belonging. Sometimes social motivation takes the form of group pressure. The individual who refuses to join the union often has a very difficult time at work. He may be ostracized, his machine may break down, or his lunch bucket may get "lost."

Cultural factors also play a part in the disposition of people to join a union. For those who have been raised in a working-class neighborhood where one's father and indeed all of the workers in the community belong to the union, acceptance of the union as a normal part of the employment situation seems natural. This condition in which union membership is simply accepted as a way of life is true in certain areas and certain industries in the United States (for example, in coal mining areas and in the garment industry in New York City). However, this condition represents a minority of the situations when one looks at the union movement in general.

Outlet When Advancement Blocked

Many employees will have nothing to do with a union as long as they are doing well in their careers. If their expectations in terms of pay increases, better jobs as they gain more experience, promotions, and greater status do actually materialize, then they may feel that there is no necessity to pay dues to a union. They may even feel that the union would impede their progress because of seniority rules and because the individual member cannot get ahead faster than the entire group. However, we often find that when a person senses that progress up the organizational ladder is blocked, when he or she can no longer get ahead on personal initiative, then he or she experiences a period of readjustment. Initially he or she may be frustrated. But often the union becomes as an outlet. Through collective action the union may obtain the economic benefits from the employer that the individual could not get on his own. If the person has aspirations for a position of responsibility and leadership, he or she may even achieve an elective union office.

Compulsion Via the Union Contract

Many agreements that are negotiated between employers and unions contain a "union shop" provision (or some variation of it) that requires that all employees must join the union and pay dues within a certain period of time after they have been hired. If they refuse to join they may be discharged. A "union shop" clause in a labor agreement is one form of union security. Other aspects of the union security issue will be discussed in Chapter 20.

MOTIVATION TO REJECT UNIONS

Since only one fourth of the labor force in the United States belongs to unions, it must be apparent that many workers either definitely oppose the prospect of unionization for themselves or at least are reluctant to join. What influences operate to cause employees to reject the union?

Cultural Factors

Many people in American society distrust unions and what they stand for. They feel that unions stand for collectivism, socialism, and the welfare state. They feel that unions stand in opposition to the traditional American concepts of free enterprise, individual freedom, and individual initiative. They feel that a person should stand on his or her own two feet and get ahead on his or her own merits. They read in the newspapers that a powerful union has shut down an essential service or industry and that the public must suffer. They resent the union, its method of action, and what it stands for. Sentiments such as the foregoing are much more common in certain segments of our society than others. Geographically, they are common in the South, in rural areas, and in small towns. Small businesspersons and farmers often hold such views. Likewise many in white-collar, professional, and executive occupations believe this.

Professionalism and Individualism

Professional employees in the private sector (such as engineers and accountants) and self-employed professionals (such as physicians) have tended not to form or join unions. Instead they have sought to advance the interests of themselves and their professions through mem-bership in professional associations. Many professionals argue that unionization and collective bargaining are appropriate for hourly paid, blue-collar workers, but that professionals have higher status and higher education and do not need (or should not need) unions to promote their interests. Also many professionals are individualistic in orientation. They feel that their employers will recognize them for their performance on the job. They feel they can bargain for themselves.

The professional associations that have been most effective in promoting the interests of their members are those that are composed of self-employed professionals such as the American Medical Association and the American Bar Association. These associations work to control entrance to the profession by rigorous educational qualifications, examinations, and state licensing. These devices keep the profession from being overcrowded and thus keep incomes high.

Certain kinds of professionals have embraced unionism and collective bargaining rather strongly in recent years. Principal among these have been public school teachers and nurses. Employed in large numbers in organizations, treated more as workers than professionals, and paid more modestly than other professionals, teachers and nurses have sought protection through union participation.

Identification with Management

White-collar, technical, and professional employees tend to identify themselves with management. Since they work in close proximity to supervisors and executives, there is a tendency to acquire the management viewpoint toward unions. These groups also feel that they can advance into management. They are looking upward. They wish to impress favorably their immediate superiors in the organization. They often feel that membership in a union might hinder their chances of promotion.

Job Satisfaction

Some people are fortunate to work for employers that provide good wages, ample employee benefits, and safe and healthful working conditions. They have supportive supervisors, and an opportunity to express their ideas and to be heard by management. They have job security. Such employees may feel no need for union protection.

Fear of Reprisal

Many employees do not join unions because they fear that management will punish them if they do so. Although the right of employees to form and join unions, free of interference by employers, has been protected by the National Labor Relations Act since 1935, the power of management in the workplace is great and pervasive. Management can discriminate in many subtle ways against prounion sympathizers in a workforce. Overt discrimination, such as a discharge or a demotion, can be appealed to the National Labor Relations Board. However, adjudication typically takes months and sometimes even years.

ATTITUDES OF WORKING PEOPLE TOWARD UNIONS

Research sheds considerable light upon the attitudes of American working people toward unionism in general, their own unions (if union members), and toward their own propensity to join a union. The 1977 Quality of Employment Survey, conducted for the U.S. Department of Labor by the Survey Research Center of the University of Michigan, offers useful insights in these regards.[1]

[1]Thomas A. Kochan, "How American Workers View Labor Unions," *Monthly Labor Review,* Vol. 102, No. 4 (April 1979), pp. 23–31.

The survey reveals that working men and women believe that unions possess considerable power. They influence who gets elected and laws that are passed. They have a real impact upon how the country is run. In workers' minds, unions got high marks for effectiveness. Of those surveyed 63 per cent agreed and 21 per cent strongly agreed that unions protect workers against unfair practices. Also 61 per cent agreed and 19 per cent strongly agreed that unions improve job security. Ratings of unions' ability to improve wages were even higher.

What factors determine whether employees would vote for union representation in their workplaces? The University of Michigan research and other investigations reveal that dissatisfactions with traditional economic issues of wages, fringe benefits, and working conditions are primarily what propel people toward unionization. Furthermore their discontent with these bread-and-butter matters must be very strong before they will take the big step of voting for a union. Whereas great dissatisfaction with wages and working conditions is the principal motivating factor for both blue- and white-collar workers to vote for union representation, white-collar people are also prone to turn to unionization in order to improve job content, scope, and organization and to exert influence in decision-making processes. In summary, Kochan says that unions are seen by a large number of workers as a strategy of last resort rather than as a natural or preferred method of improving job conditions.[2]

What do those who already belong to a union think of unions? When asked how well their unions were performing in the areas of most concern to union members, the University of Michigan study showed that unions were rated to be quite effective in the areas of wages, fringe benefits, job security, safety, handling grievances, and feedback from the union. Unions were rated rather low in helping mem-

[2]Ibid., p. 30.

bers obtain say-so on the job and in obtaining interesting jobs. See Table 19-1.

DEVELOPMENT OF UNIONS

Unions in America first appeared on the scene during the 1790s and early 1800s. They were composed of skilled craftsmen such as shoemakers, tailors, carpenters, and printers. They were formed initially as protective organizations to resist wage cuts and maintain acceptable conditions of employment. The rise of merchant capitalists as employers tended to accentuate the separate interests of employers and employees in the wage bargain. Price competition in the product market caused employers to reduce wages or at least resist wage increases. In seeking to protect and improve their lot, unions of craftsmen posted their prices (wage scales) and refused to work for less. They also resisted any influx of lesser trained workers who would undercut their wage scale.

Throughout most of the nineteenth century, unions were small and rather weak. The American Federation of Labor, officially organized in 1886 as a confederation of autonomous craft unions, proved to be an enduring and successful organization. However, its growth and impact during the closing years of the nineteenth century were rather limited. In 1890, total union membership in the United States was less than 400,000.

During the World War I period when employment levels were high, union membership increased significantly. By 1920 membership of all unions totaled slightly over 5 million. But from then until the depth of the Great Depression in 1933, the union movement lost membership. During the prosperous 1920s when conditions would ordinarily have been favorable for union growth, employer organizations launched a massive offensive against unions. This took the form of "open shop" drives, antiu-

TABLE 19-1. Evaluation of Union Performance.[1]

Issues	Not Good at All	Not Too Good	Somewhat Good	Very Good	Mean
Wages	4.7%	19.8%	42.5%	32.9%	3.04
Fringes	7.7	21.8	41.9	28.6	2.91
Job security	7.6	18.0	50.8	23.6	2.90
Safety/health	6.5	21.5	50.7	21.3	2.87
Say on job	15.2	34.3	41.9	8.6	2.44
Interesting job	22.5	43.1	29.5	4.9	2.17
Say in union	16.2	27.9	37.3	18.7	2.58
Say in business	25.8	37.7	30.1	6.3	2.16
Feedback from union	10.5	23.3	36.5	29.6	2.85
Handling grievances	8.7	15.7	40.9	4.7	3.02

Source: Thomas A. Kochan, "How American Workers View Labor Unions," *Monthly Labor Review,* Vol. 102, No. 4 (April 1979), p. 30.

[1]Union members were asked how good a job their unions were doing in addressing various issues. Ratings were valued on a 4-point scale with "not good at all" worth 1 point and "very good" worth 4. The "mean" is the average value of the responses.

nion publicity, resistance to unionization at the plant gate, and management-dominated plant unions called employee representation plans. Of course, mass layoffs and plant closings caused by the economic depression of the early 1930s caused people to lose the ability to pay dues to maintain their union memberships.

Rapid Growth—1935 Through Early 1950s

The most spectacular rate of union growth occurred during the period from the mid-1930s through the early 1950s. In 1935 total membership in the United States was 3,584,000. By 1953 it had grown to 16,948,000. This growth had a number of causes. Foremost among these was the enactment of the National Labor Relations Act in 1935 (often called the Wagner Act). This law granted workers the right to form unions of their own choosing without fear of management interference or coercion. Outlawed were blacklists, company-dominated unions, and discharges for worker participation in union activities. The act provided a peaceful and democratic means for employees to decide whether they wanted to be represented by a union or not. This mechanism was an election conducted by the National Labor Relations Board.

Another important cause for this rapid expansion of the organized labor movement was the formation of the Congress of Industrial Organizations in 1935–1936. Led by colorful and able men, such as John L. Lewis as its first president, the CIO and its constituent national unions scored spectacular successes in organizing the mass-production industries of the country such as automobile, steel, rubber, electrical, and aircraft.

Still another factor contributing to rapid union growth during this period was the high level of employment and economic prosperity during World War II and generally in the years thereafter.

Steady State in Private Sector Since Early 1950s

Although the total number of union members has increased by several million since the 1950s, the total labor force in the United States has also grown. When expressed as a percentage of the labor force, aggregate union membership has stablized in the 20–24 per cent range in the years since the mid-1950s.

A multiplicity of forces account for this stagnation in union growth. Much of the numerical strength of unions has been in manufacturing industries. Many firms in these industries have migrated from the union strongholds of the Northeast and Great Lakes areas to the Sunbelt states where antiunion sentiment is strong.

Employment in white-collar and professional occupations has increased dramatically over the past 30 years. People in these occupations have been reluctant to join unions. Employment in blue-collar occupations, where support for unionization has traditionally been strong, has increased only slowly.

Small companies of under 200 employees, in both manufacturing and service industries, have accounted for much of the growth in employment in recent years. It is very costly for unions to organize the employees and to administer contracts in these thousands of small establishments.

There has been a gradual improvement in personnel management practices throughout American business. As wages, benefit programs, working conditions, and general treatment of employees have advanced, even though slowly, employees have had less incentive to turn to unions for support.

Antiunion Pressures. Faced with a union-organizing campaign, management ordinarily opposes the unionization effort without question. Business executives believe that the collective-bargaining process restricts their power to run their firms as they see fit. Also wage costs could rise. Corporate managers have acquired considerable sophistication in the methods they use to oppose a union-organizing drive.

Since the mid-1970s there has been a thriving business in offering antiunion training seminars throughout the country. Management consultants, trade associations, and even a few universities have learned that there is a large market for such programs. These seminars are promoted with such titles as "How to Maintain Nonunion Status", "De-unionizing", "The Process of Decertification", and "Managing Without Unions."

Growth in Public Sector

Whereas union membership, expressed as a percentage of the total labor force, has not grown in the private sector, there was a very rapid expansion of unions and collective bargaining in the public sector commencing in the mid-1960s. This growth has occurred at the Federal, state, and local government levels.

In the 1960s certain employee associations, previously confined in their economic activities to lobbying and informal negotiations with units of government, shifted into full-scale collective bargaining. Among these are the National Education Association (teachers) and the New York State Civil Service Employees Association. In 1956 union membership in Federal, state, and local governments totaled 915,000. By 1978 unions and employee associations that bargained with all units of government had a total membership of 6,094,000.[3] The U.S. Census Bureau reported that in 1980 about one half of the nation's 10.3 million full-time state and local government employees belonged to unions. As of the early 1980s about 60 per cent of all civilian employees in the Federal government (excluding the Postal Service) were represented by unions.

[3]*Directory of National Unions and Employee Associations,* 1979, Bulletin 2079 (Washington, D.C.: Bureau of Labor Statistics, U.S. Department of Labor, 1980), Table 16.

About 80 per cent of Postal Service personnel were union-represented.

A major stimulus to growth of collective bargaining in the public sector was the issuance by President John F. Kennedy in 1962 of Executive Order 10988, entitled "Employee Management Cooperation in the Federal Service." This order required Federal Agencies to recognize, as exclusive bargaining agents, unions that represented a majority of the employees as determined by a vote of those in the bargaining unit. The Federal action encouraged many states to adopt laws that granted state, municipal, and public school employees the right to form unions, to have these recognized as bargaining agents, to negotiate contracts, and to process grievances. As of 1980 31 states had enacted laws providing for union recognition and bargaining for public employees. At the Federal level the Civil Service Reform Act of 1978 provides continuing support for collective bargaining in the government.

Professionals

Concurrent with the growth of unionization in public employment has been the increase in collective bargaining by professionals. A substantial portion of public school teachers throughout the country are represented by either the American Federation of Teachers or the National Education Association. College professors are organized for the purposes of collective bargaining at several hundred colleges and universities. The American Nurses Association represents nurses at hundreds of hospitals and health care agencies throughout the nation.

Professional athletes in baseball, football, basketball, and hockey are represented by unions that negotiate contracts with the owners' associations in their respective leagues.

Despite the trend toward collective bargaining by certain professionals, engineers, which constitute the largest professional occupation in private industry, have shown little inclination to form unions. A major reason for this is that engineers tend to identify with management. Many engineers hope to be promoted into management positions.

Commentary on Union Viability

The lesson of history tells us that unions in the United States thrive and grow only when supported positively by legislation or other governmental encouragement. The unionization of the mass production industries in the late 1930s and early 1940s was dependent, in large part, upon the material support given to collective bargaining by the Wagner Act. Certain AFL trade unions were able to demonstrate modest success prior to the passage of this law primarily because they represented craftspersons—notably in the building and printing trades and on the railroads—who occupied strategic positions in their industries. They established a system of job control through union agreements that made their positions reasonably strong. But the laissez-faire economic and legal environment that predominated prior to the 1930s constituted a hostile climate for the collective-bargaining aspirations of the masses of blue- and white-collar workers. In those days the employer could discharge union-minded workers with impunity. The courts of that day viewed the business and property rights of employers much more sympathetically than the job rights of workers.

Although few still claim that the Taft-Hartley Act was the principal cause for the decline in the rate of union growth that set in about 1947, it is clear that the many restrictions upon union power contained in the act have served to dampen the union advance to some extent.

Evidence in the field of public employment in the 1960s revealed that government employees have had a powerful desire to participate in decision making with respect to the terms and conditions of their employment. Following closely upon the issuance of Kennedy's Executive Order 10988 and the passage of favorable legislation in many states, they joined up by the hundreds of thousands. Without the pent-up demand, this would not have occurred. Likewise, without the sympathetic executive and legislative support, this could not have occurred. The governmental support for unionization in the mid-1930s and again in the mid-1960s (for the public sector) was initiated to meet a pressing and widespread problem.

Distribution of Union and Association Membership

More than 75 per cent of the labor force in the following industries belongs to unions: transportation, construction, and mining. Among the industries in which 50 to 74 per cent of the work force is unionized are transportation equipment, primary metals, apparel, Federal government, and paper. At the other end of the scale, we find that the following industries have a low percentage of unionized employees: chemicals, services, finance, agriculture and fishing, and trade.[4]

Figure 19-1 is a map of the Unites States which shows the percentage of employees in nonagricultural establishments who belong to unions and associations (engaged in collective bargaining) in each of the states. Inspection reveals that New York, West Virginia, and Michigan have the highest percentage of union members whereas South Carolina, North Carolina, and Florida have the lowest percentage.

UNION ORGANIZATION AND FUNCTIONS

There are about 174 national and international unions in this country (many unions call themselves "international" because they have mem-

[4]*Directory of Unions*, ibid., p. 66.

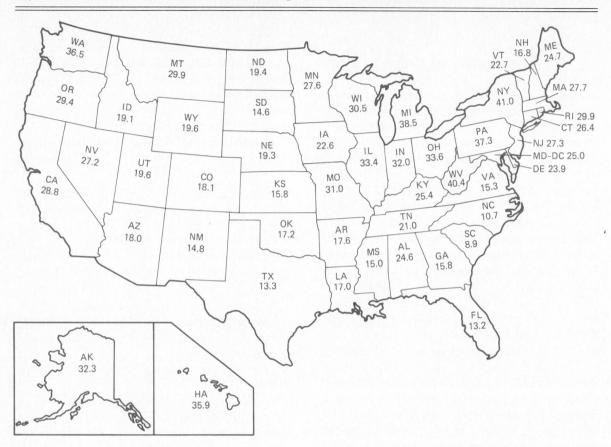

bers in Canada as well as the United States). Examples of such unions are the Automobile, Aerospace, and Agricultural Implement Workers of America, the International Association of Machinists, the United Steelworkers of America, and the International Ladies' Garment Workers Union. Each of these types of unions is composed of a national headquarters organization, intermediate bodies primarily set up for administrative purposes, and many local unions. Commonly in manufacturing, for example, each organized plant or establishment will have its own separate local union. There are about 64,000 local unions in the United States.

A simplified schematic organization chart of a union would look as shown in Figure 19-2.

Uniting the majority of national and international unions is the AFL-CIO, which was formed in 1955 through a merger of the American Federation of Labor and the Congress of Industrial Organizations. About 108 national and international unions belong to this loosely knit federation.

FIGURE 19-2 Schematic
Organization Chart of a
Union.

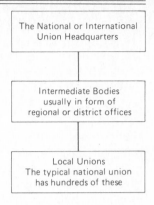

The National or International
Union Headquarters

Intermediate Bodies
usually in form of
regional or district offices

Local Unions
The typical national union
has hundreds of these

The Local Union

The local union is the basic, and a very important, unit of organization of a union. If it is a craft union, such as the carpenters', then a local may consist of all unionized carpenters in a particular town or city even though they may work for different employers; if it is an industrial union, then the local may consist of all union members in a particular factory.

Local unions are generally operated in a democratic fashion, with officers elected usually for a term of one year by the dues-paying members. Each member has one vote, and election rules ordinarily require advance notice of impending elections, open nominations, and secret ballots. The elected officials usually consist of a president, secretary-treasurer, and an executive board. Some unions also have a business agent, trustees, a negotiating committee, and a grievance committee. Every local union also has a number of shop stewards who are elected by the employees in each department of the company.

The president of a local is most commonly a worker who has been elected by the membership to be its principal leader but who devotes only part of his work time to his union duties. It is only very large locals (consisting of several thousand members) that can afford to have a full-time, salaried president. In most instances the president has a regular job, is paid a wage by the employer, and attends to his union responsibilities during the work day (for which the company grants him time off) and on his own time such as evenings and on weekends. Many unions pay these part-time union presidents a few hundred dollars a year in salary plus their necessary expenses for attending international union conventions and for other items. The local president is sometimes the chief union spokesman in contract negotiations with company representatives. He becomes involved in major union grievances, leads the members in time of a strike, and in general tries to create and maintain teamwork and solidarity among the group. His job has many political overtones to it. He often is placed in the position where he must "deliver the goods" in dealings with the company or risk being defeated for re-election. The political nature of his job is emphasized when the union is divided into factional groups.

Certain unions, especially those in the construction, clothing, and metalworking industries, have a business agent. He is a full-time, salaried union official who is usually elected by the membership. He exercises a great deal of power and in many instances overshadows the local president in authority, influence, and prestige. His duties and responsibilities are manifold. He plays a key role in contract negotiations with the employer, is alert to see that the employer and his management representatives abide by the contract, helps settle grievances, and leads the union members when there is a strike. In addition, he may also have to administer the operation of the local's headquarters, direct clerical help, handle union publicity, and make arrangements for business meetings.

A shop steward is another important person in a local union organization. Although the term *steward* is the one most commonly used, in some unions he is called a departmental representative, a committeeman, or a grievance person. The shop steward appears at the same level in the union organization structure as does a foreman in the company structure. However, he does not have the authority over the workers that a foreman has. He is usually elected for a term of one year to represent the employees in that department in the processing of their grievances to management. He represents the interests of the employees and goes to bat for them when he feels they have a justifiable grievance. He is on guard to insure that supervision lives up to the letter and spirit of the labor-management agreement. If there is no "union shop" provision in the labor agreement which requires employees to join the union, then he takes steps to increase the membership by persuading people to join. If there is no payroll checkoff of union dues, then he must also collect dues from the members.

The locals are the heart of any union. Although there is a trend in the direction of more and more contract negotiations being conducted at the national level of the union, with multiemployer bargaining becoming more prevalent, it can be said accurately that the majority of all negotiations are still conducted at the local level. Even in those situations where the top management of a multiplant company bargains a labor–management agreement with national union officials, it is common practice for each local to bargain a supplementary agreement with local plant management over local issues, such as work standards, time study, rest periods, seniority rules, and so on. In addition to carrying on contract negotiations, other functions of the local are to obtain new members, handle grievances, administer the agreement with management, and conduct strikes when other choices fail to resolve disagreements.

Intermediate Organizational Units

For purposes of coordinating the activities of a number of local unions in a given area and to act as an intermediate unit of union govern-ment, most national unions have established intermediate organizational bodies. Usually these are set up on a geographical basis. In garment-worker unions all of the locals in a city in several crafts will be grouped together in a joint board. Ordinarily the joint board will have an office or building of its own that will serve as headquarters for all of the locals in that joint board. The chairperson of the joint board will assist the business agents in contract negotiations, and in many instances he or she will actually conduct them. Other unions, such as the United Automobile Workers, are divided into regions, with each one being supervised by a director. The United Mine Workers and the United Steel Workers call their regions districts. In the railroad industry all of the locals of a single railroad company are grouped into a system federation.

National and International Unions

The top organizational entity of a union is called the national or international (if it contains branches and locals in Canada). For brevity the term *national* will be used here. A great deal of power, authority, and responsibility resides in the national. Let us look at the functions performed by the national.

First of all the national officers establish basic policies. For basic guidance in setting policy, the officers are bound by the constitution of the union. The national frequently sets the wage policy that locals must seek to accomplish. Uniformity of practice among all of the organized enterprises in a given area or industry not only on wage matters but also on seniority rules, group insurance practices, and others, is often a union goal. The national union provides a host of services to the locals. It may send out specialists to help the locals negotiate their contracts with management. It provides data to the locals on such matters as cost of living, comparable wages, and details of the contract settlements in other companies. Because the turnover of local union officers is rather high, many nationals find that they must continually train key personnel of the locals in such subjects as parliamentary procedure, grievance handling, labor law, and the administration of a local. National unions also build up strike funds in their treasuries with which to pay benefits to members when on strike and to take care of the many extra costs required during a strike.

Most nationals are continuously involved in efforts to expand their unions. This means that they are attempting to organize the unorganized or nonunion employees of certain industries. It also means that they may try to persuade the workers in a company who already belong to another union to give up their allegiance and switch membership to their own union. This activity, called "raiding," is forbidden among unions belonging to the AFL-CIO. However, an AFL-CIO union may raid a nonaffiliated union or vice versa.

Elected officials of the national consist of a president, secretary-treasurer, and several vice-presidents, who usually represent regions and who constitute the executive board. This executive board is theoretically the top policy-making body in the interval between conventions.

In addition to the elective positions, there exists at the national level a considerable number of appointed staff specialists. These include lawyers, economists, statisticians, and public relations personnel. Most unions have a research director, who, along with his or her staff, is responsible for collecting, analyzing, and disseminating economic and other information that can be of great value to the union and its locals in collective bargaining. Another key appointive position is that of educational director. His or her job is to set up training programs for local union officers and stewards so that they can conduct the affairs of the union more effectively.

International representatives or field representatives are a key group of appointive personnel. Their main responsibility is to aid the local unions both at contract negotiation time and in the day-to-day administration of the union. It is not uncommon to find the international representative acting in the role of chief union spokesman during contract bargaining. He may also have to show local officials how to set up and keep financial records, educate them as to their rights and responsibilities under the law, and perform a multitude of other services. Another prime duty of an international representative is to organize unorganized plants and establishments in his or her assigned jurisdiction.

THE AFL-CIO

AFL-CIO is the American Federation of Labor-Congress of Industrial Organizations. It is really a confederation of semiautonomous labor unions that was formed in 1955 by the merger of the American Federation of Labor and the Congress of Industrial Organizations.

The activities of the AFL-CIO are manifold. Two of its principal functions are the organization of unorganized employees and the securing of federal, state, and local legislation that is favorable to the organized labor movement and, more generally, of benefit to working men and women throughout the country. It carries on an active research program and publishes a great volume of information in the fields of economics, employment, collective bargaining, labor statistics, labor law, and so on. Through its many publications, the AFL-CIO seeks to get its message to the general public, its own union constituents, and to such special interest groups as businesspersons, farmers, consumers, and elected government leaders. The AFL-CIO has many special staff groups and committees that function in such fields as civil rights, international affairs, economic policy, safety and health, education, and social security. The Federation has, as another of its important functions, the settling of jurisdictional disputes between its member unions. Its constitution contains a "code of ethical practices" that outlaws any corruption, racketeering, communism, or fascism in member unions. It is up to the Executive Council and the president to implement this code.

Organization Structure of AFL-CIO

Figure 19-3 shows the organization structure of the AFL-CIO. It should be emphasized that this is a loose federation of independent national

FIGURE 19-3 Structure of the AFL-CIO. *From:* **Directory of National Unions and Employee Associations, 1979,** *Bulletin 2079, U.S. Department of Labor, Bureau of Labor Statistics, Washington, D.C.: 1980.*

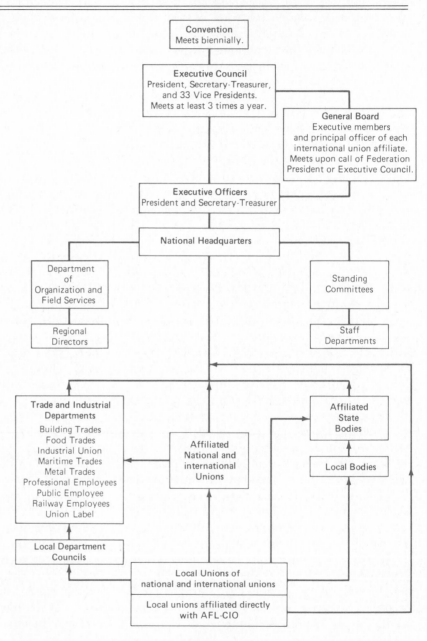

and international unions. The president of the AFL-CIO does not have the power to compel a member union to follow directives. Most of the leadership of the president and the Executive Council is exercised through persuasion, influence, and appeals to the good sense of leaders of member unions. Appeals to public opinion also play a part. The only really significant sanction that can be applied is that of suspension or expulsion from membership in the organization. This action must be approved by the Convention.

The Convention is the legislative body of the organization. It meets once every two years. The delegates are composed primarily of officials of affiliated unions. The number of persons that each union is allowed to send is determined by its total membership.

The president supervises the affairs of the organization, appoints study committees that make recommendations to the Convention, presides at conventions, calls meetings of the Executive Council, appoints staff department heads and union organizers, and serves as the official spokesperson for organized labor in the United States.

The Executive Council serves as a policy-making group. It roughly corresponds to the board of directors in a corporation. It is composed of the president, secretary-treasurer, and thirty-three vice-presidents (who in turn are presidents of their own national unions). It has the authority to direct the activities of the Federation and to make such decisions as are necessary to promote the best interests of the AFL-CIO. It keeps informed of legislative affairs affecting the labor force, makes rules that are consistent with its constitution, and can conduct investigations into the affairs of member unions that it suspects are under corrupt or totalitarian influences. The Council also has the responsibility to oversee the extension of union organization and to charter new national unions.

The "Trade and Industrial Departments" of the AFL-CIO (Building Trades, Food Trades, Industrial Union, Maritime Trades, Metal Trades, Professional Employees, Public Employees, Railway Employees, and Union Label) are composed of the member national unions that operate in these particular industries. The purpose of these departments is to help coordinate collective-bargaining activities among member unions and to settle jurisdictional work disputes. The Union Label Department promotes the sale of union-made goods by having unionized manufacturers attach "union-made" labels on items such as clothing, magazines, and books.

INDEPENDENT UNIONS

Of the 174 national unions in this country, 108 are affiliated with the AFL-CIO and 66 are unaffiliated. The two largest unions in the country—the Teamsters and the Automobile Workers—are outside the orbit of the AFL-CIO. The Teamsters Union was expelled from the AFL-CIO around 1960. The United Automobile Workers Union voluntarily disaffiliated in 1969 because of policy clashes between Walter Reuther, President of the UAW, and George Meany, President of the AFL-CIO. Other large independent unions are the International Longshoremen's and Warehousemen's Union and the United Mine Workers Union.

UNION OBJECTIVES AND BEHAVIOR

Unions basically seek to advance the interests of their members. In this sense they are no different from any other voluntary organization, such as the United States Chamber of Commerce, the Farm Bureau, or the American Legion. Unions work to achieve a better life for their membership. This means an ever-increasing standard of living, more leisure time, and financial protection against many of the risks of life—namely unemployment, injury on the job, sickness, and insufficient income in old age. Another, and a more specific, set of union goals consists of job security, job rights, and opportunity for advancement. Practically all unions have the foregoing as their goals. In addition to these, some segments of the labor movement have broader social goals. They advocate government legislation to affect improvements in educational opportunities, obtain better housing, and insure equal opportunities in employment, education, and housing regardless of race, color, or national origin. They are continually pushing for improvements in protective labor laws. Many have sought some form of federal government participation in health and medical insurance.

There exist two principal means by which unions seek to fulfill their goals. First and foremost is collective bargaining. This involves the union serving as a representative of the employees in the negotiating of a formal written agreement with management, which in turn represents the employer. Collective bargaining also includes within its compass the day-to-day administration of the agreement, the enforcement of the agreement, and the resort to collective action (such as a strike and picketing). The second principal way in which unions advance their aims is through efforts to influence government legislation. These take the form of grassroots campaigns to elect the friends of labor to political office, lobbying, and the dissemination of mass information to mold public opinion.

We have talked so far about the objectives of unionism to advance the economic and social position of its constituents. This is its principal goal. But in addition, most unions have social and fraternal goals. They provide a feeling of belonging for the members. This gives members a sense of identification and purpose. Union meetings, picnics, banquets, and the feeling of solidarity evidenced on a picket line emphasize the social and fraternal aspects of unionism. For some persons, unionism is almost a way of life in the same sense that top executives in industry tend to integrate their lives wholly with the corporation. To be sure, this way-of-life attitude holds true for only a small proportion of union members—most of these are officials and stewards.

CHARACTER OF AMERICAN LABOR MOVEMENT

Unions in America are pragmatic in their orientation and actions. They seek improvements in wages and working conditions for their members through collective bargaining with employers. They concentrate upon the bread-and-butter issues that their members want. Labor scholars characterize American unionism as "business unionism." This is in contrast to other possible orientations, such as reform, socialistic, radical, or political unionism.

The behavior of American unions contrasts with that of unions in Western Europe. European unions are socialistic in their orientations. They play a strong role in political parties. For example, there is the Labour Party in Great Britain. They advocate reform of the political and economic systems in their respective countries.

In the United States the AFL–CIO leadership and the leadership of most national and international unions have rather consistently supported the broad outlines of the capitalistic system. They seek more benefits for their members but they work for these gains within the framework of a free enterprise economy. Although union leadership upholds capitalism, it is indeed ironic that a great many corporate executives have never really accepted unionism and collective bargaining. Their actions reveal a deep-seated animus toward organized labor.

The American labor movement is a strong supporter of political democracy. George

Meany, President of the AFL–CIO from 1955 to 1979, often extolled the virtues of democracy in the U.S.A. and roundly condemned totalitarian Communism abroad. When dictators (either of the "Left" or the "Right") take control of a country, they either destroy pre-existing unions or else make them puppets of the government.

Although there is no labor party in the United States and there is unlikely to be one, union leaders have, for a great many years, supported candidates for public office who are generally sympathetic to the aims of labor and they have opposed those who are hostile to union programs. Commencing with the New Deal of Franklin D. Roosevelt in the 1930s the majority of unions (but by no means all) have endorsed Democratic Party candidates for state and Federal offices.

There have been periods in history when a few unions did embrace an anticapitalist and a prosocialist or pro-Communist political ideology. This occurred mainly during the periods 1900 to 1920 and the mid-1930s to late 1940s. These were periods of economic hardship and social upheaval as American workers were struggling to improve their lot and unions were seeking recognition from employers for purposes of collective bargaining. But such radical forces in the American labor movement lacked staying power and real support from rank-and-file working people.

A principal reason explaining the character of the American labor movement—pragmatic and supportive of the American political and economic system—is that the standard of living has risen rather steadily throughout the history of the country (with the exception of the Great Depression of the 1930s). Workers have experienced real progress in bettering their wages and living conditions. A great many workers have moved up the socioeconomic scale into the middle class. Additionally working people have always enjoyed the rights of political democracy such as voting, supporting candidates, free speech, tax-supported public education, and an independent judiciary system. The United States does not contain the strong class-consciousness so common in other parts of the world.

IMPACT OF THE UNION UPON MANAGEMENT

After a union has won bargaining rights for the employees in an organization, management finds that the way it handles employment relationships and its manner of dealing with employees is considerably altered. Let us now examine the effects of the union upon the management of people in the company.

Restriction upon Management's Freedom of Action

Unilateral action and individual dealings with workers over wage adjustments, hours, and the conditions of work are no longer possible. The first-line supervisor must be sure he does not violate the labor agreement in handling his employees. He is continuously aware of the presence of a shop steward who will go to bat for the workers in presenting their complaints and grievances. Basically the greatest change that occurs with the advent of the union on the scene is the restriction upon management's freedom of action. Its flexibility becomes limited. Management is closely bound by the conditions set forth in the union–employer agreement. At times, this loss of managerial freedom to act may impair plant efficiency. It may not be able to shift workers from one job to another as easily as before. If a person is asked to perform certain tasks that are of a higher skill than he or she has been accustomed to previously, both he or she and the union will usually demand a higher job classification. If sales decline and management finds it necessary to reduce the size of the work-force, it cannot lay off the least competent employees. Instead it must lay off those having the least seniority. If management wishes to install a profit-sharing or pension plan, it cannot do so without consulting the union and obtaining its consent. Thus we see that management has considerably less freedom to operate the business as it sees fit than before the union entered the picture.

Union Pressure for Uniformity of Treatment

Another effect of the union upon management is its insistence upon uniformity of treatment of all employees. For example, unions usually advocate that all employees who are assigned to the same job should receive exactly the same rate of pay or at least that in-grade increases in pay be based solely upon seniority. Management officials often claim that unions introduce a leveling effect upon the employees, so that individual initiative is discouraged. The psychology of individual differences tells us that among people there is a great variation in aptitudes and skills. To be sure, those on the payroll of a given company will have a much smaller range of abilities than the general population, because the employee selection process has eliminated those of inferior abilities. One of the principal reasons unions press for uniformity of treatment of all employees and for the rule of seniority to be applied to most job changes is that they do not want to introduce cliques and factionalism among the union membership. Because everyone pays the same dues, he or she is entitled to the same benefits.

Improved Personnel Policies and Practices

On the other hand, it is fair to state that the presence of the union encourages management to become fully conscious of employee wants and needs. Any omissions or faults in a company's labor policy and its manner of carrying out the policy will tend to be quickly noted by the local union officials. Thus, we find that many organizations have found it advantageous to institute supervisory- and executive-training programs that contain a strong emphasis upon sound personnel policies, labor relations, and human relations. Good leadership on the job tends to reduce the number and severity of problems about which the employees and union stewards may submit grievances. In fact, some companies have deliberately gone "all out" to provide for their employees' needs and wants, to exercise good leadership, to foster social groupings around company-sponsored recreational activities, and to maintain high morale. This is intended to blunt the union's "sword," so that the employees will feel little need for the union. Local union leadership may thereby be rendered impotent, because the employees are content and the company takes care of them.

One Spokesman for the Employees

In a sense the presence of the union simplifies management's problems in dealing with employees because it can look to the elected union leaders as spokespersons for the employees. How will the workers react to rotating instead of fixed shifts when the plant must operate around the clock? When business is slack, would the workers prefer a reduced work week (work sharing) to layoffs for a certain percentage of the work force? For these and other employee relations questions the local union leaders are generally in a good position to feel the pulse of the work force and fairly represent their attitudes to management. In those relationships that have developed to a stage of mutual respect and maturity, management often finds that it has much to gain by engaging in joint consultation with union officers on such subjects as working conditions, plant safety, suggestion system operation, and similar topics. Such action need not infringe upon management prerogatives, and many actually result in improved plant efficiency.

Centralization of Labor Relations' Decision Making

Because of the critical importance of many labor relations decisions, top executives have a tendency to take authority in labor matters away from lower ranks of supervision and centralize this in the industrial relations department. This is quite noticeable in grievance handling. Although in theory the first-level supervisor occupies the first step in the grievance procedure in all organizations, in actual practice he or she is often required to go to the industrial relations manager before he or she can give a definite answer. He or she then becomes a messenger. The power to discipline is sometimes taken away from the supervisor when there is a union. The reason for this state of affairs is that a union often does not accept the word of lower management if a decision does not meet with its approval. It goes directly to the top of the organization in many cases.

In the long run a company will develop better labor-management relations and better day-to-day leadership on the job by thoroughly training its supervisors in labor policy, personnel relations, and the elements of supervision. Top management should help foremen to do a better job instead of acquiescing in or encouraging their being bypassed.

UNION-MANAGEMENT CLIMATE

American labor history prior to the 1950s was turbulent. It was filled with such elements of strife as violent battles on the picket line, blacklisting of union sympathizers, sit-down and sympathy strikes, calling out of the state militia to maintain order, mass picketing, and importation of hired strikebreakers. The symbols of the struggle between management and labor stand out vividly on the pages of American labor history—the Homestead and Pullman strikes of the 1890s, textile strikes in Lawrence and Lowell, Mass. in 1912, the great steel strike of 1919, the open-shop drives in the 1920s launched by employers, the sit-down strikes in the automobile industry and the strikes against "Little Steel" during the 1930s—these and others are highlighted as one reviews the background of present-day labor relations. But, to a considerable extent, the relations between employers and unions have substantially improved in recent years. There is growing evidence that the managements of our business firms have come to accept the fact that unions are here to stay. Management has learned to live with unions. Unions have achieved a measure of security, for the most part they are respectable, and they have accepted the fact that higher wages and benefits for their members depend upon healthy businesses and increasing productivity.

When the management of an organization is faced with the prospect of dealing with a union as the bargaining agent for its employees, it basically has two choices: (1) opposition or (2) acceptance.[5] Within each of these choices are a variety of approaches. Opposition may take the form of forceful action to weaken the union and to break off the bargaining relationship or it may involve subtle attempts to discredit the union in the eyes of the workers and to build up respect, loyalty, and pride in the company and complete trust in management. Patterns of acceptance vary along a continuum, from grudging acceptance with strong attempts at controlling the power of the union to accommodation, to labor–management cooperation, and occasionally

[5]For a well-known classification system of bargaining relationships see Benjamin M. Selekman, Stephen H. Fuller, Thomas Kennedy, and John M. Baitsell, *Problems in Labor Relations*, 3rd ed. (New York: McGraw-Hill Book Company, 1964), pp. 2–8.

even to collusion and the making of special deals between the top leaders of the union and those of management.

The majority of the relationships in the United States, as far as management's approach is concerned, can be classified into one or the other of two forms of acceptance. It may take the form either of reluctant acceptance of the union coupled with positive management action to contain the union within certain limits, or else accommodation. In the former the employer zealously seeks to preserve the traditional management prerogatives and to use a wide range of strategies and tactics to keep the union from gaining the upper hand. It implies an acceptance of the union as a legitimate institution that possesses certain rights under the laws of the land. However, management feels that it must continuously press to keep the union from encroaching upon management's freedom to operate the business in a profitable manner. Accommodation as a characterization of a type of bargaining relationship is becoming increasingly common. It implies a rather complete acceptance of the union by management, and both union and management have considerable respect for each other. Collective bargaining is confined to the traditional areas of wages, hours, and other (well-accepted) conditions of employment. There are no excursions into labor–management consultation and cooperation on such topics as safety, cost reduction, productive efficiency, and employee suggestions. These latter joint activities are found in those bargaining relationships properly classified as labor-management cooperation. Under this setup, both the union and the management are working for the same goals. There is a maximum of joint dealings on ways to increase productivity, cut costs, eliminate waste, and improve working conditions. However, labor–management cooperation represents a very advanced stage of relationship and of working harmony and is not particularly common in the United States.

The negotiation of special deals and of collusive arrangements by management and union officials is not common, but it does occur. Sometimes employers and unions work together to keep other companies out of a particular product market. The U.S. Senate McClellan Committee hearings of 1957–59 uncovered situations in which employers signed "sweetheart" contracts with union leaders at substandard wages. The union leaders sometimes took a direct money payoff in exchange for granting a low-wage contract to the company.

Sound Labor Relations

When relations between management and union are sound, there is a substantial degree of peace between the parties. Strikes occur only infrequently. There is an acceptance by each party of the need of the other to exist as an institution. Also both management and the union believe they are getting a fair deal in their relationships with each other.

The attitudes and philosophies of the leaders in management and the union are powerful determinants of the character of the relationship. Research has shown that where harmonious relations occur, management fully accepts the union as an institution and understands its need to exist. It accepts collective bargaining as a desirable way of handling employment relationships. Management understands the political nature of the union leaders' position and their need to sometimes "play politics" to maintain rank and file members' support. Union leaders dealing with private companies accept the free enterprise system and the need of the firms to make a profit. They are concerned for the continued viability of the organization.

Both parties recognize that they have shared interests. They understand that they will continue to live and deal with each other for many years to come. A problem that is of serious concern to one party must, of necessity, be addressed by the other. It cannot be ignored. Differences and conflicts inevitably do occur between management and union leaders from time to time, but these are resolved through a rational process of problem solving and a reconciling of positions. Neither side tries to overwhelm the other by the use of power and force. Flexibility, give and take, and some compromises must occur from time to time.

Economic factors also significantly affect the probability that sound labor–management relations will exist. Harmonious relationships are more likely to exist where the employer is strong, financially viable, and where the demand for the employer's product or service is good. Competition is not cutthroat. Marginal firms struggling to survive tend to have poor labor management relations. They cannot afford to provide competitive wages and benefits. Employment conditions, generally, in such firms are mediocre or worse and such a state of affairs is bound to cause conflict between union and management.

Questions for Review and Discussion

1. Why is it important for students and practitioners of management to have a sound understanding of labor union philosophy, objectives, and behavior?
2. How does personnel management in a unionized organization differ from that in a nonunion establishment?
3. What motivates employees to form and to join a union?
4. Union membership in the private sector (expressed as a percentage of the labor force) has very gradually declined since the early 1950s. Yet union membership in the public sector increased rapidly in the late 1960s and the 1970s. How do you explain these contrasting trends?
5. "Prior to the 1940s, when wages were low, benefits were few, and workers had little defense against arbitrary treatment, unions were certainly necessary. However, in this day and age of enlightened management and of protective labor laws, there is little real need for unions. Unions no longer have a vital role to play in employee–management relations." Defend or refute the foregoing statement.
6. Describe the character and general nature of the American labor-union movement. Why does it have its distinctive features?
7. What attitudes and behavior on the part of management tend to build harmonious, constructive union–management relations?
8. From time to time the field representatives and office employees of various national unions have formed their own unions and sought collective bargaining rights with their employers (that is, the national unions). These efforts have usually been opposed by the top union leadership. How do you explain such opposition?

Suggestions for Further Reading

Barbash, Jack. "The Labor Movement After World War II," *Monthly Labor Review*, Vol. 99, No. 11 (November 1976), pp. 34–37.

Brett, Jeanne M. "Why Employees Join Unions," *Organizational Dynamics*, Vol. 8, No. 4 (Spring 1980), pp. 47–59.

Dunlop, John T. "Past and Future Tendencies in American Labor Organizations," Vol. 107, No. 1 (Winter 1978), pp. 79–96.

Dunlop, John T., and Walter Galenson, eds. *Labor in the Twentieth Century*, New York: Academic Press, 1978.

Goulden, Joseph C. *Meany*. New York: Atheneum, 1972.

Juris, Harvey A., and Myron Roomkin. *The Shrinking Perimeter: Unionism and*

Labor Relations in the Manufacturing Sector. Lexington, Mass. D. C. Heath & Co., 1979.

Justin, Jules J. *How to Manage with a Union,* Vols. I & II. New York: Van Nostrand Reinhold Co., 1979.

Levine, Marvin J., and Eugene C. Hagburg, eds. *Labor Relations in the Public Sector.* Salt Lake City: Brighton Publishing Co., 1979.

Nash, Al. *The Union Steward: Duties, Rights, and States.* Ithaca: New York State School of Industrial and Labor Relations, Cornell University, 1977.

Reuther, Victor G. *The Brothers Reuther.* Boston: Houghton Mifflin, 1976.

20

Collective Bargaining

Collective bargaining is concerned with the relations between employers acting through their management representatives, and organized labor. It is concerned not only with the negotiation of a formal labor agreement but also with the day-to-day dealings between management and the union. Because the management of people in so many organizations is so closely intertwined with union–employer relationships, it is essential that the student and the practitioner of management develop a sound knowledge of collective bargaining. Furthermore the effect of collective bargaining extends beyond those establishments that are unionized. It impacts upon the economy as a whole, upon the practices of nonunion organizations, and upon the society at large.

During the early 1980s the institution of collective bargaining was subjected to serious tensions. The American people endured the longest and deepest economic recession since the Great Depression of the 1930s. Our basic "smokestack" industries lost markets both in the United States and overseas to foreign competitors. Because of this depressed business climate, management and unions in scores of major corporations negotiated cuts in wages and benefits as a means to help the firms survive. This was the first time such "givebacks" had been negotiated on a broad scale in this country.

Wage reductions occurred widely during the Great Depression. However, the basic manufacturing industries had not yet been unionized when the cuts were instituted.

This chapter will delve into the nature of collective bargaining, the legal framework for bargaining, structure for bargaining, negotiating the labor agreement, and subject matter of union–employer agreements. We will also examine public sector collective bargaining, dispute settlement methods, and the differences found between union and nonunion organizations.

THE NATURE OF COLLECTIVE BARGAINING

Collective bargaining has existed in the United States since the early 1800s. However, it did not develop into its present form until comparatively recently. In the very early days the general practice was for either the employer or the union, depending upon their relative economic strengths, to notify the other party of the wage rates and other conditions of employment that it intended to put into effect. There was very little negotiation and discussion between the parties.

If one party refused to accept the terms imposed by the other, then either a strike or a lockout ensued.

In 1885 Samuel Gompers was called to testify at hearings into labor relations conducted by the Commissioner of Labor Statistics of the State of New York. In reporting to the state legislature on this investigation, the Commissioner used the term *arbitration* to designate the process by which employers and unions would negotiate with one another to settle their differences. In the hearings themselves Gompers used both the words *arbitration* and *conciliation* to cover the process by which unions and management bargained with one another. The modern term *collective bargaining* was actually first used by Sidney and Beatrice Webb, the well-known historians of the British labor movement, just prior to 1900.[1]

The nature, scope, and methodology of collective bargaining are continuing to evolve even today. Collective bargaining is dynamic. But in order that the reader obtain a concrete understanding of what is involved in modern-day collective bargaining, the following definition is given:

Collective bargaining is concerned with the relations between unions representing employees and employers (or their management representatives). It involves the process of union organization of employees; negotiation, administration, and interpretation of collective agreements covering wages, hours of work, and other conditions of employment; engaging in concerted economic action; and dispute settlement procedures.

The bargaining is collective in the sense that the chosen representative of the employees (that is, a union) acts as the bargaining agent for all the employees in carrying out negotiations and dealings with management. The process may also be considered collective in the case of the corporation in which the paid professional managers represent the interests of the stockholders and the board of directors in bargaining with union leaders. On the employer side, it is also collective in those common situations in which the companies have joined together in an employer association for purposes of bargaining with a union.

Characteristics of Collective Bargaining

Collective bargaining has been characterized as a form of industrial democracy and industrial government. The management and union representatives sit down at the bargaining table, where they deliberate, persuade, try to influence, argue, and haggle. Eventually they reach an agreement, which they record in the form of a labor–management contract. This is the legislative phase, in which the two parties create a type of company-wide set of laws and regulations. This "industrial law" sets forth the rights and responsibilities of the company, the union, and the employees. Ordinarily management takes on the authority and responsibility to administer and operate the agreement. Management initiates actions in conformance with the agreed-upon provisions. This corresponds to the executive function of government. When employees or the union feel they are being denied their rights under the contract, they may submit a grievance to management. This may, if conditions warrant, be eventually taken to an impartial arbitrator for a final decision. This is analogous to the judicial function of government.

Some who are not thoroughly familiar with the collective-bargaining process have asserted that there is no essential difference between the negotiating of a commercial contract (for, say, the buying or selling of a commodity) and the bargaining of a labor agreement. But this point of view is somewhat naïve. The employment of human beings cannot be handled in the same

---

[1]For the evolution of concepts and terminology in this field see Vernon H. Jensen, "Notes on the Beginnings of Collective Bargaining," *Industrial and Labor Relations Review*, Vol. 9, No. 2 (January 1956), pp. 225–234.

manner as the purchase of physical goods. If one businessman contracts with another for the purchase of a load of lumber and the seller delivers inferior merchandise, the buyer can terminate the relationship at that point. But this cannot be done in the relations between management and labor. Generally speaking, the union and the management must learn to live with one another whether they like it or not. They must accommodate to each other. Under the labor law of the land, once bargaining relationships have been commenced, both sides must honestly seek an agreement. They must bargain in good faith. Dealings cannot arbitrarily be broken off.

Further, the negotiation of a labor agreement is quite different from the handling of a commercial contract because of the human relations and political aspects of labor–management relationships. A union is a political-economic organization. Union leaders, being elected, must represent the interests of their constituents. They are often placed in a position where they must cater to the pressures of a strong faction within the union. Union leaders are interested in being re-elected. They have to contend with dissident groups within the ranks. They cannot always negotiate a contract with management according to the cold logic of an issue. In short, the social aspects of collective bargaining set it apart from the negotiation of an ordinary business contract.

THE LEGAL FRAMEWORK OF COLLECTIVE BARGAINING

Labor–management relationships are heavily regulated by both Federal and state labor laws at the present time. This state of affairs commenced in the 1930s with the passage of the Norris–LaGuardia and Wagner acts. Prior to this time the policy of the federal government was to leave the two parties—unions and employers—alone and to exert a minimum of legislative interference. Although prior to the 1930s there existed only a minimum of statute law that dealt directly with collective bargaining, there were an abundance of court decisions that did, in effect, create a common law that provided a form of regulation for labor–management relations. Thus, we find that common law and the court interpretations played a major part in expressing government labor policy from 1800 through the early 1930s, whereas since then statute law has played the dominant role. Each of the major labor relations laws has been enacted in response to pressing needs of society in general as well as needs of the direct parties involved—employees, unions, and employers. An intelligent understanding of the management of people at work and of labor–management relations is not possible without a brief study of the law of collective bargaining.

Pre-Wagner Act Era—Labor and the Courts[2]

Prior to the passage of the Wagner Act in 1935, the basic struggle of unions was for existence and recognition. They sought to exist in an environment in which the economic and political power of the business organization were dominant. Employers were strongly antiunion in their sentiments and actions. Unions, if they successfully met the struggle to survive, then had to win recognition from the employer as the bargaining agent for employees.

Employers, for their part, did not take the rise of unions complacently. They looked upon unions as a challenge to their basic rights to operate their businesses as they saw fit. They considered that unions threatened the property

[2]A comprehensive analysis of common and statute labor law and court opinions can be found in Charles O. Gregory and Harold A. Katz, *Labor and the Law*, 3rd ed. (New York: W. W. Norton & Co., Inc., 1979).

rights of ownership. It was felt that unions interfered with the relations between management and the workers.

During this era Federal and state courts tended to be sympathetic to the views of employers. As rational bases for their rulings, jurists used three principal common-law concepts: (1) the necessity for preserving free competition with a minimum of interference in the affairs of business organizations; (2) the sanctity of private property rights; and (3) the right to freedom of individual contract.

When unions sought to improve the conditions of employment for their members during the early part of the nineteenth century by calling strikes; they found their efforts frustrated by court orders that held strikes to be criminal conspiracies. It was not until 1842 that the legality of strikes per se was established. This arose as a result of a Massachusetts court decision. Henceforth, judges examined union motives and methods in strike actions to decide whether the strike should be ruled illegal or not.

In 1890 Congress passed the Sherman Act to outlaw business combinations and conspiracies in restraint of trade. Although there is real doubt as to whether Congress ever intended to include union activities within the coverage of this law, nevertheless for many years employers were successful in obtaining court orders to break union strikes under the guise that they constituted combinations and conspiracies in restraint of commerce among the states. It was not until the Apex Hosiery Company and the Hutcheson cases of 1940 and 1941 that the United States Supreme Court ruled that labor unions are not generally subject to antitrust prosecution under the Sherman Act. Later Supreme Court decisions have specified certain limited circumstances in which unions may be liable to antitrust prosecution.

For many years employers were quite successful in impeding union activities by obtaining court injunctions whenever unions called an organizational strike or a strike to improve economic conditions. An injunction is a legal device derived from English common law. It is a court order prohibiting a certain activity in order to prevent property damage when there is no other remedy at law. Courts in the United States went beyond the original English concept, because they granted injunctions to employers if there was impending or actual interference with their business even though there had been no damage to physical property. During the late nineteenth century and the first three decades of the twentieth century, the repeated and widespread use of the labor injunction served effectively to render unions impotent.

In 1932 Congress passed the Norris-LaGuardia Anti-Injunction Act, which effectively rendered the Federal judiciary neutral in labor disputes. It defined permissible union activities in very broad terms and placed such tight restrictions upon the issuance of an injunction that for all practical purposes the private injunction ceased to be used as a device to defeat strikes.

The Wagner Act—1935

Labor unrest was rampant during the 1930s. The Great Depression, which began in 1929 with the stock market crash, had caused approximately one fourth of the labor force to be unemployed by 1933. Wage cuts were widespread. Industrial workers in the mass production industries were ripe for unionism. Management during this era had not been sufficiently alert nor enlightened to adopt sound industrial relations policies in keeping with the needs of their employees.

In June 1935, the National Labor Relations Act—popularly known as the Wagner Act after its author and sponsor, Senator Robert Wagner of New York—became law. With the adoption of this far-reaching law, public policy became one of encouragement for collective bargaining as preferable to individual bargaining. The act, in effect, encouraged the unionization of employees and provided the mechanism of secret ballot elections to ascertain the free choice of workers.

If the employees voted for union representation, employers were compelled to bargain with that union over wages, rates of pay, hours of work, and other conditions of employment.

The heart of the Wagner Act was contained in Section 7, which stated that "employees shall have the right to self-organization, to form, join, or assist labor organizations, to bargain collectively through representatives of their own choosing, and to engage in concerted activities for the purpose of collective bargaining or other mutual aid or protection."

Unfair Labor Practices of Employers. To insure that employees could actually engage in collective-bargaining activities without retaliation by their employers Section 8 of the Act listed five practices that employers were forbidden to undertake. The law stated that it shall be an unfair labor practice for an employer (1) "To interfere with, restrain, or coerce employees in the exercise of the rights guaranteed in Section 7." Examples of employer conduct prohibited by this provision are (a) threatening employees with loss of jobs or benefits if they should join a union (b) threatening to close down the plant if a union should be organized in it, and (c) spying on union gatherings.

The second unfair labor practice made it illegal "to dominate or interfere with the formation or administration of any labor organization or contribute financial support to it." This provision of the law put an end to the company-dominated unions (generally called "employee representation plans") that flourished in the 1920s and early 1930s. The third unfair labor practice of employers made it illegal to discriminate in regard to hiring or tenure of employment or any term or condition of employment in order to encourage or discourage membership in a union. This provision prevented a company from demoting or discharging a worker because he was active in forming the union. It also made it illegal to refuse to hire a qualified job applicant because he belonged to a union. The fourth unfair labor practice prevented discharging or dis-criminating against an employee who filed charges or testified before the National Labor Relations Board, the agency charged with the administration of the law. The final unfair labor practice was refusal to bargain in good faith. Thus if management put into effect a unilateral wage increase without discussing it with the union, this constituted a violation of law.

National Labor Relations Board. In order to provide machinery for operating the Wagner Act, the National Labor Relations Board was established. The Board had (and still does have) two major functions. The first is to conduct representation elections to determine if the employees in a company wish to be represented by a union. An important part of this responsibility is the task of deciding which employees should be in the bargaining unit and which should be excluded. If a union wins a bargaining election, then the board certifies that it shall be the "sole and exclusive bargaining agent" for all of the employees in the unit. The second major function is that of adjudicating charges of employer unfair labor practices. If the Board decides that an unfair labor practice has occurred, it is empowered to order a cease and desist order, to order the reinstatement of a wrongfully discharged employee, or to order the payment of back wages.

Experience Under the Wagner Act. This law played a significant part in fostering the growth of organized labor. In 1935, total union membership stood at about 3.9 million, whereas in 1947, when the Taft–Harley Act was passed, it had reached 15 million. Other factors, of course, contributed to this rapid expansion as well.

Representatives of American management expressed vigorous objection to the Wagner Act on the grounds that it was very one-sided and that it tied the hands of management while giving the unions free rein. It is true that the Act sought to encourage unionization and collective bargaining and imposed no restraints whatever on union behavior. There was great unrest, and many bitter struggles occurred between labor and management during the 1935–1947 period. Much of this could be attributed to the fact that unions and management were going through the difficult process of learning to live with one another. A record number of strikes occurred in 1946. The general public and Congress tended to blame unions for the wave of strikes that occurred during this period. A reaction set in against unions, and this culminated in the passage of the Taft–Hartley act in June 1947, over President Truman's veto.

Taft–Hartley Act—1947

Officially titled the Labor–Management Relations Act, the Taft–Hartley Act amended the Wagner Act to a considerable extent. In addition, it initiated a number of new provisions completely beyond the scope of the Wagner Act. The primary purposes of this new law were to regulate and restrict the activities of unions, to protect individual employees and employers against the power of unions, and to attempt to restore a balance of power in labor relations. The Taft–Hartley Act is a very complicated law; therefore we can cover only the highlights here.

The law basically retains all of the provisions of the original Wagner Act that were designed to guarantee to employees the right to form and join unions and to engage in collective bargaining free of any restraint or coercion by the employer. Section 7, dealing with rights of employees, contains the original wording of the Wagner Act plus the statement that employees shall also have the right to *refrain* from any or all of such activities related to union organization and collective bargaining.

The five unfair labor practices of employers contained in Section 8 were retained. However, Congress added six unfair labor practices of unions.

Unfair Labor Practices of Unions. The first unfair union practice consists of restraining or coercing employees in the exercise of rights guaranteed in Section 7 of the Act. The National Labor Relations Board and the courts have interpreted this to outlaw mass picketing, which bars nonstriking employees from entering the plant. Also outlawed are violence on the picket line in connection with strikes and threats to do bodily injury to nonstrikers.

The second unfair labor practice of unions involves causing or attempting to cause the employer to discriminate against an employee in order to encourage or discourage union membership. When the second unfair union practice is combined with the original third unfair employer practice as revised by the Taft–Hartley Act, the net result is to outlaw the closed shop. (The union shop that requires union membership on or after the thirtieth day of employment is legal under the act.)

The third practice consists of a union refusal to bargain in good faith. Examples of such union conduct are the insistence upon the inclusion of illegal provisions, such as a closed shop or a discriminatory hiring hall, in a contract and adamant refusal to make a written contract of reasonable duration.

The fourth unfair practice in reality consists of four separate activities as follows:

1. Requiring an employer or self-employed person to join a union.
2. Forcing an employer to cease handling the products of or doing business with any other person. This is the ban on secondary boycotts. What is a secondary boycott? Let us assume that a union has a dispute with Company A (the primary employer). The union is unsuccessful in taking direct action against Company A, so it pickets or otherwise takes action against Company B (a secondary employer) to induce B to cease buying from or selling goods to A. This action is one type of secondary boycott.
3. Forcing an employer to bargain with one union when another union is already the certified bargaining agent.

4. Forcing the employer to assign particular work to employees in one union rather than to employees in another union. This provision outlaws the jurisdictional strike. Jurisdictional disputes are prevalent when a number of craft unions struggle for control of the same jobs. Each of the competing unions hopes to obtain employment for its own members.

The fifth unfair labor practice is that of charging excessive or discriminatory initiation fees. In judging whether a particular fee is excessive, the Board considers the practices and customs of other unions in the same industry and the wages currently paid to the employees affected.

The sixth unfair practice is that of causing or attempting to cause an employer to pay money or another thing of value for services that are not performed or not to be performed. This outlaws featherbedding. Unions tend to engage in this practice when employment opportunities for their members are declining. It is a common reaction to prevent displacement of workers due to technological advances.

As with unfair employer practices, the National Labor Relations Board has the power to issue cease and desist orders in connection with union unfair labor practices. It can order a union to reimburse an employee for any wages he may have lost as a result of union discrimination or coercion, and it can require the refund of dues and fees illegally collected. Charges of unfair employer or union practices can be filed at any of the board's regional offices by employers, unions or individual employees.

Supervisors and Professionals. The Taft–Hartley Act contains provisions that have an important effect upon certain groups of employees. It excludes supervisors from the definition of employees. They are considered to be members of management and receive no protection under the act if they choose to form a union. Professional personnel, such as engineers and scientists, are considered to be employees and do receive the full protection of the law in regard to self-organization. However, the board is not allowed to include them in the same bargaining unit as all other (nonprofessional) employees, unless a majority of them vote for inclusion in the larger unit. This provision gives recognition to the fact that professional employees feel their problems and interests are quite distinct from those of production and maintenance workers.

Free Speech. Under the Wagner Act management complained vigorously that it was not allowed to speak freely in connection with unions and their activities. To meet this situation the law states in Section 8c that "the expressing of any views, argument, or the dissemination thereof, whether in written, printed, graphic, or visual form, shall not constitute or be evidence of an unfair labor practice under any of the provisions of this Act, if such expression contains no threat of reprisal or force or promise of benefit." Employers now have considerable latitude to make antiunion speeches to their employees as long as they do not threaten workers or promise benefits. Unions also have the right of free speech.

National Emergency Disputes. In order to provide a means of settling labor–management disputes and strikes that imperil the national health and safety, a systematic procedure has been established to deal with this serious problem. Whenever, in the opinion of the President of the United States, a threatened or actual strike or lockout will affect an entire industry or substantial part thereof such that the health and safety of the nation will be endangered, he is empowered to appoint a board of inquiry that will investigate the facts in the dispute and report back to the President. Upon receiving this report, the President may direct the Attorney General to petition a federal district court for an injunction to prevent or terminate the strike or lockout. Upon the issuance of this injunction the strike must terminate, and the two parties must make every effort to settle their differences with the help of the Federal Mediation and Conciliation Service. If the strike is not settled, then at the end of 60 days the board of inquiry must make a public report on the status of the dispute and the current position of the two sides. Within 15 more days, the National Labor Relations Board must conduct a secret ballot of the employees to ascertain whether they wish to accept the employer's last offer to the union. The results must be certified to the Attorney General within 5 days. The injunction must be discharged at the end of 80 days if the strike is still not settled. The President must make a full report to Congress, together with any recommendations he wishes to make. The union has a right to strike after the 80-day injunction is lifted if no agreement has been reached.

Between 1947 and 1981 the national emergency provisions of the Act were utilized 35 times. The industries most frequently involved have been maritime, shiploading and unloading (stevedoring), atomic energy, aerospace, and coal mining.

Appraisal of the Act. The Taft–Hartley Act was passed primarily to control and restrain union activities. It has been partially successful in this respect. There has been a noticeable decline in secondary boycott and jurisdictional strikes. However, the ban on featherbedding has not been effective. The law has been a factor in retarding the organization of nonunion sectors in the South. Employers acquired a potent new device to weaken union-organizing campaigns by use of the "free speech" provision. In addition, they can delay a representation election by charging the union with an unfair labor practice if any hint of coercion occurs during the campaign. The inclusion of union unfair labor practices has required unions to exercise the same degree of responsibility in collective bargaining as has been required of employers (via employer unfair labor practices) ever since the Wagner Act became law in 1935.

Landrum–Griffin Act—1959

During the late 1950s dramatic exposes were made of racketeering, violence, lack of democratic procedures in unions, and collusion between unions and employers. A large share of these malpractices occurred in the Teamster's Union. The basic work of uncovering and publicizing these abuses was done by the Senate Select Committee on Improper Activities in the Labor or Management Field, which conducted investigations and public hearings from 1957 through 1959. The law that was passed as a result of the work of this committee is known as The Labor–Management Reporting and Disclosure Act of 1959, commonly called the Landrum–Griffin Act (after its sponsors). This law does far more than merely require the reporting of certain information by unions and management as its name implies. It establishes very detailed federal regulation of the internal affairs of unions, regulates the conduct of union officers, and drastically curtails recognition and organizational picketing.

The Act contains seven titles, each dealing with a major subject area. We shall discuss briefly all titles except title VI, which deals with miscellaneous provisions.

Bill of Rights of Union Members. A considerable number of the provisions of the Landrum–Griffin Act are designed to insure that unions are run democratically with full protection for the rights of individual members. Title I of the law, entitled "Bill of Rights," contains some of these provisions. This title stipulates that members shall have the right (1) to attend, participate in, and vote at union meetings and elections; (2) to meet, assemble, and express views at union meetings; (3) to vote on increases in dues and fees; (4) to testify and bring suit when unions infringe the rights of members; and (5) to receive notice and a fair hearing before any union disciplinary action can be taken except for nonpayment of dues.

Reporting Requirements. Title II specifies those reports that unions, union officers, employers, and labor consultants must file with the Secretary of Labor. They become public information when they are filed.

Unions must file a copy of their constitutions and bylaws with the Secretary of Labor as well as a complete explanation of their administrative practices. They must also file a detailed financial report annually.

Union officers and employees must report on any financial interests or income from a company whose employees the union represents or actively seeks to represent. This is designed to uncover or eliminate "conflict of interest" transactions in which union leaders and appointive officials take loans, gifts, and under-the-table payments from management in return for special concessions. Employers must report any payment or loan to a union or union officer, except the wages paid to a union officer who is at the same time a regular employee. Employers must report payments to employees or a group of employees designed to get them to persuade other employees to exercise or not exercise their self-organizational rights.

Trusteeships. A trusteeship is established when a national union takes over control of the operation of one of its local unions, including control of its property and funds. Although a trusteeship may be established by responsible union officials to prevent corruption and misuse of funds at the local level, Congress found, in its hearings, that some corrupt top union officials created trusteeships to thwart the growth of competing union factions and to plunder the treasuries of the seized locals.

The Act requires that the national union must file a report with the Secretary of Labor for each trusteed local every six months. The report must contain a detailed explanation of why the trusteeship was established or why it has been continued. A trusteeship is presumed valid only for 18 months. After that it is presumed invalid and the burden of proof is placed upon the national union to justify its continuance.

Election of Union Officers. Title IV of the Landrum–Griffin Act requires that elections of union officers in local unions be conducted at least once every three years, once every four years in intermediate bodies, and once every five years in a national or international union. At the local level the elections must be by secret ballot of members in good standing. For intermediate bodies and nationals it must be either a secret ballot of all members in good standing or by representatives who were chosen by a secret ballot.

To insure that democratic procedures are followed, the act stipulates that campaign literature must be distributed on equal terms for all candidates at their expense. Lists of members under union security agreements must be made available for inspection without discrimination, and any candidate has the right to have an observer at the polls and at the counting of the ballots.

Fiduciary Responsibilities. Title V restates the common law applicable to trust relations by declaring that union officers, agents, and shop stewards occupy positions of trust and that they must hold and use the funds and property of the organization solely for the benefit of the members and in accordance with the constitution and bylaws of the organization. The act makes it a Federal crime for an officer or union employee to embezzle, steal, or willfully misappropriate union assets.

Amendments to the Taft–Hartley Act. The Landrum–Griffin Act makes a number of important changes and additions to the Taft–Hartley Act. Among these are the following:

1. Tight restrictions are placed upon organizational and recognition picketing. Such picketing is prohibited if another union has been

lawfully recognized by the employer, a valid NLRB election has been conducted within the preceding 12 months, or if the picketing union has not filed an election petition within a reasonable time (not to exceed 30 days).

2. Economic strikers whose jobs have been taken by other workers are granted the right to vote in any new NLRB representation election up to 12 months after the strike has begun. This provision was added to prevent an antiunion employer from deliberately getting rid of a union by hiring new workers and then obtaining a new election.

General Observations of the Act. The Landrum–Griffin Act requires that unions conduct their affairs in a democratic fashion. Because unions are membership organizations, to which people pay dues, it is just and proper that the leaders be responsive to the wishes of the members and that the members have rights to participate in the governance of their organizations. Since the passage of this law there has been a pronounced trend toward individuals launching effective challenges to the incumbent slate of officers in union elections.

Another purpose of the Act has been to eliminate corruption by union leaders. Although corruption has traditionally been confined to only a few unions such as the Teamsters, the Act has had only modest success in reducing this corruption. This is partly due to a lack of vigor by the U.S. Departments of Labor and of Justice in investigating and prosecuting such activities.

STRUCTURE FOR COLLECTIVE BARGAINING

The listing below shows the various structures for conducting contract negotiations that exist in the United States.

A. Single-employer bargaining.
  1. Single-plant.
  2. Multiple plants.
B. Multiple-employer bargaining.
  1. Local area (city or labor market).
  2. Region-wide.
  3. Industry-wide.

The majority of agreements throughout the country are bargained by a single company dealing with a single union. However, there has been a very pronounced trend for many years toward multiemployer bargaining. Usually when companies band together to bargain with one or more unions, they set up a formal organization with a paid, professional staff. This is called an employer association. On the other hand, sometimes companies cooperate with one another during contract negotiations in order to present a united front to the union, but they do not go so far as to set up a formal or enduring association. In various negotiations with the United Automobile Workers Union, General Motors, Ford, and Chrysler have cooperated in this fashion to reduce the possibility of the union "whipsawing" one firm against another in this very competitive business field.

In single-employer bargaining in the field of manufacturing, a company may have contracts with more than one union, but negotiations are usually conducted separately with each union. Many large multiplant companies, such as General Motors and United States Steel, have practically all of their plants organized by a single union. Each local union of the United Auto Workers from each plant of General Motors, for example, elects representatives to what is known as a conference board, which meets to prepare bargaining demands and bargaining strategy. The actual negotiations are handled by the General Motors Department of the union, which is a permanent organizational branch of the union located at national headquarters in Detroit. Quite often, the president of the national union takes part in negotiations, particularly when the going gets tough. A master agreement is signed to apply to all plants. Then each plant negotiates a supplementary agreement with its local union to cover issues that apply specifically to that unit.

Multiemployer Bargaining

This type of bargaining originated with craft unions at the city level for bargaining with a number of employers under a single contract. Thus a local of the carpenters union may sign an agreement with a number of construction firms in an area. The most common practice in the construction industry at present is for all of the unions (for example, carpenters, electricians, operating engineers, laborers, and bricklayers) to bargain jointly through their building trades council with an employer association composed of all unionized contractors in the area. The negotiation process is centralized and simultaneous for all crafts. When agreement is reached, separate contracts are signed between each local of each union and each employer.

Multiemployer bargaining is extremely common in the local area in construction, hotels and restaurants, laundries, dry cleaning, retail stores, dairy products, book and job printing, and local delivery trucking.

Regional multiemployer bargaining is common in the following industries: pulp and paper, lumbering, nonferrous metal mining, maritime and longshoring, trucking, and textile manufacturing.

Industry-wide bargaining is a term used to designate that type of bargaining that covers many companies in an industry that are distributed widely throughout the nation. Although there is much talk about it, with charges that it is monopolistic, true industry-wide bargaining occurs in only a very few industries. It exists in bituminous coal, basic steel, and the trucking (not local cartage) industries.

Reasons for Multiemployer Bargaining

The basic reason for the development and spread of multiemployer bargaining is to take wages out of competition. From the viewpoint of business, this means that other companies who are competing in the same product market cannot obtain a price and cost advantage by paying lower wage rates for the same classes of labor. One firm may indeed obtain a lower-cost advantage over its competitors, but it will be achieved by better management, greater efficiency, and technological improvements and not by paying lower wage rates.

Unions have frequently been the initiators of the demand for multiemployer bargaining. They have long realized that they could not force wages up in one firm if that firm was faced with low-wage competition from other companies. Therefore, unions tend to press for uniformity of wages and conditions of employment among all unionized companies in an industry within the area of market competition.

In those industries with many small employers, unions find that contract negotiations and contract enforcement are simplified and less costly when bargaining is carried on with an employer association.

Just as individual workmen organized unions many years ago to increase their bargaining power, so have companies found it advantageous to pool their resources when confronted with a strong union at the bargaining table. By presenting a united front, they can often obtain a more favorable settlement than they could by acting individually.

NEGOTIATING THE AGREEMENT

Years ago union–employer labor agreements were generally for one year's duration. But since the 1950s there has been a pronounced trend toward contracts of two and three years' duration. This provides greater security for both sides. It is evidence of greater faith in the grievance process and in day-to-day discussions to solve problems as they arise. It demonstrates increased maturity on the part of labor and management in their bargaining relationship.

Preparations for contract-bargaining commence long before the actual negotiating sessions open. For the company the principal spadework is done by the industrial relations director. He or she and the staff must gather data on prevailing rates of pay and fringe benefit practices in the labor market area and in the industry. The company's financial situation must be analyzed carefully to determine what wage and fringe benefit improvements can be offered, if any. The experience of living with the present union agreement will undoubtedly have demonstrated a number of contract provisions that could be altered to management's benefit. The industrial relations director may hold discussions with plant supervision to collect views on problems that arose when administering the current agreement. Before entering the negotiations, management will have pretty well decided what its position will be regarding expected union demands. It will have formulated its proposals and possible demands upon the union.

Assuming that the bargaining is being conducted by a local union, the union will normally elect a bargaining committee that includes the principal elective officials plus some shop stewards. The rank and file often participate in expressing their thoughts regarding bargaining demands at a general membership meeting. Many of these stem from unresolved worker complaints and grievances. The leaders cannot simply echo the often varied and conflicting wishes of the membership; but rather they must carefully weigh the merits of each issue and consider the hard realities of what is possible. Quite frequently the international union will help guide the preparatory process. It may insist upon certain uniform union-wide demands and a standard wording of contract clauses.

At the actual negotiating sessions the company may be represented by the chief executive officer, the industrial relations director, the treasurer or the controller, and the manager of operations. The industrial relations director typically serves as chief spokesman. The chief spokesman for the union is usually either the international representative or the local union business agent. Other members of the team may include the local union president, secretary-treasurer, members of the executive board, and perhaps a few shop stewards.

Because the union demands practically always involve increased costs and sometimes restrictions on management's freedom of action, the company spokesmen generally resist or refuse to accede to these proposals. Management typically offers far less than the union demands. The union always asks for more than it really expects to get. A great many sessions may be required to reach agreement upon the issues and upon the specific contract language. The pressure on management is the threat of a strike with consequent loss of business. The union leadership will not call a strike lightly, because a lost strike can mean loss of jobs, a depleted union treasury, and a weakened union. Yet the elected union leaders are under considerable pressure from their constituents to show some gains, that is, to extract concessions from management.

Although strikes make exciting newspaper headlines, the vast majority of contracts are negotiated without a strike year after year. A strike usually occurs when one side (or both) miscalculates the other's limit.

SUBJECT MATTER OF COLLECTIVE BARGAINING

What are the issues about which management and labor negotiate when they meet at the bargaining table? Section 8(d) of the Taft–Hartley Act provides the underlying framework. It requires an employer and the representatives of his employees to meet at reasonable times, to confer in good faith about certain matters, and to put into writing any agreement reached if requested by either party. The parties must confer in good faith with respect to wages, hours, and other terms or conditions of employment, the negotiation of an agreement, or any question arising under an agreement.

Below is a list of topics commonly appearing in union-employer agreements. This is a general list; any individual agreement would necessarily contain certain items particular to that situation. The order of topics varies from one agreement to another.

SUBJECT MATTER OF UNION-EMPLOYER AGREEMENTS

1. *Union Recognition and Scope of Bargaining Unit.*
2. *Management Rights (Management Security).*
3. *Union Security.*
4. *Strikes and Lockouts.*
5. *Union Activities and Responsibilities.*
   a. Check-off of dues.
   b. Union officers and stewards.
   c. Union bulletin boards.
   d. Wildcat strikes and slowdowns.
6. *Wages.*
   a. General wage adjustments.
   b. Wage structure.
   c. Job evaluation.
   d. Wage incentives and time study.
   e. Reporting and call-in pay.
   f. Shift differentials.
   g. Bonuses.
7. *Working Time and Time-Off Policies.*
   a. Regular hours of work.
   b. Holidays.
   c. Vacations.
   d. Overtime regulations.
   e. Leaves of absence.
   f. Rest periods.
   g. Meal periods.
8. *Job Rights and Seniority.*
   a. Seniority regulations.
   b. Transfers.
   c. Promotions.
   d. Layoffs and recalls.
   e. Job posting and bidding.
9. *Discipline, suspension, and Discharge.*
10. *Grievance Handling and Arbitration.*
11. *Health and Safety.*
12. *Insurance and Benefit Programs.*
    a. Group life insurance.
    b. Health insurance.
    c. Pension program.
    d. Supplemental unemployment benefits.

Substantive Issues

We shall now examine some of the principal substantive issues and note how union and management views tend to differ.

Union Security. The term *union security* refers to both the right of a union to exist as an organization and its right to continued existence in a particular company. The first right is guaranteed by the labor laws of the nation. It is the second right that has caused so much controversy between labor and management. It has been primarily because of long-standing employer opposition to unions that unions have pressed hard to get incorporated into the labor contract some provision that formally insures the union's continued presence in the company.

Union security provisions may take any of the following forms:

1. *Union Shop.* All present employees are required to join the union. Newly hired employees must join within a specifed number of days after being hired. (The Taft–Hartley Act says this period cannot be less than thirty days, except for the construction industry, where seven days are stipulated).
2. *Modified Union Shop.* At the time the agreement is signed, present employees who do not belong to the union are not required to join. Those who already belong must continue their membership as a condition of employment, and all new hires must join within a specified number of days.
3. *Maintenance of Membership.* Workers who do not belong to the union are not required to join; however, those who do join are required to stay in the union until a brief "escape period" (usually of ten to fifteen days) just prior to the contract termination date.
4. *Agency Shop.* Employees are not required to join the union but must pay a fee to the union for the bargaining services and benefits that the union provides for all in the bargaining unit.
5. *Check-Off.* Employer deducts union dues from employees' wages if the employee signs a form authorizing it.

About 85 per cent of the employees covered by collective agreements in private industry work under some form of union security provisions.

As already indicated, unions nearly always demand contractual protection for their existence as the bargaining agent in a company. They feel that they need protection against management efforts to oust the union from the shop. Unions feel that all employees within a bargaining unit should pay to support the union, which, under the Taft–Hartley Act, bargains rates of pay and other conditions of employment for all workers regardless of whether they are union members of not. Unions are opposed to nonunion workers becoming "free riders" and enjoying benefits of union membership without supporting it financially. In an open shop the problem of maintaining union membership is extremely difficult in those organizations in which employee turnover is high.

Management views on union security (management tends to refer to it as compulsory unionism) are divided. Some companies encourage employee membership in the union because they do not want factional struggles between union and nonunion groups within the plant. Also they want all employees to belong and to participate in union affairs so that the union will faithfully represent the will of the majority of employees.

It is probably accurate to state, however, that the majority of employers oppose any form of compulsory unionism. Employer groups, such as the National Association of Manufacturers, have advocated state "right-to-work" laws that outlaw the closed shop, union shop, maintenance of membership, and all other forms of union security. As of 1982, twenty states had enacted such legislation. These are mostly Southern and Midwestern states, where antiunion sentiment is strong. The popular argument against compulsory unionism is that no person should have to join a union in order to obtain a job. However, the primary reason why many employers and associations of employers oppose union security provisions is that they feel that the union shop grants the union too much economic power. They seek to blunt the power of unions and to discourage union growth by obtaining legislative bans at the state level on all forms of compulsory unionism. Thus, this is primarily a power struggle and not a matter of principle.

Management Rights. Professional business managers as a group and as a class have viewed with some alarm the extension of union influence into subject areas that had been traditionally considered to be exclusive management prerogatives. Management has argued that it has a right and even an obligation to make its own business decisions free from union interference. This concept stems from the property rights of ownership with management acting as the representative of the stockholders in the corporation. In collective bargaining relationships, management often seeks to obtain union agreement that certain specified subject areas, such as determination of products to be made, pricing the product, deciding production methods and processes, setting up accounting methods, direction of the work force, determination of job content, and so on, are sole and exclusive management rights. Basically the management rights issue is the counterpart of the union security problem. The former grants management security and a certain management sphere of influence. The latter provides security to the union as an institution.

Unions, in the United States, have not sought to share with management the authority and responsibility to operate the business. But they generally take the position that a fence should not be built around management prerogatives. They tend to believe that labor should have a voice in all those things that affect employees and employee relationships. They tend to adopt a pragmatic view. Although certain topics may not be of concern to the union today, conditions in the future may change in such a way that the union may become interested in negotiating over a particular subject. There are many subject areas over which management and unions differ sharply over the relative amount of union and management control. Examples are the setting of production standards, imposition of disciplinary penalties, assignment of duties to jobs, subcontracting of work outside the plant, scheduling of work, and the discontinuance of a kind of work.

Management rights clauses in labor agreements take one of two forms. The first takes the form of a broad statement that asserts that the control and operation of the business is vested exclusively in the company management except insofar as these matters may be limited by provisions in the agreement. The second type attempts to list all those management functions that are not subject to joint determination, such as methods of production, planning and scheduling production, job assignments, hiring, employee discipline, and formulation of plant rules.

Wages. The topics that appear in the typical union contract under the heading of wages are many and varied. Among these are the general across-the-board wage adjustment, the pay grade structure, in-grade rate progression, special rates for learners and apprentices, job evaluation, time study, wage incentives, premium pay practice, reporting and call-in pay, cost of living or escalator clause, and productivity increments. Space does not permit an explanation and analysis of each of these items.[3]

When negotiating, management looks upon wages primarily as a labor cost. Fringe benefits are likewise translated into labor costs. A given union demand for x cents per hour increase in wages is expressed by management as a certain dollar increase in payroll for a month and a year. This affects the cost of goods sold.

In determining what its wage rates should be, management seeks (sometimes in only a general way) to pay rates equal to the average prevailing in its own labor market for each job classification. In deciding upon a wage policy, management also gives consideration to its own ability to pay (that is, profitability), future business expectations, productivity, and the relative supply of labor available in the local labor market.

Unions, for their part, seek to eliminate wages as a factor in competition among employers whom they have organized. They press for

[3]For a discussion of wage issues under collective bargaining see Daniel Q. Mills, *Labor-Management Relations*, 2nd ed. (New York: McGraw-Hill Book Company, 1982, chs. 15 and 16; also Gordon F. Bloom and Herbert R. Northrup, *Economics of Labor Relations*, 9th ed. (Homewood, Ill.: Richard D. Irwin, Inc., 1981, Chs. 5 and 10.

wage uniformity throughout an industry for the same class of work. Although this is the long-range union goal, unions frequently have to settle for something less. But certainly within each company they demand "equal pay for equal work." All employees on the same job should receive the same pay. Unions often demand a single rate for each job. Employers usually want a rate range for each job or for each labor grade in order to pay different wages to people according to variations in performance.

In making its wage-bargaining demands upon management, a union typically gives consideration to the company's profit picture, the pattern of settlements in other companies in the same and allied industries, changes in the cost of living, and prevailing wage levels in the area and in the industry. It also keeps careful watch of the wage settlements obtained by rival unions to insure that it does as well.

Job Rights. Unions try to furnish as much job security to their members as possible. In a craft union, in those common situations in which workers frequently change employers (for example, construction), the union members primarily look to their union for security. By maintaining their membership in the union they can usually obtain a job via the union hiring hall.

However, in the industrial union situation workers look to their employer for job security. This is why unions seek to have all job changes decided on the basis of company seniority. Unions feel that this is a fair and objective criterion for making transfers, promotions, and layoffs. They feel that it eliminates any likelihood of favoritism and discrimination influencing decisions on personnel changes of status.

Management typically desires the freedom to move people from one job to another and to lay off workers when business gets slack, unhampered by union-imposed restrictions. Management feels that the application of rigid seniority rules reduces efficiency and often causes unqualified workers to be assigned to

jobs. There is no close correlation between ability and length of service.

The net result of these two opposing points of view is usually a compromise. In the vast majority of companies today, layoffs are handled on the basis of seniority. This means that the most recent workers hired are the first to go in the even of a layoff. Management always retains full authority to promote a person out of the bargaining unit to an administrative or supervisory position. Criteria for promotion within the bargaining unit are frequently a combination of seniority and ability. Some contracts specify that when choosing from among several employees for a better job, seniority will be the deciding factor only when two or more candidates have equal qualifications. Other contracts state that the most senior person will receive the job, provided he or she has the minimum qualifications to do the work.

Layoffs. Most collective agreements contain provisions designed to forestall or minimize layoffs. The most common provision is some form of worksharing. Worksharing can be implemented by either a reduction in weekly hours of work or by rotation of employment. Reduction in hours of work is the most commonly used method. Where reduction in hours is used labor agreements typically specify that hours shall not be reduced beyond a certain minimum, such as 32 hours per week. If further cutbacks should be necessary when this point is reached, then layoffs can occur. Rotation of employment, the other method of worksharing, requires that short, specific periods of layoff be rotated equally among all employees.

Supplementary ways of minimizing layoffs are by restrictions on the amount of overtime worked, restrictions on subcontracting, restrictions on hiring during slack periods, and by mandating that the reduction in force shall be no faster than the rate of attrition via voluntary quits and retirements.

When layoffs actually take place, seniority

is by far the most common criterion for determining the order in which people will be laid off. A U.S. Department of Labor study of 1,845 union–employer contracts found that seniority was the sole criterion in 27.2 per cent of the agreements, the primary factor in 44.2 per cent of the agreements, and a secondary factor in 19.5 per cent.[4] When seniority is used as the primary factor in determining who shall be laid off, this means that seniority plays a predominant role but that ability and other factors are also considered. Usually this means that junior employees will be laid off provided that the senior employees can do the remaining work even if junior employees are more capable. When seniority is a secondary factor, the labor agreement specifies that only when ability and physical fitness are equal (when choosing among several employees) will length of service become the deciding factor.

The seniority provisions of a labor contract and their application in layoff, bumping, and recall often are very complex. When layoffs occur, employees may be able to exercise their seniority rights to protect their jobs according to job-family boundaries, departmental boundaries, or on a plant-wide basis. If there are fifteen machinists in a company and the lowest three in seniority are laid off when a reduction in force occurs, this is considered job or job-family seniority. It might be that the three machinists possess much higher seniority than employees who are retained in other departments, but if the contract has set up seniority units solely on the basis of job-classification boundaries, then these three must be laid off. The same principle applies to a departmental seniority system. Under plant-wide seniority the shortest-service people are let go regardless of their jobs or departments.

Bumping is the term used to denote the displacement of one employee by another who has more seniority. Under a plant-wide seniority policy, if Jones's job is eliminated, she may bump Smith from a job in another department if Jones has more seniority and if Jones can perform Smith's job. Smith, in turn, may be able to displace some other, less senior worker.

In negotiating labor agreements union leaders typically seek large or plantwide seniority units and to have layoffs occur according to strict seniority. Management, on the other hand, wants to minimize the disruptions to efficiency resulting from numerous bumpings. Hence it often seeks contract language denying bumping for temporary layoffs of short duration and language allowing bumping only within limited seniority units. It usually tries to make the criteria for layoff determination to be seniority and ability, not seniority alone.

Grievance Handling. The subject of grievances is dealt with extensively in Chapter 21, "Grievances and Arbitration." However, there are certain collective bargaining aspects of grievance handling that must be mentioned at this point. Nonunion organizations usually do not have formal grievance procedures, although it is generally understood that employees have a right to discuss their dissatisfactions and problems with their immediate supervisors. But the entry of a union into an organization nearly always brings about the establishment of a grievance procedure. Ordinarily an employee who wishes to obtain satisfaction and settlement of a grievance will present it to his supervisor or to his shop steward, who will represent him in discussions with the supervisor. The supervisor as a representative of management will give an answer to the employee and the steward. If they are not satisfied with this action, they may appeal the decision to successively higher levels of management until a mutual agreement is reached. In processing the grievance up through the management hierarchy, higher officials in the union structure enter the picture at each step. Generally, officials of the union at each

[4]U.S. Department of Labor, Bureau of Labor Statistics. *Layoff, Recall, and Worksharing Procedures,* Bulletin 1425-13 (Washington, D.C.: Goverment Printing Office, 1972.)

step occupy positions in the union hierarchy that roughly correspond to those in the management organization with whom the grievance is discussed.

Basically, in presenting grievances to management, the union is asserting that the company has not faithfully and properly administered the terms of the labor agreement. The contract establishes the *rights* of the company, the union, and the employees. The grievance procedure provides the means for adjudicating and interpreting the way in which the labor agreement is applied in practice.

Ninety-four per cent of the agreements in force in the United States provide for binding arbitration as the final step in the grievance procedure. Most agreements provide that the union, if not satisfied with top management's answer to a grievance, can appeal it to an impartial arbitrator who will hold a hearing, listen to testimony from both sides, and examine briefs and documents that may be submitted by the parties. After hearing all of the facts the arbitrator will render a decision (usually within thirty days) and submit a written statement of the award together with reasons. In submitting an unresolved grievance to arbitration both parties usually agree that the arbitrator's decision will be final and binding.

PUBLIC SECTOR COLLECTIVE BARGAINING

To this point in this chapter we have talked about collective bargaining in the private business sector of the economy. Collective bargaining in government employment, at Federal, state, and local levels, burst upon the scene in the early 1960s and has expanded rapidly since then.

Special Context of Public Collective Bargaining

Much of public sector collective bargaining is modeled after private sector bargaining because the latter emerged first and its laws and procedures are well established. However, there are unique aspects to collective bargaining by government which should be pointed out.

Sovereignty. Traditionally, public officials and writers in political science adopted the view that the government possesses sole authority that cannot be given to or shared with anyone. They held that government can establish terms and conditions of employment. Often this view was convenient for government officials who wanted to continue the unilateral establishment of terms of employment. A more recent point of view is that government has, for a very long time, negotiated contracts for personal services with doctors and teachers and for products and services with private companies. Thus, it can just as well negotiate contracts with unions representing employees. In reality, the traditional view was a manifestation in the public sector of the opposition to unions and collective bargaining that held sway among private sector employers for many years.

Finances and the Market. In private business the employer is subject to the discipline of the product or service market. He cannot readily afford to give in to union demands for higher wages and fringe benefits because he may not be able to pass these higher costs on to the customer in the form of higher prices without cutting into the company's sales volume.

In place of market restraints, the public employer must contend with budget restrictions and taxation limitations. State constitutions often place ceilings upon the taxation levels of state and local governments. Furthermore, taxpayers throughout the nation have exhibited strong resistance to higher taxes in recent years.

Separation of Powers. In private industry unions negotiate with management, which has formal authority to make binding contracts. In the public sector unions negotiate with representatives of the executive branch of government. However, authority for appropriating money and approving budgets resides in the legislative body. In school systems in many jurisdictions, the voters must authorize the budget and the tax rate.

In some governmental units the distinction between the executive and legislative branches is blurred, for both may participate in labor negotiations.

Ban on Strikes. In both common and statute law, strikes by government employees have traditionally been illegal. Although the Taft–Hartley Act deals primarily with private sector collective bargaining, it does contain a specific prohibition against strikes by employees of the United States government or any agency thereof.

In 1970 employees of the U.S. Postal Service struck in violation of the law. In August 1981 the Professional Air Traffic Controllers Organization, representing control tower employees at the nation's airports, went on strike after the members voted down a contract negotiated by their leaders with the government. When the strikers refused to return to work within 48 hours as ordered by President Reagan, the government fired all the strikers and decertified the union. These are practically the only strikes that have occurred against the U.S. government.

Strikes at the state and local level do occur occasionally. Public employee strikes usually involve teachers, sanitation workers, and clerical employees.

Some labor relations experts argue that there ought to be a limited right to strike by public employees, especially if their services are not absolutely essential to the public welfare. The states of Alaska, Hawaii, Pennsylvania, Minnesota, Oregon, and Vermont have legalized public employee strikes if no emergency or major inconveniences are involved.

Politics. Politics exerts a substantial influence upon public sector bargaining. This manifests itself in various ways. The behavior of elected public officials, or their appointed advocates, in contract negotiations is strongly affected by what they think will be acceptable to the electorate. The financial ability of a public jurisdiction to pay a given wage increase is partly based upon economic and budgetary factors and partly upon taxpayer attitudes and emotions. Often the stance a public official takes and the concessions he or she will make in bargaining are based upon what will enhance his or her popularity with the electorate. Politics also affects the behavior of union leaders. Sometimes they try to make gains through lobbying and legislation which could not be achieved through direct collective bargaining. Also duringf the course of protracted contract negotiations, a public employee union may contact individual members of the legislative body (school board, city council, etc.) to get them to influence the executive who is conducting negotiations with the union.

Federal Government

Although certain employee groups in the Federal government, notably the postal employees, had belonged to unions for many years, actual collective bargaining between the government and unions did not occur until President Kennedy issued Executive Order 10988 in 1962. This order affirmed the right of employees to join or refrain from joining unions. It created procedures for bargaining unit determination and for union recognition. It required agency heads to bargain in good faith with those unions that had achieved exclusive recognition rights.

The Civil Service Reform Act of 1978 gave statutory authority to the system of collective bargaining in the Federal government. Previously it rested upon the authority of President Kennedy's executive order and one issued by President Nixon in 1969. The Federal Service Labor–Management Relations Statute, which is one title of the Civil Service Reform Act, created the Federal Labor Relations Authority, an independent agency in the executive branch, to administer the entire program. The duties of this authority are to decide representation and unfair labor practice cases, questions of whether a particular issue is negotiable, appeals from arbitration awards, and to establish policies and procedures to make the law function effectively.

The act continued in effect the Federal Service Impasses Panel, created previously under executive order, to resolve impasses in contract negotiations between Federal agencies and unions. This panel only becomes involved after efforts of the Federal Mediation and Conciliation Service to settle a dispute have been unsuccessful.

The act also requires that grievance procedures be included in all agreements negotiated and that they provide for binding arbitration as the last step.

Certain matters are specifically excluded from collective bargaining. Wage rates are not determined by negotiations. Rather they are established by the President of the United States, upon advice of certain designated committees, for all general schedule employees and by agency heads for wage board employees (mostly craft and blue-collar personnel) based upon area wage surveys. Also excluded from bargaining are the matters of hiring, transfers, and promotions, which are covered by the civil service merit system.

State and Local Government

Of the 31 states that have statutes providing for collective bargaining by state and local government employees, there is considerable variation in their provisions. Twenty-one states allow broad-scale bargaining over wages, hours, terms, and conditions of employment. Some laws only require agency heads to "meet and confer" with unions. Some state laws spell out management rights specifically and substantially restrict the scope of bargaining. The more common practice is for the state agency that administers the public employment bargaining law to issue rulings, on a case by case basis as issues are brought to the agency, defining those matters that are mandatory and those that are nonmandatory subjects of negotiations. For example, the Public Employment Relations Board of the State of New York has ruled that such matters as the following are mandatory: retirement benefits (within defined limits), agency shop, layoff, workload, seniority rights, and discipline. Among the nonmandatory subjects are employment qualifications, class size (for teachers), faculty evaluation in colleges, staffing levels, promotion policies, and type of equipment used by firefighters and police.[5] The term mandatory means that if one party wants to negotiate the issue, the other party cannot refuse to negotiate in good faith. However, concessions are not necessarily required. An employer or union can refuse to negotiate a nonmandatory subject. However, it is still permissible to negotiate such matters.

Prior to the advent of collective bargaining, personnel policies and practices were administered by state and municipal civil service commissions. These commissions have had primary responsibility for defining jobs, pay classifications, hiring, promotions, tranfers, and grievances. Collective bargaining has been imposed upon these systems and some confusion and duplication of procedures has resulted. Unions have viewed civil service commissions as agents of the chief executive and have tried to have as many terms of employment come under the collective agreement as possible.

[5]*Mandatory/Nonmandatory Subjects of Negotiation* (State of New York: Public Employment Relations Board, 1981).

DISPUTE SETTLEMENT AND STRIKES

Often when negotiating a new contract, management and the union cannot reach agreement on the issues and an impasse occurs. The union may be holding out for a higher wage increase than management feels it can offer or management may be demanding a rollback of some employee benefits that had been negotiated in previous contracts. Conflict can also arise during the term of an existing agreement. Management may have discharged an employee and the union thinks such action is unjust. Or there may be dispute over the application of the seniority rules in the contract between the parties.

Serious differences between unions and managements can erupt into strikes, walkouts, slowdowns, picketing, or even violence.

A *strike* is a concerted withholding of labor supply in order to bring economic pressure to bear upon the employer to cause him to grant the employees and/or the union's demands. It is a test of economic strength and a contest of staying power. Generally speaking in the private sector strikes are a legal and legitimate method of applying pressure in collective bargaining. However, under our labor law secondary boycott, jurisdictional, and sympathy strikes are illegal. In most jurisdictions strikes in the public sector are illegal.

In a typical year there are about 5,000 strikes in the United States involving about 1.5 to 2 million workers in total. This level of strike activity constitutes about 0.15 to 0.17 per cent of total possible employee hours that could be worked in the economy (working time lost).[6]

A *lockout* consists of a shutdown of a plant or place of business by management in the course of a labor dispute with the employees and their union for the purpose of forcing accep-

[6]U.S. Department of Labor, Bureau of Labor Statistics, *Handbook of Labor Statistics,* Bulletin 2070, December 1980, Table 167.

tance of management's terms. Management ordinarily desires to keep its business in operation because a work stoppage can be costly. It stops production, interrupts sales, and hurts profits. Unions are usually initiators of work stoppages if progress at the bargaining table breaks down. However, we do find that management sometimes resorts to a lockout of its employees after a strike has begun. This is a way of retaliating against the union.

Dispute Settlement Methods

Various techniques have been developed over the years to resolve labor contract negotiation impasses, contract interpretation disputes, strikes, and other kinds of labor–management conflict. The principal methods used are mediation, fact finding, and arbitration. Additionally there are various forms of each of these techniques and sometimes they are used in combination.

Mediation. In mediation, a neutral third party (person) helps the union and management negotiators reach a settlement of the issues separating them. When an impasse occurs during contract negotiations mediation is practically always the first dispute resolution technique used in both the private and public sectors. In the private sector it is generally the only third party intervention used. But in the public sector fact finding and/or arbitration may follow mediation. The mediator assists the parties in reaching agreement, but has no power to dictate a settlement.

Conciliation is similar to mediation and is sometimes viewed as synonymous with it. Some authorities view conciliation as a milder process in which the neutral person calls the parties together, encourages communication, and generally serves as a procedural facilitator. Mediation includes these elements but goes further.

At the outset a mediator typically meets

with the parties jointly and/or separately to learn about the issues and rationales for each party's position. He learns the background and progress of negotiations to date and also learns the parties' feelings and attitudes. He facilitates the exchange of proposals and counterproposals. He explores privately with each negotiating team possible areas for compromise and trade-off. The mediator pushes the parties to narrow the differences. He suggests compromises. Depending upon his "reading" of the situation he may become quite vigorous in trying to persuade the negotiators to modify their positions.

Who are the mediators? The bulk of mediation is performed by the approximately 250 staff mediators employed by the Federal Mediation and Conciliation Service, an independent agency of the U.S. government created by the Taft–Hartley Act in 1947. Additionally some of the states have mediation agencies to handle labor disputes in small businesses not generally serviced by the FMCS. Public sector labor–management disputes are generally mediated by staff mediators of public employment labor–relations agencies which were created by the states to administer their laws governing public sector collective bargaining.

Fact Finding. In the public sector most state laws provide for fact finding as the next step in contract negotiation impasses if mediation has failed to obtain a settlement. Fact finding is rarely used in the private sector. However, the Taft–Hartley Act does provide for the use of a Board of Inquiry for helping to resolve national emergency disputes in the private sector.

In order to assure public employees reasonable and acceptable wages, hours, and terms of employment while denying them the right to strike, state legislatures have generally provided that outstanding differences between public employers and unions be reviewed by a qualified third party who then makes an authoritative recommendation. The fact finder (sometimes a panel of three persons) is appointed by the state labor relations agency. He or she is usually a private citizen who is an experienced labor relations specialist and who is a member of the fact-finding panel maintained by the agency. The fact finder conducts a hearing at which the negotiators for each party present their viewpoints and evidence regarding all unresolved issues. The fact finder then studies the information and issues a report containing recommendations for settlement of the issues. However, these recommendations are not binding upon the parties. Normally the recommendations of the fact finder are given to the news media so that the general public can be informed.

Arbitration. Many of the state public sector statutes provide for final and binding arbitration of contract negotiation impasses that have not been settled through mediation and fact finding. This has been primarily used for police officer and firefighter disputes. Although municipal elected officials have sometimes complained that arbitration infringes upon their legal responsibilities in the financial and taxation areas, these arbitration procedures have generally worked well. There have been practically no strikes by police officers or firefighters since enactment of these laws in the 1970s.

Wages and terms of employment awarded through arbitration have been consistent with those arrived at through direct negotiations.

This type of arbitration is called *interest arbitration* as distinguished from grievance or rights arbitration. The term *interest arbitration* means that the arbitration proceeding determines what the wages and terms of employment, which are matters of material interest to the parties, shall be. In a sense it could be said that the arbitrator legislates the terms of employment for the parties on matters which are at impasse. *Grievance or rights arbitration* is used as the last step of practically all negotiated grievance procedures. The arbitrator frames his decision based upon the evidence presented during a hearing and upon his interpretation of the labor agreement. This type of arbitration is explained in Chapter 21, "Grievances and Arbitration."

Interest arbitration is initiated by either the union or the municipality after other dispute resolution efforts have failed. The initiating party submits a demand for arbitration to the state labor relations agency. Sometimes this form of arbitration is called *compulsory arbitration* because legally the arbitration must proceed upon the demand of either party. The arbitrator may be either a single individual or there may be a tripartite arbitration panel of three persons. A tripartite panel consists of a neutral person who is the chairperson, a person appointed by the union and a person appointed by the public employer.

The arbitrator (or arbitration panel) conducts a formal quasijudicial hearing at which the union and employer negotiators present testimony of witnesses, arguments, and documentary evidence in support of their respective positions. Sometime later the arbitrator (or the panel) issues a formal award and opinion which specifies the precise terms to be adopted for settlement of all outstanding issues. The award of the arbitrator is final and binding upon the parties. Only in very limited circumstances may the decision be appealed to the courts.

There are many varieties of interest arbitration. In *conventional arbitration* the arbitrator (or panel) has full authority to select the position of the union, the position of the employer, or anything in between on each issue presented to it. In *final offer arbitration as a package* the arbitrator must select either the union's final position on all issues or the employer's final position on all issues. He or she cannot compromise and chose a settlement somewhere in between the parties' final positions. In *final offer arbitration on an issue-by-issue basis* the arbitrator must award either the union's final offer or the employer's final offer, one issue at a time. And finally, some state statutes require that all economic issues be considered as one package for final-offer determination but each noneconomic issue can be taken separately for a final-offer decision.

The theory of final-offer arbitration is that it encourages the parties to retreat from extreme positions, to move closer together in negotiations, and it is hoped, to settle the impasse via direct negotiation. As a last resort, if arbitration is required, the parties tend to adopt reasonable positions on each issue because the arbitrator is unlikely to award a party's final offer if it is extreme.

Interest arbitration is hardly ever used in the private sector. However, during World War II the War Labor Board used compulsory interest arbitration to settle thousands of labor–management disputes.

DIFFERENCES BETWEEN UNION AND NONUNION ORGANIZATIONS

That wage rates and employee benefits (pensions, insurances, holidays, vacations, etc.) tend to be higher in unionized firms than nonunion establishments may not be surprising. After all, improvement in economic conditions is a major reason employees join unions. However, the magnitude of the union/nonunion differential of 10–20 per cent for wages and 20–30 per cent for benefits (See Table 20-1) may be astonishing to many: Highly publicized nonunion companies such as IBM, Eastman Kodak, Hewlett-Packard, and Polaroid pay good wages and have liberal employee benefits. They are very well managed and have progressive personnel policies. Also some managements deliberately install professionally developed personnel programs in order to satisfy their employees and keep unions out. But for every IBM or Polaroid there are scores of companies that pay low wages, have limited fringe benefits, and have poor personnel practices. Such practices may be deliberate on the part of management. But commonly it just happens because the firm is marginal in its ability to compete and it has mediocre management.

As shown in Table 20-1, the rate of volun-

TABLE 20-1. Comparison of Personnel Practices and Outcomes in Union and Nonunion Establishments.*

Factor	Research Finding
Wage rates	Union rates 10–20 per cent above nonunion rates.
Fringe Benefits	Union fringe benefits ($cost/hour) 20–30 per cent above nonunion benefits.
Promotions	Seniority weighted more heavily in unionized establishments.
Quits	Quit rate much lower for unionized than similar nonunion employees.
Temporary layoffs	More frequent layoffs in unionized manufacturing firms.
Rules	Unionized establishments operate more with rules regarding scheduling, work assignments, discipline, and grievance handling.
Management practices	Management in unionized firms more professional and less authoritarian.
Job security	Unionized workers with long tenure have greater security.
Employee satisfaction	Unionized workers more satisfied with wages and benefits but less satisfied with supervision and working conditions.
Productivity	Higher in unionized manufacturing and construction firms, when all other factors are equal.

*Adapted, with permission from Richard B. Freeman and James L. Medoff, "The Impact of Collective Bargaining: Illusion or Reality?" in *U.S. Industrial Relations 1950–1980: A Critical Assessment* (Madison, Wis.: Industrial Relations Research Association, 1981). The findings in the Freeman and Medoff analysis are based upon their review of many research investigations.

tary exits or quits is much lower for employees in unionized firms compared with nonunion ones. A reasonable explanation for this phenomenon is that employees through collective bargaining have a voice in establishing personnel policies and have a grievance procedure to resolve complaints. Hence they stay with their employer rather than quit if dissatisfied. Furthermore, they acquire more job rights through seniority in a unionized establishment.

Labor–management agreements tend to be quite definite in spelling out how to handle transfers, layoffs, promotions, overtime assignments, job bidding, wage incentives, and grievances. Management administers the agreement. Employees can submit grievances if they feel management has not administered the agreement fairly. Hence, management must "go by the book" when managing the employees. It has much less freedom and flexibility in a unionized firm. However, employees have more job security.

The research finding that productivity tends to be higher in union than nonunion companies contradicts the conventional managerial wisdom that unions constitute an impediment to efficiency. Why is productivity generally higher? Often the quality of management practices is better in unionized enterprises. Indirectly collective bargaining contributes to the professionalization of management. If wage rates are pushed up management responds to the cost pressures by taking steps to improve efficiency. Management must run a "tighter ship." Slack practices cannot be tolerated.

Another explanation for the productivity differential is that higher wages and better employee benefits attract a better quality work force. A third reason is that the lower quit rate in unionized establishments results in a more experienced and probably more productive work force.

But clearly, those unionized companies that are beset with frequent strikes, slowdowns, and strife will tend to have lower productivity than their nonunion competitors.

Questions for Review and Discussion

1. What is meant by the term *collective bargaining?* What are its characteristics?
2. In what ways did the National Labor Relations Act (Wagner Act) aid the expansion of unions?
3. Some authorities and practitioners claim that strikes are a necessary part of collective bargaining. Without the possibility of a strike, true collective bargaining cannot occur between the union and management. Other authorities assert that the practice of collective bargaining in the United States has matured to the point that peaceful settlement of contract negotiation disputes is nearly always possible. Hence the strike is not a necessary concomitant of collective bargaining. Take a position on the issue and substantiate your views.
4. What factors have contributed to the growth of multiemployer bargaining in recent years?
5. As the president of your own company (that is, you are a principal stockholder) would you favor or oppose the granting of a union shop provision to the union with which you have been dealing for several years? Explain your position.
6. Explain differences between the context of collective bargaining in the public and the private sectors.
7. In collective bargaining what factors may bolster the union's power vis-à-vis the employer? What factors may bolster the employer's power?
8. If wage rates and employee benefits in unionized companies tend to be significantly higher than those in nonunion firms, why do not more employee groups actively seek union representation?
9. Why are fact finding and interest arbitration often used to help resolve labor contract negotiation impasses in the public sector whereas they are rarely used in the private sector?

CASE PROBLEMS

Note: Case problems for Chapter 19, "Unions and Management," and Chapter 20, "Collective Bargaining," are placed here because these two chapters deal essentially with the single subject area of labor-management relations.

PROBLEM 1: A TALK BY A PERSONNEL MANAGER

The personnel manager of a local manufacturing company was invited to speak before a class of college seniors taking a course in industrial relations at the university. He was a man of about forty-five and had arrived at his present position via the financial and accounting departments of his company. He had been personnel manager for three years at the time of his talk. As the subject of his lecture he chose to concentrate upon the relations between his company and the local union, with particular emphasis devoted to the political nature of the union. His talk, in abbreviated form, was as follows.

"Our company prides itself on having recognized unions early in the game and on having sound labor-management relations. We granted recognition to our union over forty years ago without there being a strike. I am proud to say that we have never had a single stoppage due to a labor dispute in all the years since.

"The management of our company believes in dealing honestly and in a straightforward manner with the employees and the union. We believe that common sense, logic, and sound business judgment should be all that are necessary to arrive at satisfactory agreements between union and management.

"I am continually annoyed, however, by the fact that political expediency seems to be the guidepost for the behavior of union leaders. Now, the elected officials of our local union consist of the president, vice-president, secretary-treasurer, chairman of the shop committee, and fifteen departmental stewards. All of these fellows are regular company employees who take on these union jobs as extra assignments. The union pays their president about one thousand dollars a year extra for his services. Stewards get no pay from the union. I think those people seek union jobs to be important; to be big shots in front of the men. Getting elected to a union office is nothing but a personality contest. When union election time is getting near, the incumbent officers and stewards become the biggest bunch of back-slappers and hand-shakers that can be found anywhere. They want to get re-elected. They try to show the boys that they are going to bat for them. If problems don't exist, they deliberately create them. They try to give the impression that they aren't letting the company get away with anything. At union meetings you rarely find good solid citizens in attendance. It is always the troublemakers and malcontents who go.

"It is difficult for me to understand, sometimes, why the union officers are so politically oriented. Why don't they act more responsible? Even when the company institutes some new fringe benefits or service for the employees, like new coffee machines or better washroom facilities, the union bigwigs try to claim that they had to work hard to extract these benefits from management.

"Let's take the case of the increase in pay for a special setup man's job on which two men were employed. The skill requirements of the job had increased. We offered the union fifteen cents more per hour, and they accepted. However, when the chairman of the shop committee informed the workers of their fifteen-cent raise, they complained that they should have gotten twenty-five cents per hour. The committeeman lacked the courage to tell them the increase was proper and just. Instead he returned the complaint to management and asked for a higher rate.

"Before closing I will give you students one other illustration of the political way our union officers act. Joe has been employed as a laborer for three years. He works on the evening shift, which starts at 4 P.M.. At 8 P.M., he was reported to be under the influence of liquor. I was called into the case, as I was working late that evening. The evening superintendent and I talked to Joe in the presence of two shop stewards. Joe reeked of alcohol. He could not stand straight even while hanging onto a chair. He became belligerent toward the superintendent and myself. One of the stewards agreed that Joe was very drunk. We told Joe to report to my office at 10 A.M. the next day. He came in accompanied by the chairman of the shop committee and one of the stewards from the previous evening. They claimed that he had been taking antihistamine pills for a cold and that he was doctoring with brandy to ease his cough. They even claimed that a friend of Joe's had passed away and this upset him. They clearly lied to save his job. They wanted to build themselves up in the eyes of the other workers to show how much they did for them. I recommended immediate discharge for Joe, but upon appeal by the union, top management overruled me. He was suspended for two weeks without pay and then returned to his job."

Questions

1. Do you agree that all that is required for successful labor-management dealings is "common sense, logic, and sound business judgment"?
2. Why do you feel the union officers and stewards acted in such a "political" fashion?
3. What conditions are necessary in order for union leaders to act in a truly responsible manner?
4. Do you think that politics can or should be divorced from the affairs of a local union?
5. Based upon his talk, what do you surmise regarding the experience and knowledge of labor relations possessed by the personnel manager?

PROBLEM 2: MEDIATION OF A UNION–EMPLOYER DISPUTE

Bill Smith, a staff mediator for the State Labor Relations Board, was assigned to mediate a contract negotiations impasse between the County of Clarendon and the Public Employees Union, Local 561. The county seat was located in a small city about 175 miles away from Bill's office.

Upon receiving this assignment, Bill contacted the advocates for both the county and the union. The advocate for the union was Edgar Donovan, a field representative who worked out of the union's central office. The advocate for the county was Frank Carrington, a professional labor relations consultant. In addition to setting a date for a mediation session, Bill learned what progress had been made to date in their negotiations (several issues had been settled) and the nature and seriousness of their impasse on the unresolved issues. In his telephone conversations with the two advocates, Bill Smith learned that the union and the county had thoroughly discussed all the unresolved issues across the table. It was mutually agreed that the mediator would work with the union and county negotiating teams in separate rooms when he arrived at the county office building on the agreed date.

Accordingly, at the outset of the mediation session Bill Smith met with each bargaining team in separate rooms. In addition to Frank Carrington, the county was represented by the county administrative affairs officer and three members of the board of legislators (one of whom was the chairman of the board). In addition to Edgar Donovan, the union negotiating committee was composed of the local union president plus representatives from each of the major employee groups in the county—public works (2 persons), county hospital (1), social service (1), mental health (1), custodial (1), and office (1).

Bill first met with the union negotiating committee. He made a brief explanation of the mediation process and how he would work. At this meeting Edgar Donovan, union field representative, explained each issue, as well as the union's and the county's position on the issues. For a salary increase the union's last position before mediation was 10 per cent for each of two years. Donovan stated that all the open issues were important to the union. He further stated that the union had made several concessions during the course of negotiations (which had been going on over a period of two months) and that the county had made hardly any concessions.

Then Smith met privately with the county negotiating team. Frank Carrington, the county spokesman, explained the background of negotiations and discussed each of the open or unresolved issues. The county's last salary offer before mediation was 2.5 per cent for each of two years and 4 per cent for a third year. He pointed out that when the county and the union had reached a contract settlement a year ago, the union membership had voted against ratification. The county did not want a repeat of that situation. The county felt that the union leaders had not done a good job of selling the contract settlement to the membership.

The mediator moved back and forth between the rooms occupied by the union and the county teams. He transmitted proposals and counterproposals. He suggested grouping the proposals into packages. For example, one union package dealt with five issues. In this package the union offered to drop one of its proposals, the county should drop one of its proposals, and the county should grant three of the union proposals (which represented slightly compromised positions from earlier union stances).

By the end of the first mediation session, which had lasted six hours, tentative agreement was reached on six of the twelve issues that were at impasse. However, Bill realized that these were of lesser importance and the really difficult issues were still to be settled. The next mediation session was scheduled for one week hence. Two days after the first session, Bill telephoned Edgar Donovan to find out what salary increase the union would accept. Donovan replied that the union wanted a 7 per cent increase for each of two years as a very minimum.

At the start of the second mediation session, Bill Smith talked briefly with each group separately. Then he asked to speak privately with Edgar Donovan out in the hall. After the two had been conversing in the hall for perhaps two minutes, Alice Fellows, the president of the local union, came out into the hall. She asked to join the discussion. The mediator wanted to know if the union would accept compromises on its proposals and if it would drop any items. While the three of them were standing in the hall, two of the union committee members came out of their room and walked slowly down the hall to the drinking fountain. The mediator then took the two union leaders into an empty office and closed the door. The union leaders explained the union position on the six unresolved issues and what compromises it could make. They then said that there were 200 employees in the department of public works out of a total of 700 in the bargaining unit. These people were pushing hard to have vacancies filled by awarding open jobs to the most senior qualified employees within the department. They claimed that sometimes the better jobs were filled by direct hiring from the outside and that political patronage sometimes determined who was selected. Also certain employees in the social service and mental health departments must be "on call" in the evenings and on weekends. Currently they were given one-half hour of compensatory time off at a later date for each hour of "on call" time. The county wanted to eliminate this compensatory time off because it said the employees were not actually working during "on call" time. These employee groups did not want to be "on call" if they did not receive some compensatory time off. Further, the union wanted the county to set up a disability insurance program to provide payments to those employees who were ill and had exhausted their sick leave days of entitlement.

After talking with the two union leaders, the mediator talked with the county team. He explained the union positions and possible compromises. But he did not discuss salary at this time. The county was strongly opposed to filling vacancies on the basis of the most senior qualified employee who applied. Bill Smith asked if the county would be willing, at least, to interview the three top qualified employees who apply. The mediator asked if the county would be willing to grant compensatory time off at a rate of one-third hour for each hour "on call." The county said it could not afford to set up a disability insurance plan. The mediator suggested that a sick leave bank might be adopted as a substitute for a disability insurance plan. The cost would be very small.[5]

The county wanted to caucus privately on these matters so the mediator waited in the hall. A few minutes later Frank Carrington joined Bill in the hall. Together they went into the empty office. Carrington suggested that the county would be willing to make a package offer on all open issues. Carrington asked

---

[5]In a sick leave bank each employee donates, say, one day per year of his accumulated sick leave to a fund of days to be granted to employees who are ill and who have exhausted their sick leave days of entitlement.

what salary increase the union would accept. Bill asked if the county would offer 7 per cent for each of two years. Frank Carrington said, "No." The county was willing to pay 5½ per cent for each of two years and would offer 6 per cent for a third year if the union would sign a three-year agreement. They then discussed the general outline of a package that might be acceptable to both the union and the county. Frank Carrington returned to his county team while Bill Smith met with the union. Smith explained that a package offer on all six unresolved issues was being formulated by the county team. One of the union representatives quipped that he wondered earlier, when Smith went out of the room with Edgar Donovan, whether they were going to go into the county meeting room by themselves.

In a few minutes, Bill Smith went into the county room to learn of its package offer. This offer consisted of the following: 1) 5 per cent, 5 per cent, and 6 per cent salary increase for each of three years: 2) interview top three candidates for vacancies; 3) sick leave bank; 4) one-quarter hour compensatory time off for each hour of "on call" duty; 5) no concessions on the other two union proposals.

The mediator then transmitted this package to the union group. They asked for time to caucus privately. The mediator waited in the hall.

In ten minutes Edgar Donovan and Alice Fellows came into the hall and all three went to the empty office. The union leaders said the package was partially acceptable but they insisted on more money than offered by the county. Also the union was opposed to a three-year agreement. Furthermore the department of public works people wanted two job titles increased in pay by 20 cents per hour. (This matter hadn't been mentioned before.) The public works department was the largest in the entire bargaining unit and this group had been principally responsible for voting down the contract the first time a year ago. Also, the two public works representatives were not fully satisfied with the county offer to simply interview three employees for job vacancies; however, the rest of the committee had urged them to accept this and they had reluctantly done so. Smith asked if the union would accept 6½ per cent for each of two years. They said, "Yes."

The mediator then met with the entire county team and expressed the concerns of the union. He pointed out the special interests of the public works employees. It seemed that the two issues standing in the way of a settlement were salary and the special concerns of the public works employees. (Bill Smith felt privately that both bargaining teams genuinely wished to reach an agreement this evening.) The mediator suggested that a settlement with the union could be reached with a salary offer by the county of 6½ per cent plus some concession to the public works group. The county asked to caucus privately.

A few minutes later Frank Carrington asked Smith to meet again with the county team to obtain their "final offer." This offer was for a salary increase of 6 per cent for the first year and 6½ per cent for the second year of a two-year contract. There would be no special concessions for the public works group except that the top three employee-candidates for vacancies would be interviewed. Tentative agreements on all the other issues were reviewed.

Carrington and Smith walked out into the hall together. Carrington suggested that if the union was agreeable to the terms discussed, it would be best for the union to make this package offer to the county. The county would then accept. The salary increase was slightly greater than the amount authorized by the full county legislature of seventeen members. But he was confident his committee could sell this amount to the full legislature.

Bill Smith then presented the full package to the union team. The team accepted the entire package without change. No further mention was made of the special concerns of the public works group.

Both negotiating teams then met to work out the final contract language on all the issues that had been at impasse. At 2 A.M. the mediation session was concluded and the participants all shook hands with one another.

Within two weeks both the union membership and the county legislature had ratified the agreement.

Questions
1. Why did the mediator deal with the union and county teams in separate rooms instead of together?
2. Why did the mediator hold several private meetings with the advocates?
3. What do you make of the union team's behavior when Mediator Smith invited Edgar Donovan into the hall?
4. Why did the county want the final package to be presented as an offer of settlement terms by the union?
5. How do you evaluate the special concerns of the public works group? Why were their concerns not pressed further at the end?
6. Why was mediation needed to help resolve the impasse? Why could not or did not the parties reach the same conclusion without the services of a mediator?

PROBLEM 3: WILLSONVILLE

In April 1981 several employees of the Village of Willsonville appealed to the Public Employees' Union, a statewide organization, to represent them for purposes of collective bargaining with the mayor and village board. Willsonville, with a population of 3300, is located in a rural area of a state in the Northeast. After a short organization campaign, the Public Labor–Management Board of the state conducted a secret ballot election to ascertain whether the employees in the bargaining unit wished to be represented by the union or whether they wished no union. The vote was ovewhelmingly in favor of union representation.

The bargaining unit consisted of five police officers (one captain and four patrolmen), twelve public works department employees (streets and refuse collection), three parks department employees, two village hall custodians, and two school-crossing personnel. Wages and employee benefits were low in comparison with those paid by area private-sector firms and in comparison with those paid by other villages in the region.

The village was represented in contract negotiations by the mayor and a hired professional negotiator. The union bargaining team consisted of a field representative from the Public Employees' Union headquarters and four union members elected by the membership. Negotiations dragged on for over a year without the parties ever agreeing upon contract terms. The mayor, with support from the village board, insisted upon a reduction of benefits presently accorded to employees. He demanded a reduction in annual sick leave from 10 to 5 days, a reduction in vacation days per year, and a cutback in holidays from 11 to 8. He offered a pay increase of 3 per cent with *no* retroactivity to the date negotiations commenced.

The union felt itself to be in a weak position. Because of the very protracted negotiations, employee support was slipping away. By May 1982 only 50 per cent of the employees in the unit still belonged to the union. Employee turnover was high. Many of the original union supporters had quit to take better-paying jobs elsewhere. The police captain, who had originally taken the lead in organizing the employees, was promoted by the mayor to the position of police chief with a $2,000 annual salary increase. In his new position he was out of the bargaining unit.

The union requested the services of a state mediator to help the parties resolve the impasse. During a mediation session in June 1982 the mayor told the mediator he saw no need to continue negotiations, because support for the union had dwindled. In a private session with the union bargaining team the mediator sensed that the team members' resolve to press the negotiations was weakening. The union field representative claimed that the mayor was trying to destroy the local union. The union team told the mediator they would accept a 7 per cent across-the-board wage increase, retroactivity to April 1981 when negotiations had begun, and the same employee benefits currently available to employees (no rollbacks). The mediator considered their proposals to be reasonable and rather modest.

When the mediator met with the mayor and the village negotiator, the mayor made no change in his position. He insisted that benefits be reduced and wages increased only 3 per cent. No progress was made after three hours of discussion and the mediator left.

Two weeks later the village sent a letter to the headquarters of the Public Employees' Union stating that it was withdrawing recognition of the union because it felt the local union no longer represented a majority of the employees. The union did not contest this action.

Early in July the employees, as individuals, pleaded their case for a wage increase and maintenance of existing benefits before the Village Board. The board raised wages 7½ per cent across the board, retroactive to April 1981. It announced that benefits would not be cut.

Questions
1. During the course of the protracted negotiations, is there anything that the union could have done to improve its effectiveness to successfully negotiate a fair labor agreement?

2. Should public employees have the right to strike? Would a strike, in this case, have strengthened the unions' cause?
3. Why do you suppose the mayor bargained so toughly with the union? Why did the village board offer rather generous terms to the employees after the local union was disbanded?
4. In those states having public sector collective-bargaining laws (about 31 states), it is uncommon for elected officials to pursue a campaign to destroy a local union. Why is this so? Why do private sector corporate executives generally oppose unionization?

Suggestions for Further Reading

Chauhan, D. S. "The Political and Legal Issues of Binding Arbitration in Government." *Monthly Labor Review,* Vol. 102, No. 9 (September 1979), pp. 35–41.

Elkouri, Frank, and Edna A. Elkouri. *How Arbitration Works,* 3rd ed. Washington, D.C.: Bureau of National Affairs, 1973.

Frazier, Henry B., III. "Labor–Management Relations in the Federal Government." *Labor Law Journal*, Vol. 30, No. 3 (March 1979), pp. 130–138.

Getman, Julius C. *Labor Relations: Law, Practice, and Policy,* 2nd ed. Mineola, N.Y.: The Foundation Press, 1982.

Hunt, James W. *Employer's Guide to Labor Relations,* rev. ed. Washington, D.C.: Bureau of National Affairs, 1979.

Kochan, Thomas A. *Collective Bargaining and Industrial Relations.* Homewood, Ill.: Richard D. Irwin, Inc., 1980.

Mills, Daniel Quinn. *Labor–Management Relations,* 2nd ed. New York: McGraw-Hill Book Co., 1982.

"The New Industrial Relations," *Business Week,* May 11, 1981, pp. 84–98.

Portrait of a Process: Collective Negotiations in Public Employment. Fort Washington, Pa.: Labor Relations Press, 1980.

21 Grievances and Arbitration

In the course of human events in even the best-managed company, employee discontent, gripes, and complaints will certainly arise. Thus an employee may feel that the foreman assigns him or her to do all the dirty and heavy jobs. A clerk-typist may discover that the new woman—also a clerk-typist—has just been hired at a salary ten dollars a week greater than she is getting after a full year on the job. She goes to see her supervisor about her own salary. An hourly production worker may have been handed a written disciplinary warning by the foreman because she refused to work overtime last Saturday. The worker thinks it is unfair to be disciplined for this, and goes to see the union steward.

The foregoing are but brief examples of the myriad situations that can give rise to employee anxiety and complaint. For the sake of justice to the individual and the smooth functioning of the whole organization, it behooves management to get at the root of employee dissatisfactions and to take corrective action wherever possible.

NATURE OF COMPLAINTS AND GRIEVANCES

If some problem or condition bothers or annoys an employee or if she or he thinks the treatment has been unfair, she or he may express discontent to someone else. When she or he vocalizes dissatisfaction, we can then designate such action a complaint. Usually, but not always, when a person "sounds off" about something, she or he hopes that the listener (a fellow employee or a supervisor) will do something to correct the difficulty.

But an unexpressed dissatisfaction can be just as worthy of consideration by the supervisor as the spoken complaint. Just as an untreated wound can cause dire consequences for a human being, so can a festering discontent in the shop lead to grave results.

There are many reasons why an employee may keep a problem "bottled up" inside himself. He may simply have a high tolerance limit

442

for frustration. Or he may feel that the condition may soon change in such a way that the problem will then be corrected. He may have found from past experience that it does no good to complain to his supervisor. Sometimes a person may even feel that others will criticize or condemn him if he complains. By establishing a sound and healthy relationship with his people—one of mutual trust and confidence—the supervisor can do much to dispel employee fears and encourage free expression of feelings.

What Is a Grievance?

Viewpoints as to just what constitutes a grievance vary among personnel management and industrial relations authorities. According to some a grievance is any discontent or sense of injustice, expressed or not, felt by an employee in connection with employment in an organization. This is a very broad conception. Such a definition includes all states of dissatisfaction or unhappiness whether they have been vocalized or not and whether they can be substantiated by facts or not.

A very narrow definition of a grievance is that adopted in many unionized companies. Here the labor policy may hold that a grievance is genuine only if there has been some alleged violation of the labor agreement. According to this view the only rights possessed by employees are those specifically spelled out in the contract; hence they can legitimately grieve only issues involved in the application and interpretation of the union–management agreement. As we shall see later in this chapter, such a narrow view has serious weaknesses. It is akin to a housewife's sweeping the dirt under the rug and pretending it does not exist.

Still another way of viewing this issue is to consider the act of expressing one's dissatisfaction with his supervisor as a complaint. It only becomes a true grievance if the supervisor is unable to settle the problem satisfactorily and then the employee appeals the case to the next higher

level of management according to the steps in a formal grievance procedure. Thus, some labor–management agreements specify that a complaint that has not been settled on the basis of informal discussion between foreman and worker must be put into writing and then submitted to the second step of the grievance procedure, at which point it becomes a true grievance.

The concept that will be used throughout this chapter is that a *grievance is any dissatisfaction or feeling of injustice in connection with one's employment situation that is brought to the attention of management*. This is a reasonably broad definition, but it does exclude the unexpressed dissatisfaction. It is difficult for management to act on an employee's problem if he or she does not call the matter to their attention. The emphasis on management's part should be to create a proper leadership climate, so that employees who feel they have a justifiable complaint feel free to inform management of this fact.

WHY HAVE A GRIEVANCE PROCEDURE?

Some employers, especially in nonunion companies, take the view that there is really no need for establishing a formalized grievance-handling system. They hold that all their first-line supervisors are trained to hear employee complaints and to take prompt action to settle them. As a further argument they add that the company is well managed, it has an enlightened human-relations program in operation, and employees are generally satisfied, because very little dissatisfaction or complaint ever reaches the ears of top management. Of course, to the informed student of personnel management such contentions do not really prove much.

Why is it desirable that work organizations adopt a formal means for handling employee grievances? There are a number of sound reasons.

All employee complaints and dissatisfactions are, in actual practice, not settled satisfactorily by the first-level supervisor. There are many possible reaons for this. The supervisor may lack the necessary human relations skill to deal effectively with his people. He may lack the authority to take the action that is really necessary to properly solve the problem. He may even agree with the substance of the employee's grievance but know, from past experience, that it is futile to try to get higher management to act. Some supervisors may suppress the expression of grievances by their people. In those cases where the employee feels that his immediate supervisor has discriminated against him, he may feel that the supervisor can never, during a grievance discussion, fairly and objectively judge him and the situation. In this situation the employee must be able to appeal his case to some higher official.

Another justification for having a formal grievance-handling system is that it brings employee problems to the attention of higher management. The procedure serves as a medium of upward communication. Higher management becomes more aware of employee frustrations, problems, and expectations. It becomes sensitive to employee needs and well-being. Therefore, when higher management is formulating plans that will affect employees (for example, a plant expansion or contraction, company reorganization, or installation of new labor-saving machinery), it will have become fully cognizant of employee needs and reactions; hence complaints and grievances will be less likely to arise.

A grievance-handling system serves as an outlet for employee frustrations, discontents, and gripes. It operates like a pressure release valve on a steam boiler. Employees do not have to keep their frustrations bottled up until eventually seething discontent causes an explosion. They have a legitimate, officially approved way of appealing their grievances to higher management. If dissatisfied with initial attempts to iron out the difficulty with the supervisor, employees do not have to feel that they are going over their boss's head surreptitiously, as often happens in plants lacking a grievance procedure.

The existence of an effective grievance procedure reduces the likelihood of arbitrary action by supervision, because the supervisors know that the employees are able to protest such behavior and make their protests heard by higher management.

GRIEVANCE SETTLEMENT FOR UNIONIZED EMPLOYEES

It is when a union organizes the employees that demands are made by the union to establish a formal grievance procedure. Practically all labor–management agreements contain procedures for the handling of grievances. It is understood by union and management alike that the signing of a labor contract does not automatically take care of all labor-relations problems that will arise during the life of the agreement. Therefore, a grievance procedure provides one means of settling such difficulties.

With the presence of a union, employees know that it is fully legitimate to submit complaints and grievances to management. Often the union officials will encourage the expression of grievances. This may be done to bring to the surface all underlying discontents, to demonstrate to management that all is not well in the plant, to identify issues that can strengthen the union's hand, or to show the employees that the union can successfully help them achieve their needs and wants on the job. The economic and social power of the union commonly serves to prevent lower-level supervisors from taking punitive action against those workers who have submitted grievances against management actions.

The Grievance Procedure

The general pattern for handling grievances in unionized establishments has become rather standardized, although specific details, of course, vary from company to company.

Because management is presumed to possess full authority to operate its business as it sees fit (subject of course to legal, moral, and labor agreement controls), the reasoning is that a grievance represents a request by an employee, group of employees, and/or the union for a change in some management action or lack of action. In effect management administers the business and applies the provisions of the union–management agreement. If the employees or the union do not like the way this is done, they must submit a grievance according to the procedure outlined in the labor agreement.

Table 21-1 shows the individuals or officers involved at each step of a typical grievance procedure. The exact job titles, of course, will vary from organization to organization. Although most labor agreements specify a four-step grievance procedure, some have five steps and some have only three steps. In order to prevent man-agers from stalling or sitting on grievances, most contracts show a time limit within which management must give a written reply to the union at each stage. Likewise, in order to prevent the union from stalling or appealing old grievances, contracts generally specify a time limit for appeals.

In companies the labor relations or personnel office plays a major role in representing the employer's interest. When a grievance is appealed by an employee or the union beyond the first-level supervisor step, it is the responsibility of the personnel office to investigate the facts of the case. This involves gathering written documentation and interviewing concerned persons and witnesses. The personnel or labor relations manager must decide the response to be made to the grievant by testing the events and circumstances of the case against the meaning and language of the union–employer contract. He or she will also test the response against past practice and personnel policy. In deciding the proper answer to give the grievant the personnel or labor relations manager will generally consult closely with appropriate line executives such as superintendents, department heads, and plant

TABLE 21-1. A Typical Grievance Procedure.

Step	Union Representative	Employer Representative	Time Limit for Employer Decision	Time Limit for Union Appeal
1	Employee and union steward	Supervisor	3 days	3 days
2	Chief steward or business agent	Superintendent or person-nel office	7 days	7 days
3	Grievance committee and national union representative	Personnel vice-president	10 days	10 days
4	Arbitration by Impartial Third Party			

managers. It is important for the personnel office to take a lead position in handling the employer's responses at the various steps of the grievance procedure. If this were not done, then each manager throughout the organization would develop his or her own answer to the grievances originating in his or her division. Such a procedure invites inconsistency of treatment and inequities. This could be disastrous not only to union–employer relations but also to plant human relations.

In handling grievances both union and employer representatives should view the grievance process as a means of developing solutions to problems. Oftentimes creative solutions and compromises will satisfy the grievant, the union, and the employer. Unfortunately, in too many instances the union and the management adopt a "we win/you lose" strategy. Such an attitude does not enhance the quality of labor–management relationships.

Over 90 per cent of all collective-bargaining agreements in the private sector and about 75 per cent of those in the public sector provide for binding arbitration as the final step in the grievance procedure.[1] This is the peaceful method of settling an unresolved grievance. The alternative, which does exist in some agreements, is a strike. The topic of arbitration will be covered later in this chapter.

Fair Representation. Unions possess a degree of discretion in deciding whether to serve as an employee's advocate in presenting his or her grievance to the management representative in the grievance procedure. However there are legal limits on what a union can and cannot do. The U.S. Supreme Court has ruled that a union cannot be arbitrary or discriminatory, or cannot act in bad faith in handling bargaining unit members' grievances. Also the union cannot arbitrarily ignore a meritorious grievance or process it in a perfunctory manner. However the court fully acknowledges the union's right to fairly judge a grievance on its merits and to decide which grievances to take to arbitration.[2]

With considerable frequency in recent years rank and file members have taken their unions to court charging them with failure in their legal duty of fair representation. Unions, quite naturally, are apprehensive about this development and have responded by pressing more cases to arbitration.

The Clinical Approach to Grievance Handling

A fairly common view, especially among business executives, is that the labor agreement is a legal document that spells out the rights and obligations of the company, the union, and the employees. In complaining about conditions in the plant, the employee really has a right to submit a grievance concerning only those matters that have been specifically covered in the contract. In short, as explained earlier, the contract specifies the rights of the union and the employees; hence an employee can grieve only about some alleged violation of these rights. According to this conception of the grievance process, an employee who claims that he should be classified into pay grade 7 instead of his present grade of 6, on the basis of enlarged job responsibilities, would have a legitimate grievance, because the labor agreement specifically covers the matter of job classification. On the other hand an employee who complains that his or her foreman has picked on him or her and called him or her nasty names would have no right to submit a grievance, because there is no provision in the contract covering such an issue.

The procedure just described has been called a legalistic approach to grievance handling. Many union–management agreements conform to this narrow concept of what is a proper grievance by stating that a grievance

[1]Daniel Q. Mills, *Labor–Management Relations* (New York: McGraw-Hill Book Co., 1978), p. 211.

[2]*Vaca* v. *Sipes*, 386 U.S. 171 (1967).

must be an issue that *relates to the interpretation and application of the agreement.* Other kinds of complaints are ruled out as being illegitimate or unjustified.

Benjamin Selekman has stated eloquently the argument for adopting a clinical rather than legalistic approach to the handling of grievances. The emphasis in the clinical approach is upon getting to the root of the employee's dissatisfaction regardless of whether his or her grievance, as expressed, fits some narrow mold as defined by the labor agreement. Selekman points out that emphasis should be placed upon the problems of treating grievances rather than upon the mechanics of accepting or dismissing them. In answer to the question "When is a grievance not a grievance?" Selekman says, "Never."[3] Although the grievance on its surface may not fit a strictly defined mold of what constitutes a legitimate grievance according to a contract definition, it behooves management to make every reasonable effort to find out what is bothering the employee in order to take steps to rectify the trouble. Discontent, unhappiness, and unrest do not disappear just because a supervisor pronounces them irrelevant and outside the scope of the contract.

A further argument for following a clinical approach is that numerous problem situations are bound to arise that were not foreseen at the time the company and union negotiated the contract. These trouble spots cannot be swept under the carpet until it is time to bargain the next agreement one or more years later. The labor law of the United States (for example, Taft–Hartley Act) requires bargaining between management and union at all times to settle joint problems. This supports what common sense tells us anyway, namely that there must be a good faith attempt to solve difficulties and disputes as they arise. The grievance procedure provides an effective instrument for accomplishing this objective.

[3]Benjamin M. Selekman, *Labor Relations and Human Relations* (New York: McGraw-Hill Book Company, 1947), ch. 5.

In conformity with this liberal view of grievance handling, foremen and higher-management personnel should wholeheartedly undertake to investigate and act upon *all* grievances. If a grievance cannot be tied to some provision of the labor agreement, it can certainly be judged according to psychological or sociological principles, principles of equity and justice, or according to established personnel policies of the company. This all-inclusive approach to grievances can be applied at all steps of the procedure save the last one—arbitration. Because arbitrators' decisions are generally final and binding and because management and the union, as a rule, do not choose to have arbitrators legislate for them by creating new policies and contract provisions, it seems reasonable that at this last step the arbitrator be empowered to settle only questions of contract interpretation or application. Hence use the clinical approach through all the lower stages of the grievance procedure, but be legalistic at the final arbitration step.

Role of the Supervisor

The first-line supervisor in whose department a grievance originates should take the major responsibility for trying to reach a settlement that is acceptable to all parties concerned. However, all too often in practice his or her role becomes a minor one. When unionization became widespread in the mass production industries in the 1930s and 1940s, top management in many companies feared the consequences of faulty action by foremen in handling grievances, so it centralized all grievance-handling authority in the industrial relations department. On paper the foreman was the first step in the grievance procedure. In practice the industrial relations department answered all grievances. This could be done in a number of ways. In one way the foreman might actually give an answer to the worker and/or steward, but it would be an answer he obtained as a result of consultation with the industrial relations department. Sometimes foremen would get in the habit of rejecting any and all grievances, and these would then be appealed to the industrial relations office, which appeared in the second or third step of the procedure. Often the local union would sense that the foremen were powerless and would skip the first step and immediately take its cases to the office that had the authority. In this same vein the plant industrial relations director of a large corporation once said to the author somewhat proudly. "For each and every grievance, I write out the answers that my foremen give to the union. I would no more trust them with such an important responsibility than I would a child."

It is fully sound to enter a grievance at a higher step in the regular grievance procedure if it has broad policy implications for which no precedents have been established. But for practically all other types the foreman must be granted the necessary authority to make at least an initial settlement on his or her own. He or she must be fully trained in labor policy, contract interpretation, and human relations so that he or she can properly carry out this responsibility. In recent years many companies have swung around to this way of thinking.

Because worker grievances are often intimately related to the activities and pressures involved in getting out production (for example, work assignments, transfers, workloads, job classifications, overtime distribution), the foreman is in the best position to make a full investigation of the facts of the problem. He or she can collect written data and examine records as well as interview union representatives, employees, and management staff personnel to compile a full account of the facts and history surrounding a case. When a supervisor does not feel sure, he or she should certainly consult the immediate superior or the industrial relations department. But he or she should never become merely a messenger, a front, or a figurehead. Grievances tend to be settled most expeditiously and to the satisfaction of all parties concerned in

those companies when the front-line supervisor plays an important role.

Role of Shop Steward and the Union

The position of a union steward is a difficult one. One of his prime duties is to represent workers and the union in the processing of grievances. Shall he look upon himself as a shop lawyer who goes to bat for every worker on each and every complaint? Shall he make no attempt to reject those he honestly believes have no merit? In most industrial unions the steward is elected by his fellow employees in the department where he works. They are his friends. If he wants to keep his steward's position and get re-elected, he has a powerful urge to simply go to bat for his colleagues on all complaints.

Yet there are serious disadvantages to this approach. A steward is a union leader, and he has to stand up and be counted on important issues. He must be strong enough to say no when the facts demand such a position. Most union leadership manuals for stewards tell them to perform, at least partially, a judicial role in handling employee grievances. A union's position vis-à-vis the company can be seriously weakened if it loads up the grievance machinery with a lot of cases that are so weak that the union loses them at the higher stages.

Sometimes the union steward concludes that he has a thankless job. He may overextend himself to push faithfully a large number of worker grievances to a successful conclusion. Yet once he tells the workers that they are wrong on an issue and he cannot in all fairness push their complaint, he often finds that they are vitriolic in their abuse of him.

Actually much of the legalism that has crept into collective agreements and union grievance-handling procedures has been created by union leaders to insulate themselves from rank-and-file pressures.

Political struggles within a union often have

a profound effect upon the number of grievances submitted and the vigor with which union officials push them. If there is a sharp contest for some important union office, the competing candidates will often try to demonstrate how much they can do for the rank and file by vigorously digging up issues and pursuing them to a successful conclusion. Pressure tactics such as slowdowns and brief walkouts may even be employed to force management to back down. The same kind of grievance activity may take place if the union that is "in" the company is being threatened by an outside union that seeks to win bargaining rights and unseat the incumbent union.

GRIEVANCE ARBITRATION

In the vast majority of union–employer relationships management has accepted binding arbitration as the terminal point in the grievance procedure even though this means that management does not have the "last say" in determining the outcome. In return for granting binding arbitration, management customarily receives a written "no-strike" pledge (incorporated into the agreement) from the union during the term of the union–employer agreement.

There are two basic ways of employing an arbitrator. One is the permanent arbitrator or umpire system, and the other is the *ad hoc* (from the Latin, meaning "for this case alone, or special") system. Some large corporations, such as General Motors and United States Steel, and certain trade associations, such as the needle trades in New York City, employ full-time arbitrators on a salaried basis. When the caseload is heavy there is some justification for having a permanent arbitrator. Further he can become expert in the particular problems of the industry, and there is no delay in engaging his services. Notwithstanding these considerations, however,

the most common method is to engage arbitrators on an *ad hoc* basis. An *ad hoc* arbitrator will hear either one case alone, or he may hear several cases during the course of one or two days. An advantage of the *ad hoc* system is that the individual can be selected on the basis of his expertise for the type of case to be heard.

The procedure for selecting an arbitrator is commonly spelled out in the labor agreement. Often the arbitrator is selected from a panel of qualified arbitrators listed by either the Federal Mediation and Conciliation Service or by the American Arbitration Association. If the two parties are unable to agree upon an individual, the contract will often state that an arbitrator shall be appointed by one or the other of these agencies. It is almost universal practice for the union and the company to share equally the arbitrator's fee.

Labor agreements generally specify that the decision of the arbitrator shall be final and binding upon all parties concerned—the company, the union, and the employees. Further they state, usually, that the arbitrator shall have only the authority to interpret, apply, or determine compliance with the provisions of the union–management agreement. He shall not add to, subtract, or alter the provisions of the agreement. This simply means that the parties expect the arbitrator to act in the role of judge and not a legislator.

An arbitration hearing is a quasijudicial process. It may be conducted quite formally, or the entire process may be rather informal. The desires of the arbitrator himself and the custom of the parties determine whether the hearing will be run formally, or informally. But even a formal hearing ordinarily is much less strict and structured than is a hearing in a court of law.

Quite often after the hearing has concluded both the union and the company will file a posthearing brief with the arbitrator to summarize facts and arguments of each side. Typically the arbitrator then has thirty days to make a decision and prepare the award and supporting opinion.

The award is the decision of the arbitrator regarding the issue submitted to him. The opinion summarizes the positions of the two parties and explains the reasoning of the arbitrator in arriving at his decision.

Legal Status of Arbitration

As a result of U.S. Supreme Court decisions, grievance arbitration and arbitrators' awards have acquired very substantial authority and sanctity. These Supreme Court decisions were rendered in 1960 and have become known as the "Steelworkers' trilogy" because they involved the United Steelworkers' Union and court cases with three separate companies. In essence the Court said that whether a particular grievance issue is properly arbitrable under the labor agreement between the company and union is a matter to be decided by the arbitrator not the courts. Also all questions on which the union and company disagree must come within the scope of the grievance and arbitration provisions of the collective bargaining agreement unless the two parties have specifically excluded certain matters from arbitration in the language of the agreement. Additionally the Supreme Court established a standard for only very limited review by the lower courts of an arbitrator's award. Courts should enforce an arbitration award unless it clearly is inconsistent with the labor agreement. Ordinarily a court, as a result of the trilogy decisions, will only review an arbitration award on appeal by a union or a company if the arbitrator committed fraud or was arbitrary and capricious. It might also review an award if the arbitrator exceeded his authority under the collective agreement.

Issues Arbitrated

The largest single category of issues appealed to arbitration is "discipline and discharge". The next most common issue has to do with wages.

This is a broad category that includes such matters as job classification for pay purposes, overtime pay, compensation for out-of-title work, pay increments, and wage incentives. Another common issue is the matter of arbitrability. Management may claim, at the outset of the arbitration hearing, that the issue is not properly arbitrable under the labor agreement. One common ground for raising this issue is that management may claim the employee or the union failed to file the grievance at the first step of the grievance procedure within the time limit specified in the contract. Or perhaps the union waited too long to appeal the case to arbitration. Or perhaps the issue is not clearly covered by the labor agreement and is in the area of a management prerogative. Table 21-2 gives the distribution of issues arbitrated in cases administered by the American Arbitration Association over a 13-month period.

GRIEVANCE SETTLEMENT FOR NONUNION EMPLOYEES

Only a minority of companies have created a formal grievance procedure for their nonunion employees. A 1981 survey of 374 companies revealed that 62 per cent of the firms (232 companies) had a grievance system for their nonunion production or operations employees. However only 41 per cent of these 232 companies had a formal system. The remainder had an informal "open door" policy.[4]

A 1977 survey by Ewing of 1,958 subscribers to the *Harvard Business Review* (the vast majority of the respondents were managers in private firms distributed throughout the country) showed that 14 per cent were employed in organizations having a management grievance

[4]Harriet Gorlin, *Personnel Practice III: Employee Services, Work Rules,* Information Bulletin 95 (New York: The Conference Board, 1981).

450

TABLE 21-2. Distribution of Issues Arbitrated in Cases Administered by the American Arbitration Association, September 1981–October 1982.*

Issue	Per Cent
Discipline and discharge	31.48
Wages	10.02
Arbitrability	9.99
Work assignments and schedules	7.88
Promotions and transfers	5.04
Management rights	6.45
Fringe benefits	6.77
Layoff and recall	5.25
Pension and welfare plans	2.46
Absenteeism and tardiness-control procedures	1.11
Evaluations	1.14
Working conditions	1.08
Demotions	.76
Union security	.50
Union activities	.73
Tenure and reappointment	.70
Safety and health	.50
Discrimination	.59
Strikes, work stoppages, slowdowns, and lockouts	.38
Affirmative action	.09
Other issues	7.06

*Percentages shown are based upon a total of 3412 issues arbitrated. Source: *Study Time* (January 1983), American Arbitration Association. By permission.

committee and 11 per cent were employed in firms having an ombudsman. But the majority of persons (63 per cent) stated that their companies simply had an informal "open door" policy.[5]

By and large American managements have chosen either to ignore the problem of providing

[5]David W. Ewing, "What Business Thinks About Employee Rights," *Harvard Business Review,* Vol. 55, No. 5 (September–October 1977), pp. 81–94.

a means for solving nonunion employee grievances or they have relied upon quite informal measures. But the need for programs in the nonunion sector of the working force of business firms is nevertheless pressing.

Approaches to the Problem

In comparison to the well-defined procedures and the extensive experience of American industry in grievance handling for unionized employees, the procedures for nonunion personnel are either nonexistent, or else they are ill-defined, vague, and seldom employed. We shall explore the various approaches that have been or can be instituted for nonunion people.

Open-Door Policy. Many top executives who have a genuine concern for the well-being of their employees have set up an open-door policy to solve employee grievances. The open-door policy means that any rank-and-file worker has a full right to go to the office of the chief executive officer of that company or plant to discuss a complaint. Under such a program, the executive promises to be available for such contacts with the employees. She further implies that she will investigate every grievance and take appropriate action. Although some open-door programs permit the employee to go immediately to the chief executive with a problem, it is much better to require that he discuss the issue with the immediate superior first. This procedure will solve the majority of grievances at the bottom level and will keep the supervisor fully informed of what is going on in his or her own department.

Although on the face of it the open-door policy may seem like a good system to some, it seldom works out successfully in practice. There are a number of reasons for this. The social and organizational distance between a worker in overalls and the company president in the thick-carpeted office is so great that the worker is generally fearful of going to see the "big boss." He feels that he may not express himself well or that the "big boss" may not understand his point of view.

If the president should overrule the first-level supervisor, the latter will tend to lose face in front of the workers. If the president does not act judiciously, he or she can seriously weaken the position of the supervisors.

If an employee feels that he has been mistreated by his foreman, he may get the action reversed by appealing to the chief executive. But the worker may find that although he has won that particular case, in the long run his supervisor may bear resentment against him and put him in an even worse position than he was originally.

The Inspector General Method. The military system of providing a means of correcting injustices by having a representative from the Inspector General's office visit each unit once per year to hear and investigate soldiers' grievances is an approach that is rarely employed in private industry. One large company that for many years had an open-door policy decided to establish a special vice-presidential position to relieve the president of the load of hearing and investigating worker grievances. This vice-president visits every plant at least once per year and more often if necessary. He or she in effect performs the functions of an inspector general in the military establishment.

Ombudsman. The concept of an ombudsman to process complaints of citizens against the government was first devised in Sweden in 1809. Finland also established this office in 1809 as a protector of the people. But it has not been until the 1950s and 1960s that the concept has spread elsewhere in the world. In its most precise meaning an *ombudsman* is an independent and politically neutral officer of a governmental legislature. His or her function is to handle appeals by ordinary citizens against the executive bureaucracy. He or she has the power to investigate, has access to government documents, has the right to prosecute officials for illegal acts, and can publicize his or her findings.

In its more general and looser meaning, the term ombudsman has recently been applied to any official of an organization charged with the responsibility of investigating and settling member complaints. The inspector general system of the military is a form of the ombudsman. Many universities have created ombudsman systems to handle student grievances and employee grievances.

Although this concept is just now beginning to be applied to nongovernmental organizations, its success in government–citizen relations in the Scandinavian countries reveals that it is certainly worthy of trial in private establishments.[6]

The Xerox Corporation set up an ombudsman system in 1972. The ombudsman reports directly to the president, who is the only man who has authority to reverse decisions. In creating the position, officials at Xerox were convinced that only someone outside the corporate chain of command could insure fair treatment for employees.[7]

Multistep Grievance Procedure. Some companies have established official multistep grievance procedures patterned somewhat after those for union personnel. The last avenue of appeal is generally the chief executive officer of the company, or of the division, if the company is composed of semiautonomous divisions. Arbitration is seldom provided for. There are a number of reasons for this. Management is unwilling to dilute any of its powers by having an outside party review (and perhaps reverse) its decisions. The individual employee is often ill-

[6]For an explanation of the ombudsman concept in government see Stanley V. Anderson, ed. *Ombudsmen for American Government?* prepared by the American Assembly, Columbia University (Englewood Cliffs, N.J.: Prentice-Hall, 1968).
[7]"How the Xerox Ombudsman Helps Xerox," *Business Week* (May 12, 1973), also "Where Ombudsmen Work Out," *Business Week* (May 3, 1976).

equipped to prepare adequately and to present his or her case before the arbitrator. He or she generally cannot afford to pay one half the arbitrator's fee, as is customary in unionized establishments. If management assumes the burden of assigning a person to represent the employee and if it pays the full cost of arbitration, then the claim that both the company and the individual are on an equal footing before the arbitrator can no longer be made.

Although there are plausible reasons why arbitration is not more widely used, there is still considerable justification for having some impartial and independent agency serve as a final judicial body to review the decisions of top management. Some writers have proposed a board of review or a board of neutrals.[8]

The personnel management literature contains a number of references to multistep procedures for nonunion people. In most of these procedures the employee can appeal his or her case to successively higher levels of managers in his or her direct chain of command. The industrial relations department usually plays a key part in the proceedings. Sometimes this office is the next step of appeal after the supervisor. In others, a representative from industrial relations acts in an advisory capacity to the employee.

Grievance Committee. Some organizations have created a committee of management personnel and others have set up a committee of nonmanagement personnel to hear employee grievances on appeal from lower levels. The decisions may merely be advisory to the chief executive officer or they may be final and binding. Ewing reports that the H. P. Hood Company in Boston and the Polaroid Corporation have such procedures.[9]

[8]See, for example, Walter V. Ronner, "Handling Grievances in a Nonunion Plant," *Proceedings of the Fourteenth Annual Meeting of the Industrial Relations Research Association* (Madison, Wis.: IRRA, 1961), pp. 306–314; Dale S. Beach, "An Organizational Problem: Subordinate–Superior Relations," *Advanced Management*, Vol. 25, No. 12 (December 1960), pp. 12–16.

In order for a grievance system to work successfully in a nonunion organization, the employees must be assured, by both pronouncement and actual experience, that there will be no retaliation against them for submitting and pushing a case up through the successive steps in the system. Because of the great imbalance of power between management and the worker, employees naturally tend to have a deep-seated fear of retaliation by the boss or the other members of management. In fact, this is one of the principal reasons grievance procedures for nonunion people are seldom used. The danger is that top management will thus delude itself into thinking that everyone is content, because few if any grievances are submitted.

Questions for Review and Discussion

1. What is a grievance?
2. Why is it desirable that all work organizations have an established system for hearing and adjusting employee grievances?
3. Explain how an employee's grievance would be processed through the grievance procedure in a typical large unionized company.
4. What is meant by the "clinical approach" to grievance handling? Contrast it with the legalistic approach. What are the arguments in favor of using a clinical approach?
5. Should all grievances be put in writing before management acts upon them? Discuss.
6. Discuss the proper role of the foreman in grievance settlement. Why has the foreman become powerless and a mere figurehead in grievance handling in some companies?
7. Describe the role of the union steward in grievance handling. What pressures play upon the steward?
8. Briefly describe the process of grievance arbitration. Include in your discussion the method of selecting an arbitrator, his or her

[9]David W. Ewing, *Freedom Inside the Organization* (New York: McGraw-Hill Book Co., 1978), p. 161.

authority, method of compensation, and hearing procedure.

9. Why do you think most companies have done little or nothing to establish a griev-ance-handling system for their nonunion employees?

10. What is the open-door policy? What are its merits and shortcomings?

CASE PROBLEMS

PROBLEM 1

The ABC Textile Company employs 550 production and maintenance workers who are represented by a union.

The grievance procedure in the union–employer agreement provides that the aggrieved employee and/or the union steward shall first submit the matter to the department foreman. If it is not settled at this step, it must be put in writing on a standard grievance form and submitted to the plant superintendent. Representing the union at this second step is the local union grievance committee and/or the business agent. The third step is the company president and a representative of the international union. The fourth and final step consists of binding arbitration. The company personnel director acts in an advisory capacity to plant management at all stages. In practice he or she is particularly instrumental in shaping the decision on a grievance at the second, or superintendent, step of the procedure.

During the past three months the following cases arose:

1. The company had been plagued with chronic worker absenteeism. The procedure for keeping track of absences was to have each foreman record the names of all those who were absent each day in a notebook. In an attempt to correct the problem, the superintendent and the personnel manager made a quick check of the various foremen's notebooks and then discharged six of the most serious offenders. The union immediately filed a grievance charging discrimination because some of the six people who had been fired had better attendance records than some other workers who remained on the payroll. At the second step of the grievance procedure, management decided to reduce the penalty to a one-week suspension without pay. In commenting upon the case later, the personnel manager said he expected that worker attendance would improve since the employees had learned that management was serious about improving attendance and that serious offenders might be discharged. However, several of the foremen grumbled that the incident had undermined their authority with their workers because management had backed down. They said that the six workers involved were poor performers and should have been fired.

2. A foreman in one of the production departments asked a machine operator to operate a different machine to fill in for a worker who was absent that day. When she refused, her foreman told her to punch out her time card and go

home. She would not be paid for the rest of that day. The union filed a grievance in the worker's behalf charging a violation of the labor agreement. According to the contract the machines and processes are grouped into categories. An employee cannot be assigned to a machine outside his or her category without his or her consent. In this particular case the machine involved was outside the employee's regular category. However the skill and knowledge requirements for the two different machines were essentially the same. Also the rate of pay for both operations was the same. The labor contract stated that the least senior employee in the department could be compelled to move to the other machine if more senior workers were unwilling to do so. However the foreman was unaware of this contract provision and workers had not refused in the past. At the second step of the grievance procedure, management decided that the foreman had erred and the worker was paid for the time lost.

3. A man wearing canvas sneakers was told by his foreman not to come to work again dressed in sneakers. Rather he must wear leather shoes as a safety measure to protect his feet against cuts and wounds from wire, nails, sharp projections on machines, and floor splinters. Before giving this oral warning, the foreman had consulted the superintendent and received full approval for his action. Despite the warning the man appeared for work the next day again wearing sneakers. He was sent home immediately, without pay, for the rest of the day. When he appeared for work the following day he was wearing leather shoes. However, the union filed a grievance charging discrimination because some workers in other departments had worn sneakers and had not been disciplined. The grievance was rejected at the first two steps of the grievance procedure and is now pending at the third step.

Many of the foremen complain that they repeatedly lose face in front of their employees because higher management gives in too frequently in the face of union pressure in grievance cases. The union business agent has claimed that management provokes most of the grievances by its own actions.

Questions
1. What seems to be wrong here? What measures should be taken to improve employee–management–union relations?
2. What do you think of the foremen's complaints about "undermining their authority" and "losing face in front of the employees"?

PROBLEM 2: THE ABSENT EMPLOYEE

Events of Case

At a company hearing on September 11, the Elnora Company management made a decision to discharge Thomas Kirk. Subsequently, through his union, Kirk appealed his discharge through the steps of the grievance procedure to arbitration.

Mr. Kirk had been hired as a production machine operator and continued in that job for five years until July of this year. In June the company suspended him without pay for one day for failure to follow instructions and inattention to duty. On July 12 the company suspended him with intent to discharge for failure to follow instructions. For both the June and July suspensions the company claimed the quality of his output was below standard and that he had not operated his machine according to instructions. At a hearing on July 13 the union and the company worked out a compromise. The discharge was converted to a suspension on condition that Kirk become a successful bidder on another job, for which he was qualified, within 30 days and that he be accepted on that job by the supervisor. On August 10 Kirk bid successfully for a materials handler job in the warehouse. He was placed on a 30-day trial period and was assigned to the second shift, 4:00 P.M. to midnight.

On September 6 Kirk asked George Aragona, superintendent, for a two-week leave of absence to go to Pittsburgh to visit his girlfriend who was in the hospital as a result of an automobile accident. Mr. Aragona denied the leave. On Thursday September 7, which was the regular payday, Kirk came to the guardhouse at the plant gate at 4:00 P.M. and asked the watchman-guard to obtain his paycheck for him. The guard telephoned Kirk's foreman who delivered the paycheck at the guardhouse.

While Kirk was in the guardhouse George Aragona came to the house and asked Kirk if he was going to work. Kirk replied that he would not work that day because he was too tired. Aragona then told Kirk that if he did not come to work he would be suspended with intent to discharge. Kirk asked to see his union steward at the guardhouse or at least to have the watchman-guard get the steward on the telephone. Aragona refused both requests. He told Kirk to go to work and he could see his steward in his regular department. Kirk offered to go to his doctor to obtain a medical excuse. Aragona said such action was not necessary.

Mr. Kirk did not go to work on that day. He also did not come to work on Friday. Mr. Aragona sent Kirk a letter on September 8 by certified mail stating that the company was suspending him with intent to discharge immediately. Kirk came to the plant on Monday, September 11. At a discharge hearing conducted by the personnel department that afternoon, Kirk was discharged effective immediately.

The Issue to Be Decided

Was Thomas Kirk discharged for just cause? If not, what should the remedy be?

Relevant Provisions of the Labor Agreement

Article VII: *Management*

Management of the establishment and the direction of the work force including right to hire, suspend, or discharge for just cause, or transfer, and the right to relieve employees from duty because of lack of work, or for other legitimate reasons is vested exclusively in the company, provided, however, that in the exercise of such functions the Management complies with the provisions of this Agreement.

Article XIV: *Adjustment of Grievances*

Step 1 (first two sentences only). An employee who believes he has suffered a grievance may discuss the alleged grievance with his foreman in an attempt to settle the matter. The employee may be accompanied, if he desires, by a shop steward.

Position of Company

The Company states that it discharged Thomas Kirk for two reasons. First, after denial of a leave of absence, he took it upon himself to absent himself on Thursday and Friday, September 7 and 8. Second, he was on a strict probationary status. He had to succeed on the materials handler job. Part of the requirement for succeeding was that he be on the job regularly.

After Kirk's suspension with intent to discharge on July 12 was converted to just a suspension on July 13, strict conditions were spelled out. He had to be accepted on a new job on which he bid, he had to conform to the work rules of the company, and he had to follow instructions.

Kirk refused to go to work on September 7 in the face of a direct order from his superintendent. Additionally he was absent on September 8. Kirk's reason for wanting the leave of absence (to visit his girlfriend in the hospital in Pittsburgh) was not a compelling reason to grant a two-week leave of absence.

Kirk actually went to Pittsburgh on September 8 and returned on Sunday evening, September 10. He could have waited until the weekend to visit his girlfriend.

Position of Union

The Union asserts that the burden of proof is upon the Company to justify its discharge of Kirk for just cause.

Kirk has a strong emotional attachment to his girlfriend and loves her. She was in serious condition in the hospital in Pittsburgh as a result of the automobile accident. He did not know how long he might be in Pittsburgh; hence he requested a two-week leave of absence. Kirk was very emotionally upset.

In the guardhouse incident with Mr. Aragona, Kirk indicated he would not go to work that day because he was drained physically and emotionally. He offered to get a doctor's excuse but Aragona said no. In denying Kirk's request to see his union steward in the guardhouse, Aragona violated Article XIV of the labor agreement.

Thomas Kirk had performed satisfactorily in his materials handling job. The company did not make any case that he was not performing adequately. If Kirk had not been discharged on September 11 he would have successfully completed his 30-day probationary status on the job.

This entire case should be looked upon as an absenteeism matter and not a matter of insubordination. Kirk's attendance record, while not really good, was satisfactory. He had not been warned about his attendance record within the past six months. His absences on September 7 and 8 did not generate enough absence points under the company's absenteeism control program to put him over the limit.

The Union asks that Kirk be reinstated to his job with full back pay and benefits.

Questions
1. Assume you are the arbitrator. Would you sustain the company's position and uphold the discharge? Or would you sustain the union's position and order Kirk reinstated to his job, with or without back pay?
2. Explain your reasoning in full.

Suggestions for Further Reading

Aram, John D., and Paul F. Salipante, Jr. "An Evaluation of Organizational Due Process in the Resolution of Employee/Employer Conflict," *Academy of Management Review* Vol. 6, No. 2 (April 1981), pp. 197–204.

Berenbeim, Ronald. *Nonunion Complaint Systems: A Corporate Appraisal.* Report No. 770, New York: The Conference Board, 1980.

BNA Editorial Staff. *Grievance Guide.* Washington, D.C.: Bureau of National Affairs, 1982.

Elkouri, Frank, and Edna A. Elkouri. *How Arbitration Works*, 3rd ed. Washington, D.C.: Bureau of National Affairs, 1973.

Fairweather, Owen *Practice and Procedure in Labor Arbitration*, 2nd ed. Washington, D.C.: Bureau of National Affairs, 1983.

Michael, Stephen R. "Due Process in Nonunion Grievance Systems," *Employee Relations Law Journal*, Vol. 3 (Spring 1978), pp. 516–527.

Robinson, James W., Wayne L. Deroncourt, and Ralph H. Effler. *The Grievance Procedure and Arbitration: Text and Cases.* Washington, D.C.: University Press of America, 1978.

Stacey, Frank A. *Ombudsmen Compared.* New York: Oxford University Press, 1978.

PART VI

Financial Compensation

22 Compensation Administration

Wages, as a means of providing income for employees and as a cost of doing business to the employer, constitute one of the most important subjects in the field of personnel management. Wages can provide a source of motivation for employees to perform effectively. The wage rate offered is one of the most important considerations to a person who is contemplating taking a new job.

Formerly wage rates in organizations, whether in industry or in government and nonprofit institutions, tended to be established in a haphazard fashion, with little consideration given to consistency within the organization according to differentials in job requirements or to consistency with prevailing wages paid in other establishments. The movement in industry for the development and adoption of sound principles and practices of wage and salary administration had its infancy in the 1920s and 1930s, expanded greatly during and immediately after World War II, and in the 1950s became more mature with the general acceptance of the ideas and methods initiated earlier.

This chapter explores the subject of compensation administration. We shall examine rationales for financial compensation, wage criteria, wage policy and principles, job evaluation systems, establishing the pay structure, administration of pay, wage surveys, and

compensation practices for professionals and managers.

Compensation Administration

The term *compensation administration*, or alternatively, wage and salary administration, has come to be accepted as the designation for that field of endeavor concerned with the establishment and implementation of sound policies and methods of employee compensation. It includes such areas as job evaluation, development and maintenance of wage structures, wage surveys, wage incentives, wage changes and adjustments, supplementary payments, profit sharing, control of compensation costs, and other related pay items.

The term *wage* is commonly used for those employees whose pay is calculated according to the number of hours worked. Thus, the weekly paycheck will fluctuate as the number of hours actually worked varies. The word *salary* applies to compensation that is uniform from one pay period to the next and does not depend upon the number of hours worked. *Salaried* often implies a status distinction, because those on salary generally are white-collar, administrative, professional, and executive employees, whereas wage-earners are designated as hourly or nonsupervisory, or blue-collar. Some of the distinctions between wage-earners and salary-earners have tended to disappear in recent years because wage-earners in some organizations do receive full pay if they are absent for such reasons as sickness, whereas salaried employees, especially at the lower levels, often receive overtime pay when they work over the standard work week. In this book the word *wage* will be used as the general term and will include salary except where it is desired to highlight salary in its more specific context.

RATIONALE OF FINANCIAL COMPENSATION

To design, from scratch, a comprehensive program of financial compensation for an organization requires that the designer have a rationale—a set of goals and underlying principles about compensation and how it should work. In actual practice compensation programs in the majority of establishments have grown up over the years by additions, patches, and trial and error—but without any overall grand design. Nevertheless, whether programs have been consciously planned or whether they have grown by trial and error, we can take a detached view and analyze what ongoing programs seem to be designed to accomplish.

There are four principal goals that compensation programs may seek to accomplish.

First they seek to serve a labor market function of allocating people among firms according to the perceived attractiveness of jobs as expressed by the rate of pay and associated pay supplements. Thus, wage and salary levels are an adjunct to employee recruitment. Firms must be reasonably competitive in their rates to entice job applicants to the employment office door.

Second, carefully designed compensation programs—with job evaluation, pay scales, and employee classification procedures—enable

management to control wages and salaries and control labor costs. Supervisors are not allowed to pay their people above the job rate. Many firms carefully control the distribution of rates within a given rate range. Tight controls may be placed upon the frequency and size of pay increases. A tight table of organization may be constructed for each department. Thus, a particular department manager may be permitted to have only so many machinists first class, technicians second class, and so forth. He or she cannot pad the payroll or build an empire.

A third major objective of wage and salary programs is to keep employees content, to minimize quitting, and to reduce employee complaints and grievances due to inadequate or inequitable wage rates. It is hoped that a rational program of pay administration can satisfy employees that their pay is fair and that favoritism and discrimination have played no part in the allocation of money.

A fourth and final goal of compensation is to induce and reward better performance. In other words, pay is looked upon as a motivator. It is a deeply cherished belief among American managers, generally, that increases in pay should be granted primarily on the basis of performance. Those who produce more should be paid more. Superior output and superior creativity must be rewarded.

In brief, then, wage and salary programs can have four major purposes: (1) to recruit people to the firm; (2) to control payroll costs; (3) to satisfy people—to reduce quitting, grievances, and frictions over pay; and (4) to motivate people to superior performance.

PRINCIPAL COMPENSATION ISSUES

Discussion of the multitude of topics and problems of wage and salary administration can be most conveniently organized around seven distinct but related issues. These are as follows:

scarce, the buyers bid up the price in the labor market, and the prevailing wage rises. Likewise the reverse can happen. If an organization finds that it is unable to attract and retain the labor it desires, it may be that its wage level is too low.

Ability to Pay

The ability of the employer to pay affects the general level of wages in an organization relative to the prevailing level in the labor market or industry. It does not establish rates for individual jobs or people, as such. Within the same industry, firms that are enjoying good sales and profit pictures over the long run tend to pay higher wages than those having difficulty making ends meet. Marginal firms usually pay wages lower than the average for their labor market or industry.

Cost of Living

In 1980 about nine million employees were working under union–employer agreements in which wages were adjusted automatically up or down in conformance with changes in the Consumer Price Index prepared by the Bureau of Labor Statistics of the United States Department of Labor. Such union contract provisions are commonly called escalator clauses or cost of living adjustments (COLAs). Used in this way, the purchasing power of employees' wages is maintained approximately constant, regardless of changes in the general cost of living for the country as a whole. Where there is no automatic formula for adjusting wages according to the cost of living, individual employees, unions, and employers nevertheless do give consideration to these changes and use the fact that prices are rising or falling to bolster their positions in wage discussions and bargaining.

Productivity

The key to the high standard of living that we in the United States enjoy in comparison with many other peoples of the world is our high level of productivity in the economy as a whole. Productivity is commonly measured in terms of goods and services produced or performed per employee-hour of labor. From 1947 to 1966 in the private sector of the economy, productivity increased at an annual rate of 3.2 per cent. However, from 1966 to 1977 the annual growth rate dropped to only 1.7 per cent.[1] In 1978 the productivity improvement over the previous year was only +0.6 per cent; in 1979 it was −0.9 per cent; in 1980 it was −0.7 per cent; and in 1981 it was +1.8 per cent.[2] Productivity improvements are generated by a combination of factors. These include technological improvements, greater capital investment, better methods of production, better education and job training of workers, improved worker ingenuity and skill, and more effective management.

In general highly productive industries and companies tend to pay higher wage rates than do low-productivity industries and firms. Wage increases in excess of increases in prices—that is, increases in *real* wages—can be obtained if productivity increases are greater than the rate of inflation. During the period 1947 to 1962 real hourly earnings of nonsupervisory workers in the private nonfarm economy increased at an average rate of 2.5 per cent annually. However, from 1962 to 1976 real wages increased an average of only 1.2 per cent a year.[3]

Another way of looking at the real wage sit-

[1]Gordon F. Bloom and Herbert R. Northrup, *Economics of Labor Relations*, 9th ed. Homewood, Ill.: Richard D. Irwin, Inc., 1981, p. 422.

[2]U.S. Department of Labor, *Employment and Training Report of the President, 1982* (Washington, D.C.: U.S. Government Printing Office, 1982), Table G-1.

[3]H. M. Douty, "The Slowdown in Real Wages: A Postwar Perspective," *Monthly Labor Review,* Vol. 100, No. 8 (August 1977), pp. 7–12.

Instructor's Free

Examination Copy.

Incomplete and Not

for Sale.

influence wage determination. For example, ability to pay and productivity are very closely related. In manufacturing, one company may have greater profits and lower costs because it has developed and invested in labor-saving machinery that has increased its productivity. Job requirements are listed as a wage criterion. One element of this is skill. High-skilled jobs pay more than low-skilled ones within the same company. But probably the reason more money is assigned to a high-skilled job is that there are fewer people available to fill such jobs (supply and demand).

WAGE POLICY AND PRINCIPLES

The wage policies of different firms vary somewhat. Marginal companies pay the minimum necessary to attract the required amount and type of labor. Often these companies pay only the minimum wage rates required by Federal or state law. With these rates they tend to be able to recruit only marginal labor.

At the other extreme some organizations pay well above the going rates in the labor market. They adopt such a policy because they seek to attract and retain the highest caliber labor force obtainable. By paying high rates, management is able to demand superior performance from its employees. Some managers believe in the economy of high wages. They feel that by paying good wages they can attract superior workers who will produce more than the average worker in industry. This greater production per employee, in effect, means greater output per man-hour. Hence labor costs may turn out to be lower than those existing in firms hiring only marginal-quality labor.

Some companies also pay high wage rates because of a combination of favorable product market demand, superior ability to pay, and bargaining power from a strong union. This situation has characterized the automobile industry for many years.

We have been talking about the extremes to this point. It is fair to say that the vast majority of companies seek to be competitive in their wage program. That is to say, they aim to pay somewhere near the going rate in the labor market for the various classes of labor they employ. Realistically they expect to employ a reasonably good quality of labor and to pay people fairly, with respect to one another, so that the employees feel they are paid properly. They do not want wage inequities to be a source of employee discontent. Thus, most firms give major weight to two wage criteria: job requirements and prevailing rates of pay in the labor market. Other factors, such as changes in the cost of living, supply and demand, ability to pay, and productivity are accorded subsidiary status, although special circumstances (for example, if the firm has been losing money for several years) may force one of these factors to the fore in the short run.

A generally sound policy is to adopt a job-evaluation program in order to establish fair differentials in pay based upon differences in job content. Employees are in a reasonably good position to judge whether their jobs are paid correctly in relation to other jobs in the plant. Job evaluation insures internal consistency of wage rates within the plant. External consistency—that is, reasonable equality with going rates paid by other companies in the community—can be achieved when a firm periodically surveys community rates and adjusts its general level of wages as required.

Principles of Wage and Salary Administration

The field of wage administration has been sufficiently well developed so that certain generally accepted guidelines and principles can be formulated.

FIGURE 22-1 The Elements of Job Evaluation.

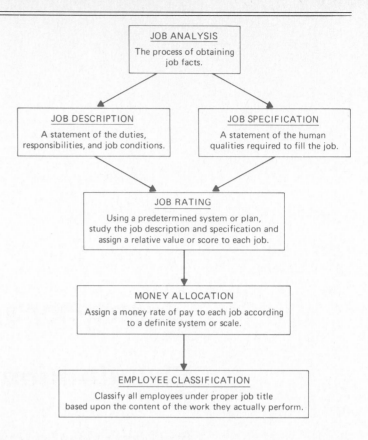

those who are doing the evaluation must rate the job, not the employee. In deciding how much money a particular job is worth, there is always a temptation to be influenced in one's judgment by the qualifications and caliber of the individual who is presently performing the work. But he may be either over- or underqualified. It is the assignment of those doing the rating to be guided by the requirements of the job. It may be that an error has been made in placing individuals on particular jobs, but this is a responsibility of supervision and the personnel department.

A second guide to keep in mind is that, whenever possible, the pooled or combined judgments of several persons should be employed in evaluating jobs. Job evaluation is a systematic, orderly, logical way of setting rates of pay within an organization or company; how-

ever, it is not exact measurement; it is grading or rating. The decisions of a number of qualified persons will reduce the likelihood of serious errors.

A third factor to bear in mind is that the accuracy of job rating is determined primarily by the accuracy of the basic job facts available. A comprehensive program of job analysis must serve as a basis for any job-evaluation program.

JOB EVALUATION SYSTEMS

There exist in current usage four main job evaluation systems plus certain other methods which tend to be variations of the four main systems. These are as follows:

468

common types of tasks, skills, knowledge, responsibilities, and job conditions can be identified and written in somewhat general language, so that these statements then become grade descriptions. When these have been developed for all grades they can then be used as a standard for assigning all other jobs to a particular pay grade.

Below are printed the first three grade descriptions for what is called the General Schedule (GS) covering professional, scientific, clerical, and administrative positions of the United States Government as defined in the Classification Act of 1949.

General Schedule

Grade GS-1 includes all classes of positions the duties of which are to perform, under immediate supervision, with little or no latitude for the exercise of independent judgment, (1) the simplest routine work in office, business, or fiscal operations, or (2) elementary work of a subordinate technical character in a professional, scientific, or technical field.

Grade GS-2 includes all classes of positions the duties of which are (1) to perform, under immediate supervision, with limited latitude for the exercise of independent judgment, routine work in office, business, or fiscal operations, or comparable subordinate technical work of limited scope in a professional, scientific, or technical field, requiring some training or experience, or (2) to perform other work of equal importance, difficulty, and responsibility, and requiring comparable qualifications.

Grade GS-3 includes all classes of positions the duties of which are (1) to perform, under immediate or general supervision, somewhat difficult and responsible work in office, business, or fiscal operations, or comparable subordinate technical work of limited scope in a professional, scientific, or technical field, requiring in either case (a) some training or experience, (b) working knowledge of a special subject matter, or (c) to some extent the exercise of independent judgment in accordance with well-established policies, procedures, and techniques; or (2) to perform other work of equal importance, difficulty, and responsibility, and requiring comparable qualifications.

The assignment of a wage rate for each grade can be accomplished by taking an average of the existing rates for all the jobs in each grade or by following a procedure similar to that of the point system, which will be described later in this chapter.

In the mid-1970s the Federal government adopted and began to install the Factor Evaluation system of job evaluation in place of the long-used grade description method. Factor Evaluation is a combination of the point and factor comparison systems.

In assessing the merits of the grade-description system, we can see that it is a definite improvement over the ranking method, because here we have a fixed written scale against which to compare all jobs. The process of rating jobs in the grade-description system involves a job-to-scale comparison. Because jobs often change in content over a period of time, one can readily see that the use of a scale is more durable and standardized. Also jobs are grouped into pay grades for administrative simplicity. A serious fault of the classification plan is that the grade description must of necessity be rather general and abstract in order to be applicable to a great variety of jobs. Also, like the ranking method it provides no way of weighting the compensable factors that make up jobs. How does one determine the worth of one job having high-skill requirements and low job hazards in comparison with one having high hazards and low skill?

Point System

The point system is, by a wide margin, the most commonly used method of job evaluation in the United States. It is more complicated than either of the preceding two that have been described. If a company chooses to adopt the point system, it can either select a universal type of plan, such as that developed by A. L. Kress for the National

FIGURE 22-2 A Point Plan of Job Evaluation for Nonmanagerial Salaried Positions Including Clerical, Technical, Service, and Professional.

Factors	Degrees and Points							
	1	2	3	4	5	6	7	8
I Education	20	40	60	80	100	120		
II Training and Experience	10	30	50	70	90	110	130	150
III Decisions	10	30	50	75	100			
IV Responsibility for Loss	5	15	25	35	45	60	75	
V Relations with Others	10	30	50	70	90			
VI Job Conditions	5	15	25	40				

I EDUCATION

This factor evaluates the general educational development, whether acquired through formal schooling or informally through life experiences, required to perform the job.

Degree	Definition	Points
1	Follow simple oral one- and two-step instructions; add, subtract, multiply, divide and count whole numbers; read and write simple sentences.	20
2	Carry out detailed but simple written or oral instructions; add, subtract, multiply, and divide including use of decimals and fractions; read simple drawings and memoranda; fill out standardized routine forms.	40
3	Compute such items as discount, interest, percentage, ratio, volume; use elementary algebra or plane geometry; draw simple graphs or charts; read mechanical drawings instructions, and specifications; write routine reports such as production and quality reports; write routine correspondence.	60
4	Use algebra including linear, quadratic and exponential functions; use plane and solid geometry; use shop mathematics including proportions, and trigonometry; prepare correspondence of a non-routine or elementary technical nature; prepare reports requiring explanations of information; apply principles of such subjects as bookkeeping, electrical wiring systems, drafting, nursing.	80
5	Use advanced algebra, calculus, statistics; apply the sciences such as biology, chemistry, physics, or economics; apply general accounting principles; read complex drawings and specifications; prepare correspondence and reports of an involved or technical nature.	100
6	Apply specialized and advanced theory in mathematics, the physical sciences, or behavioral sciences; prepare reports concerning technically involved subject; apply principles of logical and scientific thinking to a broad range of problems; deal with a variety of abstract and concrete concepts.	120

physical effort. After the weightings have been arrived at, point progressions must be given to the degrees for each factor. Although judgment plays a part in setting up the point scales, certain statistical techniques (notably linear correlation and multiple correlation methods) are often employed in addition. The method used to convert points to money will be discussed later in this chapter under the heading "Establishing the Pay Structure."

The strengths of the point system are numerous. First of all, it breaks jobs down into

472

Instructor's Free

Examination Copy.

Incomplete and Not

for Sale.

FIGURE 22-2 (Continued)

Degree	Amount	Points		Degree	Amount	Points
1	Up to $25	5		5	500 – 999	45
2	$25 to $49	15		6	1000 – 1999	60
3	50 – 99	25		7	2000 – and over	75
4	100 – 499	35				

V RELATIONS WITH OTHERS

This factor evaluates the nature and complexity of relationships and contacts with other persons.

Degree	Definition	Points
1	Dealings limited to employees and supervisor within own work unit.	10
2	Deal with persons both within own department and in other departments or organization; give and receive routine information.	30
3	Deal with persons in other departments and in other organizations; give and receive various oral and written information; tact required to obtain cooperation.	50
4	Deal with persons both within and outside the organization involving discussions, explanations, and agreements on matters of importance to the functioning of the job or department.	70
5	Deal with persons both within and outside the organization including company managers, customers, or government officials; often involves negotiation, persuasion, and making agreements affecting welfare of organization.	90

VI JOB CONDITIONS

This factor evaluates both the quality of working conditions and hazards which might cause injury or illness.

Degree	Definition	Points
1	Normal office conditions.	5
2	Infrequent exposure to one or two disagreeable conditions such as noise, heat, cold, or dirt. Little or no exposure to accident hazards.	15
3	Occasional exposure to two or more disagreeable conditions such as noise, heat, cold, dirt, fumes. Exposure to injuries such as cuts, burns, or abrasions which would require absence up to two weeks.	25
4	Frequent exposure to two or more objectionable conditions such as noise, heat, cold, fumes, vibration, etc. Frequent exposure to serious hazards such as broken bones or hernia requiring absence of two weeks or more.	40

system is its greater cost of development and installation as compared with ranking and grade description. However, the greater accuracy possible with its use usually justifies the larger expenditure of time and effort.

Factor Comparison System

Being the second most popular system after the point method, the factor comparison method is often used for evaluating white-collar, profes-

FIGURE 22-3 An Illustration of a Job Comparison Scale for Shop-Type Jobs—Factor Comparison Method.

Cents Per Hour Per Factor	Mental Requirements	Skill Requirements	Physical Requirements	Responsibility	Working Conditions
170	Electronic Tech.	Tool Maker Machinist			
	Tool Maker				
160	Electrician	Electronic Tech.		Inspector Electronic Tech. Tool Maker	
150	Machinist				
				Electrician	
140	Inspector	Electrician			
130		Engine Lathe oper.	Laborer		
				Machinist	
120		Turret Lathe oper.	Assembler Fork Lift oper.	Engine Lathe oper.	Laborer Fork Lift oper.
	Engine Lathe oper.		Turret Lathe oper.		
110		Inspector	Electrician Machinist		Assembler Janitor
100	Turret Lathe oper.		Janitor	Fork Lift oper. Turret Lathe oper.	Machinist Turret Lathe oper. Tool Maker
90	Assembler Fork Lift oper.	Assembler	Tool Maker Engine Lathe oper.	Assembler	Engine Lathe oper. Electrician
80					Inspector
		Fork Lift oper.			Electronic Tech.
70			Inspector		
	Laborer				
60	Janitor	Laborer	Electronic Tech.	Laborer Janitor	
		Janitor			
50					

rates can be found to give a figure for each grade.

With the point system a graph is plotted of all the points on the abscissa and the existing or old rates of pay on the ordinate. If the existing rates are reasonably correct and if the rating of the jobs under the point plan has been done carefully, we can expect these points to fall along a trend line with very little dispersion. On the other hand, if the existing structure is loaded with inequities and errors, we will find considerable dispersion or scatter from the trend line. There are a number of procedures available to ascertain the best-fitting trend line. The most common is to draw it by eye, carefully trying to insure that about the same number of points fall below as above the line. The other principal method is to use the statistical technique of "least squares." This is the most accurate way of finding the best-fitting straight line. For a straight line, $Y = a + bX$, where a is the Y intercept and b is the slope of the line, it is necessary to solve these two normal equations to determine the value of these constants.

$$\Sigma Y = Na + b\Sigma X$$
$$\Sigma XY = a\Sigma X + b\Sigma X^2$$

In these equations N is the number of jobs, Y is the wage for each job, and X is the point value. It must be noted that even if the points actually fall along a curve, these equations will give us the very best-fitting straight line. A similar statistical procedure can be used to find the best-fitting parabola, for example, if visual inspection leads one to suspect that the points would more faithfully be represented by such a curve. It would be best to consult a statistical textbook for the details of the exact procedure involved.

Figure 22-4 shows a trend line that has been drawn for a plotting of present wage rate against job evaluation points for seventeen hourly paid jobs. Our objective is to use this graph as a worksheet for constructing a wage structure with jobs grouped into labor grades. In this illustration vertical dashed guidelines have been

FIGURE 22-4 A Graph Showing a Trend Line Drawn Through a Plot of Points Versus Wage Rates for 17 Jobs with Single Rate Grades Constructed Thereon.

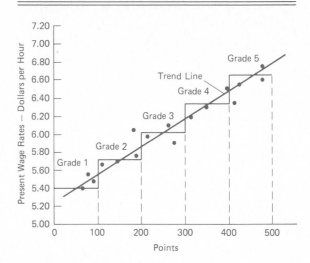

drawn in order to divide the points into five groups or grades. Horizontal lines have been drawn through the midpoints of the trend line in each grade in order to arrive at a single rate of pay for each grade. This would be the simplest kind of structure, as shown in Table 22-1.

Commonly a range of money is established for each wage grade. The content and difficulty of the job are used to decide into which grade the job falls. The skills, abilities, and lengths of service of the different employees on each job

TABLE 22-1. Wage Structure with Single Rates for Each Grade.

Grade	Point Range	Hourly Wage Rate
1	0–100	$5.40
2	101–200	5.71
3	201–300	6.02
4	301–400	6.33
5	401–500	6.64

Instructor's Free

Examination Copy.

Incomplete and Not

for Sale.

inate inequities, this solution seems sound. Should a great number of jobs require increases, thereby making the cost to the employer quite expensive, it might be practical to raise them in steps over a period of a few months. "Red circle" is a designation usually applied to those employees who are receiving more than the maximum for their grade. Mechanistically one might argue that these rates should be immediately lowered to their proper level. However, this would tend to cause a hardship for the employees affected. It certainly is no fault of theirs that management has decided to adopt a job evaluation program. They did not set the job rates in the first place. A reasonable solution would involve informing the "red circle" employees that they are being paid more than the proper rate, that they personally will continue to receive the same pay as they are now getting, but that all new persons assigned to their jobs will be paid within the grade limits. Thus, as employees are promoted to higher level jobs, and as some may eventually leave the company for reasons of retirement, resignation, and layoff, these wage rates will in the course of a few years fall into their proper slots. In addition to this solution to the problem, some organizations, when raising the entire wage structure across the board due to union bargaining or other reasons, will not grant any increases to "red circle" employees. Thus, the structure will catch up to these, and eventually they will fall within their proper limits.

Employee Classification

Regardless of which system of job evaluation is used, a decision has to be made regarding the job title to assign to every employee in the organization. For clear-cut, easily definable jobs the problem of employee classification is easy. If an employee operates a single-spindle, sensitive drill press and does nothing else, his title is self-evident, and his pay is tied to his job title.

However, many concerns have job families, such as the typist, clerk-typist, stenographer, secretarial group. A woman employed in an office may do typing, take dictation by shorthand and transcribe it, answer the telephone, sort and distribute the mail, compose routine letters for her boss, and so on. Shall she be classified as a stenographer or as a secretary? The pay differential may be $20 to $30 per week. The decision is of vital concern both to the employee and the employer. An additional example from the skilled trades should serve to emphasize the point fully. It is common in many factories to have such occupational sequences as millwright A and millwright B or machinist A and B, with the A designation receiving the higher pay and requiring somewhat greater skill and responsibility than the B.

Present Rates or Prevailing Market Rates

It should be emphasized that the entire preceding explanation concerned with establishing the pay structure has involved using existing wage rates as the basis for the new wage plan. Essentially the objective (in theory) is to iron out existing inequities and have all the rates fall upon a line when money is plotted against job difficulty points as in Figures 22-4 and 22-5. Because jobs are grouped into grades and special action is required for "red circle" rates, this theoretical goal is not achieved. However, the thoughtful reader may well question the wisdom of using present wages as a basis for building a better wage structure. If the level of the present wages is approximately correct and all that is required are some moderate adjustments of individual rates, then this procedure is sound. But if all the existing rates are out of line with the average rates prevailing in the labor market for the same class of work, then clearly it is folly to spend a large sum of money to install a job evaluation plan when the critical step of conversion to money results in the wrong answer.

A choice of one of two approaches can be

creases specifies that a person cannot be repeatedly denied an increase. If the supervisor can definitely establish that performance is decidedly unsatisfactory on a continuing basis, he or she must be discharged or else reassigned.

When the salary policy states that progression within a range is based solely upon merit, the company must have some formal program for appraising the performance of all employees on a regular basis. Some firms have clear-cut formulas for translating an individual's performance-rating score to a definite pay increase. Other companies are quite informal about the whole process. They leave both the frequency and the size of the pay increase pretty much up to the individual manager.

Especially in large organizations the problem of administering pay increases for thousands of people on a fair and honest basis has caused many managements to give some recognition to length of service. Philosophically most executives are opposed to the seniority principle, but when dealing with a very large work force, they are often forced to grant some recognition to this factor. One way of handling this problem is to count years of service as one factor in the rating plan used to set salary increases. Another method is to provide for automatic progression (length of service) to the midpoint of each range and merit progression above that point. Only those whose performance is decidedly above average can receive pay increases above the midpoint.

WAGE SURVEYS

If the wage policy of a firm is to keep competitive in the labor market, that is, pay rates that are at least approximately equal to those prevailing in the community, then it must collect accurate wage and salary data and make changes in its pay structure as may become necessary. Whereas job evaluation establishes pay differentials based upon differences in job content, wage-survey information provides a means by which management can determine whether its entire wage level is competitive.

In collecting wage data, management wants to find out the going rates for its key jobs in the area from which it recruits labor. This area is its labor market. A labor market is a geographical area within which employers recruit workers and workers seek employment. It is usually thought to consist of a central city or cities and the surrounding territory in which persons can change their jobs without changing their place of residence. This definition is especially appropriate for hourly and clerical workers. On the other hand, the labor market area for engineers, scientists, and executives tends to be regional or national in scope. This is because such individuals are much more likely to be willing to relocate if they can find a good job in another city even though it may be far removed from their home town.

Although conducting one's own survey will probably yield the most satisfactory and accurate results, this rather costly procedure is not always necessary. There are other sources of reliable information. The Bureau of Labor Statistics of the United States Department of Labor conducts comprehensive surveys at regular intervals in the larger labor markets. (See Table 22-3). Many trade and professional associations conduct wage and salary surveys and publish the results for their members. Local chamber of commerce and personnel managers' associations sometimes conduct pay surveys.

If a company conducts its own survey it must select a representative sample of its own jobs, carefully describe these jobs, and then visit other organizations in the labor market to find out what they pay for the same jobs. While job-rate information is being obtained, it is advantageous to also collect information on fringe benefits and personnel practices. The ability of a firm to attract and retain employees is influenced not only by direct wage rates but also by such items as overtime and premium pay policy,

TABLE 22-3. A Portion of the Area Wage Survey Report for the Albany-Schenectady-Troy, New York Metropolitan Area, September 1982.

Occupation and industry division	Number of workers	Average weekly hours (standard)	Weekly earnings (in dollars)[1]		
			Mean	Median	Middle range[2]
Computer systems analysts (business)	163	39.5	584.50	591.50	521.50–653.00
Nonmanufacturing	57	39.0	533.00	556.00	426.50–616.50
Computer systems analysts (business) II	68	39.5	569.50	557.00	524.00–616.00
Computer systems analysts (business) III	76	40.0	636.50	643.50	598.50–688.50
Computer programmers (business) . .	117	39.0	425.00	444.50	360.00–489.50
Manufacturing	67	39.5	443.50	451.00	395.50–489.50
Nonmanufacturing	50	38.5	400.50	394.00	288.00–489.50
Computer programmers (business) II	70	39.5	419.00	405.00	360.50–472.50
Manufacturing	41	39.5	417.00	405.00	392.50–461.00
Nonmanufacturing	29	39.0	422.00	397.00	288.00–507.00
Computer programmers (business) III	36	39.0	476.00	491.00	473.00–524.00
Computer operators	191	38.5	332.50	370.00	277.50–403.50
Nonmanufacturing	86	37.5	304.50	303.00	249.50–403.50
Computer operators I	44	36.5	319.50	403.50	217.00–403.50
Computer operators II	89	39.5	320.50	330.00	276.00–370.00
Manufacturing	57	39.5	343.50	370.00	307.00–370.00
Nonmanufacturing	32	38.5	279.50	286.00	246.50–307.50
Computer operators III	58	39.5	361.00	406.50	296.50–406.50

money worth. Thus, in a pay structure containing 12 grades for professional and managerial (lower and middle) personnel, the assistant engineer might be assigned to grade 3, the engineer to grade 5, the senior engineer to grade 7, and the project engineer to grade 9. The assignment of these general job descriptions to the different grades could be accomplished by a quantitative job evaluation plan or more simply by a ranking or grade description evaluation plan. The salary surveys of professional occupations prepared by the Bureau of Labor Statistics of the U.S. Department of Labor show these occupations grouped into several levels. Hence, a company which uses these broad categories for their professional jobs can obtain market salary data summarized in a similar fashion.

Salary administration for professionals often means rank-in-the-person more than rank-in-the-job. As a junior professional employee develops and demonstrates successful mastery of gradually larger and more complex projects, he or she is given recognition of his greater worth by merit pay increases within the grade

Instructor's Free

Examination Copy.

Incomplete and Not

for Sale.

FIGURE 22-6 Career Salary Curves Which Relate Annual Salary to Years Since Graduation from College and to Performance Rating.

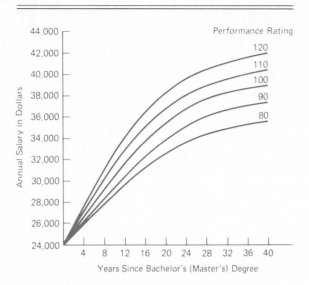

work content and create explainable job distinctions based upon differences in job duties.

The use of career salary curves has been fostered partly by the many market salary surveys which express salary data in this way. The Engineers Joint Council, which is supported by all the major engineering societies, publishes its salary survey data in the form of career curves.

A variation of the career curve approach we have been describing is to plot curves of salary vs. years in pay grade. Thus some universities prepare career curves, based upon survey data and their own salary policies, for the various academic ranks of assistant, associate, and full professor.

COMPENSATION FOR MANAGERS

The broad outlines of salary systems for managers are similar in their elements to those for lower-level groups. There are job descriptions, job evaluation, pay grades with a range of pay for each grade, and salary surveys. The specifics, of course, are quite different from employee wage administration and there are special features of managerial compensation that set it apart.

Job descriptions for management are often called position grades or responsibility guides. They do not contain detailed statements of duties and operating procedures. Rather, they cover areas of responsibility, scope of authority, and relationships with other positions and organizational functions.

Job-evaluation plans are usually tailormade to the special requirements of the organization. Sometimes point plans are used, but more commonly combination point-and-factor-comparison plans are employed. One well-known plan is the guide chart–profile method developed by Edward Hay & Associates, a management consulting organization.[6]

After all the management positions have been evaluated and points assigned, it is necessary to group these into grades. This process is guided somewhat by the hierarchy depicted in the organization chart. In a 25-grade-level system the president would be at grade 25, the executive vice-president at grade 24, and so on down to the lowest level of management. Of course, the points assigned to positions would determine in which grades particular positions belonged. An assistant plant manager might come two grades below the plant manager position and would not necessarily occupy the next grade in descending order.

To "price" the salary guide structure it is necessary to obtain salary survey data. Well-known salary services provided by management and trade associations and by consulting firms classify managerial salaries by company size, by industry, and functional responsibility. Some surveys also indicate the relationships among different jobs within firms. Thus, they may show that in a given indus-

[6]This job evaluation method is described in articles in *Personnel* (September 1951, July 1954, and January–February, 1958).

Financial Compensation

Instructor's Free

Examination Copy.

Incomplete and Not

for Sale.

to generate greater profits for the firm. Because executives must pay a high percentage of their salaries to the government in income taxes, compensation experts have tended to devote considerable (and perhaps too much) attention to tax-saving features of stock options, deferred compensation, and fringe benefits.

Here is a listing and brief explanation of the principal forms of financial incentives and supplements to direct salary that are provided for many top executives in private industry.

Incentive Bonuses. Year-end cash bonuses are a very popular form of compensation. The fund of money from which bonuses are paid is often a predetermined portion of profits. The amount granted to each executive is based upon the individual's performance and upon his salary level.

Incentive Stock Option. Created by the Economic Recovery Tax Act of 1981, the incentive stock option is a substitute for the qualified stock option which was eliminated by earlier tax legislation. The Act spells out stringent conditions on eligibility for ownership, price, length of time stock must be held, etc., in order to qualify for favored tax treatment.

Nonqualified Stock Option. When an executive buys shares of his or her company's stock under a nonqualified option plan, there is no favored tax treatment from the Internal Revenue Service. However, there is great flexibility in using such options. The option can be granted by the corporation at any price, it can be exercised any time within 10 years, and the stock can be sold by the executive after holding it only six months.

Restricted Stock Plan. With a restricted stock plan the corporation transfers stock to the manager, subject to a restriction of some kind that limits the stock's value during the period of the restriction. A typical restriction is that the individual is not allowed to sell the stock for a designated period, say five years. The executive is not required to pay income tax on the stock awarded to him until the time at which his rights to the stock become transferable.

Performance Shares. A performance share is a stock bonus that is paid to the executive several years in the future if his pre-established goals for, say, two or more years are met.

Deferred Compensation. Deferred compensation usually takes the form of a bonus in cash or stock or a pension supplement. These are paid after retirement when the person's income tax bracket is lower.

Perquisites. Perquisites include such benefits as personal use of a company automobile, personal use of a company-owned apartment, lodge, or yacht, and free medical examinations.

Questions for Review and Discussion

1. Explain why prevailing wage rates within a labor market are such an important factor influencing wages in individual companies.
2. What are reasonable goals for a comprehensive program of employee compensation? Why does compensation seldom really motivate improved performance?
3. If you had the task of persuading union officials in your organization to agree to the adoption of a job evaluation program, what arguments would you give?
4. A company president makes the statement that he or she sees no need for introducing a job evaluation plan into his company. He feels that if he conducts an annual wage survey and adjusts his own rates accordingly, there will be no need for a costly job-rating program. Do you agree or disagree? Why?

TABLE 22-4. Chart of Job Titles, Points, and Wages.

Job Title	Number of Employees	Points	Present Average Weekly Wage	Average Wage in Area
Clerk-Typist	3	118	$155.00	$140.00
Bookkeeping Machine Operator	2	123	165.00	150.00
Switchboard Operator	2	128	175.00	160.00
Stenographer	5	145	180.00	175.00
Clerk, Billing	2	148	177.00	185.00
Clerk, Payroll	3	153	191.00	200.00
Key Punch Operator	2	163	198.00	210.00
Secretary I	7	168	215.00	225.00
Accounting Clerk	2	178	220.00	235.00
Secretary II	8	196	240.00	265.00
Buyer, Assistant	2	208	252.00	285.00
Nurse, Industrial	2	216	270.00	302.00
Cashier	2	230	300.00	320.00
Draftsperson, I	12	275	300.00	360.00
Draftsperson, II	4	320	345.00	410.00
Computer Programmer	2	335	390.00	425.00
Accountant	3	355	415.00	470.00

PROBLEM 2: EVALUATING A JOB

Using the point plan shown in Figure 22-2, evaluate a job with which you are very familiar. This could be a job you have held, now hold, or one you have had a chance to observe closely. Alternatively work in groups of two to four persons. Interview one student to obtain all the essential facts about a job he has held— then evaluate it. In assigning the proper degree for each factor, select the degree which represents the highest level of job demand for the factor.

For the job that you rate, prepare a job-rating substantiation sheet. List the job title and for each factor give your selection of degree and points. Add points to obtain total. Explain with one or two sentences your reason for selecting the particular degree for each factor. Your substantiation should relate elements of job content to degree definitions.

23 Individual and Group Incentives

Wages to employees for services rendered can be paid according either to the time worked or to the amount of work produced. Those whose pay is based on time are paid a certain sum of money per hour regardless of how productive they may be—this is commonly called daywork or time work. Usually employees receive their paychecks once each week, and pay is calculated according to the number of hours the particular employee worked during that week. If, on the other hand, pay is computed according to how much work is produced (units, pounds, dozens, assemblies, tons, and so on) and if employees can earn extra money for producing more than a certain quota or norm, we say that this is a wage-incentive-payment method. If top management decides to adopt a wage-incentive program, its objectives are generally to reduce unit labor costs by increasing man-hour output, to raise worker income without increasing labor costs, and to acquire a means of effectively controlling the production process. Features that most incentive plans have in common are measurement by management of the amount of work done, establishment of a quota or standard output, and the utilization of a formula for relating pay to production or performance.

In this chapter we shall investigate direct wage incentive programs and issues. We shall look at conditions conducive to the establish-ment of wage incentives, work measurement techniques, requirements for sound incentive programs, types of incentive plans, problems caused by incentive system operation, and approaches to solutions of these problems.

In direct-wage-incentive programs there is a close relationship between the amount of work produced by the individual employee and his pay. For the most part, engineering work-measurement techniques are used to establish the production standard upon which pay and output calculations are based.

Another whole category of incentives consists of plant- and company-wide incentives that have objectives somewhat broader in scope than the higher-output-per-unit-time objective of the traditional wage-incentive installation. These plant-wide and company-wide incentives are based upon the concept of cooperation among management, employees, and the union (if the employees are represented by one). The objectives may be manifold. Included among typical objectives are a plant-wide reduction in labor costs or total payroll costs, reduction in material and supply costs, fostering of greater loyalty toward the company, improved cooperation between labor and management, and lower turnover and absenteeism.

We shall discuss three kinds of plant- or company-wide incentive programs. These are

ductivity should be attainable. Indeed a primary reason for an employer even to contemplate the installation of a pay incentive is his or her expectation that it will result in increased productivity, improved performance and efficiency, and lower unit costs.

5. The employees (and the union if the employees are organized) must accept, support, and cooperate in this method of wage payment. The reward that employees can expect to receive from participation is higher earnings than they would receive under the daywork or timework method of payment. But if such support is lacking, the incentive program will rest on a shaky foundation.

The five foregoing conditions indicate when the adoption of the incentive method of wage payment is practical and desirable. On the other hand, payment according to time worked is clearly preferable when these requirements cannot be met. Process-controlled operations, such as are found in most of the pulp and paper and chemical industries, are more properly paid by daywork. Most clerical, technical, engineering, and scientific occupations are not under incentives. However, salespersons are typically paid by commissions or at least by a guaranteed base salary plus a commission. Many organizations pay their top executives according to a salary-plus-incentive-bonus arrangement, because there is a reasonable relationship between the performance of a company president, for example, and the profits of the company.

Thus, when the work is inherently variable, when it cannot be accurately measured, standardized, and counted, when productivity is not closely related to employee skill and effort, when employees and unions strongly oppose incentive payment, and when the employer can realize no potential gain from wage incentives, it is preferable to employ time wages. Time wages have the added advantage of simplified payroll computation. Likewise employees can readily ascertain their earnings for a given pay period (the same statement cannot be made for many incentive installations). A primary disadvantage of time payment is that the labor cost per unit is variable. The employer cannot as readily control or fix direct labor costs, since different workers on the same job receive the same pay regardless of how much they turn out.

Work Measurement

Most commonly "time" is used as the standard for measuring performance of work that is on an incentive (time per piece, time per pound, time per assembly, time expressed as a percentage of maximum possible operating time for running mechanical equipment, and so on). Other bases or standards against which performance can be compared may also be used. The amount of finished or good product from a given quantity of material can give a standard expressed in terms of a percentage of maximum possible yield. Also, employees can be rewarded for a reduction in the usage of costly supply materials; in this case the standard is expressed as a budgeted money figure determined by accounting procedures. Or rewards can be tied to an improvement in quality, in which case the standard would be a permissible percentage of imperfections or rejects.

The time required to perform a given amount of work is, as was stated above, the most generally used measure upon which to base an incentive system. There are a number of methods available for establishing standards. These are (1) past performance; (2) bargaining between employer and union; (3) time study; (4) standard data; (5) predetermined elemental times; and (6) work sampling. Each of these methods will be discussed briefly.[3]

[3]Full explanations of work measurement methods can be found in Delmar W. Karger and F. M. Bayha, *Engineered Work Measurement*, 3rd ed. (New York: The Industrial Press, 1977); Benjamin W. Niebel, *Motion and Time Study*, 6th ed. (Homewood, Ill.: Richard D. Irwin, Inc., 1976).

Past Performance. Industrial engineers almost universally agree that past performance is a poor way of deciding what future performance should be. Standards derived from past performance when employees were on day work usually are much lower and easier to attain than those developed through time study and other engineered work-measurement techniques. Because no complete analysis has been made of work methods, delays, allowances, and of the skill and effort of those employees upon whom the past performance records are based, management cannot justifiably say what standard or normal performance should be.

Bargaining Between Employer and Union. Bargaining is the method followed in the men's and women's wearing apparel industries to a considerable extent. The facts upon which the negotiators base their judgments may be either past production records, their own experience, or actual time study. In the New York dress industry, as an illustration, samples of new dresses are submitted by employers to the price settlement department of the International Ladies' Garment Workers Union. The experts in this department analyze each garment in detail. Industrial engineers in the union conduct time and motion studies to provide standard time information, which is then used as a guide by the rate experts in the determination of an actual money piece rate for each garment. Then these persons meet with representatives of the manufacturers. If agreement is reached, the matter is settled. However, if there is a dispute, the office of the permanent impartial chairman (arbitrator) is requested to assign an impartial adjuster to study the garment and decide upon a piece price. Although the adjuster's word is usually taken as final, appeal may be made to the impartial chairman.

Time Study. The principal method used in industry to set work standards is stopwatch time study. The more modern and refined techniques of standard data and predetermined elemental times depend upon and are adaptations of basic time-study principles.

The basic task that is measured and standardized is the operation. An operation may consist of drilling four ½″ diameter holes through a piece of ⅜″-thick steel on a sensitive drill press; or in a garment factory it might consist of sewing a pocket on a man's white dress shirt; or in the electrical industry it might consist of spray painting the case for a circuit breaker as it hangs suspended from an overhead conveyor. In analyzing an operation, the time-study engineer will sub-divide it into work elements. He will seek to find the most efficient way to perform the work. In some cases extensive redesign of the work place layout and revamping of the hand motions may be in order. The training of the time-study engineer causes him continually to seek a better way to perform an operation or sequence of operations.

After the most efficient method has been developed (of course, in the future a still better way may be found), one or more qualified workers is timed with a stopwatch while she or he is following the prescribed work procedure. A separate time reading is taken and recorded for each work element. Since different employees exhibit considerable variation in the pace at which they work, it is necessary for the time-study engineer to adjust the actual observed time by a percentage factor to arrive at the time it should take a normal worker exhibiting normal skill and effort to perform the given operation. This process of adjusting the observed time by a percentage factor to yield a normal or base time is called leveling or performance rating. Thus, if an operator spent 0.20 minutes to perform one element of the total operation and if the time-study engineer rated the performance (that is, skill and effort) at 20 per cent above normal, the normal time for that element would be 0.24 minutes (0.20 × 120 per cent). To the sum of the times obtained for the individual elements are added allowances to compensate the employee for necessary personal time, unavoidable delays, and for rest to overcome fatigue.

The resulting figure is the standard time for the operation. Time-study authorities and practitioners claim they can achieve an accuracy of plus or minus 5 per cent of the true standard time. The true standard, of course, is never really known.

Standard Data. When similar operations have been studied repeatedly by means of stop-watch time study, it soon becomes apparent that certain patterns and uniformity of times develop for individual work elements. By tabulating and classifying times taken from a large number of studies of similar work, the initial steps toward the development of standard data are made. By use of these data it is not necessary to make a stop-watch time study in order to arrive at the proper standard time. What is required is that the engineer observe the job in question to fully comprehend what is involved (noting machine, workplace, layout, parts, fixtures, and so on). By knowing what elements are required to perform the work, the engineer can select the standard times corresponding to these elements from tables of previously prepared standard data.

Predetermined Elemental Times. Predetermined elemental times are basically a form of standard data; however, the elements of work are of the general type or order called *therbligs*. Therbligs are elements of work that were first identified and analyzed by Lillian and Frank Gilbreth in their pioneering work in motion study. Therbligs are basic finger, arm, hand, and body motions, often called basic divisions of accomplishments. Reach, move, hold, grasp, position, preposition, inspect, assemble, and select are some illustrations of these elements. Use of ordinary stop-watch time-study procedures does not permit the measurement of work elements as short as therbligs. Standard time values for these are obtained by studying a large sample of diversified operations with a timing device, such as the motion-picture camera, that is capable of measuring very short elements.

There are a great many different predetermined elemental time systems from which to choose. A considerable number have been developed as proprietary systems by industrial engineering consulting firms; others have been created by industrial companies for their own use. In order to set a standard for an operation by using such systems, it is necessary for the engineer to make an extremely detailed analysis of the motions involved and to record these on paper. He must properly classify each motion and then take the time from a table of standard times. An ordinary operation having a work cycle of one minute could very well contain over a hundred basic elements of work. The great advantage of using predetermined elemental times is that the process of establishing a standard requires that the engineer make a very detailed analysis of the motions involved. This procedure often uncovers inefficiencies and leads to significant improvements.

Work Sampling. Work sampling requires that the engineer take a great number of observations of a worker at random times throughout the working day. He records precisely what the employee is doing at the time he is being observed. No stop watch is used. The object is to find the frequency of occurrence of every work element. Even though the worker is not under observation constantly, by adequate random sampling of his or her activities, the engineer can ascertain within limits of accuracy that can be calculated statistically the percentage of time that she or he spends on each portion of the operation. Delays, allowances, and infrequently occurring noncyclic elements can also readily be measured this way. In order to set a standard by the work sampling procedure, it is necessary to level or rate the performance of the worker being studied (as with stop-watch time study) and to count the actual number of units produced during the period under study. Advantages of work sampling are that it is possible to study a considerable number of different operations at the same time, the psychological problems presented by standing over a worker for a considerable period of time as in stop-watch time study are avoided, and considerable statistical reliability can be achieved through the process of taking many observations over a period of several days.

Essential Requirements of a Sound Wage Incentive Program

Based upon the experiences derived from study of successful and unsuccessful programs in various industries through the years, writers, researchers, and others have concluded that if certain general principles or guides are followed by management in installing and administering a wage incentive plan, the chances for success are good. A successful plan is one that achieves its purpose. This is usually to increase productivity, reduce costs, improve efficiency, and increase employee earnings while at the same time maintaining or enhancing employee morale and employee relations.

1. Management, employees, and the union (if the employees are organized) should understand and support the incentive program. Since the procedures involved in methods analysis, time study, base-rate setting, and bonus calculation when taken collectively are rather complicated, explanations and training by management for employees and union leaders are essential. Discussion and participation with lower-level supervisors and union officials in the initiation and the development of the program are advantageous in creating the kind of support that is necessary for success.

2. Methods analysis of each operation should be undertaken before a work standard is established. The optimum methods and procedures for doing the work should be devised first. A standardized method should be followed. Employees must be taught how to

perform the work according to this standard procedure.

3. The standard upon which the wage incentive is based should be arrived at by carefully applied work-measurement techniques, such as time study, standard data, work sampling, or predetermined elemental times. If piece rates are bargained collectively between management and union, the decisions should be guided by engineered work-measurement techniques. Standards should not be based upon past performance. If this were done, those employees who had loafed in the past would be rewarded with easy-to-achieve standards, whereas those who had previously given an honest day's work would be penalized with a difficult-to-meet quota.

4. Each job on incentive should have a guaranteed minimum or base rate. Even if output drops to a low level, the employee can depend upon earning at least a certain minimum amount of money. Normally this base rate will be determined by job evaluation. Differences in base rates among jobs will reflect differences in skill, effort, responsibility, and job conditions. Maintenance of proper differentials between these base rates will insure that employees on jobs having low requirements will not earn more than employees on highly skilled jobs when both are on incentive.

5. The work standard (whether it be expressed in time or money per unit) should be guaranteed by management against change unless there is a change in the method, tooling, equipment, materials, or design of the product. The employee must know that the work standard or quota will not be increased just because she or he starts to make large bonus earnings. A change in the work standard is legitimate if the method of doing the job is altered. If management simplifies the operation in such a way that the time per unit is less than the previous standard, the worker should be able to earn as much money as before, provided she or he exerts equivalent

skill and effort. If the employee, through initiative and ingenuity, figures out a better way, she or he should be rewarded.

6. It should be easy for employees to calculate earnings. Even with a complicated incentive formula, management with its specialized knowledge and calculating machines can generally compute employee earnings readily. However, employees need to be able to verify the payroll department's calculations. This builds confidence and trust in the program.

7. An effective grievance procedure must be available to handle dissatisfaction and complaints on the part of employees. Grievances over incentives usually are concerned with charges by the employees that the rate or standard is too "tight" (that is, too difficult to meet) or that the time standard has been cut in violation of the labor agreement.

TYPES OF INCENTIVE PAY PLANS

Although literally scores of incentive plans have been used over the past seventy years, only a few primary types are in common usage at present. Those that will be explained here are measured daywork, piecework, standard-hour, and gains-sharing plans.[4]

Measured Daywork

The measured-daywork plan is in the twilight zone between a true direct-incentive plan and regular time payment or daywork. A work standard is set through time study or some other work-measurement technique. The worker is expected to meet this quota. If she or he exceeds the standard or falls below, she or he still receives the regular hourly rate of pay. From management's standpoint, the plan has the advantage that unit labor costs are much more predictable than with ordinary daywork, because considerable emphasis is placed upon meeting the standard. In some installations merit rating is employed. This is the classical and historical type of measured daywork. Every three months each person is rated on four factors: quantity of work, quality of work, dependability, and versatility. A high score yields an increase in hourly pay for the ensuing three months, whereas a low score results in a decrease in pay. The employee's rate of pay actually consists of two parts: a basic or guaranteed portion, which normally approximates 75 per cent of the total rate, and the personal portion, which is subject to fluctuation every three months. As an incentive plan this particular type of measured daywork has the disadvantage that the reward for improved performance is not directly and proportionately related to that behavior. The pay adjustment is too remote in point of time. Also the instrument for relating pay to performance—that is, the foreman's judgment in merit rating the employee—is subjective. On the positive side the system does encourage (in fact, it requires) the foreman to become well acquainted with every employee in order to rate her or him. Also management has greater control over labor costs than is true under ordinary daywork.

There is another kind of measured daywork program that is becoming increasingly popular in industry. Indeed, it has tended to supplant the type just described. According to Slichter, Healy, and Livernash, the kind employing merit rating that adjusts the employee's hourly rate in accordance with his performance over a period of time has become quite rare.[5] More commonly

[4]Many of the numerous other plans were created by industrial engineering consultants. Some like the Taylor Differential Piece Rate plan are of historical interest but no longer in use. Other plans are the Gantt Task and Bonus, Rowan, Barth, Emerson Efficiency, Merrick, Hayes-Manit, and Dyer.

[5]Sumner H. Slichter, James J. Healy, and E. Robert Livernash, *The Impact of Collective Bargaining on Manage-*

at present measured daywork involves simply pay by the hour accompanied by control of worker efficiency by means of production standards. The hourly rate is not adjustable. Emphasis is placed upon the establishment of accurate standards of output through time-study, standard-data, or other procedures. Then pressure is placed upon the worker to meet the standard consistently. If performance falls below standard, the industrial engineer and the supervisor investigate to determine the cause. If the materials, equipment, or process are faulty, corrective measures are taken. But if the worker is at fault, she or he is subject to disciplinary action (assuming the standard is fair and she or he has the basic capacity to do the work).

There is some evidence to indicate that measured daywork in contrast to piecework and other incentive plans results in less worker resistance to the introduction of changed methods. Also management encounters fewer union and worker grievances over the fairness of production standards. There is less likelihood of measured daywork causing sharp controversy between labor and management than with ordinary incentive arrangements, because there are fewer sensitive issues over which to clash.

Piecework

One of the simplest and most commonly used of all incentive plans is piecework. The standard is expressed in terms of a certain sum of money for every unit produced, such as $0.10 per piece or $0.77 per pound or $1.31 per dozen. The earnings of the employee are directly proportional to output. This is what industrial engineers call a 1-for-1 plan—for each 1 per cent increase in production the worker is paid a 1 per cent increase in wages. If the basic hourly rate of pay of a given job is $4.00 (as established by job evaluation) and if the industrial engineer has

set a standard time of 0.2 hours per unit (therefore 5 units per hour), we find that the piece rate then becomes $4.00 per hour divided by 5 units per hour, which is equal to $.80 per unit. Although in the early days workers were paid only for the actual work they turned out, with no guaranteed minimum, modern practice requires the payment of a certain minimum wage if the employee has not produced enough units to meet that base. Thus, as in the example just cited, if the guaranteed minimum were $4.00 per hour and if the worker's output was less than the 5 units necessary to earn the minimum, he or she would still be paid $4.00 per hour. With straight piecework (without a guaranteed minimum) many of the risks of factory management are transferred to the shoulders of the employee, because even if there are production delays, faulty materials, and machine breakdowns, the direct labor cost per unit to the employer is fixed.

For a piecework plan that has a guaranteed minimum, Figure 23-1 shows graphically the relationship between output of an individual employee and total earnings. The direct labor cost to the employer per unit of output is shown on the ordinate at the right of the graph and is portrayed by the dashed line.

The advantages of piecework are its simplicity and ease of understanding by the employees. It is eminently fair in its rewards, since earnings are directly proportional to output for all output levels in excess of standard. The guaranteed minimum protects the employee's basic income should output fall below standard due to production delays or inexperience on the employee's part. Cost accounting and control by management are facilitated by the fact that labor cost is constant for output above standard.

However, the piecework system does have serious disadvantages. If a general wage increase is put into effect for all employees, this necessitates changing all the piece rates on the books. This is a very cumbersome clerical task. Usage of piece rates for a group incentive where different employees have different hourly base

ment (Washington, D.C.: The Brookings Institution, 1960), p. 490.

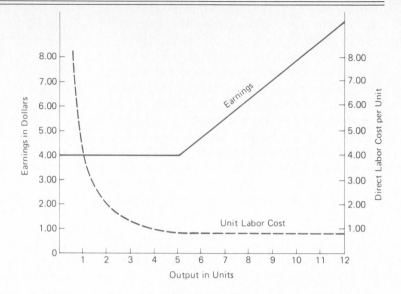

FIGURE 23-1 Piecework with a Guaranteed Minimum. The standard is $.80 per unit. For an output of 5 units or less per hour the employee is paid $4.00 per hour. For 6 units the pay is $4.80 and so on. In practice pay is calculated on basis of daily output.

rates is very cumbersome. Piece rates often lead to confusion in the minds of both management and labor in that time study is here linked rather directly with money rates. To insure objectivity, the money rate should be arrived at for every job by an evaluation of its relative amount of skill, effort, responsibility, and job conditions, whereas the standard time should be determined by an objective study of the quantity of work that can be reasonbly expected from a normal worker working under standardized conditions. The money level and the work standard should be considered separately.

Standard-Hour Plan

Sometimes called the 100 per cent bonus or standard-time plan, the standard-hour plan expresses the work standard in terms of time. It features a guaranteed base rate that the worker receives if she or he fails to meet standard performance. This plan is very widely used, and it overcomes all the disadvantages of the piecework plan while retaining its advantages. It is essentially the same as piecework with a guaranteed minimum, with the exception of the fact

that the standard is expressed in time instead of money. As defined by the Society for the Advancement of Management, it is a pay plan in which the per cent performance over standard is rewarded by equal per cent premium over base pay.[6] An example will reveal more clearly how the system works. Assume that the base rate for a job is $6.00 per hour and that the time standard for the operation upon which the employee is currently working is ¼ hour per unit. Pay would normally be calculated separately for each day. If 40 units are produced in one day, the employee would have earned 10 standard hours of pay, or $60.00. If the work day were 8 hours long, he would then have earned 10 standard hours of pay, although his clock hours were 8. His efficiency is thus 125 per cent. If, for some reason, the employee's output for the day were only 24 units (6 standard hours), he or she would be paid the base rate for the full 8 clock hours worked.

Advantages of this plan are that it is easy for employees to understand, and earnings are directly proportional to production above stan-

[6]Society for Advance of Management, *Glossary of Terms Used in Methods, Time Study, and Wage Incentives* (New York: The Society, 1953).

dard; a change in hourly wage rates for all employees has no effect upon the standards, because they are expressed in time units (rather than money units as in the piecework plan). It is readily suitable to group-incentive applications where the group may include employees on various base rates. Further it facilitates the utilization of accounting controls and departmental measures of efficiency. There appear to be no disadvantages to this system; in fact, many companies, having tried other more cumbersome plans, have dropped them in favor of the standard-hour plan.

Gains-Sharing Plans

A gains-sharing plan is one in which the money paid for increasing output above standard is not in direct proportion to the increment in production. The worker receives less than 1 per cent increase in pay for each 1 per cent increase in production. The "gains" are shared with the employer. All the gains-sharing plans are based upon the premise of rewarding the employee for saving time in the performance of the job. In one well-known plan, the Bedeaux plan, named after its creator Charles Bedeaux, 75 per cent of the gain went to the worker and 25 per cent went to indirect labor and supervision. In 1940 this plan was revised so that 100 per cent of the gain went to the worker. The Halsey 50–50 bonus plan paid 50 per cent of the value of the time saved (when a worker completed units in less than the standard time) to the worker and 50 per cent to the company.

Because the incentive payments are in less than direct proportion to output, both workers and unions have opposed gains-sharing plans. They are seldom used nowadays.

Group Incentives

Group incentives for work that is measured and standardized can be paid under any one of the foregoing types of incentive plans. Earnings are determined from the total number of units produced by the group. However, the group approach does not obviate the necessity of analysis and standardization of each job within the group. Where the workers are quite interdependent and where clear cooperation and coordination are vital to success, a group incentive plan makes a great deal of sense. On a production line, where one employee cannot get ahead of the person who precedes, a group plan may work well. If there are a number of different jobs within the group, each having a different basic hourly rate of pay, the standard-hour plan works quite well. Here the percentage increase in output above standard for the entire group can be added to the base rate for each employee to determine the amount of the bonus for that pay period.

HUMAN AND ADMINISTRATIVE PROBLEMS

The usage of wage incentives in an industrial organization often achieves management's goal of higher productivity and lower direct labor costs. Further, the total cost per unit may very well decrease too. If a particular machine or work center has an overhead (or burden) costing rate of $16.00 per direct labor hour and if output is increased, then the overhead cost per unit is decreased, because the overhead rate, within limits, does not go up if production rises. Employees, too, stand to gain from the installation of a wage incentive system. Commonly their pay will average 20 to 30 per cent higher. So far, so good.

However, the introduction of incentives brings about many administrative and human relations problems that either are not present at all under daywork or are present to only a minor extent. A larger industrial engineering staff is needed to devise the incentive plan, set work standards, and develop controls. Greater attention must be devoted to obtaining accurate piece counts of each worker and to maintaining quality and safety standards. And above all, serious human relations problems are created. Experience shows that grievance and arbitration activity is higher in plants using incentives than in nonincentive plants.

Role of the Industrial Engineer

The process of work measurement used to set standards generally requires that the engineer closely observe the detailed motions of the employee for a considerable length of time (anywhere from one half to a whole eight-hour day). The engineer often tells the employee to change his or her method of doing the work. To an experienced worker who feels he or she already knows the job well, this detailed observation and correction often cause tension and antagonism toward the engineer. But in reality this is only the start of a human relations conflict. The worker knows that the engineer is going to set a time standard on the job. This standard will determine wages. If the rate turns out to be "tight," he or she will be unable to exceed standard performance, and he or she will only be paid the hourly base rate for the time actually worked. Workers tend to feel that if they can make the work look more difficult and take longer than really necessary, they can fool the engineer and thus get a "good" or a "loose" rate. However, the engineer is often aware of the worker's objectives, so he or she adjusts the actual observed time by a percentage factor to rate or level performance. So if the employee stalls in doing the job and takes 5 minutes to perform a unit of work and if the engineer judges skill and effort to be 75 per cent of normal, he or she will allow only 3.75 minutes for the operation. Sometimes in spite of his or her awareness, the engineer is "fooled" and does establish a loose rate. On the other hand, if the resultant rate should turn out to be "tight," not only will the worker who has been studied be dissatisfied but

fellow workers who perform the same operation will blame him or her for the bad rate.

The industrial engineer, trying to do a professional job, is many times caught between two fires. There is pressure from higher management for greater efficiency, higher production, lower labor costs, and the placing of as many jobs as possible on incentive in a limited amount of time. If the engineer establishes "loose" standards, there is criticism by management. Because he or she is dependent upon management for job tenure, salary increases, and progress in the organization, he or she must conform to management's expectations. However, there are pressures on the other side of the fence, too. The workers will turn in rate grievances and express resentment if they are not satisfied with the standards. Since the engineer must frequently mingle with the employees, he or she seeks at least their passive good will and cooperation. It the employees should file a great number of grievances over the rates set, management may express dissatisfaction with the caliber of the engineer's efforts.

Restriction of Output

Restriction of output is a phenomenon that occurs with both union and nonunion employees and under both daywork and incentive situations. The problem is accentuated under an incentive system. Restriction of output means that informal group pressures and sanctions are imposed to prevent employees from producing as much as they are capable of. From the early days of the scientific management movement through to the present day, industrial engineers and management-engineering consultants have tended to believe that the installation of a wage incentive program would cause employees to try to maximize their earnings by maximizing their production. Certain individual employees indeed do just this. They work to the limit of their endurance to earn as much money as possible. But the majority control their output; they do not produce as much as they could if they worked to the limits imposed by bodily fatigue. Usually they work well below this point. In one factory the employees in the punch press department systematically produced at 27 per cent above standard, never more. This restriction was achieved through group controls. When confronted with the evidence of restriction, the informal leader, who in this case was the shop steward, vehemently denied any planned effort on the employees' part to restrict work.

Why does this phenomenon occur? There are many reasons to explain it. First, employees tend to believe that if they earn more money than management thinks they should, the piece rate will be cut. Rate cutting is a practice that arose in industry many years ago. Ill-trained "efficiency experts" who served as consultants to employers often adopted this practice. At the present time all reputable industrial engineers and employers frown upon the practice. However, it still occurs often enough to arouse the employees' fears.

Even if the employer does not intentionally cut rates when earnings reach too high a level, sometimes a worker thinks he does. This comes about through the continued auditing and re-examination of operations that some companies undertake. In the effort to reduce costs still further, operations with established rates are many times restudied for further methods improvement, and then a new and lower rate is set. Strictly speaking the employee should have as good an earnings potential as before, but frequently management's motives are mistrusted. The employees may interpret this as a form of disguised rate cutting.

There are social reasons for restriction of output also. According to the logic of management and its engineers, employees should engage in individualistic competition, should work hard, and should take pride in doing a good day's work for their employer. Primary emphasis should be upon the acquisition of more money as the fruits of hard labor. This is considered a major virtue. Concern with the reactions of one's associates to this competitive drive for more and more should not bother the individual. Yet many workers are not so strongly motivated in this direction. They are sensitive to what others in their work group think. They want to acquire and maintain the respect and friendship of their fellows. They feel that group acceptance, social participation, and group solidarity are important values. Those who seek to maximize their earnings by exceeding the group-imposed quota are labeled rate-busters. They generally are set apart from the group and its social activities. The author was once employed in a shop where one employee beat up another worker because the latter was working too fast.[7] Rate restrictors sometimes feel they are "shown up" in the eyes of management by the high output of the "rate-busters," and they resent the latter. Workers often believe that slow workers will be discharged. Thus, in many factories there are conflicts between the restrictors and the rate-busters.

Wage Inequities

Work measurement techniques such as time study have a margin of error. Authorities claim that a well-qualified engineer can set standards that are within ± 5 per cent of the true or correct values. Many critics challenge this assertion. But regardless of this controversy, it is a fact that nearly every industrial establishment has a fair number of loose and tight rates. These may be caused by inexperienced engineers, by workers figuring out short cuts so that the rates become loose over a period of many months, or because the job conditions (adjustment of machine, quality of the materials, and so on) have changed with the passage of time. The fact that the earnings potential will vary significantly from one job to another causes anxiety and jealousy

[7]The victim, only slightly bruised, was transferred to another plant. The aggressor was a local union committeeman. Management, not wanting to upset good union relations, took no disciplinary action against him.

among the employees. They naturally compete to get the jobs with "loose" standards.

Then there is the perennial problem of equity between the semiskilled worker, who is on incentive, and the highly skilled employee, such as the tool and die maker, who is paid by the hour. Industrial engineers find it very difficult to put nonrepetitive, highly variable, and complex jobs on incentive. In one electronics factory, male machine-shop craftsmen went on a one-day strike because semiskilled women on incentive in the same plant had higher take-home pay.

Fluctuations in Earnings

A common source of frustration to workers is the variation in earnings from one week to another. This is prevalent in shops where there are short runs and new operations must be continually mastered, where workers are transferred from one operation to another frequently, and where the process equipment breaks down often (down-time). In job-order shops where new and different products are continually being introduced, there naturally is a lag from the introduction of new operations until they have been placed on incentive. If workers are paid day-work rates for this interim period, they will experience a temporary lowering of their pay.

Rewards for Methods Improvements

The typical incentive plan rewards employees for physically working harder but gives them nothing for greater ingenuity and new ideas on how to improve their jobs. If employees develop methods improvements that make the work easier and reduce the time per unit, they are faced with a dilemma. If they notify their supervisor or the industrial engineer of the improvement, there is every likelihood that the operation will

be changed to conform to the better method. Then a new and lower time standard will be established. Employees often feel that their "reward" for passing on their ideas to management is a lower piece rate that will require harder work to earn as much money as they obtained previously. Even if the new rate should provide them with as much money as before the change (equivalent earnings for equivalent skill and effort), they tend to feel that they are exposing themselves to the risk of a tight rate. So we find that in many shops workers devise jigs, fixtures, and other simple methods improvements and keep them secret from management. By so doing they can increase their incentive earnings substantially without increased physical exertion. Or if they suspect that earnings of, say, 50 and 60 per cent above base rate will arouse the industrial engineer's suspicions, they use their labor-saving devices to give themselves more free time during the working day.

Many companies attempt to solve this problem by encouraging employees to submit their proposals for methods improvements and cost reductions through a formal suggestion system in order to receive monetary awards. In theory this is fine. However, the typical suggestion plan pays the employee who submitted an idea 10 to 15 per cent of the first year's net dollar savings. Many employees conclude that they will make more money by concealing their ideas from management and thereby obtain higher incentive earnings through utilization of jigs and fixtures of their own making. The central problem, in summary, is this: Should an incentive plan reward employees only for the exertion of greater physical skill and effort, or should it reward them for their own ideas and initiative as well? Would it be better to incorporate rewards for ideas into the basic incentive plan itself, or should this objective be met by means of a separate program? Possible solutions are the payment of much more liberal awards under a suggestion system or the adoption of a plant-wide incentive system, such as a Scanlon Plan.

Meeting the Problems Imposed by Incentives

Although no magic formulas exist that can solve the human problems imposed by incentives, there are certain sound approaches that, if followed, can ameliorate them. There is need for more research and experimentation to find full answers.

By assiduously applying the principles enunciated earlier in this chapter for the successful operation of an incentive program, some of these difficulties can be overcome or greatly modified. For example, employees' fears of rate cutting can be prevented by guaranteeing standards. Tight rates can be adjusted if an effective grievance procedure exists. Careful administration of the program can reduce fluctuations in earnings (for example, some firms pay the average incentive earnings that an employee has built up during the preceding three months when he or she is transferred to an unfamiliar operation or for machine down-time). If the employer adopts an easy-to-understand incentive system and if a training program is instituted to teach the employees how the plan operates, confidence will be built up and distrust and suspicion allayed.

Antagonisms between the industrial engineer and employees can be considerably reduced by a full recognition of the staff nature of the engineer's position in the organization. The employee is accustomed to having interaction originated for him or her by the foreman. In the approach to the employee for making a time study, the engineer should first obtain the authorization of the foreman. If the employees are represented by a union, the shop steward should be notified also. The foreman, steward, and engineer as a group would then approach the employee to explain the work measurement assignment in relation to his or her job. After the work standard has been determined, the engineer should present it to the foreman for reactions and approval. It should be the foreman who announces the standard to the employee. The shop steward should also be informed of developments to obtain his or her reaction.

There are still other possibilities for overcoming many of these human relations problems. When employees are represented by a union, there is considerable merit to the idea of having a degree of union participaton in the time-study and rate-setting process. Union participaton through union-employed time-study people and bargaining of piece rates accounts, in no small measure, for the full acceptance by the workers of the piecework method of payment in the garment industry. It is not proposed here that work standards and piece rates should be bargained throughout industry. Employers typically hold that setting of workloads is a management prerogative. The money paid for each job is, of course, a bargainable issue. However, there is considerable merit to the proposal that local union officlas and stewards receive training in the fundamentals of time study and incentives—even to the point where the union would have one or more fully qualified time-study experts in its membership. Various procedures could be followed for implementing this. Standards set by management would be put into effect except for those that workers have found by trial to be incorrect or unjust. They would then file a grievance. If a restudy of the operation were deemed by both parties to be advisable, it would be carried out by both the industrial engineer employed by the company and the time-study specialist working for the union. The dispute would then be resolved by a meeting of the minds of all parties involved: management as represented by the foreman and the industrial engineer and the employees as represented by the steward and the time-study specialist. Disputes unresolved at this level could be processed through the regular grievance procedure and eventually taken to arbitration if necessary.

The adoption of a plantwide incentive plan based upon the essential concept of cooperation between labor and management is another method of attempting to overcome the multitude of human problems created by wage incentives. The Scanlon Plan is one well-known method. It does not involve individual job rates but rather a standard expressed in terms of labor costs as a percentage of the sales value of the product for the plant as a whole. Employee participation in reducing costs is actively encouraged. Teamwork and cooperation instead of individualistic competition are emphasized.

INCENTIVES AND LABOR–MANAGEMENT COOPERATION

An incentive system that departs considerably from commonly accepted notions of what an incentive plan should be is the one developed by Joseph N. Scanlon. The plan is generally known as the Scanlon Plan.[8] Mr. Scanlon was an official of the United Steelworkers of America in the late 1930s and early 1940s; later he joined the faculty of the Massachusetts Institute of Technology.

The plan consists basically of two parts: (1) a plant-wide wage-incentive arrangement for which the standard is set by accounting methods and not by time study; (2) a program for implementing cooperation among the employees, the union, and the management to solve production and efficiency problems. This is accomplished through a unique suggestion plan.

[8]Descriptions and analyses of the Scanlon Plan can be found in a number of articles and books. Among them are William Foote Whyte, *Money and Motivation* (New York: Harper and Row, 1955); "Productivity and Incentive Pay," *Management Record*, Vol. 19, No. 10 (October 1957); Russell W. Davenport, "Enterprise for Everyman," *Fortune*, Vol. 41, No. 1 (January 1950), pp. 55–59; F. G. Lesieur and E. S. Puckett, "The Scanlon Plan Has Proved Itself," *Harvard Business Review*, Vol. 47, No. 5 (September–October 1969), pp. 109–118.

Although the details of the Scanlon Plan vary from one installation to another the essential features are the same. Even though the plan can work successfully in a nonunion company, Scanlon felt that if employees were represented by a union, the greatest advantages of employee participation could be obtained.

Labor-Cost Norm and Incentive Bonus

Cost-accounting records are examined to arrive at a labor-cost norm. This norm is expressed as a percentage of the total sales value of the product shipped by the company. Usually direct and indirect labor as well as supervisory payroll are included in the figures for labor cost. Sometimes even executives are included in the incentive plan. Scanlon generally recommended that all employees from worker to major executive should participate. An example will show how the plan works. Assume that labor and management after a careful examination of accounting records arrive at a labor-cost norm of 40 per cent of the sales value of the product. This figure then becomes the standard for the ensuing year. Calculations are then made on a monthly basis. If cooperative efforts reduce the actual payroll costs below that 40 per cent figure for any one month, the employees will then receive a bonus.

It has been found practical to reserve a portion of the monthly savings (25 per cent in Table 23-1) to balance against those months when the actual is in excess of the norm or standard. Likewise it should be pointed out that in some companies using the Scanlon Plan, a certain percentage of the savings is retained by the company. If major changes occur in basic wage rates, in the selling price, or in the cost of raw materials, or if the company invests in substantial technological improvements, a re-examination of the labor-cost norm may be made. A change in the percentage would be by mutual agreement between management and labor.

TABLE 23-1. An Example of the Scanlon Plan.

Sales shipped for month	$125,000
Less decrease in value of finished goods in inventory and in process	25,000
Total production value	100,000
Labor cost allowable (40%)	40,000
Actual payroll for month	36,000
Savings from improvement in production efficiency	4,000
Less 25% for contingency reserve	1,000
Net available for distribution to employees	$ 3,000
Each employee receives a bonus of 8.33 per cent for the month ($3,000 divided by actual payroll of $36,000).	

Suggestion Plan and Production Committees

It is through the suggestion plan that ideas are handled that make it possible to improve work methods, redesign products, reduce or simplify paperwork, and improve machine utilization. Every department has a production committee composed of a management representative (commonly the foreman) and an employee or union representative. The function of these committees is to process and evaluate employee suggestions. Some are accepted and put into effect at the department level. Those considered worthwhile for the entire plant or those involving major expenditures and changes are passed on to an administration or screening committee composed of an equal number of management and employee (or union) representatives. Suggestions approved by the screening committee are passed on to top management for a final decision. Because management is represented on the screening committee, it generally approves at this point. There are no individual awards under the Scanlon Plan. The payoff comes from cost-cutting ideas that benefit the organization as a whole and thus contribute to the plantwide bonus. Benefits of this participative form of suggestion plan are threefold. (1) It emphasizes cooperation between management and labor. They work together in production and screening committees to solve problems. (2) Teamwork means that often a problem that could not be solved by one person alone is successfully handled by the combined brains of a group. (3) Genuine participation by employees in the affairs of the business reduces the likelihood of restriction of output and resistance to change on their part. They tend to support that which they have initiated and designed.

It is interesting to point out the contrasts between the traditional type of suggestion plan used in industry and the type that is part and parcel of the Scanlon Plan. In the standard suggestion plan individual employees write their ideas on suggestion blanks and drop these in suggestion boxes scattered throughout the plant. The suggestion box coordinator generally either assigns the suggestions to a specialist (such as an engineer) who then studies their feasibility or turns them over to a suggestion committee that evaluates them. If, after thorough investigation, management considers a suggestion useful, it will calculate the annual dollar saving that could be realized through adoption of the idea. Then a percentage of this amount will be awarded to the employee (usually in the form of cash but sometimes in merchandise). If an employee's idea is rejected, he or she generally is notified by means of a form letter.

So we see that in the traditional suggestion system the emphasis is upon the individual, whereas in the Scanlon Plan it is upon group cooperation and group sharing in the benefits. Formal written communication is utilized in the traditional plan, whereas social interaction and discussion are key features of the Scanlon method. In the traditional setup, first-level supervisors sometimes are jealous of workers who submit cost-cutting ideas, because they fear that higher management will criticize them for not thinking of the idea themselves first. This problem is not present under the Scanlon arrangement, because both supervisor and employee work together in the production committee to initiate ideas jointly.

Evaluation of the Scanlon Plan

The Scanlon Plan is not a panacea. Just as the success of other incentive plans depends to a large extent upon the way they are administered and upon the attitudes of the parties involved, so it is with the Scanlon Plan. This plan requires a high degree of mutual confidence and cooperation between labor and management. It places a premium upon group cooperation and the initiation of ideas among the employees. If individual workers are unproductive, they will still share in the bonus earned by the entire plant. If no bonus is earned for several months running (as happens in some companies), employee dissatisfaction can mount. The underlying philosophy of the Scanlon Plan is different from that of the traditional type of incentive program. It overcomes many of the inherent difficulties of the traditional approach, but it raises new problems.

The concept of a company sharing some of the profits of its business with its employees is not new. The practice had its beginning in America in the late eighteenth century and in England and France in the middle nineteenth century. Albert Gallatin, Secretary of the Treasury under Presidents Jefferson and Madison, initiated a profit-sharing plan in 1794 at his glass works in New Geneva, Pa. Horace Greeley had a plan for certain employees of the *New York Tribune*. Pillsbury Flour Mills in Minneapolis set up a plan in 1882. In 1878 the Procter and Gamble Company adopted a plan that is still in operation although in a revised form.[9]

Profit Sharing Defined

The first formalized definition of profit sharing was that adapted by the International Cooperative Congress, Paris, France, in 1889. It reads as follows: "Profit-sharing is an agreement freely entered into, by which the employees receive a share, fixed in advance, of the profits."

The Council of Profit-Sharing Industries, which promotes the profit-sharing movement, gives the following definition: "Any procedure under which an employer makes available to all regular employees subject to reasonable eligibility rules in addition to prevailing rates of pay, special current or deferred sums based on the profits of the business."[10]

For those plans that defer the distribution of benefits to employees until some future date,

---

[9] Some of the many companies that now have profit-sharing plans are Bell and Howell Company, Dow Chemical Company, Eastman Kodak Company, Kellogg Company, The Kroger Company, The Lincoln Electric Company, S. C. Johnson and Son, Inc., Sears, Roebuck and Company, and Tappan Stove Company.

[10] Council of Profit-Sharing Industries, *Profit-Sharing Manual*, rev. ed. (Chicago: The Council, 1957).

the regulations of the United States Internal Revenue Service must be adhered to if the employer wishes to avoid paying a tax on the profit-share sums. Among these requirements are the following. (1) There must be a predetermined formula for allocating the funds to the participants. (2) There must be a trust fund established, and this must be used for the exclusive benefit of the employees or their beneficiaries. (3) The plan must be in writing and communicated to employees.[11]

A profit-sharing plan, then, distributes part of the profits of the business to the employees. The earlier definition of the International Cooperative Congress specifies that the plan must have a definite formula or method for determining the amount that goes to the employees. The definition of the Council of Profit-Sharing Industries omits any mention of an agreement by which shares are computed. Thus, under the latter's definition the percentage share going to the employees might vary from year to year. Presumably the extract amount would be determined by the board of directors. The great majority of plans actually do have a systematic formula for computing the employee's share. It is logical that greater faith and confidence will tend to be created where the employees know exactly how their shares are figured.

Objectives of Profit Sharing

Why would an entrepreneur or the board of directors choose to share some of the fruits of a business enterprise with the employees? Although in practice the motives are many and varied, a fundamental purpose is to create a sort of proprietary interest on the part of the employees in the business organization. The belief is that they will be more loyal and devoted. Presumably the prospect of a profit bonus at the end of the year will motivate the employees to work harder in the hopes of increasing the profits of the company. They will become more conscious, try to reduce waste and scrap.

Other objectives are to improve employee morale, enhance employer-employee relations, and aid in the public relations image of the corporation. A few companies, particularly in the past, looked upon profit sharing as a means of paying low wages and yet providing for adequate total employee income when profits were good. This in effect introduced a flexible wage structure to correlate with the profitability of the company. The rigidities of adequate wages through good times and bad could be avoided. Experience has shown that such plans based upon low wages (below prevailing rates for the given class of work) are generally unsuccessful.

For those plans that defer the payment of benefits until some future date, the objectives are modified somewhat from the foregoing. These plans typically provide benefits upon termination of employment, retirement, death, or disability. The goals here are to provide some financial security to meet certain risks of employment and life. Also management frequently feels that putting off the payment of the profit shares until many years in the future reduces the likelihood of employees leaving the company.

Types of Plans

Profit-sharing plans can be conveniently classified according to when the benefits are paid out to the employees. There are three categories:

1. Current Distribution—This is the oldest method historically and still quite popular. Under it benefits are paid monthly, quarterly, semiannually, and annually.
2. Deferred Distribution—Growing rapidly in popularity in recent years, this arrangement sets up a trust fund with benefits to be paid

[11]F. B. Brower, *Sharing Profits with Employees*, Studies in Personnel Policy, No. 162 (New York: National Industrial Conference Board, 1957).

out for such contingencies as retirement, permanent disability, death, and termination of employment. In some instances the money is set up as a savings fund with employees having the right to withdraw certain portions after having been on the payroll for a specified number of years.

3. A Combination Plan—Some organizations have attempted to gain the advantages of both the current and the deferred distribution plans by paying out part of the profit share in the year earned in cash to the employees. This is a tangible reward in the present that people can fully realize and appreciate. The rest of the money is placed in a trust fund to be paid out at some future date according to the provisions of the plan.

A 1965–1966 study by the Bureau of Labor Statistics of 12,771 establishments employing 8.9 million workers showed that 12 per cent of plant workers and 22 per cent of office workers were under some form of profit-sharing plan. Of these workers, 81 per cent were under a deferred distribution type plan, only 8.7 per cent were under current distribution, 7 per cent were under combined plans, and 3.7 per cent were under elective plans.[12] Bert Metzger of the Profit-Sharing Research Foundation states that as of 1972 approximately 8 million employees participated in 122,962 deferred and combination profit-sharing programs and another one million persons participated in 80,000 to 90,000 cash-type programs in the United States.[13]

Figuring the Share

Most often the share of the total profits to be distributed to employees as a whole represents a fixed percentage of corporate net profits. In some cases it is a percentage of profits before deduction for dividends and taxes, and in others it is a percentage after deduction for dividends and/or taxes. In some cases the sum paid to participants is expressed as a percentage of the dividends to stockholders.

After the size of the total fund for any one year is computed, the allocation to individuals must be made. Usually each person's share is based upon the amount of his annual earnings in relation to the total payroll of those participating in the plan. Very commonly, also, the size of the share is related to one's length of service as well as his wage level. Occasionally each person's portion is based upon a performance-rating (merit-rating) score assigned by supervision.

Requirements for a Sound Plan

Based on a relatively long history accompanied by many successes and failures of various plans, certain helpful guides can be offered to insure a successful program. Profit sharing cannot be installed as a substitute for adequate wage rates. The wages paid must be comparable to the prevailing rates for the same class of work in the labor market. The profit share distributed to each employee must be something extra. Only then will it be an incentive; only then will develop loyalty and a proprietary interest in the success of the business.

Before the plan is instituted the state of employer–employee relations must be satisfactory. Profit sharing cannot be expected to restore an unhappy situation. The entire personnel-management program should be up to date and sound. The company must already be doing the right things as far as wages, hours, working conditions, fringe benefits, supervisory climate, and employee communications are concerned.

There must be some profits available to distribute to the employees. If a company is unfortunate enough to have a number of years of financial losses or of very small profits, there

[12]Gunnar Engen, "A New Direction and Growth in Profit Sharing," *Monthly Labor Review* Vol. 90, No. 7 (July 1967), pp. 1–8.

[13]Bert L. Metzger, *Socio-economic Participation: Key to a Better World of Work in the Future* (Evanston, Ill.: Profit-Sharing Research Foundation, 1972), p. 23.

will be discontent with the program. An occasional loss will not ruin a firmly rooted plan, but continued losses have been a major factor causing the abandonment of many plans.

If the employees are represented by a union, the full support and cooperation of this organization is essential for success. According to decisions of the National Labor Relations Board, profit sharing is a bargainable issue. An employer cannot install and operate a plan unilaterally if the employees' representatives choose to bargain the point.

Some Conclusions on Profit Sharing

A fundamental weakness of profit sharing is that employees' earnings are tied to profits—something over which they have only modest control. Profits are affected by general business conditions and the state of the business cycle, extent of competition, luck, caliber of top management, and other factors beyond the control of the employees. Of course, employees as a group do have some effect upon profits to be sure. But if top management wishes to adopt such a program primarily for its incentive aspect, then this objective can be only partially realized. Nevertheless the record through the years, while fraught with ups and downs, reveals that great numbers of programs have been successful. They satisfy management. They satisfy the workers.

LINCOLN ELECTRIC INCENTIVE SYSTEM[14]

The Lincoln Electric Company of Cleveland, Ohio, is one of the world's largest producers of

[14]Much of the information on the Lincoln Electric Incentive System is derived from Bert L. Metzger, op. cit., pp. 12–15.

electric arc-welding equipment and supplies. It also manufactures electric motors. Its unique incentive plan has been in operation since 1934 with enduring and outstanding success. There is no union at Lincoln Electric. The incentive system at Lincoln has been so successful that one wonders why other companies have not been able to imitate it with corresponding success.

The program—which is really a systems type program because it encompasses a number of integrated elements—was started in 1934 by the late James F. Lincoln, the company president. He formulated the following principles as a basis for the company's incentive program:

1. Each employee's job security must be fully protected; increased productivity must not threaten his or her job.
2. Employees must learn that their increased productivity and identification with company goals lead to increased take-home pay, enhanced job security, and significant profit-sharing payments.
3. Improved productivity and lower costs shall be passed along to customers in the form of price reductions to strengthen the company in the market place and thereby further to enhance job security.
4. Management should continue to plow back earnings to develop the plant and the company's position in the market.

The incentive management program at Lincoln Electric contains the following elements:

1. *A piecework wage incentive plan with a guaranteed day rate.* Rates are set by motion- and time-study specialists. A worker can challenge a piece rate if he thinks it is unfair. The rate is then reviewed by a special committee. If the worker is still not satisfied, the time-study specialist runs the job personally for a day or two. Any re-established time is then accepted as the correct standard.

2. *Job-evaluated base rates.* Base rates upon which the piece rates are built are established by a committee of supervisors using a job evaluation procedure. The basic wage rates are competitive with other area companies.

3. *Merit Rating.* Each employee is merit-rated twice per year on four equally weighted factors: workmanship (quality), output, ideas (improvements), and supervision required. The merit-rating score substantially determines each person's portion of the annual profit-sharing fund.

4. *Cash profit sharing.* The profit fund available for distribution to all employees is equal to the total annual profit less taxes, reserve for reinvestment in the business, and a 6 per cent dividend for the stockholders. The size of an individual's profit share is equal to his annual salary times his merit-rating score times the profit-sharing factor (profit-sharing pool divided by annual payroll). Thus, in a given year if the profit-sharing factor is 105 per cent, a $12,000-per-year employee with a merit-rating score of 120 per cent would receive a cash bonus of $15,120.

5. *Job security.* Lincoln guarantees annual employment of at least 32 hours per week for fifty weeks a year for each employee after two years of service. This is a precondition for employees to expend their best efforts toward maximum productivity.

6. *Stock purchase plan for employees.*

7. *Advisory board.* There is an advisory board of elected employee representatives who suggest changes and operating policies to management.

8. *Promotions.* Promotions are primarily made by selection from within the organization. They are based upon merit not seniority.

9. *Job enrichment.* Many factory employees function almost as independent subcontractors. Each person does his or her own setups, his or her own inspection, and is responsible for his or her own production and product quality.

Results and evaluation

As of 1972 Lincoln Electric was selling its welding machines and electrodes at the same (or *slightly* higher or lower) prices as in 1934 when the comprehensive incentive-management program was begun. This has been achieved despite the fact that all cost elements such as labor rates and raw materials were three to six times as high in 1972 as in 1934. In 1969 the year-end profit-sharing fund totaled $16,544,000. This was divided among the total of 1,973 employees, making the year-end bonus equal to about 100–105 per cent of annual pay on the average.

CONCLUSIONS

The purposes of pay incentives are to generate increased productivity as well as higher take-home pay for the employees. Each technique for achieving these objectives has its advantages and disadvantages.

The historical record in countless plants shows that direct wage incentives do raise output per direct employee-hour, often significantly. However, these incentive programs demand close attention to day-to-day administration. Grievances over production standards tend to be frequent and there tends to be much conflict between management and labor in incentive shops.

Scanlon plans have shown a good record over many years. However, they tend to work best in smaller establishments. Labor-management cooperation is an essential ingredient. It seems that the collaborative spirit can be engendered more readily in the smaller organization than in the large impersonal bureaucracy.

Profit sharing rewards employees either with a year-end bonus or with a contribution to their deferred profit-share fund when the profits of the corporation are good. Profit sharing helps to generate good will and loyalty to the company. It may also keep employee turnover low. However, profit sharing alone does not induce superior day-to-day performance.

The Lincoln Electric System, combining as it does many incentive elements, would seem to be the ideal mechanism for obtaining both high productivity and high employee satisfaction. Indeed, the program works well for Lincoln. However, hardly any other firms have been able to duplicate the Lincoln system. Part of the reason is that other managements have not been willing to include all the elements of the Lincoln formula. For example, they will not provide the essential job security which serves as a foundation stone at Lincoln. Also, part of Lincoln's success is due to the culture of the organization. The work pace is fast. People who are not willing or able to work at a sustained fast pace year after year do not apply for employment at Lincoln. Or if they do apply and get hired, they find that the work demands are not to their liking and they leave.

Can good job performance be achieved when employees are paid by the hour instead of by the piece? A great many managers say yes. Measured daywork is one answer. Other answers are good supervision, a supportive and effective managerial system, and sound motivational practices. We discussed principles and practices of effective managerial leadership and motivation in earlier chapters.

Questions for review and discussion

1. What considerations would guide your decision to pay employees according to an incentive pay plan or a daywork plan?
2. Give a list of occupations for which you feel it would be very difficult to develop a fully fair and equitable incentive plan.
3. From the standpoint of employees, what are the possible advantages of working under an incentive payment plan? Disadvantages?
4. Explain the meaning of the following:
   a. Time study.
   b. Predetermined elemental time systems.
   c. Standard hour plan.
   d. Performance rating (or leveling).
5. What are the causes of organized restriction of output that often develops among work groups in industry? How can the problem be alleviated?
6. What are the relative merits of individual incentives based upon engineered time standards as compared with a plantwide incentive, such as the Scanlon Plan?
7. Explain the principal features of the Scanlon Plan. Do you feel it can be operated successfully in a large multiplant company?
8. What might motivate an employer to install a profit-sharing plan?
9. Do you feel that a deferred profit-sharing plan will appreciably alter employee productivity or attitudes? Explain.
10. How would you explain the great success of the Lincoln Electric Incentive System over such a long span of years? Why do you think it has not been copied successfully by other firms?

PROBLEM 1

The Automotive Supply Parts Company is a well-established, profitable manufacturing concern located in a large Eastern city. It makes a variety of products for the automotive industry. These are sold to the automobile manufacturers as original equipment and also sold through distributors throughout the country as replacement parts.

For several years the company has had a major portion of its production operations on individual incentives. A large, well-trained staff of industrial engineers is employed to analyze and improve production methods, standardize operations, and set time standards for individual operations by means of time-study procedures. Base rates of pay for every job are bargained with a local independent union. A standard-hour incentive plan is used throughout the plant. For output in excess of standard, the plan pays employees in direct proportion to the increase in productivity. Thus an employee whose average production for a day is 25 per cent above standard receives a 25 per cent bonus above base pay. If an operation is shut down due to a machine breakdown or lack of materials, the operator is paid the guaranteed basic hourly rate for the actual hours involved.

The incentive program works fairly well in most production departments of the plant. If an employee feels that a particular standard is unjust, he or she can file a grievance with the union time-study stewards, who will investigate and retime the job if necessary. The union time-study stewards (three in number) are members of the union who have been trained by management in the intricacies of the time-study system used. They are paid by the company but do in fact effectively try to look out for the workers' interests when a time standard is in dispute.

In one large department, the punch press department, which contains sixty employees, there is continual conflict over the operation of the incentive program. In fact, the average number of grievances over time standards emanating from this department each year is more than are filed in all of the other departments combined. The union steward in this department is very aggressive in presenting grievances to management. Those in the industrial-engineering department feel that a large part of the continuing controversy over time standards is due to the rabid antagonism of this one union steward. They feel that he keeps the workers continually stirred up and suspicious of the integrity of the industrial-engineering department. However, the employees feel that he effectively represents their interests, so they have repeatedly reelected him to office throughout the years.

The employees complain that there is too much down-time, for which they receive only their base pay. They also do not like the fact that new operations or new parts are being continually introduced. Sometimes they must work several weeks on daywork wages on these new operations before the industrial engineer who is assigned to that department gets around to timing the work and placing it on incentive. They complain, through this steward, that the standards are too "tight." They can't make a suitable bonus. There is considerable animosity toward the industrial-engineering staff members. One employee has stated, "Every time I see you time-study guys, I get so mad I see red."

The departmental foreman, who firmly allies himself with the industrial engineer assigned to the department, makes a practice of demonstrating to workers who complain about rates that the rates are in fact fair and just. He does this by sitting down at a punch press, producing at a furious pace for perhaps five minutes, and then announcing that he has no trouble meeting the standard. They complain that he could not keep up such a fast pace all day long, as they must do.

For its part the industrial-engineering department feels that the work standards in the punch press department are fair. The head of the industrial-engineering department becomes very annoyed with workers who deliberately hold back production on an operation for which the rate is in dispute. He has noticed that on more than one occasion when the standard (expressed in units per hour) has been lowered as a result of a grievance and consequent retiming of the operation, the employees have "gone to town" on the operation and produced far more than the original (disputed) standard. When workers restrict output on operations having rates they think are unfair, this also makes it very difficult, if not impossible, for the company to meet its production schedules.

On more than one occasion certain high producers (the rest of the workers call them rate-busters) have been physically shoved around and punched by other employees because the latter consider such activities detrimental to the security of the group.

With the exception of the punch press department, relations between the top leadership of the union and management are reasonably amicable. The president of the union is an electrician who remains rather aloof from the constant strife in the punch press department.

In summary, then, the employees, led by an aggressive shop steward, feel that the work standards are too tight to make a decent incentive bonus. (They have averaged 27 per cent bonus over the previous six months' period on those operations having a time standard). Further they claim that they receive only their base rate of pay for too large a portion of the time because of down-time and delay in establishing standards on new operations, and in general they resent the close controls that the incentive system imposes on their jobs. The industrial-engineering department seeks to establish accurate standards, to prevent loose rates from being created, and to have the incentive system serve as an instrument of management control. It is willing to restudy operations over which grievances have been filed and make adjustments if they are fully justified. It never loosens a rate just because of worker and union pressure—only when the objective facts justify it.

Questions
1. Diagnose the situation presented in this case.
2. What can the industrial-engineering group do to improve relations?
3. What can management do to alleviate the problem? What can the union leadership do?
4. Are problems such as these inherent in the operation of an incentive system?

PROBLEM 2

You are the president of a small manufacturing company which has total employment of 900 persons. You have been disturbed for some time about the inability of the company to earn profits on sales and on investment as good as the average for your industry as a whole. You have had a preliminary study of the problem conducted and it has been determined that your plant and equipment, while not as modern as the best firms in your industry, are at least as good as the average firm. You know that costs are too high and productivity is mediocre. You have convened a meeting of your department heads to try to figure out how to raise the performance of the company. A summary of their remarks follows.

Manager of Industrial Engineering: We should install a direct wage incentive system for all of our production operations. We should conduct a thorough methods analysis and time study of each and every operation. We should standardize in writing the detailed work methods to be followed by the worker in performing every operation. Then we should use a standard-hour wage-incentive plan.

Manager of Manufacturing Engineering: This is an era in which some other companies have been successful in introducing more mechanization and automation. I recommend that we do the same. I have begun to install several machine-paced operations in the plant. With machine-paced operations direct wage incentives are of no value. However, I favor the use of a measured daywork plan to keep people at their machines and to insure that they service them promptly.

Personnel Manager: Close worker control and regimentation by time and motion study and wage incentives are passé. I propose that we use job enrichment. We need to upgrade our front-line supervisors through better selection and training. We need better and more supportive supervision. We need more teamwork.

Manager of Manufacturing: I favor tighter controls to reduce worker absenteeism.

We also need to reduce slipshod workmanship through better inspection and quality checks. I also think a profit-sharing plan would improve employee attitudes and performance generally.

Manager of Management Development: I recommend two solutions to our problem. I think we could improve cooperation and productivity throughout the plant by the installation of a Scanlon plan. For the office and supervisory personnel I recommend training in the Managerial Grid and in team building.

Questions

1. Analyze the advantages and disadvantages of each proposed solution.
2. Can certain of the proposed solutions be used in combination? Are some incompatible with others?
3. What solution(s) would you favor and why?

Suggestions for Further Reading

Belcher, David W. *Compensation Administration.* Englewood Cliffs, N.J.: Prentice-Hall, Inc., 1974, chs. 13 & 14.

Fein, Mitchell. "Restoring the Incentive to Wage Incentive Plans," *The Conference Board Review,* Vol. IX, No. 11 (November 1972), pp. 17–21.

Henderson, Richard I. *Compensation Management,* 3rd ed. Reston Va.: Reston Publishing Co., Inc., 1982, ch. 12.

London, Manuel, and Greg R. Oldham. "A Comparison of Group and Individual Incentive Plans," *Academy of Management Journal* Vol. 20 (March 1977), pp. 34–44.

Moore, Brian E., and T. L. Ross. *The Scanlon Way to Improved Productivity.* New York: John Wiley & Sons, Inc., 1978.

Sharplin, A. D., "Lincoln Electric's Unique Policies," *Personnel Administrator,* Vol. 28, No. 6 (June 1983), pp. 8–9.

Shwinger, Pinhas. *Wage Incentive Systems.* New York: Halstead Press (Division of John Wiley & Sons, Inc.), 1976.

Tyler, Linda S., and Bob Fisher. "The Scanlon Concept: A Philosophy as Much as a System," *Personnel Administrator,* Vol. 29, No. 7 (July 1983), pp. 33–38.

PART VII

Security

24 Health and Safety

In 1982, 4,856,000 occupational illnesses and injuries occurred in the *private* sector of the economy of the United States. Of this total nearly 2,182,000 involved lost workdays, which is to say they were serious. In the same year 4,090 persons lost their lives in injuries and occupational illnesses in the private sector. These figures are generally typical of the work injury and illness experience that has occurred for all the years of the 1970s.[1] For the year 1971 the National Safety Council estimated the aggregate cost of work injuries and illnesses at $9.3 billion. This figure includes the costs of lost wages, medical expenses, insurance claims, production delays, lost time of co-workers, and equipment damage.[2] After a moment's reflection it must be evident that these figures represent a serious problem in terms of human anguish, loss of income to affected workers, and cost to employers. A half-century ago American industry did very little to protect the health and safety of its employees. Today a large portion of employers (especially medium- and large-sized organizations) operate extensive health and safety programs. Still there is a great deal more to be done

[1] *News* bulletin (U.S. Department of Labor, Bureau of Labor Statistics, November 4, 1982).

[2] Nicholas A. Ashford, *Crisis in the Workplace: Occupational Disease and Injury* (Cambridge, Mass.: The MIT Press, 1976), p. 17.

among all employers, large and small, to improve the health of their employees.

For many years employers have had two reasons for making active efforts to reduce work injuries and advance the health of their people. One is humanitarian concern for the well-being of their employees. The other reason is cost. It is more economical to maintain an accident-free plant and to have full attendance on the job than it is to have extensive lost time due to job-connected injuries and illnesses and to nonoccupational sickness. In point of fact, the real impetus for the introduction of safety programs throughout industry was the passage of workmen's compensation laws (now generally called workers' compensation) in the various states, principally between the years 1910 and 1925. These laws hold employers financially responsible for injuries incurred on the job regardless of the specific cause of any accident. Business executives may have deplored the human damage suffered in unsafe plants prior to the passage of these laws, but they were actually prodded into action, for the most part, only because of them.

Until 1971 the responsibility for regulation of health and safety in industry was vested solely in the states. But this was all changed with the passage by Congress of the Occupational Safety and Health Act of 1970, commonly called OSHA. Thus, we can say that OSHA is the third major reason for employers to take positive action for the protection of the health and safety of their employees. (This act is comprehensive and has strong enforcement powers.)

In addition to individual companies and now the Federal government since the enactment of OSHA, there are other organizations that play important roles in workplace safety and health. The National Safety Council works actively in the field of research, education, and the compilation and publication of information. Casualty insurance companies that sell workers' compensation insurance to firms generally offer certain accident-prevention consultation services to their clients. Many states maintain workplace safety inspection services within their departments of labor. Several professional societies are active in the occupational health and safety fields. Principal among these are the Industrial Medical Association (physicians), American Industrial Hygiene Association (industrial hygienists), and the American Society of Safety Engineers.

In this chapter we shall investigate the Occupational Safety and Health Act, the very serious national problem of occupational disease, occupational safety, factors in accident causation, components of a sound safety and health program, workers' compensation, stress on the job, health services, mental health, and alcoholism.

OCCUPATIONAL SAFETY AND HEALTH ACT

Background

As a result of the efforts of the organized safety movement (that is, employers, insurance companies, the National Safety Council, and state labor departments), substantial and steady progress was made throughout the country in reducing work injuries, both their frequency and severity, and death rates. Although there were continuing problems such as the high injury rates in small business generally and in certain industries such as longshoring, roofing, meat products, and lumber and wood products, by and large, professionals in the safety movement were rather satisfied with the progress that had been made. And it is fair to say that the public at large had come to believe that the problem of job safety and health had been largely solved.

But problems were brewing! During the 1951–1961 period the injury frequency rate for all manufacturing industries, combined, had declined from a high of 15.1 in 1951. However, beginning with 1961 when a rate of 11.8 was recorded, the trend was steadily upward. In 1970 the injury frequency rate was 15.2.[3] Safety professionals and government experts were never able definitely to explain why the safety record in industry had deteriorated so badly after showing rather steady improvement since the beginning of the organized safety movement in the 1915–1925 era.

Disasters in the mines stirred public concern for workers' safety. In 1968 a disaster in a mine of the Consolidation Coal Company in Farmington, West Va., took 78 lives. In that year one man died for every 550 men employed in coal mining in the country.[4] In the 1960s the problem of black lung (pneumoconiosis) came to public attention. A medical officer of the United Mine Workers Union was quoted as saying an estimated 100,000 miners (including those no longer working in the mines) had evi-

[3]Data from *Injury Rates by Industry*, BLS Report 406 (Washington, D.C.: U.S. Department of Labor, Bureau of Labor Statistics, 1972).

Injury frequency is equal to the number of disabling injuries times 1 million divided by employee-hours of exposure. This was defined by the American National Standards Institute in its Z16.1 standard. This method of measuring injury rates has been largely superseded by the OSHA system of incidence rates.

[4]*Business Week* (December 14, 1968), p. 176.

dence of the disease.[5] Congress tried to meet the serious problem of coal-mine hazards by passage of the Coal Mine Health and Safety Act of 1969, which provides for rigorous federal standards and inspections as well as for federal benefits for victims of black lung disease.

Evidence began to surface in the late 1960s concerning the pervasiveness of occupational diseases that have been previously unrecognized. Among these were pneumoconiosis (black lung), byssinosis (from cotton dust), mesothelioma (cancer from asbestos), and diseases caused by heavy metals such as lead and mercury.

Because of the foregoing conditions, Congress passed the Occupational Safety and Health Act of 1970. It became effective April 28, 1971.

Provisions of the Act

The declared Congressional purpose and policy of the act are "to assure as far as possible every working man and woman in the Nation safe and healthful working conditions and to preserve our human resources." The act authorizes the Federal government to establish and enforce occupational safety and health standards applicable to private business. Essentially, all private business firms affecting interstate commerce, even very small firms, are covered. Such coverage is broad. At the time the law became effective in 1971, it was estimated that 57,000,000 employees in more than 4,000,000 establishments were covered.

Administration and enforcement of the act are vested primarily in the Department of Labor, specifically a new agency within the Department called the Occupational Safety and Health Administration. The act established the National Institute for Occupational Safety and Health (NIOSH) within the Department of Health, Education, and Welfare. The Institute conducts

[5]*Wall Street Journal* (December 3, 1968), p. 1.

research and carries out experiments and demonstrations relating to occupational safety and health, sets up criteria for the establishment of standards in the field, publishes data on occupational illnesses, and conducts inspections necessary to carry out its responsibilities. There are approximately 13,000 potentially hazardous substances in use in industry. NIOSH has the responsibility to conduct research, or contract for the research, in order to set standards controlling the use of these substances.

The act states that each employer "shall furnish to each of his employees employment and a place of employment which are free from recognized hazards that are causing or are likely to cause death or serious physical harm to his employees." The employer has the specific duty to comply with safety and health standards promulgated under the act.

The law requires that each employee comply with occupational safety and health standards and all rules, regulations, and orders issued pursuant to the act that are applicable to his actions and conduct. Penalty provisions of the act apply only to employers. However, the wording of the law presumably strengthens the employer's right to discipline workers who violate safety rules. Employees are given certain rights. They can request a government inspection if they believe imminent danger exists or that there is a violation of a standard that threatens physical harm. An employee representative may accompany a federal compliance officer during an inspection of the establishment.

Perhaps the heart of OSHA is the system of health and safety standards. Standards are regulations for avoidance of hazards that have been proven by research and experience to be harmful to personal health and safety. For example, OSHA has set a limit for industrial noise of 90 decibels where there is continuous 8-hour-per-day exposure. Interim standards covering thousands of items and conditions were issued in 1971. There were based upon existing national consensus standards, such as those formulated by the American National Standards Institute and those applying to Federal contractors under the Walsh-Healey Act. Permanent standards are set according to the rather elaborate procedures provided in the act and according to the Administrative Procedure Act.

Enforcement is accomplished through a system of inspections, citations, and penalties (with provisions for appeals). Labor Department representatives may enter any establishment to inspect the premises, and all pertinent conditions, structures, machines, apparatus, devices, equipment, and materials. They may also question the employer, employees, and employee representatives. If there is a violation of one of the standards, a written citation is issued and a reasonable time is allowed for correcting the condition. There are various classes of citations and monetary penalties depending upon the seriousness of the infraction. The act provides for both civil and criminal penalties. An employer who willfully and repeatedly violates requirements of the law can be assessed a civil penalty of not more than $10,000. Criminal penalties could go as high as $20,000 and/or one year in prison. In actual practice the penalties assessed have been quite modest.

Employers have a right to contest a citation or penalty by filing an appeal with the Department of Labor within 15 days from receipt of the citation. They can also request a variance from a standard upon showing that the working conditions provided are just as safe and healthful as the conditions required by the standard.

All covered firms must maintain detailed injury records in the manner and form specified by the Department of Labor. The Department of Labor in consultation with the Department of Health, Education, and Welfare is required by the law to develop and maintain an effective program of collection, compilation, and analysis of statistics on work injuries and illnesses.

The states can enter into agreements with the Secretary of Labor to develop and enforce their own standards. These programs must be at least as effective as the Federal program.

Issues and Controversies over OSHA

Since its inception a great many company managements and industry associations have been vehement in their criticism of the Act and especially its administration. They have challenged the constitutionality of various sections of the law (the courts have generally upheld the law) and the engineering standards which the Occupational Safety and Health Administration has issued and required employers to meet. They have also charged that the economic cost of meeting OSHA standards is often too great and that the agency ought to consider economic impact as well as worker safety when it orders an employer to correct a particular hazard.

On the other side American unions have charged that the Occupational Safety and Health Administration has been underfunded, understaffed, and negligent in setting standards for toxic substances, carcinogens, dusts, and other disease-producing agents.

The vast majority of safety and health standards used by the OSHAdministration are known as "consensus standards." They were developed gradually over a good many years by professional engineering societies, industry and trade groups, labor, and public interest groups. In this standards-setting process, management and the engineering professions had the dominant voices and the greatest expertise. Ironically it is these very standards that many company officials have objected to. Some of these long-existing standards dealth with somewhat trivial matters. For example, often mentioned standards were the requirement that toilets have open-front seats and that fire extinguishers be hung an exact number of inches above the floor. In 1978 the OSHAdministration revoked a great many standards considered trivial and not essential to worker safety and health.

Should employers be required to meet a safety or health standard even if the cost is high? How many lives and broken bodies should be traded off for a given dollar saving in costs?

When Gerald Ford was President, he required that an economic impact analysis be made and considered in the setting of safety and health standards. The Federal courts have also ruled that economic considerations must be weighed in the establishment of standards. This is a difficult issue, for which there exist no ready criteria or guidelines for balancing human life against cost. Congressional intent has seemed to favor worker safety and health over economics; however, actual implementation of the Act has elevated economic considerations so far that the setting of new standards has been slow.

Some critics of the Act have argued that the whole concept of safety and health standards, inspections, and possible fines for violations is wrong. Rather, public policy should simply provide financial incentives and penalties for employers to induce them to create a safe and healthful workplace. This is really a free-market, free-enterprise model. However, this is precisely the program that employers have operated under with the workers' compensation insurance system for some sixty years. Insurance premiums are increased if payments to injured workers go up, and premiums go down if employers operate safe establishments and payments to injured workers are low. However, experience has demonstrated that this financial incentive induces only *some* employers to install a sound safety program. The incentive applies after the fact of injuries and losses, and it works better for measurable injuries than for diseases, which are harder to trace.

What induces an employer to comply with the Act? Is it the possibility of incurring financial penalties for violations of specific standards? Barnum and Gleason have studied the role of penalties in inducing changed behavior on the part of employers. For the period of July 1972 through December 1974, the mean fine assessed for "nonserious violations" was only $14.99. Of all violations reported during that period, 98.53 per cent were classified as nonserious. For the same time period "serious violations" resulted

in an average penalty of $618.66. Only 1.22 per cent of total violations were classified as serious. Again for the same period the average penalty for "willful violations," comprising .25 per cent of the total, was $866.44. The authors determined that the average company is likely to be inspected only once in every ten years. Also some violations will be undetected. Because the probabilities of being inspected and fined for a violation are so slight and because the actual fines levied have been so low, the authors conclude that the purely rational economic employer (who would not be motivated by humane considerations) would find it to his advantage to accept the low risk of getting caught rather than expend, perhaps, considerable money correcting the hazard.[6] It may be hoped that other motivations are affecting managements in American industry to induce them to work positively and effectively for safe and healthful workplaces.

Injury and Illness Experiences Under OSHA

Employers are required to record and report injuries and illnesses in accordance with procedures established by the Occupational Safety and Health Administration. Recordable cases include all work-related deaths and illnesses and those injuries which result in one or more of the following: loss of consciousness, restriction of work or motion, transfer to another job, or medical treatment beyond first aid. Employers must record each occurrence as fatality, an injury or illness with lost workdays, or an injury or illness without lost workdays. A case classified as a lost workday case involves one or more days following the day of injury or onset of illness on which the employee was unable to perform the duties

[6]Darold T. Barnum and John M. Gleason, "OSHA Sanctions: Implications for Public Policy," *Proceedings of 28th Annual Meeting* (Madison, Wis.: Industrial Relations Research Association, December 1975), pp. 84–92.

of his or her regular job. These days count as lost workdays even if the employee comes to work but can only do restricted activity or is temporarily assigned to a less demanding job. Also, lost workdays—not calendar days—are counted.

The OSHA formula for calculating incidence rates is as follows:

$$\frac{N}{EH} \times 200,000$$

where

N = number of injuries and illnesses, or lost workdays.

EH = total hours worked by all employees during calendar year.

$200,000$ = base for 100 full-time equivalent workers (working 40 hours per week, 50 weeks per year).

This one formula serves to give the rate for frequency of injuries and illnesses (number of cases) and the severity of injuries and illnesses (lost workdays).

Nationally, including all industries, have incidence rates improved since OSHA became operative on April 28, 1971? Table 24-1 shows incidence rates per 100 full-time workers for the entire private sector for the years 1972 through 1982. The table shows that lost-workday cases

TABLE 24-1. Occupational Injury and Illness Rates for the Private Sector of the United States (1972–1982).[1]

| | Injuries and Illnesses | | | |
	Total Cases[2]	Lost-Workday Cases	Nonfatal Cases Without Lost Workdays	Lost Workdays
1972	10.9	3.3	7.6	47.9
1973	11.0	3.4	7.5	53.3
1974	10.4	3.5	6.9	54.6
1975	9.1	3.3	5.8	56.1
1976	9.2	3.5	5.7	60.5
1977	9.3	3.8	5.5	61.6
1978	9.4	4.1	5.3	63.5
1979	9.5	4.3	5.2	67.7
1980	8.7	4.0	4.7	65.2
1981	8.3	3.8	4.5	61.7
1982	7.7	3.5	4.2	58.7

Source: *News: Occupational Injuries and Illnesses in 1982*, U. S. Department of Labor, Bureau of Labor Statistics.

[1]Data exclude self-employed individuals, farmers with fewer than eleven employees, and employees in federal, state, and local government.

[2]Includes fatalities.

have fluctuated from 3.3 to 4.3, with no discernable trend. Nonfatal cases without lost workdays (the less serious cases) have declined from 7.6 in 1972 to 4.2 in 1982. The number of lost workdays per case (an indication of severity) have generally increased since 1972. So the evidence is somewhat mixed.

Although aggregate, nationwide statistics on injuries and illnesses since the inception of OSHA show no consistent pattern, some research evidence shows that OSHA has had a very beneficial impact in those industrial plants that have been inspected by OSHA enforcement personnel. A study of industrial plants in the State of Maine having 200 or more employees showed a reduction of average days lost per worker of .29 per year after the plants had been issued citations for safety violations.[7] Of course, OSHA has a very limited budget and limited enforcement officers.

Variation by Industry and Firm Size. Figure 24-1 shows the very considerable differences in injury and illness incidence rates of the major industry classifications for the year 1982. The construction industry was the most hazardous whereas the finance, insurance, and real estate industries (largely white-collar occupations) were the least hazardous.

If one looks at statistics showing severity of injuries (excluding occupational illnesses) by specific industry classification, he finds that for 1982 the most hazardous industries in lost workdays per 100 full-time workers were: anthracite mining (409 days), bituminous mining (225 days), water transportation (269 days), trucking and warehousing (183 days), and lumber and wood products (157 days).[8]

[7]William N. Cooke and Frederick H. Gautschi, III, "OSHA, Plant Safety Programs, and Injury Reduction," *Industrial Relations*, Vol. 20, No. 3 (Fall 1980), pp. 245–257.

[8]*News* bulletin. "BLS Reports on Occupational Injuries and Illnesses for 1982," (U.S. Department of Labor, Bureau of Labor Statistics, Nov. 4, 1982), Table 3.

FIGURE 24-1 Injury and Illness Incidence Rates for Entire Private Sector and by Industry Division 1982 (Total Cases). Source:' *News: Occupational Injuries and Illnesses in 1982*, U.S. Department of Labor, Bureau of Labor Statistics.

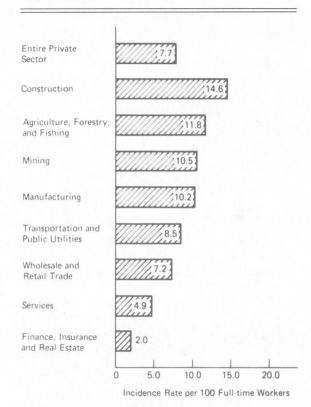

Historically, small companies have had higher injury rates than large firms. For example, for the year 1982 companies having from 100 to 249 employees had an injury incidence rate of 10.7 and those with 250 to 499 employees had a rate of 9.9 injuries per 100 full-time workers. However, establishments having 2,500 or more employees had a rate of only 5.5.[9]

Why does small business rather generally have a poor accident record? The fundamental reason is that owners and top executives in small businesses are not as safety-conscious and do not give as much effort to accident preven-

[9]U.S. Department of Labor, Ibid., Table 4.

tion as do managers of large corporations. The typical small businessman does not even compute his injury rate. The guide that he uses is the size of his workers' compensation insurance premium. The small employer does not employ a safety director and often he may not have a full-time personnel manager. In his mind, the pressing problems of production, sales, and finance overshadow the importance of workplace safety and health. His accounting system does not isolate all those costs that are directly and indirectly caused by accidents.

OCCUPATIONAL DISEASE

There is a time bomb ticking away inside the bodies of hundreds of thousands of American working men and women. That time bomb is occupational disease. Only in very recent years had the truly enormous magnitude of the problem been recognized. Occupational disease tends to be understated in the statistics of individual companies and industries because very often the diseases manifest themselves only many months or even years after worker exposure to the causative agents. By then the employees may be working for different companies, may have retired, or, if still in the same company, the cause-effect relationship may go unrecognized.

The Public Health Service estimates that each year 390,000 new cases of occupational diseases appear and 100,000 workers die from them.[10]

Illustrative of the seriousness of the problem is the following sample of headlines, with stories, which appeared in national news media in recent years:

1. *"A Grim Legacy from World War II"*

   This article explains that many of World War II's 3 million shipyard workers may have a fatal, asbestos-caused cancer. Millions of pounds of asbestos were used to insulate pipes and valves in ships. Mesothelioma, a cancer that strikes the stomach lining and chest cavity, has been showing up in those people who worked in the shipyards over three decades ago.[11]

2. *"Study Indicates Anesthetic Gas Imperils Health of Operating-Room Personnel"*

   A research study has indicated that those people who are long exposed to gases such as nitrous oxide, ether, and halogenated hydrocarbons have a higher incidence of spontaneous abortions, birth defects, cancer, and liver disease than do nonexposed people.[12]

3. *"Seminar Focuses on Cancer Risks from Working with Vinyl Chloride"*

   Vinyl chloride exposure has caused liver cancer among plastics plant workers.[13]

4. *"Workers' Exposure to Carbon Disulfide Should Be Cut Sharply, Safety Aides Say"*

   Chronic exposure causes cardiovascular disease, neurological abnormalities, and possible effects on the reproductive system.[14]

Occupational health hazards are classified into four general types: (1) physical, such as noise, heat, vibration, and radiation; (2) chemical, such as dusts, poisonous fumes, gases, toxic metals, and carcinogens; (3) biological, such as bacteria, fungi, and insects; and (4) stress, such as physical, psychological, and ergonomic factors. The effects of health hazards can be slow,

---

[10]Comptroller General of the United States, *Delays in Setting Workplace Standards for Cancer-Causing and Other Dangerous Substances* (Washington, D.C.: General Accounting Office, May 10, 1977), p. 10.

[11]*Business Week* (September 29, 1975), p. 31.
[12]*Wall Street Journal* (October 15, 1975), p. 8.
[13]*Buffalo Evening News* (March 23, 1974).
[14]*Wall Street Journal* (May 10, 1977).

cumulative, and irreversible. Also, they are complicated by nonoccupational factors such as smoking and stress.

Public health scientists have estimated that more than 80 per cent of all cancers are caused by environmental factors to which man is exposed. Precisely how much is occupationally caused is unknown. Cancer is the second leading cause of death in the United States. The rise in the incidence of cancer is rather closely correlated with the growth of industrialization. In 1900, 3.5 per cent of all deaths were caused by cancer, whereas in 1968, the figure had risen to 16.5 per cent. Because the production of petrochemicals has doubled every five years since the end of World War II, the incidence of cancer characterized by long latency periods can be expected to grow significantly over the next twenty to thirty years.[15]

It would be comforting if we could say that government officials, managers in industry, and occupational health scientists were now getting this gigantic problem under control. But in fact this is not the case. The Comptroller General of the United States has reported that about 13,000 known toxic substances are commonly used and about 500 new toxic materials are introduced by industry each year. As of 1976 the OSHAdministration had established permanent standards on only fifteen toxic substances: vinyl chloride, asbestos, and thirteen other chemicals considered to be carcinogens. Based upon this rate of progress, it would take over 100 years to establish needed standards on existing substances. But 500 new substances are introduced yearly.[16] So the job will never get done at the present rate of action. OSHAdministration is hampered not only by lack of funds, lack of manpower, and by industry resistance but also by the fact that insufficient basic research has been done in the areas of toxicology and occupational diseases.

[15]Ashford, *Crisis in the Workplace*, op. cit., pp. 10–11.
[16]Comptroller General of the United States, op. cit., pp. 9–11.

Accidents

What is an accident? Most of us tend to think of an accident as some event that causes a personal injury. But in point of fact an *accident is an unexpected occurrence that interrupts the regular progress of an activity.* In effect it is any unplanned or uncalled for break or deviation from the expected. It is a negative or unfortunate event. Many accidents take place without an injury resulting. A man may stumble while walking along an aisle yet suffer no injury. A rigger may drop a tool and narrowly miss a worker below. Both of these are accidents without injuries.

In industrial practice attention tends to be focused primarily upon accidents that cause injuries. But injury prevention should be accident prevention as well. The author is familiar with an accident involving an in-plant lift truck operator. He was using his truck, which contained a squeeze mechanism, to remove the top bale of textile fibers from a stack piled three high. The bale weighed about 1,500 pounds and was about 12 feet above the floor of the warehouse. His squeeze mechanism did not grasp the bale properly and the bale came tumbling down on top of the truck. The operator jumped to safety without a scratch. Damage to the truck was extensive. Here clearly was a serious accident calling for corrective measures by management. A commercially available protective cage was installed over the cockpit of the truck to protect the driver in the future.[17]

Costs of Accidents

In addition to the anguish and suffering experienced by injured employees, accidents are very

[17]A protective cage had previously been installed on the truck but was removed when the foreman deemed that it slowed up production.

expensive to the employer. Many executives simply look at their charges for workers' compensation insurance and lose sight of the fact that the indirect costs of an accidental injury are considerably greater than the direct costs.

Accident costs are classified into two categories. First are the insured costs. The insured cost is the money paid for doctor and hospital bills, for weekly benefits while the injured employees are absent from work, and for any scheduled payments due to death, accidental dismemberment, or permanent disability. This cost is readily apparent and is met by the insurance premium.

The second category of costs due to accidents is called the uninsured costs. Some authorities call these the indirect costs of accidents. These costs are not apparent to top management unless it assigns somebody to conduct a specific research project to isolate them. What are these uninsured costs? They include lost time of injured worker, lost time of fellow employees who render aid to the injured person, time spent by supervisory personnel to assist the injured person and to investigate the cause of the accident, lost production, possible damaged material or equipment, and administrative expenses to process paperwork connected with the accident.

The ratio of the uninsured to the insured costs varies widely from factory to factory according to the particular situation. However, investigators have found that these uninsured costs tend to average about four times those of the insured costs. In other words the insured or direct costs represent only about 20 per cent of the total costs on the average.[18]

For some companies in high-risk industries the premium for workers' compensation insurance may run as high as 15 to 20 per cent of payroll. If one estimates that the total cost for accidents in any one year is five times this fig-

ure, it can be readily appreciated that the accident rate can spell the difference between profit and loss for a company.

In addition to the financial burden imposed by accidents upon a company, those workers who are injured bear a substantial cost also. Most workers' compensation laws specify a waiting period of one week before an injured worker can collect weekly benefits to make up for his or her loss of wages. Therefore, those who lose only one to seven days from work receive no wage compensation whatever. The typical compensation law specifies that weekly benefits shall be only two thirds of the injured's wage up to a certain maximum. For permanent partial dismemberments the scheduled benefits are rarely adequate to compensate a worker for future loss of earning power.

CAUSES OF ACCIDENTS

In order to prevent accidents from taking place it is necessary, first of all, to gain an appreciation of the causes of accidents. Accidents may at times seem to occur because of chance factors that are unavoidable. But digging beneath the surface one will find that in nearly every instance measures could have been taken to prevent the accident.

Accident causes can be classified into two major categories:

1. Unsafe chemical, physical, or mechanical conditions.
2. Unsafe personal acts.

Examples of unsafe chemical, physical, or mechanical conditions are the following:

1. Inadequate mechanical guarding.
2. Defective condition of equipment or tools (for

[18]See, for example, H. W. Heinrich, *Industrial Accident Prevention: A Scientific Approach*, 4th ed. (New York: McGraw-Hill Book Company, 1959), pp. 50–51.

example, worn electrical insulation, cracked ladder, split drive belt).

3. Unsafe design or construction (for example, a pressure vessel that is too weak).
4. Hazardous atmosphere (for example, toxic substances in air, poor ventilation).
5. Inadequate or improper personal protective equipment.

Examples of unsafe personal acts are as follows:

1. Failure to follow established safe-working procedures.
2. Horseplay, fighting.
3. Taking an unsafe position, such as under a suspended load.
4. Failure to use designated protective clothing.
5. Removing safety devices or making them inoperative.

Sometimes the physical or mental condition of the person involved may contribute to the accident. Thus, a worker may be emotionally upset, inattentive, or fearful. Or he may be extremely fatigued or suffer some physical defect that makes an accident more likely.

Unsafe Condition or Human Error. Over the years attempts have been made by various groups to classify industrial injuries according to whether they were caused by an unsafe physical condition or by an unsafe personal act. Some of the earlier studies purportedly showed that 85 to 90 per cent of all injuries were caused by human error and only 10 to 15 per cent by hazardous conditions. If one did not study the matter further, one might jump to the conclusion that management could obtain the greatest gain from the dollars it spends on accident prevention by devoting its efforts to employee education and ignoring the engineering aspect of safety. But such is not the case. More recent analyses of accident statistics reveal that the vast majority are due to a combination of unsafe

physical conditions and unsafe personal acts. Basically if the hazard were not present in the first place, an injury could not occur. The traffic safety records of the modern divided, limited-access superhighways furnish ample evidence that good engineering design can reduce accident rates significantly. The people who drive on these highways are no different from those who drive on ordinary roads, so the personal behavior factor is essentially constant for both superhighway driving and ordinary driving.

A sound industrial-safety program must emphasize the engineering aspects of safety (hazard elimination) as well as employee education and training (showing people how to work safely in the presence of certain hazards).

Accident Proneness

Many years ago industrial psychologists became intrigued with the empirically observed fact that certain workers had more accidental injuries than could be expected by chance. They believed that accident rates in factories could be reduced if accident-prone people could be identified and rejected during the employment-selection process.

By administering intelligence, aptitude, and personality tests to workers and then correlating scores with injury rates, psychologists were able to determine that certain traits seemed to correlate with high injury rates. Some psychologists jumped to the conclusion that they were thus able to identify accident-prone individuals.

However, more careful investigators determined that the early researchers had studied the injury rates of individuals over too short a time span. According to the laws of probability we would expect some individuals to have several accidents in any given year whereas others would have none. Generally those who have several accidents in one year do not have several accidents in the following year. Their tendency to have frequent accidental injuries is purely a temporary phenomenon. To be truly accident-prone a person must have an inherent constitutional tendency to engage in unsafe behavior. Research has demonstrated that the percentage of truly accident-prone people in the population is very low. Management cannot solve its work-injury problems by ferreting out accident-prone workers.[19]

Accidents and Environment

The physical, psychological, and organizational environment in a plant has a powerful effect upon injury rates. Keenan, Kerr, and Sherman correlated accident rates of 7,100 personnel in a large tractor factory over a five-year period. They found that a comfortable shop environment (good working conditions) was the single most significant factor relating to a low accident rate. These researchers found that bad working conditions (noise, dirt, heat, and so on), although not directly causing accidents, cause worker tension and frustration. This physical frustration distracts the workers, causing them to have more accidents.[20] Many practicing safety engineers have for years felt, on the basis of experience, that plant housekeeping and decent working conditions are a positive encouragement to safety. Thus the research evidence supports this belief.

Substantial evidence exists to demonstrate that the total stress (internal and external) that impinges upon a worker has a strong influence upon his or her likelihood to have accidents. Internal stress consists of such conditions as disease, alcohol, anxiety, or worry, whereas external stress is built up from noise, heat, dirt, fumes, and excessive physical strain. Positive action by management to maintain not only good working conditions but also good employee health (physical and mental) is bound to pay dividends in terms of fewer accidents and lower charges for workers' compensation. The initial cost of establishing a good work environment and an occupational health program often discourages management from making the investment. Although one may fail to persuade top management to invest in such programs on the basis of their contribution to employee morale and the humanitarian objective, quite often the prospect of a long-term reduction in the cost of accidents may provide the impetus to adopt such a comprehensive program.

Management action in another broad area can have a very beneficial effect upon safety. When management directs the organization in such a way that employees have real opportunities to get ahead, to be promoted, to exercise some initiative and responsibility, to participate in controlling their own jobs, and to gain job prestige and other rewards, then accidents tend to be lower. Thus, it can be concluded that the positive, supportive, need-satisfying, autonomy-enhancing leadership that is quite generally advocated by modern researchers and writers in the field of human relations in industry is just as successful in promoting occupational safety as it is in promoting productivity, loyalty, and high morale. In other words, the elements that constitute good management in other spheres of a business enterprise also constitute sound safety management.

Age, Training, and Work Experience

Available research evidence shows quite conclusively that young workers, untrained workers, and workers who are new on the job have substantially higher frequencies of work injuries

[19]Alexander Mintz and Milton L. Blum, "A Re-examination of the Accident Proneness Concept," *Journal of Applied Psychology,* Vol. 33, No. 3 (1949), pp. 195–211; Willard Kerr, "Complementary Theories of Safety Psychology," *Journal of Social Psychology,* Vo. 45 (1957), pp. 3–9; A. G. Arbous and J. E. Kerrich, "The Phenomenon of Accident Proneness," in Edwin A. Fleishman, *Studies in Personnel and Industrial Psychology,* rev. ed. (Homewood, Ill.: The Dorsey Press, 1967), pp. 615–626.

[20]Vernon Keenan, Willard Kerr, and William Sherman, "Psychological Climate and Accidents in an Automotive Plant," *Journal of Applied Psychology,* Vol. 35, No. 2 (1951), pp. 108–111.

than older workers, trained workers, and more experienced workers. Van Zelst investigated the effect of each of these factors separately in a large plant in Indiana. He found, for example, that the average monthly accident rate of about 1,200 workers declined steadily for the first five months on the job, after which the rate remained nearly constant for approximately a five-year period. When newly hired workers were given formal job training, Van Zelst found that the initial accident frequency was lower for this trained group and that the group declined to a normal expected level of accident frequency in three months instead of the five months for untrained employees. In the third and final part of his investigation, he found that a group of 614 persons of average age 29 years and 3 years' job experience in the plant had a significantly greater accident rate than a roughly comparable-sized group age 41 years, also with three years of job experience. Van Zelst observed that age actually had a stronger effect upon accident rate than did time on the job. He tentatively concluded that immaturity of the employees was a large factor in explaining the accident experience of young workers.[21]

Management can profit from findings such as these by instituting proper job-training programs, exercising special safety monitoring of new employees, and giving attention to the possible immaturity of workers in making hazardous job assignments. A company with high labor turnover is especially vulnerable to accidents. Management is well advised to take steps to reduce such turnover. A continuous parade of new workers is a sure invitation to a high injury rate.

Matched Pairs Research

In the early 1970s Shafai-Sahrai investigated 22 pairs of companies in eleven different industrial classifications in Michigan. Within each indus-

try, two firms of similar size but markedly different injury rates were selected. All the firms studied had between 80 and 650 employees. He concentrated upon small companies because traditionally small firms have had high injury rates. He found several factors that correlated significantly with either good or bad safety performance.

In the firms that had lower injury rates there was high interest and involvement by top management in safety activity. Top management involvement included such behaviors as planning for achieving safety objectives, holding review and analysis sessions to compare results with objectives, and including safety reports on the agenda for company board meetings.

Companies that had comprehensive accident record-keeping systems in which accident costs were shown had better safety records than those firms that did not keep good records.

Good plant working conditions correlated positively with good safety performance. These included roominess, lighting, temperature, noise level, and cleanliness. Those companies that had better and more numerous safety devices and guards on machines had lower injury rates.

Shafai-Sahrai found that in firms with more married employees work injury rates were lower. Firms in which the average age level was high and worker years of service were high had lower injury rates than those firms with younger workers and fewer years of service.[22]

COMPONENTS OF SAFETY AND HEALTH PROGRAM

Assume that a company has high workers' compensation costs, and an inadequate safety and health program. What are the principal elements

[21]R. H. Van Zelst, "The Effect of Age and Experience upon Accident Rate," *Journal of Applied Psychology*, Vol. 38 (1954), pp. 313–317.

[22]Yaghoub Shafai-Sahrai, *Determinants of Occupational Injury Experience* (East Lansing, Michigan: Graduate School of Business Administration, Michigan State University, 1973).

of a sound program that top management should consider for adoption? The details of course would have to be adapted to fit the circumstances of company size, number of plants, nature of the industry, technology, and organization structure. But the content of the program could be included under the elements discussed below.

Key Elements of Program
1. Objectives and policies.
2. Top-management support.
3. Organization.
4. Establishing responsibility for safety.
5. Engineering.
6. Job-safety analysis.
7. Analysis of accidents.
8. Education and training.
9. Enforcement.
10. Healthful work environment.
11. Adequate medical treatment.
12. Rehabilitation.

Objectives and Policies

When top management decides that it wants to take steps to obtain a safe organization, it must determine just how far it wants to go and what it wants to accomplish. Does it want to have a company that ranks with the best in its industry in terms of low injury frequency and severity? Or does it simply want a safety effort that will reduce workers' compensation costs to a tolerable level. Is it willing to invest sufficient money to achieve a really nonhazardous plant? Or does it want to concentrate upon training the workers to cope moderately well in a basically dangerous environment? What policy will be adopted for those situations in which a production-oriented decision clashes with a safety-oriented decision?

Top Management Support

Top management sets the safety objectives and policies in the first place; and how top management chooses to support and implement its own policies is crucial to the effectiveness of these policies. It is top management that decides, ultimately, how extensive a safety organization to set up, the caliber of safety personnel that will be employed, and how much money, in total, it will invest in safety. The single most important element in the success or failure of any companywide program, whether it be safety, training, research, or maintenance, is the emphasis given to that program by top management.

Organization

The organizational arrangements that are created are conditioned by the size of the firm and the nature of its safety problems. In firms too small to justify a full-time safety director, the assignment may be given to the personnel director, to the plant superintendent, or to the head of industrial engineering. Larger companies will employ a full-time safety specialist. Usually he or she is part of the personnel department. Very large corporations, especially those in hazardous industries, will employ a whole staff of safety engineers, safety inspectors, and industrial hygienists.

Success in accident reduction and control requires the active involvement of operating management and of workers. Hence companies with successful safety programs usually create safety committees in each organizational unit. The principal managers in these units serve on the management committees and help in the planning and implementation of the program. Worker committees, often with rotating membership, are a useful way of identifying specific safety problems in the plant and of gaining worker support for the safety effort.

Close collaboration with the local union officers and shop stewards is desirable. In too many companies the sole involvement of the union is through the submitting of grievances about job hazards. Worker health and safety are so important that a mutuality of interests should be recognized. Shop stewards can advantageously serve on company safety committees.

Establishing Responsibility for Safety

Some industrialists think that with the appointment of a safety director they can "wash their hands" of all responsibility for safety and get on with their main business of obtaining high production, low costs, and adequate quality. Nothing could be further from the truth. The only way to achieve and maintain a safe plant is to place responsibility for safety on an equal status with responsibility for production, cost control, quality, and profit making. Whenever the responsibility for maintaining a safe plant is relegated to the position of a frill that can be attended to only after the more important objectives of production, costs, and efficiency are achieved, then injury rates will be excessive and will remain so until line management at all levels devotes adequate attention to accident prevention. The basic responsibility for injury prevention rests with line management. It starts with the company president and goes vertically downward through the entire hierarchy to the actual worker.

What then does the safety director do? Is he not responsible for safety? Yes, the safety director bears very important responsibilities for injury prevention. But he serves in a staff, not a line, capacity. He basically serves as an innovator, organizer, creator, advisor, teacher, analyzer, investigator, stimulator, and (at times) a prodder. He must organize the safety program throughout the plant, collect accident data, in-vestigate accidents, help develop engineering applications (guards and so on), conduct safety training and information meetings for management personnel, analyze jobs to develop safe working procedures, and prepare instructional material for use by foremen in conducting meetings with their employees.

The staff safety director rarely has line authority to order supervisors and workers to take a particular action in regard to safety. But he often acquires considerable influence in the establishment of plant safety policies, procedures, and the development of engineering standards for safety. He works closely in these areas with other line and staff officers. But because they recognize his proficiency and specialized competence in the field of safety, the views of the safety director are given considerable weight.

Engineering

Proper engineering to remove work hazards is fundamental to any organized safety effort. If one were to look at the typical mill of 1910 and compare it with the typical mill of the 1980s in the same industry, he would immediately perceive the vast advances that have been made in elimination and guarding of dangerous mechanical, electrical, and chemical conditions. The typical mill of 1910 was a maze of exposed pulleys, belts, chains, gears, cutters, punches, and levers. Today technology has advanced to the point where many hazardous conditions have simply been designed "out" of the equipment and processes, and most of the remaining ones have been adequately guarded. But this statement should not be interpreted to mean that further engineering for safety cannot be done. Many factories are still behind the times as far as hazard elimination is concerned. New products, processes, and machines are constantly being designed, and full attention must be given to safety engineering in both design, layout, and installation.

The most foolproof way of engineering for

safety is simply to eliminate the hazard from the machine, process, or structure. If, for example, a particular substance or material has been put into large heavy containers for movement from one operation to another throughout the plant (batch production) and if materials handlers have suffered many hernias and back injuries from lifting these containers, a basic engineering redesign of the production processes might eliminate the batch approach and substitute continuous-process production. In this case the physical handling of the containers by human labor will have been eliminated because the material will flow from one piece of equipment to another by mechanical conveyor or by blowing the substance through large pipes.

If it is not feasible to carry out a basic redesign of the production process to eliminate the hazard, then the next stage is to design and install a guard to prevent workers from coming in contact with moving parts or point of operation elements. Thus, gears on a machine are usually guarded to prevent human contact while the machine is in operation.

If it is not possible to eliminate the hazard or to guard the equipment itself, it may be possible to have the workers wear and use protective clothing and equipment. Thus, construction workers and those working around overhead cranes generally wear hard hats, machinists wear goggles, and welders wear face shields and gloves.

Job-Safety Analysis

Although job analysis for purposes of improving work methods, setting production standards, and determining pay rates is commonly carried on in many organizations, these investigations are rarely done for the purpose of identifying the hazards and figuring out ways of overcoming them. But job-safety analysis is very useful for hazard elimination and for designing safe work methods. By such study the safety engineer may note that a change in workplace layout, in the operating controls of the machine, or in work procedures may eliminate or reduce the possibility of injury to the operator.

Unfortunately most accident prevention work takes place after someone has been injured. Then the job is studied to make necessary changes to prevent a recurrence.

In addition to hazard elimination through changes in workplace, equipment, and methods, job-safety analysis produces a written statement of safe operating procedure.

Analysis of Accidents

Every accident that results in a personal injury, or could have resulted in a serious injury, whether it be simply a first-aid case or a more serious disabling one, must be investigated by the injured employee's supervisor to ascertain the cause(s) and to determine what specific remedies are required to avoid a recurrence. Although the primary reason for accident investigation is to find out what action must be taken to prevent a recurrence, accident information provides excellent case study material for use in training meetings.

Although every accident must be investigated and reported by the foreman, a more intensive investigation should be conducted by the staff safety specialist for all but the very simple and elementary accidents. This is necessary so that he or she can be fully cognizant of the accidents occurring in the plant and so that he or she can apply his or her technical skill to uncover elements of the case possibly overlooked by the foreman.

The safety department should periodically summarize all injuries that have occurred and classify them by plant, department, shift, cause, type of injury, and whether disabling or not. Injury statistics are valuable for revealing where further effort must be exerted to achieve improvement in safety performance, for comparing the record from one year to another, and for apprising management of needs for further action.

Education and Training

Safety education for all levels of management and for employees is a vital ingredient for any successful safety program. Education in this context concerns the development of proper perspective and attitudes toward safety. It deals with basic fundamentals and the reasons why. Training is more concerned with immediate job knowledge, skills, and work methods.

Top and middle management require education in the fundamentals of safety and the need for an effective accident prevention program. The costs of accidents, both human and dollar costs, must be brought to the attention of line management. Top management in large- and medium-sized companies does not need to concern itself with the detailed mechanics of accident prevention, but it must acquire a sufficient awareness of safety fundamentals so that it will actively support the work of the safety department and of middle and lower management in carrying out the program.

The safety director and his staff must undertake to provide extensive education and training for first-line supervisors. The supervisors must understand their key role in the safety effort, namely, that they are primarily responsible for preventing accidents (assuming they have adequate support from above). Each supervisor must conduct his own safety training for his employees. This takes the form of both individual on-the-job training and periodic safety meetings held right in the department.

At the employee level there are two principal objectives: (1) to develop safety consciousness and favorable attitudes toward safety and (2) to achieve safe work performance from each employee on the job. To achieve these goals, a number of things must be done. At the time a person is hired, orientation by both the personnel manager and the person's supervisor should cover such areas as the need for safe work performance, the hazards in his own department and job, the necessity for prompt reporting of any personal injuries, desirability of reporting unsafe conditions to the supervisor, and the general causes of accidents. Each new worker must be taught how to perform his job safely. This frequently takes the form of on-the-job training. Instruction in safe working procedures must be integrated with instruction designed to achieve acceptable output and quality performance.

Enforcement

Primary responsibility for enforcement of standard operating procedures and safety rules lies with the first-line supervisor. When he or she observes employees who are not performing their jobs in the approved manner he or she calls this to their attention and corrects them. This can apply to countless situations such as the operation of in-plant trucks, fire protection, wearing of safety glasses, horseplay, and removal of machine guards. With adequate indoctrination and training there should seldom be need for punitive measures for violation of safety regulations. However, when individuals deliberately refuse to cooperate, then they need to be disciplined as they would for other rule violations.

If the employees are represented by a union, one can normally expect union cooperation in these matters if there has been full communication, documentation, and proper warning of the employee.

Healthful Work Environment

Simply stated, the objective of environment control is the prevention of occupational disease. The possible causative agents in the plant environment—dusts, fumes, toxic chemicals, noise, etc.—must first be identified. Then corrective action must be taken. There are many corrective methods that may be used. The best, from a worker health standpoint, is usually to eliminate or contain the agent at its source. For example, a completely closed system may be installed to prevent the release of toxic materials into the work environment. Equipment and processes can be re-engineered to, say, cut down noise, eliminate leaks, or reduce vibration. The environment around the source can be improved. For example better plant ventilation can reduce the concentration of dust or fumes. Acoustical enclosures can be built around noisy machinery. A less expensive way of alleviating the health hazard is to provide personal protective equipment to the workers—respirators, eye goggles, gloves, and earplugs.

The diagnosis and correction of health hazards often require the services of an industrial hygienist. Industrial hygiene is the science and art devoted to the recognition, evaluation, and control of environmental factors and stresses associated with the workplace that may cause sickness, impaired health or significant discomfort and inefficiency. An industrial hygienist typically has a university bachelor's degree in engineering, chemistry, physics, or the biological sciences plus a masters degree in industrial hygiene.

Adequate Medical Treatment

Every establishment, whether large or small, should have adequate facilities and trained personnel for rendering first aid to injured employees. The small company should have a clean, adequately equipped first-aid room. Its supervisory personnel and key hourly employees should receive first-aid training so that they are skilled in rendering help to the injured. Larger establishments have need for the full-time services of an industrial nurse and a physician. The providing of first-aid treatment is but a part of a comprehensive industrial health program as described in a later section of this chapter.

Rehabilitation

If an employee has suffered a serious temporary disabling injury or a permanent disability, it behooves the employer and the workers' compensation insurance company to exercise every effort to rehabilitate that unfortunate individual. This includes helping him or her learn how to care for daily needs of living, learn how to acquire and reacquire useful job skills, helping the worker make a positive mental adjustment to the new situation, and then finding a new position for him or her in the company (if he or she cannot return to the old job).

WORKERS' COMPENSATION

Unlike most social insurance programs in the United States, workers' compensation has been almost the exclusive province of the states rather than the Federal government. The first compensation law was passed by New York State in 1910. By 1920 all but six states had passed such laws. Mississippi, the last state to do so, passed a compensation law that became effective in 1949.

Workers' compensation laws place the financial responsibility for work injuries upon the employer without regard to who was at fault or who caused the accident. The costs associated with industrial accidents are considered simply as a cost of doing business that the employer must bear. Prior to the enactment of these laws, injured workers generally had little effective recourse. They had the right to sue their employer in a court of law to try to obtain compensation for wage loss, medical costs, and compensation for the damage suffered. However, workers fared very poorly in such court actions, because they possessed insufficient funds to pursue the cases and because the common law of the period favored the employer in such cases. This sad situation has largely been changed as a result of workers' compensation legislation.

Benefits

All the compensation laws require that medical service be provided to injured employees. Although full medical treatment without any dollar limit is provided in the majority of states, about one fourth of the states place a limitation on the amount and on the period during which medical, surgical, and hospital services must be provided. In earlier years many state laws provided compensation for accidental injuries but not occupational diseases. This has changed so that all states now have coverage for occupational diseases although a few have specified limitations.

In addition to medical benefits the laws provide partial recompense for loss of wages during the period the worker is away from his job. In most jurisdictions the individual is paid two thirds of his average weekly wage up to a designated maximum, which is typically between $120 and $200 per week. To escape the administrative costs of handling numerous short disablements and to discourage employees from feigning an injury just to obtain a holiday, practically all states pay nothing to compensate for wage loss for periods of seven days or less. In other words there is a seven-day waiting period.

Administration and Financing

To make certain that funds are available to meet a company's obligation for paying claims, state laws require either that it carry compensation insurance or that it put up a bond to demonstrate financial responsibility if it wishes to be self-insuring. A company that is self-insuring pays all benefits required by the law directly out of its own pocket. Because only large companies can assume the risk involved in self-insurance, the vast majority of employers insure with either a state insurance fund or with a private insurance company.

The basic premium charged an employer is called the manual rate. This rate is based upon the various industrial classifications and occupations that exist in the establishment. This manual rate is uniform throughout a state and is set by the insurance rating board. It is based principally upon the injury experience of each industry group and upon the dollar losses (costs for claims). This basic manual rate is adjusted upward or downward annually under a system called merit rating to make the cost to the employer closely representative of true charges for payments to injured employees. The merit-rating feature of the state laws is undoubtedly a powerful stimulus to the employer to take affirmative action to reduce accidents.

HEALTH SERVICES

Historically, company health programs were inaugurated as a result of the passage of workers' compensation laws with the attendant obligation to provide first-aid treatment for work injuries. Sometime later companies began to give pre-employment physical examinations both to insure that those hired could meet the physical demands of their jobs and to prevent being charged with a compensation claim for a pre-existing ailment. Company medical services then evolved to the point that if a physician was on the premises, it was only natural that he or she would be called upon to treat minor ailments not caused at work, such as colds, sore throats, skin disorders, headaches, and gastro-intestinal upsets. Industrial medicine has grown to the point where the large corporation having a progressive personnel philosophy now takes positive steps to maintain good employee health off the job as well as on the job. Some companies have also established programs in the field of mental health. There has been a recognition by some corporate managements that it has a stake in the "whole person," not only in physical health but in mental health as well, both on and off the job. This concern for the health of employees has not led to the establishment of company clinics to provide broad treatment of nonoccupational illness. Most generally it has taken the form of health information and education services, individual counseling by physicians, referrals to private specialists, and action by management to improve hospital and doctor services in the community. Not only do comprehensive industrial health programs help the employees, but they also often result in reduced absenteeism, lower sickness insurance costs, higher productivity, and improved morale.

A comprehensive company health program will include the following features:

1. A professional staff of physicians and nurses.
2. Adequate facilities for emergency care of work injuries and for conducting pre-employment and periodic medical examinations.
3. Proper first-aid treatment for occupational injuries and diseases. Serious cases are referred to private practice physicians and hospitals.
4. Pre-employment medical examinations and periodic examinations for those exposed to special occupational hazards.
5. Reasonable first-aid to employees for non-occupational illness while on the job.
6. Information and education services for the personal health of employees.
7. Consultation with those suffering physical or emotional maladjustment to the work situation. The company medical personnel may offer advice, refer the individual to a private specialist, work with the person's supervisor, or refer the individual to an appropriate community agency.

8. Adequate and confidential medical records.
9. Cooperation by the company physician or medical director with those responsible for accident prevention and control of the work environment to achieve an integrated employee health program.
10. Cooperation with public health authorities in regard to mass inoculations and other measures for the prevention of communicable diseases.
11. Advice and supervision, where necessary, to maintain proper company sanitation.

Although the foregoing health program is most feasible for the medium- and large-sized company, the small firm can carry out may of these elements by engaging the services of a qualified physician on a retainer or consulting basis.

STRESS ON THE JOB

Although people have experienced stress and suffered from stress since the beginnings of mankind, it is only in recent years that it has been researched systematically. Dr. Hans Selye of Canada was the first medical scientist to carry out comprehensive research on stress and its treatment beginning in the 1940s and continuing for 40 years. Only in the past five to ten years have human resource managers and managers, more generally, in industry shown interest in managing stress in the workplace.

The Nature of Stress

Stress is an adaptive response, mediated by individual characteristics and/or psychological processes, that is a consequence of any external action, situation, or event that places special physical and/or psychological demands upon a person.[23] Individual characteristics may include factors such as sex, health status, and heredity. Psychological processes refer to such factors as attitudes, values, and various personality dimensions.

Although most stress is probably harmful from the physical health standpoint, not all stress is deleterious to human performance. Indeed, a certain tolerable level of stress can incite people to action and generate good performance. It ought also to be noted that stress is a universal human experience and that it can arise from outside the job as well as within one's place of employment.

Stress upon a human being causes various physiological changes including an increase in heart beat rate, blood pressure, and rate of breathing. It also can cause an increase in eye pupil size, skin temperature, perspiration, and blood glucose. Severe stress and prolonged stress can cause heart attacks, ulcers, migrane headaches, and colitis.

In addition to the physiological effects the consequences of stress can be very extensive and damaging. Stress can generate anxiety, boredom, depression, fatigue, and lowered self-esteem. Behavioral changes associated with stress include drug use, emotional outbursts, excessive drinking and smoking, impulsive behavior, impaired speech, trembling, inability to make decisions, and excessive forgetfulness. From the standpoint of the work organization, management may note excessive absenteeism, turnover, grievances, accidents, strikes, and lowered productivity.

In the typical enterprise stressful situations are common. An employee may feel excessive pressure to get work done in a limited time. Another worker may get bawled out by his or her boss for alleged errors in records. Still another person has been given a work assignment which

he or she believes is too difficult for him or her to accomplish. Three managers may have been competing for a promotion that only one can get. The two who fail feel frustrated. Perhaps the ultimate stressful situation in the world of work is to be fired from one's job.

Minimizing Stress in the Organization

Individual employees, managers, and those in charge of the human resource function should increase their awareness of stressors (stimuli which cause a stress response in people) operating in the work organization in order to devise plans to cope with the stressors and to reduce the stress impacting upon people. Managers must recognize, however, that not all plans and programs will be successful with all employees because of differences in their physical, mental, and emotional makeup.

A fruitful place to start a program of stress reduction is to improve environmental hygiene in the workplace. This includes such actions as noise abatement in both factory and office, provision for adequate rest periods, temperature control, and elimination of exposure to toxic chemicals and fumes.

Another element in stress reduction is to minimize unpredictability and ambiguity. Freedom from fear of layoff or arbitrary and capricious discharge is important to employees. Good-quality and stable supervision is also essential for providing a feeling of well-being for the employees.

Our discussion of pattern of effective supervision in Chapter 16, "Leadership, Supervision, and Management Systems," is apropos to the issue of stress reduction. People feel better satisfied in those organizations where the supervision is supportive and where management establishes an atmosphere of approval. Likewise, as demonstrated by the research of Rensis Likert and others, support by the peer group on

[23]John M. Ivancevich and Michael T. Matteson, *Stress and Work: A Managerial Perspective* (Glenview, Ill.: Scott, Foresman and Company, 1980), pp. 8–9.

the job is important for employee satisfaction and well-being.[24]

Appropriate job design can contribute to stress reduction. Such elements as vertical job loading, meaningful tasks, client relationships, and direct feedback of information on job performance are features of enriched and satisfying jobs.

Employees want reasonable autonomy and control of their activities. This can be achieved through enriched jobs and by participation in decision making in their departments through group discussions with their supervisors.

In addition to formal organization-wide programs to reduce stress, management can provide educational and informational programs to help individuals reduce their own stress. People can learn how to relax, engage in regular physical exercise, and take training in transcendental meditation.

MENTAL HEALTH

Mental health can be defined as a state wherein a person is well adapted, has an accurate perception of reality, and can reasonably successfully adjust to the stresses and frustrations of life. Solley and Munden asked fourteen senior psychiatrists and psychologists of The Menninger Foundation to describe people they knew whom they considered to be mentally healthy. From their responses five major characteristics were abstracted. First, mentally healthy persons respected others as individuals and were able to establish good relationships with them despite individual differences. They recognized that others may have different values and did not try to impose their own on them. Second, they were flexible and adaptable under stress. Third, they obtained gratification from a wide variety of sources—a variety of people, things, and events. Fourth, they accepted their own capabilities and weaknesses. They had a realistic self-concept and did not overvalue or undervalue their capacities. Finally, they were active and productive. They used their abilities for their own self-fulfillment and to serve others.[25]

Relatively few companies employ professionally trained personnel—that is, psychiatrists, clinical psychologists, and psychiatric social workers—on either a part-time or full-time basis to provide mental health services for their personnel. Those that do tend to be the very large organizations. However, quite commonly the plant physician serves as a resource person in identifying mental illnesses and referring patient employees to qualified personnel in the community. Alan McLean, a psychiatrist, asserts that there is a trend toward *some* acceptance by employers and by unions of reasonable responsibility for providing treatment for mental disorders of employees.[26]

Mental disorders are complex as to cause. They may arise from disturbances in childhood, from physical illness, from relationships with others off the job, and from interaction with the work situation. Mental illness derives from the individual personality interacting with the total life situation. Sometimes executives feel that the state of human relationships in their organizations could be enhanced if only the problem employees—the malcontents and troublemakers—could be cured by referral to counselors and psychiatrists. But as Temple Burling, a psychiatrist, has pointed out, the problems are in the relationships among people and not simply *within* the people themselves. In asking the specialist to cure problem employees the industri-

[24]Rensis Likert, *The Human Organization: Its Management and Value* (New York: McGraw-Hill Book Company, 1967), ch. 4.

[25]C. M. Solley and K. J. Munden, "Toward a Description of Mental Health," *Bulletin of the Menninger Clinic*, Vol. 26 (July 1962), pp. 178–188.

[26]Alan A. McLean, "Who Pays the Bill? A Clinical Perspective," *Journal of Occupational Medicine*, Vol. 9, No. 5 (May 1967), pp. 244–250.

alist is sometimes expecting a cure of their human nature.[27] Therefore a major thrust in a mental health program should be upon the creation of sound supervisor-subordinate relations, elimination of festering conditions causing discontent, and the development of a favorable motivational climate.

Kornhauser reports on a study of the mental health of 655 workers (mostly production workers but including some office personnel as well) employed in various firms in Detroit. In relating mental health to occupational level he found that it becomes poorer among factory workers as one moves from skilled, responsible, varied types of work down to jobs lower in these respects and that the relationship apparently is not caused in any major sense by differences of prejob background or personality of the people involved. The relationship of mental health to occupation seems to be genuine and not dependent on selection effects. Recognizing that mental health has many roots, Kornhauser demonstrates a positive correlation between job level, education, and favorable childhood economic conditions. Job characteristics relate importantly to mental health. Kornhauser found that good mental health is correlated positively with jobs that give people a chance to use their abilities, to perform worthwhile functions, to fulfill roles as competent human beings, and where they can find interest in their work and experience a sense of accomplishment. Wage rates, job security, and physical conditions of work had little or no explanatory value in accounting for poorer mental health of lower versus upper job levels.[28]

The plant physician should play a key role in the mental health program. A major responsibility is to identify persons requiring help. Because employees almost never go to him or her and directly state that they have a mental health problem, he or she must take the lead in training supervisors and the plant nurse to spot these problems. He or she can observe employee behavior during visits to the medical department. Physical complaints and emotional ailments are often intertwined. In these relationships confidentiality must be assured. The employees should not be placed in the position of jeopardizing their jobs by seeking help and acknowledging that they have an emotional, stress, or anxiety problem. If the plant doctor should find a case that calls for treatment beyond his resources, he should refer the patient to a psychiatrist in the community. He should offer information to the latter about the individual's job requirements and relationships in the organization. In some cases he may have to arrange for a leave of absence for the person.

Supervisory personnel bear important responsibilities in identifying problem employees and offering emotional first aid. They should look for signs of prolonged or excessive anxiety. An employee's usual behavior may become exaggerated. A quiet person may become more withdrawn. When the person's customary mode of response proves ineffective she may become edgy, unable to concentrate, or panicky. In a very acute condition the employee may become noisy, aggressive, or even irrational. The supervisor must be supportive in relationships and serve as a helpful listener in trying to counsel the individual. If improvement cannot be achieved with a moderate amount of counseling, the supervisor must refer the person to professional talent.

The Utah Copper Division of Kennecott Copper Corporation, employing 8,000 people, established a psychiatric counseling service in 1970 that has yielded very positive results. The program is conducted by a psychiatric social worker who provides prompt confidential help to employees. A simple phone call brings aid. The program has had considerable success with alcoholics but the counseling service deals with all sorts of problems, such as potential sui-

---

[27]Temple Burling, "Psychiatry in Industry," *Industrial and Labor Relations Review*, Vol. 8, No. 1 (October 1954), pp. 30–37.

[28]Arthur Kornhauser, *Mental Health of the Industrial Worker* (New York: John Wiley & Sons, Inc., 1965).

cides, homosexuality, racial discrimination, and drugs.[29]

Alcoholism

The National Council on Alcoholism estimates that there are about 4.5 million alcoholics in the labor force. This is about 5 per cent of the nation's work force. Trice and Roman state that between 3 and 4 per cent of an average organization's work force are deviant drinkers.[30]

Because the problem is serious more and more companies are setting up for formal programs to alleviate the problem. DuPont and Eastman Kodak have long-established programs. More recently General Motors and the United Auto Workers Union created a joint program covering 400,000 workers. Some other companies with programs are Lever Brothers, General Dynamics, Merrill Lynch, American Motors, and American Airlines.[31]

What is an alcoholic? Trice and Roman explain the matter by identifying three categories of drinking behavior. The first is normal drinking, which does not impair functioning nor interfere with efficient performance of role assignments and obligations. The second category is deviant drinking, where a person regularly drinks to excess to the point that role performance is impeded. He or she is impeded because of a hangover or because he or she tries to function while under the influence of alcohol. The third category is alcoholic addiction, which is defined as a physiological loss of control over drinking behavior. Long-term, regular drinking increases physiological tolerance so that the person must drink more to achieve the same psychological effects. Eventually the human body cannot function without the ingestion of alco-

hol. Deprivation of alcohol causes harsh physiological withdrawal symptoms.[32]

Whereas alcoholism at one time was treated as a moral and penal problem (throw the town drunk in jail overnight to dry out), a modern theory is that it is a disease. This approach tends to absolve the individual of personal responsibility for his or her behavior, at least partially. It is viewed more as a medical and a social problem. However, the cause or causes of alcoholism have not been found. A great many theories have been advanced and much research has been done but the root explanation is still lacking. Nevertheless some treatment programs have demonstrated real success, so we can see that therapy need not wait for the ultimate scientific explanation.

Deviant drinking has pronounced negative effects upon work output and quality. Sometimes the drinkers work for short periods at a fast pace but this is followed by sharp declines in performance. Absenteeism is a pronounced problem. Professional and managerial personnel often go to work even when not feeling well but their performance suffers. Hourly workers tend to just stay away from the job when under the influence of alcohol. Trice and Roman report that poor work performance and absenteeism represent the principal negative impacts upon the organization. Surprisingly, turnover and accident rates are no higher for heavy drinkers and alcoholics than for ordinary employees.[33]

Alcoholics exhibit a pervasive tendency to conceal their drinking and deny that they have a drinking problem. Because drinking is socially accepted in our society, problem drinkers and alcoholics often become adept at manipulating their colleagues and sometimes even their supervisors to cause them to cover up their behavior.

The key to correcting the problem is to confront the deviant drinker with his or her poor work performance and attendance. If he or she

---

[29]*Business Week* (April 15, 1972), pp. 113–114.
[30]Harrison M. Trice and Paul M. Roman, *Spirits and Demons at Work: Alcohol and Other Drugs on the Job* (Ithaca, N.Y.: Cornell University, 1972), p. 2.
[31]*Business Week* (November 11, 1972), p. 168.

[32]Trice and Roman, op. cit., pp. 16–117.
[33]Ibid. pp. 121–144.

is directly accused of being an alcoholic, he or she will invariably deny it. Therefore the supervisor must confront him or her with the results of alcoholism, namely poor work performance. The individual must be brought to the point at which he or she acknowledges that he or she does have a drinking problem. This may require several discussions. The person may have to be told that he or she will suffer a disciplinary suspension or even loss of the job if he or she does not respond by changing behavior. Experts in alcoholism control and therapy state that fear of job loss is generally the only deprivation that is strong enough to cause the individual to give up the pleasures of alcohol.

The supervisor plays the central role in confronting the employee with the problem, getting him or her to recognize it, and in helping him or her take corrective action. This process must be done in a constructive way. The individual must know that management wishes to help overcome dependency upon alcohol.

Trice and Roman assert that management, in formulating an alcoholism control program, should avoid labeling alcoholism a disease because this tends to give the individual the impression that his or her behavior is out of his control. Management efforts should be directed toward getting the man or woman motivated to correct his or her own problem and to improve job behavior. If this effort fails, then full-scale medical treatment may become necessary and the condition ultimately may have to be handled as a sickness.[34]

The major components of an alcoholism control program consist of the following:

1. *Policy Statement*
   Coming from the chief executive this commits the organization to a program, outlines the content of the program, and assigns responsibilities to appropriate parties in the organization. It indicates the willingness of the organization to help those in need.

[34]Ibid. pp. 173–175.

2. *Union Cooperation*
   Where the employees are represented by a union this feature is important. By being brought into the program early the union can play an important part in gaining cooperation and support from the employee group.
3. *Education*
   An organization-wide program of information and education covering the dimensions of the alcoholism problem and the features of the organization's control program is desirable.
4. *Training*
   Supervisors and managers at all levels (and union stewards, where a union is involved) must be given full training in the program and their responsibilities in it. The supervisor bears prime responsibility for identification of the problem and for working with the affected individual.
5. *Professional Services*
   Provision must be made for professional services. This may involve a nurse, counselor, personnel specialist, plant physician, or a psychiatrist. It may also involve outside medical services in the community.

Questions for Review and Discussion
1. What factors led to the passage of the Occupational Safety and Health Act?
2. Outline the principal features of the Occupational Safety and Health Act.
3. Explain the reasons for the great controversy over OSHA that has developed since the enactment of the Act.
4. What is an accident? Do all accidents result in injuries? Why must all be analyzed for effective safety effort?
5. Why is the injury experience of small companies typically worse than that of large companies in the same industry?
6. Are most injuries caused by unsafe physical or mechanical conditions or by unsafe human acts? Discuss.
7. What are the possible human consequences

of excessive stress on the job? What measures can management adopt to reduce stress in the organization?

8. How do the work environment and opportunities for recognition, advancement, and autonomy relate to accident rates in industry?

9. Give the components of a complete safety and health program.

10. Why has the seriousness of the occupational disease problem in industry been recognized only relatively recently? Why is control and reduction of the incidence of occupational disease so difficult to achieve?

11. What part does line supervision play in achieving good safety performance? What are the responsibilities of the safety department?

12. What behaviors and responsibilities must top management of a company adopt in order to achieve good occupational safety and health results?

CASE PROBLEM

In early February 1979 Frank Bradford, personnel manager of the Glen-More Processing Company, received a detailed analysis of injury experience for the period 1/1/78 through 12/31/78 for the company from the insurance company that provides workers' compensation coverage. The most striking feature of the report was the great difference in work injury rates between Plants 1 and 2, which were located directly across the street from one another. He had known for quite some time from his own data that the injury frequency rate for the company was high both in comparison with the average for all manufacturing industries and with the textile industry in particular. In addition the company president had recently been expressing concern about the high dollar losses for workers' compensation claims. Frank decided to convene a meeting of concerned management personnel to review the accident problem.

The Glen-More Processing Company produces nonwoven textile products and has been in business for over fifty years. It has a total employment of 450, of whom 397 are factory personnel including factory supervision. Plant 1 produces garnetted synthetic stock (polyester, nylon and acrylic fibers). Raw material is purchased from various large manufacturers of synthetic filaments. The plant building and processing equipment are old. Many of the machines are driven by leather belts attached to pulleys on overhead lineshafting. Operations require the employees to put certain of the belts on pulleys while the garnett machines are running. Bales of stock weigh from 400 to 1,000 pounds and are handled both by power industrial trucks and by two-wheeled hand trucks. Plant 2, although located in an old, multistory brick building, contains fairly modern production machinery. The final product consists of rolls of bonded synthetic fibers that are sold to firms making outerwear, sleeping bags, and upholstered furniture. The raw material moves through several kinds of equipment in essentially a continuous process (although there are certain batch operations as well). In certain respects the equipment in Plant 2 contains fewer hazards than that of Plant 1. Most of the machinery is driven by electric motors with enclosed "V" belt drives that are guarded. A few machines do require operators to feed material into in-running rolls and this brings their hands close to these "nip" points. Both Plants 1 and 2 have attached warehouses for receiving and shipping.

Frank showed the report from the insurance company to the general manager. They decided to use it as a resource document at the forthcoming meeting. At this meeting they hoped to uncover the causes for the high accident rate and develop a plan of corrective action. Copies of the report were given to all concerned members of top and middle management. Attending the meeting were the general manager, Frank Bradford (personnel manager), the managers of Plants 1 and 2, the chief engineer of the company, and the factory superintendents of Plants 1 and 2 (directly under the plant managers on the organization chart).

The salient information in the report "Accident Cause Analysis 1/1/78–12/31/78" prepared by the insurance company is shown below:

Total Work Injuries

	Plant 1	Plant 2
First aid only	13	25
Medical treatment only	18	68
Injuries with lost workdays	7	35
Total	38	128
Total days for all lost workday injuries	140	843
Average days/lost workday case	20.0	24.1
Incidence Rates:		
Lost workday cases	3.94	15.9
Lost workdays (severity)	78.9	383.2
Total employee hours for year	355,000	440,000
Average employment	177	220

1978 Averages for This Industry

Incidence Rates:		
Lost workday cases	3.1	
Lost workdays (severity)	65.4	
Average days per lost workday case	32	

Injuries by Type

	First Aid & Medical		Lost Workday	
	Plant 1	Plant 2	Plant 1	Plant 2
Struck against	7	11	2	7
Struck by	14	18	2	6
Caught between	8	18	2	6
Falls		8		6
Improper handling	2	4	1	4
Improper lifting		3		5
Foreign body in eye	—	31	—	1
Totals	31	93	7	35

Including *all* injuries in Plant 1, 60 per cent involved injury to the hands, 12 per cent to trunk of body, 8 per cent to arms, 8 per cent to head, and 12 per cent to legs or feet. In Plant 2, 33 per cent involved tiny particles of dust or dried chemical in eyes, 20 per cent to trunk of body, 26 per cent to hands, 8 per cent to arms, 6 per cent to head, and 7 per cent to legs or feet.

The general manager opened the meeting by explaining that the accident problem was serious, that dollar losses had mounted, and that top management wanted to cut its losses. He said that the Occupational Safety and Health Act placed direct responsibility upon management to maintain a safe and healthful work environment. He encouraged everyone present to speak freely.

Here follow key excerpts of remarks by the participants:

- *Personnel Manager:* Our wage rates are about 20–25 per cent below the going rates in the local area for occupations similar to ours. However, we are in line with other textile firms. For years we have only been able to hire people who can not qualify for jobs in other better-paying companies. The average education level of our hourly paid work force is tenth grade. We tend to hire mainly young people in the 18–25 age range. Older people usually hold better-paying jobs elsewhere and do not look for work here. In 1978 turnover of hourly help in Plant 1 was about 50 per cent while in Plant 2 it was nearly 100 per cent. The average length of service and age of employees in Plant 1 is higher than that of Plant 2. The operations in Plant 2 are rather seasonal. In that plant we lay off about 25 per cent of the force every November and rehire in the spring. Seldom do those laid off in the fall come back with us in the spring. Absenteeism is about the same for both plants and averages about 8–9 per cent.
- *Plant 1 Manager:* We cut our accident rate quite a bit over the past couple of years by doing a number of things. We follow up vigorously on every accident. If it is due to a physical hazard we try to install such devices as machine guards, interlock mechanisms on access covers, and shut-off bars as required. If due to a human error we talk to all employees working on that kind of operation and explain what was done wrong and how to do it right. We also

follow up closely on injured employees. We see that they get proper medical treatment. Sometimes a man gets a minor injury and uses it as an excuse to take a few days off. I send my superintendent (or a foreman) directly to the employee's home to investigate all questionable cases. We have been quite successful in preventing minor injuries from becoming lost-time cases. Our foremen are supposed to run short monthly safety meetings with their people but they do not do a good job of this and often will not do it at all unless I insist upon it.

- *Plant 2 Manager:* The data from the insurance company show that we had a very bad year in 1978 in incidence rates. But I do not really know why. I conduct a safety meeting with my superintendent and foremen about once every month or two to discuss machinery and equipment items that need repair or replacement and go over general safety matters. Also we try to get the foremen to conduct brief safety meetings with their people about once per month. But it is hard to get them to do this. Most claim they are unable to speak in front of a group and get their message across. A few of the foremen do tour their departments and speak to individual employees about safety matters from time to time.

- *Superintendent, Plant 2:* I think we have too many accident-prone people working here. Jake Ambrose had five accidents last year and one of these was a lost-time case. Frank Wilson had four accidents, one of which was a lost-time case where he was out for nearly a month. These are but two of the cases that come to mind now. Also our high turnover creates a serious problem. As you all know, we do not have a formal training program here for new workers but we do spend some time discussing safety rules and other matters at the time a new man is hired. I personally give each new hire a copy of the safety rules. During the first couple of days we assign new people to work under the direction of old-timers. We just about get a new man broken in on his job when he quits. Then we must start all over again breaking in a replacement. Sometimes I think we scrape the bottom of the manpower barrel when we hire people. Not only do we have a high turnover problem due to quitting but we also have to fire lots of new hires during the six-week probationary period, usually because of excessive absenteeism.

- *Personnel Manager:* I think a serious problem in both plants is that we have a lot of people on our payroll who just do not want to work. Some will fake an injury just to get a few days off. Or if they actually do get hurt on the job they may stay out for a week or two even though it is a minor injury. We must police such cases better.

- *Superintendent, Plant 1:* We have been trying to meet this problem for the last year or so. As you know we do not have a plant nurse or doctor. We are located only a half mile from the hospital. On any injuries more serious than a first-aid case we rush the person directly to the emergency room of the hospital and we stay there until the doctor has treated him and we learn exactly how serious his condition is. If someone does not show up for work some day and phones in saying he was injured the day before, we investigate thoroughly. We check with his foreman to verify or refute the claim. We even go to the worker's home if necessary. We have found some fraudulent cases and we take disciplinary action on them. Sometimes we find that a foreman has been careless and failed to make out an accident report on a real accident.

- *Chief Engineer:* The record shows that a lot of injuries occur in the shipping and receiving operations of Plant 2. These include such things as dropping a dock plate on the foot, falling off the loading dock, getting hit by a lift-truck, and getting hit by a carton. In the operations around the processing machinery we get finger and hand injuries around the machines, slips and falls on stairs and catwalks, injuries from hand tools, and particles of dust and dried chemical in the eyes. It is true we conduct our manufacturing operations in two very old multistory buildings and some of our machinery is old and not of the most modern design. Perhaps we have some inherent hazards in our materials handling and machinery operations. However, I think human error and carelessness are a major cause of our problem. I think our foremen do not do a good job of teaching safety to the men and women here.
- *General Manager:* We have discussed many aspects of our safety problem this morning but have not reached any definite conclusions. Perhaps we must reorganize our whole safety effort. As you know we do not have a safety director as such. We are not large enough for that. Frank Bradford handles the general direction of the program as part of his personnel responsibilities. In addition to the many aspects of the problem that were discussed this morning there may be others that we haven't identified yet. I am asking Frank to make a full investigation and to prepare a report that spells out just what we must do to cut down our dollar losses to a more reasonable figure. I doubt if we will ever achieve an outstanding performance here but we can certainly make improvements. Frank, I would like to know why there is such a great difference in accident frequency between Plants 1 and 2. Was this also true for 1977? Also, you might want to contact Fritz, the local union president, to get his views. I will call another meeting after we receive your report, say in about a month or so.

After the meeting Frank checked his injury records for 1977. The incidence of lost-workday cases per 100 full-time workers was 8.1 for both plants combined. Plant 1 was 3.94 and Plant 2 was 11.4.

He then invited Fritz, the union president, in for a discussion of the accident problem. Fritz was quite blunt in stating that the foremen pushed the employees very hard for production but seldom took action to correct safety hazards when these were brought to their attention by the employees. This "brush-off" practice was especially common in Plant 2. Safety meetings for the employees were held only two or three times a year in either plant. The foremen and superintendent in Plant 1 were somewhat more effective in correcting hazards than were the foremen and superintendent in Plant 2. They were more safety conscious generally. He then itemized ten separate safety problems that had not been taken care of. These ranged from lax enforcement of the safety glasses program in Plant 2 to the need to repair two plant lift-trucks that had bad brakes. He also complained about the dirty and poorly equipped lunch and locker room facilities

Security

in both plants. He felt that the better safety record in Plant 1 was due to a more conscious practice of pressing for safety by supervision on a day-to-day basis.

Questions
1. What is wrong here? Has management identified the root causes of its serious safety problem? What do you consider are the principal causes?
2. Outline a program to reorganize and improve the safety effort and include the principal action steps to be taken. What elements ought to be given first priority?

Suggestions for Further Reading

Ashford, Nicholas A. *Crisis in the Workplace: Occupational Disease and Injury*. Cambridge, Mass.: The MIT Press, 1976.

Brodeur, Paul. *Expendable Americans*. New York: Viking Press, 1974.

Cooke, William N., and Frederick H. Gautschi, II. "OSHA, Plant Safety Programs, and Injury Reduction," *Industrial Relations*, Vol. 20, No. 3 (Fall 1981), pp. 245–257.

Denenberg, Tia S., and R. V. Denenberg. *Alcohol and Drugs: Issues in the Workplace*. Washington, D.C.: Bureau of National Affairs, 1983.

Ivancevich, John M., and Michael T. Matteson. *Stress and Work: A Managerial Perspective*. Glenview, Ill.: Scott, Foresman and Co., 1980.

Levi, Lennart. *Preventing Work Stress*. Reading, Mass.: Addison-Wesley Publishing Co., 1981.

Mendeloff, John. *Regulating Safety: An Economic and Political Analysis of Occupational Safety and Health Policy*. Cambridge, Mass.: The MIT Press, 1979.

Nothstein, Gary Z. *OSHA: The Law of Occupational Safety and Health*. New York: Macmillan Publishing Co., Inc., 1982.

Pati, Gopal C., and John I. Adkins, Jr. "The Employer's Role in Alcoholism Assistance," *Personnel Journal*, Vol. 62, No. 7 (July 1983), pp. 568–572.

Tersine, Richard J., and James Hazeldine. "Alcoholism: A Productivity Hangover," *Business Horizons*, Vol. 25, (November–December 1982), pp. 68–72.

25 Benefits and Services

Nearly every organization in this country provides its employees certain tangible benefits over and above the basic paycheck. These benefits may supply financial protection against such risks as illness, accident, unemployment, and loss of income due to retirement. They may provide extra leisure, extra income, and a better work environment. Some benefits help fulfill the social and recreational needs of employees. Although benefits and services are not directly related to the productive effect of the workers, management often expects to aid its recruitment effort, raise morale, create greater company loyalty, reduce turnover and absenteeism, and, in general, improve the strength of the organization by instituting a well-conceived program in this area.

Although the term *benefits and services* is very widely used to designate this area of personnel management practice, other terms, such as *fringe benefits, employee services, supplementary compensation, indirect compensation,* and *supplementary pay* are also used. The frequently used term *fringe benefits* originated during World War II. Many management practitioners now object to this expression on the grounds that nowadays these benefits represent a very substantial portion of the total labor cost for a firm. They are no longer merely "fringe" costs or "fringe"

items. They are important to management, employees, and unions alike.

The terms *benefits* and *services* are often used interchangeably by some writers. To others the word *benefit* applies to those items for which a direct monetary value to the individual employee can be rather easily ascertained, as in the case of a pension, separation pay, major medical insurance, or holiday pay. The word *service* applies to such items as a company newspaper, athletic field, Christmas party, or company purchasing service, for which a direct money value for the individual employee cannot be readily established.

Growth of Benefits and Services

With the exception of a very small minority of companies that had adopted progressive personnel programs in the 1920s, American industry, by and large, did not provide benefits and services for hourly paid workers prior to the World War II period.[1] Pension plans were rare

[1]Salaried white-collar and managerial employees fared slightly better, because they often received paid vacations and were paid when they were absent because of illness. With these exceptions these employees generally received no more benefits and services than hourly workers during this period.

before 1940. By 1975 more than 30 million people were covered by private pension plans. Paid holidays and vacations were almost nonexistent before World War II; nowadays employees typically receive eight to nine holidays per year and from one to four weeks of vacation annually, depending upon their length of service with a particular employer. Prior to 1940 very few employees were covered by hospitalization and medical insurance; now such protection is widespread throughout industry. Some employers now provide dental insurance and prescription drug insurance.

Benefits and services represent a tangible gain to employees that is either monetary or nonfinancial, depending upon the particular item involved. They also represent a labor cost for the employer. When viewed as a cost, the dramatic increase in benefits and services over the years can be appreciated by noting benefit cost data compiled by the Chamber of Commerce of the United States. For the economy as a whole the Chamber has estimated that the total cost to employers of employee benefits (not including services) averaged 3.0 percent of direct wage and salary payments in 1929, 15.0 per cent in 1951, 21.0 per cent in 1961, 26.0 per cent in 1971, and 32.5 per cent in 1981.[2]

Causes of Growth. Several factors account for the significant increase in fringe benefits over the past fifty years. Public policy is perhaps one of the most fundamental reasons. The Social Security Act of 1935 requires employers to share equally with employees the cost of Old Age, Survivors, and Disability Insurance. Employers pay the full cost of unemployment insurance.

The great increase in fringe benefits in the United States has coincided with the growth of unionism. Union demands at the bargaining table have often forced management to grant additional benefits. Unionization combined with

[2]*Employee Benefits 1981* (Washington, D.C.: The Chamber of Commerce of the United States, 1982), Table 21, p. 30.

National Labor Relations Board and court interpretations of the Wagner and Taft–Hartley Acts have broadened the scope of mandatory bargaining, so that management must bargain such issues as pensions, Christmas bonuses, vacations, profit sharing, stock-purchase plans, and group-insurance plans.

The advanced stage of industrialization in the United States, the increasing interdependence of the people, the vital need for keeping one's job, and the general affluence and prosperity in the economy, all have served to make it both necessary and possible for employers to provide a measure of financial protection for workers against the risks of unemployment, sickness, injury, and old age.

Furthermore, employees have asked for and received longer vacations and more holidays to enable them to have time to enjoy the fruits of their good wages in leisure-time activities.

TYPES OF BENEFITS AND SERVICES

Employee benefits include programs that help provide for *employee security.* These programs provide financial reimbursement to employees and their families for costs associated with both occupational and nonoccupational injuries and illnesses, unemployment, retirement, and death (life insurance). Another category of employee benefits is *paid leave,* which includes such items as paid holidays and vacations. A third category is *premium pay* which covers extra pay for working overtime on holidays and weekends, and for shift differentials. A fourth category is *bonuses and awards* which are not related to employee production. These include profit-sharing bonuses, Christmas bonuses, and scholarships for employees and their family members. *Savings and thrift plans* comprise the last category of benefits. Some employers provide small supplements to the sums that employees voluntarily have deducted from their paychecks to be deposited in an employer-run savings plan.

Table 25-1 is from a U.S. Department of Labor survey showing employer expenditures for the principal categories of employee benefits in the economy as a whole (all industries) in 1976. The items are expressed as per cent of total compensation and as dollars per work hour. The reader will note that pay for time worked was 76.7 per cent of total compensation. Thus, employee benefits comprised 23.3 per cent of total

TABLE 25-1. Employee Benefit Categories as Per Cent and as Dollars Per Hour of Total Compensation (1977)[1].

| | All Industries | | |
| | Per Cent of Compensation | Dollars per Hour | |
Compensation Item		All Hours	Work Hours
All Workers—1977			
Total compensation	100.0	$7.43	$8.04
Pay for working time	76.7	5.70	6.17
Straight-time pay	74.8	5.56	6.02
Premium pay	1.9	.14	.15
Overtime, weekend, and holiday work	1.6	.12	.13
Shift differentials	.3	.02	.02
Pay for leave time (except sick leave)	6.1	.45	.49
Vacations	3.4	.25	.27
Holidays	2.3	.17	.19
Civic and personal leave	.2	.01	.01
Employer payments to vacation and holiday funds	.2	.01	.02
Employer expenditures for retirement programs	8.5	.63	.69
Social security	4.4	.33	.36
Private pension plans	4.1	.30	.33
Employer expenditures for health benefit programs	6.0	.45	.48
Life, accident, and health insurance	4.0	.30	.32
Sick leave	.8	.06	.07
Worker's compensation	1.2	.09	.10
Employer expenditures for unemployment benefit programs	1.3	.10	.10
Unemployment insurance	1.2	.09	.10
Severance pay	([2])	([2])	([2])
Severance pay funds and supplemental unemployment benefit funds	([2])	([2])	([2])
Nonproduction bonuses	1.1	.08	.08
Savings and thrift plans	.2	.02	.02

Source: Handbook of Labor Statistics (Washington, D.C.: U.S. Department of Labor, December 1980), Bulletin 2070, Table 132.
[1]Private nonfarm economy only.
[2]Less than 0.05 per cent, or $0.005.

compensation. Expressed differently, this 23.3 per cent represented 30.4 per cent of direct wage payments.

Employee services include *social and recreational programs* and facilities that are provided or subsidized by the company. Services also include a variety of *special aids and services* such as credit unions, loan funds, medical treatment for minor illnesses, and child care centers.

Although some businesspeople classify such items as rest periods, clean-up time, rest rooms, parking lots, and first-aid services as employee benefits, this author would not classify them as such. These things are directly associated with work activities and the needs of people in a work setting. They are essentials, not extras.

The following tabulation gives the principal kinds of benefits and services commonly found in work organizations.

Employee benefits and services

A Employee security (financial protection against certain risks)
   1. Legally required employer contributions. Old Age, Survivors, Disability, and Health Insurance.
      Unemployment Insurance.
      Workers' Compensation.
      State disability insurance.
      Railroad Retirement Tax, Railroad Unemployment Insurance.
   2. Pensions.
   3. Life insurance.
   4. Hospitalization.
   5. Medical and surgical payments.
   6. Dental insurance.
   7. Disability insurance.
   8. Paid sick leave.
   9. Supplemental unemployment benefits, separation pay, and guaranteed wages.
   10. Accident insurance.
B. Paid leave
   1. Holidays.
   2. Vacations.
   3. Personal business leave.
   4. Military service allowance.
   5. Jury duty.
   6. Voting time.
C. Premium pay
   1. Overtime, weekend, and holiday work.
   2. Shift differentials.
D. Bonuses and awards (not related directly to employee output)
   1. Profit-sharing bonus.
   2. Christmas bonus.
   3. Anniversary awards.
   4. Tuition refunds, scholarships.
E. Savings and thrift plans
F. Service programs
   1. Social and recreational programs, such as parties, picnics, athletic facilities, clubs, and dances where wholly or partially financed by the employer.
   2. Special aids and services such as credit unions, loan funds, company purchasing service, medical treatment for minor sickness, subsidy for food service, discount on purchase of company products, employee newspaper, child care center.

Prevalence of Benefits

Table 25-2 shows the percentage of full-time employees in medium and large establishments who participate in the principal kinds of employee benefits. For example, 99 per cent enjoy paid holidays and vacations, 41 per cent are covered by long-term disability insurance, 97 per cent have health insurance and 84 per cent are covered by a retirement pension plan. The percentages would be lower if small businesses were also included in the survey.

WHY ADOPT BENEFIT AND SERVICE PROGRAMS?

Let us examine the reasons that individual companies install benefits and services. We shall also note the forces causing the expansion of

TABLE 25-2. Per Cent of Full-Time Employees Participating in Selected Benefit Plans, Medium and Large Establishments (1981).

Plan	All Employees	Professional and Administrative Employees	Technical and Clerical Employees	Production Employees
Paid time off:				
Holidays	99	100	100	99
Vacations	99	100	100	99
Personal leave	23	31	32	14
Lunch period	10	4	4	15
Rest time	75	60	76	82
Sick leave	65	92	92	41
Accident and sickness insurance	50	30	35	66
Fully paid by employer	41	22	26	55
Long-term disability insurance	41	61	52	28
Fully paid by employer	32	47	40	23
Health insurance for employee	97	98	96	97
Fully paid by employer	71	67	58	79
Health insurance for dependents	94	96	91	94
Fully paid by employer	48	45	36	55
Life insurance	96	98	95	96
Fully paid by employer	81	81	78	82
Retirement pension	84	88	85	82
Fully paid by employer	79	81	80	77

Source: Robert Frumkin and William Wiatrowski, "Bureau of Labor Statistics Takes a New Look at Employee Benefits," *Monthly Labor Review* Vol. 105, No. 8 (August 1982), pp. 41–45.

existing benefits and the introduction of new ones.

A primary reason explaining why an individual company institutes certain benefits and services is competition for employees. Starting in the early twentieth century a few progressive companies in various sections of the country established such programs as private pensions, group life insurance, and profit sharing, as well as various social and recreational activities. These firms soon become known as "good" places to work. In order to recruit and retain workers, other companies began following suit.

However, the really substantial growth of various forms of supplementary compensation and benefits is due, as we have noted, to union bargaining power. Private pension rights were enjoyed by only a very small percentage of the nation's labor force prior to 1949. In that year, the United Steelworkers of America won the right to bargain for pensions in the United States Supreme Court (Inland Steel Case). Since that time most unionized workers have obtained pension rights in their collective-bargaining contracts. Unions have also taken the lead in obtaining paid holidays and vacations, health insurance, supplemental unemployment insurance, and separation pay. In recent years provisions for dental insurance, prescription drug insurance, and payments for eyeglasses have been appearing in labor-management agreements.

Some kinds of benefits are established to recruit and retain certain kinds of personnel. The opportunity to pursue advanced education programs at the master's and doctoral level is especially important to engineers and scientists. Hence, companies frequently establish tuition refund programs and will arrange for special courses and programs with nearby universities. Many firms pay membership dues to the professional society of an individual's choice and will pay expenses to attend out-of-town society conferences. In another sense, money spent for the development of professional talent ought to be viewed as an investment by the company. This should pay off in the long run in improved performance. Viewed in this way, these items are not fringe benefits but things that should be an integral part of the operation of the business.

Some benefits are provided by employers because of a concern for the welfare of their employees and because they can best be provided through the employer. Blue Cross, Blue Shield, and health insurance plans offered by insurance companies are designed primarily for groups. Costs are lower this way. Enlightened self-interest is a motivating force here also. Employers know that prompt and proper medical treatment of illnesses yields a healthier work force.

The top management of an organization may establish a comprehensive program of benefits and services because it feels this will enhance employee morale, generate greater loyalty toward the firm, and provide a positive public relations image.

When faced with the question of whether to establish a particular new benefit or service, management must weigh the following factors:

1. *Cost and ability to pay.* Will the firm be able to pay the cost of the item in both the short and long run?
2. *Union demands and power.* Both the wishes of employees as expressed by their union representatives and the bargaining power of the union are realities that must be considered.
3. *Need.* Does the contemplated program an-

swer a real need? Is it necessary in order to recruit employees?
4. *Tax consideration.* Most benefits and services are legitimate company expenses. If employees had to use part of their wages to purchase the same benefit, say from an insurance company, they would have already paid income tax on that income. Thus, for a given dollar cost it may be cheaper for a company to purchase the benefit.
5. *Administration.* Will the program be manageable or will it be unwieldy to administer?

SIGNIFICANT BENEFIT AND SERVICE PROGRAMS

Space does not permit an explanation of all the multitude of benefits and services that exist in business and industry. We shall concentrate upon those that are very widespread in usage.

Life Insurance

Group life insurance is one of the oldest and most prevalent kinds of employee benefits. The first group life-insurance policy written by an insurance company was for the Pantasote Leather Co. of Passaic, New Jersey in 1911.[3] As of 1975, 77.3 per cent of all wage and salary employees, including both private and public sectors of employment, were covered by life insurance and death benefits through their employers.[4]

Group insurance, which includes life, health, disability, and pensions, operates according to principles different from individual

[3]Robert I. Mehr and Emerson Cammack. *Principles of Insurance* (Homewood, Ill.: Richard D. Irwin, Inc., 1961), p. 553.

[4]Martha R. Yohalem, "Employee Benefit Plans, 1975," *Social Security Bulletin,* Vol. 40, No. 11 (November 1977), pp. 19–28.

insurance. With group insurance the insurance company makes no selection of individuals whom it will insure. The insurance carrier sets its premium according to the characteristics of the group as a whole. Most insurance companies require a certain minimum number of persons in the group, typically twenty-five people, to guard against adverse selection of risks and for lower administrative costs. The group to be insured must have been formed for some purpose other than to seek group insurance protection. This is to avoid a group made up solely of those in poor health or who might, for some other reason, represent expensive risks.

Group life insurance is written without a physical examination. Usually it is term insurance. This means that it has no cash surrender or paid-up value and no loan provisions.

In its survey of group life insurance practices in 1600 firms across a variety of industry classifications, The Conference Board found that life insurance benefits are usually tied to salary level. The median benefit is two times the employee's base salary. Most commonly the company pays the full premium for the coverage (this is called a noncontributory plan).[5]

Health Insurance

Private group health insurance plans pay part or all of the hospital and doctor expenses arising from illness and injury which are not job-connected. (Workers' Compensation covers expenses of occupational injury or illness.) Often the employees' dependents are also covered.

There are two kinds of health insurance plans: a base plan and a major medical plan. Often a company will have both plans. The base plan pays expenses for listed health services within the defined limits for each service. For example the base plan will typically pay for a hospital room, bed, board, and general nursing care included up to a certain dollar amount per day and up to a given maximum number of days. Some insuring organizations such as Blue Cross, established by the American Hospital Association, pay for a specified service such as semiprivate room accommodations without specifying a dollar limit.

Major medical insurance, available for an additional premium, covers a whole array of physician, hospital, laboratory, and nursing services beyond the limits of the basic plan. Generally, there are no dollar limits for specific services but there is a total dollar limit of say, $50,000 for any benefit period. The individual must typically pay the first $50 or $100 of expenses (the deductible amount). Beyond this figure the insurance company pays 80 per cent of all expenses and the employee pays 20 per cent (the coinsurance feature).

In the vast majority of organizations the employer pays the full cost of the health insurance for the employee while the premium for dependents is shared by the employer and the employee.

Dental insurance has been emerging as a new benefit over the past ten years. In The Conference Board survey mentioned earlier, 13 per cent of the companies provide dental insurance for their nonoffice employees and 9 per cent provide coverage for office employees.[6]

Another new development has been health service through a Health Maintenance Organization (HMO). A health maintenance organization provides comprehensive health services for enrolled members for a fixed prepaid annual fee. Examples are the Kaiser Foundation Plans in California, Oregon, and Hawaii which have been operating for many years. More than 7 million Americans obtain health care from HMOs.[7] The Health Maintenance Act of 1973 requires employers of 25 or more persons to offer mem-

[5]Mitchell Meyer and Harland Fox, *Profile of Employee Benefits,* Report No. 645 (New York: The Conference Board, 1974).

[6]Meyer and Fox, ibid., pp. 14–15.
[7]George E. Rejda, *Social Insurance and Economic Security* (Englewood Cliffs, N.J.: Prentice-Hall, Inc., 1976), p. 218.

bership in an HMO as an alternative to the existing health insurance plan if such a plan is available within the area.

Disability Insurance

Disability insurance compensates employees for wage loss due to nonoccupational illness and injury. There are two forms of disability insurance. The older and much more prevalent type is accident and sickness insurance. This typically pays for 50 to 70 per cent of the worker's pay for up to 26 weeks of disability. A formal disability insurance plan is most common for hourly paid workers. White-collar and managerial employees in industry are often granted sick leave at full pay by the company for a limited number of weeks. This is often done on an informal basis and the program is not insured.

A recent trend has been the introduction of long-term disability insurance to partially compensate for wage loss due to protracted or permanent disabilities. Generally employees contribute toward the cost of this insurance. Typically after a six-month waiting period, the plan will pay 60 per cent of the individual's wage up to $1500 per month.[8]

Pensions

The Social Security Act, enacted in 1935, provides basic retirement income benefits of those who have worked in covered employment for the required number of years. Over 90 per cent of the labor force are covered by old-age insurance under this law. The old-age pension program is but a part of the comprehensive Old Age, Survivors, Disability, and Health Insurance system of the Act. Retirement benefit levels are insufficient to support retired workers and their dependents at an adequate level of living; hence, retirees must augment their Social Security pay-

ments with funds from personal savings or with funds from a pension plan through their employer or both.

How much does it cost a retired couple to live? Yearly the U.S. Department of Labor surveys the annual costs for a retired husband and wife, age 65 or over, who are self-supporting and living alone in their own home in an urban area. In the autumn of 1981 the U.S. average annual cost for a lower-level budget amounted to $7,226; at an intermediate level the cost was $10,226, and at a higher level it was $15,078.[9] The family in the lower budget, compared with the intermediate budget, relies heavily on public transportation, supplemented where necessary by the use of an older car; it performs more services for itself; and it utilizes free recreational services in the community. The life style in the higher budget includes some new car ownership, more household appliances, and more paid-for services.

Let us now examine the principal characteristics of pension plans offered by employers for their employees.

Pension Benefits. There are two principal kinds of pension plans: *defined benefit* and *defined contribution*. The defined benefit plan is much more prevalent in both private industry and governmental units than is the defined contribution plan. Under the defined benefit plan the employee's retirement benefit is usually tied to years of service and earnings. A very popular formula specifies that the person shall receive 1½ per cent (the usual range is 1 to 2 per cent) times his or her years of service times average pay for the five years immediately preceding retirement. Whereas most organizations compute the pension benefit on the basis of the final three to five year's earnings, some companies base it upon career average earnings. This would yield a smaller benefit because of lower earnings early in the person's career. Whereas the white-collar

[8]Meyer and Fox, op. cit., p. 38.

[9]*Three Budgets for a Retired Couple, Autumn 1981* (Washington, D.C.: U.S. Department of Labor), July 1982.

employees overwhelmingly have their pension benefits related to pay, hourly paid workers often receive a fixed amount of pension per year of service. In The Conference Board study, 37 per cent of the firms do not relate benefit amount to pay for nonoffice workers.[10]

The money-purchase plan is a common type of defined contribution plan. This arrangement is established under a group annuity plan underwritten by an insurance company. The employer (and sometimes the employee, too) contributes a definite percentage of the individual's pay into a retirement fund. Upon retirement the principal and interest accumulated are used to pay the monthly pension. Under money purchase the contribution is fixed but the benefit varies. The variation is principally caused by changes in the interest earned on the fund over the years.

Pension benefits are sometimes also built up from deferred profit sharing plans, savings plans, and stock bonus plans. Generally these arrangements are used to supplement a basic pension plan.

In an era of continual high price inflation, retirees find their private pension benefits have eroded quite rapidly. Seldom, however, are private pension benefits adjusted upward for inflation. The Conference Board found that only 4 per cent of the firms surveyed do this.[11] Fortunately, retirement benefits under the U.S. Social Security system are adjusted upward annually according to changes in the Consumer Price Index.

Because women, on the average, live several years longer than men after retirement and thus collect monthly pension benefits for a greater number of years, it had been common practice for pension plans, using insurance industry actuarial tables, to pay women lower monthly benefits than men. However in July 1983 the U.S. Supreme Court ruled, in *Arizona Governing Committee* v. *Norris,* that a retirement plan that paid lower monthly benefits to women than men violated Title VII of the federal Civil-Rights Act which prohibits discrimination based upon sex. The court ruling requires sex-neutral benefit calculations and applies only to benefits that result from contributions (annuity premiums) applied on or after August 1, 1983. This decision applies to benefits derived from all private and public employer-sponsored pension plans.

Vesting Rights. Vesting is a nonforfeitable right to pension benefits from the employer's contributions even if the employee should terminate his employment before retirement age. Years ago the majority of pension plans granted no vesting rights to workers who were premanently laid off or who quit. By the 1960s there was a pronounced trend toward granting vesting rights after employees reached a specified age, generally 45 or 50, and had accumulated a given number of years of service, typically 15 to 20 years. Vesting much sooner is now required by the Employee Retirement Income Security Act of 1974 (ERISA) to be discussed later.

Methods of Financing. Prior to the enactment of ERISA a pension plan could be either unfunded or funded. This law requires all plans to be adequately funded. Benefits in unfunded plans were paid out of current operating income of the company. However, this was extremely risky. If the firm experienced a decline in revenue or went bankrupt, pension payments to retirees were often slashed or abolished. Many companies have funded their pensions but at an inadequate level to meet accrued liabilities.

There are two types of funded plans: *trusteed* and *insured.* A trusteed plan is administered by trustees who may be appointed by the company or jointly by the company and the union. Often a bank or trust company will administer the fund. In any case an actuary must be engaged to determine the amount of money that must be set aside each year to meet pension obligations.

---

[10]Meyer and Fox, op. cit., p. 52.
[11]Meyer and Fox, ibid., p. 52.

Insured plans are underwritten and administered by an insurance company.

Who Pays? Predominantly the employer pays the full cost of the pension benefits. In The Conference Board survey of 1600 companies 80 per cent of the plans for office employees and 81 per cent of the plans for nonoffice personnel were noncontributory. Company contributions to pensions, and the various insurances (life, health, and disability) tend, in recent years, to be viewed as a form of deferred compensation.

Retirement Age. Sixty-five has been almost universally accepted as the normal retirement age ever since that figure was adopted by the Social Security Act in 1935 as the age for commencing old age benefit payments. Prior to this, the ordinary worker could not afford to retire. He or she worked until infirmity prevented working or until death.

Beginning in the 1960s a widespread movement toward early retirement began. Whereas there are no accurate national statistics on retirement age, there are measures that show a pronounced early retirement trend. For example, the labor force participation rate of male workers aged 60 to 64 has been dropping rapidly in nonfarm industries for 20 years. In 1977 only 62.9 per cent of all men in that age group held jobs, compared with 82.6 per cent in 1955. Experts believe that the average American retires at about age 62, the age at which he or she first becomes eligible for reduced Social Security benefits. In the basic steel industry the average hourly worker retires at age 61. At General Motors Corporation the average retirement age is 59. In both the steel and auto industries the unions have negotiated pension plans providing for early retirement.[12]

In 1978 Congress amended the Age Discrimination in Employment Act of 1967 in order to ban mandatory retirement before age 70. Prior to this a majority of employers required

that their employees retire when they reached 65. (Many plans allow retirement as early as age 55 with reduced benefits.) Will many Americans opt for retirement between ages 65 and 70 now that this right is protected by law? Only time will tell. Experience shows that those possessing modest educations and holding unskilled and semiskilled jobs generally choose early retirement if their benefits are adequate. Professional and managerial personnel, who often derive intrinsic satisfaction from their jobs, will probably tend to work beyond age 65. Or they will retire early and pursue second careers.

Employee Retirement Income Security Act of 1974 (ERISA)

Background. Enactment of the Employee Retirement Income Security Act of 1974 was preceded by several years of study by Congressional committees and by the U.S. Labor and Treasury Departments. Many serious abuses and problems were uncovered. A study by the Labor and Treasury Departments for 1972 found that 1,227 pension plans terminated that year with almost $50 million of lost benefits to about 20,000 workers.[13] A U.S. Senate Labor Subcommittee in 1972 reported that many pension plans were scrapped or benefits were greatly reduced when one company was acquired by or merged with another. Workers often lost all their accumulated pension benefits when they were laid off before reaching retirement age. Some companies dipped into their pension funds when they were in need of money for acquisitions, expansion, or just for operating cash.[14]

As workers have changed employers, they have often lost pension rights built up with the former employer. The United States Senate Subcommittee on Labor in 1971 determined that, as a result of harsh vesting rules, only about one person in ten would collect pension benefits from his employer.[15]

[12]*Business Week* (June 19, 1978), pp. 73–74.

[13]*Wall Street Journal* (August 28, 1974), p. 1.
[14]*Wall Street Journal* (March 7, 1972), pp. 1 and 20.
[15]George E. Rejda, op. cit., p. 78.

In summary, the principal reason why Congress passed ERISA was to overcome problems caused by inadequate pension funding, plan terminations, restrictive vesting rules, business failures, and just plain failure of employers to provide promised pensions when workers retired.

Provisions of the law. At the outset it should be noted that ERISA does not require employers to offer or set up pension plans. But if a plan is in existence or if a new one is established then the plan must meet certain minimum standards contained in the law.

Many of the provisions of the Act also apply to employee welfare plans such as those providing benefits for health care, accident and sickness, disability, death, and unemployment. This is especially true in regard to the fiduciary provisions and the reporting and disclosure requirements. However, we will focus our discussion only on the pension features of the law.[16]

A brief summary of the provisions of this very complex law follows:

Coverage and Administration. The Act covers pension and welfare plans established and maintained by employers engaged in interstate commerce or in an industry affecting commerce. It also covers plans run by unions alone or jointly with employers. The Act is administered by both the Department of Labor and the Internal Revenue Service of the Treasury Department. The newly established Pension Benefit Guarantee Corporation handles the pension plan termination insurance program.

Participation. A plan must allow an employee to participate when he or she has completed one year of service and is at least 25 years old.

Vesting. Any employee contributions must be vested fully and immediately. Employer contributions must vest at least as fast as one of the following schedules:

1. Full (100 per cent) vesting after 10 years of service.
2. Graduated vesting. 25 per cent vesting after 5 years of service, increasing yearly until 100 per cent after 15 years.
3. 50 per cent vesting as soon as the sum of age and years of service equal 45, plus 10 per cent for each year thereafter.

Funding. The plan must fund the current year's benefit accruals. It must amortize any unfunded costs over 30 years for new plans and over 40 years for existing plans and multiemployer plans.

Fiduciary Standards. The "prudent man rule" (a legal concept) is imposed upon all persons who administer or provide investment advice for a plan. The fiduciary persons are to discharge their duties solely in the interests of the participants and beneficiaries. Various conflict-of-interest transactions are outlawed.

Reporting and Disclosure. Plan administrators must furnish each employee a summary plan description in easily understandable language. Administrators must also give the Department of Labor annual reports on various operating and financial details of the plan.

Termination Insurance. A termination insurance program is set up through the Pension Benefit Guaranty Corporation. The program pays benefits up to $750 per month to those who had vested rights in plans that were

---

[16]Further information on ERISA may be obtained by consulting the following: BNA Editorial Staff, *Highlights of the New Pension Reform Law* (Washington, D.C.: The Bureau of National Affairs, Inc., 1974); *Often-asked Questions About the Employee Retirement Income Security Act of 1974* (U.S. Department of Labor, Labor–Management Services Administration, 1975); Peter Henle and Raymond Schmitt, "Pension Reform: The Long, Hard Road to Enactment," *Monthly Labor Review* (November 1974), pp. 3–12.

terminated with insufficient assets. Insurance is funded by an annual premium on all pension plans of $1 per participant. The Guaranty Corporation can recover benefit costs from the defaulting company up to 30 per cent of the firm's net worth.

Portability. Although Congress considered making it possible for employees to take their pension credits with them when they went to a new employer, the law as enacted does not provide for true portability. It does provide that a worker, if the employer agrees, can withdraw his or her pension credits from a plan and shift them either to an Individual Retirement Account or to another employer's plan without incurring a tax liability.

Widow-Widowers' Benefit. Unless the employee specifically elects otherwise, a married person must receive a pension benefit payable for his or her lifetime with a surviving spouse to receive at least 50 per cent of that amount.

Enforcement. Both civil and criminal actions may be brought for violation of the law. Criminal penalties include fines or imprisonment or both for violations of reporting and disclosure provisions and for embezzlement, kickbacks, or false statements.

Employee Stock Ownership

Employee stock purchase plans have been around for many years. Such plans went out of favor during the depression years of the 1930s because many workers, who could ill afford it, lost money as the market value of their companies' shares declined drastically. Over the past twenty-five years or so there has been a resurgence of interest in employee stock purchase plans. Many companies operate such plans. In the typical program the corporation sets up a payroll deduction arrangement in which an employee may voluntarily have a sum of money, up to an established limit, deducted from each paycheck. This is used to purchase shares of the company's stock, in the employee's name, through a broker. Usually the only company contribution is to pay the administrative costs and the broker's fee. Sometimes stock purchase plans are combined with employee savings and thrift plans via payroll deduction. Here some companies make an added contribution of a predetermined amount in the form of cash or company stock to the individual's savings. Purposes of employee stock ownership and savings plans are to enhance employee loyalty to the corporation and to build employee savings.

ESOP. The term *employee stock ownership plan* or ESOP has come to mean, in recent years, the kind of plan devised and promoted by Louis O. Kelso, a California attorney and executive of an investment firm. Although legally possible since 1942, ESOPs did not achieve any prominence until they were given favored treatment by the Employee Retirement Income Security Act of 1974 and the Tax Reduction Act of 1975. An ESOP has particular appeal to a small- or medium-sized company that wishes to raise equity capital.

The company sets up a trust under an agreement by which the trust buys shares of the company itself. The trust borrows from a bank a sum of money sufficient to purchase an agreed number of shares of company stock which are for the benefit of participating employees. The company issues shares of its stock to the trust and receives money from the trust thereby increasing its equity capital. Generally, the bank requires the trust to turn over the shares of company stock to it as collateral for the loan. The company pays into the trust, over an agreed time period, funds to pay off the bank loan and interest. When the loan is paid off, the bank returns the stock to the trust which then credits shares to each employee's account according to a given formula (generally related to employee's salary). When the employee retires or otherwise leaves the company, he takes possession of the stock shares or he may sell them back to the trust.

The principal advantage to the company is that it can obtain loan funds indirectly through the trust which it pays back with pretax dollars. The principal of a direct bank loan would have to be paid back out of taxable earnings. Presumably the company also gains because the employees acquire an ownership stake in the business. The employee's benefit is the stock they receive without any monetary expenditure.

Employment Security and Unemployment Pay

A protracted period of unemployment can spell severe hardship for the individual and his or her family. Except for periods of wartime, the United States has been plagued by chronically high unemployment. Economists have generally considered full employment to mean an unemployment rate in the range of 4.0–4.5 per cent. Yet during all the years 1970 through 1979 the unemployment rate in the country as a whole never dropped below 4.9 per cent. Mostly it fluctuated in the 6 to 7 per cent range.

Basic protection against income loss is provided by the unemployment insurance system created by the Social Security Act of 1935. This law provided an incentive for all states to adopt unemployment insurance laws that met Federal standards. The Federal guidelines allow the states considerable latitude in setting benefit levels and durations as well as eligibility requirements. Benefits average about 50 per cent of the individuals' previous earnings up to a maximum specified in each state's law. In 1980 these maximums varied among the states from $80 to $180 per week. The maximum benefit duration in most states is 26 weeks. Unemployment insurance is financed by a payroll tax paid by the employer. In five states the employee also pays a small tax on his earnings. "Experience rating" is used to adjust each individual company's payroll tax rate. If the company has stable employment with no layoffs the rate becomes quite low (say 1.0 per cent). If an employer has unstable employment with large layoffs, his tax rate can jump up to 3–4 per cent.

Some companies have established programs to supplement the modest benefits paid by state unemployment insurance. Often these have been created as a result of union bargaining as in the steel and automobile industries where layoffs occur rather often. In some other firms the managements, on their own initiative, have set up guaranteed employment plans to remove the specter of unemployment from the workers' minds.

Supplemental Unemployment Benefits Plans. About two million employees in the automobile, steel, farm equipment, can manufacturing, rubber, and glass industries are covered by supplemental unemployment benefits (SUB) plans. These plans add to the amount of money an unemployed worker receives from the regular state unemployment compensation program to bring his total benefit up to a specified percentage of his regular wage.

There are two types of SUB plans: the insurance fund and the individual account or income-security plan. The latter is principally found in the glass industry; most of the others are insurance-fund plans.

In an insurance-fund plan the company contributes a certain number of cents per hour for all labor-hours worked to a trust fund. Company contributions continue until the trust fund reaches a designated maximum level. If withdrawals to pay benefits reduce the amount in the fund below this level, then company contributions are resumed. The liability of the employer does not extend beyond the assets in the fund and the cents per hour contribution. Benefits vary somewhat from industry to industry. The plans in the automobile industry add to the states' unemployment compensation payments to bring the laid-off worker's combined income to 95 per cent of his after-tax pay (less $7.50 for work-related expenses such as transportation and work clothing that are not incurred during layoff) up to a maximum of 52 weeks. The number of weeks of benefit each worker receives depends upon length of service and upon the company's trust fund position (the amount in the fund compared with its maximum). Benefits are paid for a genuine layoff. Employees are not paid if suspended or discharged for cause, or if out on strike. The auto industry plans also provide for lump-sum separation payments for those on layoff at least 12 months. Depending on one's length of service this can vary in amount from 50 hour's separation pay on up to 2,080 hours after 30 years of service.

The individual account plans, also called income security or savings plans, provide for an individual account being set up for each employee. A specified number of cents per hours is contributed to the account for each hour worked. Each person has a vested right to the money in his or her account and may withdraw it if he is laid off or sick, retires, or leaves the company. These plans are in no way related to the benefits received under state unemployment compensation.

SUB plans are of greatest value to employees possessing a moderate amount of seniority. Very low-seniority workers obtain either no benefits or else benefits of very limited duration. Long-service employees are rarely laid off anyway, so they have little need for a SUB program.

Separation Pay. A survey by The Conference Board of 1600 companies distributed across various industrial classifications showed that 56 per cent of the firms had separation pay plans for their office employees and 35 per cent had plans for their nonoffice personnel. Such plans were more prevalent in large than small firms.[17] To obtain separation pay the termination of employment must usually be permanent, it must be initiated by the company and it will not be paid if the individual was discharged for just cause. Separation pay benefits tend to be quite modest. For those having less than five years of service the allowance is typically just two weeks'

[17]Meyer and Fox, op. cit., pp. 78–80.

pay. For longer-service personnel the benefit is most often one week's pay for each year of service.

Guaranteed Employment Plans. So far we have been talking about private company and union programs to provide payment to unemployed workers. Now we shall talk about plans designed to keep people on the job.

Only a few corporations have seen fit to offer their employees guaranteed annual employment. Prominent among these are the Procter and Gamble Company and the Lincoln Electric Company. Although it makes no formal guarantee, the IBM Corporation has a long-standing policy of no layoffs. For over 30 years, despite recessions, it has not laid off a single employee. Among the reasons for IBM's success in avoiding layoffs are a strong management team, a growing business, careful human resource planning, extensive employee training for new job skills, and a willingness to transfer employees among departments and plants as production demands fluctuate.

The Procter and Gamble plan guarantees 48 weeks of employment each year to all hourly workers having at least two years of service. Subtracted from this 48 weeks is time lost due to holidays, vacations, disability, voluntary absence, and emergencies. The company also has the option to reduce hours of work to 75 per cent of normal. The plan makes no guarantee of an annual wage.

The Lincoln Electric Company, previously mentioned, has long been famed for its unique and highly successful wage incentive and profit-sharing systems. Less known is its guaranteed annual employment plan.

After a seven-year test of a no-layoff policy, in 1958 the Lincoln Electric Company issued a formal guarantee of continuous employment for all its regular employees. This guarantee promises 49 weeks of work each year, of at least 30 hours per week. The remaining three weeks are a paid vacation. Employees are not guaranteed a particular work assignment or wage rate. The company commitment covers all full-time employees having at least two years' continuous company service. The company has always honored this guarantee of employment. Since 1958, working hours have averaged about 2,000 per year per employee. Among the many techniques the company utilizes to maintain full employment when sales volume temporarily declines are the introduction of new products, building products for inventory, and transferring workers to other jobs.

From 1958 to 1971 productivity at Lincoln Electric grew at the rate of 5.5 per cent a year, well above the average of all manufacturing industry. Lincoln's management believes that the guarantee of annual employment stimulates workers to cooperate with management in raising productivity. They do not have to worry about being laid off as a result of cost-saving improvements.[18]

Other Benefits and Services

In the aggregate a large number of benefits and services are provided employees, with considerable variation from organization to organization in the items offered. We shall mention here some of the more prevalent ones.

Cafeterias. Employers very commonly operate cafeterias for their employees, especially where the location of the organization is not proximate to regular commercial restaurants. Often the employer will subsidize the cafeteria in order to keep food prices reasonable. Management recognizes the contribution to employee health and morale that can result from a well-run food service.

Moving Expenses. Whenever a company transfers employees to jobs at a company facility in another geographical area, it almost always pays the moving expenses of the employee and his or her family. Many employers also pay the moving expenses for newly hired employees (especially salaried ones) who must relocate to take the job.

Credit Union. A credit union is a cooperative association designed to promote thrift among its members and to make loans to members. It is similar to a bank. There are over 23,000 credit unions in the United States. Credit unions under Federal law are classified as nonprofit cooperatives and are tax exempt. Although a credit union is organized and operated primarily by a group of employees, it is considered to be a company service because management often supplies free office space and encourages its establishment and operation.

Service Awards. To reward loyalty and to build commitment to the organization, many companies award jewelry items (lapel pins, watches, rings, silver bowls, etc.), usually inscribed with the company name or logotype, upon the attainment of significant numbers of years of service such as 10, 20, and 25 years.

Social and Recreational Programs. The extent of social and recreational programs can range from establishments that have a simple Christmas party each year to those that offer a vast array of athletic facilities, hobby clubs, socials, open houses, and family get-togethers. The purpose of having such activities, from management's viewpoint, is usually to generate an enhanced feeling of belonging, to improve morale, and to develop greater company loyalty. Experience reveals that social and recreational programs are most successful when interested employees play an active part in organizing and running the individual activities.

---

[18]Further information on Lincoln Electric Company's program is contained in Robert Zager, "Managing Guaranteed Employment," *Harvard Business Review,* Vol 56, No. 3 (May–June 1978), pp. 103–115.

Holidays and Vacations

The historical trend in America has been one of declining hours of work per week and per year and greater leisure time. In the 1870s the average work week was about 53 hours. In 1930 it was 47.7 hours. After the passage of the Fair Labor Standards Act in 1938, which requires payment of rate and one half for all hours over 40 worked in one week, the work week has tended to be standardized at 40 hours.[19] During wartime periods the average work week has gone above 40 hours. During business recessions it has dropped below this figure. But it has tended to hover about the 40-hour figure for over forty years.

Prior to World War II, hourly employees were generally granted three to five holidays per year but without pay. Directives by the National War Labor Board in labor–management dispute cases during the 1942–1945 period brought about the practice of paid holidays. According to a survey by the U.S. Department of Labor, in 1981 the average number of paid holidays received by employees in establishments in the private sector was 10.[20]

Before 1940 paid vacations for hourly employees in private industry were uncommon. If they received a vacation, it was usually for one week without pay. Office and managerial personnel generally did receive a one- or two-week paid vacation in that era. Nowadays the practice of granting paid vacations in all types of employment and industries (except agriculture and construction) is nearly universal. Hourly workers usually get a one-week paid vacation after one year of service and two weeks after two or three years of service. Both hourly paid and office workers typically are entitled to three-week paid vacations after ten or fifteen years of service

and four weeks after twenty years. Some companies grant five-week vacations after twenty-five years of service and six weeks after thirty years.

Cafeteria Benefits

The cafeteria approach to benefit plan administration has been proposed as a way of meeting the differing needs and wants of employees. Under this concept each employee is granted the right to select his own benefits from among all those offered by the company. For example, a young employee with a wife and children might wish to have the most comprehensive health insurance coverage available including major medical, dental, eyeglass, and prescription drug options. On the other hand an older employee may prefer a supplement to the normal retirement benefit. Some individuals might also choose to take cash in place of a given benefit; however this may incur certain income tax obligations.

Certain constraints may be imposed. The sum total of benefits available to an individual must be within a uniform dollar limit (or percentage of salary limit) applied to all employees. Also, all employees may be required to take certain basic benefit coverages such as life insurance.

Although the idea of individual choice is intriguing, the cafeteria approach to benefit-plan administration has attracted very few corporate adherents to date. Three organizations that do have such programs are the American Can Company, TRW, Inc., and the Educational Testing Service.[21] Deterrents to the establishment of these flexible programs have been restrictive Internal Revenue Service regulations and the administrative complexity of allowing individual choice among a broad array of benefits and options.

[19]Geoffrey H. Moore and Janice N. Hedges, "Trends in Labor and Leisure," *Monthly Labor Review,* Vol. 94, No. 2 (February 1971), pp. 3–11.

[20]*Employee Benefits, 1981* (Washington, D.C.: U.S. Department of Labor), June 1982.

[21]"New Life for Flexible Compensation," *Dun's Review,* Vol. 112, No. 3 (September 1978), pp. 66–70.

ALTERNATIVE WORK SCHEDULES

Ever since the enactment of the Fair Labor Standards Act in 1938, the 5 day–40 hour work week has been widely accepted as standard in the United States. When the volume of work becomes heavy for a few weeks or months, management may require employees to work more than 40 hours or more than 5 days per week, at overtime rates of pay. Or when work is slack, a firm may reduce the hours per week below forty. But both of these conditions are considered temporary. Five days and forty hours have still been considered the normal work week. However, commencing in the late 1960s and early 1970s many private companies and government agencies have experimented with alternative work schedules. We shall discuss three of these: flexitime, compressed work week, and job sharing.

Flexitime

Flexitime, sometimes called *flexible hours*, was first introduced in 1967 at the Messerschmidt Research and Development Center near Munich, Germany. It has spread fairly rapidly throughout European countries. It is estimated that about one third of the labor force in Switzerland, 5 to 10 per cent of the white-collar labor force in West Germany, and a total of about one million workers in England, France, Scandinavia, and other European countries work under a flexitime system. Most applications in the United States have occurred since 1973.[22] In the United States flexitime is used by many companies, including Control Data Corporation, Northwestern Mutual Life Insurance Company, and the Nestle Company[23] and in many governmental agencies, including the Social Security Administration.

Flexitime works this way. Within a prescribed band of time in the morning, usually between 7:00 and 9:30 A.M., employees are free to choose their own starting time. Also they are free to leave within a prescribed band of time at the end of the workday, usually between 3:00 and 6:00 P.M. All employees are required to be at work during a core time of, say, 9:30 A.M. to 3:00 P.M. This means that the workday can vary from day to day in its length as well as the time at which it begins and ends. Each worker makes an agreement with his supervisor to put in the total required number of hours per day, per week, or per month. This time period varies from one installation to another.

The initiative in launching programs for flexible hours of work has generally come from management. Labor union leaders, particularly in the United States, have been wary of it. Because of overtime regulations of the Fair Labor Standards Act (time and one-half after 40 hours in one week) and the Walsh-Healey Act (time and one half after 8 hours per day and 40 hours per week for government contractors), the flexibility of hours worked is more limited in the United States than in many European countries.

Management's purposes in introducing flexible hours are generally to raise employee morale and to cut down on tardiness and absenteeism. Various research investigations into flexitime applications have nearly always revealed strong support from employees who have worked under the system. They can set their working hours to avoid the traffic crunch of commuters, they are better able to attend to personal business such as shopping, banking, and dealing with public agencies during regular work days. Working mothers are better able to get their children off to school in the morning. Employees like the opportunity to control their own hours of work. Several studies show that the introduction of flexitime has reduced tardiness and absenteeism.

Management is best able to apply flexible

[22]John D. Owen, "Flexitime: Some Problems and Solutions," *Industrial and Labor Relations Review*, Vol. 30, No. 2 (January 1977), pp. 152–160.

[23]*Wall Street Journal* (April 13, 1976), p. 1.

hours of work in departments where there does not need to be a continuous flow of work from one employee to another. This means that it is often easier to use in white-collar and service jobs than in direct production work.

Compressed Work Week

In the early 1970s there was a flurry of interest in the compressed work week—often called the four-day or occasionally the three-day work week. In going to a four-day week some companies retained weekly hours at 40 (thus ten-hour days), whereas others scheduled eight- or nine-hour days.

By 1972, 1,000 organizations had adopted the four-day work week.[24] However, interest soon leveled off and by mid-1974 only about 2 per cent of full-time employees of U.S. firms were working on compressed work weeks.[25]

Just as with flexitime, the principal impetus for shifting to a compressed work week has come from management. Managers have sought to reduce costs through higher productivity by reducing the percentage of total working time devoted to start-up and shut-down activities. In some instances ten-hour work days have nicely corresponded to the pattern of workload demand, as in the case of certain retail and service establishments. Other objectives have been to reduce absenteeism and turnover and to raise employee morale.

Employees have often preferred a four-day work week because this gives them three-day weekends. Also, they make fewer round trips to work each week. Thus, total commuting time and cost are reduced. Early experience with the four-day week was positive in many companies. There was better morale, lower absenteeism and

turnover, higher productivity, and lower costs. However, longer trials for some organizations demonstrated that it was really the Hawthorne effect they were witnessing.[26] The benefits were temporary.

Job Sharing

Job sharing is a pattern of work in which two employees, each working half time, share responsibility for performing one full-time job. Each person has a permanent, part-time job. Salary and fringe benefits are prorated according to the number of hours worked.

Job sharing is new. To date it has been applied in only a few organizations. It appeals to married women with family responsibilities who can really only work a few hours per day. For employers this pattern of shared jobs makes sense in times of labor shortages for particular skills and as a way of accommodating to needs of certain employees. It has been successfully used by local governments in the San Francisco Bay area for such jobs as secretary, librarian, social worker, and receptionist.[27]

Questions for Review and Discussion

1. What factors have caused benefit and service programs to grow substantially since the period around 1940?
2. Do you believe that benefits and services should be considered a part of compensation that employees have earned by working at their jobs, or do you feel that they repre-

[24]*New York Times* (July 16, 1972).

[25]U.S. Department of Labor, Bureau of Labor Statistics. *The Revised Workweek: Results of a Pilot Study of 16 Firms*, Bulletin 1846 (Washington, D.C.: Government Printing Office, 1975).

[26]This term comes from the Hawthorne studies at the Western Electric Company during 1927–1932, where gains in productivity, which had been initially attributed to improvements in working conditions, were later found to have been caused by workers' sense of involvement in a novel experiment.

[27]*Alternative Work Schedules*, EEO-Information on Equal Employment Opportunity for State and Local Governments, Issue No. 17 (Washington, D.C.: U.S. Civil Service Commission, Undated).

sent something extra that the employer is giving his employees? Justify your position.

3. Classify and give examples of the principal kinds of employee benefits and services.

4. What factors motivate the top management of a company to adopt benefit and service programs? What factors must be weighed when deciding whether a particular program should be established?

5. For a given cost for a particular group insurance program, why might it be cheaper for the company to pay the cost than for the employees to do so?

6. What factors led to the passage by Congress of the Employee Retirement Income Security Act of 1974? Give the principal provisions of the Act relating to vesting, funding,

reporting and disclosure, and plan terminations.

7. What is an ESOP (Kelso plan)?

8. How does group insurance differ from individually purchased insurance?

9. Discuss the contradictory forces at work in our society toward early retirement before age 65 and late retirement after age 65.

10. Why might the top management of an industrial company decide to establish a guaranteed annual employment program? What techniques can be used to achieve stable employment in a firm?

11. Why has there been considerable interest in recent years in alternative work schedules such as flexitime, compressed work weeks, and job sharing?

CASE PROBLEM

Your company and the union representing nonexempt white-collar employees are in the midst of negotiations for a new union–employer agreement. In addition to its wage increase proposal, the union has made the following proposals for improvements in fringe benefits.

a. Three days personal leave per year for handling personal business matters which ordinarily are difficult or impossible to attend to during nonworking hours.

b. Dental insurance, fully paid by the company, for the employee and his family.

c. Two days religious holiday leave per year. The official religious holidays for some religions, e.g. Jewish faith, fall on days other than Christmas and Easter.

d. A sick-leave bank. Each employee would contribute one day per year to a sick-leave bank out of his alloted annual sick-leave days. If any employee should use up his or her sick-leave days due to a long illness, he or she could apply for extra days from the sick-leave bank.

e. Five weeks vacation after 15 years of service. Currently the company–union labor agreement provides for two weeks after one year of service, three weeks after 10 years of service, and four weeks after 20 years of service.

Questions

1. Assuming that you are the director of industrial relations for the company, what factors would you use to guide your decision with regard to each of these bargaining proposals? What information would you seek?
2. How would you calculate the cost to the company of each item?
3. Once the union and management have agreed upon a total dollar cost for the settlement of the contract negotiations for pay increases and benefits improvement combined, would it be acceptable to management to allow the union considerable discretion in deciding the relative distribution of that total sum of money among a direct pay increase and the various benefits it has proposed?

Suggestions for Further Reading

Bell, Donald R. "Dental and Vision Care Benefits in Health Insurance Plans," *Monthly Labor Review.* Vol. 103, No. 6 (June 1980), pp. 22–26.

Bolt, James E. "Job Security: Its Time Has Come," *Harvard Business Review,* Vol. 61, No. 6 (November–December 1983), pp. 115–123.

Committee for Economic Development. *Reforming Retirement Policies.* Washington, D.C.: The Committee, 1981.

Dickman, Fred, and William G. Emener. "Employee Assistance Programs: Basic Concepts, Attributes, and Evaluation," *Personnel Administrator,* Vol. 27 No. 8 (August 1982), pp. 55–62.

Foulkes, Fred K. *Employee Benefits Handbook.* Boston: Warren, Gorham & Lamont, Inc., 1982.

McCarthy, Maureen E., and Gail S. Rosenberg. *Work Sharing Case Studies.* Kalamazoo, Mich.: W. E. Upjohn Institute for Employment Research, 1981.

Nollen, Stanley D. *New Work Schedules in Practice.* New York: Van Nostrand Reinhold, 1982.

Williams, C. Arthur Jr., John G. Turnbull, and Earl F. Cheit. *Economic and Social Security: Social Insurance and Other Approaches,* 5th ed. New York: John Wiley & Sons, Inc. 1982.

PART VIII

Employee Rights

26 Employee Rights

In the mid-1960s, George B. Geary, an experienced salesman in the United States Steel Corporation's oil and gas industry supply division in Houston, Texas, found out that test results from the company's own metallurgy department on oil-well casings produced by U.S. Steel showed a failure rate of 3.6 per cent. Geary was told by his immediate boss to sell these casings, but he knew that such a failure rate was too high and the casings would fail under high pressure. He so informed his boss. Because top management wanted to gain market position with this new product, middle-level management felt it ought to go ahead with production and sale of the oil-well casings despite the test result. Geary expressed his genuine doubts about the safety of the casings to various higher officials of the company. Eventually, he was called to the company's headquarters in Pittsburgh for a meeting with a corporate vice-president and other high officers. They decided to stop production of the steel casings. George Geary had won his point. However, a short time later, the company fired Geary. He was fired for opposing the wishes of high-level managers, even though, on the merits of the issue, he was right.[1]

A corporate vice-president in one of the public utilities in New England, in the mid 1970s, told his superiors that he did not think that an extra rate increase approved by the Rhode Island public utilities commission was justified by the factual data in the matter. He said that the company was collecting twice to offset rising fuel costs. This vice-president persisted in raising the issue within the company. To silence him, the company gave him two pay raises and a promotion. When he would not keep quiet, the company transferred him to an innocuous job in the company headquarters. Then top management tried to force him out of the company by saying he was mentally ill. It placed him on sick leave. He then resigned from the firm. The validity of his contention was later proven when the public service commission ordered the company to rebate $4 million to its customers.[2]

In 1964, Philip B. Woodroofe, Supervisor of Municipal Services at the Bethlehem Steel Corporation in Bethlehem, Pennsylvania, took an active role in founding the Community Civic League whose mission was to improve racial relations in the community. Mr. Woodroofe was the son of an Episcopal minister and was age 45

---

[1]A more complete account of the George Geary case is given in David W. Ewing, *"Do it My Way or You're Fired"* (New York: John Wiley & Sons, Inc., 1983), pp. 83–89.

[2]*Wall Street Journal*, "The Whistle Blower Chooses Hard Path, Utility Story Shows," November 8, 1978.

at the time. During World War II and the Korean War, he had been an Air Force officer. The mayor of Bethlehem was a member of the Civic League, as were other prominent citizens in the community, both white and black. In March 1964, Woodroofe was told by his boss either to resign from the League or resign from the company. When he refused, he was fired. Woodroofe believed that the purposes of the League were good and that his position in the League was not in conflict with his position in the company.[3]

Most reasonable people would say that the treatments accorded the individuals in the foregoing cases were unjust. Yet thousands of people are discharged from their jobs every year without just cause and without access to due process appeal mechanisms.

Although the Constitution, Bill of Rights, and various statutes grant Americans many rights—such as free speech, protection against unreasonable search and seizure, and due process of the law in civil and criminal proceedings—comparable protections have not, in general, extended to the workplace. For example, employees and managers, who are not protected by a union-employer contract or by government civil service regulations, are generally vulnerable to being discharged at the will (or whim) of their bosses. Employees who speak their minds freely about policies and conditions in the company may be fired if the boss dislikes what they say. Generally, employees' desks and lockers can be inspected at anytime by the boss or a member of the company security force. And if the boss suspects someone of taking an item from the premises, the employee can be subjected to seizure and search. Also, if employees take part in community or political causes which displease the boss, they may be fired summarily.

[3]There have been many published accounts of the Philip Woodroofe case. See for example: *New York Times,* March 22, 1964; David W. Ewing, *Freedom Inside the Organization* (New York: McGraw-Hill Book Co., 1977), pp. 122–123.

Gradually, employees have acquired more rights in the workplace by means of statutes, court action, collective bargaining, and personnel policies instituted by managements in some progressive firms. However, protections in important areas are still lacking or are only emerging very slowly. The thrust of this chapter is to focus upon needs for employee rights in the following areas:

- *Protection of one's job (the employment-at-will issue)*
- *Due process and just cause*
- *Freedom of speech and whistle-blowing*
- *Privacy*
- *Off-the-job behavior*
- *Protection against layoff*

Needs of the Employer

Although our focus in this chapter is on employee rights, we must first recognize that employers and managers are responsible for running enterprises and producing goods and services. In order to do this efficiently and effectively, they must be able to recruit, select, and develop productive employees; they must have the authority to assign people to jobs, to expect an adequate level of performance from these employees, to maintain discipline, to appraise performance and take corrective action if performance is inadequate, and to transfer people within the organization as may be reasonably necessary. Management has a right to expect that employees will cooperate with each other and with supervision. The employer should also expect to receive reasonable loyalty from the employees.

When conflicts occur between *employee needs* for job protection, free speech, privacy, and the like, and *employer needs* for efficiency and profit, there should be a formal mechanism for resolution of these differences.

PROTECTIONS CREATED BY LAW

Certain protections and rights have, over the years, been accorded to working men and women through federal and state laws. Let us now briefly review these protections.

Right to Organize and Bargain Collectively. The National Labor Relations Act (1935), as amended, grants employees in the private sector the right to form unions of their own choosing and to bargain collectively with their employers. If management retaliates against employees for exercising this right, the employees can seek redress through the National Labor Relations Board. As a result of Executive Orders in the 1960s and of the Civil Service Reform Act of 1978, federal government employees now enjoy the same rights (except the right to strike) as those enjoyed by employees in the private sector. State and local government employees in over half the states enjoy these same rights through state collective bargaining laws.

Health and Safety. The Occupational Safety and Health Act (1970) and the Coal Mine Health and Safety Act (1969) accord workers the right to safe and healthful working conditions. These laws also prohibit the employer from dismissing employees who institute a proceeding related to the enforcement of federal health and safety laws or for refusing to work under conditions where the employee has a good faith fear of suffering serious injury.

Equal Employment Opportunity. Title VII of the Civil Rights Act of 1964 prohibits discrimination in employment (including hiring, testing, promotion, pay, benefits, and discharge) on the basis of race, color, religion, sex, or national origin. Individuals who believe their rights have been violated can appeal to the Equal Employment Opportunity Commission, to the courts, or in some states, to the relevant state human rights commission.

Employee Retirement Income Security Act (1974). If an employer has installed a pension plan, it must meet certain standards regarding employee vesting of benefits, funding, and fiduciary standards.

Reporting a Violation of Water or Air Pollution Control Acts. The Federal Water Pollution Control Act and the Air Pollution Prevention and Contol Act (1977 Amendment) prohibit employers from discharging employees who initiate or participate in a proceeding to enforce any pollution control requirement imposed by these laws.

Wage Garnishment. The Consumer Credit Protection Act (1968) prohibits the firing of employees because their wages have been garnished due to their indebtedness.

Unemployment Compensation. Under state laws, individuals who have been laid off by their employer through no fault of their own can receive weekly unemployment payments, typically up to a maximum of 26 weeks.

Workers' Compensation. Each state has a Workers' Compensation Law which requires employers or their insurance companies to pay benefits to workers suffering from illness or injury caused at the workplace.

JOB PROTECTION

The laws outlined in the foregoing section protect employees against discharge or provide earnings protection under very specific circumstances. There is a vast area of employment circumstances not covered by these laws. A prominent authority estimates that 50 million private sector employees in the United States are unprotected against unjust discharge. He estimates that about one million nonunion private sector employees with more than six months of service are discharged each year without the right of appeal to an impartial arbitrator or tribunal. Of these, about 200,000 would have appealed their discharge if an opportunity were available, and probably 100,000 would have been reinstated to their jobs using "just cause" standards commonly applied by arbitrators.[4]

Most working Americans do not realize how vulnerable to discharge they are. If a nonunion or a nongovernmental employee should be fired from his job and if he should try to regain that job through judicial appeal, he would almost surely lose his appeal under the century-old common law doctrine of "employment-at-will." In innumerable court decisions, judges have ruled that when an employer hires a worker for an indefinite period of time, the employment relationship can be terminated by either party at any time for any reason or for no reason at all. Thus a supervisor may simply dislike a subordinate and fire him for that reason alone. Even if work performance is satisfactory, the employee would ordinarily lose if he appealed his discharge to a state court.

American judges in the 19th and early 20th centuries fashioned the employment-at-will doctrine out of the freedom-of-contract theory, which is central to the operation of our capitalistic system. The judges assumed that employers and employees entered into employment contracts (usually implied, not written) of their own free will, that bargaining power was about equal between the parties, and, therefore, that either party must be free to terminate the relationship whenever he or she wished and for whatever reason.

[4]Jack Steiber, "Nature and Significance of the Problem," in *Protecting Unorganized Employees Against Unjust Discharge* (East Lansing, Michigan: School of Labor and Industrial Relations, Michigan State University, 1983), p. 1.

Fallacies of Employment-at-Will Doctrine. Anyone who thinks carefully about the employment relationship in an organization can see that the employment-at-will doctrine is very unfair to working men and women. One's job is critically important for providing the income to support oneself and one's family. Unemployment creates an economic and psychological hardship. Prolonged unemployment can be devastating to the individual and his or her family. There exists an enormous imbalance of power between the employer and the employee. The old argument that the employee can quit at any time, and that therefore the company must be able to fire at will (even if the reason is flimsy or without merit), ignores the realities of employment. The loss of one employee does not jeopardize the organization, but the loss of one's job usually causes serious harm to the individual. Actions of corporations have extensive effects upon society. Those companies that discharge many people without just cause create extensive harm. Society expects a higher standard of conduct from American business.

Recent Developments

In recent years, courts in some states have begun to make exceptions to the employment-at-will doctrine in certain limited areas. These areas occur when the court determines that there existed an *implied contract* between the employer and the employee, and when the employee was discharged in violation of some *public policy.*

The implied contract exception to the employment-at-will doctrine can be illustrated by the cases of Charles Toussaint and Walter Ebling, both of whom were employed by Blue Cross and Blue Shield of Michigan. Both had been fired and then appealed to the court. In 1980, the Supreme Court of Michigan found that at the time of hiring, each received an oral promise that he would not be discharged as long as he did his job. Additionally, Toussaint was given an employment manual stating that it was company policy not to release nonprobationary employees except for just cause. The court ruled that both persons had been fired in violation of an implied contract and they were entitled to redress. Although the decision of the Michigan Supreme Court is precedent-setting in that state, the employment-at-will doctrine still holds in most other states. Only a few other courts have ordered redress to discharged employees under the implied contract theory.[5]

The other area of exception to the doctrine of employment-at-will occurs where management discharges an employee who is doing something directly in compliance with state law. For example, Marilyn Jo Kelsay cut her thumb while working in a factory. She was treated at a local hospital but returned to work the same day. The company personnel manager told her not to file a workers' compensation claim. He also informed her that it was company policy to discharge employees who submitted workers' compensation claims. Nevertheless, Ms. Kelsay did file such a claim and was promptly fired. Ms. Kelsay sued the company in court. The Illinois court awarded her compensatory damages, declaring that it was wrong to terminate at-will an employee who exercised her legal right to file a claim under the state's workers' compensation law.[6] State courts have also ordered discharged employees reinstated to their jobs when they were fired for serving on a jury, for refusing an order to lie when testifying in court, and for refusing to rig gasoline prices in violation of the law.

We have cited a few, narrow exceptions to the employment-at-will common law doctrine. Except for these specific instances, discharged employees usually can obtain no restitution for lost jobs if they appeal to the state courts.

[5]For contract theory limitations to employment-at-will, see Lorber, Lawrence Z., et. al., *Fear of Firing: A Legal and Personnel analysis of Employment-At-Will* (Alexandria, Virginia: American Society for Personnel Administration, 1984), pp. 7–10.

[6]*Ibid.*, p. 11.

Foreign Experience

European nations are ahead of the United States in providing, by law, protection against unfair dismissal. Let us look at the laws in Great Britain, France, and West Germany.

Great Britain. In 1978, the British Parliament enacted the Employment Protection Consolidation Act, which improved and combined the protections afforded to dismissed workers by previous laws. Under this law, employees who are to be dismissed must be given a certain minimum amount of notice, varying from only one week for those having less than two years of service to twelve weeks if the period of employment has been 12 years or more. By law, employees (except those with less than 52 weeks of continuous service and those in certain specified categories) have a right not to be unfairly dismissed by their employers. If employees feel that they have been unfairly dismissed they can appeal to an industrial tribunal which adjudicates their cases. Both the aggrieved employee and the employer present arguments and evidence to the tribunal. The burden of proof is placed upon neither; rather a neutral burden is used by the tribunal in weighing evidence. The tribunal determines the reasonableness and fairness of the employer's action, considering all the circumstances. The tribunal has the authority to order (1) reinstatement to the job held before dismissal, (2) reengagement to a different job, or (3) monetary compensation in lieu of reinstatement or reengagement.[7]

France. French labor law is based upon the concept of individual employment contracts, even if there is a union-employer agreement. The individual contract is often not in writing; rather, it is implied. Contracts of employment may be either of a definite duration (these are regulated by law) or they may be of undetermined length. Except for contracts in the enter-

[7]*Protecting Unorganized Employees Against Unjust Discharge,* op. cit. pp. 135–143.

tainment and agricultural industries, most contracts are of undetermined duration.

Dismissals can be either for economic reasons or for cause. Economic dismissals are essentially layoffs and must be approved by the Ministry of Labor. Workers so dismissed receive unemployment compensation. Our concern here is primarily with workers allegedly dismissed for cause.

Dismissal for cause is regulated by the Act of 1973. An employer has the right, under this law, to terminate an individual's employment contract of undetermined duration at any time, but in doing so the employer must follow a specified procedure and the dismissal must be for a "genuine and serious" cause. If the proper procedure is not followed or if the reason is not for a genuine and serious cause, the employer may have to pay monetary damages to the employee.

Procedurally, the employer is required to conduct a hearing for the worker prior to making the final decision. At the hearing, the grounds for possible dismissal must be explained to the employee. After the hearing, the employer must notify the employee in writing if he intends to dismiss him or her. Also, on request of the individual, the employer must state the specific grounds for dismissal in writing. If an employer fails to follow the proper procedure, the court may order him to go through the correct procedure.

The law recognizes several categories of "genuine and serious cause," such as incompetence, loss of physical aptitude, professional inadequacy, and loss of mutual confidence between an employee and a senior manager. If the court decides that a dismissal has not been for a genuine and serious cause, the dismissal is unlawful but not void. The court can propose reinstatement to the job previously held but it cannot order it. If either the employee or the employer refuses reinstatement, the court awards compensation of not less than six months' wages to the employee.[8]

Western Germany. The Works Council in Western German enterprises plays a key role in processing employee dismissal cases. A Works Council is composed of worker representatives who are elected, according to a formula, by the rank-and-file employees and by the union in the majority of German establishments. Works Councils have substantial power, especially in employee relations matters. The Act on Protection against Unfair Dismissals covers workers who have had six months or more of service in an establishment. Management must consult the Works Council on every dismissal before it occurs. If the opinion of the Council is not obtained, the dismissal is illegal. If the Council objects to a particular dismissal after it has been consulted by management, such objection does not legally prevent the dismissal. However, employers must obtain the cooperation of their Works Councils on many important matters. Because of this, they are reluctant to discharge someone in conflict with the wishes of the Council.

When a worker is discharged, with or without the concurrence of the Council, he or she has the right to appeal to a labor court. Labor courts are staffed with professional judges and with representatives of both unions and employer associations. The labor court studies all relevant aspects of each case. If it determines that the dismissal was not justified, it can order reinstatement. Rather than obtaining reinstatement to the job, in actual practice, the discharged worker is generally awarded monetary compensation in an amount determined by the court.[9]

What Can Be Done in America?

Because the problem of unjust discharges in America is serious, employers ought voluntarily to take the lead in setting up proper procedures within their own organizations to process and

[8]*Ibid.*, pp. 147–152.

[9]*Ibid.*, pp. 153–158.

adjudicate discharge cases. If private industry does not take the initiative, sooner or later, government will legislate solutions to this problem.

Some large nonunion corporations have established comprehensive personnel programs which include well-designed progressive discipline procedures as well as grievance-handling mechanisms that provide for a fair measure of due process and just cause in adverse actions against individuals.[10]

DUE PROCESS AND JUST CAUSE

Although a small minority of leading nonunion companies have created procedures providing for due process and just cause in handling potential terminations of employees, the vast preponderance of organizations has not. Employees and managers are terminated for both good and bad reasons, and with adequate notice or none. As stated before, business organizations ought voluntarily to develop procedures for investigating charges by managers that individuals should be terminated and procedures for processing appeals by employees who have been discharged.

Fair Procedures

There are many possible reasons why a supervisor or manager may want to terminate an employee. Common reasons are inadequate job performance, insubordination, alleged theft of company property, an illegal drug problem, excessive absenteeism, and conflict of interest. Sometimes groups of employees are laid off for economic reasons. It is important for management to have a procedure to prevent termination

[10]See for example, Fred Foulkes, *Personnel Policies in Large Nonunion Companies* (Englewood Cliffs, New Jersey: Prentice Hall, 1980), Chapter 15.

for some other reason (legitimate or illegitimate) from being labeled an economic layoff by the initiating manager.

In handling problems of inadequate or undesirable employee behavior, the organization should have in place sound programs of performance appraisal and employee discipline. These two topics are covered in other chapters of this book and will not be repeated here. However, it almost goes without saying that *correction* of undesirable behavior should be attempted before any initial decision to terminate is made.

In the field of collective bargaining—that is, union-management relationships—there is a well-established tradition of handling discipline, discharge, and grievances on the basis of just cause and due process. In the nonunion sector, these two important concepts are also being applied with a fair measure of frequency.

In deciding whether a particular disciplinary action was for *just cause*, arbitrators and labor relations specialists ask such questions as the following:

1. Was the employee adequately warned that this conduct could result in discipline?
2. Was the rule involved reasonably related to the safe and efficient conduct of the business?
3. Did management's investigation yield clear evidence of the employee's guilt?
4. Is the employee being treated fairly in comparison with others who have committed similar violations?

Due process procedures include the following key elements:

1. The employee who is being assessed a disciplinary penalty (including discharge) has a clear right to appeal his case through a well-defined process.
2. Management guarantees there will be no reprisal against the employee for using the appeal process.
3. The organization helps the employee obtain

an advocate or spokesperson who will assist the employee in preparing and presenting his case. In unionized organizations, this service is provided by the union. In nonunion establishments, the personnel department can make this assistance available.

4. The appeal or grievance process typically includes more than one adjudicative step. The final stage should consist of an impartial arbitrator, an impartial review committee, or in some cases a chief executive officer of the corporation who can take a detached view of the case.

Clyde W. Summers, a law professor and prominent arbitrator, argues that employees should be granted statutory protection against unjust discharge. The proposed law would require organizations to set up their own just cause and due process procedures. The final step would be binding arbitration following the model used in union-employer contracts.[11]

Several prominent American corporations have established due process grievance procedures for their nonunion personnel. These include the Pitney Bowes Corporation, Polaroid Corporation, Control Data, American Airlines, Trans World Airlines, American Optical Company, and the American Electric Power Company.

FREEDOM OF SPEECH AND WHISTLE-BLOWING

To what extent should employees, professionals, and managers be able to speak up freely about conditions and practices within the organization? By and large, work organizations have a strong authoritarian flavor. Subordinates are ex-

[11]Clyde W. Summers, "Protecting *All* Employees Against Unjust Dismissal," *Harvard Business Review,* vol. 58, no. 1 (January–February 1980), pp. 132–139.

pected to speak up about problems only when they are asked by their managers to do so. Some companies have suggestion systems in which rank-and-file workers are invited to submit written suggestions that might improve efficiency. Upper level managers often use internal auditors, industrial engineers, and personnel specialists to investigate problems and prepare reports on conditions in the organization. In unionized establishments, the grievance procedure can serve as a means of upward communication on employee complaints about employment conditions.

But, as a general practice, employees are expected to be loyal to their superiors. Those who uncover serious problems within the enterprise and who vigorously voice their concerns are usually penalized rather than rewarded for their efforts.

Let us look at the case of A. Ernest Fitzgerald. In 1965, he was hired by the U.S. Air Force as a deputy for management systems in the Office of the Assistant Secretary for Financial Management. Fitzgerald was an industrial engineer and his job responsibility centered on cost control. His Civil Service pay grade was GS-17, the next to the top Civil Service grade. Fitzgerald's performance evaluations during 1966 and 1967 were "outstanding."

Starting in 1966 and throughout 1967, Mr. Fitzgerald informed his superiors that the C-5A cargo airplane being designed and built by the Lockheed Corporation for the Air Force was experiencing huge cost overruns. Eventually, the overruns would reach $2 billion. Senator William Proxmire learned about these overruns and invited Fitzgerald to testify before a Joint Economic Subcommittee of Congress in the fall of 1968. This was the beginning of Fitzgerald's downfall in the Air Force. His bosses removed him from important projects and assigned him to trivial projects. In November 1969, despite his career Civil Service status Fitzgerald was fired. His activities had been embarrassing to Air Force officials. They accused him of not being a team player and of passing information about

Air Force matters to certain members of Congress. In effect, they accused him of being a "whistleblower" because he brought to the attention of Congress serious errors in the Air Force's procurement system.[12]

In March 1972, three engineers employed by the San Francisco Bay Area Rapid Transit District, commonly known as BART, were fired because they had uncovered serious safety flaws in the automatic control system of the vast commuter railroad then under construction. The three engineers had tried repeatedly to get their superiors to take action on the safety defects, but they were rebuffed. They then went to a member of the board of directors who listened to their concerns. This board member engaged the services of an outside consulting engineer who studied the problem and issued a report supporting the position taken by the engineers. Then the general manager fired the three engineers because the position they had taken on the serious passenger safety defects was embarrassing to him. So we see that instead of commending the engineers for their professional competence and concern for public safety, management fired all three without explanation and without a hearing.[13]

Because of the power of the employment-at-will doctrine, courageous employees who speak up or who expose malfeasance in the organization are often rewarded for their efforts with dismissal.

It is only in recent years that the courts have begun to protect the employee right of freedom of speech. To date, only employees in governmental organizations have begun to obtain free speech rights, and then only under limited circumstances. Those working in private sector establishments are unprotected.

In Pickering v. Board of Education[14], the U.S. Supreme Court ruled that it was illegal for a school board to fire a high school teacher who had written a letter to a local newspaper criticizing the way the school board had handled recent bond issues. The court ruled that public sector employees have certain constitutional rights to free speech. Since the 1968 Supreme Court decision, the lower courts have developed guidelines to determine what is proper and improper speech. In ruling on employee appeals of discharge over free speech issues, the courts examine such matters as whether the employee used obscene language (the minimum of courtesy standard), the truth or falsity of the content of his communication, and the motivation for the speech. The courts have also ruled that the employee involved must not damage the organization without good cause.[15]

Free Speech in Private Business

Within reason and with appropriate limits, employees in private sector organizations ought to have free speech rights. Free speech is part and parcel of the democratic heritage in the United States. Outside of the workplace, it has always been a deeply cherished right, protected by the U.S. Constitution. Employees should be able to exercise their social and "corporate citizenship rights" without jeopardizing their jobs. If management makes decisions without obtaining inputs from a variety of persons within the organization, it is liable to make faulty decisions. Often top management team members tend to think alike. They become homogenized. Employees, lower level managers, and professionals have much to contribute. They generally want to make their voices heard. Top management should listen.

Several corporations have set up programs

[12]Ralph Nader, Peter J. Petkas, and Kate Blackwell, eds., *Whistle Blowing: The Report of the Conference on Professional Responsibility* (New York: Grossman Publishers, 1972), Chapter 5.

[13]David Ewing, *"Do It My Way Or You're Fired,"* op. cit., pp. 118–131.

[14]Pickering v. Board of Education, 391 U.S. 563 (1968).

[15]Kenneth Walters, "Employee Freedom of Speech," *Industrial Relations*, vol. 15, (February 1976), pp. 26–43.

that provide employees with an official, legitimate method for voicing their concerns about activities within the company. Among these are Atlantic Richfield, General Electric, Dow Chemical Company, American Airlines, Pitney-Bowes, Inc., and Delta Air Lines.[16]

Employee free speech can take various forms and deal with many topics. One employee may orally express his concerns about working conditions and plant safety to an immediate superior. A staff engineer may highlight inadequacies in production equipment in a report to her boss. Another employee may write to the company president suggesting improvements in certain employee benefits. Employees who complain about improper, unethical, or unlawful activities, and who take their complaints to the government or news media if their concerns are ignored by management, are known as "whistle blowers."

To date only modest efforts have been made to protect whistle blowers from being fired. The Civil Service Reform Act of 1978 contains provisions to protect employees in the federal government who blow the whistle on illegal, corrupt, or wasteful activities. However, the Office of the Special Counsel of the Merit Systems Protection Board, the office holding the responsibility for handling whistle-blowing problems, has not functioned effectively in this field. It has been underfunded and understaffed.

In 1981, the State of Michigan enacted a law to protect whistle blowers in private industry. This law protects employees who have been fired or disciplined for reporting alleged violations of federal, state, or local law to public authorities. Such individuals can bring an action in state court for unjust reprisal. If successful in court, the employees can be reinstated to their jobs and be awarded back pay and attorney's fees.[17]

[16]David Ewing, "Constitutionalizing the Corporation," in *Corporations and their Critics*, Thornton Bradshaw and David Vogel, eds. (New York: McGraw-Hill Book Co., 1982).

[17]Alan F. Westin, "Michigan's Law to Protect the Whistle Blowers," *Wall Street Journal*, April 13, 1981.

The issue of employee privacy in the work establishment has emerged only relatively recently. Traditionally, employees have had very few privacy rights.

Here is a sampling of privacy issues that have been raised by employees, unions, legislators, and scholars in recent years.

- Forcing employees to take lie detector tests as a condition for retaining their jobs.
- Inspecting the contents of employees' desks, files, and lockers.
- Monitoring employees' telephone conversations.
- Personality testing.
- Background investigations during the hiring process.

A new form of potential privacy invasion is electronic surveillance of employees at their work stations. Such surveillance has been made possible through the use of electronic computers. The purpose is to count and record the output of the employees and to make comparisons against standards or a peer group of workers. The kinds of employees being monitored include supermarket checkers, bank tellers and check processors, discount stock brokers, insurance claims processors, airline reservation clerks, and hospital workers.[18] Some workers and health specialists have expressed concern that excessive stress is being placed upon employees through these surveillance devices.

Certainly some intrusion upon employee privacy may be legitimate and justified by the needs of the business. If management has been facing a problem of employee theft it may have to inspect employees' lunch boxes and briefcases when they leave the plant.

[18]"Corporate Big Brother Is Watching You," *Dun's Business Month*, January 1984, 36–39.

If company trade secrets have been given to a competitor or if funds have been embezzled, is it proper to subject all employees to a lie detector test? Many employers would like to do this in the hope of finding the culprits. And indeed many companies do administer lie detector tests to their employees periodically. However, many states have imposed controls upon the use of the lie detector, or polygraph, in employment situations. The rationale for the restrictive legislation is that a lie detector violates the U.S. Constitution's protection against self-incrimination. Also lie detectors are prone to error in interpretation of their measurements.

Some progressive companies have instituted policies to protect the privacy of employees in regard to information in company personnel files. For example, Chase Manhattan Bank has adopted a policy that employees may individually see identifiable information in their personnel files and must give prior approval for release of any data to outsiders except to confirm employment dates. The company promises that sensitive information, such as medical files, is kept separate from personnel files.[19]

OFF-THE-JOB BEHAVIOR

The case of Phillip Woodroofe and the steel company described in the introduction to this chapter illustrates what might happen to an employee or manager whose off-the-job community activities displease top management.

Many possible off-the-job involvements of employees can occur. Should the following activities be encouraged, tolerated, discouraged, or prohibited by management?

• An engineer is elected to the presidency of a

regional division of a national professional society.
• An employee serves on the local school board.
• An employee seeks office as a city councilwoman in the city in which the company is located.
• An employee starts up a part-time business using, in part, certain technical information gained on his or her job.
• To supplement his income, an employee works four hours each evening, Monday through Friday, on a part-time job.

Most organizations do not have detailed policies governing off-the-job behavior. They allow or even encourage certain types of community involvement under the theory that such activities enhance the establishment's image and may make the community a better place to live. They also judge each situation on its merits. Will the outside activity help the organization? Will it conflict with the employee's primary duty to the company? Will the outside activity harm the organization's reputation?

PROTECTION AGAINST LAYOFFS

A layoff is a termination for economic reasons and is generally not based upon some inadequacy of the individual. Layoffs are frequent in American industry due to the action of business cycles, fluctuations in the demand for products and services of individual companies, and management policies.

Working men and women in Japan and Europe enjoy much more stable employment than do those in the United States. Many American executives tend to be "quick on the trigger" to layoff people if the profit reports for a division or plant take a temporary downturn.

Progressive companies, such as IBM and Lincoln Electric, long ago adopted "no layoff"

[19]"Respecting Employee Privacy," *Business Week,* January 11, 1982, pp. 130–131.

policies, but these companies are the exception. Although business firms can hardly avoid some layoffs in times of general economic recession, there is much that they could do to stabilize employment in normal economic times. To avoid layoffs, management can transfer employees from one plant where business is slow to another where business is good. Concurrent with such action is the necessity of adequate training programs to train people for more than one job skill. Management can engage in strategic planning to help develop more product lines so that business may be strong in new lines if it slows down in older ones. Strong and well-managed companies can, as a matter of company policy, absorb the costs of keeping employees on the payroll for periods of weeks when sales of a given product or service may be down temporarily. Strong companies have more adequate resources to absorb such economic shocks than do individual workers.

Questions for Review and Discussion

1. Why have American business executives been so slow in developing due process and just cause procedures for employees and managers who are being discharged?
2. If you were the chief executive officer of a corporation, what policy would you adopt regarding "whistle blowing"?
3. Suggest some guidelines for the handling of whistle-blowing matters within the organization.
4. One argument in favor of the retention of the employment-at-will doctrine is that a manager should not be denied the authority to fire a subordinate even if for such a reason as not liking the subordinate. Discuss.
5. If companies adopted policies to stabilize employment, to provide for just cause and due process, and to protect employee privacy, what would be the likely consequences in terms of employee morale, productivity, and economic strength?
6. Do you think any elements of the British, French, or West German systems for handling employee dismissals could be adopted in the United States?

Suggestions for Further Reading

Coulson, Robert. "The Way It Is—Rules of the Game—How to Fire." *Across the Board*, Vol. XIX, No. 2 (February 1982), pp. 30–48.

———, *The Termination Handbook*. New York: Macmillan Publishing Co., Inc., 1981.

The Employment-at-Will Issue. Washington, D.C.: Bureau of National Affairs, 1982.

Ewing, David W., *Do It My Way or You're Fired*. New York: John Wiley & Sons, Inc., 1983.

———, "What Business Thinks About Employee Rights." *Harvard Business Review*, Vol. 55, No. 5 (September–October 1977), pp. 81–94.

Miller, Ronald L. "Worker Privacy and Collective Bargaining." *Labor Law Journal*, Vol. 33, No. 3 (March 1982), pp. 154–168.

Prentice-Hall Editorial Staff. *Employee Access to Records*. Englewood Cliffs, N.J.: Prentice-Hall, Inc., 1984.

Summers, Clyde W. "Protecting *All* Employees Against Unjust Dismissal." *Harvard Business Review*, Vol. 58, No. 1 (January–February 1980), pp. 132–139.

"Unjust Dismissal." *ILR Report*, Vol. XX, No. 1 (Fall 1982), New York State School of Industrial and Labor Relations, Ithaca, New York. (Nine articles by various authors.)

Westin, Alan F., ed., *Whistle Blowing: Loyalty and Dissent in the Corporation*. New York: McGraw-Hill Book Company, 1981.

PART IX

Perspectives

27

Personnel Management in Perspective

The process of managing any organization requires knowledge and skills in the economic, technical, and human relations spheres. The effective manager must possess real understanding of the nature of people, the determinants of interpersonal effectiveness, and the ramifications of intergroup relations.

The key to organization building is to invest in human resources. This is true whether we are talking about a university, an industrial corporation, a city government, or a military force. Many top executives are ignorant of this vital concept. They concentrate their attention so heavily upon the technical phases of the business (such as the details of new product development, financial controls, or marketing) that they neglect investment in their people.

How does an organization invest in human resources? There are many ways. At an elementary level it consists of investment in a decent, healthful, and safe working environment. Beyond this it means offering attractive wages and job opportunities so that the establishment can attract competent employees. If management pays wages well below competitive rates, it cannot hope to build a really vigorous organization. The viable company devotes continuous attention to the education and training of its employees. I have observed time and again that differences in this one dimension—education and training—correlate significantly with the degree of effectiveness and success of organizations. Emphasis upon the development of people means such things as comprehensive in-house training, reimbursement of employees' tuition costs at neighboring colleges and universities, sending managers and engineers to professional seminars, circulating professional and technical journals within the company, and sending executives to advanced-management university programs. Investment in human resources also means providing a day-to-day climate where people are encouraged to make decisions and accept responsibility. It means supportive supervision and effective appraisal and coaching. Fundamentally, effective management depends upon the existence of an underlying philosophy that people-centered and achievement-oriented management is what really counts.

We have shown in this book that the practice of personnel management comprises two stems. The first is that component—the management of people at work—which pervades the entire organization. The president cannot hire a personnel director to handle all the human problems of management so that he or she can concentrate upon financial and technical activities. Personnel management and general management are intimately related. Operating executives cannot abdicate their very considerable responsibilities for selecting, developing, motivating, and leading people as they carry on their daily activities.

The second main stem of personnel management is that carried on and guided by the staff personnel department. This work entails the development and dissemination of personnel policies, provision of specialized services and counsel to the whole corporation, and the application of control measures to regulate the human resources climate. The work content of the personnel office is centered in such prime functions as organization and human resource planning, employment, labor relations, health and safety, education, benefits and services, and pay administration. Many who study the field of personnel, organizational behavior, and industrial relations intend to make it their vocation. It holds promising career opportunities. Let us now look into personnel work as a career.

PERSONNEL (HUMAN RESOURCE) MANAGEMENT AS A CAREER

Those desiring to pursue careers in personnel (human resource) management should obtain a college education. This field has not achieved the degree of specialized professionalism that medicine and law have. Thus, there is no single pattern of education that is specified for entry into this career. Nearly all of the universities and many of the colleges in the United States offer courses and integrated programs of study in personnel management, industrial relations, and organizational behavior. Administratively these programs are given in schools of business administration, management, and industrial relations. In addition to majors in personnel, industrial relations, and organizational behavior, students ought to obtain a thorough grounding in general studies with special emphasis upon the social sciences (sociology, psychology, political science, and economics). In the applied business administration field they ought also to take courses in statistics, data processing, finance, production, business policy, and the social and legal environment of business. For those who wish to pursue careers in technical industries, a baccalaureate degree in engineering followed by a master's degree in business administration is a very sound educational plan. Some who wish to specialize in labor relations and collective bargaining may study liberal arts or business administration at the undergraduate level and then go to law school for their graduate work.

Beginning or entry-level positions in this field are such jobs as job analyst, employment interviewer, personnel trainee, training specialist, and labor-relations specialist. Actually, for the recent college graduate there are several routes for entry into personnel work. She may be hired by a company directly into one of the entry-level positions. Some of our larger corporations such as the General Electric Company and others have formal training programs in employee relations. Another very common route is for the young college graduate to be hired initially into some other activity such as manufacturing or operations and then transfer to the personnel–industrial relations department within a few years. This approach has the advantage of orienting the individual to the technology of the company, to its policies, and to its people.

Position Levels

In the large corporation there are three principal levels of positions in personnel (human resource) management. First there is the specialist level. The specialist level includes the entry-level jobs previously mentioned plus the professional specialists such as physician, nurse, psychologist, safety engineer, labor lawyer, and personnel researcher. Many of the professional specialist positions require advanced education and training. In prestige, rank, and salary certain of these, such as the physician, psychologist, and labor lawyer, are equivalent to middle management in the large company. The second or next level of positions consists of the managers in charge of the various functional branches of personnel. Thus, we find the manager or supervisor of labor relations, the manager of employment, and the manager of wage and salary administration. In the organization hierarchy these people are part of middle management. In addition to their managerial abilities, they must possess considerable knowledge and skill in the functional personnel specialty they are supervising. A manager of employment must know a great deal about sources of supply, selection testing, inteviewing, job specifications, manpower planning, and selective placement.

The third level of position in personnel in the big company is the top management or major executive level. The executive in charge of personnel-industrial relations is designated most commonly as the vice-president of personnel, vice-president of industrial relations, or director of human resources. This person typically reports to the president of the organization or to an executive vice-president and is involved in policy formulation and administration and coordination with all major units in the corporation. He or she guides the development and installation of major personnel programs.

In the smaller company there would be fewer jobs and fewer levels in the personnel department. Generally one would find the director or top executive postion plus certain of the functional positions. There would be less division of labor. One individual might handle all employment and training tasks. Another might be responsible for pay administration and labor relations. In the really small organization the personnel department might consist of only the manager of personnel plus a secretary.

Job Opportunities and Salaries

For those who have a reasonable amount of experience in personnel work, say three to five years or more, job opportunities are quite good. One need only read the advertisements in the *Wall Street Journal* or *The New York Times* to learn about job openings for labor relations manager, recruitment specialist, compensation manager, vice-president of employee relations, and a variety of other personnel occupations. Personnel opportunities with state and Federal governments are also rather abundant. Those lacking either special experience in the field or specialized education find it somewhat difficult to enter this career.

In 1976 a total of 335,000 people in the United States were engaged in personnel and labor relations work. Three fourths of these were employed in the private sector and one fourth worked for Federal, state, and local governments. The U.S. Department of Labor has forecasted that the number of persons employed in the field of personnel and labor relations will grow faster than the average for all occupations through 1985.[1] A major force causing growth in the field has been Federal legislation in the areas of equal employment opportunity, occupational safety and health, and pension plan regulation. Another important factor has been the greater recognition by managers of the need for sound human resource programs to insure the viability and strength of their enterprises.

Salaries for entry-level positions are essentially the same as those offered business administration graduates generally. This is a little lower than beginning pay for engineers and scientists. Supervisory and executive posts in employee relations command pay that is essentially equivalent to that paid other managerial positions of similar rank within the organization.

[1]U.S. Department of Labor, Bureau of Labor Statistics *Occupational Outlook Handbook, 1978–79 Edition,* Bulletin 1955 (Washington, D.C.), pp. 150–153.

Salaries for these managerial jobs correlate highly with the size of the company. The top personnel executive in a small company (under 1,000 employees) will typically be paid from $30,000 to $45,000 per year. But in the large corporation salaries will lie in the $60,000 to $85,000 range with a few going even higher.

Some familiarity with the kinds of jobs available in the personnel field can be gained by mentioning job titles given in the "Positions Available" section of recent issues of the *Job Placement Newsletter* of the American Society for Personnel Administration Employment Service.[2] The following titles are illustrative:

Director for Personnel & Training
Benefits & Compensation Manager
Senior Compensation Analyst
Recruiter
Human Resources Administrator
Staffing Manager
Employee Relations Manager
Manager, Employee Benefits
Management Development Specialist
Personnel/Labor Relations Director
Personnel Data Analyst
Manager of Human Resources

Status and Professionalism

In many companies the personnel director serves as a key member of the top management group. Often he or she enjoys vice-presidential status. In many companies the personnel director serves as a key advisor to the president and to the whole top-management team, carrying great weight in shaping personnel policy, labor policy, formulating executive development programs, and in designing employee and executive compensation plans.

²*Job Placement Newsletters, ASPA Employment Service,* Alexandria, Va.: American Society for Personnel Administration, Issues. April 1983, June–July 1983, October–November 1983, January–February 1984.

In the area of professionalism, personnel practitioners have made considerable progress. Educational programs at the university level have been mentioned previously. There are a number of professional associations that are national in scope. Among these are the Industrial Relations Research Association, the International Personnel Management Association, American Society for Personnel Administration, the American Society for Training and Development, the College and University Personnel Association, and the Personnel Division of the American Management Associations. Active in most of the major metropolitan areas are local personnel managers associations.

In the mid-1970s the American Society for Personnel Administration set up a program to accredit personnel and industrial relations practitioners based upon a series of examinations plus education and work experience standards. Their program provides for two types of accreditation: Professional in Human Resources and Senior Professional in Human Resources.

Yet there is another side to this whole picture. In far too many situations, and especially in small-sized organizations, top management staffs the personnel department with individuals of only modest capabilities and skills. Too often a person gets the position of personnel manager because he is loyal, has worked for the company a long time, is familiar with company traditions, and gets along well with others. Such an individual generally looks upon his job as one of hiring and firing workers, keeping records, and administering the cafeteria, charity drives, and company parties and picnics. One can usually recognize whether the personnel manager and his staff are assigned a low status when the personnel functions for the executive, professional, and sales groups are handled by someone else attached to the chief executive's office and collective bargaining is handled by the company's legal counsel.

When placed in proper perspective, the executive in charge of the personnel function should be of major executive caliber and should serve as a member of the top-management team. His counsel should play a significant part (along with that of those in other functional parts of the business) in shaping decisions pertaining to company expansion or contraction, new facilities, plant relocation, organization planning, personnel policy, labor policy, executive development, and community relations policy.

The responsibility for insuring that the chief personnel executive sits in the halls of top management rests both with the personnel profession and with chief executive officers throughout industry. The personnel profession must continuously strive to educate and train its members for higher standards of competence, and it must educate top management regarding the values and contributions of personnel management. In staffing the personnel-industrial relations department, the chief executive officer must select people with demonstrated professional competence and then give them the necessary support to be really effective.

Is personnel (human resource) management a distinct profession in the same sense as engineering and law? Or is it but a part of the broader, emerging profession of management? Does a manager who has been successful in marketing, production, or general management necessarily possess the qualifications to be a successful personnel director? Have the technical and knowledge requirements for personnel management grown to the point where only those who have had college preparation plus specific work experience in the field are qualified to assume the responsibilities of personnel director? In selecting individuals to manage engineering, accounting, and research functions, top management invariably chooses those who have professional education and work experience in these respective fields.

The author finds that the specialist and first-level supervisory positions in personnel are coming to demand specialized professional training. Thus, in this sense, personnel work is becoming a distinct profession in itself. On the other hand, the position of director of personnel

demands skills, abilities, and aptitudes that are common to nearly all top-management work. Thus, at this level in the organization, the position requires general management talent. A top-level manager should consider that his or her profession is management. He or she may be equally effective in various managerial posts at this level. However, the executive in charge of the personnel function should have had considerable professional education and experience in personnel work before being placed in the position.

ACCOMPLISHMENTS AND CONTINUING NEEDS

As we come to the end of this book it is pertinent to review briefly the accomplishments in the personnel field to date and to highlight some of the principal unsolved or persistent problems that must command the attention of theorists, policy makers, and practitioners in the future.

In discussing progress that has been achieved, it should be borne in mind that we are making generalizations. The actual state of affairs in particular enterprises may deviate widely from the levels depicted. Specifically, many companies do fall short of the levels described.

Personnel Practices

The practice of personnel management in business and public institutions has grown from infancy to young adulthood in the past sixty years. For the most part organized hiring, training, and wage administration programs were nonexistent sixty years ago. Most of these functions were done very haphazardly by line supervision. The organized safety movement was just getting started in 1913. Pensions and health insurance were provided by only a handful of companies throughout the nation. Paid vacations for hourly workers generally did not exist.

Today employee selection is handled by means of planned interviews, validated selection tests, medical examinations, and background investigations. Many of the large corporations are using assessment centers to identify persons with management potential. Management recognizes that new employees do not learn well by looking over the shoulders of older workers, but rather they must go through a planned training effort. Management also recognizes that long years of experience as an individual contributor do not automatically qualify one for promotion to supervision. Nowadays both potential and practicing supervisors are given classroom and on-the-job training in management fundamentals. Rational wage determination via job evaluation, formal pay structures, and wage surveys has become well accepted throughout industry. Ten paid holidays and two to three weeks paid vacation per year are now commonplace. Four weeks vacation after fifteen years of service is becoming increasingly popular. Comprehensive health and dental insurance, paid partially or entirely by the employer, is now widespread. Group life insurance, weekly disability benefits, pensions, and separation pay have all become well established by the mid-1980s.

Whereas a few years ago personnel specialists devoted most of their attention to the problems of blue-collar workers, more recently they have properly taken cognizance of the change in the composition of the work force and are now achieving a sophistication in developing programs for managerial and professional personnel.

Problems and Needs. There is need for small business firms to upgrade their personnel practices and benefit programs. Lacking specialized personnel staffs, many small companies have only a rudimentary personnel program. Millions of Americans who are employed in small businesses have no pension plan coverage whatever (other than legally mandated Social Security).

Personnel executives need to examine their various programs and practices to determine if they continue to meet contemporary needs and goals. Much "me-too-ism" prevails in the personnel field. It is not always necessary to follow the latest fashion in regard to training and motivational techniques. For example, zero-defects programs that were so popular in the 1960s are all but forgotten now.

Whereas many companies have built sound financial compensation programs from the standpoint of equity and consistency, relatively few have done a good job of designing their pay programs from a motivational or total systems incentive framework. Also they have not adequately integrated nonfinancial with financial incentives.

A persistent problem in many companies and many industries is that of periodic employee layoffs. In attitude surveys workers always rate job security as an important need. Yet this motive is frustrated quite frequently. Company officials need to give more thought to methods of regularizing employment. Some layoffs are inevitable, however. Better and more liberal income maintenance benefits ought to be provided for the affected employees.

Health and Safety

Unquestionably American industry has accomplished a great deal over the years toward providing a safe workplace. However, serious problems remain.

National statistics show that the injury frequency rate climbed steadily throughout the 1960s. A rising awareness of a serious workplace safety and health problem caused Congress to pass the Occupational Safety and Health Act in 1970. However, national injury statistics do not reveal any substantial improvement in national injury experience since enactment of this law.

During the 1970s authorities began to recognize that hundreds and even thousands of workers in many occupations and many industries were becoming victims of occupational diseases. Mesothelioma (caused by asbestos dust), byssinosis (caused by cotton dust), and pneumoconiosis (caused by coal dust) are just a few diseases that have received prominent attention in recent years. Hundreds of new chemicals are put on the market each year. Many of these are toxic. The latency period for the emergence of symptoms for the diseases caused by these substances often is long. Hence it can be hard to prove cause and effect. Far more effort and resources must be directed to the occupational disease problem.

Another area for concern is the generally poor performance of small business in job health and safety.

Mental health as it may be affected by one's job is an area that has been insufficiently recognized. The real stake that the employer has in controlling worker alcoholism is just beginning to be understood.

Personnel Research

A great deal of research—both university- and company-based—has been conducted over the past thirty to forty years. Research findings are available in many areas of concern to the people-oriented manager. To identify just a few, significant research-based knowledge has been developed in the areas of absenteeism, motivation, morale, performance appraisal, the problems of the professional employee in industry, organization design, communication, accident causes, industrial toxicology and medicine, and pay incentives.

Some of the larger corporations have established their own research units to conduct investigations into human resource areas. Prominent among these is the Behavioral Research Service of the General Electric Company. Texas Instruments, Procter and Gamble, and General Motors also have units devoted to behavioral and personnel research.

The problems encountered in such research are complex and the results obtained are occasionally contradictory; nevertheless, substantial progress is being made. Managers nowadays need rely less upon trial and error and rule of thumb.

Problems and Needs. Despite the progress much more research in the human resources field needs to be done by corporations themselves. Compared with funds spent on products and hardware the amounts spent on organizational social systems are minuscule. "In-house" research results need to be more adequately reported in professional and scientific journals so that others may benefit and so that dialogue between university contributors and industry researchers may be enhanced.

Here are a few of the more pressing needs for more research. In the area of selection testing we need culture-fair tests to overcome the problem of unintentional discrimination against minorities. The state of the art of personality testing is still inadequate. We need to know much more about how to make the interview contribute to the validity of a hiring decision. Job design is developing into an exciting area for research. Job design and organizational design must be related in a more effective way. The accounting profession is trying to develop a useful system of human resource valuation so that human assets can be more objectively figured into corporate planning. The personnel profession must work closely with the accountants to help accomplish this difficult task.

Knowledge about conflict resolution is just beginning to be generated. This needs to focus upon all facets—interpersonal, intragroup, intergroup, and interorganization.

The relationship between the culture of the organization and of groups within the organization to styles of leadership and organizational practices needs to be more thoroughly explored. Despite the outpouring of articles and monographs about worker alienation, much more research needs to be done in this area.

Union-Management Relations

Until the late 1930s union-management relations, for the most part, featured labor spies, strikebreakers, discharge of union sympathizers, picket line violence, uncompromising employers, and militant union leaders.

Today, thanks to a generous assist from Federal labor legislation, organized labor has won its battles for recognition and acceptance as equals in dealings with management spokesmen. The old-time deep-seated hostility on the part of management and militancy on the part of union officials has largely disappeared. To the casual observer the modern sophisticated union official is indistinguishable from his management counterpart when seated at the conference table.

The union movement has largely won most of its longtime struggles for decent wages, shorter hours, seniority and job rights, a voice in workload determination, and employee security benefits. Agricultural employment is an exception. Disagreements arising over the administration and interpretation of the labor agreement are settled peacefully by use of voluntary labor arbitration.

Problems and Needs. Although the days of open warfare between organized labor and management have happily passed into history, and although countless relationships have matured into a cooperative atmosphere, to a considerable extent the picture bears many of the characteristics of an uneasy truce. Many American managements have never really accepted unionism as a necessary and permanent institution. Indeed, they yearn for the day when management can rid itself of the interferences and challenges caused by unionism. Many managements feel that they know what is best for their employees and that union leaders do not truly represent the interests of their constituents.

For their part many union leaders have not altered their philosophy, derived from the days of open conflict, to conform to the realities of the 1980s. They have not been sufficiently adaptable to meet the problems of a newer age. At times they have ignored the long-range consequences of their actions upon the prosperity of business, wage-price levels, and employment. Organized labor has been slow to advance educated young men and women with new ideas to positions of leadership.

Increasingly in recent years, because of the interdependent nature of our society, union strikes against employers tend also to become strikes against the general public because its goods and services are shut off.

Collective bargaining in the public sector has now become an accepted institution for the Federal government and for about half of the states. Yet experience in the private sector has not always been the best guide for policy in the public sector. For example, the unit of government that negotiates labor agreements—the executive branch—does not have authority to appropriate the funds to pay for the settlement. This is a legislative function. The issue of sovereignty of government and what to do about strikes has not been worked out effectively. Public-employee strikes are banned by statute in most jurisdictions yet strikes occasionally occur anyway. How should these be handled and how should striking public employees be treated? Several states have legalized public employee strikes if no emergency or major inconvenience is involved. Should other states follow their lead? Members of management, from foremen on up, are generally denied the right of collective-bargaining representation in private industry. Yet lower- and middle-level administrators in government often are unionized. Should this pattern continue in the future?

Ethics and Values

Problems and Needs. The whole field of ethics and values in management and in human relations practices in work organizations has received insufficient attention. Periodically there is a public outcry about deceptive business practices, stock manipulations, conflict-of-interest transactions, and fraud perpetrated by buccaneer businesspeople. But these affairs concern mostly investors, corporate officers, customers, suppliers, and government regulatory agencies. There is less public knowledge of unethical and improper practices in the management of people within enterprises.

There needs to be a much more careful examination of values within the organization, that is, of values and standards of conduct among managers, employees, and union. What are the value implications of the internal struggles for power within the organization? Can executives justify the sabotaging of another person's career in order to advance their own? Is it right for top management to seek to destroy the very union that the employees have chosen, in a democratic election, to represent them in dealings with management?

What should management do with the faithful, long-service employee who can no longer cope with an enlarged and complex job? Changes in technology and advances in the state of an art often proceed faster than some engineers and supervisors can accommodate. Should management discard these people? Or should it give them a sinecure and design the organization so that the work flows away from them?

How can ethical standards be adopted, accepted, and enforced? How can they be upgraded? Do managers as a leadership elite have a mission to develop higher standards of conduct? Or is their day-to-day behavior merely a reflection of the prevailing standards of society?

Some measures would help in these matters. We need searching examinations of the current situation by associations representing management generally. We also need a similar study by the personnel-industrial relations profession. Codes of ethics and standards of conduct need to be formulated, agreed upon, promulgated, and enforced. These actions are much easier said than done. There are several professional societies active in the general management field and in the personnel-industrial area. Lacking is a unified voice as exists in medicine, law, psychology, architecture, and other professions. In 1958 the American Society for Personnel Administration adopted a code of ethics. However, this statement is very general and it has not been widely publicized.

In the traditional self-employed professions the client, who needs to be protected by standards of conduct, is well known and easily identified. But who is the client of the personnel officer in a bureaucratic organization? Is it the employer or is it the employee?

Constitutionalism and Organizational Justice

Historically in the United States employee rights were accorded a status distinctly subservient to the rights of employers. The property rights of ownership reigned supreme. The unilateral right of an employer to hire and fire at will and to operate the business as the employer saw fit was largely assumed and unchallenged. Today, the "employment-at-will" concept is being widely questioned.

But in recent years private business has begun to accord greater protection, security and rights to employees. This change has developed as a consequence of protective labor legislation, unionism, and a changed social attitude on the part of management. As a consequence of the laws and regulations governing equal employment opportunity and age discrimination, it is illegal for employers to discriminate against individuals in regard to hiring, compensation, or terms of employment because of race, color, religion, sex, national origin, or age.

The presence of unions has resulted in greater job rights for workers. Layoffs are generally determined by seniority. An employee can appeal grievances through a formal grievance procedure and even get a hearing before an impartial arbitrator. Discipline and discharge must be handled by due process procedures.

The labor-relations law of the land prevents discrimination or discharge solely because of a person's union activities. In recent years court decisions have tended to grant greater recognition to job rights in cases of plant shutdowns and relocations.

The foregoing comments do not mean that employers cannot discharge someone for just cause. No one is guaranteed absolute job security regardless of transgressions.

Problems and Needs. Despite the progress that has been made there are serious deficiencies. Some writers argue that we need to establish corporate constitutionalism or organizational justice.[3] Collective-bargaining rights cover only about one quarter of the labor force. Except for those in government service, salaried personnel are not represented by unions. Administrators, managers, and professionals are vulnerable to discharge by whim in many organizations. Honest disagreements over salary, job assignments, workloads, and promotion opportunities tend to be settled by power and authority rather than by reference to corporation policies and impartial dispute settlement procedures. Arbitration of such disagreements is almost never used.

Constitutionalism in work organizations means basically the rule of law with dispute settlement by an impartial judiciary. Written policies are the laws of an enterprise. They must deal with all the major rights, responsibilities, and problems likely to be encountered in the management of a work force. Voluntary arbitration or something comparable can serve as the impartial judiciary for the organization. The process is well established in the unionized sector. Something comparable needs to be set up in the nonunion sector.

The matters of protecting employee's privacy and providing guidelines for employee free speech within the organization have only very recently been given consideration by a few leaders in the field of human resource management.

The issue of "whistle blowers" within work organizations has received national publicity in recent years, and deservedly so. The persecution of A. Ernest Fitzgerald, a high-level civil service management systems expert, by U.S. Department of Defense officials because he reported vast cost overruns in the Lockheed C-5A air cargo plane program in the late 1960s is a cause célèbre. A whistle blower is an employee who tries to correct or make known improper or illegal practices often committed by upper level managers. Instead of being rewarded for his actions, the whistle blower is usually downgraded, transferred, or fired.

Most employees are afraid to report possible improper actions within their own organizations. Even a high-level official can have difficulty in correcting possible wrongdoing as evidenced by the two-year struggle of a public utility vice-president to rectify an improperly large (he thought) electric rate increase.[4]

The adoption of policies and procedures to provide for organizational justice would go a long way to solve this important problem.[5]

---

[3]See, for example, Robert G. Wright, "Managing Management Resources Through Corporate Constitutionalism," *Human Resource Management*, Vol. 12, No. 2 (Summer 1973), pp. 15–23.

[4]*Wall Street Journal*, "The Whistle Blower Chooses Hard Path, Utility Story Shows," (November 8, 1978).

[5]Issues of organization justice and freedoms within an organization are addressed in Ralph Nader, Peter J. Petkas, and Kate Blackwell, *Whistle Blowing* (New York: Grossman Publishers, 1972) and David W. Ewing, *Freedom Inside the Organization* (New York: McGraw-Hill Book Company, 1978).

Equal Employment Opportunity

Since the mid-1960s substantial progress has been made by blacks, other ethnic minorities, and by women in obtaining more and better jobs. Under prodding by governmental equal employment opportunity enforcement officials and because of pressures by organized groups of blacks and of women, employers have substantially increased the number of minorities and women in a great many occupational classifications. The real push in recent years has been to upgrade these people into better-paying skilled jobs and into management. The old stereotypes of women's jobs (nurses, secretaries, airline stewardesses) and men's jobs (policemen, managers, and engineers) are disappearing fast.

In very recent years there has been a pronounced backlash by white males. When corporations strive to meet affirmative action goals and timetables they naturally reject many qualified white males. These people, some corporate executives, and some social philosophers are charging that past wrongs must not be righted by engaging in reverse discrimination. This is a serious problem for which there are no easy answers.

Productivity Improvement

During the 1970s and early 1980s productivity growth in the economy as a whole was insignificant. In both domestic and overseas markets the percentage of the total sales volume going to American firms in many key industries was smaller in the 1980s than in the 1960s. Major inroads were made by Japanese and Western European companies. The personnel or human resource function can make very important contributions to productivity improvement in the enterprise.

Proper human resource planning can utilize and allocate employees to work assignments more effectively. Good planning can minimize layoffs of experienced people. An expansion of training activities is essential for upgrading employee skills and enhancing productivity. Increased emphasis upon manager training can improve the performance of the entire management team. This should be ultimately reflected in productivity improvement.

Personnel managers need to create programs that enhance employee involvement in production and quality decisions. These programs may include quality circles, labor-management cooperation, and other forms of participative management.

In the area of collective bargaining, personnel executives can work with local union officials to find ways of making their enterprises more competitive. Possible methods are greater flexibility in job assignments, adjustments in crew sizes, reduction in time away from the job, wider use of wage incentives, and facilitating adjustments to technological change.

Health and safety programs and morale-building programs can reduce work injuries, absenteeism, and turnover. All of these conditions have a harmful effect upon productivity.

Quality of Working Life

A great many establishments have comprehensive personnel programs that are well managed and that provide many of the conditions that comprise a high quality of working life. Their employees are productive and they experience a considerable measure of job satisfaction.

Unfortunately, far too many enterprises badly neglect even the rudiments which make up a good quality of working life. Day-to-day treatment, pay, work loads, and promotion opportunities may be inconsistent or perceived to be unfair. Opportunities for employee growth and advancement may be minimal. Managerial leadership may be incompetent. Those engaged in the practice of personnel management ought to be more vigorous in working for improvements in the quality of working life in their organizations.

1. Discuss careers in personnel-industrial relations. Include fields of specialization, qualifications for employment, and status of personnel-industrial relations within the organization.
2. Is personnel-industrial relations a profession in itself or is it but a part of the larger (emerging) profession of management?
3. Explain how the prevailing practices in "the management of people at work" have matured over the past half century.
4. Give and discuss current and emerging problems in the management of people at work.
5. How do you feel the issue of "whistle blowers" should be handled by personnel executives and other top policy-making managers?
6. How might action in the quality of working life be supportive of efforts to improve productivity?

Suggestions for Further Reading

Carroll, Stephen J., and Randall S. Schuler, eds. *Human Resources Management in the 1980s.* Washington, D.C.: Bureau of National Affairs, Inc. 1983.

Coleman, Charles J. "The Personnel Director: A Cautious Hero Indeed," *Human Resource Management,* Vol. 18, No. 4, (Winter 1979), pp. 14–20.

English, Jack W. "The Road Ahead for the Human Resources Function," *Personnel,* Vol. 57 (March–April 1980), pp. 35–39.

Foulkes, Fred K. "How Top Nonunion Companies Manage Employees," *Harvard Business Review.* Vol. 59, No. 5 (September–October 1981), pp. 90–96.

Herman, Georgianna (ed.). *Personnel and Industrial Relations Colleges: An ASPA Directory.* Alexandria, Va.: American Society for Personnel Administration, 1974.

Miles, Raymond E., and Howard R. Rosenberg. "The Human Resources Approach to Management: Second-Generation Issues," *Organizational Dynamics,* Vol. 10, No. 3 (Winter 1982), pp. 26–41.

Ritzer, George, and Harrison M. Trice. *An Occupation in Conflict: A Study of the Personnel Manager.* Ithaca: New York State School of Industrial and Labor Relations, Cornell University, 1969.

Name Index

Appley, Lawrence, 7
Argyris, Chris, 20, 32, 67, 302
Arvey, Richard D., 165

Babbage, Charles, 13
Barnum, Darold T., 525
Bedeaux, Charles, 501
Bennis, Warren, 67
Berne, Eric, 276
Binet, Alfred, 158
Blake, Robert R., 20, 283–285, 312
Bloom, Gordon F., 9
Blum, Milton L., 149
Bowers, David G., 338, 339
Bradley, Omar, 351
Brown, Paula, 216
Burling, Temple, 542
Burtt, Harold E., 266

Campion, James E., 165
Carroll, Stephen J. Jr., 223
Cook, Morris L., 13
Craf, John R., 271–272
Cronbach, Lee J., 148–149
Cummings, Thomas G., 359

Davis, Sheldon A., 34–35
Deming, W. Edwards, 363

Ebling, Walter, 578

Eels, Richard, 27–28
Emerson, Harrington, 13
Evans, M.G., 341
Ewing, David W., 450, 453

Fayol, Henri, 65
Ferber, Robert, 166
Fiedler, Fred E., 340
Fitzgerald, A. Ernest, 582–583, 600
Fjerstad, Robert L., 187
Fleishman, Edwin A., 266
Ford, Gerald, 525
Ford, Henry, 86
Form, W.H., 139
Freeman, Douglas Southall, 345
French, John R.P. Jr., 219, 336

Galbraith, John Kenneth, 28
Gallatin, Albert, 508
Gantt, Henry L., 13
Geary, George B., 575
Ghiselli, Edwin E., 33
Gilbreth, Frank, 13, 496
Gilbreth, Lillian, 13, 496
Gleason, John M., 525
Gomersall, Earl R., 257
Gompers, Samuel, 12, 410
Gottier, Richard F., 163
Greeley, Horace, 508
Griffin, Ricky W., 89, 90
Guion, Robert M., 163
Gulick, Luther, 65

Hackman, J. Richard, 88
Haire, Mason, 33
Hall, Douglas T., 233
Harbison, Frederick, 6
Harris, Edwin F., 266
Harris, Thomas A., 276
Hay, Edward N., 477, 486
Healy, James J., 498
Herzberg, Frederick, 20, 32, 67, 87, 89, 300–302
Hobbes, Thomas, 30
Hodges, Luther, 25
House, Robert J., 339, 341

James, Muriel, 276
Jerdee, Thomas H., 187
Johnson, Lyndon B., 185
Jongeward, Dorothy, 276
Juran, J.M., 363

Kahn, Robert, 323
Kallejian, Verne, 216
Katz, Robert L., 264
Kay, E., 219
Keenan, Vernon, 532
Kelsay, Marilyn Jo, 579
Kelso, Louis O., 563
Kennedy, John F., 17, 181, 394, 427
Kerr, Willard, 532
King, Martin Luther Jr., 177
Koontz, Harold, 6
Kornhauser, Arthur, 543
Kress, A.L., 470

Lewin, Arie Y., 208–209
Lewin, Kurt, 359
Lewis, John L., 12, 393
Likert, Rensis, 20, 27, 32, 67, 302, 308, 311, 347–348, 351, 541
Lincoln, James F., 511
Lippitt, Ronald, 337, 359
Livernash, E. Robert, 498
Livingston, Sterling, 345

McClelland, David, 300, 303, 309
McCormick, Charles P., 271, 364
McGregor, Douglas, 20, 31, 32, 67, 218, 221, 302, 305, 311, 351, 363
Machiavelli, Niccolò, 30
McLean, Alan, 542
Maier, Norman, 89
Marrow, Alfred J., 351, 359
Maslow, Abraham, 20, 297, 305, 363
Massarik, Fred, 333
Mayfield, Eugene C., 165
Mayo, Elton, 20, 66
Meany, George, 12, 401, 402
Metzger, Bert, 510
Meyer, H.H., 219
Meyers, M. Scott, 257
Miller, Delbert C., 139
Mitchell, Terence R., 339, 341
Molloy, Edmond S., 359
Mooney, James D., 65
Moreno, J.L., 253
Mouton, Jane S., 20, 32, 283–285
Munden, K.J., 542
Munsterberg, Hugo, 15
Murray, Philip, 12
Myers, Charles A., 6

Nixon, Richard, 428
Northrup, Herbert R., 9

O'Donnell, Cyril, 6
Oldham, Greg R., 88
Owen, Robert, 12–13

Porter, Lyman W., 33
Purves, Dale, 477

Raven, Bertram, 336
Reagan, Ronald, 427
Reiley, Alan C., 65
Reuther, Walter, 12, 401
Revans, Reginald W., 272
Roadman, Harry E., 208
Roman, Paul M., 544, 545
Roosevelt, Franklin D., 181, 403
Rorschach, Hermann, 162
Rosen, Benson, 187
Rosenstein, Eliezer, 369
Rowe, Mary P., 197

Scanlon, Joseph, 366, 506
Schein, Edgar H., 232, 282
Schneider, Benjamin, 142
Scott, Walter D., 165
Seashore, Stanley E., 338, 339
Selekman, Benjamin, 447
Selye, Hans, 540
Shafai-Sahrai, Yaghoub, 533
Sherman, William, 532
Silberman, Laurence H., 200
Skinner, B.F., 300, 304, 305
Slichter, Sumner H., 498
Smith, Adam, 13, 26, 30, 85
Solley, C.M., 542
Spencer, Herbert, 30
Stogdill, Ralph M., 334
Strauss, George, 369
Summers, Clyde W., 582

Tannenbaum, Robert, 34–35, 332–333
Taylor, Frederick W., 3, 13–15, 64, 86
Thurstone, L.L., 158
Tito, Marshall, 368
Tosi, Henry L. Jr., 223
Toussaint, Charles, 578–579
Trice, Harrison M., 544, 545

Ure, Andrew, 13
Urwick, Lyndall, 65

Van Maanen, John, 232
Van Zelst, R.H., 533
Vroom, Victor H., 302, 306, 307

Wagner, Robert, 412
Wales, Hugh, 166
Walker, James W., 117
Walton, Clarence, 25, 27–28
Walton, Richard E., 325–326
Webb, Beatrice, 410
Webb, Sidney, 410
Weber, Brian, 200
Weber, Max, 30, 65, 320
Weschler, Irving R., 216, 332–333
White, Ralph K., 337, 359
Wolfe, Dael, 248
Wonderlic, E.F., 158, 167
Woodroofe, Philip B., 575–576

Yukl, Gary, 359

Zwany, Abram, 208–209

Subject Index

Academy of Management, 43
Accidents
  age, training, and experience and, 532–533
  analysis of, 536–537
  causes, 530–531
  costs, 530
  defined, 529
  environment and, 532
  proneness, 531–532
  research on, 533
  See also Health and Safety
Accreditation in personnel field, 594
Achievement, leadership and, 335
Achievement motivation, 303
Achievement tests, 158, 159, 161
Acquired needs, 296
  characteristics, 298
Action interview, 167
Action learning, 272
Ad hoc arbitrators, 449
Adaptability test, 158
Administrative justice, 330
Administrative management theory, 65
Adverse impact, 131, 163, 186, 187, 191
Advertising as recruitment method, 136
Advice, as personnel role, 45
Affective orientation, 306
Affirmative action, 194, 200, 201
  Executive Order 11246 and, 185–186
  key features, 185–186
AFL–CIO, 396, 399–401, 402, 406
  organizational structure, 400–401
Age discrimination, 177–178, 187–189

Age Discrimination in Employment
  Act of 1967, 18, 50–51, 181–183, 188–189, 561
    1978 amendments, 122, 188
Agency shop, 422
Aggression, 299
Air Pollution Prevention and Control
  Act, 577
Albermarle Paper Co. v. Moody (1975), 192
Alcoholism, 544–545, 597
  control program components, 545
Alienation, 321–322
Alternative ranking, 214
Alternative work schedules, 329, 568–569
Amalgamated Clothing and Textile
  Workers, 365
American Can Company, 567
American Federation of Labor, 392
American Industrial Hygiene Association, 16, 522
American Management Association, 19
American Quality of Work Center, 319
American Society for Personnel
  Administration, 55, 594, 599
American Society of Safety Engineers, 522
Appeal, right of, 378–379
Application blank, 141–142
  weighted, 142–143
Appraisal, performance. *See* Performance appraisal
Apprentice training, 257–258
Aptitude tests, 157–159
Arbitration, 430–431

  grievance, 430, 449–450
Arizona Governing Committee v. Norris
  (1983), 560
Assembly line, 86
Assessment centers, 148, 171–172, 240
Assistants to staff, 78–79
AT & T, 51, 171, 275
Attitudes, learning, 249
Auditing
  of human resource plan, 122
  in job analysis, 103
  of recruitment and selection program, 146
Authoritarian management philosophy, 29–32
  vs. traditional, 34–35
Authority
  defined, 335
  power and, 335–336
Autonomous work groups, 91, 327

Background investigation of potential
  employees, 144–145
Baltimore and Ohio Railroad, 365
Bank of America, 133
Battery of tests, 157
Bedeaux plan, 501
Behavior modification, 304–305
Behavioral research as personnel function, 51
Behavioral science
  approach to organization, 66–67
  development, 20
  job design and, 87

Behaviorally anchored rating scale (BARS), 211–214
Benchmark position, 487
Benefits and services, 552–570
    alternative work schedules, 568–570
    growth of, 552–553
    as personnel function, 49
    prevalence, 555
    reasons for adopting, 555–557
    significant kinds, 557–567
        cafeteria benefits, 567
        disability insurance, 559
        employee security, 564–566
        health insurance, 558–559
        holidays and vacations, 567
        life insurance, 557–558
        other, 566
        pensions, 559–563
        stock ownership, 563–564
    types, 553–555
Bennett Tests of Mechanical Competence, 158
Bias
    interpersonal, in rating scales, 210, 216–217
    of interviewers, 166, 171
Biographical information blank, 142–143
Black Americans, equal employment opportunity and, 177–179
Blue-collar workers, work conditions, 322–323
Boards of directors
    junior, 271–272, 364
    trusteeship function of, 74–75
Bonuses, cash, 488
Brown vs. Board of Education (1954), 177
Budgetary planning, 118
Bumping, 425
Burden of proof, 376
Bureau of Apprenticeship, 258
Bureau of Labor Statistics, 464, 465, 482, 484, 510
Bureau of National Affairs, 55
    Survey No. 46 (1982–1983), 51–53
Bureaucracy, 79–81
    advantages and disadvantages, 80–81
    features of, 79–80
    as model of organization, 65–66
Business Ethics Advisory Council (1961), 25
Business game, 276
Business Roundtable, 387

Business Week, 132

Cafeteria benefits, 567
Career counseling, 240
Career development, 121, 231–242, 328–329
    career management, 237–241
    career planning, 234–237
    processes and concepts, 232–234
    reasons for career development programs, 231–232
    smaller organization, 241–242
Career paths, 237–238
Career salary curves, 485–486
Career stages, 232–233
Career workshop, 236–237, 240
Case study as training method, 253
Central tendency, 210, 216
Centralization, factors governing, 76–77
CETA programs, 258
Chain of command, 65, 80
Change agent, 280
Check list
    for employee appraisal, 215
    for job analysis, 100
Check-off, 422
Civil Rights Act of 1964, 17–18, 50
    Pregnancy Disability Amendments, 181
    See also Title VII—Equal Employment Opportunity
Civil Service Reform Act of 1978, 394, 427–428, 477, 577, 584
Classical theories of organization, 64–66
    critique of, 66
Classification system of job evaluation, 469–470
Classroom instruction, 251–255
Clerical aptitude tests, 159
Client, organization by, 70
Clinical approach to grievance handling, 446–447
Closed shop, 414
Clothing Manufacturers Association, 365
Coaching as management development technique, 271
Coal Mine Health and Safety Act of 1969, 523, 577
Codetermination system in West Germany, 367–368, 369

Coefficient of correlation, 152, 153–154
Collective bargaining, 10, 402, 409–433, 577, 598, 601
    characteristics, 410–411
    defined, 410
    development, 394
    differences between union and nonunion organizations, 431–433
    dispute settlement and strikes, 429–431
    legal framework, 411–418
    nature of, 409–410
    negotiating agreement, 419–420
    as participation system, 364–365
    public sector, 426–428
    structure, 418–419
    subject matter, 421–426
        grievance handling, 425–426
        job rights, 424
        layoffs, 424–425
        management rights, 422–423
        union security, 421–422
        wages, 423–424
College graduates, lack of jobs for, 5
Colleges as personnel source, 136
Committee for Economic Development, 28
Committees, 362–363
Comparable worth, 197–199
Compensation administration, 461–488
    administration of pay within ranges, 481–482
    development, 18
    establishing pay structure, 477–481
    human resource planning and, 122
    job evaluation, 467–477
        factor comparison, 474–475, 476
        factor evaluation system, 477
        factor guide chart-profile method, 477
        grade description, 469–470
        point, 470–474
        ranking system, 469
    for managers, 486–489
    as personnel function, 48
    principle issues, 462–463
    for professionals, 483–486
        career salary curves, 485–486
        job descriptions, 483
        salary structure, 483–485
    rationale, 462
    terminology, 461–462
    wage criteria, 463–466

wage policy and principles, 466–467

wage surveys, 482–483

Competition as motivation, 310

Comprehensive Employment and Training Act (1973), 258

Compressed work week, 9–10, 329, 569

Compromise reactions, 300

Compulsory arbitration, 431

Computer-assisted instruction, 254

Computerized system for manpower information management, 117

Concepts, learning, 249

Conciliation, 429–430

Concurrent validity, 152–192

Conference Board, 19, 113, 137, 149, 205, 558, 560, 561, 565

Conference of experts technique of job analysis, 100–101

Conference as training method, 252–253

Congress of Industrial Organizations, 393

Constitutionalism and organizational justice, 599–600

Construct validity, 153, 191, 192

Consultative management, 10, 348, 362

Consumer Credit Protection Act (1968), 577

Consumer Price Index, wage adjustment and, 464

Content validity method, 95, 153, 191–193

Contingency approach to organizational design, 81–82

Contract
 implied, 578
 union shop clause, 389

Control as personnel role, 45–46

Conventional arbitration, 431

Conventional rating scale technique, 210

Corporate Excellence Rubric (Blake and Mouton), 285

Corporate institutes, 275

Cost of living adjustments (COLAs), 464

Council of Profit-Sharing Industries, 508, 509

Country-club management, 284

County of Washington v. Gunther, 199

Credentialitis, 131

Credentials barrier, 131–132

Credit union, 566

Criterion-related validity, 95, 191, 192

Critical incident system, 215

Criticism in interviews, 219, 220

Customer, organization by, 70

Daily diary method of job analysis, 100

Daywork, 493
 measured, 498–499
 wage incentive or, 493–494

Decentralization, 76–77

Decision making, participation in, 311–312

Decision rules in human resource forecasting, 118

Defense mechanisms, 299–300

Deferred compensation, 488

Delegation, 75–76

Delphi technique, 118

Demand analysis, 119

Demand forecast in human resource planning, 117

Democratic management, 10, 362

Demotion, 377

Dental insurance, 558

Depth interview, 167

Development plan, 268
 performance appraisal, 217–218

Diagnostic Interviewer's Guide, 167

Dictionary of Occupational Titles (U.S. Department of Labor), 97, 102

Disability insurance, 559

Disadvantaged, training, 258–259

Discharge
 employee rights and, 577–582
 as grievance issue, 450
 as penalty, 380–381
 as personnel function, 49

Discipline, 371–381
 approaches, 372–374
  negative, 372–373
  positive, 373–374
 and discharge as grievance issue, 450
 meaning, 371–372
 as personnel function, 48–49
 program administration, 374–379
  administrative justice, 374–375
  burden of proof, 376
  circumstances of case, 377
  communication of rules, 376
  consistency of treatment, 377
  policy and procedure, 375–376
  principles, 375

progressive discipline, 377–378

reasonable rules and standards, 378

right of appeal, 378–379

right of representation, 378

rules and penalties, 379–381
 discharge as penalty, 380–381
 uniform, published scale of penalties, 378

Discrimination. *See* Equal employment opportunity

Disease. *See* Occupational disease

Division of labor, 85–86

Due process procedures, 374, 375, 581–582

Dynamic equilibrium, 68

Early Identification of Management Potential (Exxon), 172

Economic Recovery Tax Act of 1981, 488

Education
 attainment
  increase in, 10
  as selection criteria, 131, 132
 career management and, 241
 distinguished from training, 244
 employee training, 18–19
 management development, 18
 safety, 537
 See also Management development; Training

Educational Test Bureau, 159

Educational Testing Service, 567

Edwards Personal Preference Schedule, 162

Ego states, 276–277

80 per cent rule, 191

Eli Lilly, 351

Employee records, privacy of, 133

Employee referrals, 136–137

Employee relations, meaning of, 42, 43

Employee Retirement Income Security Act of 1974 (ERISA), 560, 561–563, 577
 background, 561–562
 provisions, 562–563

Employee rights, 5, 575–586, 599–600
 due process and just cause, 581–582
 employee privacy, 584–585
 freedom of speech and whistle-blowing, 582–584

Employee rights (cont.)
    job protection, 577–581
    needs of employer, 576
    off-the-job behavior, 585
    problems and needs, 600
    protection against layoffs, 585–586
    protections created by law, 577
Employee stock ownership plan
    (ESOP), 563–564
Employees
    classification, 480
    over and underpaid, 479–480
Employment agencies, 135–136
Employment as personnel function, 47
Employment-at-will doctrine, 578–599
    exceptions, 578–579
    fallacies, 578
Engineering, safety and, 535–536
Engineering, Science, and Manage-
    ment War Training program, 243
Engineering approach to job design,
    86–87
Environment
    accidents and, 532
    healthful, 537–538
Equal employment opportunity,
    177–201, 577, 601
    application blanks and, 143
    career development programs
        and, 231–232
    comparable worth, 197–199
    handicapped, 189
    human resource planning and, 110
    impact on personnel activities,
        189–194
        performance appraisal, 193
        promotions, 194
        recruitment, 190
        selection, 190–191
        seniority, 194
        testing, 191–193
    increases in litigation, 5
    issues in the 1980s, 5
    job analysis and, 95
    laws and regulations, 181–187
        enforcement guidelines and
            remedies, 186–187
        Equal Pay Act of 1983, 184
        Executive Order 11246 and af-
            firmative action, 185–186
    nonwhites and Hispanic Ameri-
        cans, 178–179
    older workers and age discrimina-
        tion, 187–189
    as personnel function, 50–51

recruitment and selection policies
    and, 131
reverse discrimination, 199–201
sexual harassment, 194–197
    implications for personnel
        management, 197
    nature of, 195
    remedies and legal consider-
        ations, 195–196
    testing and, 163
    women, 179–181
        married, 180–181
        pregnancy disability, 181
Equal Employment Opportunity Act of
    1972, 17–18, 181–184
Equal Employment Opportunity Com-
    mission, 143, 163, 184–185, 188,
    190–194, 197, 200, 232, 577
    *Guidelines on Discrimination on the
        Basis of Sex* (1980), 195, 196
Equal Pay Act of 1963, 17, 50, 177,
    181–183, 184, 198, 199, 465
Escalator clauses, 464
Essay method of performance ap-
    praisal, 215
Ethics
    managerial philosophy and, 24–25
    problems and needs, 599
Europe
    flexitime, 568
    job protection, 579–580
    participative management, 358,
        367–369
    unions, 402
Executive Order 10988 (Employee
    Management Cooperation in the
    Federal Service), 17, 394, 395, 427
Executive Order 11246 (discrimina-
    tion), 17–18, 50, 181–183, 185–186
    enforcement guidelines and reme-
        dies, 186–187
Executive Order 11375, 181, 182–183
Executive recruitment firm, 136
Exempt employees, 96–97
Expectancy model of motivation,
    306–307, 341
Expectations, increase in, 10
Expected utility, 306
Extinction, 304, 305
Extrinsic motivation, 247, 302
Exxon, 172

Face-to-face program at Pacific North-
    west Bell, 326–327

Face validity, 153
Facilitator, 280
Fact finding in strike settlement, 430
Factor comparison system of job evalu-
    ation, 474–475, 476
Factor evaluation system of job evalua-
    tion, 470, 476
Factor guide chart–profile method of
    job evaluation, 477
Fair Employment Practices Committee,
    181
Fair Labor Standards Act (1938), 17,
    97, 184, 465, 568
Featherbedding, 415, 416
Federal Committee on Apprenticeship,
    258
Federal government, collective bar-
    gaining and, 427–428
Federal Labor Relations Authority, 428
Federal Mediation and Conciliation
    Service, 365, 416, 428, 430, 449
Federal Service Impasses Panel, 428
Federal Service Labor–Management
    Relations Statute, 428
Federal Water Pollution Control Act,
    577
Feedback, 68
    job design and, 88, 90
Final offer arbitration, 431
Finland, 452
First aid, 538
First-level outcome, 307
Fitzgerald Act (1937), 258
Fixation, 300
Flexitime, 329, 568–569
Followership, 333
Force and power as motivation, 309
Forced distribution procedure, 214
Ford Motor Company, 329–330, 365
Forecast, human resources, 117–121
    budgetary planning, 118
    judgment and experience, 117–118
    key predictive factors, 118–120
    management succession planning,
        120–121
    work standards data, 118
Four-fifths rule, 191
France, 369
    job protection, 579–580
Freedom-of-contract theory, 578
Freedom of speech, 582–584
Fringe benefits, 463, 552
    See also Benefits and services
Function, grouping work activities by,
    69

Functional foremanship, 65
Functional job analysis, 102–103
Functional job descriptions, 483

Gains-sharing plan, 501
Games as training method, 255, 276
General Clerical Test, 159
General Electric, 51, 69, 70, 72, 171,
    221, 222, 231, 351, 584
    Management Research and Devel-
        opment Institute, 275
General job descriptions, 483
General Motors, 51, 319, 327–330, 351,
    364, 365, 418, 449, 544, 561
General staff, 79
Geographical area, organization by, 69
Germany, works council system,
    367–368, 369
Goal setting
    in management-by-objectives,
        221–223
    in organization development,
        285–286
Goals. See Organization objectives
Grade-description system of job evalu-
    ation, 469–470
Great Britain, 369, 402
    job protection, 579
Grievance arbitration, 430, 449–450
    issues arbitrated, 450
    legal status, 450
Grievance committee, 453
Grievances, 442–458
    arbitration, 449–450
    collective bargaining aspects,
        425–426
    defined, 443
    discipline and, 374–375
    nature of, 442–443
    over incentives, 498
    personnel function in, 49
    reasons for system, 443–444
    settlement for nonunion employ-
        ees, 450–453
        grievance committee, 453
        inspector general method, 452
        multistep grievance proce-
            dure, 452–453
        ombudsman, 452
        open-door policy, 451–452
    settlement for unionized employ-
        ees, 444–449
        clinical approach to handling,
            446–447

fair representation, 446
    procedure, 445–446
    role of shop steward and
        union, 448–449
    role of supervisor, 447–448
Griggs v. Duke Power Company (1971),
    184, 191–192
Group appraisal method, 209
Group incentives, 501
Group relationships and participation,
    supervision and, 346
Grouping of work activities
    by kind, 69–70
    by level, 72–73
Guide chart-profile method, 486

Halo effect, 170–171, 210, 216
Halsey 50-50 bonus plan, 501
Hand-Tool Dexterity Test, 159
Handbook for Analyzing Jobs (U.S. De-
    partment of Labor), 102
Handicapped persons, equal employ-
    ment opportunity and, 178, 189, 193
Harvard Advanced Management Pro-
    gram, 275
Harvard Business School, 275
Harwood Manufacturing Company,
    359
Hawthorne effect, 569
Hawthorne Works of Western Electric
    Company, 66
Health insurance, 558–559
Health maintenance organization
    (HMO), 558–559
Health and safety, 5, 15–17, 521–545,
    577
    accidents, 529–533
    accomplishments and needs,
        596–597
    health services, 539–540
    mental health, 542–545
    occupational disease, 528–529
    Occupational Safety and Health
        Act, 522–528
    as personnel function, 48
    program components, 533–538
    stress on the job, 540–542
    workers' compensation, 538–539
Heelan v. Johns-Manville Corporation, 196
Hewlett-Packard Company, 237, 351
Hierarchy of systems, 68
Hispanic Americans, equal employ-
    ment opportunity and, 177, 178–179

Histadrut, 369
Holidays, 567
Horizontal job loading, 89
Human adjustment, 298–300
Human behavior fundamentals,
    293–295
Human factors analysis, 15
Human needs
    acquired, characteristics of, 298
    classification of, 296–297
    hierarchy of, 297–298
    See also Motivation
Human relationists, 66
Human relations movement, 66–67
    development of, 19–20
Human resource management, 3
    philosophy, 32–34
    terminology, 43
    vs. tradition, 34–35
    See also Personnel management
Human resource planning, 109–123
    career management and, 237
    defined, 109–110
    job analysis and, 93–94
    as personnel function, 50
    planning process, 111–123
        audit and adjustment, 122–123
        current human resource situa-
            tion, 113–117
        goals and plans of organiza-
            tion, 111–113
        human resource forecast,
            117–121
        implementation programs,
            121–122
        reasons for, 110–111
Human resources, terminology, 43
Human Rights Commission, 143
Hygiene theory of motivation, 300–302

IBM, 51, 133, 171, 275, 329, 351, 431,
    565, 585
Implementation programs in human
    resource planning, 121–122
Implied contract, 579–580
In-basket test, 161–162
Incentive stock option, 488
Incentives. See Wage incentives
Indoctrination, 47
Industrial democracy, 358
Industrial engineer, role in wage in-
    centives, 502
Industrial hygiene, 16, 538

Industrial Medical Association, 16, 522
Industrial medicine, 16, 539–540
Industrial psychology, 15
Industrial relations, meaning of, 42, 43
    See also Personnel management
Industrialization in America, 9
Industries, declining, 4
Industry-wide bargaining, 419
Information systems, 51
Injunctions, 412
Inspector general method of grievance
    handling, 452
Institute for Social Research at Univer-
    sity of Michigan, 338, 344, 347
Instrumentality, 306
Integrated work groups, 91, 327
Integration of goals, motivation and,
    311
Intelligence, 158
    leadership and, 335
Intelligence tests, 158
Interdependency, 68
Interest arbitration, 430–431
International Cooperative Congress,
    508, 509
International Harvester Company, 266,
    275
Interpersonal bias in rating scales, 210,
    216–217
Interpersonal comparisons, 214
Interview, 163–171
    appraisal, 219–221, 224
    conducting, 168, 170
    defined, 164
    in hiring, 143
    limitations, 164–165
    objectives, 164
    pitfalls, 170–171
    postappraisal, 218–219
    preliminary, 141
    preparing for, 168, 169
    psychological foundations,
        165–167
    research findings, 165
    salary, 224
    types, 167–168
Interview method of job analysis, 100
Intrinsic motivation, 247, 302
Israel, 369

Jamestown, New York, 365–366
Japanese system of management,
    348–351

applicability to America, 350–351
characteristics, 348–350
contrasted with American man-
    agement, 350
quality circles, 363
Job, defined, 97
Job analysis
    administration of program, 103
    defining, 92–93
    functional, 102–103
    job categories, 96–97
    obtaining information, 97–101
        content of information, 101
        methods, 97–101
    for safety, 536
    terms used, 97
    for testing program development,
        155
    uses, 93–96
Job categories, 96–97
Job characteristics theory, 88–89
Job descriptions
    career paths and, 238
    for management, 486
    for professionals, 483
Job design, 85–92
    contemporary orientation, 87–89
    engineering approach, 86–87
    motivation and, 89–91, 310
    perspective on, 91–92
Job dimension scales, 210–211
Job enlargement, 89–90
Job enrichment, 90, 286, 328
Job evaluation, 465, 467–477
    factor comparison, 474–475, 476
    factor evaluation, 470, 476
    factor guide chart-profile method,
        477
    grade description, 469–470
    point system, 470–474
    ranking system, 469
Job openings, publicizing, 239
Job posting, 135
Job protection, employee rights in,
    577–581
Job redesign, 328
Job rotation, 89, 270–271
Job satisfaction
    analysis and explanation, 324–325
    unionization and, 391
    workers-are-dissatisfied thesis,
        321–323
    workers-are-satisfied thesis,
        323–324
Job security, 329–330, 351

collective bargaining and, 424
    in Japan, 349
Job sharing, 329, 569
Job skills training, 257
Job Training Partnership Act (1982),
    258–259
Judgment and experience in human
    resource forecasting, 117–118
Junior-board-of-executives system,
    271–272, 364
Just cause procedures, 581
Justice, administrative, 330

Key predictive factors technique,
    118–119
Kuder Preference Record, 161

Labor force in America, 9–12
    changing composition, 10–12
    rising status of labor, 9–10
Labor laws, chronological listing, 17–18
    See also under specific laws
Labor–management cooperation, 10,
    365–366, 406
    wage incentives and, 506–508
Labor–Management Relations Act. See
    Taft–Hartley Act
Labor–Management Reporting and
    Disclosure Act of 1959. See Lan-
    drum–Griffin Act
Labor market, 128–129
    defined, 482
Labor movement, American, character
    of, 402–403
Labor relations
    management reaction to unionism,
        16–17
    as personnel function, 49
Labor supply
    to company, 129–130
    source of people, 134–137
Laboratory training, 282
Landrum–Griffin Act (1959), 17, 364,
    416–418
    amendments to Taft–Hartley Act,
        417–418
    bill of rights of union members,
        416
    election of union officers, 417
    fiduciary responsibilities, 417
    reporting requirements, 417
    trusteeships, 417

Layoffs, 329
  collective bargaining and, 424–425
  human resource planning and, 122
  as personnel function, 47
  protection against, 585–586
  threat of, 321
Leaderless group discussion, 161, 162, 172
Leadership, 332–341
  authority and power, 335–337
  foundations of, 333–335
  nature of, 332–333
  situational factors, 339–341
  style, 337–339
Learner–controlled instruction (LCI), 254–255
Learning process, 246–250
  defined, 246
  principles, 247–250
Lecture, 249, 251–252
Lee's Lieutenants: A Study in Command (Freeman), 345
Legalistic approach to grievance handling, 446–447
Leniency in rating scales, 210, 216
Levels of management, 73–75
  grouping activities by, 72–73
Leviathan (Hobbes), 30
Lie detector, 132
Life insurance, 557–558
Lincoln Electric company, 329, 565–566, 585
  incentive system, 511–512, 513
Line management, 43, 77
  relations between staff and, 79
  responsibilities in hiring, 145
  training responsibilities, 245–246
Line project management, 71, 72
Litigation in employment relationship, increasing, 5
Location, organization by, 69
Lockheed Missiles and Space Company, 351, 363
Lockout, 429
Longevity, work satisfaction and, 323
Lower management, 74

McClellan Committee Hearings (1957-59), 406
McCormick and Company, 364
Machinists Union, 365
McMurray Patterned Interview Form, 167

Major medical plan, 558
Mallinckrodt, 329
Management
  defining, 6, 263
  functions, 6–7
  human interaction in, 7
  impact of union on, 403–405
  levels, 73–75
  participative, 326–327, 357–369
  philosophies, 29–35
    modern (human resource), 32–34
    traditional (authoritarian), 29–32
    traditional vs. modern, 34–35
  as profession, 264–265
  in public administration, 6
  reaction to unionism, 16–17
  scientific, 13–14
  separation of ownership from, 6
  –union climate, 405–407
Management development, 19, 262–277
  defined, 262
  formal training courses, 272–277
    corporate institutes, 275
    management games, 276
    subject matter and course content, 273–274
    transactional analysis, 276–277
    university nondegree programs, 274–275
  job analysis and, 95
  nature of, 262–266
  program planning and administering, 266–268
  through work experience, 269–272
    action learning, 272
    coaching, 271
    job rotation, 270–271
    multiple management, 271–272
    understudies, 269–270
Management games, 276
Management by integration and self-control, 32, 311
Management by objectives, 34, 121, 205, 210, 221–223, 286, 345
Management Progress Study (AT & T), 171–172
Management rights in collective bargaining, 422–423
Management succession planning, 120–121
Management systems, 332, 347–352

Japanese, 348–351
  Likert's systems, 347–348
Managerial grid, 283–285
Managers
  compensation for, 463, 486–488
    supervisory pay issues, 487
    top management compensation, 487–488
  defining, 263
  job descriptions for, 486
  knowledge and skills of, 263–264
Manpower information system, 113
Manpower planning, 50
  See also Human resource planning
Manufacturing, decline in, 4
Married women, special problems of, 180–181
Mass picketing, 414
Mass production, 86
Massachusetts Institute of Technology, 275
Materials Research Corporation, 378
Maternity leave, 181
Matrix organization, 70–72
Measured-daywork plan, 498–499
Mechanical aptitude tests, 158
Mediation, 429–430
Medical examination, pre-employment, 144
Medical treatment, 538
Medical-ability tests, 158
Mental-ability tests, 158
Mental health, 540, 542–545, 597
Messerschmidt Research and Development Center, 568
Middle management, 74
Minnesota Rate of Manipulation Test, 159
Modern management philosophy, 32–34
Modified union shop, 422
Money as motivator, 309–310
Morale
  defined, 307
  productivity and, 307–308
Motivation, 293–312
  acquired needs, characteristics of, 298
  applying concepts, 308–312
    competition, 310
    integration of goals, 310–311
    job design and work flow, 310
    money as motivator, 309–310
    participation, 311–312
    power and force, 309
  classification of needs, 296–297

Motivation (cont.)
    hierarchy of needs (Maslow),
        297–298
    human adjustment, 298–300
    human behavior fundamentals,
        293–295
    human resource planning and, 122
    of interviewees, 165–166
    job designs and, 87–91
    learning and, 247
    morale and productivity, 307–308
    nature of, 295–296
    theories, 300–307
        achievement motivation, 303
        behavior modification,
            304–305
        expectancy model, 306–307
        hygiene theory, 300–302
        intrinsic and extrinsic motiva-
            tion, 302–303
Motor skills, learning, 249
Moving equilibrium, 68
Moving expenses, 566
Multiemployer bargaining, 418, 419
    reasons for, 419
Multiple-correlation approach in selec-
    tion, 140, 157
Multiple management, 271–272, 364
Multiple regression analysis, 154

National Alliance of Businessmen, 28
National Association of Chain Drug
    Stores survey, 132
National Association of Manufacturers,
    389
National Association of Suggestion
    Systems (NASS), 367
National Center for Production and
    Quality of Working Life, 319
National Council on Alcoholism, 544
National Education Association, 394
National Institute for Occupational
    Safety and Health (NIOSH), 523
National Labor Relations Act. See Wag-
    ner Act
National Labor Relations Board, 5, 16,
    17, 364, 391, 393, 413–416, 553, 577
National Safety Council, 16, 521, 522
National War Labor Board, 567
Natural work units, 90
Negative reinforcement, 305–306
New Industrial State, The (Galbraith), 28
New Lanark, Scotland, 13

New View of Society, A (Owen), 12–13
New York State Civil Service Employ-
    ees Association, 394
Nonexempt employees, 96–97
Nonprofit organizations, 29
Nonqualified stock option, 488
Nonwhites, equal employment oppor-
    tunity and, 177, 178–179
Norris-LaGuardia Anti-Injunction Act
    (1932), 411, 412
North America Rockwell Corporation,
    115

Objective personality tests, 162
Objectives. See Organization objectives
Observation in job analysis, 97
Occupation, defined, 97
Occupational disease, 523, 525, 527,
    528–529, 597
    classification, 528
    environment and, 537–538
Occupational health and safety. See
    Health and safety
Occupational Outlook Handbook (U.S.
    Department of Labor), 236
Occupational safety. See Accidents;
    Health and safety; Safety
Occupational Safety and Health Act of
    1970, 16, 18, 48, 521–528, 577, 596
    background, 522–532
    injury and illness experiences un-
        der, 525–528
    issues and controversies over,
        524–525
    provisions, 523–524
Occupational Safety and Health
    Administration, 523, 524, 525
Office of Federal Contract Compliance
    Programs (OFCCP), 185, 191, 194,
    232
Office Skills Tests, 159, 160
Office of the Special Counsel of the
    Merit Systems Protection Board, 584
Ohio State University, 338
Older Americans, equal employment
    opportunity and, 177–178, 187–189
Ombudsman, 452
On the Economy of Machinery and Manu-
    facturers (Babbage), 13
On-the-job training, 47, 250–251,
    269–272
    action learning, 272
    coaching, 271

job rotation, 270–271
multiple management, 271–272
understudies, 269–270
100 per cent bonus plan, 500
Open-door policy, 451–452
Open shop, 422
Open systems, 68
Opinion Research Corporation, 324
Organic system of organization, 81
Organization, 63–82
    approaches to study, 64–68
        behavioral science, 66–67
        classical, 64–66
        systems view, 67–68
    bureaucratic and organic systems,
        79–82
    defined, 64
    delegation and decentralization,
        75–77
    job analysis and, 93–94
    line and staff, 77–79
    for personnel function, 54–56
    structure, 68–75
        grouping activities by kind,
            68–69
        grouping activities by level,
            72–73
        levels of management, 73–75
        project and matrix organiza-
            tion, 70–72
    for training, 245
Organization development, 262,
    277–287
    defined, 278
    elements, 280–281
    interventions, 281–286
        goal setting and planning,
            285–286
        managerial grid, 283–285
        others, 286
        process consultation, 282
        sensitivity training, 282–283
        survey feedback, 281–282
        team building, 286
    objectives, 279
    overview, 19
    as personnel function, 50
    process, 279–280
    values, 278–279
Organization objectives, 25–29
    fallacy of profit as sole objective,
        26–27
    importance, 26
    of modern publicly owned corpo-
        ration, 27–28

proper role of profit, 27
public and nonprofit organizations, 29
social responsibilities, 28–29
Organization planning as personnel function, 49–50
Organizational climate, 360
leadership and, 339–340, 347
Organizational influences in performance appraisal, 217
Organizational justice, 330
Organizational reward, 306
Orientation, 47, 255–257
Output, restriction of, 502–503

Pacific Northwest Bell face-to-face program, 326–327
Paired-comparison technique, 214
Panel interview, 168
Part-time employment, 329
Participation, motivation and, 311–312
Participative management, 286, 326–327, 339, 346, 348, 351, 357–369
conditions for effective participation, 360–361
in Japan, 349
research into participation, 358–360
role in organization, 358
types of participation, 361–367
collective bargaining, 364–365
committees, 362–363
junior boards of executives, 364
quality circles, 363–364
suggestion plans, 366–367
union–management cooperation, 365–366
workers', European style, 367–369
Past performance as work measurement method, 495
Paternalism, 31–32, 347
in Japanese management, 350
Path–goal theory of leadership, 341
Patterned interview, 167
Pay. See Compensation administration; Wages
Pearsonian product–moment method, 154
Peer ratings, 208–209
Pensions, 552–553, 559–563
benefits, 560
Employee Retire Income Security Act (1974), 561–563

methods of financing, 560–561
retirement age, 561
types, 559–560
vesting rights, 560
who pays, 561
Performance appraisal, 115, 121, 204–223
applications, 205–206
basic considerations, 206–209
defined, 205
equal employment opportunity and, 193
issues and perspectives, 223–224
job analysis and, 95
methods, 209–215
check list, 215
critical incident, 215
essay, 215
interpersonal comparisons, 214
management by objectives, 214, 221–223
rating scales, 210–214
personal development and, 217–221
problems in rating, 215–217
Performance goals, 345
Performance shares, 488
Perquisites, 488
Personal Audit, 162
Personal development, performance appraisal and, 217–221
Personal fulfillment career orientation, 233–234
Personal traits and behavior scale, 210
Personality, 294
Personality tests, 158, 162–163
Personnel and behavioral research, 50
Personnel departments
development, 15
organization for large divisionalized companies, 56
organization for medium-size, single-establishment company, 54–55
staff role, 44–46
terminology, 42–43
top executive of, 54
Personnel function, 42–58
benefits and services, 49
compensation administration, 48
discipline and discharge, 48–49
employment, 47
equal employment opportunity, 50–51

health and safety, 48
human resource planning, 50, 110–111
labor relations, 49
organization development, 50
organization for, 54–56
large divisionalized companies, 56
medium-size, single-establishment company, 54–55
organization planning, 49–50
people performing, 43–44
personnel and behavioral research, 51
personnel department, staff role of, 44–46
advice, 45
control, 45–46
policy initiation and formulation, 44–45
service, 45
personnel information systems, 51
survey data, 51–53
terminology, 42–43
training and development, 47
transfer, promotion, layoff, 47
Personnel information systems, 51
Personnel management
accomplishments and continuing needs, 595–602
as career, 54, 592–595
job opportunities and salaries, 593–594
position levels, 592–593
status and professionalism, 594–595
evolution of theory and practice, 12–20
job information and, 92–97
overview, 7–9
recent emergence, 3–4
terminology, 42, 43
Personnel policies, 35–37
communicating, 37
distinguished from objectives and procedures, 35
formulating, 36–37
personnel department function in, 44–45
reasons for adopting, 35–36
written, importance of, 36
Personnel practices, accomplishments and needs, 595–596
Personnel tests, 141
Philosophy of Manufacturers (Ure), 13

Pickering v. Board of Education (1968), 583
Picketing, 414, 417–418
Piecework, 499–500
Planned interview, 167
Point system of job evaluation, 470–474
Policies. *See* Personnel policies
Politics, public sector collective bargaining and, 427
Polygraph, 132
Position, defined, 97
Positive reinforcement, 304
Postappraisal interview, 218–219
Power
    and force as motivation, 309
    leadership and 337–338, 340
Predetermined elemental times, 496
Predictive validity, 153, 192
Preference in expectancy model of motivation, 306
Pregnancy disability, 181
Pregnancy Disability Amendments to Title VII of Civil Rights Act of 1964, 181
Principles of Scientific Management (Taylor), 13
Privacy, employee, 584–585
    interviews, 168
    records, 133
Private Industry Council (PIC), 259
Probation period, 134–135
Procedural controls, 46
Procedure, distinguished from policy, 35
Process consultation, 282
Procter and Gamble, 51, 565
Product, organization by, 69–70
Product management, 70
Product manager, role of, 70
Productivity
    improvement in, 601
    in Japanese economy, 349
    morale and, 307–308
    in union vs. nonunion organizations, 433
    as wage criterion, 464–465
Professional associations, 136, 390, 594
Professional maturity curves, 485
Professionals
    compensation for, 463, 483–486
        career salary curves, 485–486
        job descriptions, 483
        salary structure, 483–485
    in Taft–Hartley Act, 415
    unions and, 390, 394–395

Professions, characteristics, 264–265
Profit
    proper role of, 27
    as sole objective, fallacy of, 26–27
Profit sharing, 508–513
    defined, 508–509
    figuring share, 510
    objectives, 509
    requirements, 510–511
    types of plans, 509–510
Program management, 70
Programmed instruction, 254
Project management, 70–72
Projection, 300
Projective personality tests, 162–163
Promotion
    equal employment opportunity and, 194
    human resource planning and, 122
    as personnel function, 47
    from within or without company, 130–131
Protestant ethic, 320
Psychological Corporation, The, 158, 159, 162
Psychological tests, 141, 158
    defined, 148–149
    See also Tests and testing
Psychology, industrial, 15
Psychology and Industrial Efficiency (Munsterberg), 15
Psychomotor tests, 158–159
Public Health Service, 528
Public organizations, 29
Public sector
    collective bargaining, 426–428
    unions, 394
Punishment in behavior modification, 304, 305
Purdue Pegboard, 159

Quality circles, 363–364
    in America, 351
    in Japan, 349
Quality of Employment Survey (1977), 391
Quality of working life, 319–330
    characteristics of good quality, 325–326
    job satisfaction, workers' attitudes and, 321–325

nature of work, 320–321
perspective on, 601–602
strategies for improvement, 326–330
    alternative work schedules, 329
    career development, 328–329
    effective leadership and supervisory behavior, 328
    job redesign and enrichment, 328
    job security, 329–330
    participative management, 326–327
    self-managed work teams, 327–328
Quantitative techniques for human resource forecasting, 119–120
Questionnaire, use in job analysis, 97–100

Raiding, 399
Rand Corporation, 118
Ranking method
    of job evaluation, 469
    of performance appraisal, 241
Rate cutting, 503
Rating scales, 210–214
    behaviorally anchored, 211–214
    job dimension, 210–211
    personal traits and behavior, 210
Rationalization, 300
Real wages, standard of living and, 9
Recreational programs, 566
Recruitment and selection, 121, 128–147
    auditing, 146
    employment process, 133–135
    equal employment opportunity and, 190
    job analysis and, 94–95
    labor market considerations, 128–130
    policy issues, 130–133
        equal employment opportunity, 131
        filling vacancies from within or without, 130–131
        lie detector, 132
        privacy of employee records, 133
        quality of persons hired, 133

relatives of employees, 133
selection standards, 131–132
selection procedure, 140–146
application blank, 141–143
background investigation,
144–145
interview, 143
medical examination, 144
rejecting applicants, 145–146
responsibilities of line management, 145
tests, 143
selection process, 137–140
sources of people, 135–137
inside, 135
outside, 135–137
See also Selection
Red circle employees, 480
Regression, 300
Rehabilitation, 538
Rehabilitation Act of 1973, 18, 95,
181–183, 189, 193
Reinforcement, positive and negative,
304–305
Rejection of applicants, 145–146
Relatives of employees, hiring policies
and, 133
Reliability of tests, 151–152
Replacement tables and charts,
267–268
Representation, right of, 378
Research in personnel, problems and
needs, 597–598
Resignation as defense mechanism,
300
Respondeat superior doctrine, 196
Restricted stock plan, 488
Restriction of output, 502–503
Retirement, human resource planning
and, 122
See also Pensions
Retirement age, 188–189, 561
Reverse discrimination, 199–201
Revised Minnesota Paper Form Board
Test, 158
Right of appeal, 378–379
Right arbitration, 430
Right of representation, 378
Rockwell International, 115
Role playing as training method,
253–254
Rorschach test, 162
Rotation of employment, 424
Rules
communication of, 376

and penalties, listing of, 379–381
reasonable, 378
of thumb in human resource forecasting, 118

Safety, 5, 16–17, 529–538
accidents, 529–533
job analysis and, 196
program components, 533–538
See also Accidents; Health and
safety
Salary
annual interview, 224
defined, 461
Salary maturity curves, 485
Scanlon plan, 365, 366, 504, 506–508,
512
evaluation of, 508
labor-cost norm and incentive bonus, 506
suggestion plan and production
committees, 507–508
Schools as personnel source, 136
Science Research Associates, Inc., 158,
159, 162
Mechanical Aptitudes Test, 158
Test of Mechanical Concepts, 158
Verbal Form, 158
Scientific management movement,
13–14, 64–65, 86
Sears, 171
Second careers, 328–329
Secondary boycotts, 414
Selection
equal employment opportunity
and, 191–192
interview, 163–171
procedure, 140–146
process, 137–140
standards, 131–132
testing, 141, 143, 148–149
See also Interview; Recruitment
and selection; Tests and testing
Selection ratio, 156
Self-concept, 293–294
Self-employed persons, job satisfaction
of, 324
Self-managed work teams, 91, 327–328
Senate Select Committee on Improper
Activities in the Labor or Management Field, 416

Seniority, 424–425
equal employment opportunity
and, 194
Sensitivity training, 282–283
Separation pay, 565
Service awards, 566
Service Delivery Areas (SDAs), 259
Service industries, shift toward, 4
Service as personnel role, 45
Service staff, 77–78
Sexual harassment, 194–197
implications for personnel man-
agement, 197
nature of, 195
remedies and legal considerations,
195–196
Sherman Act (1890), 412
Shop steward, 397–398
role in grievances, 448–449
Short Employment Tests, 159
Short Tests of Clerical Ability, 159
Simulation as training method, 255
Single employer bargaining, 418–419
Situational tests, 158, 161–162
Skills inventory, 113–117, 135
Sloan Fellowship program, 275
Social Darwinism, 30
Social and recreational programs, 566
Social responsibilities of corporations,
28–29
Social Security Act of 1935, 553, 559,
561, 564
Social skills
job performance and, 139
leadership and, 335
Soldier's Story, A (Bradley), 351
Span of control, 65
Staff personnel, 77–79
assistant-to, 78–79
general, 79
relations between line and, 79
specialized and service, 77–78
Staff project/product manager, 71
Standard data as work measurement
method, 496
Standard-hour plan, 500–501
Standard of living, 9
Standard-time plan, 500
Standardized interview, 167
Standards of performance, 207
State employment service, 135–136
State and local government, collective
bargaining and, 428
Statistical correlation, 119
Steelworkers' trilogy, 450

Stochastic analysis, 119
Stock purchase plans, 563–564
Strategic planning, human resource
  planning and, 110
Stress, on the job, 540–542
  accidents and, 532
  minimizing, 541–542
  nature of, 540–541
Stress interview, 167–168
Strictness in rating scales, 210, 216
Strikes, 420, 429–431
  ban on in public sector, 427
  defined, 429
  settlement methods, 429–431
Strokes, 276, 277
Strong–Campbell Interest Inventory,
  161
Strong Vocational Interest Blank, 161
Structure of organization, 68–75
Sublimination, 300
Successive-hurdles technique, 139–140
Suggestion plans, 10, 366–367, 504,
  507–508
Supervision, 332, 341–346
  duties and responsibilities,
    343–344
  effective, 328, 344–347
    concentration upon manage-
      ment functions, 346–347
    facilitation of work, 345
    group relationships and par-
      ticipation, 346
    influence in hierarchy,
      345–346
    organizational climate, 347
    performance goals, 345
    supportive behavior, 344–345
  nature of, 342–343
  pay issues, 487
  role in grievances, 447–448
  in Taft-Hartley Act, 415
Supplemental unemployment benefits
  (SUB) plans, 564–565
Supportive behavior, effective supervi-
  sion and, 344–345
Supportive management, 32
Survey feedback in organization devel-
  opment, 281–282
Survey Research Center (University of
  Michigan), 391
Survey of Values, 162
Sweatshops, 322–323
Sweden, 369, 452
System 4 management, 311
Systems theory of organization, 67–68

T-group programs, 282–283
Taft–Hartley Act (1947), 342, 395, 413,
  414–416, 420, 422, 427, 430, 553
  amendments to Landrum–Griffin
    Act, 417–418
  appraisal of, 416
  free speech, 415
  national emergency disputes,
    415–416
  supervisors and professionals, 415
  unfair labor practices of unions,
    414–415
Task, defined, 97
Tax Reduction Act of 1975, 563
Team building, 286
Teamsters Union, 401, 416, 418
Teamwork development, 285
Technology industries, growth in, 5
Tennessee Valley Authority, 365
Termination. See Discharge
Terminology in employment relationships, 42–43
Tests and testing, 148–163
  concepts, 151–154
    coefficient of correlation,
      153–154
    reliability, 151–152
    validity, 152–153
  contributions to selection, 149
  equal employment opportunity
    and, 163, 191
  guides to, 149, 151
  program development, 154–157
  as selection aid, 143
  types, 157–163
    achievement, 159, 161
    aptitude, 157–159
    personality, 162–163
    situational, 161–162
    vocational, 161
  usage, 148, 150
Texaco, 329
Texas Instruments, 51, 256, 319
Thematic Apperception Test, 162, 303
Theory X, 31, 34
Theory Y, 32, 33, 34, 311
Therbligs, 496
3M Company, 231, 329
Thurstone Temperament Schedule, 162
Thurstone Test of Mental Alertness,
  158
Time study as work measurement
  method, 495–496
Time work, 492
Title VII of Civil Rights Act of 1964—

Equal Employment Opportunity,
  17–18, 50, 177, 181–185, 190, 191,
  194, 197, 199, 200, 577
  enforcement guidelines and reme-
    dies, 186–187
  Pregnancy Disability Amend-
    ments, 181
Tomkins v. Public Service Electric and Gas
  Company, 196
Top management, 74
Toxic substances, 5
Traditional management. See Authoritarian management philosophy
Training, 18–19, 122, 241, 243–260
  accidents and, 532–533
  benefits, 244–245
  defined, 244
  discovering needs, 246
  distinguished from education, 244
  establishing programs, 268
  evaluation of program, 259–260
  in evolution of personnel manage-
    ment, 18–19
  formal, 272–277
  job analysis and, 95
  learning process, 246–250
  lining responsibilities, 245–246
  methods, 250–255
    classroom, 251–255
    on-the-job, 250–251
    vestibule, 251
  on-the-job, 269–272
  organization for, 245
  as personnel function, 47
  programs, 255–259
    apprentice, 257–258
    disadvantaged, 258–259
    job skills and knowledge, 257
    orientation, 255–257
  in safety, 537
  See also Management development
Training-Within-Industry (TWI) program, 18, 243, 257
Transactional analysis (TA), 276–277
Transactions, 276, 277
Transfer
  human resource planning and, 122
  as personal function, 47
Travelers Insurance Company, 231
Trusteeship management, 74–75
TRW Systems, 72, 231, 567
Umpire system, 449
Understudies, 269–270
Unemployment, declining industries
  and, 4

Unemployment insurance system, 564–565, 577
Unemployment rates for blacks, 178–179
Uniform Guidelines on Employee Selection Procedures (Equal Employment Opportunity Commission, Civil Service Commission, Office of Federal Contract Compliance Programs), 191
Union Carbide Corporation, 189
Union of Japanese Scientists and Engineers, 363
Union–management cooperation. *See* Labor–management cooperation
Union security, 389, 421–422
Union shop, 389, 422
Unions, 136, 387–407
    AFL–CIO, 399–401
    American labor movement, 402–403
    attitudes of working people towards, 391–392
    development, 392–395
    discipline and, 374–376
    fringe benefits and, 553, 556, 557
    impact on management, 403–405
    independent, 401
    –management climate, 405–407
    management reaction, 16–17
    –management relations, problems and needs, 598
    motivation to join, 388–389
    motivation not to join, 390–391
    objectives and behavior, 401–402
    organization and functions, 395–399
        intermediate organizational units, 398
        local, 397–398
        national and international, 398–399
    role in authoritarian management, 32
    role in grievances, 448–449
    role in modern management philosophy, 34
    See also Arbitration; Collective bargaining; Grievances
United Automobile Workers, 365, 401, 418, 544
U.S. Civil Service, 191, 469–470, 477
U.S. Department of Defense, 70
U.S. Department of Health, Education, and Welfare, 523, 524
U.S. Department of Justice, 191

U.S. Department of Labor, 200, 258, 391, 523, 524, 554, 559, 593
    Training and Employment Service, 102
    See also Office of Federal Contract Compliance Programs
U.S. Employment Service, 135
U.S. Steel Corporation, 189
U.S. Training and Employment Service of Department of Labor, 102
United Steelworks of America, 556
Unity of command, 65
Universities, nondegree programs in management, 274–275
University of Michigan, 275, 324, 338, 344, 347, 391
University of Iowa, 337–338, 359
Unweighted check list, 215
Utah Copper Division of Kennecott Copper Corporation, 543–544

Vacancies, filling from within or from outside company, 130–131
Vacations, 567
Valence, 306
Validity of tests, 152–153, 191–193
Vertical job loading, 90
Vestibule training, 251
Vesting, 560, 562
Vocational tests, 161

Wage and Hour Law, 184
Wage incentives, 3, 465, 492–513
    direct, 493–498
        program requirements, 497–498
        wage incentive or daywork, 493–494
        work measurement, 494–497
    for executives, 487–488
    human and administrative problems, 501–506
    labor-management cooperation and, 506–508
    Lincoln Electric systems, 511–512
    profit sharing, 508–511
    types, 498–501

        gains-sharing plan, 501
        group incentives, 501
        measured daywork, 498–499
        piecework, 499–500
        standard-hour plan, 500–501
Wages
    collective bargaining and, 423–424
    comparable worth issues, 197–199
    criteria, 463–466
    defined, 461
    establishing proper rates, 95
    garnishment, 577
    as grievance issues, 450
    inequities, 503–504
    policy and principles, 466–467
    surveys, 482–483
    variation in for same kind of work, 129
    See also Compensation administration
Wagner Act (1935), 16, 17, 378, 391, 393, 395, 411–414, 553, 577
    experience under, 413–414
    National Labor Relations Board, 413
    unfair labor practices of employees, 413
Walsh-Healy Act, 568
War Labor Board, 18, 431
Watergate, 25
Wealth of Nations (Smith), 13, 30, 85
Weighted application blank, 142–143
Weighted check list, 215
Welfare movement, 14–15
Wesman Personnel Classification Test, 158
West Germany
    job protection, 580
    works council system, 367–368
Western Electric Company, 66
Westinghouse, 275
Whistle-blowing, 582–584, 600
White-collar employment
    increase in, 10–11
    work conditions, 323
Wholism, 68
Withdrawal, 299–300
Women
    assimilation in workplace, 5
    comparable worth, 197–199
    compensation of, 465
    equal employment opportunity and, 177, 179–181, 184
    increasing percentage in labor force, 11–12

married, special problems of, 180–181
pensions and, 560
pregnancy disability, 181
sexual harassment, 194–197
Wonderlic Personnel Test, 158
Work
alternative schedules, 329, 568–569
conditions of, 322–323
defined, 320
nature of, 320–321
pressures and health, 323
See also Quality of working life
Work in America Institute, 319
Work Environment Preference Schedule, 162

Work measurement methods, 494–497
Work organization, use of term, 6
Work-planning-and-review method, 221
Work sampling, 161, 496–497
Work standards data, human resource planning and, 118
Workers' compensation, 15–16, 521, 538–539, 577
administration and financing, 539
benefits, 539
Workers' participation, European style, 367–369
Works Constitution Act (1952), Germany, 368
Works council, 367

Worksharing, 424
Workweek, compressed, 9–10, 329, 569
Wyeth Laboratories, 329

Xerox Corporation, 28, 115, 117, 231, 452

Yugoslavia, self-management system, 367, 368–369

Zia Corporation, 193